BARRON'S
BUSINESS
TRAVELERS

GERMAN

FOR THE

BUSINESS
TRAVELER

Henry Strutz, M.A.

Former Associate Professor of Languages
SUNY Agricultural and Technical College
at Alfred, New York

BARRON'S

All inquiries should be addressed to:
Barron's Educational Series, Inc.
250 Wireless Boulevard
Hauppauge, NY 11788

Library of Congress Catalog Card No. 93-20912

International Standard Book No. 0-8120-1769-2

Library of Congress Cataloging-in-Publication Data

Strutz, Henry.
    German for the business traveler / Henry Strutz. — 2nd ed.
    p.cm. — (Bilingual business guides)
    English and German.
    Rev. ed. of: Talking business in German. 1987.
    ISBN 0-8120-1769-2
    1. Commerce—Dictionaries. 2. Commerce—Dictionaries—German.
    3. Business—Dictionaries. 4. Business—Dictionaries—German. 5.
    English language—Dictionaries—German. 6. German language—
    Dictionaries—English. I. Strutz, Henry. Talking business in German.
    II. Title. III. Series: Barron's bilingual business guides.
HF1002.S79   1994   93-20912
650'.03—dc20   CIP

PRINTED IN THE UNITED STATES OF AMERICA

4567   9692   987654321

CONTENTS

PREFACE

It is the nature of business to seek out new markets for its products, to find more efficient ways to bring its goods to more people. In the global marketplace, this often means travel to foreign countries, where language and customs are different. Even when a business person knows the language of the host country, the specific and often idiosyncratic terminology of the business world can be an obstacle to successful negotiations in a second language. Pocket phrase books barely scratch the surface of these problems, while standard business dictionaries prove too cumbersome.

Now there is a solution—Barron's *German for the Business Traveler.* Here is the essential pocket reference for all international business travelers. Whether your business be manufacturing or finance, communications or sales, this three-part guide will put the right words in your mouth and the best expression in your correspondence. It is a book you'll carry with you on every trip and take to every meeting. But it is also the reference you'll keep on your desk in the office. This is the business dictionary for people who do business in German.

This book is one of a new series of business dictionaries. We welcome your comments on additional phrases that could be included in future editions.

Acknowledgments

We would like to thank the following individuals and organizations for their assistance on this project:

John Downs, Business Development Consultant, Office for Economic Development, New York, New York; Petra Durach of the Commercial Department of the Consulate General of Switzerland in New York; Thomas Missong of the Austrian Trade Commission in the United States; the German Information Center in New York; the German-American Chamber of Commerce in New York.

Portions of this book are reprinted with permission from *German at a Glance* by Henry Strutz and from *Travel Diary—German,* both published by Barron's Educational Series, Inc.

I. PRONUNCIATION GUIDE

This book assumes you are already somewhat familiar with the basic pronunciation rules of German, but for those whose knowledge is a little rusty, here are some tips.

German pronunciation is not difficult because in German spelling, letters consistently represent the same sounds. The phonetic transcriptions in this book are English approximations of the German sounds and should be read as you would normally read them in English. Capitalized syllables indicate stress and should be pronounced with more emphasis than lower-case syllables in the same word.

Vowels

Vowels may be long or short. A vowel is long when:
1. doubled (B*ee*thoven, B*oo*t, W*aa*ge);
2. followed by an *h* Br*a*hms, *O*hm, F*e*hler);
3. followed by a single consonant (Sch*u*bert, M*o*zart, T*o*n).

When followed by two or more consonants, a vowel is usually short, as in Bach.

VOWEL	SOUND IN ENGLISH	EXAMPLE
a	aa (long; f*a*r)	h*a*ben (H*AA*-ben)
	ah (short; h*o*t)	h*a*tte (H*AH*-teh)
ä	ay (long; w*ay*)	B*ä*der (B*AY*-duh)
	eh (short; m*e*t)	Gep*ä*ck (geh-P*EH*K)
e	ay (long; hay)	l*e*ben (L*AY*-ben)
	eh (short; end)	h*e*lfen (H*EH*L-fen)
	e (unstressed syllables ending in -*n*, -*l*, and -*t* (like -*en* in hidd*en*)	li*e*ben (LEE-b*e*n)
	uh (unstressed syllables ending in -*er*, moth*er*)	Ritt*er* (RIT-*uh*)
i	ee (long; fl*ee*t)	*I*hnen (*EE*-nen)
	i (short; w*i*t)	w*i*ssen (V*I*ss-en)
ie	ee (always long; mart*ini*)	L*ie*be (L*EE*-beh)
o	oh (long; r*o*se)	R*o*se (R*OH*-zeh)
	o (short; l*o*ve)	k*o*mm (k*o*m)
ö	er (like h*er*, but sounded with the lips forward and rounded)	h*ö*ren (H*ER*-en)

VOWEL	SOUND IN ENGLISH	EXAMPLE
u	oo (long; bl*oo*m)	Sch*u*h (sh*oo*)
	u (short; b*u*ll)	B*u*lle (B*U*L-eh)
ü	ew (like dr*ea*m, but with lips forward and rounded)	Br*ü*der (BR*EW*-duh)
y	ew (like the German *ü*)	l*y*risch (L*EW*-rish)

Diphthongs

DIPHTHONGS	SOUND IN ENGLISH	EXAMPLE
ai, ay	ey (*eye*)	schr*ei*ben
ei, ey		(SHR*EYE*-ben)
au	ow (br*ow*nn)	br*au*n (br*ow*n)
ä, eu	oy (j*oy*)	tr*eu* (tr*oy*)

NOTE: German is pronounced more vigorously and with sharper vowels than English.

Consonants

CONSONANTS	SOUND IN ENGLISH	EXAMPLE
f, h, k, l, m, n, p, t, x	usually pronounced as in English	
b	p (between vowel and consonant or at end of word: ma*p*)	Lei*b* (leye*p*)
	b (elsewhere as in English)	*b*in (*b*in)
c	ts (before *e*, *i*, *ö*, and *ä*: wi*ts*)	*C*äsar (*TS*AY-zahr)
	k (elsewhere; *c*old)	*C*oburg (*K*OH-boork)
ch	kh strongly aspirated (breathy) sound; ("*H*a-waiian" or "*H*ugh")	

CONSONANTS	SOUND IN ENGLISH	EXAMPLE
chs	k (*k*ind)	La*chs* (lahks)
d	t (between vowel and consonant and at end of word; ca*t*)	Hun*d* (hun*t*)
	d (otherwise *d*ollar)	*D*ank (*d*ank)
g	g (hard; *g*ods)	*G*eist (*g*eyest)
	k (at the end of word; ba*ck*pa*ck*)	Ta*g* (taa*k*)
	kh (words ending in *ig*; see *ch* above)	windi*g* (VIN-di*kh*)
j	y (*y*ear)	*J*ahr (*y*aar)
qu	kv (*k*, followed by *v* as in *v*eal)	*Qu*ell (*kv*ehl)
r	r preferably rolled in the throat, as in French, or trilled with the tip of the tongue, as in Spanish or Irish or Scottish brogues)	*R*eise (*R*EYE-zeh)
s	z (preceding vowels or between them; *z*ap)	*S*ee (*z*ay)
	sh (at beginning of syllable, before *p* and *t*; *sh*ell)	*s*pielen (*SH*PEE-len)
	s, ss (elsewhere; *s*ing)	Wa*s* ist da*s*? (vahs ist dahs)
ß, ss	s, ss (always: *s*ell)	(wei*ß* veye*s*) wi*ss*en (VI-*ss*en)
sch	sh (*sh*ow)	*sch*lau (*sh*low)
tsch	ch (*ch*eer)	Ki*tsch* (ki*ch*)
tz	ts (wi*ts*)	Ka*tze* (KAH-*ts*eh)
v	f (*f*ather)	*V*ater (*F*AA-tuh)
	v (words of non-Germanic origin: *v*iolin)	*V*ioline (*v*ee-o-LEE-neh)
w	v (*v*est)	*W*asser (*V*ah-suh)
z	ts (gri*ts*)	*Z*eit (*ts*eyet)

II. INTRODUCTION

DOING BUSINESS IN GERMAN-SPEAKING COUNTRIES

Doing business with another culture and in another language can be a difficult and mystifying experience. Customs and procedures may be quite different from what is perceived as the "normal" way of conducting oneself in a business circumstance.

In this introduction, some of the customs and economic aspects of German-speaking countries are outlined, in order to assist you in effectively conducting business in these areas. Basic knowledge of these factors will help in becoming more accustomed to the business situation of the German-speaking world.

Usual Hours of Operation

Hours of operation can vary considerably in each country, and the following are only general guidelines. It will be wise to telephone in advance to determine the precise hours of the business or government office you plan to visit.

Germany: Monday to Friday 8:00 AM–4:00 PM, with 1–2 hours lunch.
Switzerland: Monday to Friday 7:30 AM–5:30 PM, with 1–2 hours lunch.
Austria: Monday to Friday 8:00 AM–6:00 PM, with 1 hour for lunch.

Business Customs

Germany: Business people in Germany tend to be formal and reserved, but many will be more open when they become familiar with you. An increasing number have had contact with Americans and will try to behave like an American business person. It's best to let your German business partner set the tone to avoid unnecessary friction. German business people are usually very efficient and they will expect you to be well-informed, particularly because they are very interested in American techniques. It's very important to be punctual.

The addition of new federal states (the former GDR, East Germany) has strained the German economy. Nevertheless, inflation-fearing Germans continue to maintain a strong deutsch mark to ensure economic stability. Particularly eager for foreign investment are areas in the former GDR, where a few of the old bureaucratic structures of the German Democratic Republic have been retained. Of these, some will probably be phased out after a transition period of a few years. The German Ministry of Economics, as well as Chambers of Commerce (see "Useful Addresses") will supply addresses of local agencies in the new German Federal *Länder* (states) where privatization is proceeding.

In Germany, as in Austria, Switzerland, and much of Europe, it is customary to shake hands at the beginning and end of business contracts.

Austria: For centuries Austria has been a gateway to Southeastern Europe. In former Hapsburg domains such as Slovenia, Bohemia, and Hungary, some nostalgia for the old empire persists and remains a factor in business dealings. Although Austrians consider themselves much more affable and outgoing then allegedly standoffish "Prussians" to the north, business relationships tend to be quite formal. Business people in Austria are polite and formal, though they may become more open in an on-going relationship.

Switzerland: Switzerland continues to be an important international financial and business center. The Swiss, like the Austrians, are not members of the EC. Still, they both trade extensively with EC countries and strive to be competitive in world markets. Swiss people are usually very formal and serious. Their businesses are generally efficiently managed, and you will be expected to be well-informed and well-organized. As in Germany, it is best to let your business partner set the tone of your meetings.

General Government Policy and Economic Situation

Germany: The German economy is based on free enterprise but the German federal and state governments, as well as the European Community, have considerable influence over economic affairs. Germany has one of the world's largest economies and foreign trade is an extremely important component. The German economy (particularly in the West) grew spectacularly in the 1950s and '60s, but economic growth has slowed in the 1980s and unemployment has increased. Major manufacturing products include motor vehicles, iron and steel, chemicals, machinery, processed food, clothing, and electrical and electronic equipment.

With unification, former large export surpluses have decreased sharply. Privatization of GDR enterprises has led to the establishment of a variety of funds and agencies. Through labor-management councils, workers have a voice in management. Workers also enjoy a 37-hour workweek plus six weeks of paid vacation. Despite rising costs, German industry has counted on quality to remain competitive in world markets. Global recession, however, coupled with local problems, have destabilized the economy and some inflation is likely.

Main imports: crude and refined petroleum, food, machinery, chemicals, clothing.

Main exports: machinery, motor vehicles, chemical and electrical engineering products, iron and steel products, textiles, and clothing.

Principal trade partners: France, the Netherlands, Belgium and Luxembourg, Italy, United Kingdom, the United States, Russia, Japan.

Population: 79.5 million.

Language: German.

Religion: Protestant (44%), Roman Catholic (37%)

Gross Domestic Product: $1,554 billion.

Switzerland: The Swiss economy is based on free enterprise, with relatively little government regulation. The Swiss have long been noted as efficient business people, and today the country's economy is highly developed. Manufactures are important, and so are financial services and tourism. Principal products of Switzerland include precision machinery, tools, timepieces, textiles and clothing, chemicals and pharmaceuticals, foodstuffs, refined metal, banking, and tourism. The famous secret-numbered bank accounts are being discounted, although the Swiss maintain that banking confidentiality is still safeguarded. Despite famed Swiss cheese and chocolates, agriculture plays a relatively small role in the Swiss economy.

Main imports: machinery, transportation equipment, crude and refined petroleum, textiles and clothing, metals.

Main exports: machinery, chemicals and pharmaceuticals, timepieces, electronic equipment, precision instruments, chocolate.

Principal trade partners: Germany, France, Italy, Great Britain, United States.

Population: 6.8 million.

Language: German (65%), French (18%), Italian (12%), Romansh (1%).

Religion: Roman Catholic (49%), Protestant (48%).

Gross Domestic Product: $126 billion.

Austria: The state plays an important role in the Austrian economy, with most major industries controlled by the government. Manufacturing is key to the economy, though agriculture and tourism also are important. Major industries are iron and steel, machinery, electrical and optical equipment, transportation equipment, forestry products, glassware, sporting goods, paper, handicrafts, processed food, textiles and clothing, chemicals, and cement.

Main imports: machinery, transportation equipment, chemicals, petroleum, foodstuffs.

Main exports: forest products, textiles, machinery, chemicals, handicrafts.

Principal trade partners: Germany, Italy, Switzerland, Great Britain.

Population: 7.6 million.

Language: German.

Religion: Roman Catholic (85%), Protestant (6%).

Gross Domestic Product: $11 billion.

BEFORE YOU GO...

Passports

All permanent U.S. residents must carry a valid passport in order to travel to, from, and within Europe. Application should be made by mail or in person at least eight and preferably twelve weeks in advance to either (1) a U.S. Passport Agency office located in thirteen major cities in the U.S.; (2) designated U.S. post offices throughout the country; or (3) State and Federal courthouses. You may also consult your travel agent or international airline office. All of these offices will let you know what documents you need and the proper procedures to follow. Requirements for citizens and non-citizens differ somewhat. No international travel tickets will be issued by an airline or travel agent to persons without valid passports.

Visas

No visas are required by western European countries for travelers with U.S. passports whose stay does not exceed three months. If planning to stay longer, contact the consulate or national tourist organization of the country in the nearest major city or in New York City, or ask your travel agent or international airline office about visa applications. Visas may also be acquired while abroad before the 3-month limit expires.

Immunizations

There are no immunization requirements (for smallpox or other diseases) for entry into western European countries or upon return to the United States. If you plan to include travel outside Europe to Asia, Africa, or the Middle East, consult your doctor or the nearest U.S. Public Health Service office.

Customs and Currency Regulations

In general, travelers to and within western Europe with U.S. passports are allowed to bring in fairly generous amounts of duty-free items for their own personal use. These items include tobacco, alcohol, and perfumes and are typically allowed in the following quantities (despite local variation):

200 cigarettes or 50 cigars or 250 grams of tobacco (about 1½ lb.)
2 liters of wine
1 liter of liquor
2 ounces of perfume

If you are not well in excess of these amounts, a simple statement of "nothing to declare" will be respected by most customs officials.

For gifts whose final destination is the country you are entering, the rules are a bit stricter and vary greatly among the different countries. If you are planning to bring a large number of such gifts, it would be wise to check on the duty-free limits beforehand and to declare whatever is in excess.

For personal valuables, like jewelry or furs and foreign-made items like watches, cameras, typewriters or tape recorders (acquired before your trip), you should have proof possession or register with U.S. Customs before departure. This will ensure that they are not subject to duty either by the United States upon return or by the country you visit.

Upon return to the United States, each person (including children) has a duty-free allowance of $400, including 100 cigars and 1 carton of cigarettes. Each adult may bring in only 1 liter of wine or other liquor duty free. Gifts worth $50 or less may be sent home subject to certain restrictions. For further up-to-date details ask your travel agent or airline to provide a copy of U.S. Customs regulations or write: U.S. Customs, P.O. Box 7407, Washington, DC 20044 (202-566-8195).

There are usually no restrictions on the amounts of foreign currency (or checks) which foreign nationals may bring into western Europe. Some countries, however, do restrict the amount of local currency that may be brought in or out. Consult a travel agent or national tourist organization office either in the United States or abroad on these restrictions.

Traveler's Checks, Credit Cards, Foreign Exchange

Although all major international traveler's checks and credit cards are accepted by large travel agencies and most of the better (more expensive) hotels, restaurants and shops in Europe, it is always best to check at each establishment beforehand. The checks most recognized are: American Express, Barclays, Visa, CitiBank, Bank of America, and Thomas Cook & Sons. The cards most acceptable are: American Express, Bank Americard, Master Card, Visa, Diners Club, and Carte Blanche.

However, be advised that the exchange rate on dollar traveler's checks is almost always disadvantageous. If you want, you can buy foreign currency checks and/or actual currency in the United States before leaving at rates equivalent to or better than the bank rate you will get over there. Currency or checks may be purchased from retail foreign currency dealers. The largest of these, Deak-Perera, will send information if you write them at: 29 Broadway, New York, NY 10006.

A warning to credit card users. When charging make sure that the following information appears on the original and all copies of your bill: the correct date; the type of currency being charged (francs, marks, kroner, etc.); the official exchange rate for that currency on that date (if possible); and the total amount of the bill. Without this information, you may end up paying at an exchange rate less favorable to you and more favorable to your European host, and for a larger bill than you thought!

Drivers' Licenses

A valid American (state) license is usually respected throughout Europe, if you are 18 years old or over. However, if you have time, and want to avoid language problems on the road, it is a good idea to get an international drivers' document through the AAA or a local automobile club. Also, despite local rules, car rental agencies may restrict rentals to people 21 years old or over. And remember, drive on the left in Great Britain and Ireland!

III. BASIC WORDS AND PHRASES

Fundamental Expressions

Yes.	Ja. (yaa)
No.	Nein. (neyen)
Maybe.	Vielleicht. (fee-LEYEKHT)
Please.	Bitte. (BIT-eh)
Thank you very much.	Vielen Dank. (FEEL-en-dahnk)
Excuse me.	Verzeihung! (fehr-TSEYE-ung)
I'm sorry.	Es tut mir leid. (ehs toot meer leyet)
Just a second	Augenblick mal! (OW-gen-blik maal)
It doesn't matter.	Das macht nichts. (dahs mahkht nikhts)
That'll be fine.	Schon gut. (shon goot)
Good morning.	Guten Morgen. (GOOT-en MORG-en)
Good afternoon.	Guten Tag. (GOOT-en taak)
Good evening.	Guten Abend. (GOOT-en AAB-ent)
Good night.	Gute Nacht. (GOOT-eh nahkht)
Good-bye!	Auf Wiedersehen! (owf VEED-uh-zayen) auf Wiederschauen! (owf VEED-uh-show-en) Uf Wiederluege! (Swiss)(uf VEED-uh-leuh-geh)
How are you? (How do you do?)	Wie geht es Ihnen? (vee gayt ehs EEN-en)
How are things?	Wie geht's? (vee gayts)
Fine, thank you. And you?	Gut, danke. Und Ihnen? (goot DAHNK-eh)(unt EEn-en)
See you later.	Bis später. (bis-SHPAYT-uh)
See you soon.	Bis bald. (bis bahlt)
Do you speak English?	Sprechen Sie Englisch? (SHPREHKH-en-zee EHNG-lish)
I don't speak German.	Ich kann kein Deutsch sprechen. (ikh kahn keyen doytsh SPREHKEN-en)
Do you understand?	Verstehen Sie? (fehr-SHTAY-en zee)
I (don't) understand.	Ich verstehe (nicht). (ikh fehr-SHTAY-eh [nikht])

What was that you said?	Wie bitte? (vee BIT-eh)
I speak little German.	Ich spreche wenig Deutsch. (ikh SHPREHKH-eh VAYN-ikh doytch)
Does anyone here speak English?	Spricht hier jemand Englisch? (shprikht heer YAY-mahnt EHNG-lish)
Please write it down.	Bitte schreiben Sie es auf! (BIT-eh SHREYEB-en-zee ehs owf)
Please speak more slowly.	Bitte sprechen Sie langsamer! (BIT-eh SHPREKH-en zee LAHNG-zaam-uh)
Please repeat.	Wiederholen Sie bitte! (VEED-uh-hoh-len zee BIT-eh)
What does that mean?	Was bedeutet das? (vahss be-DOYT-et dahs)
How do you say that in German?	Wie heißt das auf deutsch? (vee heyest dahs owf doytch)
What's your name?	Wie heißen Sie? (vee HEYESS-en zee)
(The) gentlemen, Mr.	(Der) Herr, ([dehr] hehrr)
(The) lady, Mrs.	(Die) Frau. ([dee] frow)
(The) girl, Miss.	(Das) Fräulein. ([dahs] FROY-leyen)
Here's my address and telephone number.	Hier ist meine Adresse und Telefon Nummer. (heer ist meyen-eh aa-DRESS-eh unt TAY-leh-fohn NUM-uh)
Where are you staying?	Wo sind Sie einquartiert? (voh zint zee EYEN-kwaa-teert)
Where can I reach you?	Wo kann ich Sie erreichen? (voh kahn ikh zee ehr-REYEKH-en)
I'll pick you up at your house (hotel).	Ich hole Sie in Ihrem Haus (Hotel) ab. (ikh HOHL-eh zee in EER-em hows [ho-TEL] ahp)
Nice to have met you.	Nett, daß ich Sie kennengelernt habe. (neht dahss ikh zee KEHN-en-geh-lehrnt HAAB-eh)

Common Questions and Phrases

Where is _____?	Wo ist _____ (voh ist)
When?	Wann? (vahn)
How?	Wie? (vee)

How much does that cost?	Wieviel kostet das? (VEE-feel KOST-et dahs)
Who?	Wer? (vayr)
Why?	Warum? (vah-RUM)
Which?	Welcher? (VEHLKH-uh)
Here is _____. .	Heir ist _____ . (heer ist)
There is _____ .	Dort ist _____ . Da ist _____ . (dort ist)(daa ist)
That is _____ .	Das ist _____ . (dahs ist)
It is _____ .	Es ist _____ . (ehs ist)
Arrival/Hotel	Hotelankunft. (hoh-TEL-ahn-kunft)
My name is _____	Ich heiße _____ (ikh HEYESS-eh)
I am an American.	Ich bin Amerikaner. (ikh bin aa-meh-ri-KAAN-uh)
I'm staying at _____ .	Ich bin im _____ . (ikh bin im)
Here is my passport.	Hier ist mein Paß. (heer ist meyen pahss)
I'm on a business trip.	Ich bin auf Geschäftsreise hier. (ikh bin owf geh-SHEHFTS-reye-zeh heer)
I'm just passing through.	Ich bin nur auf der Durchreise. (ikh bin noor owf dehr DOORKH-reye-zeh)
I'll be staying _____ .	Ich bleibe _____ . (ikh BLEYEB-eh)
• a few days	• einige Tage (EYEN-ig-eh TAAG-eh)
• a few weeks	• einige Wochen (EYEN-ig-eh VOKH-ehn)
• a month	• einen Monat (EYEN-en MOHN-aat)
I have nothing to declare	Ich habe nichts zu verzollen. (ikh HAAB-eh nikhts tsoo fehr-TSOL-en)

Useful Nouns

address	die Adresse (dee ah-DRESS-seh)
amount	der Betrag (dehr beh-TRAHK)
appointment	die Verabredung (dee fehr-AHP-ray-dung)
bill	die Rechnung (dee REKH-nung)
business	das Greschäft (dahs geh-SHEHFT)
car	der Wagen, das Auto (dehr VAA-gen)(dahs OW-toh)
cashier	die Kasse (de KAHSS-eh)
check	der Scheck (dehr shehk)

city	die Stadt (dee shtaht)
customs	der Zoll (dehr tsol)
date	das Datum (dahs DAA-tum)
document	das Dokument (dahs doh-koo-mehnt)
elevator	der Aufzug (dehr OWF-tsook)
flight	der Flug (dehr flook)
friend	der Freund, die Freundin (dehr froynt)(dee FROYN-din)
hanger	der Kleiderbügel (dehr KLEYE-duh-bew-gel)
key	der Schlüssel (dehr SHLEWSS-el)
list	die Liste (dee LISS-teh)
maid	das Dienstmädchen (dahs DEENST-mayt-khen)
mail	die Post (dee post)
magazine	die Zeitschrift (dee TSEYET-shrift)
manager	der Geschäftsführer (dehr geh-SHEHFTS-few-ruh)
map	die Karte (dee KAAR-teh)
mistake	der Fehler (dehr-FAY-luh)
money	das Geld (dahs gelt)
name	der Name (dehr NAA-meh)
newspaper	die Zeitung (dee TSEYE-tung)
office	das Amt, das Büro (dahs ahmt) (dahs bew-ROH)
package	das Paket (dahs pah-KAYT)
paper	das Papier (dahs pah-PEER)
passport	der Paß (dehr pahss)
pen	der Kugelschreiber (dehr KOO-gel-shreye-buh)
pencil	der Bleistift (dehr BLEYE-shtift)
porter	der Gepäckträger, der Hausdiener (dehr geh-PEHK-tray-guh)(dehr HOWSS-dee-nuh)
post office	das Postamt (dahs POST-ahmt)
postage	die Postgebühr (dee POST-geh-BEWR)
price	der Preis (der preyess)
raincoat	der Regenmantel (dehr RAY-gen-mahn-tel)
reservation	die Reservierung (dee reh-zehr-VEE-rung)
rest room	die Toilette (dee toy-LET-te)
restaurant	das Restaurant (dahs res-toh-RANG)
road	die Straße (dee SHTRAHS-seh)

room	das Zimmer (dahs TSIM-muh)
shirt	das Hemd (dahs hehmt)
shoe	der Schuh (dehr shoo)
shower	die Dusche (dee DOOSH-eh)
store	der Laden (dehr LAA-den)
street	die Straße (dee SHTRAHS-seh)
suit	der Anzug (dehr AHN-tsook)
suitcase	der Koffer (dehr KOF-fuh)
taxi	die Taxe (dee TAHK-seh)
telegram	das Telegramm (dahs tay-leh-GRAHM)
telephone	das Telefon (dahs TAY-leh-fon)
terminal	die Endstation (dee END-stah-tzee-ohn)
ticket	die Karte, die Fahrkarte (dee KAAR-teh)(dee FAAR-kaar-teh)
time	die Zeit (dee tseyet)
tip	das Trinkgeld (dahs TRINK-gelt)
train	der Zug (dehr tsook)
trip	das Reise (dee REYE-zeh)
umbrella	der Schirm (dehr shirm)
waiter	der Kellner (dehr KEL-nuh)
watch	die Uhr (dee oor)
water	das Wasser (dahs VAHS-suh)

Useful Verbs (infinitive forms)

accept	annehmen (AHN-nay-men)
answer	antworten (AHNT-vor-ten)
arrive	ankommen (AHN-kom-men)
ask	fragen (FRAA-gen)
assist	beistehen, helfen (BEY-shtay-en)(HEL-fen)
be	sein, werden (zeyen) (VEHR-den)
begin	beginnen (beh-GIN-nen)
bring	bringen (BRING-en)
buy	kaufen (KOW-fen)
call	rufen (ROO-fen)
carry	tragen (TRAA-gen)
change	wechseln (VEHK-seln)
close	schließen (SHLEES-sen)
come	kommen, ankommen (KOM-men)(AHN-kom-en)
confirm	bestätigen (beh-SHTAY-tee-gen)
continue	fortsetzen (FORT-zet-sen)
cost	kosten (KOS-ten)
deliver	bringen (BRING-en)

direct	anweisen, leiten (AHN-vey-sen) LEY-ten)
do	tun (toon)
eat	essen (EHS-sen)
end	beenden (beh-EN-den)
enter	betreten, hereinkommen (beh-TRAY-ten)(hehr-EYEN-kom-en)
examine	erwägen, untersuchen (ehr-VAY-gen)(un-tuh-ZOO-khen)
exchange	wechseln (VEHK-seln)
feel	fühlen (FEW-len)
finish	beenden (beh-EHN-den)
fix	reparieren (reh-paa-REE-ren)
follow	folgen (FOL-gen)
forget	vergessen (fehr-GEHS-sen)
forward	schiken (SHI-ken)
get	bekommen (beh-KOM-men)
give	geben (GAY-ben)
go	gehen (GAY-en)
hear	hören (HER-en)
help	helfen (HEL-fen)
keep	behalten (be-HAHL-ten)
know	kennen (KEN-en)
learn	lernen (LEHR-nen)
leave	lassen (LAHS-sen)
like	mögen (MERG-en)
listen	hören (ER-en)
look at	ansehen (AHN-zay-en)
lose	verlieren (fehr-LEE-ren)
make	machen (MAHKH-en)
mean	bedeuten (beh-DOY-ten)
meet	treffen (TREF-en)
miss	versäumen (fehr-ZOY-men)
need	brauchen (BROWKH-en)
open	aufmachen (OWF-mahkh-en)
order	bestellen (beh-SHTEL-en)
park	parken (PAHRK-en)
pay	zahlen (TSAA-len)
prefer	vorziehen (FOR-tsee-hen)
prepare	vorbereiten (FOR-beh-reye-ten)
present	vorlegen (FOR-lay-gen)
prove	beweisen (beh-VEYE-zen)
pull	ziehen (TSEE-en)
purchase	kaufen (KOW-fen)
put	stellen (SHTEHL-en)
read	lesen (LAY-zen)
receive	bekommen (beh-KOM-men)

recommend	empfehlen (ehmp-FAY-len)
remain	bleiben (BLEYE-ben)
repair	reparieren (reh-pah-REE-ren)
repeat	wiederholen (VEE-duh-hoh-len)
return	zurückbringen (tsoo-REWK-bring-en)
run	laufen (LOW-fen)
say	sagen (ZAA-gen)
see	sehen (ZAY-en)
send	senden (ZEN-den)
show	zeigen (TSEYE-gen)
sit	sitzen (ZIT-sen)
speak	sprechen (SHPREHKH-en)
stand	stehen (SHTAY-en)
start	anfangen (AHN-fahng-en)
stop	anhalten (AHN-hahl-ten)
take	nehmen (NAY-men)
talk	sprechen (SHPREHKH-en)
tell	sagen, erzählen (ZAA-gen) (ehr-TSAY-len)
think	denken, glauben (DEHNK-en) (GLOW-ben)
try	versuchen (fehr-ZOOKH-en)
turn	drehen, wenden (DRAY-en, VEHN-den)
use	benutzen (beh-NUTS-en)
visit	besuchen (beh-ZOOKH-en)
wait	warten (VAAR-ten)
walk	gehen (GAY-en)
want	mögen (MERG-en)
wear	tragen (TRAAG-en)
work	arbeiten (AHR-beye-ten)
write	schreiben (SHREYE-ben)

Useful Adjectives and Adverbs

above/below	über/unter (EW-buh/un-tuh)
ahead/behind	vorwärts/hinter (FOR-vayrts/ HIN-tuh)
best/worst	beste/am schlechtesten (BEH-ste/am SHLEHKH-te-sten)
big/small	groß/klein (grohss/kleyen)
early/late	früh/spät (frew/shpayt)
easy/difficult	einfach/schwierig (EYEN-fahkh/SHVEE-rikh) leicht/ schrer (leyekht/shreyr)
few/many	einige/viele (eye-nee-ge/VEE-le)
first/last	erstens/letztens (EHRS-tens/ LEHTS-tens)
full/empty	voll/leer (foll/layr)

good/bad	gut/schlecht (goot/shlehkht)
hot/cold	heliß/kalt (heyess/kahlt)
high/low	hoch/niedrig (hohk/NEE-rikh)
large/small	groß/klein (grohss/kleyen)
more/less	mehr/weniger (mayr/VAYN-ikh-uh)
old/new	alt/neu (ahlt/noy)
open/shut	offen/geschlossen (OFF-en/geh-SHLOSS-en)
right/wrong	richtig/falsch (RlHKH-ikh/fahlsh)
slow/fast	langsam/schnell (LAHNG-zaam/shnell)
thin/thick	dünn/dick (dewn/dik)

Other Useful Words

a, an	ein, eine, einer (eyen) (EYE-neh) (EYE-nuh)
across	über (EW-buh)
after	nach (nahkh)
again	wieder (VEED-uh)
all	alle, ganz (AHL-leh)(gahns)
almost	fast (fahst)
also	auch (owkh)
always	immer (IM-uh)
among	unter (UN-tuh)
and	und (unt)
another	andere (AHN-de-reh)
around	um (um)
away	weg (vek)
back	zurück (tsoo-REWK)
because	weil (veyel)
before	vor (for)
behind	hinter (HlN-tuh)
between	zwischen (TSVI-shun)
both	beide (BEYE-deh)
but	aber (AAB-uh)
down	unter (UN-tuh)
each	jede, jeder, jedes (YAY-deh) (YAY-duh) (YAY-des)
enough	genug (geh-NOOK)
every	jede (YAY-deh)
except	sonst, ausser (zonst) (OWSS-uh)
few	wenig (vaye-nikh)
for	für (fewr)
from	von (fon)
however	jedoch (yay-dohkh)
if	wenn (vehn)
in	in (in)

instead	anstatt (ahn-SHTAHT)
into	in (in)
maybe	vielleicht (fee-LEYEKHT)
more	mehr (mayr)
much	viel (feel)
next to	neben (NAYE-ben)
not	nicht (nikht)
now	jetzt (yetst)
of	von (fon)
often	oft (oft)
only	nur (noor)
or	oder (OHD-uh)
other	andere, anderer, anderes (AHND-eh-reh) (AHND-eh-ruh) (AHND-eh-res)
perhaps	vielleicht (feel-LEYEKHT)
same	dasselbe (dahs-ZEHL-beh)
since	seit (zeyet)
some	einige (EYEN-ig-eh)
still	noch (nokh)
that	daß, das (dahs) (dahs)
these	diese (DEE-seh)
this	dies (dees)
to	zu, nach (tsoo) (nahkh)

Directions

Which way do I go?	In welche Richtung soll ich gehen? (in VELKH-eh RIKHT-ung zol ikh GAY-en)
• straight ahead	• geradeaus (ge-RAAD-eh-OWS)
• north	• der Norden (NOR-den)
• south	• der Süden (dehr ZEW-den)
• east	• der Osten (dehr OS-ten)
• west	• der Westen (dehr VEHS-ten)
• left	• links (links)
• right	• rechts (rehkhts)
Is this the road to _____?	Ist dies die Straße nach _____ (ist dees dee SHTRAASS-eh nahkh)
Am I on the right road now?	Bin ich jetzt auf der richtigen Straße? (bin ikh yetst owf dehr RIKHT-ig-en SHTRAASS-eh)
Can you show it to me on the map?	Können Sie ihn mir auf der Karte zeigen? (KF.RN-en zee een meer owf dehr KAART-eh TSEYEG-en)

Days of the Week

Today is _____ .

- Monday
- Tuesday
- Wednesday
- Thursday
- Friday
- Saturday

- Sunday

yesterday
the day before
  yesterday
tomorrow
the day after
  tomorrow
in the morning
- afternoon

- evening

tonight

this afternoon

every day

Heute ist _____ . (HOYT-eh ist)

- Montag (MOHN-taak)
- Dienstag (DEENS-taak)
- Mittwoch (MIT-vokh)
- Donnerstag (DON-ehrs-taak)
- Freitag (FREYE-taak)
- Samstag/Sonnabend (ZAHMS-
  taak / ZON- aab -ent)

- Sonntag (ZON-taak)

gestern (GEST-ehrn)
vorgestern (FOHR-gest-ehrn)

morgen (MORG-en)
übermorgen (EWB-ehr-
  morg-en)
am Morgen (ahm MORG-en)
- Nachmittag (NAHKH-mit-
  taak)

- Abend (AAB-ent)

heute abend (HOYT-eh
  AAB-ent)
heute nachmittag (HOYT-eh
  NAHKH-mit-taak)
jeden Tag (YAYD-en taak)

Months of the Year

January

February
March
April
May
June
July
August
September
October
November
December
What is today's
  date?
Today is May 3.

monthly
this month

Januar/Jänner (Austria)
  (YAA-noo-aar/YEH-nehr)
Februar (FAY-broo-aar)
März (mehrts)
April (ah-PRIL)
Mai (meye)
Juni (YOON-ee)
Juli (YOOL-ee)
August (ow-GUST)
September (zep-TEHM-buh)
Oktober (ok-TOH-buh)
November (no-VEHM-buh)
Dezember (deh-TSEHM-buh)
Der wievielte ist heute? (dehr
  VEE-feelt-eh ist HOYT-eh)
Heute ist der 3. Mai. (HOYT-eh
  ist dehr DRIT-eh meye)
monatlich (MOHN-aat-likh)
in diesem Monat (in DEEZ-em
  MOHN-aat)

next month	im nachsten Monat (im NAYKHST-en MOHN-aat)
last month	im letzten Monat (im LETST-en MOHN-aat)

The Four Seasons

spring	der Frühling (dehr FREW-ling)
summer	der Sommer (dehr ZOM-uh)
autumn	der Herbst (dehr hehrpst)
winter	der Winter (dehr VINT-uh)
during the spring	während des Frühlings (VEHR-ent dehs FREW-lings)
every summer	jeden Sommer (YAYD-en ZOM-uh)
in the winter	im Winter (im VINT-uh)

Time

What time is it?	Wieviel Uhr ist es? (VEE-feel oor ist ehs)
• hour	• Stunde (SHTUND-eh)
• minute	• Minute (mi-NOOT-eh)
• second	• Sekunde (zeh-KUN-deh)
• half an hour	• eine halbe Stunde (EYEN-eh HAHLB-eh SHTUND-eh)
• an hour and a half	• anderthalb Stunden (AHN-dehrt-haalp SHTUND-en)
twenty after twelve	zwanzig nach zwölf (TSVAHNTS-ikh nahkh tsverlf)
OR	
twelve-twenty	zwölf Uhr zwanzig (tsverlf oor TSVAHNTS-ikh)
one-thirty	ein Uhr dreißig (eyen oor DREYSS-ikh)
OR	
half an hour (30 minutes to two)	halb zwei (hahlp tsveye)
9:37	neun Uhr siebenunddreißig (noyn oor ZEEB-en-unt-drevess-ikh)
eight to three (2:52)	acht vor drei (ahkht for drey)
five to seven (6:55)	fünf vor sieben (fewnf for ZEEB-en)
nine after four (4:09)	neun nach vier (noyn nahkh feer)
a quarter after three (3: 15)	viertel nach drei (FEERT-el nahkh dreye) drei

| At what time shall we meet? | Um wieviel Uhr treffen wir uns? (um VEE-feel oor TREHF-en veer uns) |
| We'll eat at eight (o'clock). | Wir essen um acht (Uhr). (veer ESS-en um ahkht [oor]) |

Arrival/Hotel

My name is…	Ich heiße… (ikh HEYESS-eh)
Here is my passport.	Hier ist mein Paß. (heer ist meyen pahss)
I'm on a business trip.	Ich bin auf Geschäftsreise hier. (ikh bin owf geh-SHEHFTS-reye-zeh heer)
I'm just passing through.	Ich bin nur auf der Durchreise. (ikh bin noor owf dehr DOORKH-reye-zeh)
I'll be staying _____ .	Ich bleibe _____ . (ikh BLEYEB-eh)
• a few days	• einige Tage (EYEN-ig-eh TAAG-eh)
• a few weeks	• einige Wochen (EYEN-ig-eh VOKH-ehn)
• a month	• einen Monat (EYEN-en MOHN-aat)
I have nothing to declare.	Ich habe nichts zu verzollen. (ikh HAAB-eh nikhts tsoo fehr-TSOL-en)
I'm looking for the hotel.	Ich suche das Hotel . (ikh ZOOKH-eh dahs hoh-TEL)
Where is the taxi stand?	Wo ist der Taxistand? (voh ist dehr TAHK-see-shtahnt)
Please call a taxi for me.	Rufen Sie bitte eine Taxe für mich ROOF-en zee BIT-eh EYEN-eh TAHKS-eh fewr mikh)
I (don't) have a reservation.	Ich habe (nicht) reservieren lassen. (ikh HAAB-eh [nikht] reh-zehr-VEER-en LASS-en)
I'd like a single (double) room for tonight.	Ich möchte ein Einzelzimmer (Doppelzimmer) für heute nacht. (ikh MERKHT-eh eyen EYEN-tsel-tsim-uh (DOP-el-tsim-uh) fewr HOYT-eh nahkht)
Is breakfast included in the price of the room?	Ist der Zimmerpreis mit Frühstück? (ist dehr TSIM-uh-preyes mit FREW-shtewk)

Where is the elevator?	Wo ist der Aufzug? (voh ist dehr OWF-tsook)
Please wake me tomorrow at ____ o'clock.	Bitte wecken Sie mich morgen um ____ Uhr. (BIT-eh VEHK-en zee mikh MORG-en um oor)
Are there any letters (messages) for me?	Gibt es Briefe (Nachrichten) für mich? (gipt ehs BREEF-en [NAHKH-rikht-en] fewr mikh)
May I leave this in your safe?	Darf ich dies in Ihrem Tresor lassen? (dahrf ikh dees in EE-rem treh-ZOHR LASS-en)
Please send someone up for the bags.	Bitte schicken Sie jemanden für das Gepäck hoch. (BIT-ch SHIK-en zee YAY-mahnd-en fewr dahs geh-PEHK hohkh)
Please prepare my bill.	Bitte bereiten Sie meine Rechnung vor. (BIT-eh beh-REYET-en zee MEYEN-en REKH-nung for)

Transportation

Streetcar	Straßenbahn (SHTRAASS-en-baan)
Buses	Busse (BUSS-eh)
Suburban commuter trains of German Rail	S-Bahn (EHS-baan)
Subway	U-Bahn (OO-baan)
• the men's room	• die Herrentoilette (de HEHR-en-toy-let-eh)
• the ladies' room	• die Damentoilette (dee DAAM-en-toy-let-eh)
• the bus stop	• die Bushaltestelle (dee BUS-hahl-teh-shteh-leh)
• the nearest subway station	• die nächste U-Bahn Station (Untergrundbahn) (dee NAYKH-steh oo-baan shtah-TSYOHN [UNT-uh-grunt-baan])
Where can I buy a ticket?	Wo kann ich eine Fahrkarte kaufen? (voh kahn ikh EYEN-eh FAAR-kahr-teh KOWF-en)
Do I have to change trains?	Muß ich umsteigen? (muss ikh UM-shteyeg-en)

Drive me to the hotel.	Fahren Sie mich zum Hotel. (FAAR-en zee mikh tsoom ho-TEL)
• railroad station	• Bahnhof (BAAN-hohf)
• airport	• Flughafen (FLOOK-haa-fen)
Let me off at the next corner.	Lassen Sie mich an der nächsten Ecke aussteigen! (LASS-en zee mikh ahn dehr NAYKST-en EK-oh OWS-shteye-gen)
Please wait for me.	Warten Sie auf mich bitte. (VAART-en zee owf mikh BIT-eh)
Please tell me arrival and departure time again.	Bitte sagen Sie mir noch einmal Ankunft-und Abflugzeiten. (BIT-eh ZAAG-en zee meer noch EYEN-maal AHN-kunft mt AHP-flook-tseye-ten)
I want a seat next to the window in the (non) smoking section.	Ich möchte einen Fensterplatz (Nicht) Raucher haben. (ikh MERKH-teh EYEN-en FEHNST-uh-plahts [nikht] ROWKH-uh HAAB-en)
When do I have to check in?	Wann muß ich mich melden? (vahn muss ikh mikh MEHLD-en)
May I take this with me as carry-on luggage?	Darf ich dies als Handgepäck mitnehmen? (daarf ikh dees ahls HAHNT-ge-pehk MIT-nay-men)
Is there a car rental office nearby?	Gibt es eine Autovermietung in der Nähe? (gipt chs EYEN-eh OW-toh-fehr-meet-ung in dehr NAY-eh)
What sort of cars do you have available?	Was für Wagen haben Sie zu vermieten? (vahs fewr VAAG-en HAAB-en zee tsoo fehr-MEET-en)
How much does it cost per _____?	Wieviel kostet es pro _____? (VEE-feel KOST-et ehs proh)
• day	• Tag (taak)
• week	• Woche (VOKH-eh)
• month	• Monat (MOH-naat)
• kilometer	• Kilometer (kee-loh-MAYT-uh)
How much is the insurance?	Was kostet die Versicherung? (vahs KOST-et dee fehr-ZIKH-ehr-ung)

Do I have to pay for gas?	Muß ich das Benzin bezahlen? (muss ikh dahs behn-TSEEN beh-TSAAL-en)
Do I have to leave a deposit?	Muß ich etwas hinterlegen? (muss ikh EHT-vahs hin-tehr-LAYG-en)
I want to rent the car here and leave it in Munich.	Ich will das Auto hier mieten und es in München wieder abgeben. (ikh vil dahs OW-toh heer MEET-en unt ehs in MEWN-khen VEED-uh AHP-gayb-en)
Is there an additional charge for that?	Entstehen mir dadurch zusätzliche Kosten? (ehnt-SHTAY-en meer daa-DURKH TSOO-zehts-likh-eh KOST-en)
Here is my driver's license.	Hier haben Sie meinen Führerschein. (heer HAAB-en zee MEYEN-en FEWR-ehr-sheyen)
Where is the nearest gas station (with service)?	Wo ist die nächste Tankstelle (mit Bedienung)? (voh ist dee NAYKST-eh TAHNK-shtehl-eh [mit beh-DEEN-ung])
Fill it up, please.	Voll, bitte. (fol, BIT-eh)

Drivers should recognize these international road signs.

Guarded railroad crossing

Yield

Stop

Right of way

Dangerous intersection ahead

Gasoline (petrol) ahead

Parking

No vehicles allowed

Dangerous curve

Pedestrian crossing

Oncoming traffic
has right of way

No bicycles allowed

No parking allowed

No entry

No left turn

No U-turn

No passing

Border crossing

Traffic signal ahead

Speed limit

Traffic circle (roundabout)
ahead

Minimum speed limit

All traffic turns left

End of no passing zone

One way street   Detour

Danger ahead   Entrance to expressway   Expressway ends

Leisure Time

I'd like to go to an interesting nightclub tonight.	Ich möchte gerne in ein interessantes Nachtlokal heute abend gehen. (ikh MERKHT-eh GEHRN-eh in eyen in-teh-ress-AHNT-es NAKHT-lo-kaal HOYT-eh AAB-ent GAY-en)
Is a reservation necessary?	Muß man reservieren lassen? (muss mahn reh-zehr-VEER-en LASS-en)
I'd like a good table.	Ich möchte einen guten Tisch. (ikh MERKHT-eh EYEN-en GOOT-en tish)
Where is the check-room?	Wo ist die Garderobe? (voh ist dee gahr-deh-ROHB-eh)
May I smoke?	Darf ich rauchen? (dahrf ikh ROWKH-en?)
Where can I buy English newspapers?	Wo kann ich englische Zeitungen kaufen? (voh kahn ikh EHNG-lish-eh TSEYET-ung-en KOWF-en?)
I'm looking for _____ .	Ich suche _____ . (ikh ZOOKH-eh)
• a tennis court	• einen Tennisplatz (EYEN-en TEN-is-plahts)
• a golf course	• einen Golfplatz (EYEN-en GOLF-plahts)
Where can I find a swimming pool?	Wo kann ich ein Schwimmbad finden? (voh kahn ikh eyen SHVIM-baat FIND-en)

Restaurants

Breakfast	Frühstück (FREW-shtewk)
Lunch	Mittagessen (MIT-aak-ehs-en)
Dinner	Abendessen (AAB-ehnt-ehs-en)
spoon	einen Löffel (EYEN-en LERF-el)
fork	eine Gabel (EYEN-eh GAAB-el)
knife	ein Messer (eyen MESS-uh)
glass	ein Glas (eyen glaas)
plate	einen Teller (EYEN-en TEL-uh)
chair	einen Stuhl (EYEN-en shtool)
ashtray	einen Aschenbecher (EYEN-en AHSH-en-bekh-uh)
napkin	eine Serviette (EYEN-eh zehr-VYEHT-eh)
Is there a good, not too expensive, German restaurant around here?	Gibt es ein gutes, nicht zu teures deutsches Restaurant in der Nähe? (gipt ehs eyen GOOT-es nikht tsoo TOYR-es DOY-ches restow-RAHNG in dehr NAY-eh)
Waiter!	Kellner! (KELN-uh)
Waitress!	Fräulein! (FROY-leyen)
Do you have a table for me?	Haben Sie einen Tisch für mich? (HAAB-en zee EYEN-en tish fewr mikh)
May we see the menu, please?	Können wir die Speisekarte haben? (KERN-en veer dee SHPEYEZ-en-kaart-eh HAAB-en)
What do you recommend?	Was empfehlen Sie? (vahs ehmp-FAYL-en zee)
May I take a look at the winc list please?	Darf ich mir bitte die Wein-karte ansehen? (daarf ikh meer BIT-eh dee VEYEN-kaart-eh AHN-zay-en)
Beer, please.	Ein Bier, bitte. (eyen beer BIT-eh)
Where can I wash my hands?	Wo kann ich mir die Hände waschen? (voh kahn ikh meer dee HEHND-eh VAHSH-en)
The check, please.	Die Rechnung, bitte! (dee REKH-nung BIT-eh)

Shopping

I must do some shopping today.	Ich muß heute einige Einkäufe machen. (ikh muss HOY-teh EYE-ni-geh EYEN-koy-feh MAH-khen)
I'm looking for _____ .	Ich suche _____ . (ikh ZOOKH-eh)
• a department store	• ein Warenhaus (eyen VAAR-en-hows)
• a camera shop	• ein Photogeschäft (eyen FOH-toh-geh-shehft)
• a book store	• eine Buchhandlung (EYEN-eh BOOKH-hahnt-lung)
• a china shop	• einen Porzellanladen (EYEN-en por-tseh-LAAN-laad-en)
How much does that cost?	Wieviel kostet das? (VEE-feel KOST-et dahs)
Will you accept this credit card?	Nehmen Sie diese Kreditkarte an? (NAYM-en zee DEEZ-eh kray-DIT-kaar-teh ahn)

Medical Care

I don't feel well.	Ich fühle mich nicht wohl. (ikh FEWL-eh mikh nikht vohl)
I think I'm sick.	Ich glaube, ich bin krank. (ikh GLOWB-eh ikh bin krahnk)
I need a doctor.	Ich brauche einen Arzt. (ikh BROWKH-eh EYEN-en ahrtst)
Is there a doctor here who speaks English?	Gibt's hier einen Arzt, der Englisch spricht? (gipts heer EYEN-en ahrtst dehr EHNG-lish shprikht)
I've had this pain since yesterday.	Seit gestern habe ich diese Schmerzen. (zeyet GEHST-ehrn HAAB-eh ikh DEEZ-eh SHMEHRTS-en)
I am a diabetic and take insulin.	Ich bin Diabetiker und nehme Insulin. (ikh bin dee-ah-BEH-tik-uh unt NAYM-eh in-zoo-LEEN)
I have heart trouble.	Ich bin herzkrank. (ikh bin HEHRTS-krahnk)
Unfortunately I must go to the dentist.	Leider muß ich zum Zahnarzt. (LEYED-uh muss ikh tsoom TSAAN-ahrtst)

Do you know a good one?	Kennen Sie einen guten? (KEN-en zee EYEN-en GOOT-en)
Where can I find the nearest (all-night) pharmacy?	Wo finde ich die nächste Apotheke (mit Nachtdienst)? (voh FIND-eh ikh dee NAYKST-eh ah-poh-TAYK-eh [mit NAHKHT-deenst])
I'm looking for something for _____ .	Ich suche etwas gegen . ikh ZOOKH-eh EHT-vahs GAYG-en _____ .

- a cold
- constipation
- cough
- a fever
- diarrhea
- a hangover
- indigestion
- headache
- insomnia

- eine Erkältung (EYEN-eh ehr-KEHLT-ung)
- Verstopfung (fehr-SHTOPF-ung)
- Husten (HOOST-en)
- Fieber (FEEB-uh)
- Durchfall (DOORKH-fahl)
- Kater (KAAT-uh)
- Magenverstimmung (MAAG-en-fehr-shtim-ung)
- Kopfschmerzen (KOPF-shmehrts-en)
- Schlaflosigkeit (SHLAAF-loh-zikh-keyet)

Telephones

I'm looking for _____ .	Ich suche _____ . (ikh ZOOKH-eh)

- a telephone booth
- a telephone directory

- eine Telefonzelle (EYEN-eh tay-leh-FOHN-tsel-eh)
- ein Telefonbuch (eyen tay-leh-FOHN-bookh)

May I use your phone?	Darf ich Ihr Telefon benutzen? (dahrf ikh eer tay-leh-FOHN beh-NUTS-en)
Here is the number.	Hier ist die Nummer. (heer ist dee NUM-uh)
Can you help me?	Können Sie mir helfen? (KERN-en zee meer HELF-en)
It's a local call.	Es ist ein Ortsgespräch. (ehs ist eyen ORTS-geh-shpraykh)

- a long-distance call
- a person-to-person call

- ein Ferngespräch (eyen FEHRN-geh-shpraykh)
- ein Gespräch mit Voranmeldung (eyen geh-SHPRAYKH mit FOHR-ahn-mehld-ung)

- a collect call
- ein R-Gespräch (eyen ehr-geh-SHPRAYKH)

Can you dial direct?
Kann man durchwählen? (kahn mahn DOORKH-vayl-en)

May I speak to Mr. (Mrs., Miss) ?
Darf ich bitte Herrn (Frau Fräulein) ____ sprechen? (dahrf ikh BIT-eh hehrn [frow, FROY-leyen] SHPREHKH-en)

Speak louder (more slowly).
Sprechen Sie lauter (langsamer). (SHPREHKH-en zee LOWT-uh [LAHNG-zaam-uh])

Don't hang up.
Bleiben Sie am Apparat. (BLEYEB-en zee ahm ah-pah-RAAT)

I'll call again later.
Später rufe ich noch einmal an. (SHPAYT-uh roof ikh nokh EYEN-maal ahn)

I'd like to leave a message.
Ich möchte etwas ausrichten lassen. (ikh merkht EHT-vahs OWSS-rikht-en LAHSS-en)

Where is the post office?
Wo ist das Postamt? (voh ist dahs POST-ahmt)

Where can I find a mailbox?
Wo finde ich einen Briefkasten? (voh FIND-en ikh EYEN-en BREEF-kahst-en)

Where is the stamp window?
Wo ist der Schalter für Brief-marken? (voh ist dehr SHAHLT-uh fewr BREEF-mahrk-en)

Where can I send a telegram?
Wo kann ich ein Telegramm aufgeben? (vo kahn ikh eyen tay-leh-GRAHM OWF-gayb-en)

I want to send it collect.
Ich möchte, daß der Empfänger es bezahlt. (ikh MERKHT-eh dahs dehr ehmp-FEHNG-uh ehs beh-TSAALT)

At what time will it arrive?
Um wieviel Uhr wird's ankommen? (um VEE-feel oor veerts AHN-kom-en)

Signs

Abtahrten	Departures
Aufzug	Elevator
Ausgang	Exit
Auskunft	Information

Belegt	Filled Up
Besetzt	Occupied
Betreten des Rasens verboten	Keep off the grass
Damentoilette	Ladies' room
Drücken	Push
Eingang	Entrance
Gefahr	Danger
Geschlossen	Closed
Herrentoilette	Men's room
Nicht berühren	Do not touch
Nichtraucher	Nonsmoking section
Notausgang	Emergency exit
Rauchen verboten	No smoking
Ziehen	Pull

Numbers

Cardinal Numbers

0	null (nul)
1	eins (eyenss)
2	zwei, zwo (tsveye), (tsvoh)
3	drei (dreye)
4	vier (feer)
5	fünf (fewnf)
6	sechs (zehks)
7	sieben (ZEEB-en)
8	acht (ahkht)
9	neun (noyn)
10	zehn (tsayn)
11	elf (elf)
12	zwölf (tsverlf)
13	dreizehn (DREYE-tsayn)
14	vierzehn (FEER-tsayn)
15	fünfzehn (FEWNF-tsayn)
16	sechzehn (ZEHKH-tsayn)
17	siebzehn (ZEEP-tsayn)
18	achtzehn (AHKHT-tsayn)
19	neunzehn (NOYN-tsayn)
20	zwanzig (TSVAHN-tsikh)
21	einundzwanzig (EYEN-unt-tsvahn-tsikh)
22	zweiundzwanzig (TSVEYE-unt-tsvahn-tsikh)
23	dreiundzwanzig (DREYE-unt-tsvahn-tsikh)
24	vierundzwanzig (FEER-unt-tsvahn-tsikh)
25	fünfundzwanzig (FEWNF-unt-tsvahn-tsikh)

26	sechsundzwanzig (ZEHKS-unt-tsvahn-tsikh)
27	siebenundzwanzig (ZEEB-en-unt-tsvahn-tsikh)
28	achtundzwanzig (AHKHT-unt-tsvahn-tsikh)
29	neunundzwanzig (NOYN-unt-tsvahn-tsikh)
30	dreißig (DREYESS-ikh)
31	einundreißig (EYEN-unt-dreyess-ikh)
40	vierzig (FEER-tsikh)
41	einundvierzig (EYEN-unt-fccr-tsikh)
50	fünfzig (FEWNF-tsikh)
60	sechzig (ZEHKH-tsikh)
70	siebzig (ZEEP-tsikh)
80	achtzig (AHKH-tsikh)
90	neunzig (NOYN-tsikh)
100	(ein)hundert ([eyen]HUN-dehrt)
101	hunderteins (HUN-dehrt-eyenss)
102	hundertzwei (HUN-dehrt-tsveye)
200	zweihundert (TSVEYE-hun-dehrt)
300	dreihundert (DREYE-hun-dehrt)
400	vierhundert (FEER-hun-dehrt)
500	fünfhundert (FEWNF-hun-dehrt)
600	sechshundert (ZEHKS-hun-dehrt)
700	siebenhundcrt (ZEEB-en-hun-dehrt)
800	achthundert (AHKHT-hun-dehrt)
900	neunhundert (NOYN-hun-dehrt)
1,000	(ein)tausend (Leyen] TOW-zehnt)
2,000	zweitausend (TSVEYE-tow-zehnt)
3,000	dreitausend (DREYE-tow-zehnt)
4,000	viertausend (FEER-tow-zehnt)
5,000	fünftausend (FEWNF-tow-zehnt)
6,000	sechstausend (ZEHKS-tow-zehnt)

7,000	siebentausend (ZEEB-en-tow-zehnt)
8,000	achttausend (AHKHT-tow-zehnt)
9,000	neuntausend (NOYN-tow-zehnt)
10,000	zehntausend (TSAYN-tow-zehnt)
20,000	zwanzigtausend (TSVAHN-tsikh-tow-zehnt)
30,000	dreißigtausend (DREYESS-ikh-tow-zehnt)
40,000	vierzigtausend (FEER-tsikh-tow-zehnt)
50,000	fünfzigtausend (FEWNF-tsikh-tow-zehnt)
60,000	sechzigtausend (ZEHKH-tsikh-tow-zehnt)
70,000	siebzigtausend (ZEEP-tsikh-tow-zehnt)
80,000	achtzigtausend (AHKH-tsikh-tow-zehnt)
90,000	neunzigtausend (NOYN-tsikh-tow-zehnt)
100,000	(ein)hunderttausend (eyen)HUN-dehrt-tow-zehnt)
200,000	zweihunderttausend (TSVEYE-hun-dehrt-tow-zehnt)
300,000	dreihunderttausend (DREYE-hun-dehrt-tow-zehnt)
400,000	vierhunderttausend (FEER-hun-dehrt-tow-zehnt)
500,000	fünfhunderttausend (FEWNF-hun-dehrt-tow-zehnt)
600,000	sechshunderttausend (ZEHKS-hun-dehrt-tow-zehnt)
700,000	siebenhunderttausend (ZEEB-en-hun-dehrt-tow-zehnt)
800,000	achthunderttausend (AHKHT-hun-dehrt-tow-zehnt)
900,000	neunhunderttausend (NOYN-hun-dehrt-tow-zehnt)
1,000,000	eine Million (EYEN-eh mil-YOHN)
2,000,000	zwei Millionen (TSVEYE mil-YOHN-en)
10,000,000	zehn Millionen (TSAYN mil-YOHN-en)

100,000,000	(ein)hundert Millionen (eyen)HUN-dehrt-mil-YOHN-en
1,000,000,000	eine Milliarde (EYEN-eh mil YAHRD-eh)

Examples

540	fünfhundertvierzig (FEWNF-hunehrt-feer-tsikh)
1,540	eintausendfünfhundertvierzig (EYEN-tow-zehnt-fewnf-hun-dehrt-feer-tsikh)
11,540	elftausendfünfhundertvierzig (ELF-tow-zehnt-fewnf-hun-dehrt-feer-tsikh)
611,540	sechshundertelftausendfünfhundertvierzig (ZEHKS-hun-dehrt-elf-tow-zehnt-fewnf-hun-dehrt-feer-tsikh)
1,611,540	eine Million sechshundertelftausendfünfhundertvierzig (EYEN-eh mil-yohn zehks-hun-dehrt-elf-tow-zehnt-fewnf-hun-dehrt-feer-tsikh)

Years

1900	neunzehnhundert (NOYN-tsayn-hun-dehrt)
1987	neunzehnhundertsiebenundachtzig (NOYN-tsayn-hun-dehrt-seeb-en-unt-ahkh-tsikh)
1988	neunzehnhundertachtundachtzig (NOYN-tsayn-hun-dehrt-ahkht-unt-ahkh-tsikh)
1989	neunzehnhundertneunundachtzig (NOYN-tsayn-hun-dehrt-noyn-unt-ahkh-tsikh)
1990	neunzehnhundertneunzig (NOYN-tsayn-hun-dehrt-noyn-tsikh)

Ordinal Numbers

first	erst- (ayrst)
second	zweit- (tsveyet)
third	dritt- (drit)
fourth	viert- (feert)
fifth	fünft- (fewnft)

sixth	sechst- (zehkst)
seventh	siebt- (zeept)
eighth	acht- (ahkht)
ninth	neunt- (noynt)
tenth	zehnt- (tsaynt)

In writing, ordinals are abbreviated by placing a period after the number.

the first day	der erste Tag (der 1. Tag) (dehr AYRST-eh taak)
for the second time	zum zweiten Mal (zum 2. Mal) (tsoom TSVEYET-en maal)
once	einmal (EYEN-maal)
twice	zweimal (TSVEYE-maal)

German Abbreviations

Abt.	Abteilung	compartment
ACS	Automobil-Club der Schweiz	Automobile Association of Switzerland
ADAC	Allgemeiner Deutscher Auto-mobil Club	General Automo-bile Association of Germany
Bhf	Bahnhof	railway station
BMW	Bayerische Motorenwerke	Bavarian Motor Works
CDU	Christlich-Demokratische Union	Christian Demo-cratic Union
DZT	Deutsche Zentrale fur Tourismus	German National Tourist Board
d.h.	das heißt	that is (i.e.)
e.V.	eingetragener Verein	registered associa-tion, corporation
FKK	Freikörperkultur	Free Physical Culture (nudism)
Frl.	Fräulein	Miss
GmbH	Gesellschaft mit beschränkter Haftung	limited-liability corporation
Hr.	Herr	Mr.
JH	Jugendherberge	youth hostel
km	Kilometer	kilometer
KG	Kommandit-gesellschaft	limited partnership
LKW	Lastkraftwagen	truck
Mill.	Million	million

ÖAMTC	Österreichischer Automobil-Motorrad-und Touring-Club	Austrian Automobile, Motorcycle, and Touring Assocation
ÖBB	Österreichische Bundesbahnen	Austrian Federal Railroad
PKW	Personenkraft-wagen	passenger car
PTT	Post, Telefon, Telegraph	Postal, Telephone, and Telegraph Office
SSB	Schweizerische Bundesbahnen	Swiss Federal Railways
SPD	Sozialdemokra-tische Partei Deutschlands	Social Democratic Party of Germany
Str.	Straße	street
TCS	Touring-Club der Schweiz	Swiss Touring Association
usf./usw.	und so fort/und so weiter	et cetera (etc.)
Ztg.	Zeitung	newspaper
z.Z.	zur Zeit	at the present time

IV. BUSINESS DICTIONARY

All nouns in German are capitalized. They come in three genders: masculine feminine, and neuter. **Der, die,** and **das** all mean *the* and indicate the noun's gender—masculine, feminine and neuter, respectively. *The,* for all nouns in the plural is **die**. The feminime forms for nouns of agent usually end in -**in** and sometimes they take an amlaut.

der Anwalt lawyer (m)   **die Anwältin** lawyer (f)

A few nouns, like **das Firmenmitglied**, do double duty for males and females. But few such nouns exist. For the sake of simplicity and space, we've limited the definitions to masculine forms when necessary. When referring to a female in this position, use the feminine form, as illustrated above.

Many of the definitions in this dictionary contain a noun modified by an adjective or an adverb. Fortunately, adverbs always stay the same. But German adjectivves are variable, depending on the gender and grammatical usage of the noun. The English-German dictionary defines *competitive price* as **der konkurrenzfähige Preis**. The ending on the adjective is *e* because the word for *the* is given. In the German-English dictionary, however, *competitive price* is listed without the word *the* and is therefore **konkurrenzfähiger Preis** (note the final **r** on the adjective). The English-German dictionary gives you the word *the*, thus indicating gender. If there is an adjective, it has the correct ending necessary when *the* is used.

Verbs change endings, too, depending, as in English, on the subject and the time (tense). But that need not concern you here since verb forms are given in the infinitive, which in German usually ends in **en**.

kaufen to buy   **verkaufen** to sell

German has an abundance of commercial terms. Many are of Latin origin by way of Italian or French. There are usually Germanic synonyms. Note:

die Gleichheit   **die Herstellung**
parity   production
die Parität   **die Produktion**

If you don't know the German term, use an English one and it's probable that you'll be understood. Whether you use the Germanic or Germanized term in German, try to pronounce the word distinctly and sharply, since German is a more strongly accented language than English (see Pronunciation Guide). You will note that in both the key industries and dictionary sections, we have included the phonetic pronunciations of the German words.

abandon (v)	aufgeben	*(OWf-gAY-ben)*
abandonment	die Ausbuchung	*(dee OWs-bOO-khunk)*
abatement (reduction)	der Abschlag	*(duh AHB-shlAHk)*
abatement (suspension)	die Einstellung	*(dee EYEn-shtEHL-lunk)*
ability-to-pay concept	die Zahlungsfähigkeit	*(dee tsAA-lunks-fEHig-keyet)*
above mentioned	obenerwähnt, obengenannt	*(OH-behn-AYr-vAYnt), (OH-behn-geh-nAHnt)*
above par	über pari	*(EW-buh pah-rEE)*
above-the-line (short term)	kurzfristig	*(kURTS-frist-tikh)*
above-the-line	über der Linie	*(EW-buh duh lEE-nee-eh)*
absentee owner	der Eigentümer ohne Leitungsfunktion	*(duh EYE-gen-tEW-muh OH-neh lEYE-tunks-funk-tsEE-ohn)*
absenteeism	die Abwesenheit	*(dee AHB-vAY-zen-heyet)*
absorb (v)	absorbieren	*(ahb-zor-bEE-ren)*
absorb the loss (v)	den Verlust auffangen	*(dehn fuh-lOOst OWf-fAAn-gehn)*
absorption costing	das Kostenaufteilungsverfahren	*(dahs kOS-ten-OWf-tEYE-lungs-fuh-fAA-rehn)*
accelerated depreciation	die erhöhte Abschreibung	*(dee ayr-hER-teh AHB-shrEYE-bunk)*
accelerating premium	die produktivitätsabhängige Leistungsprämie	*(dee proh-dUK-ti-vee-tAYts-ahb-hAYng-ikh-eh lEYEs-tungs-PRAY-mee-eh)*
acceleration clause	die Fälligkeitsklausel	*(dee fEHl-likh-keyts-klOW-zel)*
accept (v)	annehmen	*(AHN-nAY-men)*
acceptable quality level	das annehmbare Qualitätsniveau	*(dee AHN-naym-bAA-reh kvah-li-tAYts-nee-voh)*
acceptance (bill of agreement)	das Akzept	*(dahs ahk-tsEPt)*
acceptance agreement	der Annahmevertrag	*(die AHN-nah-meh-fuh-trAHk)*

A

acceptance bill	das Akzept, der Wechsel	*(dahs ahk-tsEPt), (duh vEHk-sehl)*
acceptance credit	der Wechselkredit	*(duh vEHk-sehl-kray-dIT)*
acceptance house	das Akzepthaus	*(dahs ahk-tsEPt-hOWs)*
acceptance sampling	die Stichprobenprüfung	*(dee shtIKH-proh-ben-prEW-funk)*
acceptor	der Akzeptant	*(duh ahk-tsEP-tahnt)*
accession rate	die Einstellungsquote	*(dee EYEn-shtEHL-lunks-kvOH-teh)*
accident damage	der Unfallschaden	*(duh un-fAHl-shAA-den)*
accommodation bill	der Gefälligkeitswechsel	*(duh geh-fEH-lig-keyets-vEHk-sehl)*
accommodation credit	der Gefälligkeitskredit	*(duh geh-fEH-lig-keyets-kray-dIT)*
accommodation endorsement	das Gefälligkeitsindossament	*(dahs geh-fEH-lig-keyets-IN-dohs-sah-ment)*
accommodation paper	das Gefälligkeitsakzept	*(dahs geh-fEH-lig-keyets-ahk-tsEPt)*
accommodation parity	die Gefälligkeitsparität	*(dee geh-fEH-lig-keyets-paa-ree-tAYt)*
accommodation platform	die Gefälligkeitsplattform	*(dee geh-fEH-lig-keyets-plAAt-fohrm)*
accompanied goods	die begleiteten Waren	*(dee beh-glEYE-ten vAA-ren)*
accord and satisfaction	der außergerichtliche Vergleich	*(duh OWs-uh-geh-rIKHt-lIKH-eh fuh-glEYEkh)*
account	das Konto	*(dahs kON-toh)*
account balance	der Kontostand	*(duh kON-toh-shtAHnt)*
account day	der Abrechnungstag	*(duh AHB-rEHKH-nungs-taak)*
account executive	der Kundenbetreuer	*(duh kUN-dehn-beh-trOY-uh)*
account for (v)	Rechenschaft ablegen	*(rEHKH-en-shAHft AHB-lAY-gen)*
account number	die Kontonummer	*(duh kON-toh-num-muh)*
accountable	rechenschaftspflichtig	*(rEHKH-en-shAHfts-pflIKH-tig)*
accountant (CPA)	der Wirtschaftsprüfer	*(duh vEErt-shAHfts-prEW-fuh)*
accountant	der Buchhalter	*(duh bOOkh-hAAl-tuh)*

A

accountant, chief	der Buchhaltungsleiter	*(duh bOOkh-hAAl-tuh-lEYE-tuh)*
accounting department	die Buchhaltung	*(dee bOOkh-hAAl-tunk)*
accounting method	die Buchungsmethode	*(dee bOOkh-unks-meh-tOH-deh)*
accounting period	der Buchungszeitraum	*(duh bOOkh-unks-tsEYEt-rOWm)*
accounting principles	die Bilanzierungsrichtlinien	*(dee bee-lAHn-tsEE-runks-rIKHt-lee-nee-ehn)*
accounting, cost	die Kostenrechnung	*(dee kOS-rEHKH-nunk)*
accounting, management	das Rechnungswesen für Betriebsführungs-bedürfnisse	*(dahs rEHKH-nungs-vAY-zen fEWr beh-trEEps-fEW-runks-beh-dEWrf-nis-seh)*
accounts payable	die Buchschulden	*(dee bOOkh-shUl-den)*
accounts receivable	die Buchforderungen	*(dee bOOkh-FOHR-duh-run-gen)*
accretion	der Zuwachs	*(duh tsOO-vahkhs)*
accrual	das Auflaufen	*(dahs OWf-low-fen)*
accrue (v)	auflaufen, anwachsen	*(OWf-low-fen), (AHN-vahkh-zen)*
accrued assets	die antizipativen Aktiva	*(dee ahnti-tsi-pah-tEE-fehn ahk-tEE-vah)*
accrued depreciation	die entstandene Abschreibung	*(dee EHNT-shtAAnt-endeh AHB-shrEYE-bunk)*
accrued expenses	der antizipative Aufwand	*(duh ahnti-tsi-pah-tEE-feh OWf-vahnt)*
accrued interest	die aufgelaufenen Zinsen	*(dee OWf-geh-lOW-feh-nen tsIN-zen)*
accrued revenue	der antizipative Ertrag	*(duh ahnti-tsi-pah-tEE-feh uh-trAHk)*
accrued taxes	die aufgelaufenen Steuern	*(dee OWf-geh-lOW-feh-nen shtOY-uhn)*
accumulated depreciation	die Wertberichtigung auf das Anlagevermögen	*(dee vEHRt-beh-rIKH-ti-gunk OWf dahs AHN-laa-geh-fuh-mER-gen)*
acetic acid	die Azetatsäure	*(dee Ah-TSEH-taht-ZOY-reh)*
acid	die Säure	*(dee ZOY-reh)*
acid content	der Säuregehalt	*(duh ZOY-reh-geh-hahlt)*

acid-test ratio	der Barliquiditätsgrad	*(dahs BAHR-lee-kvee-dee-tAYts-grahd)*
acknowledge (v)	bestätigen	*(beh-shtAY-ti-gen)*
acknowledgment	die Anerkennung	*(dee ahn-EHR-ken-nunk)*
acknowledgment of payment	die Zahlungsbestätigung	*(dee tsAA-lungs-beh-shtAY-ti-gunk)*
acoustic coupler	die akustische Koppelung	*(dee ah-kUS-ti-sheh-kOP-peh-lunk)*
acquire (v)	erwerben, gewinnen	*(ayr-vAYr-ben), (geh-vIN-nen)*
acquired rights	die erworbenen Rechte	*(dee ayr-vOHr-benen rehkh-teh)*
acquisition	der Erwerb	*(duh ayr-vAYrb)*
acquisition profile	das Erwerbungsprofil	*(dahs ayr-vAYr-bunks-proh-fEEl)*
acre	die Anbaufläche	*(dee AHN-bow-flehkheh)*
acreage allotment	die Parzellierung	*(dee pahr-tseh-lEE-runk)*
acronym	das Akronym	*(dahs ah-kro-nEWm)*
across the board	generell, allgemein	*(gen-AY-rehl), (AHl-geh-mEYEn)*
act of God	die höhere Gewalt	*(dee hER-uh-reh geh-vAAlt)*
action, legal	die Klage, der Prozeß	*(dee klAA-geh), (duh proh-tsEHs)*
active account	das Aktivkonto	*(dahs ahk-tEEf-kON-toh)*
active assets	die Aktiva	*(dee ahk-tEE-vah)*
active debts	die Außenstände	*(dee OWs-en-shtehn-deh)*
actual cash value	der effektive Geldwert	*(duh ehf-fehk-tEE-fuh gehlt-vEHrt)*
actual costs	die Selbstkosten	*(dee zehlbst-kOS-ten)*
actual liability	die tatsächliche Haftpflicht	*(dee taht-sEHKH-likh-eh hAHft-pflikht)*
actual total loss	der tatsächliche Gesamtverlust	*(dee taht-sEHKH-likh-eh geh-zAAmt-fuh-lOOst)*
actuals	die Effektiveinnahmen	*(dee ehf-fehk-tEEf-EYEn-nAA-men)*
actuary	der Versicherungsstatistiker	*(duhfuh-zIkheh-runks-shtAH-tis-ti-kuh)*
ad valorem duty	der Wertzoll	*(duh vEHRt-OOm-zAHts)*
add-on sales	der Mehrumsatz	*(duh mAYr-OOm-zAHts)*

addendum	der Zusatz	*(duh tsOO-zAHts)*
address commission	die Provision des Verladers	*(dee pro-vzEE-on dehs fayr-lAA-duhs)*
adjudge (v)	gerichtlich entscheiden	*(geh-rIKHt-likh-ent-shEYE-den)*
adjudication	das Urteil	*(dahs OOr-teyel)*
adjust (v) (correct)	berichtigen	*(beh-rIKH-tee-gen)*
adjust (v)	anpassen	*(AHN-pAS-sen)*
adjusted CIF price	der berichtigte cif-Preis	*(duh beh-rIKH-tee-teh TSAY-EE-EHF prEYEs)*
adjusted gross income	das steuerpflichtige Bruttoeinkommen	*(dahs shtOY-uh-pflIKH-tik-eh BRU-toh-EYEn-kOM-mehn)*
adjusted rate	der angepaßte Kurs	*(duh AHN-geh-pAS-teh koors)*
adjusting entry	die Berichtigungsbuchung	*(dee beh-rIHKH-tee-gunks-bOO-khunk)*
adjustment account	das Berichtigungskonto	*(dahs beh-rIKH-tee-gunks-kON-toh)*
adjustment trigger	der Regelungsauslöser	*(duh RAY-geh-lunks-OWs-lER-suh)*
administration	die Verwaltung	*(dee fuh-vAHl-tunk)*
administrative	verwaltungsmäßig	*(fuh-vAHl-tunks-mEH-sig)*
administrative expenses	die Verwaltungskosten	*(dee fuh-vAHl-tunks-kOS-ten)*
administrator	der Verwalter	*(duh fuh-vAHl-tuh)*
advance (v) (money)	vorschieben	*(FOHR-shEE-sehn)*
advance (v) (promote)	fördern	*(fER-duhn)*
advance freight	die vorausbezahlte Fracht	*(dee FOHR-OWs-beh-tsAAl-teh fRAKHT)*
advance notice	die Vorankündigung	*(dee FOHR-ahn-kEWn-di-gunk)*
advance payment	die Vorauszahlung	*(dee FOHR-OWs-tsAA-lung)*
advance refunding	die Rückerstattung im voraus	*(dee rEWk-uh-shtAA-tunk im-FOHR-ows)*
adverse balance	der Sollsaldo	*(duh zol-sAHl-doh)*
advertisement	die Werbung	*(dee vAYr-bunk)*

advertising agency	die Werbeagentur	*(dee vAYr-beh-ah-gen-tOOR)*
advertising budget	das Werbebudget	*(dahs vAYr-beh-bew-tshEH)*
advertising campaign	die Werbekampagne	*(dee vAYr-beh-kahm-pAHn-yeh)*
advertising expenses	die Werbekosten	*(dee vAYr-beh-kOS-ten)*
advertising manager	der Werbeleiter	*(dee vAYr-beh-lEYE-tuh)*
advertising media	die Werbeträger	*(dee vAYr-beh-trAY-guh)*
advertising rate	der Anzeigentarif	*(duh AHN-tseye-gen-taa-rIF)*
advertising research	die Werbeforschung	*(dee vAYr-beh-fOHR-shunk)*
advice note	das Benachrichtigungsschreiben	*(dahs beh-nAKH-reekh-tee-gunks-shrEYE-ben)*
advise (v)	beraten	*(beh-rAA-ten)*
advisory council	der Beirat	*(duh BEYE-raat)*
advisory service	der Beratungsdienst	*(duh beh-rAA-tuns-deenst)*
affidavit	die eidesstattliche Erklärung	*(dee EYEd-ehs-shtAAt-likh-eh AYr-klAY-runk)*
affiliate	die Konzerngesellschaft	*(dee kon-tsAYrn-geh-zEL-shaht)*
affirmative action	die Vorschriften über die Anstellung von Frauen und Minoritäten	*(dee FOHR-shrif-ten EW-buh dee AHn-shtEL-lung fon frOW-en unt mEE-noh-ree-tAY-ten)*
affreightment	der Schiffsfrachtvertrag	*(duh shIFs-frAHKHt-fuh-trAHk)*
afloat (debt-free)	schuldenfrei	*(SHUL-dehn-frEYE)*
afloat (in circulation)	im Umlauf	*(im UM-lowf)*
after-hours trading	die nachbörslichen Umsätze	*(dee nakh-bERs-likh-eh UM-zAY-tseh)*
after-sales service	der Kundendienst	*(duh kUN-dehn-dEEnst)*
after-sight	das nach Sicht Akzept	*(dahs nAHKH zikht ahk-tsEPt)*
after-tax real rate of return	der Realgewinn nach Steuern	*(duh rAY-AAl-geh-vIN nAKH shtOY-uhn)*

afterdate (v)	nachdatieren	*(nAKH-daa-tEE-ren)*
against all risks	gegen alle Gefahren	*(gAY-gen AHL-leh geh-fAA-ren)*
agency	die Agentur, die Vertretung	*(dee a-gen-tOOr), (dee fuh-trAY-tunk)*
agency fee	die Vertretungsgebühr	*(dee fuh-trAY-tunks-geh-bEWr)*
agenda	die Tagesordnung	*(dee tAA-gehs-ORd-nunk)*
agent	der Vertreter	*(duh fuh-trAY-tuh)*
aggregate demand	die Gesamtnachfrage	*(dee geh-zAHmt-nAKH-frah-geh)*
aggregate risk	das Gesamtrisiko	*(dahs geh-zAHmt-rEE-zEE-koh)*
aggregate supply	das Gesamtangebot	*(dahs geh-zAHmt-AHN-geh-bot)*
aging	das Altern	*(dahs AHL-tehrn)*
agreement (written)	der Vertrag	*(duh fuh-trAHk)*
agreement	die Vereinbarung	*(dee fuh-EYEn-bAA-runk)*
agricultural paper	das landwirtschaftliche Akzept	*(dahs LAHnd-vEErt-shahft-likh-eh ahk-tsEPt)*
agricultural products	die landwirtschaftlichen Erzeugnisse	*(dee LAHnd-vEErt-shahft-likh-eh ayr-tsOYg-nis-seh)*
agriculture	die Landwirtschaft	*(dee LAHnd-vEErt-shahft)*
air express	der Luftexpress	*(duh LOOft-EX-prehs)*
air filter	der Luftfilter	*(duh LUFT-FIL-tuh)*
air freight	die Luftfracht	*(dee LOOft-frAKHt)*
air shipment	die Luftfrachtsendung	*(dee LOOft-frAKHt-zEN-dunk)*
alcohol	der Alkohol	*(duh AHL-ko-hol)*
alcoholic content	der Alkoholgehalt	*(duh AHL-ko-hol-geh-hahlt)*
algorithm	der Algorithmus	*(duh ahl-go-rIT-mus)*
alien corporation	die ausländische Gesellschaft	*(dee OWS-lehn-di-sheh geh-zEL-shahft)*
all in cost	der Gesamtpreis	*(duh geh-zAHmt-prEYEs)*
all or none	alles oder nichts	*(AHl-lehs oduh nIKHts)*
allocation of costs	die Kostenzuteilung	*(dee kOS-ten-tsoo-tEYE-lunk)*

allocation of responsibilities	die Verantwortungsverteilung	*(dee fuh-AHnt-vOHr-tunks-fuh-tEYE-lunk)*
allocation, resource	die Mittelverwendung	*(dee mit-tEL-fayr-vEHn-dunk)*
allonge	der Verlängerungsabschnitt	*(duh fuh-lEHng-uh-runks-AHB-shnIT)*
allot (v)	verteilen, zuweisen	*(fuh-tEYE-len), (tsOO-vEYE-zen)*
allotment	die Verteilung	*(dee fuh-tEYE-lunk)*
allotment letter	der Zuteilungsschein	*(duh tsOO-tEYE-lunks-shEYEn)*
allow (v)	erlauben	*(ayr-lOW-ben)*
allowance (discount)	der Rabatt	*(duh rah-bAAt)*
allowance (subsidy)	der Zuschuß	*(duh tsOO-shUs)*
allowance, depreciation	der Abschreibungsbetrag	*(duh AHB-shrEYE-bungs-beh-trAHk)*
alloy steel	der Legierstahl	*(duh leh-gEEr-shtAAL)*
alongside	neben, daneben	*(nAY-ben), (dah-nAY-ben)*
alteration	die Änderung	*(dee EHn-deh-runk)*
alternating current	der Wechselstrom	*(duh vEHk-sel-shtrOHm)*
alternative order	die Alternativbestellung	*(dee ahl-tuh-nah-tEEf-beh-shtEL-lunk)*
alternator	der Wechselstromgenerator	*(duh vEHk-sel-shtrOHm-geh-neh-rAH-tor)*
aluminum	das Aluminium	*(dahs ah-lu-mEE-nEE-um)*
amalgamation	die Fusion	*(dee foo-zEE-ohn)*
amend (v)	abändern, ändern	*(AHB-EHn-duhn), (EHn-duhn)*
amendment	die Abänderung, die Änderung	*(dee AHB-EHn-duh-runk), (dee EHn-duh-runk)*
ammonia	das Ammoniak	*(dahs a-MOH-nee-ahk)*
amortization	die Amortisation	*(dee ah-mor-ti-zah-tsEE-ohn)*
amount	der Betrag	*(duh beh-trAHk)*
amount due	der Schuldbetrag	*(duh SHULT-beh-trAHk)*
amplifier	der Verstärker	*(duh fuh-shtEHR-kuh)*

amplitude modulation	(AM) die Amplituden-Modulation	*(dee ahm-pli-TOO-den-moh-DU-lah-TSI-ohn)*
anaesthetic	das Betäubungsmittel	*(dahs beh-tOY-bungs-mit-tel)*
analgesic	das Analgetikum	*(dahs ahn-ahl-gAY-ti-kum)*
analog computer	der Analogcomputer	*(duh ah-nah-lOg-kom-pyU-tuh)*
analysis	die Analyse	*(dee a-naa-LEW-zeh)*
analysis, breakeven	die Deckungsbeitrags-rechnung	*(dee dEHKH-unks-beye-trAAgs-rEHKH-nunk)*
analysis, competitor	die Konkurrenzstudie	*(dee kon-koor-rEHnts-shtoo-di-eh)*
analysis, cost	die Kostenanalyse	*(dee kOS-ten-ah-nah-lEW-zeh)*
analysis, cost-benefit	die Kostennutzenanalyse	*(dee kOS-ten-nU-tsen-ah-nah-lEW-zeh)*
analysis, critical path	die Analyse der Netzplantechnik	*(dee ah-nah-lEW-zeh duh nets-plAAn-tekh-nik)*
analysis, financial	die Finanzanalyse	*(dee fee-nAHnts-ah-nah-lEW-zeh)*
analysis, functional	die Funktionsanalyse	*(dee funk-tsEE-ohns-ah-nah-lEW-zeh)*
analysis, input-output	die Eingaben-Ausgaben Analyse	*(dee EYEn-gAA-ben-OWs-gAA-ben-ah-nah-lEW-zeh)*
analysis, investment	die Anlagenanalyse	*(dee AHN-lAA-gen-ah-nah-lEW-zeh)*
analysis, job	die Arbeitsplatzuntersuchung	*(deeAHR-beyets-plahts-ah-nah-lEW-zeh)*
analysis, needs	die Bedarfsanalyse	*(dee beh-dAArfs-ah-nah-lEW-zeh)*
analysis, product	die Warenanalyse	*(dee vAA-ren-ah-nah-lEW-zeh)*
analysis, profitability	die Rentabilitätsanalyse	*(dee ren-tah-bi-lee-tAYts-ah-nah-lEW-zeh)*
analysis, risk	die Risikoanalyse	*(dee REE-see-koh-ah-nah-lEW-zeh)*
analysis, sales	die Absatzanalyse	*(dee AHB-zAHts-ah-nah-lEW-zeh)*
analysis, systems	die Systemanalyse	*(dee zew-stAYm-ah-nah-lEW-zeh)*

analyst	der Analytiker	*(duhah-nah-lEW-ti-kuh)*
analytic chemistry	die analytische Chemie	*(dee a-naa-LEW-ti-sheh KHAY-mee)*
anchorage dues	die Ankergebühr	*(dee ahn-kuh-geh-bEWr)*
ancillary operation	der Nebenbetrieb	*(duh nAY-ben-beh-trEEp)*
angora	die Angorawolle	*(dee ahn-GOH-rah-vOL-leh)*
ankle boots	die Halbstiefel	*(dee hAHLb-shtEE-fel)*
annealing	das Ausglühen, die Härtung	*(dahs OWs-gLEW-en), (dee HEHR-tunk)*
annual	jährlich	*(yAYr-likh)*
annual accounts	die Jahresabrechnung	*(dee yAAr-ehs-beh-rEHKH-nunk)*
annual audit	die Jahresprüfung	*(dee yAAr-ehs-prEW-funk)*
annual report	der Jahresbericht	*(duh yAAr-ehs-beh-rIKHt)*
annuitant	der Leibrentenempfänger	*(duh lEYEb-rEHn-ten-em-pfAYng-uh)*
annuity	die Jahresrente	*(dee yAAr-ehs-rEHn-teh)*
antacid	das Antiacidum	*(dahs AHN-ti-AH-tsidum)*
anti-inflammatory	entzündungshemmend	*(ent-tsEWn-dungs-hEHM-ment)*
antibiotic	das Antibiotikum	*(dahs AHN-ti-BEE-o-ti-kum)*
anticoagulant	das Gegengerinnungsmittel	*(dahs gEH-gen-geh-rin-nungs-mit-tel)*
antidepressant	depressionshemmend	*(deh-pres-sI-ONs-hEHM-ment)*
antidumping duty	der Antidumpingzoll	*(duh ahnti-dum-ping-tsOL)*
antique authenticity certificate	die Echtheitsbescheinigung für Antiquitäten	*(dee eKHT-heyets-beh-shEYE-ni-gunk fEWr ahnti-kvee-tAY-ten)*
antiseptic	das Antiseptikum	*(dahs AHN-ti-sEHp-ti-kum)*
antitrust laws	die Kartellgesetze	*(deekahr-tEHL-geh-zEHt-seh)*
apparel	die Kleidung	*(dee klEYE-dunk)*
application form	das Antragsformular	*(dahs AHN-trahgs-for-mu-lAAr)*
applied proceeds swap	der angewandte Erlöstausch	*(duh AHN-geh-vAHnd-teh AYr-lERs-tOWsh)*

appointment (engagement)	die Verabredung	*(dee fuh-AHB-rAY-dunk)*
appointment (nomination)	die Ernennung	*(deeayr-nEHN-nunk)*
appraisal	die Bewertung	*(dee beh-vAYr-tunk)*
appraise (v)	bewerten, abschätzen	*(beh-vAYr-ten), (AHB-shEH-tsen)*
appreciation	die Wertsteigerung	*(dee vEHRt-shtEYE-guh-runk)*
apprentice	der Lehrling	*(duh lAYr-ling)*
appropriation	der Bereitstellungfonds	*(duh beh-rEYEt-shtEHL-lunk-fOH)*
approval	die Bewilligung	*(dee beh-vIL-ee-gunk)*
approve (v)	billigen	*(BIL-li-gen)*
approved securities	die genehmigten Wertpapiere	*(dee geh-nAY-mig-tehn vEHRt-pah-pEEr-eh)*
arbitrage	die Arbitrage	*(deeahr-bi-trAAsh)*
arbitration	das Schiedsverfahren	*(dahs shEEds-fuh-fAA-ren)*
arbitration agreement	das Schiedsabkommen	*(dahs shEEds-AHB-kOM-men)*
arbitrator	der Schiedsrichter	*(duh shEEds-rIKH-tuh)*
area manager	der Gebietsleiter	*(duh geh-bEETs-lEYE-tuh)*
arithmetic mean	das arithmetische Mittel	*(dahs ah-rIT-meh-ti-shehs-mit-tEL)*
armaments	die Rüstung	*(dee REWs-tunk)*
arrears	die Rückstände	*(dee rEWk-shtEHn-deh)*
art	die Kunst	*(dee kUNst)*
as is goods	die Waren ohne Gewähr	*(dee vAA-ren ohneh geh-vAYr)*
as per advice	laut Bericht	*(lowt beh-rIKHt)*
as soon as possible	so schnell wie möglich	*(zoh shnehl vEE mER-glikh)*
asked price	der Briefkurs	*(duh brEEf-koors)*
assay	die Feinheitgehaltsbestim-mung	*(dee feyen-heyet-geh-hAHlts-beh-shtIM-munk)*
assay (v)	prüfen	*(prEW-fen)*
assemble (v) (people)	versammeln	*(fuh-zAHm-meln)*

assemble (v) (things)	zustammenstellen	*(tsOO-zAH-men-shtEL-len)*
assembly	die Versammlung	*(dee fuh-zAHm-lunk)*
assembly line	das Fließband	*(dahs flEES-bahnt)*
assess (v)	bewerten	*(beh-vAYr-ten)*
assessed valuation	die steuerliche Veranlagung	*(dee shtOY-uh-likh-eh fayr-AHn-lAA-gunk)*
assessment	die Veranlagung	*(dee fayr-AHn-lAA-gunk)*
asset	das Vermögensstuck	*(dahs fuh-mER-gens-shtEWk)*
asset turnover	der Vermögensumsatz	*(duh fuh-mER-gens-um-zAHts)*
asset value	der Vermögenswert	*(duh fuh-mER-gens-vEHRt)*
assets, accrued	die antizipativen Aktiva	*(dee ahnti-tsi-pah-tEE-ven ahk-tEE-vah)*
assets, current	das kurzfristige Umlaufvermögen	*(dahs kURts-frist-tikh-eh Um-lOWf-fuh-mER-gen)*
assets, fixed	die Sachanlagen	*(dee zahkh-AHN-lAA-gen)*
assets, intangible	die immateriellen Werte	*(dee im-mAA-tayr-ee-EL-leh vAYr-teh)*
assets, liquid	das Umlaufvermögen	*(dee Um-lOWf-fuh-mER-gen)*
assets, net	das Reinvermögen	*(dee REYEN-fuh-mER-gen)*
assets, tangible	das Sachanlagevermögen	*(dahs zahkh-AHN-lAA-geh-fuh-mER-gen)*
assign (v)	übertragen, zuweisen	*(EW-buh-trAA-gen), (tsOO-vEYE-sen)*
assignee	der Übernehmer	*(duh EW-buh-nAY-muh)*
assignor	der Abtretende	*(duh AHB-trAY-ten-deh)*
assistant	der Assistent	*(duh as-sis-tENt)*
assistant general manager	der stellvertretende Generaldirektor	*(duh shtEHL-fuh-trAY-ten-duh gehn-eh-rAAl-di-rEHK-tohr)*
assistant manager	der stellvertretende Geschäftsführer	*(duh shtEHL-fuh-trAY-ten-duh geh-shEHfts-fEW-ruh)*
associate company	die Tochtergesellschaft	*(dee tOKH-tuh-geh-zEL-shahft)*
assumed liability	die übernommene Verpflichtung	*(dee EW-buh-nom-meh-neh fuh-pflIKH-tunk)*

astrakan	der Astrachan	*(duh ahs-trah-khAHN)*
at and from	zu und von	*(tsoo unt fon)*
at best	bestens	*(beh-stens)*
at or better	zum Bestkauf	*(tsum bEHst-kowf)*
at par	zu pari	*(tsoo pah-rEE)*
at sight	bei Sicht	*(beye sIKHt)*
at the close	bei Börsenschluß	*(beye bER-zen-shlUs)*
at the market	zum Marktpreis	*(tsum mAHrkt-prEYEs)*
at the opening	bei Börsenöffnung	*(beye bER-zen-EWf-nunk)*
atom	das Atom	*(dahs a-TOHm)*
atomic	atomar	*(a-toh-MAAr)*
attach (v) (affix, adhere)	anhängen	*(AHN-hehn-gen)*
attach (v) (seize)	beschlagnahmen	*(beh-shlAHg-nAA-meh)*
attaché case	die Aktentasche	*(dee AHk-ten-tAH-SHeh)*
attachment (contract)	das Anhängsel	*(dahs AHN-hehn-gsel)*
attended time	die Wartezeit	*(dee vAAr-teh-tsEYEt)*
attestation	die Bescheinigung	*(dee beh-shEYE-ni-gunk)*
attorney	der Anwalt	*(duh AHN-vahlt)*
attorney, power of	die Vollmacht	*(die FOL-makht)*
attrition	die Abnutzung	*(dee AHB-nU-tsunk)*
audit (v)	prüfen	*(prEW-fen)*
audit trail	der Prüfungsweg	*(duh prEW-funks-vAYk)*
audit, internal	die innerbetriebliche Revision	*(dee IN-nuh-beh-trEEp-likh-eh rAY-vEE-zee-ohn)*
auditing balance sheet	die Bilanzprüfung	*(dee bee-lAHnts-prEW-funk)*
auditor	der Buchprüfer	*(duh bOOkh-prEW-fuh)*
autarchy	die Autarkie	*(dee ow-tAAR-kee)*
authority, to have (v)	berechtigt sein	*(beh-rehkh-tIGT seyen)*
authorize (v)	ermächtigen	*(ayr-mAYkh-ti-gehn)*
authorized dealer	der bevollmächtigte Händler	*(duh beh-fol-mAYKH-tig-teh hEHnd-luh)*

A

authorized shares	die genehmigten Aktien	*(dee geh-nAY-mig-teh ak-tsEE-en)*
authorized signature	die autorisierte Unterschrift	*(dee OW-toh-ree-seer-tuh un-tuh-shrift)*
automatic	automatisch	*(OW-toh-mAA-tish)*
automatic gearshift	die Schaltautomatik	*(dee shAHLt-OW-to-mah-tik)*
automation	die Automation	*(dee OW-toh-maa-tsEE-ohn)*
automobile	das Auto	*(dahs OW-to)*
autonomous	selbständig	*(zehlbst-shtEHn-dikh)*
availability, subject to	vorbehaltlich der Verfügbarkeit	*(FOHR-beh-hahlt-likh duh fuh-fEWg-bAAr-keyet)*
average	der Durchschnitt	*(duh dURKH-shnIT)*
average cost	die Durchschnittskosten	*(dee dURKH-shnITs-kOS-ten)*
average life	die durchschnittliche Lebensdauer	*(dee dURKH-shnIT-likh-eh lAY-benz-dOW-uh)*
average price	der Durchschnittspreis	*(duh dURKH-shnITs-prEYEs)*
average unit cost	die durchschnittlichen Einheitskosten	*(dee dURKH-shnIT-likh-en EYEn-heyets-kOS-ten)*

B

back date (v)	zurückdatieren	*(tsOO-rEWk-dah-tEE-ren)*
back order	der noch nicht erledigte Auftrag	*(deh nOHKH nIKHt AYr-lAY-dig-tuh OWf-trAHk)*
back pay	der Lohnrückstand	*(duh LOHN-rEWk-shtAHnd)*
back selling	das Rückverkaufen	*(dahs rEWk-fuh-kOW-fen)*
back taxes	die Steuerrückstände	*(dee shtOY-uh-rEWk-shtAYn-deh)*
back-to-back credit	das Gegenakkreditiv	*(dahs gAY-gen-ah-kray-di-tEEf)*
back-to-back loan	die völlig gedeckte Anleihe	*(dee fER-likh geh-dEHK-teh AHN-leye-eh)*
backlog	der Rückstand	*(deh rEWk-shAHnt)*
backup bonds	die Pfandbriefe	*(dee pfAHnd-brEE-feh)*
backwardation	der Deport	*(duh day-pOHrt)*

bad debt	die uneinbringliche Forderung	*(dee un-eyen-brING-likh-eh FOHR-deh-run-gen)*
balance	die Bilanz	*(dee bee-lAHnts)*
balance, bank	das Bankguthaben	*(dahs BAHNK-gOOT-hAA-ben)*
balance, credit	der Kreditsaldo	*(duh kray-dIT-zAAl-doh)*
balance of payments	die Zahlungsbilanz	*(dee tsAA-lungs-bee-lAHnts)*
balance of trade	die Handelsbilanz	*(dee hAHN-dehls-bee-lAHnts)*
balance sheet	die Bilanz	*(dee bee-lAHnts)*
balanced budget	der ausgeglichene Haushalt	*(duh OWs-geh-glIkh-eneh hOWs-haalt)*
bale capacity	die Ballenkapazität	*(dee BAAL-en-kaa-pah-tsEE-tayt)*
bale cargo	die Ballenladung	*(dee BAAL-en-lAA-dunk)*
ballast bonus	der Ballastbonus	*(duh bahl-LAAst-boh-noos)*
balloon payment (loan repayment)	die größte Zahlung	*(dee grER-steh tsAA-lung)*
bank	die Bank	*(dee BAHNK)*
bank acceptance	das Bankakzept	*(dahs BAHNK-ahk-tsEPt)*
bank account	das Bankkonto	*(dahs BAHNK-kON-toh)*
bank balance	das Bankguthaben	*(dahs BAHNK-gOOt-hAA-ben*
bank charges	die Bankgebühren	*(dee BAHNK-geh-bEW-ren)*
bank check	der Bankscheck	*(duh BAHNK-shek)*
bank deposit	die Bankeinlage	*(dee BAHNK-eyen-lAA-geh)*
bank draft	die Banktratte, der Wechsel	*(dee BAHNK-trAH-teh), (duh vEHk-sehl)*
bank examiner	der Bankrevisor	*(duh BAHNK-rAY-vee-zohr)*
bank exchange	der Bankwechsel	*(duh BAHNK-vEHk-sehl)*
bank holiday	der Bankfeiertag	*(duh BAHNK-fEYE-uh-tAAk)*
bank letter of credit	das Bankakkreditiv	*(dahs BAHNK-ah-kray-di-tEEf)*
bank loan	das Bankdarlehen	*(dahs BAHNK-daar-lAY-en)*
bank money order	die Bankgeldanweisung	*(dee BAHNK-gehlt-ahn-vEYE-zung)*

B

bank note	die Banknote	*(dee BAHNK-nOH-teh)*
bank rate	der Bankzins	*(duh BAHNK-tsINs)*
bank release	die Bankfreigabe	*(dee BAHNK-frEYE-gAA-beh)*
bank statement	der Kontoauszug	*(duh kon-tOH-OWs-tsOOg)*
bankbook	das Bankbuch	*(dahs BAHNK-bOOkh)*
bankruptcy	der Bankrott	*(duh BAHNK-rOT)*
bar chart	das Saülendiagramm	*(duh zOY-lehn-dee-ah-grAHm)*
bareboat charter	der Bootsverleih ohne Mannschaft und Verpflegung	*(duh bohts-fAYr-leye ohneh mAAn-shahft unt fuh-pflAY-gunk)*
bargain	der Gelegenheitskauf	*(duh geh-lAY-gen-heyets-kOWf)*
bargaining power	die Verhandlungsstärke	*(dee fuh-hAHnd-lunks-shtEHr-keh)*
barratry	die vorsätzliche Ladungsbeschädigung, die Anstifung zum Prozessieren	*(dee FOHR-zehts-lIKH-eh lAA-dunks-beh-shEH-di-gunk), (deeAHN-shtIF-tunk tsoom pro-tses-sEE-ren)*
bars	die Stangen	*(dee shtAHN-gen)*
barter	der Tauschhandel	*(duh tOWsh-hAHn-dehl)*
barter (v)	tauschen	*(tOW-shen)*
base	die Base	*(dee BAA-zeh)*
base currency	die Grundwährung	*(dee grUNd-vAY-runk)*
base price	der Grundpreis	*(duh grUNd-prEYEs)*
base rate	der Grundtarif	*(duh grUNd-taa-rIF)*
base year	das Basisjahr	*(dahs BAA-zis-yAAr)*
basis point	der Basispunkt	*(duh BAA-zis-pUnkt)*
batch processing	die Schubverarbeitung	*(dee SHUb-fuh-ahr-bEYE-tunk)*
batch production	die Serienproduktion	*(dee ZAY-ree-ehn-proh-duk-tsEE-ohn)*
batten fitted	mit Latten versehen	*(mit-lAHt-tehn fAYr-zeh-en)*
baud	das Baud	*(dahs bowd)*
beam	die Strahlung	*(dee shtRAA-lunk)*
bear (v)	tragen	*(trAA-gen)*

bear market	die Baissebörse	*(dee bayss-eh-bER-zeh)*
bearer	der Inhaber	*(duh IN-hah-buh)*
bearer bond	die Inhaberobligation	*(dee IN-hah-buh-ob-li-gah-tsEE-ohn)*
bearer security	das Inhaberpapier	*(dahs IN-hah-buh-pah-pEEr)*
beaver	der Biber	*(duh bEE-buh)*
bell-shaped curve	die Glockenkurve	*(dee glok-en-kOOr-veh)*
below par	unter pari	*(un-tuh pah-rEE)*
below the line	unter dem Strich	*(un-tuh daym shtrIKH)*
belt	der Gürtel	*(duh gEWR-tel)*
beneficiary	der Begünstigte	*(duh beh-gEWns-tig-tuh)*
benzene	das Benzol	*(dahs BEHN-tsol)*
bequest	das Vermächtnis	*(dahs fuh-mEHkht-nis)*
berth terms	die Stückgutfracht	*(dee shtEWk-gOOt-frahkht)*
bid and asked	Brief und Geld	*(breef unt gehlt)*
bid price	der Geldkurs	*(duh gehlt-koors)*
bid, takeover	das Übernahmeangebot	*(dahs EW-buh-nAA-meh-AHN-geh-boht)*
bill (currency)	die Banknote, der Geldschein	*(dee BAHNK-nOH-teh), (duh gehlt-shEYEn)*
bill (invoice)	die Rechnung	*(dee rEHKH-nunk)*
bill broker	der Wechselmakler	*(duh vEHk-sehl-mAHk-luh)*
bill of exchange	der Wechsel	*(duh vEHk-sehl)*
bill of lading	der Frachtbrief	*(duh frAHKHt-brEEf)*
bill of sale	die Verkaufsurkunde	*(dee fuh-kOWfs-OOr-kun-deh)*
bill of sight	der Sichtwechsel	*(duh zikht-vEHk-sehl)*
billboard	die Anschlagetafel	*(dee AHN-shlaa-geh-tAA-fel)*
billets	die Barren	*(dee bAHR-ren)*
billfold	die Brieftasche	*(dee brEEF-tAH-SHeh)*
binary code	der Binärkode	*(duh bee-nAYR-koh-deh)*
binary notation	die binäre Zahlendarstellung	*(dee bee-nAY-reh tsAAl-en-dAAr-shtEL-lunk)*
binder	der Vorvertrag	*(duh FOHR-fuh-trAHk)*

B

biochemistry	die Biochemie	*(dee BEE-o-KHAY-mee)*
biological deacidizing	die biologische Entsäuerung	*(dee bee-oh-LOHG-ish-eh ent-ZOY-eh-runk)*
biologist	der Biologe	*(duh BEE-o-LOH-geh)*
biology	die Biologie	*(dee bee-o-LOH-gee)*
black and white	schwarzweiß	*(shvarts-vEYES)*
black market	der Schwarzmarkt	*(duh shvAArts-mAHrkt)*
blanket insurance	die Kollektivversicherung	*(dee koh-lehk-tEEf-fuh-zIkheh-runk)*
blanket order	der Blankoauftrag	*(duh blAHn-koh-OWf-trAHk)*
blast furnace	der Hochofen	*(duh hOHKH-ohfen)*
bleed	über den Rand gedruckt	*(EWbuh den rAHNt geh-drUKt)*
bleed (v)	bluten	*(blOO-ten)*
blend (v)	verschneiden	*(fuh-shnEYE-den)*
blockage of funds	die Geldsperre	*(dee gehlt-shpEH-reh)*
blocked currency	die nicht frei konvertierbare Währung	*(dee nIKHt frEYE kon-fayr-tEEr-baa-reh vAY-runk)*
blood	das Blut	*(dahs blOOT)*
blotter	der (Tinten) Löscher	*(duh [TIN-Ten] lERSH-uh)*
blowup	die Vergrößerung	*(dee fuh-gRER-seh-runk)*
blue-chip stock	das erstklassige Wertpapier	*(dahs ayrst-klAHS-si-gehs vEHRt-pah-pEEr)*
blue-collar worker	der Fabrikarbeiter	*(duh fah-brEEk-ahr-bEYE-tuh)*
blueprint	die Blaupause	*(dee blOW-pOW-zeh)*
board, executive	der Vorstand	*(duh FOHR-shtAHnt)*
board meeting	die Vorstandssitzung	*(dee FOHR-shtAHnts-zI-tsunk)*
board of directors	der Vorstand	*(duh FOHR-shtAHnt)*
board of supervisors	der Aufsichtsrat	*(duh OWf-zikhts-raat)*
boardroom	der Sitzungsraum	*(duh ZIts-unks-rOWm)*
body	der Körper	*(duh KER-puh)*
boldface	der Fettdruck	*(duh fET-drUK)*
bond	die Obligation	*(dee ob-li-gah-tsEE-ohn)*

bond issue	die Anleiheemission	*(dee AHN-lEYE-eh-eh-mi-see-OHn)*
bond power	die Schuldverschreibungs-vollmacht	*(dee SHULT-fuh-shrEYE-bunks-fOL-makht)*
bond rating	die Anleihebewertung	*(dee AHN-lEYE-eh-beh-vAYr-tunk)*
bonded carrier	der versicherte Bote	*(deh fuh-zIkheh-teh bOH-teh)*
bonded goods	die zollpflichtigen Waren	*(dee tsOL-pflIKH-ti-gen vAA-ren)*
bonded warehouse	das Zollagerhaus	*(dahs tsOl-lAA-guh-hOWs)*
bone china	das feine Porzellan	*(dahs fEYE-neh por-TSEl-lahn)*
bonus (premium)	die Prämie	*(dee prAY-mee-eh)*
book	das Buch	*(dahs bOOKH)*
book inventory	das Buchinventar	*(dahs bOOkh-in-vehn-tAAr)*
book value	der Buchwert	*(dahs bOOkh-vAYrt)*
book value per share	der Buchwert pro Aktie	*(duh bOOkh-vAYrt proh ak-tsEE-eh)*
bookkeeping	die Buchhaltung	*(dee bOOkh-hAAl-tunk)*
boom	die Hochkonjunktur	*(dee hOHkh-kon-yunk-tOOr)*
boot shop	der Stiefelladen	*(duh shtEE-fel-laa-den)*
bootmaker	der Stiefelmacher	*(duh shtEE-fel-mahkh-uh)*
boots	die Stiefel	*(dee shtEE-fel)*
border	die Grenze	*(dee grEHn-tseh)*
border tax adjustment	die Grenzsteuerberichtigung	*(dee grEHnts-shtOY-uh-beh-rIKH-ti-gunk)*
borrow (v)	borgen	*(bohr-gen)*
botanic	botanisch	*(bo-tAA-nish)*
bottle	die Flasche	*(dee flAH-sheh)*
bouquet	das Bukett	*(dahs bU-ket)*
bow tie	die Fliege	*(dee fLEE-geh)*
bowl	die Schale	*(dee SHAA-leh)*
boycott	der Boykott	*(dahs boy-KOT)*
brake	die Bremse	*(dee brEHM-zeh)*
brake pedal	das Bremspedal	*(dahs brEHMs-PEH-dahl)*
branch office	die Filiale	*(dee fi-lee-AA-leh)*

B

brand acceptance	die Annahme als Markenartikel	*(dee AHN-nAA-neh ahls mAHr-ken-ahr-ti-kel)*
brand	die Marke	*(dee mAHr-keh)*
brand image	das Markenimage	*(dahs mAHr-ken-EE-mah-djeh)*
brand loyalty	die Markentreue	*(dee mAHr-ken-trOY-eh)*
brand recognition	die Markenanerkennung	*(dee mAHr-ken-ahn-ayr-kEHn-unk)*
breadbasket	der Brotkorb	*(duh brOT-korb)*
break even (v)	die Gewinnschwelle erreichen	*(dee geh-vIN-shvEL-leh ayr-rEYE-khen)*
break-even point	die Gewinnschwelle	*(dee geh-vIN-shvEL-leh)*
breakeven analysis	die Deckungsbeitragsrechnung	*(dee dEH-kunks-beye-trAHks-rEHKH-nunk)*
briefcase	die Aktenmappe	*(dee ahk-tEN-mAHP-peh)*
broadcast (v)	senden, ausstrahlen	*(zEN-den), (OWs-shtrAA-len)*
broken stowage	die Staulücken	*(dee shtOW-lEW-ken)*
broker	der Makler	*(duh mAHk-luh)*
budget appropriation	die Haushaltsmittelbereitstellung	*(dee hOWs-hahlts-mit-tEL-beh-rEYEt-shtEL-lunk)*
budget	das Budget	*(dahs bew-djEH)*
budget, advertising	das Werbebudget	*(dahs vAYr-beh-bew-djEH)*
budget, balanced	der ausgeglichene Haushalt	*(duh OWs-geh-glIKH-eh-neh hOWs-hahlt)*
budget, capital	das Investitionsbudget	*(dahs in-vehs-ti-tsi-OHnz-bew-djEH)*
budget, cash	der Kassenvoranschlag	*(duh kAH-sehn-FOHR-ahn-shlAHk)*
budget forecast	der Haushaltsvoranschlag	*(duh hOWs-hahlts-FOHR-ahn-shlAHk)*
budget, investment	das Investitionsbudget	*(dahs in-vehs-ti-tsi-OHnz-bew-djEH)*
budget, marketing	das Absatzbudget	*(dahs AHB-zAHTS-bew-djEH)*
budget, sales	der Absatzplan	*(duh AHB-zAHTS-plAAn)*
bug (computers)	der Fehler	*(duh fAY-luh)*

bull	der Haussespekulant	*(duh hOWs-seh-shpEHk-OO-lahnt)*
bull market	die Haussebörse	*(dee hOWs-seh-bER-zeh)*
bumper	die Stoßstange	*(dee shtOS-shtAHN-geh)*
burden rate	der Gemeinkostensatz	*(duh geh-mEYEn-kOS-ten-zahts)*
bureaucrat	der Bürokrat	*(duh bEW-roh-krAAt)*
business activity	die Geschäftstatigkeit	*(dee geh-shEHfts-tAY-tig-keyet)*
business card	die Geschäftskarte	*(dee geh-shEHfts-kAAr-teh)*
business cycle	der Konjunkturzyklus	*(duh kon-yunk-tOOr-tsEW-klus)*
business management	die Betriebsleitung	*(dee beh-trEEps-lEYE-tunk)*
business plan	der Geschäftsplan	*(duh geh-shEHfts-plAAn)*
business policy	die Betriebspolitik	*(dee beh-trEEps-po-li-tEEk)*
business strategy	die Geschäftsstrategie	*(dee geh-shEHfts-straa-teh-gEE)*
butter dish	die Butterdose	*(dee BUTuh-do-zeh)*
button	der Knopf	*(duh knOpf)*
buttonhole	das Knopfloch	*(dahs knOpf-lOKH)*
buy at best (v)	bestens kaufen	*(beh-stehns kOW-fen)*
buy back (v)	zurückkaufen	*(tsOO-rEWk-kOW-fen)*
buy on close (v)	bei Börsenschluß kaufen	*(beye bER-zen-shlUS kOW-fen)*
buy on opening (v)	bei Börsenöffnung kaufen	*(beye bER-zen-ERf-nunk kOW-frn)*
buyer	der Käufer	*(duh kOY-fuh)*
buyer's market	der Käufermarkt	*(duh kOY-fuh-mAHrkt)*
buyer's option	die Käuferoption	*(dee kOY-fuh-op-tsEE-ohn)*
buyer's premium	das Käuferaufgeld	*(dahs kOY-fuh-OWf-gehlt)*
buyer's responsibility	die Verantwortung des Käufers	*(dee fuh-AHNt-vOHr-tunk dehs kOY-fuhs)*
buyout (takeover)	die Übernahme	*(dee EW-buh-nAA-meh)*
by-laws	die Vorschriften	*(dee FOHR-shrIF-ten)*
by-product	das Nebenprodukt	*(dahs nAY-ben-proh-dUKt)*
byte	das Byte	*(dahs beyet)*

C

cable	das Kabel	*(dahs kAA-behl)*
cable television	das Kabelfernsehen	*(dahs KAA-bel-fehrn-zay-hen)*
cable transfer	die telegraphische Überweisung	*(dee tay-leh-grAA-fish-eh EW-buh-vEYE-zunk)*
calculator	der Rechner	*(duh rEHKH-nuh)*
calfskin	das Kalbsleder	*(dahs kAHLbs-lAY-duh)*
call (v)	anrufen	*(AHN-ROO-fen)*
call back (v)	abrufen	*(AHB-ROO-fen)*
call feature	die Kündigungsklausel	*(dee kEWn-di-gunks-klOW-sehl)*
call loan	der vorzeitig kündbare Kredit	*(duh FOHR-tsEYE-tik kEWnd-bAA-reh kray-dIT)*
call money	das täglich kündbare Geld	*(dahs tEHg-likh kEWnd-bAA-reh gehlt)*
call option	die Bezugsoption	*(dee beh-tsOOgs-op-tsEE-OHn)*
call price	der Kündigungspreis	*(duh kEWn-di-gunks-prEYEs)*
call protection	der Kündigungsschutz	*(duh kEWn-di-gunks-shUts)*
call rate	der Kündigungstarif	*(duh kEWn-di-gunks-taa-rIF)*
call rule	die Kündigungsregel	*(dee kEWn-di-gunks-rAY-gel)*
camel's hair	das Kamelhaar	*(dahs kah-mAYL-HAAr)*
campaign, advertising	die Werbekampagne	*(dee vAYr-beh-kahm-pAHn-yeh)*
camshaft	die Nockenwelle	*(dee nOK-ken-vEL-leh)*
cancel (v)	abbestellen	*(ABH-beh-stEL-en)*
cancelled check	der eingelöste Scheck	*(duh EYEn-geh-lERs-teh shehk)*
candlestick	der Kerzenständer	*(duh kuh-tsen-shTEHN-duh)*
capacity	die Kapazität	*(dee kah-pah-tsee-tAYt)*
capacity, manufacturing	die Produktionskapazität	*(dee proh-dUK-tsee-ohns-kah-pah-tsee-tAYt)*

capacity, plant	die betriebliche Leitsungsfähigkeit	*(dee beh-trEEp-likh-eh lEYE-stunks-fAY-hig-keyet)*
capacity utilization	die Kapazitätsausnutzung	*(dee kah-pah-tsee-tAYt-OWs-nU-tsunk)*
cape	der Umhang	*(duh UM-hahnk)*
capital	das Kapital	*(dahs kah-pi-tAAL)*
capital account	das Kapitalkonto	*(dahs kah-pi-tAAL-kON-toh)*
capital asset	das Anlagevermögen	*(dahs AHN-lAA-geh-fuh-mER-gen)*
capital budget	das Investitionsbudget	*(dahs in-vehs-ti-tsi-OHnz-bew-djEH)*
capital expenditure	der Kapitalaufwand	*(duh kah-pi-tAAL-OWf-vahnt)*
capital exports	die Kapitalausfuhr	*(dee kah-pi-tAAL-OWs-foor)*
capital gain (loss)	der Kapitalertrag, der Kapitalverlust	*(duh kah-pi-tAAL-uh-trAHk), (duh kah-pi-tAAL-fuh-lUst)*
capital goods	die Anlagewerte	*(dee AHN-lAA-geh-vAYr-teh)*
capital increase	die Kapitalerhöhung	*(dee kah-pi-tAAL-uh-hER-unk)*
capital market	der Kapitalmarkt	*(duh kah-pi-tAAL-mAHrkt*
capital spending	die Kapitalaufwendungen	*(dee kah-pi-tAAL-OWf-vehn-dOOng-ehn)*
capital stock	die Stammaktie	*(dee shtAHm-ak-tsEE-eh)*
capital structure	die Kapitalstruktur	*(dee kah-pi-tAAL-strook-tOOr)*
capital surplus	der Kapitalüberschub	*(duh kah-pi-tAAL-EW-buh-shUs)*
capital, raising	die Kapitalaufnahme	*(dee kah-pi-tAAL-Owf-nAA-meh)*
capital, return on	die Kapitalrendite	*(dee kah-pi-tAAL-ren-di-teh)*
capital, risk	das Risikokapital	*(dahs REE-see-koh-kah-pi-tAAL)*
capital, working	das Betriebskapital	*(dahs beh-trEEps-kah-pi-tAAL)*
capital-intensive	kapitalintensiv	*(kah-pi-tAAL-in-ten-sEEv)*
capital-output ratio	der Kapitalkoeffizient	*(duh kah-pi-tAAL-ko-ayf-fEE-tsEE-ehnt)*

C

capitalism	der Kapitalismus	*(duh kah-pi-tAAL-lis-mus)*
capitalization	die Kapitalisierung	*(dee kah-pi-tAAL-EE-zEE-runk)*
capsule	die Kapsel	*(dee kAP-sel)*
car	das Auto	*(dahs OW-to)*
carbon	der Kohlenstoff	*(duh KOH-len-shtOF)*
carbon steel	der Kohlenstoffstahl	*(duh KOH-len-shtOF-shtAAL)*
carburetor	der Vergaser	*(duh fuh-gAA-suh)*
card case	das Visitenkartentäschchen	*(dahs vi-zEE-ten-kahr-ten-tEHSH-khen)*
cargo	die Ladung	*(dee lAA-dunk)*
carload	die Wagenladung	*(dee vAA-gen-lAA-dunk)*
carnet	das Zollpapier fur vorüber-gehende zollfreie Einfuhr	*(dahs tsOL-pah-pEE-fEWr-FOHR-EW-buh-gAY-hehn-deh tsOL-frEYE-eh EYEn-fOOr)*
carrier	der Spediteur	*(duh shpeh-dee-tEWr)*
carrier's risk	die Transporthaftung	*(dee trahns-pOHrt-hAHf-tunk)*
carry back (v)	zurückbringen	*(tsOO-rEWk-brING-en)*
carry forward (v)	übertragen	*(EW-buh-trAA-gen)*
carrying charges	die Betriebskosten	*(dee beh-trEEps-kOS-ten)*
carrying value	der Buchwert	*(uh bOOkh-vAYrt)*
carryover	der Verlustvortrag	*(duh fAYr-lUst-FOHR-trAHk)*
cartel	das Kartell	*(dahs kahr-tEHl)*
carving knife	das Tranchiermesser	*(dahs trahn-shEER-MEHS-suh)*
case	die Kiste	*(dee kIS-teh)*
cash	das Bargeld	*(dahs BAHR-gehlt)*
cash balance	der Geldbestand	*(duh GEHLT-beh-shtAHnt)*
cash before delivery	die Barzahlung im voraus	*(dee BAHR-tsAA-lung im FOHR-ows)*
cash book	das Kassabuch	*(dahs kAH-sah-bOOkh)*
cash budget	der Kassenvoranschlag	*(duh kAH-sehn-FOHR-ahn-shlAHk)*

cash delivery	die Bargeldzustellung	*(dee BAHR-gehlt-tsOO-shtEL-lunk)*
cash discount	das Kassaskonto	*(duh kAH-sah-kON-toh)*
cash dividend	die Bardividende	*(dee BAHR-dee-vee-dEHN-deh)*
cash entry	der Kasseneintrag	*(duh kAH-sehn-eyen-trAHk)*
cash flow	der Finanzfluß	*(duh fee-nAHnts-flus)*
cash flow statement	die Kapitalflußrechnung	*(dee kah-pi-tAAL-flus-rEHKH-nunk)*
cash in advance	die Vorausbezahlung	*(dee FOHR-OWs-beh-tsAA-lung)*
cash management	die Kassenhaltung	*(dee kAH-sehn-hAHl-tunk)*
cash on delivery	die Zahlung bei Lieferung	*(dee tsAA-lung beye lEE-feh-runk)*
cash surrender value	der Rückkaufswert	*(duh rEWk-kOWfs-vEHrt)*
cash-and-carry	der Verkauf gegen Barzahlung und Selbstabholung	*(duh fuh-kOWf gAY-gen bAAr-tsAA-lung unt zehlbst-AHB-hOH-lunk)*
cash-basis accounting	die Buchführung der bar durchgeführten Geschäfte	*(dee bOOkh-fEW-runk- duh bahr dURKH-geh-fEWr-ten-geh-shEHf-teh)*
cashier's check	der Bankscheck	*(duh BAHNK-shehk)*
cashmere	die Kaschmirwolle	*(dee kah-shmEER-vOL-leh)*
cask (225 litres)	das Faß	*(dahs fAHS)*
cassette	die Kassette	*(dee kah-SEH-teh)*
cast iron	das Gußeisen	*(dahs gUS-EYE-zen)*
casualty insurance	die Unfallversicherung	*(dee un-fAHL-fuh-zIkheh-runk)*
catalog	der Katalog	*(duh kah-tah-lOHg)*
catalyst	der Katalysator	*(duh kah-tah-LEW-zah-tohr)*
catalytic converter	der Katalysator	*(duh Kah-tah-LEW-zah-tohr)*
cathode	die Kathode	*(dee kah-TOH-deh)*
ceiling	die Höchstgrenze	*(dee hERkhst-greEHn-tseh)*
centiliter	der Zentiliter	*(duh tsen-ti-LEE-tuh)*
central bank	die Zentralbank	*(dee tsEHn-trAAl-bahnk)*
central processing unit	die Zentralrecheneinheit	*(dee tsEHn-trAAl-rEHKH-en-EYEn-heyet)*

C

central rate	der Leitkurs	*(duh lEYEt-koors)*
centralization	die Zentralisierung	*(dee tsEHn-trAA-li-zEE-runk)*
certificate	die Bescheinigung	*(dee beh-shEYE-ni-gunk)*
certificate of deposit	das Depositenzertifikat	*(dahs deh-poh-zIT-ehn-tsEHR-ti-fi-kaat)*
certificate of incorporation	die Gründungsurkunde	*(dee grEWn-dunks-OOr-kun-deh)*
certificate of origin	das Ursprungszeugnis	*(dahs OOr-shprUnks-tsOYg-nis)*
certified check	der bestätigte Scheck	*(duh beh-shtAY-tikh-teh shek)*
certified public accountant	der Wirtschaftsprüfer	*(duh vEErt-shahfts-preEW-fuh)*
chain of command	die Befehlskette	*(dee beh-FAYLs-keh-teh)*
chain store	das Filialgeschäft	*(dahs fi-lee-AAl-geh-shEHft)*
chain store group	das Zweigstellenunternehmen	*(dahs tsvEYEg-shtEHL-len-un-tuh-nAY-men)*
chairman of the board	der Vorstandsvorsitzender	*(duh FOHR-shtahnts-fohr-zIT-tsen-duh)*
chamber of commerce	die Handelskammer	*(dee hAHn-dehls-kAM-muh)*
champagne glass	das Champagnerglas	*(dahs shahm-pAHN-yuh-glAAs)*
channel	der Kanal	*(duh kah-nAAL)*
channel of distribution	der Absatzweg	*(duh AHB-zAHts-vAYg)*
chapter	das Kapitel	*(dahs kah-PI-tel)*
character	der Charakter	*(duh kah-rAHK-tuh)*
charge account	das Kreditkonto	*(dahs kray-dIT-kON-toh)*
charge off (v)	abbuchen	*(AHB-bOOkh-en)*
charges	die Spesen	*(dee shpAY-zen)*
chart, bar	das Säulendiagramm	*(dahs zOY-lehn-dee-ah-grAHm)*
chart, flow	das Schaubild	*(dahs shOW-bild)*
chart, management	die Geschäftsleitungstabelle	*(dee geh-shEHfts-lEYE-tunks-tAA-behl-leh)*

charter (mercantile lease)	die Befrachtung	*(dee beh-frAHKH-tunk)*
charter (written instrument)	das Statut	*(dahs shtah-tOOt)*
chartered accountant	der Wirtschaftsprüfer	*(duh vEErt-shahfts-preEW-fuh)*
charterparty agent	der Frachtvertragsagent	*(duh frAHKHt-fuh-trAHks-ah-gEHnt)*
chassis	das Fahrgestell	*(dahs fAAR-geh-shtel)*
chattel	die Fahrnis	*(dee fAAr-nis)*
chattel mortgage	die Mobiliarhypothek	*(dee moh-bi-lee-AAr-hew-poh-tAYk)*
cheap	billig	*(BIL-ikh)*
check	der Scheck	*(duh shehk)*
check in (v)	sich anmelden	*(zikh AHN-mel-den)*
checking account	das Scheckkonto	*(dahs shEHk-kON-toh)*
checklist	die Kontrolliste	*(dee kon-trohl-lIS-teh)*
cheese-tray	das Käsebrett	*(dahs KAY-zeh-breht)*
chemical	chemisch	*(KHAY-mish)*
chemistry	die Chemie	*(dee KHAY-mee)*
chief accountant	der Buchhaltungsleiter	*(duh bOOkh-hAHl-tunks-lEYE-tuh)*
chief buyer	der Haupteinkäufer	*(duh hOWpt-eyen-kOY-fuh)*
chief executive	der Vorstandsvorsitzender	*(duh FOHR-shtAHnts-fohr-zI-tsen-duh)*
china	das Porzellan	*(dahs por-TSEl-lahn)*
chinaware	die Porzellanwaren	*(dee por-TSEl-lahn-VAAren)*
chip	der Mikrochip	*(duh mEE-kroh-ship)*
chloride	das Chlorid	*(dahs khlOH-rit)*
chloroform	das Chloroform	*(dahs khlOH-ro-FOrm)*
chromium	das Chrom	*(dahs khrOHm)*
cigarette case	das Zigarettenetui	*(dahs tsEE-gah-ret-ten-e-tuEE)*
circuit	die Schaltung	*(dee shAHL-tunk)*
circulation	die Auflage	*(dee OWf-lah-geh)*
civil action	die Zivilklage	*(dee tsee-vEEl-klAA-geh)*

civil engineering	das Bauingenieurwesen	*(dahs bOW-een-shen-EEewr-vAY-zen)*
claim	der Anspruch	*(dee AHN-shprUKH)*
classified advertisement	die Kleinanzeige	*(dee klEYEn-AHN-tsEYE-geh)*
classified sparkling wine	der Qualitätsschaumwein	*(duh kvah-li-tehts-shOWm-vEYEN)*
clean document	die uneingeschränkte Urkunde	*(dee un-eyen-geh-shrEHnk-teh OOr-kOOn-deh)*
cleanup (waste waters)	Abwasserreinigung	*(AHB-vahsser-reyen-igoong)*
clearinghouse	die Girozentrale	*(dee djEE-rOH-tsEN-trAA-leh)*
climate	das Klima	*(dahs kLEE-mah)*
closed account	das abgeschlossene Konto	*(dahs ahb-geh-shlOS-seh-neh kON-toh)*
closed-end fund	der Investmentfonds mit begrenzter Emissionshöhe	*(duh in-vehs-mEHnt-fOH mit-beh-grEHNts-tuh ehmi-see-OHns-hER-heh)*
closely held corporation	die personenbezogene Aktiengesellschaft	*(dee payr-sOH-nen-beh-tsOH-gen-neh ak-tsEE-en-geh-zEL-shahft)*
closing entry	die Abschlußbuchung	*(dee AHB-shlUS-bOO-khunk)*
closing price	der Schlußkurs	*(duh shlUS-koors)*
clutch	die Kupplung	*(dee kUP-lunk)*
clutch pedal	das Kupplungspedal	*(dahs kUP-lunks-peh-dahl)*
co-ownership	das Miteigentum	*(dahs MIT-eye-gen-tOOm)*
coal	die Kohle	*(dee KOH-leh)*
coat	der Mantel	*(duh mAHN-tel)*
coated paper	das gestrichene Papier	*(dahs geh-shtRI-KHeh-neh pah-pEER)*
coaxial cable	das Koaxialkabel	*(dahs ko-ahxi-AAL-KAA-bel)*
codicil	das Kodizill	*(dahs koh-dee-tsIL)*
coffee break	die Kaffeepause	*(dee kAH-fay-pOW-zeh)*
coffeepot	die Kaffekanne	*(dee kahf-fAY-kAHN-neh)*
coil	die Spule	*(dee shpOO-leh)*
coinsurance	die Mitversicherung	*(dee mIT-fuh-zIkheh-runk)*

cold call	der Überraschungsanruf	*(duh EW-buh-rAHsh-unks-AAN-rOOf)*
cold rolling	das Kaltwalzen	*(dahs kAHLT-vAL-tsen)*
collar	der Kragen	*(duh kRAH-gen)*
collateral	die Deckung	*(dee DEK-unk)*
colleague	der Kollege	*(duh koh-lAY-geh)*
collect on delivery	die Nachnahme	*(dee nAHKH-nAA-meh)*
collection period	die Einziehungszeit	*(dee EYEn-tsEE-unks-tsEYEt)*
collective agreement	der Tarifvertrag	*(duh taa-rIF-fuh-trAHk)*
collective bargaining	die Tarifverhandlungen	*(dee taa-rIF-fuh-hAHndl-lunk-en)*
color	die Farbe	*(dee fAHR-beh)*
color separation	der Farbauszug	*(duh fAHRb-OWs-tsOOk)*
combination	die Vereinigung	*(dee fuh-EYE-ni-gunk)*
commerce	der Handel	*(duh hAHn-dehl)*
commercial (broadcasting)	die Werbesendung	*(dee vAYr-beh-zEN-dunk)*
commercial bank	die Handelsbank	*(dee hAHn-dehls-bahnk)*
commercial grade	die handelsübliche Qualität	*(deehAHn-dehls-EWb-likheh kvah-li-tAYt)*
commercial invoice	die Faktura	*(dee fAHK-tOO-rah)*
commission (agency)	der Ausschuß	*(duh OWs-shUs)*
commission (fee)	die Provision	*(dee proh-vi-zEE-ohn)*
commitment	die Verpflichtung	*(dee fuh-pflIKH-tunk)*
commodity	die Handelsware	*(dee hAHn-dehls-vAA-reh)*
commodity exchange	die Warenbörse	*(dee vAA-ren-bEWr-seh)*
common carrier	das öffentliche Verkehrsunternehmen	*(dahs ERf-fehnt-likh-eh fuh-kAYrs-un-tuh-nAY-men)*
common market	der gemeinsame Markt	*(duh geh-mEYEn-zAA-muh mAHrkt)*
common market (European Common Market)	die Europäische Wirtschaftsgemeinschaft	*(dee OY-roh-pAY-ish-eh vEERt-shahfts-geh-mEYEn-shahft)*
common stock	die Stammaktie	*(dee shtAHm-ak-tsEE-eh)*

company	die Gesellschaft, die Firma	*(dee geh-zEL-shahft), (dee fIR-mah)*
company goal	das Gesellschaftsziel	*(dahs geh-zEL-shahfts-tsEEl)*
company policy	die Betriebspolitik	*(dee beh-trEEps-po-li-tIK)*
compensating balance	das Kontokorrentguthaben	*(dahs kON-toh-kor-rEHnt-gOOt-haa-ben)*
compensation	die Vergütung	*(dee fuh-gEW-tunk)*
compensation (salary)	das Gehalt	*(dahs geh-hAHlts)*
compensation trade	der Kompensationshandel	*(duh kom-pehn-zaa-tsEE-OHns-hAHn-dehl)*
competition	die Konkurrenz	*(dee kon-koor-rEHnts)*
competitive advantage	der Wettbewerbsvorteil	*(duh vEHt-beh-vAYrbs-FOHR-teyel)*
competitive price	der konkurrenzfähige Preis	*(duh kon-koor-rEHnts-fAY-hi-guh preEYEs)*
competitive strategy	die Wettbewerbsstrategie	*(dee vEHt-beh-vAYrbs-shtrAH-teh-gee)*
competitor	der Konkurrent	*(duh kon-koor-rEHnt)*
competitor analysis	die Konkurrenzstudie	*(dee kon-koor-rEHnt-shttoo-di-eh)*
complimentary copy	das Freiexemplar	*(dahs frEYE-ex-em-plAAr)*
component	die Komponente	*(dee kom-PO-nen-tEH)*
composite index	der Mischindex	*(duh MISH-in-dex)*
composition	der Schriftsatz	*(duh shrIFT-zAHTS)*
compound	die Verbindung	*(dee fuh-BIN-dunk)*
compound interest	der Zinseszins	*(duh tsIN-zeh-tsINs)*
compounds	die Verbindungen	*(dee fuh-BIN-dun-gen)*
comptroller	der Rechnungsprüfer	*(duh rEHKH-nungs-prEW-fuh)*
computer	der Computer	*(duh kom-pyU-tuh)*
computer, analog	der Analogcomputer	*(duh ah-nah-lOHg-kom-pyU-tuh)*
computer center	die Datenverarbeitungs-zentrale	*(dee dAA-ten-fuh-ahr-bEYE-tungs-tsen-trAA-leh)*
computer, digital	der Digitalrechner	*(duh di-gi-tAAl-rEHKH-nuh)*

computer input	die Computereingabe	*(dee kom-pyU-tuh-EYEn-gAA-beh)*
computer language	die Computersprache	*(deekom-pyU-tuh-shprAAHkh-eh)*
computer memory	der Speicher des Computers	*(duh spEYE-khuh dehs kom-pyU-tuhs)*
computer output	das Computerergebnis	*(dahs kom-pyU-tuh-ayr-gAYb-nis)*
computer program	das Computerprogramm	*(dahs kom-pyU-tuh-proh-grAAm)*
computer storage	die Datenspeicherung	*(dee dAA-ten-shpEYE-khch-runk)*
computer terminal	das Computerterminal	*(dahs kom-pyU-tuh-tayr-mEE-nahl)*
concentration	die Konzentration	*(dee kon-tsen-trAH-TSI-on)*
condensor	der Kondensator	*(duh kon-den-ZAA-tor)*
conditional acceptance	die Annahme mit Vorbehalt	*(dee AHN-nAA-meh mit FOHR-beh-hAHlt)*
conditional sales contract	der bedingte Verkaufsvertrag	*(duh beh-dING-teh fuh-kOWfs-fuh-trAHk)*
conference room	der Konferenzraum	*(duh kon-fuh-rEHnts-rOWm)*
confidential	vertraulich	*(fuh-trOW-likh)*
confirmation of order	die Auftragsbestätigung	*(dee OWf-trAHks-beh-shtEH-tee-gunk)*
conflict of interest	der Interessenkonflikt	*(duh in-teh-rEHs-seh)*
conglomerate	der Großkonzern	*(duh grOHs-kon-tsayrn)*
connecting rod	die Pleuelstange	*(dee plOY-el-shtAHN-geh)*
consideration (contract law)	die Gegenleistung	*(dee gAY-gen-lEYEs-tunk)*
consignee	der Empfänger	*(duh em-pfAYnk-uh)*
consignment	die Sendung	*(dee zEN-dunk)*
consignment note	der Frachtbrief	*(duh frAHKHt-brEEf)*
consolidated financial statement	der konsolidierte Finanzbericht	*(duh kon-soh-lee-dEEr-tuh-fee-nAHnts-beh-rIKHt)*
consolidation	die konsolidierte Bilanz	*(dee kon-soh-lee-dEEr-teh bee-lAHnts)*
consortium	das Konsortium	*(dahs kon-sohr-tEE-um)*

consular invoice	die Konsulatsfaktura	*(dee kon-soo-lAAts-fahk-tOO-rah)*
consultant	der Berater	*(duh beh-rAA-tuh)*
consultant, management	der Unternehmensberater	*(duh un-tuh-nAY-mens-beh-rAA-tuh)*
consumer	der Verbraucher	*(duh fuh-brOW-khuh)*
consumer acceptance	die Verbraucherannahme	*(dee fuh-brOW-khuh-ahn-nAA-meh)*
consumer credit	der Konsumentenkredit	*(duh kon-soo-mEHn-ten-kray-dIT)*
consumer goods	die Konsumgüter	*(dee kon-zOOm-gEW-tuh)*
consumer price index	der Verbraucherpreisindex	*(duh fuh-brOW-khuh-prEYEs-in-dEHx)*
consumer research	die Verbraucherforschung	*(dee fuh-brOW-khuh-FOHR-shung)*
consumer satisfaction	die Verbraucherzufriedenstellung	*(dee fuh-brOW-khuh-tsOO-frEE-den-shtEL-lunk)*
container	der Container	*(duh kon-tAY-nuh)*
contango	die Reportprämie	*(dee ray-pOHrt-PRAY-mee-eh)*
content	der Inhalt	*(duh IN-hahlt)*
contingencies	die unvorhergesehenen Ausgaben	*(dee un-FOHR-hehr-geh-zeh-heh-neh OWs-gAA-ben)*
contingent fund	der Reservefonds	*(duh reh-sAYrv-fOH)*
contingent liability	die Eventuellverbindlichkeit	*(dee eh-fEN-tOO-el-fuh-bINt-likh-heyet)*
continuous mill	die kontinuierliche Walzstraße	*(dee kon-TEE-noo-EER-li-kheh vALTS-shtrAA-seh)*
contract	der Vertrag	*(duh fuh-trAHk)*
contract carrier	der vertragliche Frachtführer	*(duh fuh-trAHk-likh-eh frAHKHt-fEW-ruh)*
contract month	der Vertragsmonat	*(duh fuh-trAHks-mOH-naht)*
controllable costs	die wechselnden Kosten	*(dee vEHk-sehl-dehn kOS-ten)*
controller	der Leiter des Rechnungswesens	*(duh lEYE-tuh dehs rEHKH-nungs-vAY-sens)*
controlling interest	die Aktienmehrheit	*(dee ak-tsEE-en-mAYr-hEYEt)*
convertible	das Kabriolett	*(dahs kahb-ri-o-LET)*

convertible debentures	die konvertierbaren Obligationen	*(dee kon-fuh-tEEr-bAA-ren ob-li-gah-tsEE-ohn-nen)*
convertible preferred stock	die konvertierbare Vorzugsaktie	*(dee kon-fuh-tEEr-bAA-reh FOHR-tsoogs-ak-tsEE-eh)*
conveyor	das Fördergerät	*(dahs FER-duh-geh-rEHt)*
conveyor belt	das Förderband	*(dahs FER-duh-bahnt)*
cooper	der Küfer	*(duh kEW-fuh)*
cooperation agreement	das Kooperationsabkommen	*(dahs koh-op-eh-rah-tsEE-OHns-AHB-kOM-men)*
cooperative	die Genossenschaft	*(dee geh-nOS-sen-shahft)*
cooperative advertising	die Gemeinschaftswerbung	*(dee geh-mEYEn-shahfts-vAYr-bunk)*
copper	das Kupfer	*(dahs kup-fEHR)*
copy	die Kopie	*(dee ko-PEE)*
copy (advertising text)	der Werbetext	*(duh vAYr-beh-tEHxt)*
copy (v)	Abzüge machen	*(ahb-tsEW-geh ma-khen)*
copy testing	die Werbetextprüfung	*(dee vAYr-beh-tEHxt-prEW-funk)*
copyright	das Urheberrecht	*(dahs OOr-hay-beh-rehkht)*
cork	der Korken	*(duh kor-ken)*
corkscrew	der Korkenzieher	*(duh kor-ken-tsEE-huh)*
corporate growth	das Unternehmenswachstum	*(dahs un-tuh-nAY-mens-vAHKHs-tum)*
corporate image	das Gesellschaftsbild	*(dahs geh-zEL-shahfts-bild)*
corporate planning	die Gesellschaftsplanung	*(dee geh-zEL-shahfts-plAA-nunk)*
corporate structure	die Gesellschaftsstruktur	*(dee geh-zEL-shahfts-shtrOOk-toor)*
corporate tax	die Körperschaftssteuer	*(dee kER-puh-shahfts-shtOY-uh)*
corporation	die Aktiengesellschaft	*(dee ak-tsEE-en-geh-zEL-shahft)*
corpus	das Stammkapital	*(dahs shtAHm-kah-pi-tAAl)*
correspondence	die Korrespondenz	*(dee koh-rehs-pon-dEHnts)*
correspondent bank	die Korrespondenzbank	*(dee koh-rehs-pon-dEHnts-bahnk)*

C

cost	die Kosten	*(dee kOS-ten)*
cost accounting	die Kostenrechnung	*(dee kOS-ten-rEHKH-nunk)*
cost analysis	die Kostenanalyse	*(dee kOS-ten-ah-nah-lEW-zeh)*
cost and freight	Kosten und Fracht	*(kOS-ten unt frAHKHt)*
cost control	die Kostenüberwachung	*(dee kOS-ten-EW-buh-vAAkh-unk)*
cost effective	kostenintensiv	*(kOS-ten-in-ten-zEEf)*
cost factor	der Kostenfaktor	*(duh kOS-ten-FAHK-tohr)*
cost of capital	die Kapitalkosten	*(dee kah-pi-tAAL-kOS-ten)*
cost of goods sold	die Umsatzselbstkosten	*(dee um-zAHts-zehlbst-kOS-ten)*
cost of living	die Lebenshaltungskosten	*(dee lAY-benz-kOS-ten)*
cost reduction	die Kosteneinsparung	*(dee kOS-ten-EYEn-shpAA-runk)*
cost-benefit analysis	die Kostennutzenanalyse	*(dee kOS-ten-nU-tsen-ah-nah-lEW-zeh)*
cost-plus contract	der Auftrag auf Basis Selbstkosten plus Gewinn	*(duh OWf-trahk owf bAA-zis ZEHLbst-kOS-ten plOOs geh-vIN)*
cost-price squeeze	die Kostenpreisschere	*(dee kOS-ten-prEYEs-shAY-reh)*
cotton	die Baumwolle	*(dee BOWm-voleh)*
cough (v)	husten	*(hUS-ten)*
cough drop	der Hustentropfen	*(duh hUS-ten-trOP-fen)*
cough syrup	der Hustensaft	*(duh hUS-ten-sahft)*
counter check	der Kassenscheck	*(duh kAH-sehn-shehk)*
counterfeit	die Fälschung	*(dee fEHl-shunk)*
countervailing duty	der Ausgleichszoll	*(duh OWs-glEYEkhs-tsOL)*
country	das Gebiet	*(dahs geh-bEET)*
country of origin	das Ursprungsland	*(dahs OOr-shprunks-lAHnt)*
country of risk	das Risiko übernehmende Land	*(dahs REE-see-koh-EW-buh-nAY-mehn-dehs lAHnd)*
coupon (bond interest)	der Zinskoupon	*(duh tsINs-koo-pon)*
courier service	der Kurier	*(duh koo-REER)*

covenant (promises)	der Vertrag	*(duh fuh-trAHk)*
cover	die Titelseite	*(dee TI-tel-zEYE-teh)*
cover charge	der Mindestbetrag	*(duh MIN-dehst-beh-trAHk)*
cover letter	der Begleitbrief	*(duh beh-glEYEt-brEEf)*
cover ratio	das Deckungsverhältnis	*(dahs dEH-kunks-fuh-hEHlt-nis)*
coverage (insurance)	der Versicherungsschutz	*(duh fuh-zIkheh-runks-shUTs)*
cowhide	das Rindsleder	*(dahs RINds-lAY-duh)*
cracking	das Krachverfahren	*(dahs KRAHKH-fuh-fAA-ren)*
crankshaft	die Kurbelwelle	*(dee kUR-bel-vEL-leh)*
credit	der Kredit	*(duh kray-dIT)*
credit (v)	gutschreiben	*(gOOt-shrEYE-ben)*
credit balance	der Kreditsaldo	*(duh kray-dIT-zAAl-doh)*
credit bank	die Kreditbank	*(dee kray-dIT-bahnk)*
credit bureau	die Kreditanstalt	*(dee kray-dIT-ahn-shtAAlt)*
credit buyer	der Kreditkäufer	*(duh kray-dIT-kOY-fuh)*
credit card	die Kreditkarte	*(dee kray-dIT-kAAr-teh)*
credit control	die Kreditkontrolle	*(dee kray-dIT-kON-trol-leh)*
credit insurance	die Kreditversicherung	*(dee-kray-dIT-fuh-zIkheh-runk)*
credit line	die Kreditlinie	*(dee kray-dIT-lEE-nee-eh)*
credit management	die Kreditverwaltung	*(dee kray-dIT-fuh-vAAl-tunk)*
credit note	die Gutschriftsanzeige	*(dee gOOt-shrifts-AHN-tseye-geh)*
credit rating	die Krediteinschätzung	*(dee kray-dIT-shEH-zung)*
credit reference	die Kreditreferenz	*(dee kray-dIT-reh-feh-rEHnts)*
credit terms	die Kreditbedingungen	*(dee kray-dIT-beh-dEEn-gunk-ehn)*
credit union	der Kreditverein	*(duh kray-dIT-fuh-EYEn)*
creditor	der Gläubiger	*(duh glOY-bi-guh)*
critical path analysis	die Analyse der Netzplantechnik	*(dee ah-nah-lEW-zeh duh nets-plAAn-tehkh-nik)*

C

crop	die Masse	*(dee MAHs-seh)*
cross-licensing	der Lizenzaustausch	*(duh lee-tsEHnts-OWs-tOWsh)*
crucible	der Schmelztiegel	*(duh shmEHLTS-tEE-gel)*
crude	roh, unbearbeitet	*(roh), (UN-beh-ahr-beye-tet)*
crystal glass manufacturing	die Kristallglasherstellung	*(dee kris-tAHL-glAAs-huh-shTEL-lunk)*
crystallization	die Kristallisierung	*(dee kris-tAHL-li-ZEE-runk)*
cuff link	der Manschettenknopf	*(duh mAHN-shET-ten-knOpf)*
cultural export permit	die Ausfuhrlizenz für Kulturgüter	*(dee OWs-foor-lee-tsEHnts fEWr kul-TOOR-gew-tuh)*
cultural property	der Kulturbesitz	*(duh kul-TOOR-beh-zITs)*
cum dividend	mit Dividende	*(mit di-vi-dEHn-deh)*
cumulative	anhäufend, kumulativ	*(AHN-hoy-fend), (koo-moo-lah-tEEf)*
cumulative preferred stock	die kumulative Vorzugsaktie	*(dee koo-moo-lah-tEE-feh FOHR-tsoogs-ak-tsEE-eh)*
cup	die Tasse	*(dee TAHs-seh)*
cupola	die Beobachtungskuppel	*(dee beh-OH-bahkh-tungs-kUP-pel)*
currency	das Geld	*(dahs gehlts)*
currency band	die Währungsgruppe	*(dee VAY-runks-grUP-peh)*
currency clause	die Währungsklausel	*(dee VAY-runks-klOW-sehl)*
currency exchange	der Geldwechsel	*(duh gehlt-vEHk-sehl)*
current	der Strom	*(duh shtrOHm)*
current assets	das kurzfristige Umlaufvermögen	*(dahs kURts-fris-tikh-eh Um-lOWf-fuh-mER-gen)*
current liabilities	die kurzfristigen Verbindlichkeiten	*(dee kURts-fris-tikh-en fuh-bINd-likh-keye-ten)*
current ratio	der Liquiditätsgrad	*(duh li-kvi-dee-tAYts-grAAd)*
current yield	die laufende Rendite	*(dee lOW-fehn-deh ren-di-teh)*
curriculum vitae	der Lebenslauf	*(duh lAY-behns-lOWf)*
customer	der Kunde	*(duh kUn-deh)*
customer service	der Kundendienst	*(duh kUN-dehn-dEEnst)*

customs	der Zoll	*(duh tsOL)*
customs broker	der Zollagent	*(duh tsOL-ah-gEHnt)*
customs collector	der Zolleinnehmer	*(duh tsOL-EYEn-nAY-muh)*
customs duty	die Zollgebühr, der Zoll	*(dee tsOL-geh-bEWr), (duh tsOL)*
customs entry	die Zollerklärung	*(dee tsOL-AYr-kleh-runk)*
customs union	der Zollverein	*(duh tsOL-fuh-EYEn)*
cut (v)	zuschneiden	*(tsOO-shnEYE-den)*
cutback	die Verminderung	*(dee fuh-mIN-duh-runk)*
cutlery	das Eßbesteck	*(dahs EHS-beh-shtek)*

≡ **D** ≡

D

daily	täglich	*(tAY-glikh)*
dairy products	die Molkereiprodukte	*(dee MOl-kuh-reye-proh-dUKt)*
damage	der Schaden	*(duh shAA-dehn)*
data	die Daten	*(dee dAA-ten)*
data acquisition	der Datenerwerb	*(duh dAA-ten-ayr-vAYrb)*
data bank	die Datenbank	*(dee dAA-ten-bahnk)*
data base	die Angabengrundlage	*(dee AHN-gAA-ben-grUNd-lAA-geh)*
data processing	die Datenverarbeitung	*(dee dAA-ten-fuh-ahr-bEYE-tunk)*
date of delivery	der Liefertermin	*(duh LEE-fuh-tAYr-meen)*
day loan	das Tagesgeld	*(dahs tAA-gehs-gehlt)*
day order	der Tagesauftrag	*(duh tAA-geh-OWf-trahk)*
dead freight	die Leerfracht	*(dee lAYr-frAHKHt)*
dead rent	der feste Pachtzins	*(duh FEHs-teh pAHKHt-tsINs)*
deadline	der Stichtag	*(duh shtIKH-taak)*
deadlock	die Pattsituation	*(dee PAHT-si-too-ah-tsEE-ohn)*
deal (agreement)	das Abkommen	*(dahs AHB-kOM-men)*
deal (transaction)	der Handel	*(duh hAHn-dehl)*
dealer	der Händler	*(duh hEHnd-luh)*

dealership	die Handlung	*(dee hAHnd-lunk)*
debenture	die Obligation	*(dee ob-li-gah-tsEE-ohn)*
debit	das Soll	*(dahs zol)*
debit entry	der Debetposten	*(dee deh-beht-pOS-ten)*
debit note	die Lastschriftanzeige	*(dee lAHst-shrift-AHN-tseye-geh)*
debt	die Schuld	*(dee shult)*
debug (v) (computers)	einen Fehler beseitigen	*(EYE-nen fAY-luh beh-zEYE-ti-gen)*
decanter	die Karaffe	*(dee kah-rAHF-feh)*
deductible	abzugsfähig	*(AHB-tsOOks-fAY-ikh)*
deduction	der Abzug	*(duh AHB-tsOOk)*
deed	die Urkunde	*(dee OOR-kun-deh)*
deed of sale	der Kaufbrief	*(duh kOWf-brEEf)*
deed of transfer	die Übertragungsurkunde, die Auflassungsurkunde	*(dee EW-buh-trAA-gunks-OOr-kun-deh), (dee OWf-lah-sungs-OOr-kun-deh)*
deed of trust	der Treuhandvertrag	*(duh trOY-hahnd-fuh-trAHk)*
default (v)	zahlungsunfähig werden	*(tsAA-lung-un-fAY-ikh vAYr-den)*
defective	mangelhaft, fehlerhaft	*(mAHng-ehl-hAHft), (fAY-luh-hAHft)*
deferred annuities	die aufgeschobenen Renten	*(dee OWf-geh-shOH-beh-nen REN-ten)*
deferred assets	die zeitweilig nicht einlösba-ren Aktiva	*(dee tsEYEt-vEYE-lik nIKHt EYEn-lERs-bAA-ren ahk-tEE-vah)*
deferred charges	die gestundeten Zahlungen	*(dee geh-shtun-deh-ten tsAA-lung-en)*
deferred deliveries	die aufgeschobenen Lieferungen	*(dee OWf-geh-shOH-beh-nen lEE-fuh-rung-en)*
deferred income	die im voraus eingegange-nen Erträge	*(dee im FOHR-ows EYEn-geh-gahng-en-nen uh-trEH-geh)*
deferred liabilities	die aufgeschobenen Schulden	*(dee OWf-geh-shOH-ben-nen shUl-ten)*
deferred tax	die zurückgestellte Steuerzahlung	*(dee tsoo-rEWk-geh-shtEL-teh shtOY-uh-tsAA-lung)*
deficit	das Defizit	*(dahs DEH-fi-tsIT)*

D

deficit financing	die Defizitfinanzierung	*(dee DEH-fi-tsIT-fee-nahn-tsEE-runk)*
deflation	die Deflation	*(dee day-flAA-tsEE-ohn)*
defroster	der Entfroster	*(duh ent-frOS-tuh)*
degree	der Grad	*(duh graht)*
delay	der Aufschub	*(duh OWf-shub)*
delinquent account	das rückständige Konto	*(dahs rEWk-shtEHn-dikh-eh kON-toh)*
delivered price	der Lieferpreis	*(duh LEE-fuh-prEYEs)*
delivery	die Lieferung	*(dee LEE-fuh-runk)*
delivery date	der Liefertermin	*(duh LEE-fuh-tAYr-meen)*
delivery notice	der Lieferschein	*(duh LEE-fuh-shEYEn)*
delivery points	die Erfüllungsorte	*(dee ayr-fEW-lunks-sOHR-teh)*
delivery price	der Lieferpreis	*(duh LEE-fuh-prEYEs)*
demand	die Nachfrage	*(dee nAHKH-frAA-geh)*
demand (v)	verlangen	*(fuh-lAAng-en)*
demand deposit	das tägliche Geld	*(dahs tAY-glikh-eh gehlt)*
demand line of credit	die Kontokorrentkreditlinie	*(dee kON-toh-kor-rEHnt-kray-dIT-lee-nEE-eh)*
demographic	demographisch	*(day-moh-grAA-fish)*
demotion	die Zurückstufung	*(dee tsOO-rEWk-shtOO-funk)*
demurrage (fee for)	das Liegegeld	*(dahs lEE-geh-gehlt)*
demurrage (period of)	die Überliegezeit	*(dee EW-buh-lEE-geh-tsEYEt)*
density	die Dichte	*(dee DIKH-teh)*
department	die Abteilung	*(dee AHB-teye-lunk)*
department store	das Kaufhaus	*(dahs kOWf-hOWs)*
depletion allowance	die Abschreibung für Substanzverringerung	*(dee AHB-shrEYE-bunk fEWr zub-stAHnts-fuh-rin-guh-runk)*
depletion control	die Verringerungskontrolle	*(dee fuh-rin-guh-runks-kon-trOL-leh)*
deposit	die Einlage	*(dee EYEn-lAA-geh)*
deposit account	das Depositenkonto	*(dahs deh-poh-zIT-ehn-kON-toh)*

D

deposit, bank	die Bankeinlage	*(dee BAHNK-eyen-lAA-geh)*
depository	das Depot	*(dahs day-pOH)*
depreciation	die Abschreibung	*(dee AHB-shrEYE-bunk)*
depreciation allowance	der Abschreibungsbetrag	*(dee AHB-shrEYE-bunks-beh-trAHk)*
depreciation of currency	die Geldentwertung	*(dee gehlt-ent-vEHt-tunk)*
depression	die Depression	*(dee deh-preh-sEE-ohn)*
deputy chairman	der stellvertretende Vorsitzende	*(duh shtEL-fuh-trAY-ten-deh FOHR-zIT-sen-deh)*
deputy manager	der stellvertretende Geschäftsführer	*(duh shtEL-fuh-trAY-ten-deh geh-shEHfts-fEW-ruh)*
design	der Entwurf	*(duh EHNt-vOOrf)*
design (v)	entwerfen	*(ent-vER-fen)*
designer	der Entwerfer	*(duh ent-vEHR-fuh)*
dessert plate	der Dessertteller	*(duh dehs-sEHah-tel-luh)*
devaluation	die Abwertung	*(dee AHB-vEHr-tunk)*
digital	digital	*(di-gi-tAAl)*
digital computer	der Digitalrechner	*(duh di-gi-tAAl-rEHKH-nuh)*
dilution equity	die Aktienverwässerung	*(dee ak-tsEE-en-fuh-vEHs-suh-runk)*
dilution of equity	die Eigenkapital-verwässerung	*(dee EYE-gen-kah-pi-tAAl-fuh-vEHs-suh-runk)*
dilution of labor	die Einstellung ungelernter Arbeitskräfte	*(dee EYEn-shtEHl-lunk Un-geh-lAYrn-tuh AHR-beyets-krehf-teh)*
dinner plate	der Teller	*(duh tel-luh)*
direct access storage	der Schnellspeicher	*(duh shnEHl-shpEYE-khuh)*
direct cost	die direkten Kosten	*(dee dee-REK-ten kOS-ten)*
direct current	der Gleichstrom	*(duh glEYEKH-shtrOHm)*
direct expenses	die direkten Auslagen	*(dee dee-REK-ten OWs-lAA-gen)*
direct investment	die Direktinvestition	*(dee dee-REKT-in-vehs-ti-tsi-OHn)*
direct labor	die unmittelbar geleistete Arbeitszeit	*(dee un-mit-tEL-bAAr geh-lEYEs-teh-teh AHR-beyets-tsEYEt)*

direct labor cost	die Fertigungslöhne	*(dee fEHr-ti-gunks-lER-neh)*
direct mail	die Postversandwerbung	*(dee pOSt-fuhr-zAHnt-vAYr-bunk)*
direct paper	der gezogene Wechsel	*(duh geh-tsOH-geh-neh vEHk-sehl)*
direct quotation	die direkte Preisangabe	*(dee dee-REK-teh prEYEs-gAA-beh)*
direct quotation (stocks)	die direkte Kursnotierung	*(dee dee-REK-teh koors-no-tEE-runk)*
direct selling	der Direktverkauf	*(duh dee-REKT-fuh-kOWf)*
director	der Geschäftsführer	*(duh geh-shEHfts-fEW-ruh)*
disbursement	die Auslage	*(dee OWs-lAA-geh)*
disc brake	die Scheibenbremse	*(dee shEYE-ben-brEHM-zeh)*
discharge (v) (dismiss)	entlassen	*(EHNt-lAH-sen)*
discharge (v) (obligation)	ablösen	*(AHB-lER-sen)*
discount	der Diskont	*(duh dIS-kont)*
discount rate	der Diskontsatz	*(duh dIS-kont-zAHts)*
discount securities	die Diskontwertpapiere	*(dee dIS-kont-vEHRt-pah-pEEr-eh)*
discounted cash flow	die interne Zinsflußrechnung	*(dee in-tAYr-neh tsINs-flus-rEHKH-nunk)*
discounting	die Diskontierung	*(dee dIS-kon-tEE-runk)*
discretionary order	die Vertrauensorder	*(dee fuh-trOW-ens-OR-duh)*
disease	die Krankheit	*(dee KRAHNK-heyet)*
dish	die Schüssel, der Teller	*(dee SHEWs-sel), (duh tel-luh)*
dishonor	nicht honorieren	*(nIKHt on-oh-rEE-rehn)*
disincentive	der hemmende Faktor	*(duh hEHm—mehn-deh FAHK-tohr)*
disk	die Magnetplatte	*(dee mahg-nAYt-plAH-teh)*
disk drive	der Magnetplattenantrieb	*(duh mahg-nAYt-plAH-ten-AHN-trEEb)*
dispatch	der Versand	*(duh fuh-zAHnt)*
displacement	der Hubraum	*(duh hOOb-rOWm)*
disposable income	das verfügbare Einkommen	*(dahs fuh-fEWg-bAA-reh EYEn-kOM-men)*

D

dispute	der Konflikt	*(duh kon-flIKT)*
dispute (v)	streiten	*(shtrEYE-ten)*
distribution	der Vertrieb	*(duh fuh-trEEB)*
distribution channel	der Absatzweg	*(duh AHB-zAHTs-vAYk)*
distribution costs	die Vertriebskosten	*(dee fuh-trEEps-kOS-ten)*
distribution network	das Verteilungsnetz	*(dahs fuh-tEYE-lunks-nehts)*
distribution policy	die Vertriebspolitik	*(dee fuh-trEEps-po-li-tEEk)*
distributor	der Verteiler	*(duh fuh-tEYE-luh)*
distributor (wholesale)	der Großhändler	*(duh grOHs-hEHnd-luh)*
diuretic	das Diuretikum	*(dahs dEE-U-reh-ti-kum)*
diversification	die Diversifikation	*(dee dee-vayr-si-fi-kah-tsEE-OHn)*
divestment	die Desinvestition	*(dee dehs-in-vehs-ti-tsi-OHn)*
dividend	die Dividende	*(dee di-vi-dEHn-deh)*
dividend yield	der Dividendenertrag	*(duh di-vi-dEHn-den-uh-trAHk)*
division of labor	die Arbeitsteilung	*(dee AHR-beyets-tEYE-lunk)*
dock (ship's) receipt	der Docklagerschein	*(duh DOK-lAA-guh-shEYEn)*
dock handling charges	die Dockgebühren	*(dee DOK-geh-bEW-ren)*
document	das Dokument	*(dahs dok-OO-ment)*
domestic bill	der Inlandwechsel	*(duh IN-lahnt-vEHk-sehl)*
domestic corporation	die inländische Gesellschaft	*(dee in-lEHn-dish-eh geh-zEL-shahft)*
door-to-door sales	der Verkauf durch Vertreter	*(duh fuh-kOWf durkh fuh-trAY-teuh)*
dosage	die Dosierung, die Dosis	*(dee doh-ZEE-runk), (dee DOH-zis)*
dose	die Dosis	*(dee DOH-zis)*
double dealing	die Doppelzüngigkeit	*(dee DOP-el-tsEWng-ig-keyet)*
double taxation	die Doppelbesteuerung	*(dee DOP-el-beh-shtOY-uh-runk)*

D

double time	der Lohnzuschlag	*(duh lOHn-tsOO-shlahk)*
double-entry bookkeeping	die doppelte Buchführung	*(dee DOP-el-teh bOOkh-fEW-runk)*
down payment	die Anzahlung	*(dee AHN-tsAA-lung)*
down period	die Baisse	*(dee behs)*
down period (factory)	das Stilliegen	*(dahs shtIL-lAY-gen)*
down the line	auf der ganzen Linie	*(OWF duh GAN-tsen lEE-nee-eh)*
downtime	die Ausfallzeit einer Maschine oder eines Betriebs	*(dee OWs-fahl-tsEYEt EYE-nuh MAA-shee-nuh oh-duh EYE-nehs beh-trEEps)*
downturn	die Flaute	*(dee flOW-teh)*
draft	der Entwurf	*(duh ehnt-vOOrf)*
drape (v)	drapieren	*(drah-PEE-ren)*
draw off	ausdestillieren	*(OWs-dehs-ti-lEE-ren)*
drawback (disadvantage)	der Nachteil	*(duh nAKH-tEYEl)*
drawback (export premium)	die Erstattung	*(dee ayr-shtAH-tunk)*
drawback (money)	die Rückerstattung	*(dee rEWK-ayr-shtAH-tunk)*
drawdown	herabziehen	*(hAYr-AHB-tsEE-ehn)*
drawee	der Akzeptant	*(duh ahk-tsEPt-tahnt)*
drawer	der Aussteller	*(duh OWs-shtEL-luh)*
drayage	das Rollgeld	*(dahs ROL-gehlt)*
dregs	die Hefe	*(dee hay-feh)*
dress	die Kleidung	*(dee klEYE-dunk)*
dressing	der Verband	*(duh fuh-bahnt)*
drink (v)	trinken	*(trINK-en)*
driver	der Fahrer	*(duh fAA-ruh)*
drop	der Tropfen	*(duh trOP-fen)*
drop shipment	die direkte Verschiffung	*(dee dee-REK-teh fuh-shIF-funk)*
drug	die Droge, das Medikament	*(dee drOH-geh), (dahs meh-di-KAH-ment)*
drugstore	die Apotheke	*(dee ah-po-tAY-keh)*
dry cargo	die Trockenladung	*(dee trOK-en-lAA-dunk)*

dry goods	die Schnittwaren	*(dee shnIT-vAA-ren)*
dry wine	der trockene Wein	*(duh tRO-keh-neh vEYEN)*
dummy	der Probeband	*(duh pro-beh-bahnt)*
dumping (goods in foreign market)	die Schleuderausfuhr	*(dee shOY-duh-OWs-foor)*
dun (v)	mahnen	*(mAA-nen)*
duopoly	das Duopol	*(dahs doo-oh-pOHl)*
durable goods	die dauerhaften Verbrauchsgüter	*(dee dOW-uh-hAHf-ten fuh-brOWkhs-gEW-tuh)*
duress	der Zwang	*(duh tsvAHng)*
duty (customs)	der Zoll	*(duh tsOL)*
duty (free)	die Gebühr	*(dee geh-bEWr)*
duty (obligation)	die Pflicht	*(dee pflikht)*
duty (tax)	die Steuer	*(dee shtOY-uh)*
dutyfree	zollfrei	*(tsOL-freye)*
dye (v)	färben	*(fAYR-ben)*

E

earmark (v)	bestimmen	*(beh-shtIM-men)*
earnings	die Einnahmen	*(dee EYEn-nAA-men)*
earnings on assets	der Aktivenertrag	*(duh ak-tEEf-en-fuh-trAHk)*
earnings per share	der Gewinn pro Aktie	*(duh geh-vIN proh ak-tsEE-eh)*
earnings performance	die Ertragsleistung	*(dee ayr-trAHks-lEYEs-tunk)*
earnings report	der Gewinnbericht	*(duh geh-vIN-beh-rIKHt)*
earnings, retained	die thesaurierten Gewinne	*(dee tay-zow-rEEr-tehn-geh-vIN-neh)*
earnings yield	das Ertragsergebnis	*(dahs ayr-trAHks-ayr-gAYb-nis)*
earthenware	die Töpferware	*(dee TERp-fuh-VAAreh)*
ecology	die Umweltforschung	*(dee UM-velt-four-shoong)*
econometrics	die Ökonometrie	*(dee ER-ko-noh-meh-trEE)*
economic	wirtschaftlich	*(vEErt-shahft-likh)*
economic indicators	die Konjunkturindikatoren	*(dee kon-yunk-tOOr-in-dee-kAA-toh-rehn)*

economic life	die wirtschaftliche Nutzungsdauer	*(dee vEErt-shahft-likh-eh nU-tsungs-dOW-uh)*
economics	die Wirtschaftslehre	*(dee vEErt-shahfts-lAY-reh)*
economy of scale	die Kostenherabsetzung bei Betriebsvergrößerung	*(dee kOS-ten-hAYr-AHB-zeh-tsunk beye beh-trEEps-fuh-grER-suh-runk)*
edit (v)	herausgeben	*(heh-rOWs-gay-ben)*
edition	die Ausgabe	*(dee OWs-gah-beh)*
editor	der Redakteur	*(duh re-dahk-tER)*
effective yield	die Effektivverzinsung	*(dee ehf-fek-tEEf-fuh-tsIN-tsunk)*
efficiency	die Leistungsfähigkeit	*(dee lEYEs-tunks-fAY-ikh-keyet)*
elasticity (of supply or demand)	die Elastizität von Angebot und Nachfrage	*(dee eh-lahs-ti-tsee-tAYt fon AHN-geh-boht unt nAHKH-frAA-geh)*
electric arc furnace electrodes	die Elektroden	*(dee eh-lEHk-tROH-den)*
electrical engineering	die Elektrotechnik	*(dee eh-lehk-troh-tEHKH-nik)*
electricity	die Elektrizität	*(dee eh-lEHk-tri-tsee-TAYt)*
electrode	die Elektrode	*(dee eh-lEHk-tROH-deh)*
electrolysis	die Elektrolyse	*(dee eh-lEHk-tro-LEW-zeh)*
electrolytic process	der Elektrolyseprozeß	*(duh eh-lEHk-tro-LEW-zeh-pRO-tsehs)*
electron	das Elektron	*(dahs eh-lEHk-trOHN)*
electronic	elektronisch	*(eh-lEHk-trOH-nish)*
electronic whiteboard	das elektronische Weißbrett	*(dahs eh-lehk-trOH-ni-shes vEYEs-breht)*
electrostatic	elektrostatisch	*(eh-lEHk-tro-stAH-tish)*
element	das Element	*(dahs eh-leh-MENt)*
embargo	die Handelssperre	*(dee hAHn-dehls-shpEH-reh)*
embezzlement	die Unterschlagung	*(dee un-tuh-shlAH-gunk)*
employee	der Angestellte	*(duh AHN-geh-shtEL-teh)*
employee counseling	die Angestelltenberatung	*(dee AHN-geh-shtEL-tehn-beh-rAA-tunk)*

E

employee relations	die innerbetrieblichen Beziehungen	*(dee IN-nuh-beh-trEEp-likh-en beh-tsEE-hun-gen)*
employment agency	das Stellenvermittlungsbüro	*(dahs shtEHL-len-fuh-mIT-lunks-bEW-roh)*
encumbrance	die Belastung	*(dee beh-lAHs-tunk)*
end of period	der Rechnungsschluß	*(duh rEHKH-nungs-shlUs)*
end product	das Fertigprodukt	*(dahs fEHr-tikh-proh-dUKt)*
end-use certificate	der Zweck-Gebrauch Schein	*(duh tsvEHk-geh-brOWkh-sheyen)*
endorsee	der Girat	*(duh djEE-rAAt)*
endorsement	das Indossament	*(dahs in-dos-sAH-meh)*
endorsement (approval)	die Zustimmung	*(dee tsOO-shtIM-munk)*
endowment	die Dotation	*(dee doh-tah-tsEEohn)*
energy consumption	der Energieverbrauch	*(duh e-ner-GEE-fuh-browkh)*
energy source	der Energiequelle	*(duh e-ner-GEE-kvEL-eh)*
engine	der Motor	*(duh mOH-tor)*
engineer	der Ingenieur	*(duh in-sheh-NEE-er)*
engineering	das Ingenieurwesen	*(dahs EEn-shen-EEewr-vAY-zen)*
engrave (v)	gravieren	*(grah-vEE-ren)*
enlarge (v)	vergrößern	*(fuh-grER-sen)*
enterprise	das Unternehmen	*(dahs un-tuh-nAY-men)*
entrepreneur	der Unternehmer	*(duh un-tuh-nAY-muh)*
entry permit	die Einreisebewilligung	*(dee EYEn-reye-zeh-beh-vIL-lee-gunk)*
environmental protection	der Umweltschutz	*(duh UM-velt-shuts)*
enzyme	das Enzym	*(dahs ehn-TSEWm)*
equal pay for equal work	der gleiche Lohn für die gleiche Arbeit	*(duh glEYE-kheh LOHN fEWr dee glEYE-kheh AHR-beyet)*
equipment	die Ausrüstung	*(dee OWs-rEWs-tunk)*
equipment leasing	das Ausrüstungsmietung	*(dee OWs-rEWs-tunks-MEE-tunk)*
equity	das Eigenkapital	*(dahs EYE-gen-kah-pi-tAAl)*

E

equity investments	die Beteiligung an Kapitalgesellschaften	*(dee beh-tEYE-li-gunk ahn kah-pi-tAAl-geh-zEL-shahf-ten)*
equity share	der Eigenkapitalanteil	*(duh EYE-gen-kah-pi-tAAl-AHN-teyel)*
ergonomics	die Ergonomie	*(dee AYR-goh-noh-mEE)*
error	der Irrtum, der Fehler	*(duh EEr-toom), (duh FAY-luh)*
escalator clause	die Steigerungsklausel	*(dee shtEYE-guh-runks-klOW-sehl)*
escape clause	die Ausweichklausel	*(dee OWs-vEYEkhs-klOW-zehl)*
escheat	der Heimfall einer Erbschaft an den Staat	*(duh hEYEm-fahl eye-nuh AYrb-shahft ahn dehn shtAAt)*
escrow	der Treuhandvertrag	*(duh trOY-hahnd-fuh-trAHk)*
escrow account	das Treuhandkonto	*(dahs trOY-hahnd-kON-toh)*
espresso cup	die Espressotasse	*(dee ehs-prEHS-so-TAHs-seh)*
estate	die Erbschaft	*(dee AYrb-shahft)*
estate (or chateau)	das Gut	*(dahs gOOt)*
estate (testamentary)	der Nachlaß	*(duh nAHKH-laas)*
estate agent	der Grundstücksverwalter	*(duh grUnd-shtEWks-fuh-vAAl-tuh)*
estate bottled	die Erzeugerabfüllung	*(dee AYR-tsOY-guh-ahb-fewl-lunk)*
estate tax	die Nachlaßsteuer	*(dee nAHKH-laas-shtOY-uh)*
estimate	die Schätzung	*(dee shEH-tsunk)*
estimate (v)	schätzen	*(shEH-tsen)*
estimated price	der Schätzwert	*(duh shEHts-vEHrt)*
estimated time of arrival	die voraussichtliche Ankunft	*(duh FOHR-OWs-zIKHt-llKH-eh AHn-kunft)*
estimated time of departure	die voraussichtliche Abfahrt	*(dee FOHR-OWs-zIKHt-llKH-eh AHb-faart)*
ethane	das Äthan	*(dahs AY-taan)*
ether	der Äther	*(duh AY-tuh)*
Eurobond	die Euroanleihe	*(dee OY-roh-AHN-leye-eh)*

E

Eurocurrency	das Guthaben in konvertier-barer Währung	*(dahs gOOt-haa-ben in kon-fuh-tEEr-bAA-ruh VAY-runk)*
Eurodollar	der Eurodollar	*(duh OY-roh-dOHl-laar)*
evaluation	die Bewertung	*(dee beh-vAYr-tunk)*
evaporation	die Verdampfung	*(dee fuh-dAHM-pfunk)*
ex dividend	ohne Dividende, dividendlos	*(oh-neh di-vi-dEHn-deh), (di-vi-dEHnd-lohs)*
ex dock	ab Dock	*(ahb dOK)*
ex factory	ab Fabrik	*(ahb fah-brEEk)*
ex mill	ab Betrieb	*(ahb beh-trEEp)*
ex mine	ab Grube	*(ahb gROO-beh)*
ex rights	ohne Rechte	*(ohneh rEHKH-teh)*
ex ship	ab Schiff	*(ahb shIF)*
ex warehouse	ab Lager	*(ahb LAA-guh)*
ex works	ab Werk	*(ahb vehrk)*
exchange (commodity)	die Warenbörse	*(dee vAA-ren-bER-zeh)*
exchange (stock)	die Börse	*(dee bER-zeh)*
exchange (v)	tauschen	*(tOW-shen)*
exchange control	die Devisenkontrolle	*(dee deh-vEE-zen-kon-trOL-leh)*
exchange discount	der Wechseldiskont	*(duh vEHk-sehl-dIS-kont)*
exchange loss	der Kursverlust	*(duh koors-fuh-lOOst)*
exchange rate	der Wechselkurs	*(duh vEHk-sel-kOOrs)*
exchange risk	das Währungsrisiko	*(dahs VAY-runks-ree-zEE-koh)*
exchange value (on stock exchange)	der Börsenwert	*(duh bER-zen-vEHrt)*
exchange value	der Tauschwert	*(duh tOSsh-vEHrt)*
excise duty	die Verbrauchsabgabe	*(dee fuh-brOWkhs-AHb-gAA-beh)*
excise license	die Schankkonzession	*(dee shAAnk-kon-tseh-tsEE-ohn)*
excise tax	die Verbrauchssteuer	*(dee fuh-brOWkhs-shtOY-uh)*
executive	der leitende Angestellte	*(duh lEYE-ten-deh AHN-geh-shtEHL-teh)*

E

executive board	der Vorstand	*(dee FOHR-shtAHnt)*
executive committee	der geschäftsführende Vorstand	*(duh geh-shEHfts-fEWr-en-deh FOHR-shtAHnt)*
executive compensation	die Vergütung für leitende Angestellte	*(dee fuh-gEW-tunk fEWr lEYE-ten-deh AHN-geh-shtEHL-teh)*
executive director	der Geschäftsführer	*(duh geh-shEHfts-fEW-ruh)*
executive search	die Suche von Führungskräften	*(dee zOO-kheh fon fEW-runks-krEHf-ten)*
executor (of an estate)	der Testamentsvollstrecker	*(duh tehs-tah-mEHnts-FOL-shtrEH-kuh)*
exemption	die Befreiung	*(dee beh-frEYE-unk)*
exemption (tax exemption)	der Steuerfreibetrag	*(duh shtOY-euh-beh-trAHk)*
expectations, up to our	unseren Erwartungen entsprechend	*(un-zEHren AYr-vAAr-tunk-en ehnt-shprEHKH-ent)*
expected result	das erwünschte Ergebnis	*(dahs ayr-vEWnsh-tes ayr-gAYb-nis)*
expenditure	der Aufwand	*(duh OWf-vahnt)*
expense account	das Spesenkonto	*(dahs shpAY-zehn kON-toh)*
expenses	die Auslagen	*(dee OWs-lAA-gen)*
experiment	das Experiment	*(dahs EHX-peh-RI-mehnt)*
experimental	experimentell	*(EHX-peh-RI-mehn-tel)*
expiry date	der Verfalltag	*(duh fuh-fAAl-tAAk)*
export (v)	ausführen	*(OWs-fEW-ren)*
export agent	der Ausfuhragent	*(duh OWS-foor-ah-gent)*
export credit	der Ausfuhrkredit	*(duh OWS-foor-kray-dIT)*
export duty	der Ausfuhrzoll	*(duh OWS-foor-tsOL)*
export entry	die Ausfuhrzollerklärung	*(dee OWS-foor-tsOL-ayr-klAY-runk)*
export house	das Exportgeschäft	*(dahs ehx-pOHrt -geh-shEHft)*
export manager	der Leiter der Exportabteilung	*(duh lEYE-tuh ehx-pOHrt-AHB-tEYE-lunk)*
export middleman	der Exportmakler	*(duh ehx-pOHrt-mAHk-luh)*
export permit	die Ausfuhrbewilligung	*(dee OWS-foor-beh-vIL-i-gunk)*
export quota	die Ausfuhrquote	*(dee OWS-foor-KVOH-teh)*

export regulation	die Ausfuhrbestimmung	*(dee OWS-foor-beh-shtIM-munk)*
export sales contract	der Exportverkaufsvertrag	*(duh ehx-pOHrt-fuh-kOWfs-fuh-trAHk)*
export tax	die Ausfuhrsteuer	*(dee OWS-foor-shtOY-uh)*
Export-Import bank	die Export-Import Bank	*(dee ehx-pOHRt-im-pOHRt bahnk)*
expropriation	die Enteignung	*(dee ehnt-EYEg-nunk)*
extra dividend	die Zusatzdividende	*(dee tsOO-zAHTs-di-vi-dEHn-deh)*
eyedrop	der Augentropfen	*(duh OW-gen-trop-fen)*
eyeglass case	das Brillenetui	*(dahs brIL-len-e-tuEE)*

E

F

fabric	der Stoff, das Gewebe	*(duh shtOF), (dahs geh-vAY-beh)*
face value	der Nennwert	*(duh NEHN-vEHRt)*
facilities (means of production)	die Produktionsmittel	*(dee proh-duk-tsEE-ohns-mit-tEL)*
facilities (possibilities)	die Möglichkeiten	*(dee mER-glikh-keye-ten)*
factor (agent)	der Kommissionär	*(duh kom-mi-sEE-oh-nAYr)*
factor (component, element)	der Faktor	*(duh FAHK-tohr)*
factor analysis	die Faktorenanalyse	*(dee FAHK-tohr-en-an-ah-lEW-zeh)*
factor rating	die Faktorenbewertung	*(dee FAHK-tohr-en-beh-vEHr-tunk)*
factoring	das Faktoring	*(dahs fEHK-toh-ring)*
factory	die Fabrik	*(dee fah-brEEk)*
factory overhead	die Fertigungsgemeinkosten	*(dee fEHr-ti-gunks-kOS-ten)*
fail (v)	mißlingen	*(mis-lING-en)*
fail (v) (go bankrupt)	Bankrott machen	*(bahnk-rOT mAHKH-en)*
failure	der Mißerfolg	*(duh MIS-ayr-folg)*
fair market value	der angemessene Marktpreis	*(duh AHN-geh-mES-seh-nuh mAHrkt-prEYEs)*

fair return	der angemessene Ertrag	*(duh AHN-geh-mES-seh-nuh AYR-trAHk)*
fair trade	die Preisbindung	*(dee prEYEs-bIN-dunk)*
farm out (v)	verpachten	*(fuh-pAHKH-ten)*
fashion	die Mode	*(dee mOH-deh)*
fashionable	modisch, elegant	*(mOH-dish), (eh-leh-gAHNt)*
feed ratio	das Zuführungsverhältnis	*(dahs tsoo-fEW-runks-fuh-hEHLt-nis)*
feedback	die Rückwirkung	*(dee rEWk-vEEr-kunk)*
fender	der Kotflügel	*(duh kot-flEW-gel)*
ferment	die Gärung	*(dee gAY-runk)*
ferroalloys	die Eisenlegierungen	*(dee EYE-zen-leh-gEE-run-gen)*
ferromanganese	das Manganeisen	*(dahs mahn-gAAN-EYE-zen)*
ferronickel	das Nickeleisen	*(dahs ni-KEl-EYE-zen)*
fidelity bond	die Betriebstreuhand-versicherung	*(dee beh-trEEps-trOY-hahnd-fuh-zIkheh-runk)*
fiduciary	der Treuhänder	*(duh trOY-hEHnd-uh)*
fiduciary issue	die Notenausgabe ohne Deckung	*(dee nOH-ten-OWs-gAA-beh oh-neh DEK-unk)*
fiduciary loan	das treuhänderische Darlehen	*(dahs trOY-hEHnd-uh-rish-ehs dAAr-lAY-en)*
field warehousing	die Lagerung sicherungs-übereigneter Waren	*(dee laa-geh-runk zIKH-uh-runks-EW-buh-EYEg-neh-tuh vAA-ren)*
file (v)	ablegen	*(AHB-lAY-gen)*
file (v) (papers)	zu den Akten legen	*(tsoo dehn AHk-ten lAY-gen)*
file (v) (submit forms)	einreichen	*(EYEn-reye-khen)*
filter	der Filter	*(duh FIL-tuh)*
finalize (v)	abschließen	*(AHB-shlEE-sen)*
finance (v)	finanzieren	*(fee-nahn-tsEE-ren)*
finance company	die Finanzierungsgesellschaft	*(dee fee-nahn-tsEE-runks-geh-zEL-shahft)*
financial analysis	die Finanzanalyse	*(dee fee-nAHnts-ah-nah-lEW-zeh)*
financial appraisal	die Finanzbewertung	*(dee fee-nAHnts-beh-vEHr-tunk)*

F

financial control	die Finanzkontrolle	*(dee fee-nAHnts-kon-trOL-leh)*
financial director	der Finanzdirektor	*(duh fee-nAHnts-di-rEHK-tohr)*
financial highlights	finanzielle Höhepunkte	*(fee-nahn-tsee-EL-leh hER-heh-pUnk-teh)*
financial incentive	der finanzielle Anreiz	*(duh fee-nahn-tsee-EL-leh AHN-rEYEts)*
financial management	die Finanzverwaltung	*(dee fee-nAHnts-fuh-vAAl-tunk)*
financial pages, newspaper	der Wirtschaftsteil	*(duh vEERt-shahfts-tEYEl)*
financial period	die Bilanzperiode	*(dee bee-lAHnts-pAY-rEE-oh-deh)*
financial planning	die Finanzplanung	*(dee fee-nAHnts-plAA-nunk)*
financial services	die Finanzdienstleistungen	*(dee fee-nAHnts-dEENst-lEYEs-tunk-en)*
financial statement	der Finanzstatus	*(duh fee-nAHnts-stAH-toos)*
financial year	das Geschäftsjahr	*(dahs geh-shEHfts-yAAr)*
fine (penalty)	die Geldstrafe	*(dee GEHLT-shtAA-feh)*
finished goods inventory	der Bestand an Fertigwaren	*(duh beh-shtAHnt ahn fEHr-tikh-vAA-ren)*
finished products	die Endprodukte	*(dee EHnd-Pro-dUk-teh)*
finishing mill	der Schlichfräser	*(duh shLIKH-frAY-zuh)*
fire (v)	feuern	*(FOY-uhn)*
firm	die Firma	*(dee fIR-mah)*
first in-first out (FIFO)	die Zuerstentnahme der ältc-ren Vorräte und deren Bilanzierung zum Buchwert	*(dee tsoo-AYrst-ehnt-nAA-meh duh EHl-tuh-rehn FOHR-reh-teh)*
first preferred stock	die Vorzugsaktien erster Ausgabe	*(dee FOHR-tsoogs-ak-tsEE-en AYR-stuh OWs-gAA-beh)*
fiscal agent	die Zahlstelle	*(dee tsAAL-stEL-leh)*
fiscal drag	die Steuerbremse	*(dee shtOY-uh-brEHm-zeh)*
fishyback service	der Land-Seewegverkehr	*(duh LAHnd-zAY-vAYg-fuh-kAYr)*
fitch hair	das Iltishaar	*(dahs IL-tIS-hAAR)*
fitch hair brush	die Iltishaarbürste	*(dee IL-tIS-hAAR-bEWR-steh)*

F

fixed assets	die Sachanlagen	*(dee zahkh-AHN-lAA-gen)*
fixed capital	das Anlagekapital	*(dahs AHN-lAA-gen-kah-pi-tAAl)*
fixed charges	die Festkosten	*(dee fEHSt-kOS-ten)*
fixed costs	die Fixkosten	*(dee fIx-kOS-ten)*
fixed expenses	die laufenden Ausgaben	*(dee lOWf-en-den-OWs-gAA-behn)*
fixed income security	das festverzinsliche Wertpapier	*(dahs FEHst-vuh-tsINs-likh-es vEHRt-pah-pEEr)*
fixed investment	die festverzinsliche Anlage	*(dee FEHst-vuh-tsINs-likh-eh AHN-lAA-geh)*
fixed liability	die langfristige Verbindlichkeit	*(dee lAAng-fris-tikh-eh fuh-bINd-likh-keyet)*
fixed rate of exchange	der feste Wechselkurs	*(duh fEHs-teh vEHk-sehl-koors)*
fixed term	die festgelegte Frist	*(dee fEHSt-geh-layg-teh frist)*
fixture	das Inventarstück	*(dahs in-vehn-tAAr-shtEWk)*
flat bond	die Obligation ohne aufge-laufene Zinsen	*(dee ob-li-gah-tsEE-ohn ohneh OWf-geh-lOWf-ehneh tsIN-zen)*
flat rate	der einheitliche Satz, die Pauschale	*(duh EYEn-heyet-likh-eh zAHts), (dee pow-shAA-leh)*
flat yield	der Pauschalbetrag	*(duh pow-shAAl-beh-trAHk)*
flatcar	der offene Güterwagen	*(duh OF-feh-neh gEW-tuh-vAA-gehn)*
fleet policy	die Gruppenpolice	*(dee grUP-pen-po-lee-sAY)*
flexible tariff	der Staffeltarif	*(duh shtAH-fel-taa-rIF)*
float (outstanding checks)	die im Einzug befindlichen Schecks	*(dee im EYEn-tsOOk beh-find-lIKH-en shehks)*
float (v) (issue stock)	eine Emission begeben	*(EYE-neh eh-mi-see-OHn beh-gAY-ben)*
floater	die Pauschalversicherung	*(dee pow-shAAL-fuh-zIkheh-runk)*
floating assets	das kurzfristige Umlaufvermögen	*(dahs kURts-fris-tikh-eh um-lOWf-fuh-mER-gen)*
floating charge	die schwebende Belastung	*(dee shvAY-behn-deh beh-lah-stunk)*
floating debt	die schwebende Schuld	*(dee shvAYbehn-deh shUlt)*

floating exchange rate	der gleitende Wechselkurs	*(duh glEYE-ten-duh vEHk-sehl-koors)*
floating rate	der freie Kurs	*(duh frEYE-eh kOOrs)*
floor (stock exchange)	der Börsensaal	*(duh bER-zen-zaal)*
floppy disk	die Diskette	*(dee dis-kEH-teh)*
flow chart	das Schaubild	*(dahs shOW-bild)*
flute	die Flöte	*(dee FLER-teh)*
follow up (v)	verfolgen	*(fuh-FOL-gen)*
follow-up order	der Anschlußauftrag	*(duh AHN-shlUs-OWf-trAHk)*
font	der Schriftsatz	*(duh shrIFT-zAHTS)*
foodstuffs	die Nahrungsmittel	*(dee nAA-runks-mit-tEL)*
footage	die Gesamtlänge	*(dee geh-zaHMT-LEHN-geh)*
footing (accounting)	die Addition	*(dee ah-dI-tsEE-ohn)*
for export	zur Ausfuhr	*(tsoor OWS-foor)*
forecast	die Prognose	*(dee prog-nOH-zeh)*
forecast (v)	voraussagen	*(FOHR-OWS-zAA-gen)*
foreign bill of exchange	der Fremdwährungswechsel	*(duh frehmd-vAY-runks-vEHk-sehl)*
foreign corporation	die ausländische Gesellschaft	*(dee OWS-lehn-di-shuh geh-zEL-shahft)*
foreign currency	die Auslandswährung	*(dee OWs-lahnds-vAY-runk)*
foreign debt	die Auslandsverschuldung	*(dee OWs-lahnds-fuh-shUl-dunk)*
foreign exchange	die Devisen	*(dee deh-vEE-zen)*
foreign security	das ausländische Wertpapier	*(dahs OWs-lEHn-dish-eh vEHRt-pah-pEEr)*
foreign tax credit	die Auslandssteuergutschrift	*(dee OWs-lahnds-shtOY-uh-gOOt-shrift)*
foreign trade	der Außenhandel	*(duh OWs-en-hahn-dehl)*
foreman	der Vorarbeiter	*(duh FOHR-ahr-bEYE-tuh)*
forgery	die Fälschung	*(dee fEHl-shunk)*
fork	die Gabel	*(dee GAA-bel)*
form	die Gestalt	*(dee geh-shtAHlt)*
form letter	der Formularbrief	*(duh fohr-moo-lAAr-brEEf)*

F

format	das Format	*(dahs for-mAAT)*
formula	die Formel	*(dee FOR-mehl)*
forward (v)	befördern	*(beh-fER-duhn)*
forward contract	der Terminabschluß	*(duh tayr-mEEn-AHB-shlUs)*
forward cover	die Kurssicherung	*(dee kOOrs-zikh-uh-runk)*
forward margin	die Termindeckung	*(dee tayr-mEEN-DEK-unk)*
forward market	der Terminmarkt	*(duh tayr-mEEN-mAHrkt)*
forward purchase	der Terminkauf	*(duh tayr-mEEN-kOWf)*
forward shipment	die Terminsendung	*(dee tayr-mEEn-zEN-dunk)*
forwarding agent	der Spediteur	*(duh shpeh-dee-tEWr)*
foul bill of lading	das unreine Konnossement	*(dahs un-rEYE-neh kon-nos-seh-mEH)*
foundry	die Gießerei	*(dee gEE-seh-rEYE)*
four-color	vierfarbig	*(fEER-fAHR-bik)*
four-cylinder engine	der Vierzylindermotor	*(duh fEER-tsew-lin-duh-mOH-tor)*
fox	der Fuchs	*(duh fUKS)*
franchise	der Konzessionsbetrieb	*(duh kon-tsehs-sEE-OHns-beh-trEEp)*
fraud	der Betrug	*(duh beh-trOOg)*
free alongside ship	frei Seeschiffsseite	*(frEYE zAY-shIFs-zEYE-teh)*
free and clear	(debt free) schuldenfrei	*(SHUL-dehn-frEYE)*
free and clear (unencumbered)	lastenfrei	*(lAHs-ten-frEYE)*
free and clear (unmortgaged)	hypothekenfrei	*(hew-poh-tAYk-en-freye)*
free enterprise	die freie Marktwirtschaft	*(dee fEYE-eh mAHrkt-vEErt-shahft)*
free list	die Freiliste	*(dee frEYE-li-teh)*
free market	der freie Markt	*(duh frEYE-eh mAHrkt)*
free of particular average	frei von besonderer Havarie	*(frEYE fon beh-zON-duh-ruh hah-vAA-ree)*
free on board (fob)	frei Schiff	*(frEYE shIF)*
free on rail	frei Eisenbahn	*(frEYE EYE-zen-baan)*
free port	der Freihafen	*(duh frEYE-hAA-fen)*
free time	die Freizeit	*(dee frEYE-tsEYEt)*

F

free trade	der Freihandel	*(duh frEYE-hAHn-dehl)*
free trade zone	die Freihandelszone	*(die frEYE-hAHn-dehls-tsOH-neh)*
freelance writer	der freischaffende Schriftsteller	*(duh frEYE-shAHf-en-duh shrift-shtEHl-luh)*
freight	die Fracht	*(dee frAHKHt)*
freight all kinds	der Frachtbetrieb	*(duh frAHKHt-beh-trEEp)*
freight allowed	Fracht gestattet	*(frAHKHt geh-shtAH-teht)*
freight collect	die Fracht gegen Nachnahme	*(dee frAHKHt gAY-gen nAHKH-nAA-meh)*
freight forwarder	der Frachtführer	*(duh frAHKHt-fEW-ruh)*
freight included	Fracht inbegriffen	*(frAHKHt in-beh-grIF-fen)*
freight prepaid	vorausbezahlte Fracht	*(FOHR-OWs-beh-tsAAl-teh frAHKHt)*
frequency	die Frequenz	*(dee frEH-kvehnts)*
frequency curve	die Frequenzkurve	*(dee freh-kvENTS-kOOr-veh)*
frequency modulation (FM)	die Frequenzmodulation	*(dee frEH-kvehnts-moh-DU-lah-TSI-ohn)*
fringe benefits	die Zusatzleistungen	*(dee tsOO-zAHts-lEYEs-tun-gen)*
fringe market	der Randmarkt	*(duh rAHnt-mAHrkt)*
front-end fee (front-end load)	die Anfangsprovision	*(dee AHN-fahngs-proh-vi-zee-OHn)*
front-wheel drive	der Frontantrieb	*(duh front-AHN-treeb)*
frozen assets	die eingefrorenen Guthaben	*(dee EYEn-geh-frOH-reh-nehn gOOt-hAA-ben)*
fruity	fruchtig	*(frUKH-tik)*
functional analysis	die Funktionsanalyse	*(dee funk-tsee-OHns-ah-nah-lEW-zeh)*
fund	der Fonds, die Mittel	*(duh fOH), (die Mit-tEL)*
fund, contingent	der Reservefonds	*(duh reh-sAYrv-fOH)*
fund, sinking	der Tilgungsfonds	*(duh tIL-gunks-fOH)*
fund, trust	der Treuhandfonds	*(duh trOY-hahnd-fOH)*
funded debt	die verbriefte Schuld	*(dee fuh-brEEf-teh shUlt)*
funds, public	die öffentlichen Mittel	*(dee ERf-fehnt-likh-en MIT-tel)*
funds, working	die Betriebsmittel	*(dee beh-trEEps-mit-tEL)*

fungible	vertretbar, ersetzbar	*(fuh-trAYt-bAAr), (ayr-zEHts-bAAr)*
furnace	der Hochofen	*(duh hOHKH-ohfen)*
futures	die Termingeschäfte	*(dee tayr-mEEn-geh-shehf-teh)*
futures option	die Terminoption	*(dee tayr-mEEn-op-tsEE-ohn)*

G

galley proof	die Fahnenabzug	*(dee fAA-nehn-ahb-tsOOk)*
galvanizing	die Galvanisierung	*(dee gahl-vAA-nEE-zEE-runk)*
garbage	der Müll	*(mewl)*
garbage collection	die Müllabfuhr	*(mEWL-ahp-foor)*
garbage dump	der Müllabladeplatz	*(mewl-ahp-lahd-eh-PLAHTS)*
garnishment	die Beschlagnahme	*(dee beh-shlAHg-nAA-meh)*
gas	das Gas	*(dahs gaas)*
gas consumption	der Benzinverbrauch	*(duh ben-tsEEn-fuh-brOWkh)*
gasoline	das Benzin	*(dahs ben-tsEEn)*
gasoline tank	der Benzintank	*(duh ben-tsEEn-tahnk)*
gearing	der festverzinsliche Anteil am Gesamtkapital	*(duh FEHst-fuh-tsINs-likh-es AHN-teyel ahm geh-zAHmt-kah-pi-tAAL)*
gearless	die Kapitalanlage ohne geborgte Mittel	*(dee kah-pi-tAAl-AHN-lAA-geh oh-neh geh-bOHrg-teh mit-tEL)*
gearshift	die Gangschaltung	*(dee gAHnk-shahl-tunk)*
general acceptance	das Blankoakzept	*(dahs blAAnk-oh-ahk-tsEPt)*
general average loss	der Schaden aus allgemeiner Havarie	*(duh shAA-dehn OWS AHl-geh-mEYE-nuh hah-vAA-rEE)*
general manager	der Generaldirektor	*(duh gen-ah-rAAl-di-rEHK-tohr)*
general meeting	die Generalversammlung	*(dee gen-ah-rAAl-fuh-zAHM-lunk)*
general partnership	die offene Handelsgesellschaft	*(dee OF-fen-neh hAHn-dehls-geh-zEL-shahft)*

general strike	der Generalstreik	*(duh gen-ah-rAAl-shtrEYEk)*
generator	die Lichtmaschine	*(dee LIKHT-mah-SHEE-neh)*
gentleman's agreement	die Vereinbarung auf Treu und Glauben, das Gentleman's Agreement	*(fuh-EYEn-bAa-runk OWf troy unt glOW-ben), (dahs djEHntl-mahns eh-grEE-mehnt)*
gilt-edged investment	die mündelsichere Anlage	*(dee MEWnd-likh-zikh-eh-reh AHN-lAA-geh)*
glass	das Glas	*(dahs glAAs)*
glossy	glänzend	*(glEHN-tsent)*
gloves	die Handschuhe	*(dee HAHNd-shOO-eh)*
glut	das Überangebot	*(dee EW-buh-AHN-geh-boht)*
go around (v)	herumgehen	*(hAYr-um-gAY-hehn)*
go public (v)	umwandeln in eine Aktiengesellschaft	*(um-vahn-dEHln in EYE-neh ak-tsEE-en-geh-zEL-shahft)*
godown	das Lager	*(dahs lAA-guh)*
going concern value	der Ertragswert	*(duh ayr-trAHks-vEHrt)*
going rate (going price)	der übliche Satz	*(duh EWb-likh-uh zAHts)*
gold clause	die Goldklausel	*(dee GOLT-klOW-zel)*
gold price	der Goldpreis	*(duh GOLT-prEYEs)*
gold reserves	die Goldbestände	*(dee GOLT-beh-shtEHn-deh)*
good delivery	die einwandfreie Überbringung	*(dee EYEn-vahnd-frEYE-eh EW-buh-brING-unk)*
goods	die Güter	*(dee gEW-tuh)*
goodwill	der Goodwill	*(duh GOOD-wil)*
government	die Regierung	*(dee reh-gEE-runk)*
government agency	die Regierungstelle	*(dee reh-gEE-runks-shtEHL-leh)*
government bank	die Staatsbank	*(dee shtAAts-bahnk)*
government bonds	die Staatspapiere	*(dee shtAAts-pah-pEE-reh)*
grace period	die tilgungsfreie Zeit	*(dee tIL-gunks-frEYE-eh tsEYEt)*

graduated tax	die gestaffelte Steuer	*(dee geh-shtAHf-fel-teh shtOY-uh)*
graft	die Bestechung	*(dee beh-shtEHKH-unk)*
grain	die Faserung	*(dee fAH-zeh-runk)*
grape	die Weinrebe, die Weinbeere	*(dee vEYEN-ray-beh), (dee vEYEN-bay-reh)*
grape bunch	die Weintraube	*(dee vEYEN-trOW-beh)*
grape harvest	die Weinlese	*(dee vEYEN-leh-zeh)*
graph	die graphische Darstellung	*(dee grAH-fisheh dAAr-shtEHL-lunk)*
gratuity	die Vergütung, die Abfindung	*(dee fuh-gEW-tunk), (dee AHB-fin dunk)*
gravy boat	die Soßenschüssel	*(dee ZOH-sen-SHEWs-sel)*
gray market	der graue Markt	*(duh grOW-eh mAHrkt)*
greenhouse effect	Treibhauseffekt	*(TREYEB-howse-eh-fekt)*
grievance procedure	das Schlichtungsverfahren	*(dahs shlIKH-tunks-fuh-vAA-rehn)*
grille	das Kühlerschutzgitter	*(dahs kEW-luh-shuts-git-tuh)*
grinding	das Mahlen, das Schleifen	*(dahs mAA-len), (dahs shlEYE-fen)*
gross domestic product	das Bruttosozialprodukt	*(dahs BRU-toh-zoh-tsEE-aal-proh-dUKt)*
gross income	das Bruttoeinkommen	*(dahs BRU-toh-eyen-kOM-men)*
gross investment	die Bruttoanlageninvestition	*(dee BRU-toh-AHN-lAA-gen-in-vehs-ti-tsi-OHn)*
gross loss	der Bruttoverlust	*(duh BRU-toh-fuh-lUst)*
gross margin	die Bruttogewinnspanne	*(dee BRU-toh-geh-vIN-shpAHn-neh)*
gross national product	das Bruttosozialprodukt	*(dahs BRU-toh-zoh-tsEE-aal-proh-dUKt)*
gross price	der Bruttopreis	*(duh BRU-toh-prEYEs)*
gross profit	der Bruttogewinn	*(duh BRU-toh-geh-vIN)*
gross receipts	die Bruttoeinnahmen	*(dee BRU-toh-eyen-nAA-men)*
gross sales	der Bruttoumsatz	*(duh BRU-toh-um-zAHts)*
gross spread	der Bruttopreisunterschied	*(duh BRU-toh-prEYEs-un-tuh-shEEd)*

G

gross weight	das Rohgewicht	*(dahs ROH-geh-vikht)*
gross yield	der Bruttoertrag	*(duh BRU-toh-uh-trAHk)*
group account	der Konzernabschluß	*(duh kon-tsAYrn-AHB-shUs)*
group dynamics	die Gruppendynamik	*(dee grUP-pen-dew-nAAm-ik)*
group insurance	die Gruppenversicherung	*(dee grUP-pen-fuh-zIkheh-runk)*
growth	das Wachstum	*(dahs vAHkhs-toom)*
growth area	das Wachstumsgebiet	*(dahs vAHkhs-tooms-geh-bEET)*
growth index	der Wachstumsindex	*(dahs vAHkhs-tooms-in-dEHx)*
growth industry	die Wachstumsindustrie	*(dee vAHkhs-tooms-in-dus-trEE)*
growth potential	das Wachstumspotential	*(dahs vAHkhs-tooms-poh-ten-tsI-AAL)*
growth rate	die Zuwachsrate	*(dee tsOO-vahks-rAA-teh)*
growth stock	die Wachstumsaktie	*(dee vAHkhs-tooms-ak-tsEE-eh)*
guarantee	die Garantie	*(dee gah-rahn-tEE)*
guaranty bond	die gesicherte Obligation	*(dee geh-zIKH-uh-teh ob-li-gah-tsEE-ohn)*
guaranty company	die Kautionsversicherungsges ellschaft	*(dee kow-tsEE-ohns-fuh-zIkheh-runks-geh-sEHl-shahft)*
guesstimate (v)	vermuten	*(fuh-mOO-ten)*
guideline	die Richtlinie	*(dee RIKHt-lee-nee-eh)*

H

half-life	das Halbleben	*(dahs hAHlb-lAY-ben)*
handbag	die Handtasche	*(dee HAHNd-tAH-SHeh)*
handblown (glass)	das handgeblasene Glas	*(dahs hAHNd-geh-bLAA-zeh-neh gLAAs)*
handpainted	handbemalt	*(hAHNd-beh-maalt)*
handicap	der Nachteil	*(duh nAHKH-teyel)*
handkerchief	das Taschentuch	*(dahs tAH-SHen-TOOkh)*
handling	die Abwicklung	*(dee AHB-vIK-lunk)*

G

harbor dues	die Hafengebühren	*(dee hAA-fen-geh-bEW-ren)*
hard copy	der Klartext	*(duh klAAr-text)*
hard currency	die Hartwährung	*(dee hAArt-vAY-runk)*
hard sell	die Holzhammermethode	*(dee hOHlts-hAAm-muh-meh-tOH-deh)*
hardcover	das Hardcover	*(dahs hart-kah-vah)*
hardware	die Mettalwaren	*(dee meh-tAAl-vAA-ren)*
hardware (computer)	die Hardware	*(dee hAHrt-vayr)*
head office	das Hauptbüro	*(dahs hOWpt-bEW-roh)*
headhunter	der Kopfjäger	*(duh KOpf-yay-guh)*
headline	die Überschrift	*(dee EW-buh-shrIFT)*
headquarters	die Zentrale	*(dee tsehn-trAA-leh)*
heat	der Schmelzgang	*(duh shmEHLTS-gahnk)*
heavy industry	die Schwerindustrie	*(dee shvAYr-in-dus-trEE)*
heavy lift charge	der Schwergutaufschlag	*(duh shvAYr-gOOt-OWf-shlAHk)*
hectare	das Hektar	*(dahs hehk-tAAR)*
hedge (v)	sich gegen Verluste sichern	*(zikh gAY-gen fuh-lUs-teh zIKH-uhn)*
hem	der Saum	*(duh zOWm)*
hidden asset	die stille Reserve	*(dee shtIL-leh reh-sAYr-veh)*
high fashion designer	der Couturier	*(duh ku-tEW-ree-ay)*
high fidelity	die High-Fidelity	*(dee HEYE fi-dEH-li-ti)*
highest bidder	der Meistbietende	*(duh mEYEst-bEE-ten-deh)*
hire (v)	anstellen	*(AHN-shtEHL-len)*
hoard (v)	horten	*(hOHr-ten)*
holder	der Inhaber	*(duh IN-haa-buh)*
holder in due course	der ausgewiesene Inhaber	*(duh OWS-geh-vEE-zen-eh IN-haa-buh)*
holding company	die Dachgesellschaft	*(dee daaKH-geh-zEL-shahft)*
holding period	die Haltezeit	*(dee hAHl-teh-tsEYEt)*
hole (in ozone layer)	ozonloch	*(O-tsohn-lokh)*
holiday	der Ruhetag	*(duh rOO-heh-taak)*

holster	das Pistolenhalfter	*(dahs pis-tOH-len-hAHLf-tuh)*
home market	der Binnenmarkt	*(duh BIN-nen-mAHrkt)*
homogeneity	die Homogenität	*(dee homo-gehnI-tAYT)*
hood	die Kapuze	*(dee kah-PU-tseh)*
horsepower	die Pferdestärke	*(dee pfEHR-deh-shtEHR-keh)*
hot money	heiße Geld	*(hEYE-seh gehlt)*
hot rolling	das Warmwalzen	*(dahs vahrm-vAL-tsen)*
hourly earnings	der Stundenlohn	*(duh shtUn-dehn-lOHn)*
house-to-house selling	der Direktverkauf an der Haustür	*(duh di-REHKT-fuh-kOWf ahn duh hOWs-tEWr)*
housing authority (construction)	die Baubehörde	*(dee BOW-beh-hER-deh)*
housing authority (residential)	das Wohnungsamt	*(dahs vOH-nunks-AHmt)*
human resources	das Angestelltenpotential	*(dahs AHN-geh-shtEHL-ten-poh-ten-tsEE-AAL)*
hybrid computer	der Hybridrechner	*(duh hEW-brid-rEHKH-nuh)*
hydrocarbon	der Kohlenwasserstoff	*(duh KOH-len-vAHS-suh-shtOF)*
hydrochloric acid	die Salzsäure	*(dee ZAHlts-ZOY-reh)*
hydrolysis	die Hydrolyse	*(dee HEW-dro-LEW-zeh)*
hypertension	die Hypertonie	*(dee hEW-puh-to-nee)*
hyphenate (v)	mit Bindestrich schreiben	*(mit bIN-deh-shtrIKH shrEYE-ben)*
hypothecation	die Verpfändung, die Beleihung	*(dee fuh-pfEHn-dunk), (dee beh-lEYE-unk)*

I

idle capacity	die ungenutzte Kapazität	*(dee un-geh-nUts-teh kah-pah-tsee-tAYt)*
ignition	die Zündung	*(dee tsEWnd-dunk)*
illegal	gesetzwidrig	*(geh-zEHTs-vEE-drig)*
illegal shipments	die gesetzwidrigen Sendungen	*(dee geh-vEE-dri-gen zEN-dun-gen)*

imitation	die Nachahmung	*(dee nAHKH-ah-munk)*
impact on (v)	wirken auf	*(vEEr-ken OWf)*
impending change	die bevorstehende Änderung	*(dee beh-FOHR-shteh-en-deh EHN-deh-runk)*
implication (conclusion)	die Folgerung	*(dee FOL-guh-runk)*
implication (involvement)	die Verwicklung	*(dee fuh-vIK-lunk)*
implied agreement	die stillschweigend verstandene Zustimmung	*(dee shtIL-shvEYE-gend fuh-shtAHn-deh-neh tsOO-shtIM-munk)*
import	die Einfuhr, der Import	*(dee EYEn-foor), (duh im-pOHrt)*
import (v)	einführen	*(EYEn-fEW-ren)*
import declaration	die Einfuhrerklärung	*(dee EYEn-foor-ayr-klAY-runk)*
import deposits	die Einfuhrdepots	*(dee EYEn-foor-day-pOHs)*
import duty	der Einfuhrzoll	*(duh EYEn-foor-tsOL)*
import entry	die Einfuhrdeklaration	*(dee EYEn-foor-deh-klah-rah-tsEE-ohn)*
import license	die Einfuhrerlaubnis	*(dee EYEn-foor-ayr-lOWb-nis)*
import quota	die Einfuhrquote	*(dee EYEn-foor-kvOH-teh)*
import regulations	die Einfuhrvorschriften	*(dee EYEn-foor-FOHR-shrif-ten)*
import tariff	der Einfuhrzoll	*(dee EYEn-foor-tsOL)*
import tax	die Einfuhrsteuer	*(dee EYEn-foor-shtOY-uh)*
importer of record	der protokollierte Importeur	*(duh proh-toh-ko-lEEr-teh im-pohr-tEWr)*
impound (v)	beschlagnahmen	*(beh-shlAHg-nAA-mehn)*
improve upon (v)	verbessern	*(fuh-bEHs-sun)*
improvement	die Verbesserung	*(dee fuh-bEHs-suh-runk)*
impulse purchase	der Spontankauf	*(duh shpon-tAAn-kOWf)*
impurity	die Unreinheit	*(dee UN-rEYEn-heyet)*
imputed	zugeschrieben	*(tsoo-geh-shrEE-behn)*
in the red	im Debet	*(im deh-beht)*
in transit	unterwegs	*(un-tuh-vAYgs)*
inadequate	unzulänglich	*(un-tsoo-lEHng-likh)*

I

incentive	der Ansporn	*(duh AHN-shporn)*
inch	der Zoll	*(duh tsOL)*
inchoate interest	das Anwartschaftsrecht	*(dahs AHN-vahrt-shahfts-rEHKHt)*
incidental expenses	die Nebenausgaben	*(dee nAY-ben-OWs-gAA-ben)*
income	das Einkommen	*(dahs EYEn-kOM-men)*
income account	das Ertragskonto	*(dahs ayr-trAHks-kON-toh)*
income bonds	die Gewinnobligationen	*(dee geh-vIN-ob-li-gah-tsEE-ohn-nen)*
income bracket	die Einkommensgruppe	*(dee EYEn-kOM-menz-grUp-peh)*
income, gross	das Bruttoeinkommen	*(dahs BRU-toh-EYEn-kOM-mehn)*
income, net	das Nettoeinkommen	*(dahs NEH-toh-EYEn-kOM-mehn)*
income statement	die Gewinn und Verlustrechnung	*(dee geh-vIN unt fuh-lUst-rEHKH-nunk)*
income tax	die Einkommensteuer	*(dee EYEn-kOM-mehnz-shtOY-uh)*
incorporate (v)	gesellschaftlich organisieren und gründen	*(geh-zEL-shahft-likh ohr-gaa-nee-zEE-ren unt grEWn-den)*
increase	der Aufschlag	*(duh OWf-shlAHk)*
increase (v)	vermehren	*(fuh-mAY-ren)*
increased costs	die gestiegenen Kosten	*(dee geh-shtEE-gen-en kOS-ten)*
incremental cash flow	der Geldumlaufzuwachs	*(duh GEHLT-um-lOWf-tsOO-vahks)*
incremental costs	die Grenzkosten	*(dee grEHNts-kOS-ten)*
indebtedness	die Verschuldung	*(dee fuh-shUl-dunk)*
indemnity	die Entschädigung	*(dee EHNt-shAY-di-gunk)*
indenture	die Vertragsurkunde	*(dee fuh-trAHks-OOr-kun-deh)*
index	der Index	*(duh IN-dehx)*
index (v)	registrieren	*(ray-gis-trEEr-ehn)*
index option	die Indexoption	*(dee IN-dehx-op-tsEE-ohn)*
indexing	die Indexierung	*(dee IN-dehk-sEE-runk)*

indirect claim	der indirekte Anspruch	*(dee in-di-REK-teh AHN-shprUkh)*
indirect costs	die Gemeinkosten	*(dee geh-mEYEn-kOS-ten)*
indirect expenses	die Fertigungsgemeinkosten	*(dee fEHr-ti-gunks-geh-mEYEn-kOS-ten)*
indirect labor	die Gemeinkostenlöhne	*(dee geh-mEYEn-kOS-ten-lER-neh)*
indirect tax	die indirekte Steuer	*(dee in-di-REK-teh shtOY-uh)*
induction	die Induktion	*(dee IN-duk-TSI-On)*
induction furnace	der Induktionsofen	*(duh IN-duk-TSI-Ons-ohfen)*
industrial accident	der Arbeitsunfall	*(duh AHR-beyets-un-fahl)*
industrial arbitration	die gewerbliche Schiedsgerichtbarkeit	*(dee geh-vAYrb-likh-eh shEEds-geh-rIKHts-baar-keyet)*
industrial engineering	die Gewerbetechnik	*(dee geh-vAYr-beh-tEHKH-nik)*
industrial goods	die Industrieprodukte	*(dee in-dus-trEE-proh-dUK-teh)*
industrial insurance	die Betriebsversicherung	*(dee beh-trEEps-fuh-zIkheh-runk)*
industrial planning	die Industrieplanung	*(dee in-dus-trEE-plAA-nunk)*
industrial relations	die Arbeitsbeziehungen	*(dee AHR-beyets-beh-tsEE-hun-gen)*
industrial union	die Industriegewerkschaft	*(dee in-dus-trEE-geh-vAYrk-shahft)*
industry	die Industrie	*(dee in-dus-trEE)*
industrywide	die gesamte Industrie betref-fend	*(dee geh-zAHm-teh in-dus-trEE-beh-trEH-fehnt)*
inefficient	ineffizient	*(in-ehf-fi-tsEE-ehnt)*
inelastic demand	starre Nachfrage	*(shtAH-reh nAHKH-frAA-geh)*
inelastic supply	starres Angebot	*(shtAH-rehs AHN-geh-boht)*
infant industry	die schutzzollbedürftige Industrie	*(dee shUts-tsOL-beh-dEWrf-ti-geh in-dus-trEE)*
inflation	die Inflation	*(die in-flah-tsee-OHn)*
inflationary	inflationär	*(in-flah-tsee-oh-nAYr)*
infrastructure	die Infrastruktur	*(dee in-frah-struk-tOOr)*
ingot mold	die Gußform	*(dee gUS-FORm)*

I

ingots	die Gußblöcke	*(dee gUS-bLER-keh)*
inheritance tax	die Nachlaßsteuer	*(dee nAHKH-lahss-shtOY-uh)*
injection	die Spritze	*(dee shpRI-tseh)*
injector	der Einspritzer	*(duh EYEn-shprIT-tsuh)*
injunction	die gerichtliche Anordnung	*(dee geh-rIKHt-likh-eh AHN-ord-nunk)*
ink	die Tinte	*(dee TIN-Teh)*
inland bill of lading	der inländische Frachtbrief	*(duh in-layn-dISH-eh geh-zEL-shahft)*
innovation	die Neuerung	*(dee NOY-uh-runk)*
inorganic chemistry	die unorganische Chemie	*(dee ahn-or-gAA-ni-she KHAY-mee)*
input	die Eingabe	*(dee EYEn-gAA-beh)*
input-output analysis	die Eingaben-Ausgaben Analyse	*(dee EYEn-gAA-ben-OWs-gAA-ben ah-nah-lEW-zeh)*
insert	die Einlage	*(dee EYEn-laa-geh)*
insolvent	insolvent	*(IN-sohl-vehnt)*
inspection	die Inspektion	*(dee in-spehk-tsEE-ohn)*
inspector	der Inspektor	*(duh in-spehk-tOHr)*
instability	die Unbeständigkeit	*(dee un-beh-shtEHn-dikh-keyet)*
installment credit	der Teilzahlungskredit	*(duh teyel-tsAA-lungs-kray-dIT)*
installment plan	der Teilzahlungsplan	*(duh teyel-tsAA-lungs-plAAn)*
institutional advertising	die Firmenwerbung	*(dee fIR-men-vAYr-bunk)*
institutional investor	der institutionelle Investor	*(duh in-sti-tu-tsee-oh-nEL-leh in-vEHs-tohr)*
instruct (v) (order)	anordnen	*(AHN-ord-nen)*
instruct (v) (teach)	unterrichten	*(un-tuh-rIKH-ten)*
instrument (document)	die Urkunde	*(dee OOr-kun-deh)*
instrumental capital	das Produktivkapital	*(dahs proh-duk-tEEf-kah-pi-tAAl)*
insufficient assets	die unzureichenden Aktiva	*(dee un-tsoo-rEYEkh-en-den ahk-tEE-vah)*

I

insulator	der Isolator	*(duh EE-zo-LAA-tor)*
insurance	die Versicherung	*(dee fuh-zIkheh-runk)*
insurance broker	der Versicherungsmakler	*(duh fuh-zIkh-eh-runks-mAHk-luh)*
insurance company	die Versicherungsgesell-schaft	*(dee fuh-zIkh-eh-runks-geh-zEL-shahft)*
insurance fund	die Versicherungskasse	*(dee fuh-zIkh-eh-runks-kAH-seh)*
insurance policy	die Versicherungspolice	*(dee fuh-zIkh-eh-runks-poh-lee-sAY)*
insurance premium	die Versicherungsprämie	*(dee fuh-zIkh-eh-runks-PRAY-mee-eh)*
insurance underwriter	der Versicherer	*(duh fuh-zIkh-eh-ruh)*
intangible assets	die immateriellen Werte	*(dee im-mah-tayr-ree-EL-en vEHr-teh)*
integrated circuit	der integrierte Schaltkreis	*(duh in-teh-gREER-tuh shAHLt-krEYES)*
integrated management system	das eingegliederte Führungssystem	*(dahs EYEn-geh-glEE-uh-teh fEW-runks-zew-stAYm)*
interact (v)	aufeinander wirken	*(OWf-eyen-AHN-duh vEEr-ken)*
interbank	zwischen Banken	*(tsvISH-en bahnk-en)*
interest	das Interesse (general	*(dahs in-tayr-reh-sEH)*
interest (return on capital)	die Verzinsung	*(dee fuh-tsIN-zunk)*
interest (share)	der Anteil	*(duh AHN-teyel)*
interest arbitrage	die Zinsarbitrage	*(dee tsINs-ahr-bi-trAAsh)*
interest expenses	die Zinsaufwendungen	*(dee tsINs-OWf-vEHn-dunk-en)*
interest income	der Zinsertrag	*(duh tsINs-uh-trAHk)*
interest parity	der Interessenausgleich	*(duh in-tayr-reh-sEHnts-OWs-gleyekh)*
interest period	der Verzinsungszeitraum	*(duh fuh-tsINs-zunks-tsEYEt-rOWm)*
interest rate	der Zinssatz	*(duh tsINs-zAHts)*
interim	einstweilig	*(EYEnst-vEYE-likh)*
interim budget	der Zwischenhaushalt	*(duh tsvISH-en-hOWs-hAHlt)*

I

interim statement	die Zwischenbilanz	*(dee tsvISH-en-bee-lAHnts)*
interlocking directorate	der Schachtelaufsichtsrat	*(duh shAHkh-tel-OWf-zikhts-raat)*
intermediary	der Vermittler	*(duh fuh-mIT-luh)*
intermediary goods	die Zwischenwaren	*(dee tsvISH-en-vAA-rehn)*
internal	intern	*(in-tAYrn)*
internal audit	die innerbetriebliche Revision	*(dee IN-nuh-beh-trEEp-likh-eh rAY-vi-zEE-ohn)*
internal funding	die Innenfinanzierung	*(dee IN-nen-fee-nahn-tsEE-runk)*
internal rate of return	die interne Rendite	*(dee in-tAYr-neh ren-di-teh)*
internal revenue tax	die inländischen Steuern und Abgaben	*(dee in-layn-dISH-en shtOY-uhn unt AHB-gAA-ben)*
International Date Line	die internationale Datumsgrenze	*(dee in-tayr-nah-tsee-oh-nAAL-eh DAA-tumz-grEHn-tseh)*
International Development Agency	Die Internationale Entwicklungsstelle	*(dee in-tayr-nah-tsee-oh-nAAL-eh ehnt-vIK-lunks-shtEHL-leh)*
International Monetary Fund	Der Weltwährungsfonds	*(duh VEHLT-vAY-runks-fOH)*
interstate commerce	der zwischenstaatliche Handel	*(duh tsvISH-en-shtAAt-lIKH-eh hAHn-dehl)*
intervene (v)	dazwischenkommen	*(dah-tsvISH-en-kOM-men)*
interview	die Unterredung	*(dee un-tuh-rAY-dunk)*
intestate	ohne Testament	*(oh-neh tehs-tah-mEHnt)*
intrinsic value	der innere Wert	*(duh IN-nuh-reh vEHRt)*
introduction	die Einführung	*(dee EYEn-FEWR-runk)*
invalidate (v)	ungültig machen	*(un-gEWl-tikh mAA-khen)*
inventory	das Inventar	*(dahs in-vehn-tAAr)*
inventory control	die Bestandsüberwachung	*(dee beh-shtahnts-EW-buh-vAAkh-unk)*
inventory turnover	der Lagerumschlag	*(duh lAA-guh-um-shlAHk)*
inverted market	der umgekehrte Markt	*(duh um-geh-kAYr-teh mAHRkt)*
invest (v)	anlegen	*(AHN-lay-gen)*
invested capital	das angelegte Kapital	*(dahs AHN-geh-layg-teh kah-pi-tAAL)*

I

investment	die Investition	*(dee in-vehs-ti-tsi-OHn)*
investment adviser	der Anlageberater	*(duh AHN-laa-geh-buh-rAA-tuh)*
investment analysis	die Anlagenanalyse	*(dee AHN-lAA-gen-ah-nah-lEW-zeh)*
investment bank	die Emissionsbank	*(dee eh-mi-see-OHns-bahnk)*
investment budget	das Investitionsbudget	*(dee in-vehs-ti-tsi-OHnz-bew-djEH)*
investment company	die Investmentgesellschaft	*(dee in-vehs-mEHnt-geh-zEL-shahft)*
investment credit	der Anlagekredit	*(duh AHN-lAA-geh-kray-dIT)*
investment criteria	die Investitionskriterien	*(dee in-vehs-ti-tsi-OHnz-kree-tAY-ree-en)*
investment grade	die Investitionseinstufung und Bewertung	*(dee in-vehs-ti-tsi-OHnz-eyen-shtOO-funk unt geh-vEHr-tunk)*
investment letter	der Anlagebrief	*(duh AHN-laa-geh-brEEf)*
investment policy	die Investitionspolitik	*(dee in-vehs-ti-tsi-OHnz-po-li-tEEk)*
investment program	das Investitionsprogramm	*(dahs in-vehs-ti-tsi-OHnz-proh-grAHm)*
investment strategy	die Investitionsstrategie	*(dee in-vehs-ti-tsi-OHnz-strah-teh-gEE)*
investment trust	die Investmenttreuhand-gesellschaft	*(dee in-vehs-mEHnt-trOY-hahnd-geh-zEL-shahft)*
investor relations	die Beziehungen zu den Anlegern	*(dee beh-tsEE-hun-gen tsoo dehn AHN-lay-guhn)*
invisible	unsichtbar	*(UN-zikht-baar)*
invitation to bid	die Ausschreibung	*(dee OWs-shrEYE-bunk)*
invoice	die Faktura	*(dee fAHk-tOO-rah)*
invoice cost	der Fakturenpreis	*(duh fAHk-tOOr-en-prEYEs)*
iodine	das Jod	*(dahs yOHt)*
iron	das Eisen	*(dahs EYE-zen)*
iron ore	das Eisenerz	*(dahs EYE-zen-EHRTS)*
isotope	das Isotop	*(dahs EE-zo-tohp)*
issue (v)	ausgeben	*(OWs-gay-behn)*
issue, stock	die Ausgabe	*(dee OWs-gAA-beh)*
issue price	der Ausgabekurs	*(duh OWs-gAA-beh-kOOrs)*

issue stock	die Emission	*(dee eh-mi-see-OHn)*
issued shares	die ausgegebenen Aktien	*(dee OWs-geh-gAY-beh-nen ak-tsEE-en)*
italic	kursiv	*(kur-zEEF)*
item	der Eintrag	*(duh EYEn-trAHk)*
itemize (v)	aufgliedern	*(OWf-glee-duhn)*
itemized account	die spezifizierte Rechnung	*(dee speh-tsee-fee-tsEEf-teh rEHKH-nunk)*

J

jacket	die Jacke	*(dee yAH-Keh)*
Jason clause	die Jasonsklausel	*(dee yAH-zohns-klOW-zehl)*
jawbone (v)	gründlich besprechen	*(grEWnd-likh beh-shprEHKH-en)*
jet lag	die Nachflugerschöpfung	*(dee nAHKH-floog-ayr-shERp-funk)*
jewelry	der Schmuck	*(duh shmUK)*
job	die Arbeit	*(dee AHR-beyet)*
job analysis	die Arbeitsstudie	*(dee AHR-beyets-shtOO-dee-eh)*
job description	die Arbeitsbeschreibung	*(dee AHR-beyets-beh-shrEYE-bunk)*
job evaluation	die Arbeitsbewertung	*(dee AHR-beyets-beh-vEHR-tunk)*
job hopper	der häufige Stellenwechsler	*(duh hOY-fi-geh shtEHL-len-vEHKHs-luh)*
job lot	der Restposten	*(duh rEHSt-pOS-ten)*
job performance	die Arbeitsleistung	*(dee AHR-beyets-lEYEs-tunk)*
job security	die Arbeitsplatzsicherheit	*(dee AHR-beyets-plahts-zikh-huh-heyet)*
job shop	der Einzelfertigungsbetrieb	*(duh EYEn-tsel-fEHr-ti-gunks-beh-trEEp)*
jobber	der Grossist	*(duh groh-SISt)*
jobber's turn	der Lagerumschlag des Grossisten	*(duh lAA-guh-um-shlAHk dehs groh-SIS-ten)*
joint account	das gemeinschaftliche Konto	*(dahs geh-mEYEn-shahft-likh-eh kON-toh)*

joint cost	die Umlagekosten	*(dee um-lAA-geh-kOS-ten)*
joint estate	der gemeinsame Besitz	*(duh geh-mEYEn-zAA-meh beh-zITs)*
joint liability	die gesamtschuldnerische Haftung	*(dee geh-zAHmt-shUlt-neh-rish-eh hAHf-tunk)*
joint owner	der Miteigentümer	*(duh MIT-eye-gen-tEW-muh)*
joint stock company	die Aktiengesellschaft	*(dee ak-tsEE-en-geh-zEL-shahft)*
joint venture	das gemeinschaftliche Unternehmen	*(dahs geh-mEYEn-shahft-likh-eh un-tuh-nAY-men)*
journal	das Geschäftstagebuch, das Journal	*(dahs geh-shEHfts-tAA-geh-bOOkh), (dahs djoor-naal)*
journeyman	der Geselle	*(duh geh-zEL-leh)*
joystick	der Steuerknüppel	*(duh shtOY-uh-knEWp-pel)*
junior partner	der Juniorpartner	*(duh djOO-nee-ohr pAHrt-nuh)*
junior security	das Wertpapier nachgeord-neter Sicherheit	*(dahs vEHRt-pah-pEEr nAHKH-geh-OHrd-neh-tuh zIKH-uh-heyet)*
jurisdiction	der Amtsbereich	*(duh AMts-beh-rEYEkh)*
justify (v)	justieren	*(yus-tEE-ren)*

K

keep posted (v)	auf dem laufenden halten	*(OWf dehm lOW-fen-den hAHl-ten)*
key case	das Schlüsseletui	*(dahs shlEWS-sel-e-tuEE)*
key exports	die Hauptausfuhrwaren	*(dee hOWpt-OWs-foor-vAA-ren)*
key man insurance	die Versicherung für Personen in Schlüsselstellungen	*(dee fuh-zIkheh-runk fEWr pAYr-soh-nen in shlEW-sehl-shtEHL-lunk-en)*
Keynesian economics	die Keynessche Wirtschaftslehre	*(dee kEHns-sheh vEErt-shahfts-lAY-reh)*
keypuncher	der Locher	*(duh lOKH-uh)*
kickback	das Schmiergeld	*(dahs shmEEr-gehlt)*
kidskin	das Ziegenleder	*(dahs tsEE-gen-lAY-duh)*

kilowatt	das Kilowatt	*(dahs KI-loh-vaht)*
kiting	die Wechselreiterei	*(deevEHk-sehl-reye-tuh-rEYE)*
knife	das Messer	*(dahs MEHS-suh)*
knot (nautical)	die Seemeile	*(dee ZAY-mEYE-leh)*
know-how	das Können	*(dahs kER-nen)*

L

label	das Etikett	*(dahs eh-TI-ket)*
labor code	die Arbeitsverfassung	*(dee AHR-beyets-fuh-fAHS-sunk)*
labor die	Arbeiterschaft	*(ahr-bEYE-tuh-shahft)*
labor dispute	die Tarifstreitigkeit	*(dee taa-rIF-shtrEYE-tikh-keyet)*
labor force	die Arbeitskräfte	*(dee AHR-beyets-krehf-teh)*
labor law	das Arbeitsrecht	*(dahs AHR-beyets-rEHKHt)*
labor leader	der Arbeiterführer	*(duh AHR-beyet-uh-fEW-ruh)*
labor market	der Arbeitsmarkt	*(duh AHR-beyets-mAHrkt)*
labor relations	das Arbeitgeber-Arbeitnehmerverhältnis	*(dahs AHR-beyet-gAY-buh-AHR-beyet-nAY-muh-fuh-hEHLt-nis)*
labor turnover	der Personalwechsel	*(duh payr-soh-nAAl-vEHk-sehl)*
labor union	die Gewerkschaft	*(dee geh-vAYrk-shahft)*
labor-intensive	arbeitsintensiv	*(AHR-beyets-in-ten-zEEf)*
labor-saving	arbeitsparend	*(AHR-beyet-shpAA-rent)*
laboratory	das Labor	*(dahs lah-bOHR)*
laboratory technician	der Labortechniker	*(duh lah-bOHR-tehkh-ni-kuh)*
laborer	der Arbeiter	*(duh AHR-beyet-uh)*
lace	die Spitze	*(dee SHPIT-tseh)*
lagging indicator	der nachhängende Konjunkturindikator	*(duh nAHKH-hehn-gen-deh kon-yunk-tOOr-in-di-KAH-tohr)*
laissez-faire	der freie Wettbewerb	*(duh frEYE-eh veht-beh-vAYrb)*

lamb	das Schafleder	*(dahs shAAF-lAY-duh)*
land	das Land	*(dahs lahnd)*
land grant	die Landzuteilung	*(dee LAHnd-tsOO-teye-lunk)*
land reform	die Bodenreform	*(dee BOH-den-reh-fOHrm)*
land tax	die Grundsteuer	*(dee grUNd-shtOY-uh)*
landed cost	die Gesamtkosten für importierte Waren	*(dee geh-zAHmt-kOS-ten fEWr im-pOHr-tEEr-teh vAA-ren)*
landfill	die Deponie	*(dee DEH-poh-nee)*
landing certificate	der Löschschein	*(dahs lERsh-shEYEn)*
landing charges	die Landungsgebühren	*(dee LAHn-dunks-geh-bEW-ren)*
landing costs	die Löschkosten	*(dee lERsh-kOS-ten)*
landowner	der Grundbesitzer	*(duh grUnd-beh-zIT-suh)*
large-scale	großangelegt	*(grOHs-AHN-geh-laygt)*
laser	der Laser (strahl)	*(duh LAA-zuh [shtRAAl])*
last in-first out (LIFO)	die Zuerstentnahme der neuen Vorräte	*(dee tsoo-AYrst-ehnt-nAA-meh duh NOY-en FOHR-reh-teh)*
law	das Gesetz	*(dahs geh-zEHts)*
law of diminishing returns	das Gesetz vom abnehmenden Ertrag	*(dahs geh-zEHts fom ahb-nAY-men-den uh-trAHk)*
lawsuit	der Prozeß	*(duh proh-tsEHs)*
lawyer	der Rechtsanwalt	*(duh REHKHTS-AHN-vahlt)*
laxative	das Abführmittel	*(dahs ahb-fEWR-mit-tel)*
lay off (v)	entlassen	*(EHNt-lAH-sen)*
lay time	die Liegezeit	*(dee LEE-geh-tsEYEt)*
lay up (v)	ein Schiff außer Dienst stellen	*(eyen shIF OWs-uh dEEnst shtEL-len)*
laydays	die Liegetage	*(dee LEE-geh-tAA-geh)*
layout	das Layout	*(dahs LAY-owt)*
lead time	die Vorlaufzeit	*(dee FOHR-lOWf-tseyet)*
leader	der Führer	*(duh fEW-ruh)*
leading indicator	der Vorindikator	*(duh FOHR-ahr-tIK-el)*
leads and lags	gut und schlecht verkaufte Artikel	*(gOOt unt shlEHKHt fuh-kOWf-teh ahr-tIK-el)*

L

leakage	die Leckage	*(dee lehk-AAdj)*
learning curve	die Lernkurve	*(dee lAYrn-kOOr-feh)*
lease	der Mietvertrag	*(duh MEET-fuh-trAHk)*
lease (v)	mieten	*(MEE-ten)*
leased department	die gemietete Abteilung	*(dee geh-MEE-teh-teh AHB-tEYE-lunk)*
leather	das Leder	*(dahs lAY-duh)*
leather goods	die Lederwaren	*(dee lAY-duh-VAAren)*
leather jacket	die Lederjacke	*(dee lAY-duh-yAH-Keh)*
leave of absence	der Urlaub	*(duh OOr-lOWb)*
ledger	das Hauptbuch	*(dahs hOWpt-bOOkh)*
ledger account	das Hauptbuchkonto	*(dahs hOWpt-bOOkh-kON-toh)*
ledger entry	die Hauptbucheintragung	*(dee hOWpt-bOOkh-EYEn-traa-gunk)*
legacy	das Vermächtnis	*(dahs fuh-mEHkht-nis)*
legal action	die Klage	*(dee klAA-geh)*
legal capital	das festgesetzte Eigenkapital	*(dahs FEHst-geh-zEHts-teh EYE-gen-kah-pi-tAAL)*
legal entity	die juristische Person	*(dee yoor-IS-tish-eh payr-zOHn)*
legal holiday	der gesetzliche Feiertag	*(duh geh-zEHts-likh-eh fEYE-uh-tAAk)*
legal list (fiduciary investments)	die Investitionsliste	*(dee in-vehs-ti-tsi-OHnz-lis-teh)*
legal monopoly	das gesetzliche Monopol	*(dahs geh-zEHts-likh-eh mo-noh-pOHl)*
legal reserve (banking)	die gesetzliche Rücklage	*(dee geh-zEHts-likh-eh rEWk-laa-geh)*
legal tender	das gesetzliche Zahlungsmittel	*(dahs geh-zEHts-likh-eh tsAA-lungs-mit-tEL)*
lending margin	die Kreditsicherungsgrenze	*(dee kray-dIT-zikh-uh-runks-grEHN-tseh)*
length	die Länge	*(dee LEHN-geh)*
less-than-carload	die Stückgutsendung	*(dee shtEWk-gOOt-zEN-dunk)*
lessee	der Mieter	*(duh MEE-tuh)*
lessor	der Vermieter	*(duh fuh-mEE-tuh)*

L

letter	der Brief	*(duh brEEf)*
letter of credit	der Kreditbrief	*(duh kray-dIT-brEEF)*
letter of guaranty	der Mietsvertrag	*(duh MEEts-fuh-trAHk)*
letter of indemnity	die Konnossementsgarantie	*(dee kon-no-seh-mEHnts-gah-rahn-tEE)*
letter of introduction	das Empfehlungsschreiben	*(dahs em-pfAY-lunks-shrEYE-ben)*
letterhead	der Geschäftsbogen	*(duh geh-shEHfts-bOH-gen)*
level out (v)	ausgleichen, abflachen	*(OWs-gleyekh-en), (AHB-flah-khen)*
leverage	die Hebelwirkung	*(dee hAY-bel-vEEr-kunk)*
leveraged lease	der Mietsvertrag mit Bestimmungen für Einrichtungsfinanzierung und eventuellem Ankauf	*(duh MEEts-fuh-trAHk mit beh-shtIM-mun-gen fEWr EYEn-rikh-tunks-fee-nAHn-tsEE-runk unt eh-vehn-too-EL-lem AHN-kOWf)*
levy taxes (v)	Steuern erheben	*(shtOY-uhn ayr-hAY-ben)*
liability	die Haftung	*(dee hAHf-tunk)*
liability, actual	die tatsächliche Haftpflicht	*(dee taht-sEHKH-likh-eh hAHft-pflIKHt*
liability, assumed	die übernommene Verpflichtung	*(dee EW-buh-nom-meh-neh fuh-pflIKH-tunk)*
liability, contingent	die Eventuellverbindlichkeit	*(dee eh-vehn-too-EL-fuh-bINd-likh-keyet)*
liability, current	die kurzfristige Verbindlichkeit	*(dee kURts-fris-tikh-eh fuh-bINd-likh-keyet)*
liability, fixed	die langfristige Verbindlichkeit	*(dee lAHng-fris-tikh-eh fuh-bINd-likh-keyet)*
liability insurance	die Haftpflichtversicherung	*(dee hAHft-pflIKHt-fuh-zIkheh-runk)*
liability, secured	die gesicherte Haftung	*(dee geh-ZIKH-uh-teh hAHf-tunk)*
liability, unsecured	die ungesicherte Haftung	*(dee un-geh-ZIKH-uh-teh hAHf-tunk)*
liable for tax	steuerpflichtig	*(shtOY-uh-pflIKH-tik)*
liable to (responsible)	verantwortlich	*(fuh-AHnt-vOHrt-likh)*
liaison	die Verbindung	*(dee fuh-bIN-dunk)*
libel	die Verleumdung	*(dee fuh-lOYm-dunk)*

L

license	die Lizenz	*(dee lee-tsEHnts)*
license fees	die Lizenzgebühren	*(dee lee-tsEHnts-geh-bEWr-en)*
licensed warehouse	das genehmigte Lagerhaus	*(dahs geh-nAY-mig-teh lAA-guh-hOWs)*
lien	das Pfandrecht	*(dahs pfAHnt-rehkht)*
life cycle	die Lebensdauer	*(dee lAY-benz-dOW-uh)*
life insurance policy	die Lebensversicherungs-police	*(dee lAY-benz-fuh-zIkheh-runks-poh-lee-sAY)*
life member	das Mitglied auf Lebenszeit	*(dahs MIT-gleed OWf lAY-benz-tsEYEt)*
life of a patent	die Dauer eines Patentes	*(dee dOW-uh EYE-nehs pah-tEHn-tes)*
lighterage	der Schutentransport	*(duh SHOO-ten-trAHnz-port)*
limestone	der Eisenbitterkalk	*(duh EYE-zen-bIT-tuh-kahlk)*
limit order (stock market)	die limitierte Börsenorder	*(dee li-mee-tEEr-teh bER-zen-OR-duh)*
limited liability	die beschränkte Haftung	*(dee beh-shrAYnk-teh hAHf-tunk)*
limited partnership	die Kommanditgesellschaft	*(dee kom-mahn-dIT-geh-zEHl-shahft)*
line	die Linie	*(dee LEE-ni-eh)*
line drawing	die Federzeichnung	*(dee fAY-duh-tsEYEKH-nunk)*
line executive	der Liniendirektor	*(duh LEE-nee-ehn-di-rEHK-tohr)*
line management	das Linienmanagement	*(dahs LEE-nee-ehn-mehn-EHdj-mehnt)*
line of business	der Geschäftsbereich	*(duh geh-shEHfts-beh-rEYEkh)*
lineal estimation	die lineare Schätzung	*(dee lin-ay-AA-reh shAY-tsunk)*
linear	gradlinig	*(grAAd-li-nig)*
linear programming	die lineare Programmierung	*(dee lin-ay-AA-reh proh-grAH-mee-runk)*
linear terms	die linearen Bedingungen	*(dee lin-ay-AA-ren beh-dING-unk-en)*
linen	das Leinen	*(dahs LEYE-nen)*

L

lingerie	die Feinwäsche	*(dee fEYEN-vEH-sheh)*
lining	das Futter	*(dahs fUT-tuh)*
liquid assets	das Umlaufvermögen	*(dahs um-lOWf-fuh-mER-gen)*
liquidation	die Auflösung	*(dee OWf-ler-zung)*
liquidation value	der Auflösungswert	*(duh OWf-ler-zungs-vEHrt)*
liquidity	die Liquidität	*(dee li-kvi-dee-tAYt)*
liquidity preference	die Liquiditätsbevorzugung	*(dee li-kvi-dee-tAYts-beh-FOHR-tsoo-gunk)*
liquidity ratio	der Liquiditätsgrad	*(duh li-kvi-dee-tAYts-grAHd)*
list price	der Listenpreis	*(duh lIS-ten-prEYEs)*
listed securities	die amtlich notierten Werte	*(dee AHmt-likh noh-tEEr-ten vEHr-ten)*
listing	die Katalogisierung	*(dee kah-tah-loh-gee-zEE-runk)*
liter	der Liter	*(duh LEE-tuh)*
litigation	der Rechtsstreit	*(duh REHKHt-shrEYEt)*
living trust	das Treuhandverhältnis unter Lebenden	*(dahs trOY-hAHnd-fuh-hEHlt-nis un-tuh lAY-ben-den)*
lizard (skin)	das Eidechsenleder	*(dahs EYE-dekh-sen-lAY-duh)*
load (sales charge)	die Verkaufsgebühr	*(dee fuh-kOWfs-geh-bEWr)*
load factor	der Kapazitätsausnutzungs-grad	*(duh kah-pah-tsee-tAYts-OWs-nUts-unks-grAAd)*
loan	das Darlehn	*(dahs dAAr-layn)*
loan agreement	der Darlehnsvertrag	*(dahs dAAr-layns-fuh-trAHk)*
loan value	der Lombardwert	*(duh lom-bAArd-vEHrt)*
lobbying	die Meinungsbeeinflussung der Abgeordneten durch Interessengruppen	*(dee mEYE-nunks-beh-EYEn-flus-sunk duh AHB-geh-ORd-neh-ten durkh IN-teh-rehs-sen-grUP-pen)*
local customs	die Ortsgebräuche	*(dee OHRts-geh-brOYkh-eh)*
local tax	die Gemeindesteuer	*(dee geh-mEYEn-deh-shtOY-uh)*
lock in	Kapital blockieren	*(kah-pi-tAALblo-kEE-rehn)*

L

lock out (v)	aussperren	*(OWs-shpehr-en)*
logistics	die Logistik	*(dee loh-gIS-tik)*
logo	das Firmenzeichen	*(dahs fIR-men-tsEYE-khen)*
long hedge	der langfristige Terminkauf	*(duh lAAng-fris-tikh-eh tayr-mEEn-kOWf)*
long interest	die langfristige Verzinsung	*(duh lAAng-fris-tikh-eh fuh-tsIN-zunk)*
long sleeves	die langen Armel	*(dee LAHN-gen AYR-mel)*
long ton	die englische Tonne	*(dee AYN-glish-eh-tON-neh)*
long-range planning	die langfristige Planung	*(dee lAAng-fris-tikh-eh plAA-nunk)*
long-term capital account	das langfristige Kapitalkonto	*(dahs lAAng-fris-tikh-eh kah-pi-tAAL-kON-toh)*
long-term debt	die langfristige Schuld	*(dee lAAng-fris-tikh-eh shUlt)*
loss	der Verlust	*(duh fuh-lUst)*
loss, gross	der Bruttoverlust	*(duh BRU-toh-fuh-lUst)*
loss leader	der Lockartikel	*(duh lOK-ahr-ti-kel)*
loss, net	der Reinverlust	*(duh REYEN-fuh-lUst)*
loss, total	der Totalverlust	*(duh toh-tAAl-fuh-lUst)*
loss-loss ratio	das Gesamtverlustverhältnis	*(dahs geh-zAHmt-fuh-lUst-fuh-hEHlt-nis)*
lot	das Los	*(dahs lOHs)*
low income	die niedrige Einkommenstufe	*(dee nEE-dri-geh EYEn-kOM-mehn-shtOO-feh)*
low interest loans	die niedrigverzinslichen Darlehen	*(dee nEE-drig-fuh-tsINS-likh-eh dAAr-lAY-hen)*
low-yield bonds	die niedrigverzinslichen Schuldverschreibungen	*(dee nEE-drig-fuh-tsINS-likh-ehn shUlt-fuh-shrEYE-bunk-ehn)*
lower case	Kleinbuchstaben	*(klEYEn-bOOKH-shtah-behn)*
lubrication	die Schmierung	*(dee shmEE-runk)*
lump sum	die einmalige Summe	*(dee EYEn-maa-li-geh tsOOm-meh)*
luxury goods	die Luxuswaren	*(dee LOOks-us-vAAr-ehn)*
luxury tax	die Luxussteuer	*(dee LOOks-us-shtOY-uh)*
lynx	der Luchs (pelz)	*(duh LUKHs[pELTS])*

L

M

machinery	der Maschinenpark	*(duh mAH-shEE-nen-pAAfk)*
macroeconomics	die Makroökonomie	*(dee mahk-roh-ew-ko-noh-mEE)*
magnetic memory	der Magnetspeicher	*(duh mahg-nAYt-shpEYE-khuh)*
magnetic tape	das Magnetband	*(dahs mahg-nAYt-bahnd)*
magnum	die Zweiquartflasche	*(dee tsveye-kvAHRT-flah-sheh)*
mail order	der Versandhandel	*(duh fuh-zAHnt-hAHn-dehl)*
mail-order sales	der Verkauf durch Versandgeschäft	*(duh fuh-kOWf durkh fuh-zAHnt-geh-shEHft)*
mailing list	die Adressenkartei	*(dee ah-dreEHS-sen-kahr-teye)*
mainframe computer	der Hauptrechner	*(duh hOWpt-rEHKH-nuh)*
maintenance	die Instandhaltung	*(dee in-shtAHnt-hahl-tunk)*
maintenance contract	der Instandhaltungsvertrag, der Wartungsvertrag	*(duh in-shtAHnt-hahl-tunks-fuh-trAHk), (duh vAAr-tunks-fuh-trAHk)*
maintenance margin	die Erhaltungsspanne	*(dee ayr-hAHl-tunks-shpAH-neh)*
maize	der Mais	*(duh meyez)*
majority interest	die Anteilmehrheit	*(dee AHN-teyel-mayr-heyet)*
make available (v)	zur Verfügung stellen	*(tsOOr fuh-fEW-gunk shtEL-en)*
make-or-buy decision	die Entscheidung über Eigenfertigung oder Ankauf	*(dee EHNT-shEYE-dunk EW-buh- EYE-gen-fAYr-ti-gunk OH-duh AHN-kOWf)*
make-ready	die Zurichtung	*(dee tsOO-rIKH-tunk)*
makeshift	der Notbehelf	*(duh NOHt-beh-hehlf)*
makeup case	das Kosmetiktäschchen	*(dahs kos-mAY-tik-tEHSH-khen)*
malleability	die Formbarkeit	*(dee FORm-baar-kEYET)*
man (gal) Friday	der treue Gehilfe, die treue Gehilfin	*(duh trOY-eh geh-hIL-feh), (dee trOY-eh geh-hIL-fin)*
man hours	die Arbeitsstunden	*(dee AHR-beyet-shtun-den)*

M

manage (control)	kontrollieren	*(kon-troh-lEE-ren)*
manage (v) (administrate)	verwalten	*(fuh-vAHl-ten)*
managed costs	die kontrollierten Kosten	*(dee kon-troh-lEEr-ten kOS-ten)*
managed economy	die gelenkte Wirtschaft	*(dee geh-lAYnk-teh vEErt-shahft)*
managed float	der kontrollierte Kassenvorschuß	*(duh kon-troh-lEEr-teh kah-sEHn-FOHR-shUS)*
management	die Verwaltung, die Leitung	*(dee fuh-vAHl-tunk), (dee lEYE-tunk)*
management accounting	das Rechnungswesen für Betriebsführungsbedürfnisse	*(dahs rEHKH-nungs-vAY-sen fEWr beh-trEEps-fEW-runks-beh-dEWrf-nis-seh)*
management, business	die Betriebsleitung	*(dee beh-trEEps-lEYE-tunk)*
management by objectives	die Betriebsführung durch Zielvorgabe	*(dee beh-trEEps-fEW-runk durkh tsEEl-FOHR-gAA-beh)*
management chart	die Geschäftsleitungstabelle, das Betriebsführungsschaubild	*(dee geh-shEHfts-lEYE-tunks-tah-bEHl-leh), (dahs beh-trEEps-fEW-runks-shOW-bild)*
management consultant	der Unternehmensberater	*(duh un-tuh-nAY-menz-buh-rAA-tuh)*
management, credit	die Kreditverwaltung	*(dee kray-dIT-fuh-vAAl-tunk)*
management fee	die Verwaltungsgebühr	*(dee fuh-vAHl-tunkz-geh-bEWr)*
management, financial	die Finanzverwaltung	*(dee fee-nAHnts-fuh-vAAl-tunk)*
management group	die Führungsgruppe	*(dee fEW-runks-grUP-peh)*
management, line	das Linienmanagement	*(dahs LEE-nee-en-meh-nEHdj-mehnt)*
management, market	die Marktleitung	*(dee mAHrkt-lEYE-tunk)*
management, office	die Büroleitung	*(dee bEW-roh-lEYE-tunk)*
management, personnel	die Personalleitung	*(dee payr-zoh-nAAl-lEYE-tunk)*
management, product	das Produktmanagement	*(dahs proh-dUKt-meh-nEHdj-mehnt)*

M

management, sales	die Vertriebsleitung	*(dee fuh-trEEps-lEYE-tunk)*
management, systems	die Systemsteuerung	*(dee zews-stAYm-shtOY-uh-runk)*
management team	die Leitungsschicht	*(dee lEYE-tunks-shIKHt)*
management, top	die oberste Führungsschicht	*(dee OH-buh-steh fEW-runks-shikht)*
manager	der Leiter, der Geschäftsführer	*(duh lEYE-tuh), (duh geh-shEHfts-fEW-ruh)*
mandate	der Befehl	*(duh beh-FAYL)*
mandatory redemption	die Zwangseinziehung	*(dee tsvAHngs-EYEn-tsee-unk)*
manganese ore	das Manganerz	*(dahs mahn-gAAN-EHRTS)*
manifest	die Frachltliste	*(dee frAHKHt-lIS-teh)*
manmade	die synthetischen Stoffe	*(dee zewn-tAY-ti-shen shtOF-feh)*
manmade fibers	die künstlichen Fasern	*(dee kEWnst-likh-en fAA-zuhn)*
manpower	die Arbeitskräfte	*(dee AHR-beyets-krEHf-teh)*
manual worker	der Handarbeiter	*(duh hAHnd-ahr-bEYE-tuh)*
manufacturer	der Hersteller	*(duh hAYr-shtEHL-luh)*
manufacturer's agent	der Herstellervertreter	*(duh hAYr-shtEHL-luh-fuh-trAY-tuh)*
manufacturer's representative	der Handlungsreisende	*(duh hAHnd-lunks-rEYE-zen-deh)*
manufacturing	die Produktionskapazität	*(dee proh-duk-tsee-OHnz-kah-pah-tsee-tAYt)*
manufacturing capacity	die Herstellungskapazität	*(dee hAYr-shtEHL-lunks-kah-pah-tsee-tAYt)*
manufacturing control	die Fertigungssteuerung	*(dee fEHr-ti-gunkz-shtOY-uh-runk)*
margin call	die Kreditkündigung mit Geldforderung	*(dee kray-dIT-kEWn-di-gunk mit GEHLT-FOHR-duh-runk)*
margin	der Mindesteinzahlungsbetrag	*(duh MIN-dehst-EYEn-tsAA-lungs-beh-trAHk)*
margin, gross	die Bruttogewinnspanne	*(dee BRU-toh-geh-vIN-shpAH-neh)*
margin, net	die Nettogewinnspanne	*(dee nEH-toh-geh-vIN-shpAHn-neh)*
margin, profit	die Gewinnspanne	*(dee geh-vIN-shpAHn-neh)*

M

margin of safety	die Sicherheitskoeffizient	*(dee zIKH-uh-heyets-koh-ehf-fee-tsEE-ehnt)*
margin requirements	der Mindesteinschuß	*(duh MIN-dehst-EYEn-shUs)*
marginal account	das Einschußkonto	*(dahs EYEn-shUs-kON-toh)*
marginal cost	die Grenzkosten	*(dee grEHnts-kOS-ten)*
marginal pricing	die marginale Preisfestsetzung	*(dee mahr-gee-nAA-leh prEYEs-fehst-zEHts-unk)*
marginal productivity	die Grenzproduktivität	*(dee grEHnts-proh-duk-ti-vee-tAYt)*
marginal revenue	der Grenzertrag	*(duh grEHnts-uh-trAHk)*
marine cargo insurance	die Seetransportversicherung	*(dee ZAY-trahns-pohrt-fuh-zIkheh-runk)*
marine underwriter	der Seeversicherer	*(duh ZAY-fuh-zIkheh-ruh)*
maritime contract	der Schiffahrtsvertrag	*(duh shIF-fAArts-fuh-trAHk)*
markdown	die Preisherabsetzung	*(dee prEYEs-hayr-AHB-zeht-tsunk)*
market	der Markt	*(duh mAHrkt)*
market (v)	vertreiben	*(fuh-trEYE-ben)*
market, stock	die Börse	*(dee bER-zeh)*
market access	der Marktzugang	*(duh mAHrkt-tsoo-gank)*
market appraisal	die Markteinschätzung	*(dee mAH,rkt-EYEn-shEH-tsunk)*
market concentration	die Marktkonzentration	*(dee mAHrkt-kon-tsen-trah-tsEE-ohn)*
market dynamics	die Marktdynamik	*(dee mAHrkt-dew-nAA-mik)*
market forces	die Marktkräfte	*(dee mAHrkt-krEHf-teh)*
market forecast	die Marktprognose	*(dee mAHrkt-prog-nOH-zeh)*
market index	der Börsenindex	*(duh bER-zen-IN-dex)*
market letter	der Börsenbrief	*(duh bER-zen-brEEf)*
market management	die Marktleitung	*(dee mAHrkt-lEYE-tunk)*
market penetration	die Marktdurchdringung	*(dee mAHrkt-durkh-drING-unk)*
market plan	der Marktplan	*(duh mAHrkt-plAAn)*
market planner	der Absatzplan	*(duh AHB-zATS-plAAn)*

market position	die Marktlage	*(dee mAHrkt-lAA-geh)*
market potential	das Marktpotential	*(dahs mAHrkt-po-teh-tsee-AAL)*
market price	der Marktpreis	*(duh mAHrkt-prEYEs)*
market rating	die Börsenmarkteinstufung	*(dee bER-zen-mAHrkt-eyen-shtOO-funk)*
market report	der Marktbericht	*(duh mAHrkt-beh-rIKHt)*
market research	die Marktforschung	*(dee mAHrkt-fOHr-shunk)*
market saturation	die Marktsättigung	*(dee mAHrkt-shtEH-ti-gunk)*
market share	der Marktanteil	*(duh mAHrkt-AHN-teyel)*
market survey	die Marktübersicht	*(dee mAHrkt-EW-buh-zikht)*
market trends	die Markttendenzen	*(dee mAHrkt-ten-dEHn-tsehn)*
market value (general)	der Marktwert	*(duh mAHrkt-vEHrt)*
market value (stocks)	der Kurswert	*(duh kOOrs-vEHrt)*
market-maker	der Börsenmakler	*(duh bER-zen-mAHk-luh)*
marketable securities	die börsengängigen Werte	*(dee bER-zen-gEHng-ikh-ehn vEHR-teh)*
marketing	der Absatz	*(duh AHB-zAHts)*
marketing budget	das Absatzbudget	*(dahs AHB-zATS-bew-djEH)*
marketing concept	das Absatzkonzept	*(dahs AHB-zATS-kon-tsEHPt)*
marketing plan	der Absatzplan	*(duh AHB-zATS-plAAn)*
marketplace	der Marktplatz	*(duh mAHrkt-plAHts)*
markup	der Aufschlag	*(duh OWf-shlAHk)*
marmot	das Murmeltier	*(dahs mur-mEL-tEER)*
mass communications	die Massenkommunikation	*(dee MAHS-sehn-ko-moo-ni-kah-tsEE-ohn)*
mass marketing	der Massenabsatz	*(duh MAHS-sehn-AHB-zATS)*
mass media	die Massenmedien	*(dee MAHS-sehn-mAY-dee-ehn)*
mass production	die Massenproduktion	*(dee MAHS-sehn-proh-duk-tsEE-ohn)*
master agreement	das Manteltarifabkommen	*(dahs mAHn-tel-taa-rIF-AHB-kOM-mehn)*

M

matched samples	die abgestimmten Vergleichsproben	*(dee AHB-geh-shtIM-ten fuh-glEYEKHs-proh-ben)*
materials	die Materialien	*(dee maa-tay-ree-AAl-EE-ehn)*
maternity leave	der Mutterschaftsurlaub	*(duh MU-tuh-shahfts-OOr-lowb)*
mathematical model	das mathematische Modell	*(dahs mah-teh-mah-tISH-eh moh-dEL)*
matrix	die Matrize	*(dee ma-TRI-tseh)*
matrix management	die Matrizenüberwachung	*(dee maa-trEEts-en-EW-buh-vahkh-unk)*
maturity	die Reife	*(dee rEYE-feh)*
maturity (due debts)	der Verfall	*(duh fuh-fAHl)*
maturity date	der Verfalltag	*(duh fuh-fAHl-tAAk)*
maximize (v)	steigern	*(shtEYE-guhn)*
mean (average)	der Durchschnitt	*(duh dURKH-shnIT)*
measure (v)	messen	*(mehs-sehn)*
mechanical engineering	der Maschinenbau	*(duh mah-shEE-nen-bOW)*
mechanic's lien	das Zurückbehaltungsrecht des Handwerkers	*(dahs tsOO-rEWk-beh-hAHl-tunks-rehkht dehs hAHnd-vEHr-kuhs)*
media	die Medien	*(dee mAY-dee-ehn)*
median	der Zentralwert	*(duh tsehn-trAAl-vEHrt)*
mediation	die Vermittlung	*(dee fuh-mIT-lunk)*
medication	die medizinische Behandlung	*(dee meh-di-tsEE-ni-sheh beh-hAHN-dlunk)*
medicine	die Medizin	*(dee meh-di-tsEEN)*
medium of exchange	das Tauschmittel	*(dahs tOWsh-mit-tEL)*
medium term	mittelfristig	*(mit-tEL-fris-tig)*
meet the price (v)	dem Preis entsprechen	*(dehm prEYs ehnt-shrEHKH-en)*
meeting	die Tagung	*(dee tAA-gunk)*
member firm	die Mitgliedsfirma	*(dee MIT-gleeds-fIR-mah)*
member of a firm	das Firmenmitglied	*(dahs fIR-men-MIT-gleed)*
memorandum	das Rundschreiben	*(dahs RUnt-shrEYE-ben)*

M

mercantile	handelsbezogen	*(hAHn-dehls-beh-tsOH-gen)*
mercantile agency	die Handelsagentur	*(dee hAHn-dehls-ah-gen-tOOR)*
mercantile law (a specific law)	das Handelgesetz	*(dahs hAHn-dehls-geh-zEHts)*
mercantile law (in general)	das Handelsrecht	*(dahs hAHn-dehls-rehkht)*
merchandise	die Waren	*(dee vAA-ren), die Güter (dee gEW-tuh)*
merchandising	die Absatztätigkeiten	*(dee AHB-zATS-tAY-tig-keye-ten)*
merchant	der Händler	*(duh hENd-luh)*
merchant bank	die Handelsbank	*(dee hAHn-dehls-bhank)*
merchant guild	die Handelskammer	*(dee hAHn-dehls-kAHM-muh)*
merger	die Vereinigung	*(dee fuh-EYE-ni-gunk)*
metals	die Metalle	*(dee meh-tAHl-leh)*
method	das Verfahren	*(dahs fuh-fAA-ren)*
metrification	die Metrifikation	*(dee meh-tri-fe-kah-tsEE-ohn)*
microchip	der Mikrochip	*(duh mEE-kroh-ship)*
microcomputer	der Mikrocomputer	*(duh mEE-kroh-kom-pyU-tuh)*
microfiche	das Mikrofiche	*(dahs mEE-kroh-feesh)*
microfilm	der Mikrofilm	*(duh mEE-kroh-film*
microphone	das Mikrofon	*(dahs mee-kroh-fOHN)*
microprocessor	der Mikroprozessor	*(duh mEE-kroh-proh-tsehs-sOHr)*
microwave	die Mikrowelle	*(dee mee-kroh-vEL-leh)*
middle management	die mittlere Führungsschicht	*(dahs MIT-luh-reh fEW-funks-shikht)*
middleman	der Vermittler	*(duh fuh-MIT-luh)*
mileage	die Meilenlänge	*(dee mEYE-lehn-LEHN-geh)*
milling	die Müllerei	*(dee MEWl-luh-reye)*
minicomputer	der Minicomputer	*(duh mI-nee-kom-pyU-tuh)*
minimum reserves	die Mindestreserven	*(dee MIN-dehst-reh-zAYr-fen)*
minimum wage	der Mindestlohn	*(duh MIN-dehst-lohn)*

M

mink	der Nerz	*(duh nEHRTS)*
minority interest	der Minderheitsanteil	*(duh MIN-duh-heyets-AHN-teyel)*
mint	die Münzstätte	*(dee MEWnts-shtEH-teh)*
miscalculation	der Rechenfehler	*(duh rEHKH-en-fAY-luh)*
miscellaneous	Verschiedenes	*(fuh-shEE-deh-nehs)*
misleading	irreführend	*(EEr-reh-fEW-rent)*
misunderstanding	das Mißverständnis	*(dahs MIS-fuh-shEHnd-nis)*
mixed costs	die Mischkosten	*(dee MISH-kOS-ten)*
mixed sampling	die ungleichartige Stichprobenauswahl	*(dee un-glEYEKH-ahr-ti-geh shtIKH-proh-ben-OWs-vaal)*
mobility of labor	die Beweglichkeit der Arbeitskräfte	*(dee beh-vAYg-likh-keyet duh AHR-beyets-krEHf-teh)*
mock-up	das Lehrmodell	*(dahs LAYr-moh-dEL)*
mode	die Weise	*(dee vEYE-zeh)*
model	das Modell	*(dahs moh-dEL)*
modem	der Modem	*(duh moh-dEM)*
modular production	die Vorfertigung	*(dee FOHR-fEHr-ti-gunk)*
moiré	die Moireseide	*(dee moh-EER-zeYE-deh)*
mole	das Grammolekül	*(dahs grAM-mo-leh-kEWL)*
molybdenum	das Molybdän	*(dahs mo-LEWB-dAYN)*
monetary base	die Geldmenge	*(dee GEHLT-mAYng-eh)*
monetary credits	die Währungskredite	*(dee VAY-runks-kray-dIT-eh)*
monetary policy	die Geldpolitik	*(dee GEHLT-po-li-tEEk)*
monetary standard	die Währungseinheit	*(dee VAY-runk-eyen-heyet)*
money	das Geld	*(dahs GEHLT)*
money broker	der Geldmakler	*(duh GEHLT-mAHk-luh)*
money manager	der Geldverwalter	*(duh GEHLT-fuh-vAHl-tuh)*
money market	der Geldmarkt	*(duh GEHLT-mAHrkt)*
money order	die Geldanweisung	*(dee GEHLT-AHN-vEYE-zung)*
money shop	der "Geldladen"	*(duh "GEHLT-lAA-den")*

M

money supply	die Geldversorgung	*(dee GEHLT-fuh-zOHr-gunk)*
monitor	der Abhörer	*(duh AHB-hER-uh)*
monopoly	das Monopol	*(dahs mo-noh-pOHl)*
monopsony	die Monopsonie	*(dee mo-nohp-so-nEE)*
Monte Carlo technique	die Monte Carlo Methode	*(dee MON-tay kAAr-loh meh-tOH-deh)*
moonlighting	die Ausübung einer Zusatzbeschäftigung	*(dee OWs-EW-bunk eye-nuh tsOO-zATS beh-shEHf-ti-gunk)*
morale	die Arbeitsmoral	*(dee AHR-beyets-moh-rAAL)*
moratorium	der Zahlungsaufschub	*(duh tsAA-lungs-OWf-shUb)*
morphine	das Morphium	*(dahs mOR-fi-um)*
Morroco leather	das Saffianleder	*(dahs zahf-fi-AAn-lAY-duh)*
mortgage	die Hypothek	*(dee hew-poh-tAYk)*
mortgage bank	die Hypothekenbank	*(dee hew-poh-tAYk-en-bahnk)*
mortgage bond	der Hypothekenbrief	*(duh hew-poh-tAYk-en-brEEf)*
mortgage certificate	der Hypothekenschein	*(duh hew-poh-tAYk-en-sheyen)*
mortgage debenture	der Hypothekenpfandbrief	*(duh hew-poh-tAYk-en-pfAHnd-brEEf)*
most-favored nation	das meistbegünstigte Land	*(dahs mEYEst-beh-gEWnz-tig-teh lAHnd)*
motion	die Bewegung	*(dee beh-vAY-gunk)*
motion (parliamentary)	der Antrag	*(duh AHN-trAHk)*
motivation study	die Motivationsstudie	*(dee mo-ti-vah-tsEE-ohnz-shtoo-dee-deh)*
movement of goods	der Gütertransport	*(duh gEW-tuh-trahns-pOHrt)*
moving average	der gleitende Durchschnitt	*(duh glEYE-ten-deh dURKH-shnIT)*
moving expenses	die Umzugskosten	*(dee um-tsOOgs-kOS-ten)*
moving parity	die veränderliche Parität	*(dee fuh-EHN-duh-likh-eh pah-ree-tAYt)*
multicurrency	die Multiwährung	*(dee MUL-tee-VAY-runk)*

M

multilateral agreement	das mehrseitige Abkommen	*(dahs mAYr-zEYE-ti-geh AHB-kOM-men)*
multilateral trade	der mehrseitige Handel	*(dee mAYr-zEYE-ti-geh hAHn-dehl)*
multinational corporation	die multinationale Gesellschaft	*(dee MUL-tee-nah-tsee-oh-nAA-leh geh-zEL-shahft)*
multiple exchange rate	die gespaltenen Wechselkurse	*(dee geh-shpAAl-teh-nuh vEHk-sehl-koor-seh)*
multiple taxation	die Mehrfachbesteuerung	*(dee mAYr-fahkh-beh-shtOY-uh-runk)*
multiples	die Preis-Gewinn Verhältnisse	*(dee prEYEs-geh-vIN fuh-hEHlt-nis-seh)*
multiplier	der Multiplikator	*(duh mul-tee-pli-kAA-tohr)*
multiprogramming	die Mehrprogrammverarbeitung	*(dee mAYr-proh-grAHm-fuh-ahr-bEYE-tunk)*
municipal bond	die Kommunalobligation	*(dee kom-moo-nAAl-ob-lí-gah-tsEE-ohn)*
mutual	der Investmentfonds	*(duh in-vehs-mEHnt-fOH)*
mutual fund	die Investmentgesellschaft	*(dee in-vehs-mEHnt-geh-zEL-shahft)*
mutual savings bank	die Sparkasse	*(dee shpAAr-kAH-seh)*
mutually exclusive types	die gegenseitig sich ausschließenden Gattungen	*(dee gAY gen-zeye-tig zikh OWs-shlEE-zen-deh GAHT-tun-gen)*

N

named point of destination	der genannte Bestimmungsort	*(duh geh-nAAn-teh beh-shtIM-mungs-ohrt)*
named point of exportation	der genannte Ausfuhrort	*(duh geh-nAAn-teh OWs-foor-ohrt)*
named point of origin	der genannte Ursprungsort	*(duh geh-nAAn-teh OOr-shprunks-ohrt)*
named port of importation	der genannte Einfuhrhafen	*(duh geh-nAAn-teh EYEn-foor-hAA-fen)*
named port of shipment	der genannte Versandhafen	*(duh geh-nAAn-teh fuh-zAHND-hAA-fen)*
napkin	die Serviette	*(dee zuh-VI-et-teh)*
napkin ring	der Serviettenring	*(duh zuh-VI-et-tehn-rINk)*

narcotic	das Narkotikum	*(dahs nahr-kOH-ti-kum)*
national bank	die Staatsbank	*(dee shtAAts-bahnk)*
national debt	die Staatsverschuldung	*(dee shtAAts-fuh-shUL-tunk)*
nationalism	der Nationalismus	*(duh nah-tsee-oh-nah-lIS-mus)*
nationalism (economic)	der Staatssozialismus	*(duh shtAAts-zoh-tsee-ah-lIS-mus)*
nationalization	die Verstaatlichung	*(dee fuh-shtAAt-likh-unk)*
native produce	das Inlandserzeugnis	*(dahs IN-lahnds-ay-tsOYg-nis)*
natural gas	das Erdgas	*(dahs AYrd-gaas)*
natural resources	die Naturschätze	*(dee nah-tOOr-shEH-tseh)*
near money	die geldähnliche Forderung	*(dee GEHLT-AYn-likh-eh FOHR-duh-runk)*
neck (of bottle)	der Flaschenhals	*(duh flAH-shen-hahls)*
necktie	die Krawatte	*(dee kRAH-vAT-teh)*
needle	die Nadel	*(dee nAA-del)*
needs analysis	die Bedarfsanalyse	*(dee beh-dAArf-ah-nah-lEW-zeh)*
negative	negativ	*(nay-gah-tEEF)*
negative cash flow	der negative Zahlungsstrom	*(duh nAY-gah-tee-veh tsAA-lungs-shtrOHm)*
negative pledge	das Unterlassungsversprechen	*(dahs un-tuh-lAA-sunks-fuh-shprEHKH-en)*
negligent	nachlässig	*(nAHKH-leh-sig)*
negotiable (convertible transferable)	übertragbar	*(EW-buh-trAHk-bAAr)*
negotiable (subject to discussion)	verhandlungsfähig	*(fuh-hAHnd-lunks-fAY-ig)*
negotiable securities	dic übertragbaren Wertpapiere	*(dee EW-buh-trAHk-bAA-ren vEHRt-pah-pEEr-eh)*
negotiate (v)	verhandeln	*(fuh-hAHn-dehln)*
negotiated sale	der getätigte Verkauf	*(duh geh-tAY-tig-teh fuh-kOWf)*
negotiation	die Verhandlung	*(dee fuh-hAHnd-lunk)*

N

net asset value	der Reinvermögenswert	*(duh REYEN-fuh-mER-genz-vEHrt)*
net asset worth	das Eigenkapital	*(dahs EYE-gen-kah-pi-tAAL)*
net assets	das Reinvermögen	*(dahs REYEN-fuh-mER-gen)*
net borrowed reserves	die Nettofremdkapital-reserven	*(dee nEH-toh-frehmt-kah-pi-tAAL-reh-zAYr-fehn)*
net cash flow	der Nettobargeldstrom	*(duh nEH-toh-bAAr-gehlt-shtrOHm)*
net change	die Nettoänderung	*(dee nEH-toh-EHn-deh-runk)*
net equity assets	das Nettoeigenkapital	*(dahs nEHt-toh-EYE-gen-kah-pi-tAAL)*
net income	das Nettoeinkommen	*(dahs nEH-toh-EYEn-kOM-men)*
net investment	die Nettoinvestition	*(dee nEHt-toh-in-vehs-ti-tsi-OHn)*
net loss	der Reinverlust	*(duh REYEN-fuh-lUSt)*
net margin	die Nettogewinnspanne	*(dee nEH-toh-geh-vIN-shpAHn-neh)*
net position of a trader	der Nettostand eines Maklers	*(duh nEH-toh-shtahnd-EYE-nehs mAHk-luhs)*
net present value	der Nettobarwert	*(duh nEH-toh-bAAr-vEHrt)*
net profit	der Nettogewinn	*(duh nEH-toh-geh-vIN)*
net sales	der Nettoumsatz	*(duh nEH-toh-um-zAHts)*
net working capital	das Nettobetriebskapital	*(dahs nEH-toh-beh-trEEps-kah-pi-tAAl)*
net worth	der Nettowert	*(duh nEH-toh-vEHrt)*
network	das Netz	*(dahs nehts)*
new issue	die Neubegebung	*(dee NOY-beh-gAY-bunk)*
new money	das neue Geld	*(dahs NOY-eh gehlt)*
new product development	die Entwicklung eines neuen Produkts	*(dee ehnt-vIK-lunk EYE-nes noy-en proh-dUKts)*
newsprint	das Zeitungspapier	*(dahs tsEYE-tungs-pah-pEER)*
nickel	der Nickel	*(duh ni-KEl)*
night depository	das Nachtdepot	*(dahs nAHKHt-day-pOH)*

N

nitric acid	die Salpetersäure	*(dee zahl-PEH-tuh-ZOY-reh)*
nitrogen	der Stickstoff	*(duh shtIK-shtOF)*
no par value	die nennwertlose Aktie	*(dee NEHN-vEHRt-lOH-zeh-ak-tsEE-eh)*
no problem	kein Problem	*(keyen proh-blAYm)*
no-load fund	der gebührenfreie Investmentfonds	*(duh geh-bEW-ren-frEYE-eh in-vehs-mEHnt-fOH)*
nominal price	der Nominalpreis	*(duh noh-mi-nAAl-prEYEs)*
nominal yield	der Nennertrag	*(duh NEHN-uh-trAHk)*
noncumulative preferred stock	die nichtkumulative Vorzugsaktie	*(dee nIKHt-ku-mu-lah-tEE-feh FOHR-tsoogs-ak-tsEE-eh)*
noncurrent assets	die langfristigen Vermögenswerte	*(dee lAAng-fris-ti-gen fuh-mER-genz-vEHr-teh)*
nondurable goods	die Verbrauchsgüter	*(dee fuh-brOWkhs-gEW-tuh)*
nonfeasance	die pflichtwidrige Unterlassung	*(dee pflIKHt-vI-dri-geh un-tuh-lAH-sunk)*
nonmember	das Nichtmitglied	*(dahs nIKHt-MIT-gleed)*
nonprofit	gemeinnützig	*(geh-meyen-nEWts-ig)*
nonresident	der Devisenausländer	*(duh deh-vEE-zen-hEHnd-luh)*
nonvoting stock	die Aktien ohne Stimmberechtigung	*(dee ak-tsEE-en oh-neh shtIM-beh-rEHKH-ti-gunk)*
norm	die Norm	*(dee nohrm)*
not otherwise indexed by name	nicht sonst im Namenregister verzeichnet	*(nIKHt zonst im nAA-men-ray-gis-tuh fuh-tsEYEkh-neht)*
notary	der Notar	*(duh noh-tAAr)*
note, credit	die Gutschriftsanzeige	*(dee gOOt-shrifts-AHN-tseye-geh)*
note, debit	die Lastschriftanzeige	*(dee lAHst-shrift-AHN-tseye-geh)*
note, promissory	der Eigenwechsel	*(duh EYE-gen-vEHk-sehl)*
note receivable	der Besitzwechsel	*(duh beh-zIts-vEHk-sehl)*
novation	die Novation	*(dee noh-vAA-tsee-ohn)*
nuclear power station	das Kernkraftwerk	*(kern-kraft-verk)*

N

null and void	null und nichtig	*(nUl unt nIKH-tik)*
nullify (v)	aufheben	*(OWf-hAY-ben)*
numerical control	die zahlenmäßige Steuerung	*(dee tsAA-len-mAY-si-geh shtOY-uh-runk)*
nutria (skin)	das Nutriafell	*(dahs nOO-triah-fEL)*

O

obligation	die Verpflichtung	*(dee fuh-pflIKH-tunk)*
obsolescence	das Veralten	*(dahs fuh-AHl-ten)*
occupation	der Beruf	*(duh beh-rOOf)*
occupational hazard	das Berufsrisiko	*(dahs beh-rOOfs-REE-zee-koh)*
odd lot	die ungerade Menge	*(dee un-geh-rAA-deh mEHn-geh)*
odd lot broker	der Börsenmakler in kleinen Mengen	*(duh bER-zen-mAHk-luh in klEYE-nen mAYn-gen)*
odometer	der Kilometerzähler	*(duh KI-loh-mAY-tuh-tsAY-luh)*
off line	in unabhängiger Datenverarbeitung	*(in un-ahb-hEHn-gi-guh dAA-ten-fuh-AHR-beye-tunk)*
off-the-books	ohne Geschäftsbucheintragung	*(oh-neh geh-shEHfts-bOOkh-EYEn-trAAg-unk)*
offer (v)	bieten	*(bEE-ten)*
offer for sale	zum Verkauf anbieten	*(tsum fuh-kOWf AHN-bee-ten)*
offered price	der Angebotspreis	*(duh AHN-geh-bohts-prEYEs)*
offered rate	der Briefkurs	*(duh brEEf-kOOrs)*
office	das Büro	*(dahs bEW-roh)*
office, branch	das Zweiggeschäft	*(dahs tsvEYEg-geh-shEHft)*
office, head	das Hauptbüro	*(dahs hOWpt-bEW-roh)*
office management	die Büroleitung	*(dee bEW-roh-lEYE-tunk)*
offset printing	der Offsetdruck	*(duh OFF-seht drOOk)*
offshore company	die offshore Gesellschaft	*(dee OFF-shohr geh-zEL-shahft)*
oilcloth	das Wachstuch	*(dahs VAHKs-TOOkh)*

ointment	die Salbe	*(dee zAHL-beh)*
oligopoly	das Oligopol	*(dahs o-li-goh-pOHl)*
oligopsony	die Oligopsonie	*(dee o-li-gop-zoh-nEE)*
omit (v)	auslassen	*(OWs-laa-sen)*
on account	auf Rechnung	*(OWF rEHKH-nunk)*
on consignment	kommissionsweise	*(ko-mi-sEE-ohnz-vEYE-zeh)*
on cost	die laufenden Ausgaben	*(dee lOW-fehn-dehn-OWs-gAA-ben)*
on demand	auf Verlangen	*(OWF fuh-lAAng-en)*
on line (computer)	mit der Datenverarbeitung verbunden	*(mit duh dAA-ten-fuh-AHR-beye-tunk fuh-bUn-den)*
on-sale date	der Verkaufstermin	*(duh fuh-kOWfs-tayr-mEEn)*
on-the-job training	die Ausbildung am Arbeitsplatz	*(dee OWs-bil-dunk ahm AHR-beyets-plahts)*
open account	das laufende Konto	*(dahs lOW-fehn-deh kON-toh)*
open cover	die Generalversicherung	*(dee gen-ah-rAAl-fuh-zIkheh-runk)*
open door policy	die Politik der offenen Tür	*(dee po-li-tEEk duh OF-fen-nen tEWr)*
open market	der Offenmarkt	*(duh OF-fen-mAHrkt)*
open market operations	die Offenmarktpolitik der Notenbank	*(dee OF-fen-mAHrkt-po-li-tEEk duh nOH-ten-bahnk)*
open order	die unbefristete Order	*(dee un-beh-frIS-teh-teh OHR-duh)*
open shop	der offene Betrieb	*(duh of-feh-neh beh-trEEp)*
opening balance	der Anfangsbestand	*(duh AHN-fanks-beh-shtAHnt)*
opening price	der Eröffnungskurs	*(duh ayr-ERf-nunks-koors)*
operating budget	das Betriebsbudget	*(dahs beh-trEEps-bew-djEH)*
operating expenses	die Betriebskosten	*(dee beh-trEEps-kOS-ten)*
operating income	das Betriebseinkommen	*(dahs beh-trEEps-EYEn-kOM-mehn)*
operating loss	der Betriebsverlust	*(duh beh-trEEps-fuh-lUst)*
operating profit	der Betriebsgewinn	*(duh beh-trEEps-geh-vIN)*
operating statement	die Betriebsergebnisrechnung	*(dee beh-trEEps-ayr-gAYb-nis-rEHKH-nunk)*

operating unit	die Betriebseinheit	*(dee beh-trEEps-eyen-heyet)*
operations audit	die Betriebstätigkeitsprüfung	*(dee beh-trEEps-tAY-tikh-keyets-prEW-funk)*
operations headquarters	die Betriebszentrale	*(dee beh-trEEps-tsen-trAA-leh)*
operations management	die Betriebsführung	*(dee beh-trEEps-fEW-runk)*
opium	das Opium	*(dahs OH-pi-um)*
opossum	das Opossum	*(dahs o-pOS-sum)*
opportunity cost	die Opportunitätskosten	*(dee op-pohr-too-ni-tAYts-kOS-ten)*
optic	optisch	*(OP-tish)*
option	die Option	*(dee op-tsEE-ohn)*
option (put or call options)	das Börsentermingeschäft	*(dahs bER-zen-tayr-mEEn-geh-shEHft)*
order	die Bestellung	*(dee beh-shtEHL-lunk)*
order (command)	der Befehl	*(duh beh-fAYl)*
order form	der Bestellschein	*(duh beh-stEHL-shEYEn)*
order number	die Bestellnummer	*(dee beh-shtEHL-nU-muh)*
order of the day	die Tagesbestellung	*(dee tAA-gehs-beh-shtEHL-lunk)*
order, to place an (v)	einen Auftrag erteilen	*(EYE-nen OWf-trAHk ayr-tEYE-len)*
ordinary capital	das Stammkapital	*(dahs shtAHm-kah-pi-tAAL)*
ore	das Erz	*(dahs AYRTS)*
organic	organisch	*(or-gAA-nish)*
organic chemistry	die organische Chemie	*(dee or-gAA-ni-she KHAY-mee)*
organic farming	der biologische Anbau	*(duh bee-oh-LOHG-ish-eh AHN-bow)*
organization	die Organisation	*(dee ohr-gah-ne-zah-tsee-OHn)*
organization chart	der Organisationsplan	*(duh ohr-gah-ne-zah-tsee-OHnz-plAAn)*
original cost	die Anschaffungskosten	*(dee AHN-shAHF-funks-kOS-ten)*
original entry	die Grundbuchung	*(dee grUnd-bOO-khunk)*
original maturity	die ursprüngliche Fälligkeit	*(dee OOr-shprewnk-lIKH-eh fEHl-lig-keyet)*

oscillator	der Oszillator	*(duh os-tsi-LAH-tor)*
ostrich	der Strauß	*(duh shtrOWS)*
other assets (other liabilities)	das sonstige Vermögen, die sonstigen Verbindlichkeiten	*(dahs ZONS-ti-geh fuh-mER-gen), (dee ZONS-ti-gen fuh-bIND-likh-keye-ten)*

otter (fur)	der Otterpelz	*(duh OT-tuh-pELTS)*
otter (skin)	das Otterfell	*(dahs OT-tuh-fEL)*
out of style	außer Mode	*(OWs-suh mOH-deh)*
out-of-pocket expenses	die Barauslagen	*(dee BAAR-ows-laa-gen)*
outbid (v)	überbieten	*(EW-buh-bEE-ten)*
outlay	die Auslage	*(dee OWs-laa-geh)*
outlet	der Absatz	*(duh AHB-zAHTs)*
outlook	die Aussicht	*(dee OWs-zikht)*
outlook (philosophy)	die Anschauung	*(dee AHN-show-unk)*
output	die Arbeitsleistung	*(dee AHR-beyets-lEYEs-tunk)*
outsized articles	die übergroßen Artikel	*(dee EW-buh-grOH-sehn ahr-TI-kel)*
outstanding contract	der noch rechtskräftige Vertrag	*(duh nOHKH REHKHts-krehf-ti-geh fuh-trAHk)*
outstanding debt	die Außenstände	*(dee OWs-en-shtehn-deh)*
outstanding stock	die ausstehenden Aktien	*(dee OWs-steh-hen-dehn ahk-tsEE-en)*
outturn	der Ausstoß	*(duh OWs-shtohs)*
outturner	der Ertrag	*(duh ayr-trAHk)*
over the counter	freihändig	*(frEYE-hAYn-dig)*
over-the-counter quotation	der freihändige Kurs	*(duh frEYE-hAYn-di-geh koors)*
overage	der Überbetrag	*(duh EW-buh-be-trAHk)*
overbought	zu stark gekauft	*(tsoo shtAHrk geh-kOWft)*
overcapitalized	überkapitalisiert	*(EW-buh-kah-pi-tAA-li-zEErt)*
overcharge	zuviel fordern	*(tsOO-vEEl fOHr-duhn)*
overcharge (v)	überfordern	*(EW-buh-fOHR-duhn)*
overdraft	die Überziehung	*(dee EW-buh-tsEE-unk)*
overdue	überfällig	*(EW-buh-fEH-lig)*

overhang	überhängen	*(EW-buh-hehn-gen)*
overhead	die Generalkosten	*(dee gen-ah-rAAl-kOS-ten)*
overlap	überlappen	*(EW-buh-lAHp-pen)*
overnight	über Nacht	*(EW-buh nAHKHt)*
overpayment	die Überzahlung	*(dee EW-buh-tsAA-lung)*
overseas common point	der Gemeinpunkt in Übersee	*(duh geh-mEYEn-pUnkt in EW-buh-zAY)*
oversold	zu stark verkauft	*(tsoo shtAHrk fuh-kOWft)*
overstock	der Überfluß	*(duh EW-buh-flUs)*
oversubscribe (v)	überzeichnen	*(EW-buh-tsEYEkh-en)*
oversupply	das Überangebot	*(dahs EW-buh-AHN-geh-boht)*
overtime	die Überstunden	*(dee EW-buh-shtun-den)*
overvalue (v)	überbewerten	*(EW-buh-beh-vEHr-ten)*
owner	der Besitzer	*(duh beh-zITs-uh)*
owner's equity	das Eigenkapital	*(dahs EYE-gen-kah-pi-tAAL)*
ownership	das Eigentum, der Besitz	*(dahs EYE-gen-toom), (duh beh-zITs)*

P

package deal	das Kopplungsgeschäft	*(dahs kOP-lunks-geh-shEHft)*
packaging	die Verpackung	*(dee fur-PAHK-unk)*
packing case	die Packkiste	*(dee PAHK-kIS-teh)*
packing list	der Packzettel	*(duh PAHK-tsEH-tel)*
page makeup	die Seitenaufmachung	*(dee zEYE-ten-owf-mah-khunk)*
pagination	die Paginierung	*(dee pah-gi-nEE-runk)*
paid holiday	der bezahlte Feiertag	*(deh beh-tsAAl-teh fEYE-uh-taak)*
paid in full	voll bezahlt	*(fol beh-tsAAlt)*
paid up capital	das voll eingezahlte Kapital	*(dahs fol EYEn-geh-tsAAl-teh kah-pi-tAAL)*
paid up shares	die eingezahlten Anteile	*(dee EYEn-geh-tsAAl-teh AHN-teye-leh)*

paid-in surplus	der nicht entnommene Gewinn	*(duh nIKHt ehnt-nOM-mehn-uh geh-vIN)*
paint	die Farbe	*(dee fAHR-beh)*
pallet	die Palette	*(dee pah-lEH-teh)*
palletized freight	die palettierte Ladung	*(dee pah-leh-tEEr-teh lAA-dunk)*
pamphlet	die Broschüre	*(dee bro-shEW-reh)*
panel	das Schaltfeld	*(dahs shAHLt-felt)*
paper	das Papier	*(dahs pah-pEEr)*
paper profit	der Buchgewinn	*(duh bOOkh-geh-vIN)*
paper tape	der Lochstreifen	*(duh lOKH-shtrEYE-fehn)*
par, above	über pari	*(EW-buh pah-rEE)*
par, below	unter pari	*(un-tuh pah-rEE*
par value	der Pariwert	*(duh pah-rEE-vEHrt)*
parallel circuit	die Parallelschaltung	*(dee pah-rah-LEL-shahl-tunk)*
parcel post	die Paketpost	*(dee paa-kAYt-pOSt)*
parent company	die Muttergesellschaft	*(dee MU-tuh-geh-zEL-shahft)*
parity	die Parität	*(dee pah-ri-tAYt)*
parity income ratio	das Paritätseinkommen-verhältnis	*(dahs pah-ri-tAYts-EYEn-kOM-mehn-fuh-hEHElts-nis)*
parity price	der Paritätspreis	*(duh pah-ri-tAYts-prEYEs)*
part	der Teil	*(duh teyel)*
part cargo	die Teilladung	*(dee tEYEl-lAA-dunk)*
partial payment	die Teilzahlung	*(dee teyel-tsAA-lung)*
participation fee	die Beteiligungsgebühr	*(dee beh-tEYE-li-gunks-geh-bEWr)*
participation loan	die Beteiligungsanleihe	*(dee beh-tEYE-li-gunks-AHN-leye-eh)*
particular average loss	der Schaden in besonderer Havarie	*(duh shAA-den in beh-zON-duh-ruh hah-fah-rEE)*
partner	der Teilhaber	*(duh tEYEl-hAA-buh)*
partnership	die Teilhaberschaft	*(dee tEYEl-hAA-buh-shahft)*
party (contract)	die Vertragspartei	*(dee fuh-trAHks-pahr-tEYE)*
pass (written permit)	der Personalausweis	*(duh payr-zoh-nAAl-OWs-vEYEs)*

passbook	das Bankbuch	*(dahs BAHNK-bOkh)*
passed dividend	die nicht ausgeschüttete Dividende	*(dee nIKHt OWS-geh-shEW-teh-teh di-vi-dEHN-deh)*
passport case	das Paßetui	*(dahs pAHS-e-tuEE)*
past due	überfällig	*(EW-buh-fEH-lig)*
pasteurized	pasteurisiert	*(pahs-tOY-REE-zEErt)*
pastry server	der Tortenheber	*(duh TOR-ten-hay-buh)*
patent	das Patent	*(dahs pah-tEHnt)*
patent application	die Patentanmeldung	*(dee pah-tEHnt-mEHl-dunk)*
patent infringement	die Patentverletzung	*(dee pah-tEHnt-fuh-lEHts-unk)*
patent law	das Patentrecht	*(dahs pah-tEHnt-rehkht)*
patent pending	das angemeldete Patent	*(dahs AHN-geh-mel-deh-teh pah-tEHnt)*
patent royalty	die Patentabgabe	*(dee pah-tEHnt-AHB-gAA-beh)*
patented process	das patentierte Verfahren	*(dahs pah-tEHn-tEEr-teh fuh-fAA-ren)*
pattern	das Muster	*(dahs MUS-tuh)*
pay (v)	zahlen	*(tsAA-len)*
pay off (v)	tilgen	*(tIL-gehn)*
pay up (v)	vollständig bezahlen	*(FOL-shtEHn-dikh beh-tsAA-len)*
payable on demand	zahlbar bei Sicht	*(tsAAl-bAAr beye zIKHT)*
payable to bearer	an den Inhaber zahlbar	*(ahn dehn IN-hah-buh tsAAl-bAAr)*
payable to order	an Order zahlbar	*(ahn OR-duh tsAAl-bAAr)*
payback period	der Zurückzahlungszeitraum	*(duh tsOO-rEWks-tsAA-lungs-tsEYEt-rOWm)*
payee	der Zahlungsempfänger	*(duh tsAA-lungs-em-pfEHn-guh)*
payer	der Zahler	*(duh tsAA-luh)*
payload	die Nutzlast	*(dee nUts-lahst)*
paymaster	der Zahlungsmeister	*(duh tsAA-lungs-mEYE-stuh)*
payment	die Zahlung	*(dee tsAA-lung)*
payment in full	die volle Zahlung	*(dee fOL-leh tsAA-lung)*

payment in kind	die Sachleistung	*(dee zahkh-lEYEs-tunk)*
payment, refused	die verweigerte Zahlung	*(dee fuh-vEYE-guh-teh tsAA-lung)*
payout period	die Kapitalrückflußdauer	*(dee kah-pi-tAAL-rEWk-flus-dOW-uh)*
payroll	die Lohnliste	*(dee LOHN-lIS-teh)*
payroll tax	die Lohnsteuer	*(dee LOHN-shtOY-uh)*
peak load	die Spitzenbelastung	*(dee shpI-tsehn-beh-lAHs-tunk)*
pegged price	der Stützpreis	*(duh shtEWts-prEYEs)*
pegging	die Preisstützung	*(dee prEYEs-shtEW-tsunk)*
pellet	die Pille, das Dragée	*(dee pIL-leh), (dahs drah-SHAY)*
penalty clause	die Strafklausel	*(dee shtrAAf-klOW-zehl)*
penalty-fraud action	das Strafverfahren wegen Unterschlagung	*(dahs shtrAAf-fuh-fAA-ren VAY-gen un-tuh-shlAH-gunk)*
penicillin	das Penizillin	*(dahs peh-ni-tsi-LEEN)*
penny stock	die Kleinaktie	*(dee klEYEn-ak-tsEE-eh)*
pension fund	die Pensionskasse	*(dee pen-zee-OHns-kAH-seh)*
pepper mill	die Pfeffermühle	*(dee pfEHF-fuh-mEW-leh)*
pepper shaker	der Pfefferstreuer	*(duh pfEHF-fuh-shtROY-uh)*
per capita	pro Kopf	*(proh kopf)*
per diem	pro Tag	*(proh tAAk)*
per share	pro Anteil	*(proh AHN-teyel)*
percent	das Prozent	*(dahs proh-tsEHnt)*
percentage earnings	die Provisionseinkünfte	*(dee pro-vi-zee-OHnz-EYEn-kEWnf-teh)*
percentage of profit	der Gewinnanteilprozentsatz	*(duh geh-vIN-AHN-teyel-proh-tsEHNt-zahts)*
percentage point	der Prozentpunkt	*(duh proh-tsEHnt-pUnkt)*
perfect binding	die perfekte Bindung	*(dee puh-fehk-teh BIN-dunk)*
performance bond	die Gewährleistungsgarantie	*(dee geh-vAYr-lEYEs-tunkgs-gah-rahn-tEE)*
period	die Periode	*(dee pay-ree-OH-deh)*
period (time)	der Zeitraum	*(duh tsEYEt-rOWm)*

periodic inventory	die periodische Bestandsaufnahme	*(dee pay-ree-OH-dish-eh beh-shtAHnds-OWf-nAA-meh)*
peripherals	die Randmaschinen	*(dee rAHnt-mah-shEE-nen)*
perks	die Nebeneinkünfte	*(dee nAY-ben-EYEn-kEWnf-teh)*
permit	der Zulassungsschein	*(dee tsoo-lahs-soonks-shEYEn)*
perpetual inventory	die permanente Buchinventur	*(dee payr-mah-nEHn-teh bOOkh-in-vehn-tOOr)*
personal deduction	der persönliche Abzug	*(duh payr-sERn-likh-eh AHB-tsOOk)*
personal exemption	der persönliche Freibetrag	*(duh payr-sERn-likh-eh frEYE-beh-trAHk)*
personal income tax	die persönliche Einkommensteuer	*(dee payr-sERn-likh-eh EYEn-kOM-mehn-shtOY-uh)*
personal liability	die persönliche Haftpflicht	*(dee payr-sERn-likh-eh hAHft-pflIKHT)*
personal property	das Privateigentum	*(dahs pree-vAAt-EYE-gen-tOOm)*
personality test	die Persönlichkeitsprüfung	*(dee payr-sERn-likh-keyets-prEW-funk)*
personnel	das Personal	*(dahs payr-zoh-nAAL)*
personnel department	die Personalabteilung	*(dee payr-zoh-nAAL-AHB-tEYE-lunk)*
personnel management	die Personalleitung	*(dee payr-zoh-nAAL-lEYE-tunk)*
petrochemical	petrochemisch	*(peh-troh-KHAY-mish)*
petrodollars	die Petrodollars	*(dee peh-troh-dOHl-laars)*
petroleum	das Erdöl	*(dahs AYrd-ERl)*
pharmaceutical	pharmazeutisch	*(fahr-ma-tsOY-tish)*
pharmacist	der Apotheker	*(duh ah-po-tAY-kuh)*
phase in (v)	stufenweise einführen	*(shtOO-fen-vEYE-zeh EYEn-fEW-ren)*
phase out (v)	stufenweise einstellen	*(shtOO-fen-vEYE-zeh EYEn-stEHL-len)*
phosphate	das Phosphat	*(dahs FOS-faht)*
physical inventory	die körperliche Inventur	*(dee kER-puh-likh-eh in-vehn-tOOr)*

physician	der Arzt	*(duh ARtst)*
pica	die Pica	*(dee pi-kah)*
picket line	die Streikpostenkette	*(dee shtrEYEk-pOS-ten-keh-teh)*
pickling	das Abbeizen	*(dahs ahb-bEYE-tsen)*
pickup and delivery	die Abholung und Lieferung	*(dee AHB-hOH-lunk unt LEE-fuh-runk)*
pie chart	das Kreisdiagramm	*(dahs krEYEs-dee-ah-grAHm)*
piecework	die Stückarbeit	*(dee shtEWk-AHR-beyet)*
pig iron	das Gußeisen	*(dahs gUS-EYE-zen)*
piggyback service	der Huckepackverkehr	*(duh hU-keh-pahk-fuh-kAYr)*
pigment	das Pigment	*(dahs PIG-ment)*
pigskin	das Schweinsleder	*(dahs shvEYEns-lAY-duh)*
pilferage	der kleine Diebstahl	*(duh klEYE-neh dEEb-shtaal)*
pill	die Pille	*(dee pIL-leh)*
pilotage	das Lotsengeld	*(dahs lOt-zehn-gehlt)*
pinion	das Antriebsrad	*(dahs AHN-treebs-raht)*
pipage	das Röhrensystem	*(dahs RER-en-zew-stAYm)*
piston	der Kolben	*(duh kOL-ben)*
pitcher	der Krug	*(duh krUk)*
place an order (v)	einen Auftrag erteilen	*(EYE-nen OWf-trAHk ayr-tEYE-len)*
place of business	das Geschäftslokal	*(dahs geh-shEHfts-loh-kAAL)*
place setting	die Tischordnung	*(dee TISH-ORd-nunk)*
placement (personnel)	die Stellenvermittlung	*(dee shtEHL-en-fuh-mIT-lunk)*
plan	der Plan	*(duh plaan)*
plan, market	der Marktplan	*(duh mAHrkt-plAAn)*
planned obsolescence	die geplante Überalterung	*(dee geh-plAAn-teh EW-buh-ahl-tAY-runk)*
plant capacity	die betriebliche Leistungsfähigkeit	*(dee beh-trEEp-likh-eh lEYEs-tungs-fAY-ikh-keyet)*
plant location	die Fabriklage	*(dee fah-brEEk-lAA-geh)*

P

plant manager	der Werkleiter	*(duh vEHrk-mEYEs-tuh)*
plants	die Pflanzen	*(dee pflAHN-tsen)*
plate	die Platte	*(dee plAHT-teh)*
pleat	die Falte	*(dee fAHL-teh)*
pleated	gefaltet	*(geh-fAHL-teht)*
pledge	das Pfand	*(dahs pfahnt)*
plenary meeting	die Plenarsitzung	*(dee plehn-AAr-zIT-sunk)*
plow back earnings (v)	selbstfinanzieren	*(zehlbst-fee-nAHn-tsEE-ren)*
plus accrued interest	zuzüglich aufgelaufener Zinsen	*(tsOO-tsEW-glikh OWf-geh-lOW-feh-nuh tsIN-zen)*
pocketbook	die Handtasche	*(dee HAHNd-tAH-SHeh)*
point, breaker	die Gewinnschwelle	*(dee geh-vIN-shvEL-leh)*
point, breakeven	der Kostendeckungspunkt	*(duh kOS-ten-DEK-unks-pUnkt)*
point, percentage	der Prozentpunkt	*(duh proh-tsEHnt-pUnkt)*
point of order	die Verfahrensfrage	*(dee fuh-fAA-renz-frAA-geh)*
point of sale	der Verkaufspunkt	*(duh fuh-kOWfs-pUnkt)*
policy (action)	die Politik	*(dee po-li-tEEk)*
policy (insurance)	die Police	*(dee po-li-sAY)*
policy (principle)	der Grundsatz	*(duh grUNd-zahts)*
policyholder	der Policeinhaber	*(duh po-li-sAY-IN-hah-buh)*
polymer	die polymeren Körper	*(dee po-lEW-meh-ren KER-puh)*
pool (v)	zusammenlegen	*(tsOO-zAHM-men-lAY-gen)*
pool of funds	der Sammelfonds	*(duh zAH-mehl-fOH)*
pooling of interests	eine Interessengemeinschaft bilden	*(EYE-neh IN-teh-rehs-sens-geh-mEYEn-shahft bIL-den)*
poplin	der Popelin	*(duh po-pEH-lin)*
portfolio	die Aktentasche	*(dee AHk-ten-tAH-SHeh)*
portfolio management	die Portefeuilleverwaltung	*(dee port-FOY-fuh-vAHl-tunk)*
portfolio theory	die Portfeuilletheorie	*(dee port-FOY-tay-oh-rEE)*
position limit	das Orderlimit	*(dahs OR-duh-li-mit)*
positive	das Positiv	*(dahs po-zi-tEEF)*

positive cash flow	der positive Zahlungsstrom	*(duh po-zee-tEE-fuh tsAA-lungs-shtOHm)*
post (v) (bookkeeping)	verbuchen	*(fuh-bOOkh-en)*
postdated	nachdatiert	*(nAHKH-daa-teert)*
postpone (v)	aufschieben	*(OWf-shEE-ben)*
potential buyer	der Kaufinteressent	*(duh kOWf-in-teh-rehs-sENT)*
potential sales	die Absatzmöglichkeiten	*(dee AHB-zAHts-mER-glikh-keye-ten)*
pottery	die Töpferware	*(dee TERp-fuh-VAAreh)*
powder	das Pulver	*(dahs pUL-fuh)*
power	die Arbeitsleistung	*(dee AHR-beyets-lEYEs-tunk)*
power consumption	der Stromverbrauch	*(duh shtrOHm-fuh-brOWkh)*
power of attorney	die Vollmacht	*(dee FOL-mahkht)*
power steering	die Servolenkung	*(dee zEHR-vo-len-kunk)*
practical	praktisch, zweckmäßig	*(PRAHK-tish), (tsvEHK-mAY-sig)*
practice	die Praktik	*(dee PRAHK-tik)*
preemptive	das Bezugsrecht	*(dahs beh-tsOOgs-rehkht)*
preemptive right	das Vorkaufsrecht	*(dahs FOHR-kOWfs-rehkht)*
prefabricated house	das Fertighaus	*(dahs fEHr-tig-hOWs)*
prefabrication	die Vorfertigung	*(dee FOHR-fEHR-ti-gunk)*
preface	das Vorwort	*(dahs FOHR-vort)*
preferential debts	die bevorrechtigten Forderungen	*(dee beh-FOR-rehkht-tIG-ten FOHR-duh-run-gen)*
preferential tariff	der Vorzugszoll	*(duh FOHR-tsoogs-tsOL)*
preferred stock	die Vorzugsaktie	*(dee FOHR-tsoogs-ak-tsEE-eh)*
preliminary prospectus	der Vorprospekt	*(duh FOHR-pros-pEHkt)*
premises	das Grundstück	*(dahs grUnd-shtEWk)*
premium, insurance	die Versicherungsprämie, der Versicherungsbeitrag	*(dee fuh-zIkh-eh-runks-PRAY-mee-eh), (duh fuh-zIkh-eh-runks-bEYE-trAHk)*

premium offer	das Zugabenangebot	*(dahs tsoo-gAA-ben-AHN-geh-boht)*
premium payment	die Prämienzahlung	*(dee PRAY-mee-ehn-tsAA-lung)*
premium pricing	die Spitzenpreisansetzung	*(dee shpI-tsehn-prEYEs-AHn-zEH-tsunk)*
prepaid expenses (balance sheet)	die vorausgezahlten Aufwendungen	*(dee FOHR-OWs-geh-tsAAl-ten OWf-vEHn-dunk-en)*
prepay (v)	vorauszahlen	*(FOHR-OWs-tsAA-len)*
prescription	das Rezept	*(dahs reh-tsEHPt)*
president	der Präsident	*(duh pray-zee-dEHnt)*
press book	das Pressebuch	*(dahs prehs-zeh-bUKH)*
pressure	der Druck	*(duh drUK)*
preventive maintenance	die vorbeugende Instandhaltung	*(dee FOHR-bOY-gen-deh in-stAHnt-hahl-tunk)*
price	der Preis	*(duh prEYEs)*
price (v)	auspreisen	*(OWs-prEYEs-en)*
price abatement	der Preisnachlaß	*(duh prEYEs-nAKH-lahs)*
price cutting	die Preissenkung	*(dee prEYEs-zAYn-kunk)*
price differential	der Preisunterschied	*(duh prEYEs-un-tuh-shEEd)*
price elasticity	die Preiselastizität	*(dee prEYEs-eh-lahs-ti-tsee-tAYt)*
price fixing	die Preisbindung	*(dee prEYEs-bIN-dunk)*
price freeze	der Preisstop	*(duh prEYEs-stop)*
price increase	die Preiserhöhung	*(dee prEYEs-uh-hER-unk)*
price index	der Preisindex	*(duh prEYEs-IN-dehx)*
price limit	die Preisgrenze	*(dee prEYEs-grEHN-tseh)*
price list	die Preisliste	*(dee prEYEs-lIs-teh)*
price range	die Preislage	*(dee prEYEs-lAA-geh)*
price support	die Preisstützung	*(dee prEYEs-shtEW-tsunk)*
price tag	der Preiszettel	*(duh prEYEs-tsEH-tel)*
price war	der Preiskrieg	*(duh prEYEs-krEEg)*
price/earnings (p/e) ratio	das Preis-Einnahmen Verhältnis	*(dahs prEYEs-EYEn-nAA-men fuh-hEHlt-nis)*
primary market	der Hauptmarkt	*(duh hOWpt-mAHrkt)*
primary reserves	die Primärreserven	*(dee pree-mAYr-reh-zAYr-fehn)*

prime costs	die Selbstkosten	*(dee zehlbst-kOS-ten)*
prime rate	der Leitzinssatz	*(duh lEYEt-tsIN-zAHts)*
prime time	die Hauptsendezeit	*(dee hOWpt-zEN-deh-tsEYEt)*
principal (capital)	das Grundkapital	*(dahs grUNd-kah-pi-tAAL)*
principal (employer of an agent)	der Auftraggeber	*(duh OWf-trAHk-gAY-buh)*
print	der Druck	*(duh drUK)*
print run	der Drucklauf	*(duh drUK-lowf)*
printed circuit	die gedruckte Schaltung	*(dee geh-drUK-teh shAHL-tunk)*
printed matter	die Drucksache	*(dee drOOk-sakh-eh)*
printing	der Druck	*(duh drUK)*
printout	der Computerausdruck	*(duh kom-pyU-tuh-OWs-druk)*
priority	die Priorität	*(dee pree-ohr-ee-tAYt)*
private fleet	die Privatflotte	*(dee pree-vAAt-flOT-teh)*
private label (or brand)	die Privatmarke	*(dee pree-vAAt-mAHR-keh)*
private placement (finance)	die Privatplazierung	*(dee pree-vAAt-plah-tsEE-runk)*
pro forma invoice	die Proformarechnung	*(dee proh-FOHR-mah-rEHKH-nunk)*
pro forma statement	die Proformabilanz	*(dee proh-FOHR-mah-bee-lAHnts)*
probate	die Testamentseröffnung und Bestätigung	*(dee tehst-ta-mEHnt-uh-ERf-nunk unt beh-shtEH-ti-gunk)*
problem	das Problem	*(dahs proh-blAYm)*
problem analysis	die Problemanalyse	*(dee proh-blAYm-ah-nah-lEW-zeh)*
problem solving	die Problemlösung	*(dee proh-blAYm-lER-zunk)*
proceeds	die Erlöse	*(dee AYr-lER-seh)*
process	der Arbeitsvorgang	*(duh ahr-bEYEts-fOHR-gahnk)*
process (v)	bearbeiten	*(beh-AHR-beye-ten)*
processing error	der Bearbeitungsfehler	*(duh beh-AHR-beye-tunks-fAY-luh)*

procurement	die Beschaffung	*(dee beh-shAF-funk)*
product	das Produkt	*(dahs pro-dUkt)*
product analysis	die Warenanalyse	*(dee vAA-ren-ah-nah-lEW-zeh)*
product design	die Produktgestaltung	*(dee proh-dUKt-geh-shtAHl-tunk)*
product development	die Produktentwicklung	*(dee proh-dUKt-ehnt-vIK-lunk)*
product dynamics	die Produktdynamik	*(dee proh-dUKt-dew-nAA-mIk)*
product group	die Produktgruppe	*(dee proh-dUKt-grUP-peh)*
product life	die Lebensdauer	*(dee lAY-benz-dOW-uh)*
product line	das Produktsortiment	*(dahs proh-dUKt-sohr-tee-mEH)*
product management	das Produktmanagement	*(dahs proh-dUKt-meh-nEHdj-mehnt)*
product profit-ability	die Produktrentabilität	*(dee proh-dUKt-rehn-tah-bi-lee-tAYt)*
production	die Produktion	*(dee Pro-duk-TSI-On)*
production control	die Produktionslenkung	*(dee proh-duk-tsEE-ohns-lAYnk-unk)*
production costs	der Produktionsaufwand	*(duh proh-duk-tsEE-ohns-OWf-vahnt)*
production line	die Produktion am laufenden Band	*(dee proh-duk-tsEE-ohn ahm lOW-fehn-dehn bahnt)*
production process	das Fertigungsverfahren	*(dahs fEHR-ti-gunks-fuh-fAA-ren)*
production schedule	der Fertigungsplan	*(duh fEHR-ti-gunks-plAAn)*
productivity	die Produktivität	*(dee proh-duk-ti-vee-tAYt)*
profession	der Beruf	*(duh beh-rOOf)*
professional	der Fachmann	*(duh fAKH-mahn)*
profit	der Gewinn	*(duh geh-vIN)*
profit factor	der Gewinnfaktor	*(duh geh-vIN-FAHK-tohr)*
profit, gross	der Rohgewinn	*(duh ROH-geh-vIN)*
profit impact	die Gewinnwirkung	*(dee geh-vIN-vEEr-kunk)*
profit margin	die Gewinnspanne	*(dee geh-vIN-shpAA-neh)*

profit, net	der Reingewinn	*(duh REYEN-geh-vIN)*
profit projection	die Gewinnprognose	*(dee geh-vIN-prog-nOH-zeh)*
profit sharing	die Gewinnbeteiligung	*(dee geh-vIN-beh-tEYE-li-gunk)*
profit-and-loss account	das Gewinn- und Verlustkonto	*(dahs geh-vIN unt fuh-lUst-kON-toh)*
profit-and-loss statement	die Gewinn- und Verlustrechnung	*(dee geh-vIN unt fuh-lUst-rEHKH-nunk)*
profit-taking	die Gewinnrealisierung	*(dee geh-vIN-ray-ahl-li-zEE-runk)*
profitability	die Rentabilität	*(dee ren-tah-bi-lee-tΛYt)*
profitability analysis	die Rentabilitätsanalyse	*(dee ren-tah-bi-lee-tAYts-ah-nah-lEW-zeh)*
program	das Programm	*(dahs proh-grAHm)*
program (v)	programmieren	*(proh-grahm-mEE-ren)*
prohibited goods	die Schmuggelwaren	*(dee shmOOg-gehl-vAA-rehn)*
project	das Vorhaben	*(dahs FOHR-hAA-ben)*
project (v)	planen	*(plAA-nen)*
project planning	die Projektplanung	*(dee proh-yEHKt-plAA-nunk)*
promissory note	der Eigenwechsel	*(duh EYE-gen-vEHk-sehl)*
promotion	die Förderung	*(dee fER-duh-runk)*
promotion, sales	die Verkaufsförderung	*(dee fuh-kOWfs-fER-duh-runk)*
proof of loss	der Schadennachweis	*(duh shAA-den-nAHKH-vEYEs)*
proofreading	das Korrekturlesen	*(dahs kor-rehk-tOOR-lay-zen)*
property	der Besitz	*(duh beh-zITs)*
proprietary	gesetzlich geschützt	*(geh-zEHts-likh geh-shEWtst)*
proprietor	der Eigentumer	*(duh EYE-gen-tOOm-uh)*
prospectus	der Prospekt	*(duh pros-pEKt)*
protectionism	der Protektionismus	*(duh proh-tek-tsee-oh-nIS-mus)*
protest (banking, law)	der Wechselprotest	*(duh vEHk-sehl-proh-tEHst)*

P

proxy	die Bevollmächtigung	*(dee beh-fol-mAYKH-ti-gunk)*
proxy statement	das Vollmachtsformular	*(dahs FOL-mahkhts-for-mu-lAAr)*
public auction	die öffentliche Versteigerung	*(dee ERf-fent-likh-eh fuh-shtEYE-guh-runk)*
public company	die Aktiengesellschaft	*(dee ak-tsEE-en-geh-zEL-shahft)*
public domain	das Gemeingut	*(dahs geh-mEYEn-gOOt)*
public funds	die öffentlichen Mittel	*(dee ERf-fehnt-likh-eh mit-tEL)*
public offering	das öffentliche Angebot	*(dahs ERf-fehnt-likh-eh AHN-geh-boht)*
public opinion poll	die Meinungsforschung	*(dee mEYE-nunks-fOHr-shunk)*
public property	das Staatseigentum	*(dahs shtAAts-EYE-gen-tOOm)*
public relations	die Öffentlichkeitsarbeit	*(dee ERf-fehnt-likh-keyets-AHR-beyet)*
public sale	der öffentliche Verkauf	*(duh ERf-fehnt-likh-eh fuh-kOWf)*
public utility	der Versorgungsbetrieb	*(duh fuh-zOR-gunks-beh-trEEp)*
public works	die öffentlichen Arbeiten	*(dee ERF-fehnt-likh-en AHR-beye-ten)*
publicity	die Publizität	*(dee pu-bli-tsi-tAYt)*
publisher	der Verleger	*(duh fuh-LAY-guh)*
pump priming	die Konjunkturspritze	*(dee kon-yunk-tOOr-shprI-tseh)*
punch card	die Lochkarte	*(dee lOKH-kAAr-teh)*
purchase (v)	kaufen	*(kOW-fen)*
purchase money mortgage	die Restkaufgeldhypothek	*(dee rehst-kOWf-gehlt-hew-poh-tAYk)*
purchase order	der Kaufauftrag	*(duh kOWf-OWf-trAHk)*
purchase price	der Kaufpreis	*(duh kOWf-prEYEs)*
purchasing agent	der Einkaufsleiter	*(duh EYEn-kOWfs-lEYE-tuh)*
purchasing power	die Kaufkraft	*(dee kOWf-krahft)*
pure risk	das reine Risiko	*(dahs rEYE-neh REE-zee-koh)*

purgative	das Abführmittel	*(dahs ahb-fEWR-mit-tel)*
purification	die Purifikation	*(dee PU-ri-fi-kah-TSI-on)*
purse	die Geldbörse	*(dee gELt-bER-zeh)*
put and call	das Stellagegeschäft	*(dahs shtEHL-lAA-geh-geh-shEHft)*
put in a bid (v)	ein Angebot machen	*(EYEn AHN-geh-boht mAA-khen)*
put option	die Verkaufsoption	*(dee fuh-kOWfs-op-tsee-OHn)*
pyramid selling	das Schneeballverkaufs-system	*(dahs shnAY-bahl-fuh-kOWfs-zew-shAYm)*
pyramiding	die Nutzung noch nicht rea-lisierter Gewinne	*(dee nUts-unk nOHKH nIKHt ray-aal-lee-zEEr-tuh geh-vIN-neh)*

Q

qualification	die Qualifikation	*(dee kvah-li-fi-kah-tsee-OHn)*
qualified acceptance endorsement	das eingeschränkte Indossament	*(dahs EYEn-geh-shrAYnk-tes-in-dos-ah-mEH)*
quality control	die Qualitätskontrolle	*(dee kvah-li-tAYts-kon-trOL-leh)*
quality goods	die Qualitätswaren	*(dee kvah-li-tAYts-vAA-ren)*
quantity	die Menge	*(dee mAYng-eh)*
quantity discount	der Mengenrabatt	*(duh mAYng-en-rah-bAAt)*
quasi-public company	der quasi-öffentliche Betrieb	*(duh kvAA-zee ER-fent-likh-eh beh-trEEp)*
quick assets	die flüssigen Anlagen	*(dee flEW-sig-en AHN-lAA-gen)*
quit claim deed	die Verzichturkunde	*(dee fuh-tsIKHts-OOr-kund-deh)*
quorum	die beschlußfähige Anzahl	*(dee beh-shlUS-fAY-hi-geh AHN-tsAAl)*
quota	das Kontingent	*(dahs kon-tin-gEHnt)*
quota (export)	die Ausfuhrquote	*(dee OWs-foor-kvOH-teh)*
quota (import)	die Einfuhrquote	*(dee EYEn-foor-kvOH-teh)*
quota (sales)	die Verkaufsquote	*(dee fuh-kOWfs-kvOH-teh)*

| **quota system** | das Kontingentierungssystem | *(dahs kon-tin-gehn-tEE-runks-zew-stAYm)* |
| **quotation (stock exchange)** | die Notierung | *(dee noh-tEE-runk)* |

R

rabbit	das Kaninchen	*(dahs kah-nEEN-khen)*
raccoon	der Waschbär(pelz)	*(duh vahsh-bAYR [pELTS])*
rack jobber	der Großlieferant	*(duh grOHs-lEE-fuh-rahnt)*
radial tire	der Gürtelreifen	*(duh gEWR-tel-rEYE-fen)*
rail shipment	die Bahnsendung	*(dee BAAN-zEN-dunk)*
railroad	die Eisenbahn	*(dee EYE-zen-bAAn)*
rain check	die Gültigkeitsverlängerung	*(dee gEWl-tikh-keyets-fuh-lAYn-guh-runk)*
raincoat	der Regenmantel	*(duh RAY-gen-mAHN-tel)*
raising capital	die Kapitalaufnahme	*(dee kah-pi-tAAL-OWf-nAA-meh)*
rally	die Erholung	*(dee ayr-hOH-lunk)*
rally (v)	sich sammeln	*(zikh zAA-meln)*
random access memory	der wahlfreie Speicherzugriff	*(duh vAAl-freye-eh shpEYEkh-uh-tsOO-grif)*
random sample	die Stichprobe	*(dee shtIKH-proh-beh)*
rate	der Kurs, die Rate	*(duh koors), (dee rAH-teh)*
rate of growth	die Wachstumsrate	*(dee vAHks-tooms-rAH-teh)*
rate of increase	die Zuwachsrate	*(dee tsOO-vahks-rAH-teh)*
rate of interest	der Zinsfuß, der Zinssatz	*(duh tsINs-foos), (duh tsINs-zAHts)*
rate of return	die Rentabilitätsrate	*(dee ren-tah-bi-li-tAYts-rAH-teh)*
rating (credit)	die Krediteinschätzung	*(dee kray-dIT-EYEn-shEHts-zunk)*
rating (market)	die Börsenmarkteinstufung	*(dee bER-zen-mAHrkt-eyen-stOO-funk)*
ratio	das Verhältnis	*(dahs fuh-hEHlt-nis)*
rationing	die Rationierung	*(dee rah-tsee-oh-nEE-runk)*
raw materials	die Rohstoffe	*(dee ROH-shtof-feh)*

rayon	die Kunstseide	*(dee kUNst-zeYE-deh)*
reactant	der Verbrennungshilfsstoff	*(duh fuh-brEHN-nungs-hilfs-shtOF)*
ready cash	das verfügbare Bargeld	*(dahs fuh-fEWg-bAA-reh bAAr-gehlt)*
ready-to-wear	von der Stange	*(fon duh shtAHN-geh)*
real assets	das Grundvermögen	*(dahs grUNd-fuh-mER-gen)*
real estate	der Grundbesitz	*(duh grUnd-beh-zITs)*
real income	das Realeinkommen	*(dah ray-AAl-EYEn-kOM-mehn)*
real investment	die Realinvestition	*(dee ray-AAl-in-vehs-ti-tsi-OHn)*
real price	der Effektivpreis	*(duh eh-fehk-tEEv-prEYEs)*
real time	die Echtzeit	*(dee eKHT-tsEYEt)*
real wages	die Reallöhne	*(dee ray-AAl-lER-neh)*
ream	das Ries	*(dahs rees)*
rear axle	die Hinterachse	*(dee hIN-tuh-akh-seh)*
reasonable care	die angemessene Sorgfalt	*(dee AHN-geh-mES-seh-neh zORG-fahlt)*
rebate	der Preisnachlaß	*(duh prEYEs-nAHKH-lahs)*
recapitalization	die Neufinanzierung	*(dee NOY-fee-nahn-tsEE-runk)*
receipt (paper)	die Quittung	*(dee kvIT-tunk)*
receipt (reception)	der Empfang	*(duh em-pfAHnk)*
receiver	der Empfänger	*(duh ehm-pfEHN-guh)*
recession	der Rückgang	*(duh REWK-gahnk)*
reciprocal training	die gegenseitige Ausbildung	*(dee gAY-gen-zEYE-tig-eh OWs-bil-dunk)*
record	die Schallplatte	*(dee shAHL-plaht-teh)*
record (v)	aufnehmen	*(OWf-nay-men)*
record date	das Protokolldatum	*(dahs proh-toh-kOL-DAA-tum)*
record player	der Schallplattenspieler	*(duh shAHL-plaht-ten-shPEE-luh)*
recourse	der Rückgriff	*(duh REWK-grif)*
recovery	der Aufschwung	*(duh OWf-shvunk)*
recovery of expenses	die Ausgabenvergütung	*(dee OWs-gAA-ben-fuh-gEW-tunk)*

R

recyclable	recyclingsfähig	*(ree-SEYEK-lings-FAY-ikh)*
recycling economy	Kreislaufwirtschaft	*(KREYES-lowf-veert-shahft)*
red tape	der Amtsschimmel	*(duh AHMt-shIM-mel)*
redeemable bond	die kündbare Obligation	*(dee kEWnd-bAA-reh ob-li-gah-tsEE-ohn)*
redemption allowance	die Einlösungsvergütung	*(dee EYEn-lER-zungz-fuh-gEW-tunk)*
redemption fund	der Tilgungsfonds	*(duh tIL-gunks-fOH)*
redemption premium	die Einlösungsprämie	*(dee EYEn-lER-zunks-PRAY-mee-eh)*
rediscount rate	der Rediskontsatz	*(duh RAY-dis-kONt-zahts)*
reduction	die Reduktion	*(dee reh-duk-TSI-On)*
reexport (v)	wieder ausführen	*(vEE-duh OWs-fEW-ren)*
reference, credit	die Kreditreferenz	*(dee kray-dIT-reh-feh-rEHnts)*
reference number	das Aktienzeichen	*(dahs ak-tsEE-en-tsEYE-khen)*
refinancing	die Refinanzierung	*(dee RAY-fee-nahn-tsEE-runk)*
refine (v)	raffinieren	*(RAf-fi-nee-ren)*
refinery	die Raffinerie	*(dee RAf-fi-neh-ree)*
reflation	die Reflation	*(dee RAY-flah-tsEE-ohn)*
refractories	die Schamottesteine	*(dee shah-mOT-eh-shTEYE-neh)*
refund	die Rückzahlung	*(dee rEWk-tsAA-lung)*
refuse acceptance (v)	die Annahme verweigern	*(dee AHN-nah-meh fuh-vEYE-guhn)*
refuse payment (v)	die Zahlung verweigern	*(dee tsAA-lung fuh-vEYE-guhn)*
registered check	der eingetragene Scheck	*(duh EYEn-geh-trAA-gen-eh shek)*
registered mail	die Einschreibepost	*(dee EYEn-shrEYE-beh-pOSt)*
registered representative	der eingetragene Vertreter	*(duh EYEn-geh-trAA-geh-neh fuh-trAY-tuh)*
registered security	das Namenspapier	*(dahs nAA-menz-pah-pEEr)*
registered trademark	das eingetragene Warenzeichen	*(dahs EYEn-geh-trAA-geh-neh vAA-ren-tsEYE-khen)*

regression analysis	die Regressionsanalyse	*(dee ray-grehs-sEE-ohns-ah-nah-lEW-zeh)*
regressive tax	die rückwirkende Steuer	*(dee rEWk-vEEr-ken-deh shtOY-uh)*
regular warehouse	das eingetragene Lagerhaus	*(dahs EYEn-geh-trAA-geh-neh lAA-guh-hOWs)*
regulation	die Vorschrift	*(dee FOHR-shrift)*
reimburse (v)	entschädigen	*(EHNt-shAY-di-gen)*
reinsurer	der Rückversicherer	*(duh rEWk-fuh-zIKH-uh-uh)*
reliable source	die zuverlässige Quelle	*(dee tsOO-fuh-lEH-si-geh kvEH-leh)*
remainder	der Rest, das Übrige	*(duh rehst), (dahs EWb-ri-geh)*
remedies	die Heilmittel	*(dee hEYEL-mit-tel)*
remedy (law)	das Rechtsmittel	*(dahs REHKHTs-mit-tEL)*
remission of a customs duty	der Zollerlaß	*(duh tsOL-AYr-lahs)*
remission of a tax	der Steuernachlaß	*(duh shtOY-uh-nAHkh-lahs)*
remuneration	die Vergütung	*(dee fuh-gEW-tunk)*
renegotiate (v)	neu verhandeln	*(noy fuh-hAHn-dehln)*
renew (v)	erneuern	*(ayr-nOY-uhn)*
renovation	die Sanierung	*(Zah-nee-ROONG)*
rent	die Miete	*(dee mEE-teh)*
rent (v) (rent from)	mieten	*(mEE-ten)*
rent (v) (rent to)	vermieten	*(fuh-mEE-ten)*
reorganization	die Umorganisierung	*(dee um-ohr-gah-ni-zEE-runk)*
repay (v)	zurückzahlen	*(tsOO-rEWk-tsAA-len)*
repeat order	die Nachbestellung	*(dee nAKH-beh-shtEHL-lunk)*
replacement cost	die Wiederbeschaffungs-kosten	*(dee vEE-duh-beh-shAF-funks-kOS-ten)*
replacement parts	die Ersatzteile	*(dee AYr-zahts-tEYE-leh)*
reply (v)	beantworten	*(beh-AHNt-vohr-ten)*
report	die Nachricht	*(dee nAKH-rikht)*
repossession	die Wiederinbesitznahme	*(dee vEE-duh-in-beh-zITs-nAA-meh)*

R

representative	der Vertreter	*(duh fuh-trAY-tuh)*
reproduction	die Reproduktion	*(dee reh-proh-duk-tsEE-ohn)*
request for bid	die Ausschreibung	*(dee OWs-shrEYE-bunk)*
requirement	die Anforderung	*(dee AHN-FOHR-duh-runk)*
resale	der Wiederverkauf	*(duh vEE-duh-fuh-kOWf)*
research	die Forschung	*(dee FOR-shunk)*
research and development	die Forschung und Entwicklung	*(dee FOHr-shunk unt ehnt-vIK-lunk)*
reserve	die Rücklage	*(dee rEWK-lAA-geh)*
resident buyer	der ansässige Einkäufer	*(duh AHN-sehs-si-geh EYEn-kOY-fuh)*
resistance	der Widerstand	*(duh VI-duh-shtahnt)*
resolution	der Beschluß, die Resolution	*(duh beh-shlUS), (dee reh-zoh-loo-tsEE-ohn)*
resonance	die Resonanz	*(dee REH-zo-nahnts)*
resource allocation	die Mittelverwendung	*(dee mit-tEL-fuh-vEHn-dunk)*
restore (v)	restaurieren	*(rehst-ow-rEE-ren)*
restrictions on export (import)	die Ausfuhrbeschränkungen, die Einfuhrbeschränkungen	*(dee OWs-foor-beh-shrAYNK-unk-en), (dee EYEn-foor-beh-shrAYNK-unk-en)*
restructure (v)	umstrukturieren	*(um-strook-tOO-rEE-ren)*
resume (v)	wiederaufnehmen	*(vEE-duh-OWf-nAY-men)*
retail	der Einzelhandel	*(duh EYEn-tsehl-hAHn-dehl)*
retail bank	die Handelsbank	*(dee hAHn-dehls-bahnk)*
retail merchandise	die Einzelhandelswaren	*(dee EYEn-tsehl-hAHn-dehls-vAA-ren)*
retail outlet	die Einzelhandelsverkaufs-stelle	*(dee EYEn-tsehl-hAHn-dehls-fuh-kOWf-stEHL-leh)*
retail price	der Einzelhandelspreis	*(duh EYEn-tsehl-hAHn-dehls-prEYEs)*
retail sales tax	die Einzelhandelsumsatz-steuer	*(dee EYEn-tsehl-hAHn-dehls-um-zAHts-shtOY-uh)*

retail trade	der Einzelhandel	*(duh EYEn-tsehl-hAHn-dehl)*
retained earnings	die thesaurierten Gewinne	*(dee tay-zow-rEEr-ten geh-vIN-neh)*
retained profits	die zurückbehaltenen Gewinne	*(dee tsOO-rEWk-beh-hAHl-teh-nen geh-vIN-neh)*
retirement	der Ruhestand	*(duh rOO-heh-shtAHnt)*
retirement (debt)	die Schuldentilgung	*(dee shUL-den-tIL-gunk)*
retroactive	rüickwirkend	*(rEWK-vEEr-kehnt)*
return on assets managed	die Anlagenrendite	*(dee AHN-lAA-geh-ren-di-teh)*
return on capital	die Kapitalrendite	*(dee kah-pi-tAAL-ren-di-teh)*
return on investment	die Kapitalverzinsung	*(dee kah-pi-tAAL-fuh-tsINs-zunk)*
return on sales	die Umsatzrendite	*(dee um-zAHts-ren-di-teh)*
return, rate of	die Rentabilitätsrate	*(dee ren-tah-bi-li-tAYts-rAH-teh)*
reutilize	wieder verwerten	*(vee-deer fuh-VEHR-tern)*
revaluation	die Umwertung	*(dee um-vEHR-tunk)*
revenue	die Einnahme	*(dee EYEn-nAA-meh)*
revenue bond	die Ertragsobligation	*(dee ayr-trAHks-ob-li-gah-tsEE-ohn)*
reverse stock split	die Aktienzusammenlegung	*(dee ak-tsEE-en-tsoo-zAHM-men-lay-gunk)*
revocable trust	das widerrufliche Treuhandverhältnis	*(dahs vi-duh-rOOf-likh-eh trOY-hAHnd-fuh-hEHlt-nis)*
revolving credit	der revolvierende Kredit	*(duh reh-fol-vEE-ren-deh kray-dIT)*
revolving fund	die rückzahlbare Staatsubvention	*(dee rEWk-tsAAl-bAA-reh shtAAt-zub-vehn-tsEE-ohn)*
revolving letter of credit	das revolvierende Akkreditiv	*(dahs reh-fol-vEE-ren-deh ak-kray-di-tEEf)*
reward	die Belohnung	*(dee beh-lOH-nunk)*
rider (contracts)	die Zusatzklausel	*(dee tsOO-zAHts-klOW-zel)*
right of recourse	das Regreßrecht	*(dahs ray-grEHs-rehkht)*
right of way	die Vorfahrt	*(dee FOHR-fAArt)*
ripe	reif	*(rEYEF)*

R

risk	die Gefahr, das Risiko	*(dee geh-fAAr), (dahs REE-zee-koh)*
risk analysis	die Risikoanalyse	*(dee REE-zee-koh-ah-nah-lEW-zeh)*
risk assessment	die Risikoeinschätzung	*(dee REE-zee-koh-EYEn-shEH-tsunk)*
risk capital	das Risikokapital	*(dahs REE-zee-koh-kah-pi-tAAL)*
rod	die Rundstange	*(dee rund-shtAHN-geh)*
rollback	die Preissenkung	*(dee prEYEs-zAYn-kunk)*
rolling mill	der Walzwerkbetrieb	*(duh vALTS-vehrk-beh-trEEb)*
rolling stock	die Eisenbahnbetriebsmittel	*(dee EYE-zen-bAAn-beh-trEEps-mit-tEL)*
rollover	die automatische Erneuerung	*(dee ow-toh-mAA-tish-eh AYR-noy-ayr-runk)*
rough draft	der Vorentwurf	*(duh FOHR-ehnt-vOOrf)*
rough estimate	die Überschlagsrechnung	*(dee EW-buh-shlAHgs-rEHKH-nunk)*
round lot	das Hundertaktienpaket	*(dahs hUn-duht-ak-tsEE-en-paa-kAYt)*
routine	der Programmablauf	*(duh proh-grAHm-AHB-lowf)*
royalty (book)	der Autorenanteil	*(duh OW-tohr-en-AHN-teyel)*
royalty (patent)	die Lizenzgebühr	*(dee lee-tsEHnts-geh-bEWr)*
running expenses	die laufenden Unkosten	*(dee lOW-fen-den OOn-kOS-ten)*
rush order	der Eilauftrag	*(duh EYEl-OWf-trAHk)*

S

sable	der Zobel (pelz)	*(duh tsOH-bel [pELTS])*
saddle	der Sattel	*(duh zaHT-tel)*
saddler	der Sattler	*(duh zaHT-tluh)*
safe deposit box	das Bankfach	*(dahs BAHNK-fahkh)*
safeguard (v)	schützen	*(shEW-tsehn)*
salad plate	der Salatteller	*(duh zah-lAAT-tel-luh)*

salary	das Gehalt	*(dahs geh-hAHlt)*
sales	der Umsatz	*(duh um-zAHts)*
sales analysis	die Absatzanalyse	*(dee AHB-zATS-ah-nah-lEW-zeh)*
sales budget	der Absatzplan	*(duh AHB-zATS-plAAn)*
sales estimate	die Umsatzschätzung	*(dee um-zAHts-shEH-tsung)*
sales force	das Verkaufspersonal	*(dahs fuh-kOWfs-payr-zoh-nAAl)*
sales forecast	die Verkaufsprognose	*(dee fuh-kOWfs-prog-nOH-zeh)*
sales management	die Vertriebsleitung	*(dee fuh-trEEps-lEYE-tunk)*
sales promotion	die Verkaufsförderung	*(dee fuh-kOWfs-fER-duh-runk)*
sales quota	die Verkaufsquote	*(dee fuh-kOWfs-kvOH-teh)*
sales tax	die Umsatzsteuer	*(dee um-zATS-shtOY-uh)*
sales territory	das Absatzgebiet	*(dahs AHB-zATS-geh-bEET)*
sales turnover	der Warenumsatz	*(duh vAA-ren-um-zAHTs)*
sales volume	das Verkaufsvolumen	*(dahs fuh-kOWfs-vol-OO-men)*
salt	das Salz	*(dahs ZAHlts)*
salt shaker	der Salzstreuer	*(duh ZAHlts-shtROY-uh)*
salts	das Salz	*(dahs ZAHlts)*
salvage (v)	bergen, retten	*(BAYr-gehn), (REHT-ten)*
salvage charges	die Bergungskosten	*(dee BAYr-gunks-kOS-ten)*
salvage value (junk, scrap)	der Schrottwert	*(duh shrOt-vEHRt)*
salvage value (recovery)	der Bergungswert	*(duh BAYr-gunks-vEHRt)*
salve	die Salbe	*(dee zAHL-beh)*
sample	die Probe	*(dee pROH-beh)*
sample (v)	probieren	*(pROH-bEE-ren)*
sample line	die Musterkollektion	*(dee MUS-tuh-ko-layk-tsEE-OHn)*
sample size	der Stichprobenumfang	*(dee shtIKH-proh-behn-OOm-fank)*
saponification	die Verseifung	*(dee fuh-zEYE-funk)*
saucer	die Untertasse	*(dee UN-tuh-TAHs-seh)*

S

savings	die Ersparnisse	*(dee ayr-shpAAr-nIS-seh)*
savings account	das Sparkonto	*(dahs shpAAr-kON-toh)*
savings bank	die Sparkasse	*(dee shpAAr-kAH-seh)*
savings bond	die Staatsschuld-verschreibung	*(dee shtAAts-shUlt-fuh-shrEYE-bunk)*
scale	die Gußhaut	*(dee gUS-hOWT)*
scalper	der Weiterverkaufsgewinnler	*(duh VEYE-tuh-fuh-kOWfs-geh-vIN-luh)*
scanner	der Abtaster	*(duh AHB-tahs-tuh)*
scanning	die (Bild) Abtastung	*(dee [Bild] AHB-tahs-tunk)*
scarf	der Schal	*(duh SHAAl)*
schedule	der Zeitplan	*(duh tsEYEt-plAAn)*
schedule (v)	ansetzen	*(AHN-zeh-tsen)*
scissor case	das Scherenetui	*(dahs shAY-ren-e-tuEE)*
scrap	der Abfall	*(duh ahb-fAHL)*
screen	der Bildschirm	*(duh Bild-SHIrm)*
screen (v)	sieben	*(ZEE-behn)*
script	das Manuskript	*(dahs mah-noo-skrIpt)*
sealed bid	das versiegelte Angebot	*(dahs fuh-zEE-gehl-teh AHN-geh-boht)*
sealskin	das Seehundsfell	*(dahs ZAY-hunds-fEL)*
seasonal	jahreszeitlich	*(yAA-rehs-tsEYEt-likh)*
seat	der Sitz	*(duh zITS)*
second mortgage	die zweite Hypothek	*(dee tsvEYE-teh hew-poh-tAYk)*
second position	zweitstellig	*(tsvEYEt-shtEHL-lig)*
second rate	zweitrangig	*(tsvEYEt-rAHng-ig)*
secondary market (securities)	der Wertpapierhandel	*(duh vEHRt-pah-pEEr-hAHn-dehl)*
secretary	die Sekretärin	*(dee zeh-kreh-tEH-rin)*
secured accounts	die gesicherten Konten	*(dee geh-ZIKH-uh-ten kON-ten)*
secured liability	die gesicherte Haftung	*(dee geh-ZIKH-uh-teh hAHf-tunk)*
securities	die Effekten	*(dee eh-fEHk-ten)*
security	die Sicherheit	*(dee zIKH-uh-heyet)*

sedative	das Beruhigungsmittel	*(dahs beh-rOO-I-gungs-mit-tel)*
self-appraisal	die Selbstschätzung	*(dee zehlbst-shEH-tsung)*
self-employed	selbständig	*(zehlbst-shtEHn-dikh)*
self-service	die Selbstbedienung	*(dee zehlbst-beh-dEE-nunk)*
sell (v)	verkaufen	*(fuh-kOW-fen)*
sell and lease back	verkaufen und anschließend mieten	*(fuh kOW-fen unt AHN-shlEE-sent mEE-ten)*
sell direct (v)	direkt verkaufen	*(di-REHKT-fuh-kOWf)*
semiconductor	der Halbleiter	*(duh hAHLb-leye-tuh)*
semivariable costs	die Sprungkosten	*(dee shprUng-kOS-ten)*
senior issue	die mit Vorrechten ausge-stattete Wertpapieremission	*(dee mit FOIIR-rehkh-ten OWs-geh-shtAH-teh-teh vEHRt-pah-pEEr-eh-mi-see-OHn)*
seniority	das Dienstalter	*(dahs dEENst-AAl-teuh)*
separation	die Trennung	*(dee trEHn-nunk)*
serial bonds	die Serienanleihen	*(dee ZAY-ree-ehn-AHN-leye-en)*
serial storage	die Serienspeicherung	*(dee ZAY-ree-ehn-shpEYEkh-uh-runk)*
serum	das Serum	*(dahs ZAY-rum)*
service (v)	versorgen	*(fuh-zOR-gen)*
service, advisory	der Beratungsdienst	*(duh beh-rAA-tunks-deenst)*
service contract	der Dienstvertrag	*(duh dEEnst-fuh-trAHk)*
service, customer	der Kundendienst	*(duh kUN-dehn-dEEnst)*
set-up costs	die Rüstkosten	*(dee REWst-kOS-ten)*
settlement	die Regelung	*(dee RAY-geh-lunk)*
settlement in full	der vollständige Ausgleich	*(duh FOL-shtEHn-dikh-eh OWS-gleykh)*
severance pay	die Entlassungsabfindung	*(dee EHNT-lAH-sunks-AHB-fin-dunk)*
sew (v)	nähen	*(NAY-hen)*
sewage	das Abwasser	*(dahs AHB-vah-sehr)*
sewing kit	das Nähtäschchen	*(dahs nAY-tEHSH-khen)*
sewing machine	die Nähmaschine	*(dee NAY-mah-SHEE-neh)*
sewn	geheftet, broschiert	*(geh-hEHF-tet), (bro-shEERt)*

S

shareholder	der Aktionär	*(duh ak-tsEE-oh-nAYR)*
shareholders' equity	das Eigenkapital	*(dahs EYE-gen-kah-pi-tAAL)*
shareholders' meeting	die Aktionärsversammlung	*(dee ak-tsEE-oh-nAYRz-fuh-zAM-lunk)*
shares	die Aktien	*(dee ak-tsEE-en)*
sheet	die Platte	*(dee plAHT-teh)*
shift (working hours)	die Schicht	*(dee shikht)*
shipment	die Sendung	*(dee zEN-dunk)*
shipper	der Versender	*(duh fuh-zEN-duh)*
shipping agent	der Spediteur	*(duh speh-dee-tEWr)*
shipping charges	die Versandkosten	*(dee fuh-zAHndt-kOS-ten)*
shipping container	der Versandbehälter	*(duh fuh-zAHndt-beh-hEHEl-tuh)*
shipping expenses	die Verladekosten	*(dee fuh-lAA-deh-kOS-ten)*
shipping instructions	die Versandanweisungen	*(dee fuh-zAHndt-AHN-vEYE-zun-gen)*
shirt	das Hemd	*(dahs hEHmt)*
shock absorber	der Stoßdämpfer	*(duh shtOS-dEHm-pfuh)*
shoe	der Schuh	*(duh shOO)*
shopping center	das Geschäftszentrum	*(dahs geh-shEHfts-tsEHN-troom)*
short delivery	die Minderlieferung	*(dee MIN-duh-LEE-fuh-runk)*
short of cash	knapp bei Kasse	*(knahp beye duh kAH-seh)*
short position	die Leerverkaufsposition	*(dee lAYr-fuh-kOWfs-po-zi-tsEE-OHN)*
short sale	der Leerverkauf	*(duh lAYr-fuh-kOWf)*
short shipment	die Mindersendung	*(dee MIN-duh-zEN-dunk)*
short sleeves	die kurzen Ärmel	*(dee KUr-tsen AYR-mel)*
short supply	die Unterversorgung	*(dee un-tuh-fuh-zOR-gunk)*
short wave	die Kurzwelle	*(dee KUrts-vEL-leh)*
shortage	der Mangel	*(duh mAHn-ehl)*
short-term capital account	das kurzfristige Kapitalkonto	*(dahs kURts-fris-tikh-eh kah-pi-tAAL-kON-toh)*
short-term debt	die kurzfristige Verschuldung	*(dee kURts-frist-tikh-eh fuh-shUl-dunk)*

short-term financing	die kurzfristige Finanzierung	*(dee kURts-fris-tikh-eh fee-nahn-tsEE-runk)*
sick leave	die Krankheitsabwesenheit	*(duh krAHnk-heyets-AHB-vAY-zen-heyet)*
sight draft	der Sichtwechsel	*(duh zikht-vEHk-sehl)*
signature	die Unterschrift	*(dee un-tuh-shrIft)*
silent partner	der stille Gesellschafter	*(duh shtIL-leh geh-zEL-shahft-uh)*
silicon	das Silizium	*(dahs zi-LEE-tsi-um)*
silk	der Seidenstoff	*(duh zeYE-den-shtOF)*
silk factory	die Seidenfabrik	*(dee zeYE-den-fah-brIK)*
silk goods	die Seidenwaren	*(dee zeYE-den-VAAren)*
silk manufacturers	die Seidenhersteller	*(dee zeYE-den-huh-shTEL-luh)*
silkworm	die Seidenraupe	*(dee zeYE-den-ROW-peh)*
silverware	das Tafelsilber	*(dahs TAH-fel-zil-buh)*
simulate (v)	vorgeben	*(FOHR-gAY-ben)*
sinking fund	der Tilgungsfonds	*(duh tIL-gunks-fOH)*
sinus	der Sinus	*(duh zEE-nus)*
six-cylinder engine	der Sechszylindermotor	*(duh zEKHs-tsew-lin-duh-mOH-tor)*
size	die Größe	*(dee gRER-seh)*
skilled labor	die gelernten Arbeitskräfte	*(dee geh-lAYrn-ten AHR-beyets-krehf-teh)*
skin	der (Wein) Schlauch	*(duh [vEYEN] shlowkh)*
skirt	der Rock	*(duh rOK)*
slabs	die Metallplatten	*(dee meh-tAHL-plaht-ten)*
slacks	die lange Hose	*(dee LAHN-geh hOH-zeh)*
sleeping pill	die Schlaftablette	*(dee shlAAF-tah-bleh-teh)*
sliding parity	die veränderliche Parität	*(dee fuh-EHn-duh-likh-eh pah-ri-tAYt)*
sliding price scale	die bewegliche Preisskala	*(dee beh-vAYg-li-kheh prEYEs-skAA-lah)*
slippers	die Pantoffel	*(dee pAHN-tOF-fel)*
slump	die Flaute	*(dee flOW-teh)*
small business	der Kleinbetrieb	*(duh klEYEn-beh-trEEp)*
snakeskin	das Schlangenleder	*(dahs shlAHN-gen-lAY-duh)*

S

sneeze (v)	niesen	*(nEE-zen)*
socks	die Socken	*(dee ZO-ken)*
soft currency	die weiche Währung	*(dee vEYE-kheh vAY-runk)*
soft goods	die Textilien	*(dee tehks-tIL-lee-ehn)*
soft loan	das zinsbegünstigte Darlehen	*(dahs tsINs-beh-gEWns-tig-teh dAAr-layn)*
soft sell	die weiche Verkaufstour	*(duh vEHE-kheh fuh-kOWfs-tOOr)*
software	die Software	*(dee soft-vAYr)*
sole agent	der Alleinvertreter	*(duh ahl-lEYEn-fuh-trAY-tuh*
sole proprietorship	die Einzelfirma	*(dee EYEn-tsehl-fIR-mah)*
sole rights	das Alleinrecht	*(dahs ahl-lEYEn-rehkht)*
solubility	die Löslichkeit	*(dee LEWS-likh-kEYET)*
solute	der aufgelöste Stoff	*(duh OWf-geh-LER-stehr shtOF)*
solution	die (Auf) Lösung	*(dee [OWf-ler] LER-zunk)*
solvency	die Zahlungsfähigkeit	*(dee tsAA-lungs-fAY-hig-keyet)*
solvent	das Lösungsmittel	*(dahs LER-zunks-mit-tel)*
sound	der Ton	*(duh tOHn)*
soup dish	der Suppenteller	*(duh ZUP-pen-tel-luh)*
spare tire	der Ersatzreifen	*(duh ayr-zAHTS-rEYE-fen)*
spark plug	die Zündkerze	*(dee tsEWnd-kuh-tseh)*
sparkling wine	der Schaumwein	*(duh shOWm-vEYEN)*
speaker	der Lautsprecher	*(duh LOWt-shpreh-khuh)*
specialist (stock exchange)	der Börsenspezialist	*(duh bER-zen-shpay-tsEE-ah-list)*
specialty goods	die Spezialerzeugnisse	*(dee spay-tsee-AAl-AYr-tsOYg-ni-seh)*
specialty steels	der Spezialstahl	*(duh shpeh-tsIAAL-shtAAL)*
specific duty	der Stückzoll	*(duh shtEWk-tsOL)*
speculator	der Spekulant	*(duh shpeh-koo-lAHnt)*
speed up (v)	beschleunigen	*(beh-shlOY-ni-gen)*
speedometer	der Geschwindigkeitsmesser	*(duh geh-shvIN-dig-kEYETs-MEHS-suh)*

spin off	die Vermögemsübertragung gegen Aktien	*(deefuh-mER-gens-EW-buh-trAA-gunk gAY-gen ak-tsEE-en)*
spine	der Buchrücken	*(duh bOOKH-rEW-ken)*
split, stock	die Aktienaufteilung	*(dee ak-tsEE-en-OWf-tEYE-lunk)*
spoilage	der Verderb	*(duh fh-dAYrb)*
sponsor (of a fund or partnership)	der Förderer	*(duh fER-duh-ruh)*
spoon	der Löffel	*(duh LERF-fel)*
sportswear	die Sportkleidung	*(dee shpORT-klEYE-dunk)*
spot delivery	die Platzlieferung	*(dee plahts-lEE-fuh-runk)*
spot market	der Kassamarkt	*(duh kAH-sah-mAHrkt)*
spread	die Spanne	*(dee shpAHn-neh)*
spreadsheet	die Matrixbilanz	*(dee mah-trIKs-bee-lAHnts)*
spring	die Feder	*(dee fAY-duh)*
staff	der Stab	*(duh shtahp)*
staff and line	Stab und Linie	*(shtahp unt lEE-nee-eh)*
staff assistant	der Stabsassistent	*(duh shtahps-ah-sis-tEHnt)*
staff organization	die Stabsorganisation	*(dee shtahps-or-gah-nee-zah-tsEE-ohn)*
stagflation	die Stagflation	*(dee shtAHg-flaa-tsEE-ohn)*
stainless steel	der rostfreie Stahl	*(duh rost-frEYE-uh shtAAL)*
stale check	der veraltete Scheck	*(duh fuh-AHl-teh-teh shek)*
stand in line (v)	Schlange stehen	*(shlAHn-geh shtAY-hen)*
stand-alone word processor	der alleinstehende Datenverarbeiter	*(duh ahl-lEYEn-shtay-hen-deh dAA-ten-fuh-ahr-beye-tuh)*
stand-alone workstation	der unabhängige Arbeitsplatz	*(duh un-ahb-hEHn-gi-guh AHR-beyets-plahts)*
standard costs	die Plankosten	*(dee plAAn-kOS-ten)*
standard deviation	die Standardabweichung	*(dee shtahn-dahrd-AHB-vEYE-khunk)*
standard of living	der Lebensstandard	*(duh lAY-benz-shtahn-dahrd)*
standard practice	das übliche Verfahren	*(dahs EWb-likh-eh fuh-fAA-ren)*
standard time	die Normalzeit	*(dee nor-mAAl-tsEYEt)*

S

standardization	die Normung	*(dee NOR-mung)*
standing charges	die laufenden Kosten	*(dee lOW-fen-den kOS-ten)*
standing costs	die Fixkosten	*(dee fIX-kOS-ten)*
standing order	der Dauerauftrag	*(duh dOW-uh-OWf-trAHk)*
starch	die Stärke	*(dee shtEHR-keh)*
start-up costs	die Anfangskosten	*(dee AHN-fahngs-kOS-ten)*
starter	der Anlasser	*(duh AHN-lahs-suh)*
statement	die Angabe	*(dee AHN-gAA-beh)*
statement, financial	der Bilanzabschluß	*(duh bee-lAHnts-ahb-shlUS)*
statement of account	der Kontoauszug	*(duh kON-toh-OWs-tsOOk)*
statement, pro forma	die Proformabilanz	*(dee proh-FOHR-mah-bee-lAHnts)*
statement, profit-and-loss	die Gewinn- und Verlustrechnung	*(dee geh-vIN unt fuh-lUst-rEHKH-nunk)*
statistics	die Statistik	*(dee shtah-tIS-tik)*
statute	die Satzung	*(dee zAH-tsunk)*
statute of limitations	das Verjährungsgesetz	*(dahs fuh-yAY-runks-geh-zEHts)*
steel mill	das Hüttenwerk	*(dahs hEWT-ten-vehrk)*
steering	die Steuerung	*(dee shtOY-eh-runk)*
steering wheel	das Steuerrad	*(dahs shtOY-uh-raht)*
stereophonic	stereophonisch	*(shtAY-reh-o-FO-nish)*
stimulant	das Anregungsmittel	*(dahs AHN-reh-gungs-mit-tel)*
stitch	der Stich, die Masche	*(duh shtIKH), (dee mAH-sheh)*
stock (inventory)	der Vorrat	*(duh FOHR-rAAt)*
stock (share)	die Aktie	*(dee ak-tsEE-eh)*
stock certificate	das Aktienzertifikat	*(dahs ak-tsEE-en-tsEHr-ti-fi-kaat)*
stock exchange	die Börse	*(dee bER-zeh)*
stock index	der Börsenindex	*(duh bER-zen-IN-dex)*
stock issue	die Ausgabe	*(dee OWS-gAA-beh)*
stock market	der Aktienmarkt	*(duh ak-tsEE-en-mAHrkt)*

stock option	das Aktienbezugsrecht	*(dahs ak-tsEE-en-beh-tsOOgs-rehkht)*
stock portfolio	das Aktienportefeuille	*(dahs ak-tsEE-en-port-fOY)*
stock power	die Börsenvollmacht	*(dee bER-zen-fOL-mahkht)*
stock profit	der Aktiengewinn	*(duh ak-tsEE-en-geh-vIN)*
stock purchase	der Aktienkauf	*(duh ak-tsEE-en-kOWf)*
stock split	die Aktienaufteilung	*(dee ak-tsEE-en-OWf-tEYE-lunk)*
stock takeover	der Erwerb der Aktienmehrheit	*(duh ayr-vAYrb duh ak-tsEE-en-mayr-heyet)*
stock turnover	der Lagerumschlag	*(duh LAA-guh-um-shlAHk)*
stockbroker	der Börsenmakler	*(duh bER-zen-mAHk-luh)*
stockholder	der Aktionär	*(duh ak-tsEE-oh-nAYR)*
stockholders' equity	das Aktienkapital	*(dahs ak-tsEE-en-kah-pi-tAAL)*
stockings	die Strümpfe	*(dee shtrEWM-PFeh)*
stock-in-trade	der Warenbestand	*(duh vAA-ren-beh-shtAHnt)*
stoneware	das Steingut	*(dahs shtEYEn-gOOt)*
stop-loss order	der limitierte Börsenauftrag	*(duh li-mee-tEEr-teh bER-zen-OWf-trAHk)*
storage	die Aufbewahrung	*(dee OWf-beh-vAA-runk)*
storage (computer)	die Speicherung	*(dee shpEYE-khuh-runk)*
store (computer)	speichern	*(shpEYE-khuhn)*
store (v)	aufbewahren	*(OWf-beh-vAA-ren)*
store	der Laden	*(duh LAA-dehn)*
stowage	die Verstauung	*(dee fuh-shtOW-unk)*
stowage charges	der Stauerlohn	*(duh shtOW-uh-lOHn)*
straddle	die Stellage	*(dee shtEHL-lAA-geh)*
strapping	die Ladungsriemen	*(dee LA-dunks-rEE-men)*
strategic articles	die strategischen Artikel	*(dee strah-tAY-gi-shehn ahr-tIK-el)*
streamline (v)	modernisieren	*(moh-dayr-ni-zEE-ren)*
stress management	die Streßbewältigung	*(dee shtres-beh-vEHl-ti-gunk)*
strike (v)	streiken	*(shtrEYE-ken)*
strike, wildcat	der Spontanstreik	*(duh shpon-tAAn-shtreyek)*

S

strikebreaker	der Streikbrecher	*(duh shtrEYEk-brehkh-uh)*
structural shapes	das Profileisen	*(dahs pro-fEEL-EYE-zen)*
stuffing	die Füllung	*(dee fEW-lunk)*
style	der Stil	*(duh shtEEL)*
stylist	der Stilist	*(duh shtEEL-ist)*
subcontract	der Nebenvertrag	*(duh nAY-behn-fuh-trAHk)*
subject to availability	vorbehaltich der Verfügbarkeit	*(FOHR-beh-hahlt-likh duh fuh-fEW-bAAr-keyet)*
sublease	die Untervermietung	*(dee un-tuh-fuh-mEE-tunk)*
subscription price (periodicals)	der Bezugspreis	*(duh beh-tsOOgs-prEYEs)*
subscription price (securities)	der Zeichnungspreis	*(duh tsEYEkh-nunks-prEYEs)*
subsidiary	die Konzerngesellschaft	*(dee kon-tsAYrn-geh-zEL-shahft)*
subsidy	die Subvention	*(dee zub-vehn-tsee-OHn)*
substandard	unter der Norm	*(un-tuh duh nohrm)*
suede	das Wildleder	*(dahs vILd-lAY-duh)*
suede jacket	die Wildlederjacke	*(dee vILd-lAY-duh-yAH-Keh)*
sugar bowl	die Zuckerdose	*(dee TSU-ker-do-zeh)*
sugar content	der Zuckergehalt	*(duh TSU-ker-geh-hahlt)*
suit	der Anzug	*(duh AHN-tsook)*
suitcase	der Koffer	*(duh kOF-fuh)*
sulfuric acid	die Schwefelsäure	*(dee shvay-fel-ZOY-reh)*
sulphamide	das Sulfamid	*(dahs zul-fah-mEEt)*
sum-of-the-years digits	die digitale Jahressummen-abschreibung	*(dee di-gi-tAA-leh yAAr-ehs-zum-men-AHB-shrEYE-bunk)*
super alloys	die Superlegierungen	*(dee zOO-puh-leh-gEE-run-gen)*
supersede (v)	aufheben	*(OWf-hAY-ben)*
supervisor	die Aufsichtsperson	*(dee OWf-zikhts-payr-zOHn)*
supplier	der Lieferant	*(duh lee-fuh-rAHnt)*
supply and demand	(das) Angebot und (die) Nachfrage	*(dahs AHN-geh-boht unt dee nAKH-fraa-geh)*

support activities	die Unterstützungstätig- keiten	*(dee un-tuh-shtEW-tsunks- tAY-tikh-keye-ten)*
surcharge	der Aufschlag	*(duh OWf-shlAHk)*
surety company	die Kautionsversicherungs- gesellschaft	*(dee kow-tsEE-ohns-fuh- zIkheh-runks-geh-zEL- shahft)*
surplus capital	der Kapitalüberschuß	*(duh kah-pi-tAAl-EW-buh- shUs)*
surplus goods	der Warenüberschuß	*(duh vAA-ren-EW-buh- shUs)*
surtax	die Zusatzsteuer	*(dee tsOO-zAHts-shtOY-uh)*
suspend payment (v)	die Zahlungen einstellen	*(dee tsAA-lun-gen EYEn- shtEHL-len)*
suspension	die Aufhängung	*(dee OWf-hehn-gunk)*
swear	vereidigen	*(fuh-EYE-di-gen)*
swear (v)	schwören	*(shvER-ehn)*
sweater	der Pullover	*(duh PUL-ovah)*
switch	die Umschaltung	*(dee UM-shahl-tunk)*
switching charges	die Rangiergebühren	*(dee rAHn-djeer-geh-bEW- ren)*
syndicate	das Syndikat	*(dahs zewn-di-kAAt)*
synthesis	die Synthese	*(dee sewn-tAY-seh)*
synthetic	synthetisch	*(ZEWN-teh-tish)*
syringe	die Spritze	*(dee shpRI-tseh)*
systems analysis	die Systemanalyse	*(dee zew-stAYm-ah-nah- lEW-zeh)*
systems design	die Systemgestaltung	*(dee zew-stAYm-geh-shtAHl- tunk)*
systems engineering	die Systemerarbeitung	*(dee zew-stAYm-uh-AHR- beye-tunk)*
systems management	die Systemsteuerung	*(dee zew-stAYm-shtOY-uh- runk)*

T

table of contents	das Inhaltsverzeichnis	*(dahs IN-hahlts-fuh- tsEYEKH-nis)*
tablecloth	das Tischtuch	*(dahs TISH-TOOkh)*

tablespoon	der Eßlöffel	*(duh EHS-lERF-fel)*
tablet	die Tablette	*(dee tah-bleh-teh)*
taffeta	der Taft	*(duh tahft)*
tailor	der Schneider	*(duh shnEYE-duh)*
take down (v)	aufschreiben	*(OWf-shrEYE-ben)*
take off (v)	abziehen	*AHB-tsEE-hen)*
take out (v)	herausnehmen	*(hAYr-OWs-nAY-men)*
take out (v) (insurance)	abschließen	*(AHB-shlEE-sen)*
take-home pay	das Nettogehalt	*(dahs nEH-toh-geh-hAHlt)*
takeover	die Übernahme	*(dee EW-buh-nAA-meh)*
takeover bid	das Übernahmeangebot	*(dahs EW-buh-nAA-meh-AHN-geh-boht)*
tan (v)	(Leder) gerben	*([lAY-duh] gEHR-ben)*
tangible assets	das Sachanlagevermögen	*(dahs zahkh-AHN-laa-gen-fuh-mER-gen)*
tanker	der Tanker	*(duh tAAnk-uh)*
tanner	der Gerber	*(duh gEHR-buh)*
tannery	die Gerberei	*(dee gEHR-beh-rEYE)*
tannin	das Tannin	*(dahs tahn-nEEN)*
tape recorder	das Tonbandgerät	*(dahs tOHn-bahnd-geh-rEHt)*
target price	der Richtpreis	*(duh RIKHT-prEYEs)*
tariff	der Tarif, der Zoll	*(duh taa-rIF), (duh tsOL)*
tariff adjustment	die Zollangleichung	*(dee tsOL-AHN-glEYE-khunk)*
tariff barriers	die Zollschranken	*(dee tsOL-shrAHnk-en)*
tariff charge	die Zollgebühr	*(dee tsOL-geh-bEWr)*
tariff classification	die Zolleinstufung	*(dee tsOL-EYEn-stOO-funk)*
tariff commodity	die Zollware	*(dee tsOL-vAA-reh)*
tariff differential	der Zollunterschied	*(duh tsOL-un-tun-shEEd)*
tariff war	der Zollkrieg	*(duh tsOL-krEEg)*
task force	der Arbeitsausschuß	*(duh AHR-beyets-OWs-shUS)*
tasting	die Weinprobe	*(dee vEYEN-pro-beh)*
tax	die Steuer	*(dee shtOY-uh)*

T

tax, excise	die Verbrauchssteuer	*(dee fuh-brOWkhs-shtOY-uh)*
tax, sales	die Umsatzsteuer	*(dee um-zAHTs-shtOY-uh)*
tax abatement	der Steuernachlaß	*(duh shtOY-uh-nAKH-laas)*
tax allowance	der Steuerfreibetrag	*(duh shtOY-uh-frEYE-beh-trAHk)*
tax base	die Besteuerungsgrundlage	*(dee beh-shtOY-uh-runks-grUNd-laa-geh)*
tax burden	die Steuerlast	*(dee shtOY-uh-lAHst)*
tax collector	der Steuereinnehmer	*(duh shtOY-uh-EYEn-nAY-muh)*
tax deduction	der Steuerabzug	*(duh shtOY-uh-AHB-tsOOk)*
tax evasion	die Steuerhinterziehung	*(dee shtOY-uh-hin-tuh-tsEE-unk)*
tax haven	die Steueroase	*(dee shtOY-uh-oh-AA-zeh)*
tax relief	die Steuervergünstigung	*(dee shtOY-uh-fuh-gEWns-ti-gunk)*
tax shelter	die steuerbegünstigte Anlagemöglichkeit	*(dee shtOY-uh-beh-gEWns-tig-teh AHN-laa-geh-mER-glikh-keyet)*
tax-free income	das steuerfreie Einkommen	*(dahs shtOY-uh-frEYE-eh EYEn-kOM-men)*
tax-free	steuerfrei	*(shtOY-uh-frEYE)*
taxation	die Besteuerung	*(dee beh-shtOY-uh-runk)*
taxpayer	der Steuerzahler	*(duh shtOY-uh-tsAA-luh)*
team management	das Gruppenmanagement	*(dahs grUP-pen-mehn-EHdj-ment)*
teapot	die Teekanne	*(dee TAY-KAHN-neh)*
teaspoon	der Teelöffel	*(duh TAY-lERF-fel)*
technical	technisch	*(tehkh-nish)*
technology	die Technologie	*(dee tehkh-noh-loh-gEE)*
telecommunications	die Telekommunikation	*(dee tay-leh-kom-moo-ni-kah-tsEE-ohn)*
telegram	das Telegramm	*(dahs tay-leh-grAHm)*
telemarketing	der Fernvertrieb	*(duh fEHrn-fuh-trEEp)*
telephone	das Telefon	*(dahs tay-leh-FOHN)*
television	das Fernsehen	*(dahs fEHrn-zay-hen)*

television, cable	das Kabelfernsehen	*(dahs kAA-behl-fEHrn-zay-hen)*
telex	das Telex	*(dahs tay-lehx)*
teller	der Schalterbeamter	*(duh shAAl-tuh-beh-AHm-tuh)*
temperature	die Temperatur	*(dee tehm-peh-rah-tOOR)*
temporary	vorläufig, zeitweilig	*(FOHR-lOY-fig), (tsEYEt-vEYE-lig)*
tenant	der Mieter	*(duh MEE-tuh)*
tender offer	das Lieferungsangebot	*(dahs LEE-fuh-rungs-AHN-geh-boht)*
term bond	die Festobligation	*(dee FEHSt-ob-li-gah-tsEE-ohn)*
term insurance	die Kurzversicherung	*(dee kURts-fuh-zIkheh-runk)*
terminal	das Terminal	*(dahs tayr-mi-nAAl)*
terminate (v)	beenden	*(beh-EHn-den)*
terminate (v) (employment)	kündigen	*(kEWn-di-gen)*
terms of sale	die Verkaufsbedingungen	*(dee fuh-kOWfs-beh-dING-unk-en)*
terms of trade	die Handelsbedingungen	*(dee hAHn-dehls-beh-dING-unk-en)*
territorial waters	das Hoheitsgewässer	*(dahs HOH-heyets-geh-vEH-suh)*
territory	das Gebiet	*(dahs geh-bEET)*
test tube	das Reagenzglas	*(dahs reh-AH-gents-glAAs)*
thermometer	das Thermometer	*(dahs tEHR-mo-mEH-tuh)*
thin market	der schwache Markt	*(duh shvAA-kheh mAHrkt)*
third-party exporter	der Drittexporteur	*(duh drit-ex-pohr-tEWr)*
thread	der Faden	*(duh FAH-den)*
through bill of lading	das Transitkonnossement	*(dahs trahn-zeet-kon-nos-seh-mEH)*
throughput	der Durchsatz	*(duh dURKH-zAHts)*
ticker (stock prices)	der Börsenfernschreiber	*(duh bER-zen-fayrn-shrEYE-buh)*
ticker tape	das Papierband	*(dahs pah-pEEr-bahnd)*
tied aid	die gebundene Hilfe	*(dee geh-bUn-dehn-eh hIL-feh)*

T

tied loan	die zweckgebundene Anleihe	*(dee tsvEHK-geh-bUn-dehn-eh AHN-leye-eh)*
tight market	die angespannte Marktlage	*(dee AHN-geh-shpAHN mAHrkt-laa-geh*
time and motion study	die Zeit- und Bewegungsstudie	*(dee tsEYEt unt beh-vAY-gunks-shtoo-di-eh*
time bill of exchange	der Zeitwechsel	*(duh tsEYEt-vEHk-sehl)*
time deposit	die befristete Einlage	*(dee beh-frIS-teh-teh EYEn-laa-geh)*
time order	der zeitlich bestimmte limitierte Börsenauftrag	*(duh tsEYEt-likh beh-shtIM-teh li-mee-tEEr-teh bER-zen-OWf-trAHk)*
time sharing	die gemeinschaftliche Computerbenutzung	*(dee geh-mEYEn-shahft-likh-eh kon-pyU-tuh-beh-nU-tsunk)*
time zone	die Zeitzone	*(dee tsEYEt-tsOH-neh)*
timetable (airplanes)	der Flugplan	*(duh flOOg-plAAn)*
timetable (schedule)	der Zeitplan	*(duh tsEYEt-plAAn)*
timetable (trains)	der Fahrplan	*(duh fAAR-plAAn)*
tip (inside information)	der Börsentip	*(duh bER-zen-tip)*
tire	der Reifen	*(duh rEYE-fen)*
titanium	das Titan	*(dahs ti-tAAn)*
title	der Titel	*(duh TI-tel)*
title insurance	die Rechtsmängel-versicherung	*(dee REHKHts-mEHn-gehl-fuh-zIkheh-runk)*
titration	die Titrierung	*(dee ti-trEE-runk)*
tombstone advertisement	die Wertpapieremission-sanzeige	*(dee vEHRt-pah-pEEr-eh-mi-see-OHns-AHN-tseye-geh)*
tone	der Ton	*(duh tOHn)*
tonnage	die Tonnage	*(dee ton-nAA-djeh)*
tools	die Werkzeuge	*(dee vEHrk-tsOY-geh)*
top management	die oberste Führungsschicht	*(dee OH-buh-steh fEW-runks-shikht)*
top price	der Höchstpreis	*(duh hERkhst-prEYEs)*
top quality	die Spitzenqualität	*(dee shpI-tsehn-kva-li-tAYt)*

torque	der Drehmoment	*(duh drAY-mo-ment)*
tort	die Delikthandlung	*(dee deh-lIKt-hAHnd-lunk)*
total loss	der Totalverlust	*(duh toh-tAAL-fuh-lUst)*
tote bag	die Einkaufstasche	*(dee EYEn-kOWfs-tAH-SHeh)*
toughness	die Zähigkeit	*(dee TSAY-hig-kEYET)*
tourism	der Fremdenverkehr	*(duh frehmd-en-fuh-kAYr)*
toxic waste	Sondermüll	*(ZON-duh-mewl)*
toxicology	die Toxikologie	*(dee to-xi-ko-loh-gee)*
toxin	das Toxin	*(dahs to-xEEN)*
trade	der Handel	*(duh hAHn-dehl)*
trade (v)	handeln	*(hAHn-dehln)*
trade acceptance	das Handelsakzept	*(dahs hAHN-dehls-ahk-tsEPt)*
trade agreement	das Handelsabkommen	*(dahs hAHn-dehls-AHB-kOM-mehn)*
trade association	der Handelsverband	*(duh hAHn-dehls-fuh-bahnd)*
trade barrier	die Handelsschranke	*(dee hAHn-dehls-shrAAn-keh)*
trade commission	die Handelskommission	*(duh hAHn-dehls-ko-mi-sEE-ohn)*
trade credit	der Handelskredit	*(duh hAHn-dehls-kray-dIT)*
trade date	das Handelsdatum	*(dahs hAHn-dehls-DAA-tum)*
trade discount	der Händlerrabatt	*(duh hEHnd-luh-rah-bAAt)*
trade fair	die Gewerbeausstellung	*(dee geh-vAYr-beh-OWs-shtEHL-lunk)*
trade house	das Gewerbehaus	*(dahs geh-vAYr-beh-hOWs)*
trade union	die Gewerkschaft	*(dee geh-vEHrk-shahft)*
trademark	die Schutzmarke	*(dee shUts-mAHr-keh)*
trader	der Händler	*(duh hEHnd-luh)*
trader (stocks)	der Börsenmakler	*(duh bER-zen-mAHk-luh)*
trading company	die Handelsgesellschaft	*(dee hAHn-dehls-geh-zEL-shahft)*
trading limit	die Handelsgrenze	*(dee hAHn-dehls-grEHn-tseh)*

T

trainee	der Volontär	*(duh fol-on-tAYr)*
tranche	die Tranche	*(dee trAHn-sheh)*
tranquilizer	das Beruhigungsmittel	*(dahs beh-rOO-I-gungs-mit-tel)*
transaction	das Geschäft	*(dahs geh-shEHft)*
transfer	der Übertrag	*(duh EW-buh-trAHk)*
transfer (v)	übertragen	*(EW-buh-trAA-gen)*
transfer agent	der Effektenüberträger	*(duh ehf-fEHK-ten-EW-buh-trAY-guh)*
transformer	der Umwandler	*(duh UM-vAHN-dluh)*
transit, in	unterwegs	*(un-tuh-vAYgs)*
translator	der Übersetzer	*(duh EW-buh-zEH-suh)*
transmitter	der Übermittler	*(duh EWbuh-mIT-luh)*
transportation	das Verkehrswesen	*(dahs fuh-kAYrs-vAY-zen)*
travel agency	das Reisebüro	*(dahs REYE-zeh-bEW-roh)*
traveler's check	der Reisescheck	*(duh REYE-zeh-shehk)*
treasurer	der Schatzmeister	*(duh shahts-mEYE-stuh)*
treasury bills	die Schatzwechsel	*(dee shahts-vEHk-sehl)*
treasury bonds	die Staatsanleihen	*(dee shtAAts-AHN-leye-en)*
treasury notes	die Staatsobligationen	*(dee shtAAts-ob-li-gah-tsEE-ohn-nen)*
treasury stock	die Vorratsaktien	*(dee FOHR-rAAts-ak-tsEE-en)*
treaty	der Vertrag	*(duh fuh-trAHk)*
trend	die Tendenz	*(dee tehn-dEHnts)*
trial balance	die Vorbilanz	*(dee FOHR-bee-lAHnts)*
troubleshoot (v)	Störungen auffinden und beseitigen	*(stER-ung-en OWf-fin-dehn unt beh-zEYE-ti-gehn)*
truckload	die Lastwagenladung, die LKW-Ladung	*(dee lAHst-vAA-gen-lAA-dunk), (dee EL-KAA-VAY lAA-dunk)*
trunk	der Koffer	*(duh kOF-fuh)*
trust	das Treuhandverhältnis	*(dahs trOY-hahnd-fuh-hEHlt-nis)*
trust company	die Treuhandgesellschaft	*(dee trOY-hahnd-geh-zEL-shahft)*
trust fund	der Treuhandfonds	*(duh trOY-hahnd-fOH)*

T

trust receipt	der Hinterlegungsschein	*(duh hin-tuh-lAY-gunks-shEYEn)*
trustee	der Treuhänder	*(duh trOY-hehn-duh)*
tune	einstellen	*(EYEn-shtel-len)*
tungsten	das Wolfram	*(dahs volf-rAAM)*
tureen	die Terrine	*(dee tuh-rEEN-neh)*
turn-key contract	der schlüsselfertige Vertrag	*(duh shlEW-sehl-fuh-tI-guh-fuh-trAHk)*
turnover	der Umschlag	*(duh um-shlAHk)*
tuxedo	der Smoking	*(duh smOH-king)*
two-tiered market	der zweistufige Markt	*(duh tsvEYE-shtoo-fi-geh mAHrkt)*
type of vine	die Weinart	*(dee vEYEN-ahrt)*
typist	der Maschinenschreiber	*(duh mah-shEE-nen-shrEYE-buh)*

U

ultra vires act	die Vollmachtsüberschreitung	*(dee FOL-mahkhts-EW-buh-shrEYE-tunk)*
unaccompanied goods	die unbegleiteten Waren	*(dee un-be-glEYE-teh-ten vAA-ren)*
unbleached linen	das ungebleichte Leinen	*(dahs UN-geh-blEYEKH-teh LEYE-nen)*
uncollectible accounts	die uneinbringlichen Forderungen	*(dee un-eyen-brING-likh-en FOHR-duh-run-gen)*
undercapitalized	unterkapitalisiert	*(un-tuh-kah-pi-taa-li-zEErt)*
undercut (v)	unterbieten	*(un-tuh-bEE-ten)*
underdeveloped nations	die Entwicklungsländer	*(dee EHNt-vIK-lunks-lAYn-duh)*
underestimate (v)	unterschätzen	*(un-tuh-shEH-tsen)*
underpaid	unterbezahlt	*(un-tuh-beh-tsAAlt)*
undersigned	unterzeichnet	*(un-tuh-tsEYEkh-net)*
understanding (agreement)	das Übereinkommen	*(dahs EW-buh-EYEn-kOM-mehn)*
undertake (v)	unternehmen	*(un-tuh-nAY-men)*
undervalue (v)	unterbewerten	*(un-tuh-beh-vEHr-ten)*

underwriter	der Versicherer	*(duh fuh-zIKHeh-ruh)*
underwriter (securities)	die Emissionsbank	*(dee eh-mi-see-OHns-bahnk)*
undeveloped	unentwickelt	*(un-ehnt-vI-kehlt)*
unearned increment	der nicht verdiente Wertzuwachs	*(duh nIKHt fuh-dEEn-teh vEHrt-tsOO-vahks)*
unearned revenue	die transitorischen Passiva	*(dee trahn-zEE-tohrish-eh pahs-sEE-vaa)*
unemployment	die Arbeitslosigkeit	*(dee AHR-beyets-loh-zig-keyet)*
unemployment compensation	die Arbeitslosenunterstützung	*(dee AHR-beyets-loh-zen-un-tuh-shtEWt-tsunk)*
unfair competition	der unlautere Wettbewerb	*(duh un-lOW-tuh-ruh vEHt-beh-vAYrb)*
unfavorable	ungünstig	*(un-gEWns-tig)*
unfeasible	undurchführbar	*(un-durkh-fEWr-bAAr)*
unfermented grape juice	der unfermentierte Rebensaft	*(duh UN-fuh-men-tEEr-tuh ray-ben-zahft)*
union, labor	die Gewerkschaft	*(dee geh-vEHrk-shahft)*
union contract	der Tarifvertrag	*(duh taa-rIF-fuh-trAHk)*
union label	das Gewerkschaftsetikett	*(dahs geh-vEHrk-shahfts-ti-keht)*
unit costs	die Stückkosten	*(dee shtEWk-kOS-ten)*
unit load discount	der Rabatt je Verladeeinheit	*(duh rah-bAAt yay fuh-lAA-deh-EYEn-heyet)*
unit price	der Stückpreis	*(duh shtEWk-prEYEs)*
unlisted	nicht eingetragen	*(nIKHt EYEn-geh-trAA-gehn)*
unload (v)	entladen	*(EHNt-lAA-den)*
unsecured liability	die ungesicherte Haftung	*(dee un-geh-zikh-uh-teh hAHf-tunk)*
unsecured loan	die ungesicherte Anleihe	*(dee un-geh-zikh-uh-teh AHN-leye-eh)*
unskilled labor	die ungelernten Arbeitskräfte	*(dee un-geh-lAYrn-ten AHR-beyets-krehr-teh)*
up to our expectations	unseren Erwartungen entsprechend	*(un-zEHren AYr-vAAr-tunk-en ehnt-shprEKH-ent)*
upmarket	der Haussemarkt	*(duh hOWs-seh-mAHrkt)*
upturn	der Aufschwung	*(duh OWf-shvunk)*

U

urban renewal	die Stadterneuerung	*(dee shtAHt-ayr-nOY-uh-runk)*
urban sprawl	die Stadtausbreitung	*(dee shtAHt-OWs-brEYE-tunk)*
urgent	dringend	*(drING-ent)*
use tax	die Gebrauchssteuer	*(dee geh-brOWkhs-shtOY-uh)*
useful life	die Nutzungsdauer	*(dee nUts-unks-dOW-uh)*
user-friendly	benutzerfreundlich	*(beh-nU-tsuh-frOYNd-likh)*
usury	der Wucher	*(duh vOO-khuh)*
utility	der Versorgungsbetrieb	*(duh fuh-zOR-gunks-beh-trEEp)*

V

V8 engine	der V8-Motor	*(duh fOW AKHT mOH-tor)*
vaccine	die Vakzine	*(dee vak-tsEE-neh)*
vacuum melting furnace	der Vakuumschmelzofen	*(duh vAA-ku-um-shmEHLTS-ohfen)*
valid	gültig	*(gEWl-tikh)*
validate (v)	validieren	*(vah-li-dEE-ren)*
valuation	die Bewertung	*(dee beh-vEHr-tunk)*
value	der Wert	*(duh vehrt)*
value, asset	der Vermögenswert	*(duh fuh-mER-gens-vEHrt)*
value, book	der Buchwert	*(duh bOOkh-vEHRt)*
value, face	der Nennwert	*(duh NEHN-vEHrt)*
value, market (general)	der Marktwert	*(duh mAHrkt-vEHrt)*
value, market (stocks)	der Kurswert	*(duh kOOrs-vEHrt)*
value engineer	die Wertplanungstechnik	*(dee vEHrt-plAA-nungs-tehkh-nik)*
value engineering	die Wertanalyse	*(dee vEHrt-ah-nah-lEW-zeh)*
value for duty	der Zollwert	*(duh tsOL-vEHrt)*
value-added tax (VAT)	die Mehrwertsteuer	*(dee mAYr-vEHrt-shtOY-uh)*

U

valve	das Ventil, die Klappe	*(dahs ven-tEEL), (dee klAHP-peh)*
vanadium	das Vanadium	*(dahs va-nAA-di-um)*
variable annuity	die veränderliche Jahresrente	*(dee fuh-EHn-duh-likh-eh yAAr-es-rEHn-teh)*
variable costs	die veränderlichen Kosten	*(dee fuh-EHn-duh-likh-en kOS-ten)*
variable import levy	die schwankende Einfuhrabschöpfung	*(dee shvAHnk-ehn-deh EYEn-foor-AHB-shERp-funk)*
variable margin	der variable Erlösüberschuß	*(duh vaa-ree-AHb-luh ayr-lERs-EW-buh-shUs)*
variable rate	der schwankende Kurs	*(duh shvAHnk-ehn-deh koors)*
variable rate mortgage	die Staffelhypothek	*(dee shAH-fehl-hew-poh-tAYk)*
variance	die Abweichung	*(dee AHB-vEYE-khunk)*
vat	das große Faß	*(dahs grO-Seh fAHS)*
veil	der Schleier	*(duh shlEYE-uh)*
velocity of money	die Geldumlauf-geschwindigkeit	*(dee GEHLT-um-lOWf-geh-shvIN-dikh-keyet)*
vendor	der Verkäufer	*(duh fuh-kOY-fuh)*
vendor's lien	das Eigentumsvorbehalt des Verkäufers	*(dahs EYE-gen-tOOms-FOHR-beh-hahlt dehs fuh-kOY-fuhs)*
venture capital	das Risikokapital	*(dahs REE-zee-koh-kah-pi-tAAL)*
vertical integration	die vertikale Verflechtung	*(dee fayr-ti-kLL-leh fuh-flEHKH-tunk)*
vest	die Weste	*(dee vEH-steh)*
vested interests	die wohlerworbenen Rechte	*(dee vOHl-uh-vOHr-beh-neh REHKH-teh)*
vested rights	die verbrieften Rechte	*(dee fuh-brEEf-ten REHKH-teh)*
veto	der Einspruch, das Veto	*(duh EYEn-shprUKH), (dahs vAY-toh)*
vice-president	der Vizepräsident	*(duh vEE-tseh-pray-zi-dEHnt)*
videocassette player	das Videokasettengerät	*(dahs vEE-deh-o-kahs-SEHt-ten-geh-rEHt)*

V

videocassette recording	die Fernsehbandaufnahme	*(dee fEHrn-zay-bahnd-OWf-nAA-meh)*
vine	die Weinrebe	*(dee vEYEN-ray-beh)*
vineyard	der Weinberg	*(duh vEYEN-behrk)*
vintage	die Weinernte	*(dee vEYEN-EHRn-teh)*
vintage year	der Jahrgang	*(duh yAAR-gahnk)*
vintner	der Winzer	*(duh vIN-tsuh)*
visible balance of trade	die sichtbare Handelsbilanz	*(dee zikht-bAA-reh hAHn-dehls-bee-lAHnts)*
vitamin	das Vitamin	*(dahs vi-tah-mEEn)*
voice-activated	stimmaktiviert	*(shtIM-ahk-tee-vEErt)*
voiced check	der mündlich bestätigte Scheck	*(duh MEWnd-likh beh-shtAY-tikh-teh shehk)*
void	nichtig	*(nikh-tik)*
volatile market	die sprunghafte Börsenmarktlage	*(dee shprOOng-hAAf-teh bER-zen-mAHrkt-lAA-geh)*
voltage	die Stromspannung	*(dee shtrOHm-shpAN-nunk)*
volume	der Umfang, das Volumen	*(duh um-fank), (dahs fo-lU-men)*
volume discount	der Mengenrabatt	*(duh mAYng-ehn-rah-bAAt)*
voluntary	freiwillig	*(frEYE-vil-lig)*
voting right	das Stimmrecht	*(dahs shtIM-rehkht)*
voucher	der Beleg	*(duh beh-lAYg)*

W

wage	der Lohn	*(duh lohn)*
wage differential	der Lohnunterschied	*(duh LOHN-un-tuh-sheed)*
wage dispute	der Lohnstreit	*(duh LOHN-shtreyet)*
wage drift	die Lohnrichtung	*(dee LOHN-rIKH-tunk)*
wage earner	der Lohnempfänger	*(duh LOHN-emp-fAYng-uh)*
wage freeze	der Lohnstopp	*(duh LOHN-shtop)*
wage level	das Lohnniveau	*(dahs LOHN-nee-voh)*
wage scale	die Lohnskala	*(dee LOHN-skAA-lah)*
wage structure	die Lohnstruktur	*(dee LOHN-strUk-toor)*

wage-price spiral	die Lohn-Preis-Spirale	*(dee LOHN-prEYEs-shpEE-rAA-leh)*
wages	die Löhne	*(dee lER-neh)*
waiver clause	die Verzichtsklausel	*(dee fuh-tsIKHts-klOW-zel)*
walkout	die Arbeitsniederlegung	*(dee AHR-beyets-nee-duh-lAY-gunk)*
want-ad	die Kleinanzeige	*(dee klEYEn-AHN-tseye-geh)*
warehouse	das Lagerhaus	*(dahs LAA-guh-hOWs)*
warehousekeeper	der Lageraufseher	*(duh LAA-guh-OWf-zAY-uh)*
warrant (guarantee)	die Gewähr	*(dee geh-vAYr)*
waste disposal	die Entsorgung	*(dee ehnt-ZOHR-goong)*
wasting asset	das kurzlebige Wirtschaftsgut	*(dahs kUrts-lAY-bi-geh vEErt-shahfts-gOOt)*
watch strap	das Uhrenarmband	*(dahs OO-ren-ahrm-bahnt)*
water pump	die Wasserpumpe	*(dee VAHS-suh-pUM-peh)*
wave	die Welle	*(dee vEL-leh)*
waybill	der Frachtbrief	*(duh fRAKHT-brEEf)*
wealth	das Vermögen	*(dahs fuh-mER-gen)*
wear and tear	der Verschleiß	*(duh fuh-shlEYEs)*
weaver	der Weber	*(duh vEH-buh)*
weight	das Gewicht	*(dahs geh-vIKHt)*
weighted average	der gewogene Durchschnitt	*(duh geh-vOH-gen-eh dURKH-shnIT)*
wharf	der Kai	*(duh keye)*
wharfage	die Löschungskosten	*(dee lERsh-unks-kOS-ten)*
wharfage charges	die Kaigebühren	*(dee kEYE-geh-bEW-ren)*
wheel	das Rad	*(dahs raht)*
when issued	zur Emissionszeit	*(tsoor eh-mi-see-OHns-tsEYEt)*
whip	die Peitsche	*(dee pEYE-tSHEH)*
white-collar worker	der Büroangestellte	*(duh bEW-roh-AHN-geh-shtEHL-teh)*
wholesale market	der Großhandel	*(duh grOHs-hAHn-dehl)*
wholesale price	der Großhandelspreis	*(duh grOHs-hAHn-dehls-prEYEs)*

W

wholesale trade	der Großhandel	*(duh grOHs-hAHn-dehl)*
wholesaler	der Großhändler	*(duh grOHs-hEHnd-luh)*
wildcat strike	der Spontanstreik	*(duh shpon-tAAn-shtreyek)*
will	der Wille	*(duh VIL-leh)*
windfall profit	der unerwartete Gewinn	*(duh un-ayr-vAAr-teh-teh geh-vIN)*
window dresser	der Schaufensterdekorateur	*(duh SHOW-fen-stuh-deh-ko-rah-TER)*
window dressing	die Schaufensterdekoration, die Bilanzverschleierung	*(dee shOW-fehn-shuh-day-koh-rah-tsEE-ohn), (dee bee-LAHnts-fuh-shlEYE-uh-runk)*
windshield	die Windschutzscheibe	*(dee vINd-shuts-shEYE-beh)*
wine	der Wein	*(duh vEYEN)*
wine cellar	der Weinkeller	*(duh vEYEN-kel-luh)*
wine cooperative	die Winzergenossenschaft	*(dee vIN-tsuh-geh-nos-sen-shahft)*
wine steward	der Weinkellner	*(duh vEYEN-kel-nuh)*
winegrower	der Weinbauer	*(duh vEYEN-bow-uh)*
winemaker	der Weinhersteller	*(duh vEYEN-huh-shTEL-luh)*
winepress	die Weinpresse	*(dee vEYEN-prehs-zeh)*
wire	der Draht, das Telegramm	*(duh drAAt), (dahs tay-leh-grAHM)*
wire transfer	die telegraphische Überweisung	*(dee tay-leh-grAA-fish-eh EW-buh-vEYE-zunk)*
with average	mit Durchschnittsberechnung	*(mit dURKH-shnITs-beh-rehkh-nunk)*
with regard to	betreffs	*(beh-trehfs)*
withdrawal	die Zurücknahme	*(dee tsOO-rEWk-nAA-meh)*
withholding tax	die Quellensteuer	*(dee kvEL-ehn-shtOY-uh)*
witness	der Zeuge	*(duh tsOY-geh)*
witness (v)	bezeugen	*(beh-tsOY-gen)*
wool	die Wolle	*(dee vOL-leh)*
word processor	das Textverarbeitungsgerät	*(dahs text-fuh-AHR-beye-tunks-guh-rayt)*
work (v)	arbeiten	*(AHR-beye-ten)*

W

work by contract	vertragsgemäß arbeiten	*(fuh-trAHks-geh-mEHs AHR-beye-ten)*
work cycle	der Arbeitsgang	*(duh AHR-beyets-gahnk)*
work day	der Arbeitstag	*(duh AHR-beyets-tAAk)*
work in progress	die Arbeit im Gang	*(dee AHR-beyet im gahnk)*
work load	die Arbeitsbelastung	*(dee AHR-beyets-beh-lah-stunk)*
work order	der Arbeitsauftrag	*(duh AHR-beyets-OWf-trAHk)*
work station	die Arbeitsstätte	*(dee AHR-beyets-shtEH-teh)*
workforce	die Arbeitskräfte	*(dee AHR-beyets-krehf-teh)*
working assets	das Betriebsvermögen	*(dahs beh-trEEps-fuh-mER-gen)*
working balance	die Betriebsbilanz	*(dee beh-trEEps-bee-lAHnts)*
working capital	das Betriebskapital	*(dahs beh-trEEps-kah-pi-tAAl)*
working class	die Arbeiterklasse	*(dee AHR-beye-tuh-klAA-seh)*
working funds	die Betriebsmittel	*(dee beh-trEEps-mit-tEL)*
working hours	die Arbeitszeit	*(dee AHR-beyets-tsEYEt)*
working papers	die Arbeitspapiere	*(dee AHR-beyets-pah-pEE-reh)*
working tools	die Arbeitsmittel	*(dee AHR-beyets-mit-tEL)*
workplace	der Arbeitsplatz	*(duh AHR-beyets-plahts)*
workshop	die Werkstatt	*(dee vEHrk-shtaht)*
World Bank	Die Weltbank	*(dee VEHLT-bahnk)*
worth, net	der Nettowert	*(duh nEH-toh-vEHrt)*
worthless	wertlos	*(vEHRt-lOHs)*
writ	der Gerichtsbefehl	*(duh geh-rIKHts-beh-fAYl)*
write off (v)	abschreiben	*(AHB-shrEYE-ben)*
write-off	die Abschreibung	*(dee AHB-shrEYE-bunk)*
writedown	die Herabsetzung	*(dee hAYr-ahb-zET-tsunk)*
written agreement	der schriftliche Vertrag	*(duh shrIFt-likh-eh fuh-trAHk)*

W

Y

yardstick	der Maßstab	*(duh mAAs-shtahp)*
yarn	das Garn	*(dahs Gahrn)*
year	das Jahr	*(dahs yaar)*
year, fiscal	das Geschäftsjahr	*(dahs geh-shEHfts-yAAr)*
year-end	das Jahresende	*(dahs yAAr-ehs-AYn-deh)*
yeast	die Hefe	*(dee heh-feh)*
yield	der Weinertrag	*(duh vEYEN-ayr-trahk)*
yield (v)	einbringen	*(EYEn-bRIN-gehn)*
yield to maturity	die Effektivverzinsung	*(dee ehf-fehk-tEEv-fuh-tsIN-zung)*

Z

zero coupon	die Anleihe ohne Zinskoupon	*(dee AHN-leye-eh ohneh tsINs-ku-pon)*
zinc	das Zink	*(dahs tsINK)*
ZIP code	die Postleitzahl	*(dee pOSt-lEYEt-tsAAl)*
zipper	der Reißverschluß	*(duh rEYES-fuh-shlUS)*
zone	die Zone	*(dee tsOH-neh)*
zoning law	die Wohn- und Industrie-baubestimmungen	*(dee vOHn unt in-dus-trEE bOW-beh-shtIM-mun-gen)*

ab Betrieb	*(ahb beh-trEEp)*	ex mill
ab Fabrik	*(ahb fah-brEEk)*	ex factory
ab Grube	*(ahb gROO-beh)*	ex mine
ab Lager	*(ahb LAA-guh)*	ex warehouse
ab Schiff	*(ahb shIF)*	ex ship
ab Werk	*(ahb vEHrk)*	ex works
abändern	*(AHB-EHn-dehrn)*	amend (v), renegotiate (v)
Abänderung (f)	*(AHB-EHndeh-roong)*	amendment
abandonnieren	*(ah-bahn-do-nEE-ren)*	abandon (v)
Abbeizen (n)	*(ahb-bEYE-tsen)*	pickling
abbestellen	*(AHB-beh-shtEHL-len)*	cancel (v)
abbuchen	*(AHB-bOO-khen)*	charge off (v), write off (v)
Abbuchung (f)	*(AHB-bOO-khunk)*	write-off
Abfall (m)	*(ahb-fAHL)*	scrap
Abfindung (f)	*(AHB-fIN-dunk)*	gratuity
abflachen	*(AHB-flah-khen)*	level out (v)
Abführmittel (n)	*(ahb-fEWR-mit-tel)*	laxative, purgative
Abgabe (f)	*(AHB-gaa-beh)*	tax
Abgeordnetenbe-einflussung durch Interessengruppen (pl)	*(AHB-ge-ORd-neh-ten-beh-EYEn-flus-sunk durkh in-tay-rEHs-sens-grUP-pen)*	lobbying
abgeschlossenes Konto (n)	*(ahb-geh-shlOS-seh-nehs kON-toh)*	closed account
abgestimmte Vergleichsproben (pl)	*(ahb-geh-shtIM-teh fuh-glEYEKHs-proh-ben)*	matched samples
Abhebung (f)	*(AHB-hAY-bunk)*	withdrawal
Abholung und Lieferung (f)	*(AHB-hOH-lunk unt LEE-fuh-runk)*	pickup and delivery
Abhörer (m)	*(AHB-hER-ruh)*	monitor
ablegen	*(AHB-lAY-gen)*	file (v)
ablösen	*(AHB-lER-zen)*	discharge (v)
Ablösungsfonds (m)	*(AHB-lER-zungs-fOH)*	redemption fund

Abnehmer (m)	*(AHB-nAY-muh)*	buyer
Abnutzung (f)	*(AHB-nU-tsunk)*	attrition
Abrechnungstag (m)	*(AHB-rEHKH-nungs-taak)*	account day
Abrechnungstelle (f)	*(AHB-rEHKH-nungs-shtEHL-leh)*	clearinghouse
abrufen	*(AHB-ROO-fen)*	call back (v)
Absatz (m)	*(AHB-zAHTS)*	marketing, outlet
Absatzanalyse (f)	*(AHB-zAHTS-ah-nah-lEW-zeh)*	sales analysis
Absatzbudget (n)	*(AHB-zAHTS-bew-djEH)*	marketing budget
Absatzgebiet (n)	*(AHB-zAHTS-geh-bEET)*	sales territory
Absatzkalkulation (f)	*(AHB-zAHTS-kal-ku-lah-tsEE-OHn)*	sales estimate
Absatzkonzept (n)	*(AHB-zAHTS-kon-tsEHPt)*	marketing concept
Absatzleitung (f)	*(AHB-zAHTS-lEYE-tunk)*	sales management
Absatzmöglichkeiten (pl)	*(AHB-zAHTS-mER-glikh-keye-ten)*	potential sales
Absatzplan (m)	*(AHB-zAHTS-plAAn)*	marketing plan, sales budget
Absatzposition (f)	*(AHB-zAHTS-po-zi-tsee-OHN)*	market position
Absatztätigkeiten (pl)	*(AHB-zAHTS-tAY-tig-keye-ten)*	merchandising
Absatzweg (m)	*(AHB-zAHTS-vAYk)*	channel of distribution
abschätzen	*(AHB-shEH-tsen)*	appraise (v)
Abschlag (m)	*(AHB-shlAHk)*	abatement (reduction)
abschließen	*(AHB-shlEE-sen)*	finalize (v)
Abschlußbuchung (f)	*(AHB-shlUS-bOO-khunk)*	closing entry
Abschnitt (m)	*(AHB-shnIT)*	tranche
abschreiben	*(AHB-shrEYE-ben)*	charge off (v), write off (v)
Abschreibung (f)	*(AHB-shrEYE-bunk)*	depreciation, write-off
Abschreibung für Substanzverringerung (f)	*(AHB-shrEYE-bunk fEWr zub-stAHNts-fuh-rin-guh-runk)*	depletion allowance
Abschreibungsbetrag (m)	*(AHB-shrEYE-bungs-beh-trAHk)*	depreciation allowance
Absendung (f)	*(AHB-zEN-dunk)*	dispatch

absetzen	*(AHB-zet-tsen)*	charge off (v), market
absorbieren	*(ahb-zor-bEE-ren)*	absorb (v)
Abtaster (m)	*(AHB-tahs-tuh)*	scanner
Abteilung (f)	*(AHB-tEYE-lunk)*	department
Abtretende (m)	*(AHB-trEH-ten-deh)*	assignor
Abwasser (n)	*(AHB-vah-sehr)*	sewage
Abwasserreinigung (f)	*(AHB-vahsser-reyen-igoong)*	cleanup of waste waters
Abweichung (f)	*(AHB-vEYE-khunk)*	variance
Abwertung (f)	*(AHB-vEHR-tunk)*	devaluation
Abwesenheit (f)	*(AHB-vAY-zen-heyet)*	absenteeism
Abwicklung (f)	*(AHB-vIK-lunk)*	handling
abziehen	*(AHB-tsEE-hen)*	take off (v)
Abzug (m)	*(AHB-tsOOk)*	deduction
Abzüge (pl) machen	*(ahb-tsEW-geh ma-khen)*	copy (v)
abzugsfähig	*(AHB-tsOOks-fAY-hik)*	deductible
Addition (f)	*(ah-di-tsEE-ohn)*	footing (accounting)
Adressenkartei (f)	*(ah-drEHS-sen-kahr-teye)*	mailing list
Agentur (f)	*(a-gen-tOOR)*	agency
aggressive Verkaufspolitik (f)	*(ah-greh-zEE-fuh fuh-kOWfs-po-li-tEEk)*	hard sell
Akkordarbeit (f)	*(ah-kORd-ahr-beyet)*	piecework
Akkreditiv (n)	*(ah-kray-di-tEEf)*	letter of credit
Akronym (n)	*(ah-kro-nEWm)*	acronym
Aktenkoffer (m)	*(AHk-ten-kof-fuh)*	attaché case
Aktenmappe (f)	*(AHk-ten-mAHP-peh)*	briefcase
Aktentasche (f)	*(AHk-tEN-tAH-SHeh)*	portfolio
Aktenzeichen (n)	*(AHk-ten-tsEYE-khen)*	reference number
Aktie (f)	*(ak-tsEE-eh)*	stock (share)
Aktien (pl)	*(ak-tsEE-en)*	shares
Aktien ohne Stimmberechtigung (pl)	*(ak-tsEE-en ohneh shtIM-beh-rehkh-ti-gunk)*	nonvoting stock
Aktienaufteilung (f)	*(ak-tsEE-en-OWf-tEYE-lunk)*	stock split

Aktienbezugsrecht (n)	*(ak-tsEE-en-beh-tsOOgs-REHKHT)*	stock option
Aktiengesellschaft (f)	*(ak-tsEE-en-geh-zEHL-shahft)*	corporation, joint stock company
Aktiengesellschaft (f)	*(ak-tsEE-en-geh-zEHL-shahft)*	public company
Aktiengewinn (m)	*(ak-tsEE-en-geh-vIN)*	stock profit
Aktienkapital (n)	*(ak-tsEE-en-kah-pi-tAAL)*	stockholders' equity
Aktienkauf (m)	*(ak-tsEE-en-kOWf)*	stock purchase
Aktienmarkt (m)	*(ak-tsEE-en-mAHrkt)*	stock market
Aktienmehrheit (f)	*(ak-tsEE-en-mayr-heyet)*	controlling interest
Aktienportefeuille (n)	*(ak-tsEE-en-port-fOY)*	stock portfolio
Aktiensplit (m)	*(ak-tsEE-en-shplit)*	stock split
Aktienverwässerung (f)	*(ak-tsEE-en-fuh-vEHS-seh-runk)*	dilution equity
Aktienzertifikat (n)	*(ak-tsEE-en-tsEHR-ti-fi-kaat)*	stock certificate
Aktienzusammenlegung (f)	*(ak-tsEE-en-tsoo-zAHM-men-lay-gunk)*	reverse stock split
Aktionär (m)	*(ak-tsEE-oh-nAYR)*	shareholder, stockholder
Aktionärsversammlung (f)	*(ak-tsEE-o-nAYRs-fuh-zAM-lunk)*	shareholders' meeting
Aktiva (f)	*(ahk-tEE-vah)*	active assets
aktive Rechnungsabgrenzungen (pl)	*(ahk-tEE-veh rEHKH-nungs-ahb-gren-tsun-gen)*	deferred charges
aktive Rechnungsabgrenzungsposten (pl)	*(rahk-tEE-veh rEHKH-nungs-ahb-gren-tsungs-pOS-ten)*	prepaid expenses
Aktivenertrag (m)	*(ahk-tEE-ven-uh-trAHk)*	earnings on assets
Aktivkonto (n)	*(ahk-tEEf-kON-toh)*	active account
akustische Kopplung (f)	*(ah-kUS-ti-sheh kOP-peh-lunk)*	acoustic coupler
Akzept (n)	*(ahk-tsEPt)*	acceptance (bill of agreement)
Akzeptant (m)	*(ahk-tsEP-tahnt)*	acceptor, drawee
Akzepthaus (n)	*(ahk-tsEPt-hOWs)*	acceptance house
akzeptieren	*(ahk-tsep-tEE-ren)*	accept (v)

A

Algorithmus (m)	*(ahl-go-rIT-mus)*	algorithm
Alkohol (m)	*(AHL-ko-hol)*	alcohol
Alkoholgehalt (m)	*(AHL-ko-hol-geh-hahlt)*	alcoholic content
Alleinrecht (n)	*(ahl-lEYEn-REHKHT)*	sole rights
alleinstehender Datenver- arbeiter (m)	*(ahl-lEYEn-shtay-hen-duh dAA-ten-fuh-ahr-beye- tuh)*	stand-alone word processor
Alleinvertreter (m)	*(ahl-lEYEn-fuh-trAY-tuh)*	sole agent
alles oder nichts	*(AHl-lehs oduh nIKHts)*	all or none
allgemein	*(AHl-geh-mEYEn)*	across the board
allmählich abschaffen	*(AHl-mAY-likh AHB-shAF- fen)*	phase out (v)
Altern (n)	*(AHL-tehrn)*	aging
Alternativbestel- lung (f)	*(ahl-tuh-nah-tEEf-beh- shtEHL-lunk)*	alternative order
alternative Kosten (pl)	*(ahl-tuh-nah-tEE-veh kOS- ten)*	opportunity cost
Ammoniak (n)	*(a-MOH-nee-ahk)*	ammonia
Amortisation (f)	*(ah-mor-ti-zah-tsEE-ohn)*	amortization
Amplituden- modulation (f)	*(ahm-pli-TOO-den-moh- DU-lah-TSI-ohn)*	amplitude modulation (AM)
Amt (n)	*(AHmt)*	office (official)
amtlich notierte Werte (pl)	*(AHmt-likh no-tEER-teh vEHR-teh)*	listed securities
Amtsbereich (m)	*(AHmts-beh-rEYEkh)*	jurisdiction
Amtsschimmel (m)	*(AHmts-shIM-mel)*	red tape
an den Inhaber zahlbar	*(ahn dehn IN-hah-buh tsAAl-buh)*	payable to bearer
an Order zahlbar	*(ahn OR-duh tsaal-buh)*	payable to order
Analgetikum (n)	*(ahn-ahl-gAY-ti-kum)*	analgesic
Analogcomputer (m)	*(ah-nah-lOHg-kom-pyU- tuh)*	analog computer
Analyse (f)	*(a-naa-LEW-zeh)*	analysis
Analyse der Netz- plantechnik (f)	*(ah-nah-lEW-zeh duh nets- plAAn-tehkh-nik)*	critical path analysis
Analytiker (m)	*(ah-nah-lEW-ti-kuh)*	analyst
analytische Chemie (f)	*(a-naa-LEW-ti-sheh KHAY- mee)*	analytic chemistry

Anbaufläche (f)	*(AHN-bow-flehkh-eh)*	acre
ändern	*(EHn-dehrn)*	amend (v)
Änderung (f)	*(EHndeh-runk)*	alteration, amendment
Anerkennung (f)	*(ahn-EHR-ken-nunk)*	acknowledgment
Anfangsbestand (m)	*(AHN-fahngs-beh-shtahnt)*	opening balance
Anfangskosten (pl)	*(AHN-fahngs-kOS-ten)*	start-up costs
Anfangskurs (m)	*(AHN-fahngs-koors)*	opening price
Anfangsprovision (f)	*(AHN-fahngs-pro-vi-zee-OHn)*	front-end fee (front-end load)
Anforderung (f)	*(AHN-for-deh-runk)*	requirement
Angabe (f)	*(AHN-gaa-beh)*	statement, data
Angabengrundlage (f)	*(AHN-gAH-ben-grUNd-laa-geh)*	data base
Angebot (n)	*(AHN-geh-boht)*	supply and demand
Angebot und Nach-frage	*(AHN-geh-boht unt nAKH-fraa-geh)*	bid and asked
Angebotsaufforde-rung (f)	*(AHN-geh-bohts-OWf-for-deh-runk)*	request for bid
Angebotspreis (m)	*(AHN-geh-bohts-prEYEs)*	offered price
angelegtes Kapital (n)	*(AHN-geh-layg-tes kah-pi-tAAL)*	invested capital
angemeldetes Patent (n)	*(AHN-geh-mel-deh-tes PAH-tent)*	patent pending
angemessene Sorg-falt (f)	*(AHN-geh-mES-seh-neh zORg-fahlt)*	reasonable care
angemessener Ertrag (m)	*(AHN-geh-mES-seh-nuh uh-trAHk)*	fair return
angemessener Marktpreis (m)	*(AHN-geh-mES-seh-nuh mAHrkt-prEYEs)*	fair market value
angepaßter Kurs (m)	*(AHN-geh-pAHS-tuh koors)*	adjusted rate
angespannte Marktlage (f)	*(AHN-geh-shpAHN-teh mAHrkt-laa-geh)*	tight market
Angestelltenberat-ung (f)	*(AHN-geh-shtEHL-ten-beh-rAA-tunk)*	employee counseling
Angestelltenpoten-tial (n)	*(AHN-geh-shtEHL-ten-poh-ten-tsee-AAL)*	human resources
Angestellter (m)	*(AHN-geh-shtEHL-tuh)*	employee

angewandter Erlöstausch (m)	*(AHN-geh-vahn-tuh AYr-lERs-tOWsh)*	applied proceeds swap
Angorawolle (f)	*(ahn-GOH-rah-vOL-leh)*	angora
anhängen	*(AHN-hehn-gen)*	attach (v) (affix, adhere)
Anhängsel (n)	*(AHN-hehn-gsel)*	attachment (contract)
anhäufend	*(AHN-hOY-fend)*	cumulative
Ankauf (m)	*(AHN-kOWf)*	leveraged lease
Ankauf offener Buchforderungen (m)	*(AHN-kOWf OF-feh-nuh bOOkh-FOHR-duh-run-gen)*	factoring
Ankergebühr (f)	*(ahn-kehr-geh-bEWr)*	anchorage dues
Anlage (f)	*(AHN-laa-geh)*	layout (of premises)
Anlageberater (m)	*(AHN-laa-geh-buh-rAA-tuh)*	investment adviser
Anlagebrief (m)	*(AHN-laa-geh-brEEf)*	investment letter
Anlagekapital (n)	*(AHN-laa-geh-kah-pi-tAAL)*	fixed capital
Anlagekredit (m)	*(AHN-laa-geh-kray-dIT)*	investment credit
Anlagenanalyse (f)	*(AHN-laa-gen-ah-nah-lEW-zeh)*	investment analysis
Anlagenrendite (f)	*(AHN-laa-gen-ren-di-teh)*	return on assets managed
Anlagevermögen (n)	*(AHN-laa-ge-fuh-mER-gen)*	capital asset
Anlagewerte (pl)	*(AHN-laa-ge-vEIIR-teh)*	capital goods
Anlasser (m)	*(AHN-lahs-suh)*	starter
Anlasserwelle (f)	*(AHN-lahs-suh-vEL-leh)*	crankshaft
anlegen	*(AHN-lay-gen)*	invest (v)
Anlegestelle (f)	*(AHN-lay-geh-shtEHL-leh)*	wharf
Anleihe (f)	*(AHN-leye-eh)*	bond, loan
Anleihe ohne Zinskoupon (f)	*(AHN-leye-eh ohneh tsINs-ku-pon)*	zero coupon
Anleiheausgabe (f)	*(AHN-leye-eh-OWs-gAA-beh)*	bond issue
Anleihebewertung (f)	*(AHN-leye-eh-beh-vEHR-tunk)*	bond rating
Anleihegarant (m)	*(AHN-leye-eh-gah-rahnt)*	underwriter
Annahme (f)	*(AHN-nah-meh)*	acceptance (agreement)
Annahme als Markenartikel (f)	*(AHN-nah-meh ahls mAHR-ken-ahr-tiIK-el)*	brand acceptance

A

Annahme mit Vor-behalt (f)	*(AHN-nah-meh mit FOHR-beh-hahlt)*	conditional acceptance
Annahme verwei-gern (f)	*(AHN-nah-meh fuh-vEYE-guhn)*	refuse acceptance (v)
Annahmevertrag (m)	*(AHN-nah-meh-fuh-trAHk)*	acceptance agreement
annehmbares Qua-litäsniveau (n)	*(AHN-naym-bah-rehs kvah-li-tAYts-nee-voh)*	acceptable quality level
annehmen	*(AHN-nAY-men)*	accept (v)
anordnen	*(AHN-ord-nen)*	instruct (v) (order)
anorganische Che-mie (f)	*(ahn-or-gAA-ni-she KHAY-mee)*	inorganic chemistry
anpassen	*(AHN-pAHS-sen)*	adjust (v)
Anpassung an das Dezimalsystem (f)	*(AHN-pAHS-sunk ahn dahs det-SEE-mahl-zews-taym)*	metrification
Anregungsmittel (n)	*(AHN-reh-gungs-mit-tel)*	stimulant
Anreiz (m)	*(AHN-rEYEts)*	incentive
anrufen	*(AHN-ROO-fen)*	call (v)
ansässiger Einkäu-fer (m)	*(AHN-sehs-si-guh eyen-kOY-fuh)*	resident buyer
Anschaffungsko-sten (pl)	*(AHN-shAHF-fungs-kOS-ten)*	original cost
Anschauung (f)	*(AHN-show-unk)*	outlook (philosophy)
Anschauungs-modell (n)	*(AHN-show-ungs-mo-dEL)*	mock-up
Anschlagetafel (f)	*(AHN-shlaa-geh-tAA-fel)*	billboard
Anschlußauftrag (m)	*(AHN-shlUS-OWf-trAHk)*	follow-up order
Ansehen einer Firma (n)	*(AHN-zeh-hen eye-nuh fIR-mah)*	goodwill
ansetzen	*(AHN-zeh-tsen)*	schedule (v)
Ansporn (m)	*(AHN-shporn)*	incentive
Anspruch (m)	*(AHN-shprUKH)*	claim
anstellen	*(AHN-shtEHL-len)*	hire (v)
Anstiftung (f) zum Prozessieren	*(AHN-shtIF-tunk tsum pro-tses-sEE-ren)*	barratry
Anteil (m)	*(AHN-teyel)*	interest (share)
Anteilmehrheit (f)	*(AHN-teyel-mayr-heyet)*	majority interest

Antiacidum (n)	*(AHN-ti-AH-tsidum)*	antacid
Antibiotikum (n)	*(AHN-ti-BEE-o-ti-kum)*	antibiotic
Antidumpingzoll (m)	*(ahnti-dum-ping-tsOL)*	antidumping duty
Antiseptikum (n)	*(AHN-ti-sEHp-ti-kum)*	antiseptic
antizipative Aktiva (pl)	*(ahnti-tsi-pah-tEE-fuh ahk-tEE-vah)*	accrued assets
antizipativer Auf-wand (m)	*(ahnti-tsi-pah-tEE-fuh OWf-vahnt)*	accrued expenses
antizipativer Ertrag (m)	*(ahnti-tsi-pah-tEE-fuh uh-trAHk)*	accrued revenue
Antragsformular (n)	*(AHN-trahgs-for-mu-lAAr)*	application form
Antriebsrad (n)	*(AHN-treebs-raht)*	pinion
anwachsen	*(AHN-vahkh-zen)*	accrue (v)
Anwalt (m)	*(AHN-vahlt)*	attorney
Anwartschafts-recht (n)	*(AHN-vahrt-shahfts-REHKHT)*	inchoate interest
Anwesenheitszeit (f)	*(AHN-vAY-zen-heyets-tsEYEt)*	attended time
Anzahlung (f)	*(AHN-tsAA-lunk)*	down payment
Anzeigentarif (m)	*(AHN-tseye-gen-tah-rIF)*	advertising rate
Anzug (m)	*(AHN-tsook)*	suit
Apotheke (f)	*(ah-po-tAY-keh)*	pharmacy
Apotheker (m)	*(ah-po-tAY-kuh)*	pharmacist
Arbeit (f)	*(ahr-bEYEt)*	job
Arbeit im Gang (f)	*(ahr-bEYEt im gahnk)*	work in progress
arbeiten	*(ahr-bEYE-ten)*	work (v)
Arbeiter (m)	*(ahr-bEYE-tuh)*	laborer
Arbeiterführer (m)	*(ahr-bEYE-tuh-fEW-ruh)*	labor leader
Arbeiterklasse (f)	*(ahr-bEYE-tuh-klAS-seh)*	working class
Arbeiterschaft (f)	*(ahr-bEYE-tuh-shahft)*	labor
Arbeitgeber-Arbeitnehmer-verhältnis (n)	*(ahr-bEYEt-geh-buh-ahr-bEYEt-nAY-muh-fuh-hEHLt-nis)*	labor relations
Arbeitsauftrag (m)	*(AHR-beyets-OWf-trAHk)*	work order

A

Arbeitsausschuß (m)	*(AHR-beyets-OWs-shuS)*	task force
Arbeitsbelastung (f)	*(AHR-beyets-beh-lah-stunk)*	work load
Arbeitsbeschreibung (f)	*(AHR-beyets-beh-shrEYE-bunk)*	job description
Arbeitsbewertung (f)	*(AHR-beyets-beh-vEHR-tunk)*	job evaluation
Arbeitsbeziehungen (pl)	*(AHR-beyets-beh-tsEE-hun-gen)*	industrial relations
Arbeitsfolge (f)	*(AHR-beyets-fol-geh)*	work order (sequence)
arbeitsfreier Tag (m)	*(AHR-beyets-frEYE-uh tAAk)*	holiday
Arbeitsgang (m)	*(AHR-beyets-gahnk)*	work cycle
arbeitsintensiv	*(AHR-beyets-in-ten-zEEf)*	labor-intensive
Arbeitskräfte (pl)	*(AHR-beyets-krehf-teh)*	labor force, manpower, workforce
Arbeitsleistung (f)	*(AHR-beyets-lEYEs-tunk)*	job performance, output
Arbeitsleistung (f)	*(AHR-beyets-lEYEs-tunk)*	power
Arbeitslosenunterstützung (f)	*(AHR-beyets-loh-zen-un-tuh-shtEWt-tsunk)*	unemployment compensation
Arbeitslosigkeit (f)	*(AHR-beyets-loh-zig-keyet)*	unemployment
Arbeitsmarkt (m)	*(AHR-beyets-mAHrkt)*	labor market
Arbeitsmittel (pl)	*(AHR-beyets-mit-tEL)*	working tools
Arbeitsmoral (f)	*(AHR-beyets-mo-rAAL)*	morale
Arbeitsniederlegung (f)	*(AHR-beyets-nee-duh-lAY-gunk)*	walkout
Arbeitspapiere (pl)	*(AHR-beyets-pah-pEE-reh)*	working papers
arbeitsparend	*(AHR-beyets-shpAA-rent)*	labor-saving
Arbeitsplatz (m)	*(AHR-beyets-plahts)*	workplace
Arbeitsplatzanalyse (f)	*(AHR-beyets-plahts-ah-nah-lEW-zeh)*	ergonomics
Arbeitsplatzsicherheit (f)	*(AHR-beyets-plahts-zikh-huh-heyet)*	job security
Arbeitsplatzuntersuchung (f)	*(AHR-beyets-plahts-un-tuh-zOO-khunk)*	job analysis
Arbeitsrecht (n)	*(AHR-beyets-REHKHT)*	labor law
Arbeitsschema (n)	*(AHR-beyets-sheh-ma)*	layout

Arbeitsstab (m)	*(AHR-beyets-shtahp)*	task force
Arbeitsstätte (f)	*(AHR-beyets-shtEHT-teh)*	work station
Arbeitsstudie (f)	*(AHR-beyets-shtu-di-eh)*	job analysis
Arbeitsstunden (pl)	*(AHR-beyets-shtun-den)*	man hours
Arbeitstag (m)	*(AHR-beyets-taak)*	work day
Arbeitsteilung (f)	*(AHR-beyets-tEYE-lunk)*	division of labor
Arbeitsunfall (m)	*(AHR-beyets-un-fAHL)*	industrial accident
Arbeitsverfassung (f)	*(AHR-beyets-fuh-fAHS-sunk)*	labor code
Arbeitsvorgang (m)	*(ahr-bEYEts-fOHR-gahnk)*	process
Arbeitszeit (f)	*(AHR-beyets-tsEYEt)*	working hours
Arbitrage (f)	*(ahr-bi-trAAsh)*	arbitrage
arithmetisches Mittel (n)	*(ah-rIT-meh-ti-shehs mit-tEL)*	arithmetic mean
Art (f)	*(ahrt)*	mode
Artikel (m)	*(ahr-tIK-el)*	item
Arzneimittel (n)	*(ahr-tsnEYE-mit-tel)*	medicine
Arzneiverordnung (f)	*(ahr-tsnEYE-fuh-ORd-nunk)*	medication
Arzt (m)	*(ARtst)*	physician
Assistent (m)	*(as-sis-tENt)*	assistant
Astrachan (m)	*(ahs-trah-khAHN)*	astrakan
Äthan (n)	*(AY-taan)*	ethane
Äther (m)	*(AY-tuh)*	ether
Atom (n)	*(a-TOHm)*	atom
atomar	*(a-toh-MAAr)*	atomic
Attest (n)	*(ah-TEHst)*	attestation
auf dem laufenden halten	*(OWf dehm lOW-fen-den hAHl-ten)*	keep posted (v)
auf der ganzen Linie	*(OWf duh GAN-tsen LEE-nee-eh)*	down the line
(Auf) Lösung (f)	*([OWf] LER-zunk)*	solution
auf Rechnung	*(OWf rEHKH-nunk)*	on account
auf Verlangen	*(OWf fuh-lAHng-en)*	on demand
auf Ziel	*(OWf TSEEL)*	on account

aufbewahren	*(OWf-beh-vAA-ren)*	store (v)
Aufbewahrung (f)	*(OWf-beh-vAA-runk)*	storage
aufeinander wirken	*(OWf-eyen-AAN-duh VEER-ken)*	interact (v)
Aufforderung zur Einreichung von Angeboten (f)	*(OWf-FOHR-duh-runk tsoor EYEn-reyekh-unk fon AHN-geh-boh-ten)*	invitation to bid
aufgeben	*(OWf-gay-ben)*	abandon (v)
aufgelaufene Steuern (pl)	*(OWf-ge-lowfen-uh STOY-ern)*	accrued taxes
aufgelaufene Zinsen (pl)	*(OWf-ge-lowfen-uh tsIN-zen)*	accrued interest
aufgelöster Stoff (m)	*(OWf-geh-LER-stehr shtOF)*	solute
aufgeschobene Lieferungen (pl)	*(OWf-ge-shoh-be-nuh LEE-feh-rung-en)*	deferred deliveries
aufgeschobene Renten (pl)	*(OWf-ge-shoh-be-nuh REN-ten)*	deferred annuities
aufgeschobene Schulden (pl)	*(OWf-ge-sho-be-nuh SHOOl-den)*	deferred liabilities
aufgliedern	*(OWf-glee-dehrn)*	itemize (v)
Aufhängung (f)	*(OWf-hehn-gunk)*	suspension
aufheben	*(OWf-hay-ben)*	nullify (v), supersede (v)
Auflage (f)	*(OWf-lah-geh)*	circulation, print run, printing
Auflassungsurkunde (f)	*(OWf-lah-sungs-OOr-kun-deh)*	deed of transfer
Auflaufen (n)	*(OWf-lowfen)*	accrual
auflaufen	*(OWf-lowfen)*	accrue (v)
Auflösung (f)	*(OWf-ler-zunk)*	liquidation
Auflösungswert (m)	*(OWf-ler-zoongs-vEHRt)*	liquidation value
aufnehmen	*(OWf-nay-men)*	record (v)
aufs Höchstmaß bringen	*(OWfs HERKHST-maass BRING-en)*	maximize
aufschieben	*(OWf-shee-ben)*	postpone (v)
Aufschlag (m)	*(OWf-shlAHk)*	increase, markup, surcharge
aufschreiben	*(OWf-shrEYE-ben)*	take down (v)

A

Aufschub (m)	*(OWf-shoob)*	delay
Aufschwung (m)	*(OWf-shvunk)*	rally, recovery, upturn
Aufsichtsperson (f)	*(OWf-zikhts- payr-zOHn)*	supervisor
Aufsichtsrat (m)	*(OWf-zikhts-raat)*	board of supervisors
Aufstellungskosten (pl)	*(OWf-shtEHL-lunks-kOS-ten)*	set-up costs
Auftrag (m)	*(OWf-trAHk)*	order
Auftrag auf Basis Selbstkosten plus Gewinn (m)	*(OWf-trAHk owf BAA-zis zEHLbst-kOS-ten plOOs geh-vIN)*	cost-plus contract
Auftraggeber (m)	*(OWf-trAHk-gAY-buh)*	principal (employer of an agent)
Auftragsbestätig-ung (f)	*(OWf-trAHks-beh-shtAY-tee-gunk)*	confirmation of order
Auftragssendung (f)	*(OWf-trAHks-zEN-dunk)*	drop shipment
Aufwand (m)	*(OWf-vahnt)*	expenditure
Aufwärtsbewegung (f)	*(OWf-vehrts-be-VAY-gunk)*	upturn
Augentropfen (m)	*(OW-gen-trop-fen)*	eyedrop
Ausbeute (f) schneiden	*(OWs-boy-teh shnEYE-den)*	crop
Ausbildung am Arbeitsplatz (f)	*(OWS-bil-dunk ahm AHR-beyets-plahts)*	on-the-job training
ausbuchen	*(OWS-bOO-khen)*	abandon (v)
Ausbuchung (f)	*(bOO-khunk)*	abandonment
ausdestillieren	*(OWs-dehs-ti-lEE-ren)*	draw off
ausfahren	*(OWS-faar-en)*	export (v)
Ausfallzeit einer Maschine (f)	*(OWS-fahl-tsEYEt eye-nuh MAA-shee-nuh)*	downtime of a machine
Ausfuhragent (m)	*(OWS-foor-ah-gent)*	export agent
Ausfuhrbeschrän-kungen (die Ein-fuhrbeschrän-kungen) (pl)	*(OWS-foor-beh-shrAYNK-unk-en dee EYEn-foor-be-shrAYNK-unk-en)*	restrictions on export (import)
Ausfuhrbestim-mung (f)	*(OWS-foor-beh-shtIM-munk)*	export regulation
Ausfuhrbewilli-gung (f)	*(OWS-foor-beh-vIL-i-gunk)*	export permit

Ausfuhrkredit (m)	*(OWS-foor-kray-dIT)*	export credit
Ausfuhrlizenz für Kulturgüter (f)	*(OWS-foor-lee-tsEHnts fEWr kul-TOOR-gew-tuh)*	cultural export permit
Ausfuhrprämie (export premium) (f)	*(OWS-foor-pRAY-mee-eh)*	drawback
Ausfuhrquote (f)	*(OWS-foor-kvOH-teh)*	export quota
Ausfuhrsteuer (f)	*(OWS-foor-shtOY-uh)*	export tax
Ausfuhrzoll (m)	*(OWS-foor-tsOL)*	export duty
Ausfuhrzollerklärung (f)	*(OWS-foor-tsOL-ayr-klAY-runk)*	export entry
Ausfütterung (f)	*(OWs-fEWT-teh-runk)*	lining
Ausgabe (f)	*(OWS-gah-beh)*	expenditure, stock issue
Ausgabe (f)	*(OWs-gah-beh)*	edition
Ausgabekurs (m)	*(OWS-gah-beh-koors)*	issue price
Ausgabenvergütung (f)	*(OWS-gah-behn-fuh-gEW-tunk)*	recovery of expenses
ausgeben	*(OWS-gay-behn)*	issue (v)
ausgegebene Aktien (pl)	*(OWS-ge-gay-ben AK-tsee-en)*	issued shares
ausgeglichener Haushalt (m)	*(OWS-ge-glikh-enuh-hOWs-haalt)*	balanced budget
ausgewiesener Inhaber (m)	*(OWS-ge-vEE-zenuh IN-haa-buh)*	holder in due course
Ausgleich (m)	*(OWS-gleyekh)*	settlement
ausgleichen	*(OWS-gleyekh-en)*	adjust (v), level out (v)
Ausgleichszoll (m)	*(OWS-gleyekh-tsOL)*	countervailing duty
Ausglühen (n)	*(OWs-gLEW-en)*	annealing
Auslage (f)	*(OWS-laa-geh)*	disbursement, outlay
Auslagen (pl)	*(OWS-laa-gen)*	charges, expenses
Auslagenabrechnung (f)	*(OWS-lah-gen-AHB-rEHKH-nunk)*	expense account
ausländische Gesellschaft (f)	*(OWS-lehn-di-shuh geh-zEL-shahft)*	alien corporation, foreign corporation
ausländisches Wertpapier (n)	*(OWS-lehn-di-shuh-uhs vEHRt-pah-pEEr)*	foreign security
Auslandssteuergutschrift (f)	*(OWS-lahndz-shtOY-uh-gOOt-shrift)*	foreign tax credit

Auslandsverschul-dung (f)	*(OWS-lahndz-fuh-shUL-dunk)*	foreign debt
Auslandswährung (f)	*(OWS-lahndz-vAY-runk)*	foreign currency
auslassen	*(OWS-laa-sen)*	omit (v)
auspreisen	*(OWS-prEYE-sen)*	price (v)
Auspuff (m)	*(OWs-pUF)*	exhaust
Ausrüstung (f)	*(OWS-rews-tunk)*	equipment
Ausrüstungsmie-tung (f)	*(OWS-rews-tunks-MEE-tung)*	equipment leasing
Ausschreibung (f)	*(OWS-shrEYE-bunk)*	invitation to bid, request for bid
Ausschuß (m)	*(OWs-shuS)*	commission (agency)
Ausschußwaren (pl)	*(OWs-shUS-vAA-rehn)*	as is goods
Außenhandel (m)	*(OWs-en-hahn-dehl)*	foreign trade
Außenstände (pl)	*(OWs-en-shtehn-deh)*	active debts
Außenwirtschaft (f)	*(OWs-en-vEErt-shahft)*	foreign trade
außer Mode	*(OWs-suh mOH-deh)*	out of style
außergerichtlicher Vergleich (m)	*(OWs-uh-geh-RIKHT-likh-eh fuh-glEYEKH)*	accord and satisfaction
außerordentliche Rücklage (f)	*(OWs-uh-OHR-dehnt-likheh REWk-laa-geh)*	contingent fund
Aussicht (f)	*(OWs-seekht)*	outlook
aussperren	*(OWs-shpehr-en)*	lock out (v)
ausstehende Aktien (pl)	*(OWs-shtay-hen-deh ak-tsEE-en)*	outstanding stock
ausstehende Forde-rungen (pl)	*(OWs-shtay-hen-deh FOHR-duh-run-gen)*	accounts receivable, out-standing debt
Aussteller (m)	*(OWs-shtEHL-luh)*	drawer
Ausstoß (m)	*(OWs-shtohs)*	outturn (v)
ausstrahlen	*(OWs-shtrAA-len)*	broadcast (v)
Ausübung einer Zusatzbeschäfti-gung (f)	*(OWs-ew-bunk eye-nuh tsOO-zahts-beh-shEHf-ti-gunk)*	moonlighting
Auswahl (f)	*(OWs-vaal)*	sample line
Auswahlgröße (f)	*(OWs-vaal-grer-suh)*	sample size

Ausweichklausel (f)	*(OWs-vEYEkh-klOW-zel)*	escape clause
Autarkie (f)	*(ow-tAAR-kee)*	autarky
Auto (n)	*(OW-to)*	automobile, car
Automation (f)	*(ow-toh-maa-tsEE-ohn)*	automation
automatisch	*(ow-toh-mAA-tish)*	automatic
automatische Erneuerung (f)	*(ow-tOH-maa-tishuh AYR-noy-ay-runk)*	rollover
Autorenanteil (m)	*(OW-tohr-en-AHN-teyel)*	royalty
Autorenhonorar (n)	*(OW-tohr-en-OH-noh-raar)*	royalty (book)
autorisierte Unterschrift (f)	*(OW-toh-ree-seer-tuh un-tuh-shrift)*	authorized signature
Azetatsäure (f)	*(ah-TSEH-taht-ZOY-reh)*	acetic acid

B

(Bild) Abtastung (f)	*([Bild] AHB-tahs-tunk)*	scanning
Bahn (f)	*(baan)*	railroad
Bahnsendung (f)	*(BAAN-zEN-dunk)*	rail shipment
Baisse (f)	*(behss)*	down period, slump
Baissebewegung (f)	*(bayss-uh-buh-vAY-gunk)*	downturn
Baissebörse (f)	*(bayss-uh-bER-suh)*	bear market
Ballastbonus (m)	*(bahl-LAAst-boh-noos)*	ballast bonus
Ballenkapazität (f)	*(BAAL-en-kah-pah-tsee-tAYt)*	bale capacity
Ballenladung (f)	*(BAAL-en-laa-dunk)*	bale cargo
Bank (f)	*(bahnk)*	bank, money shop
Bankakkreditiv (n)	*(BAHNK-ah-kreh-di-tEEf)*	bank letter of credit
Bankakzept (n)	*(BAHNK-ahk-tsEPt)*	bank acceptance
Bankbuch (n)	*(BAHNK-bOOkh)*	bankbook, passbook
Bankdarlehen (n)	*(BAHNK-daar-lAY-en)*	bank loan
Bankeinlage (f)	*(BAHNK-eyen-laa-geh)*	bank deposit
Bankfach (n)	*(BAHNK-fahkh)*	safe deposit box
Bankfeiertag (m)	*(BAHNK-fEYE-uh-taak)*	bank holiday

Bankfreigabe (f)	*(BAHNK-frEYE-gaa-beh)*	bank release
Bankgebühren (pl)	*(BAHNK-geh-bEW-ren)*	bank charges
Bankgeldanweisung (f)	*(BAHNK-gehlt-ahn-vEYE-zunk)*	bank money order
Bankguthaben (n)	*(BAHNK-gOOt-haa-ben)*	bank balance
Bankkonto (n)	*(BAHNK-kON-toh)*	bank account
Bankkreditbrief (m)	*(BAHNK-kray-dIT-brEEf)*	bank letter of credit
Banknote (f)	*(BAHNK-nOH-teh)*	bank note, bill (currency)
Bankrevisor (m)	*(BAHNK-rAY-vee-zohr)*	bank examiner
Bankrott (m)	*(bahnk-rOT)*	bankruptcy
Bankrott machen (v)	*(bahnk-rOT MAA-khen)*	fail (go bankrupt)
Bankscheck (m)	*(BAHNK-shek)*	bank check, cashier's check
Banktratte (f)	*(BAHNK-tRAH-teh)*	bank draft
Bankwechsel (m)	*(BAHNK-vEHk-sel)*	bank exchange
Bankzins (m)	*(BAHNK-tsINs)*	bank rate
Barauslagen (pl)	*(BAAR-ows-lah-gen)*	out-of-pocket expenses
Bardividende (f)	*(BAAR-di-vi-dEHN-deh)*	cash dividend
Bargeld (n)	*(BAAR-geld)*	cash
Bargeldzustellung (f)	*(BAAR-geld-tsOO shtEHL-lunk)*	cash delivery
Barliquiditätsgrad (m)	*(BAAR-lee-kvee-dee-tAYts grahd)*	acid-test ratio
Barren (pl)	*(bAHR-ren)*	billets
Barzahlung im voraus (f)	*(BAAR-tsAA-lunk im FOHR-ows)*	cash before delivery
Barzahlungsrabatt (m)	*(BAAR-tsAA-lungs-rAA-baht)*	cash discount
Base (f)	*(BAA-zeh)*	base
Basisjahr (n)	*(BAA-zis-yaar)*	base year
Basispunkt (m)	*(BAA-zis-pUnkt)*	basis point
Baubehörde (f)	*(BOW-beh-hER-deh)*	housing authority (construction)
Baud (n)	*(bowd)*	baud
Bauingenieurwesen (n)	*(BOW-een-shen-EEewr-vAY-zen)*	civil engineering

Baumwolle (f)	*(BOWm-voleh)*	cotton
Bauteil (m)	*(BOW-teyel)*	component
beantworten	*(beh-AHnt-vohr-ten)*	reply (v)
bearbeiten	*(beh-ahr-bEYE-ten)*	process (v)
Bearbeitungsfehler (m)	*(beh-ahr-bEYE-tungs-fAY-luh)*	processing error
Bedarfsanalyse (f)	*(beh-dAARFs-ah-nah-lEW-zeh)*	needs analysis
bedingte Annahme (f)	*(beh-dEENK-teh AAN-naameh)*	conditional acceptance
bedingter Ver-kaufsvertrag (m)	*(beh-dEENK-tuh fuh-kOWfs-fuh-trAHk)*	conditional sales contract
beenden	*(beh-EHn-den)*	terminate (v)
Befähigung (f)	*(beh-fAY-hee-gunk)*	qualification
Befehl (m)	*(beh-FAYL)*	mandate, order (command)
Befehlskette (f)	*(beh-FAYLs-ket-teh)*	chain of command
befördern	*(beh-FER-duhn)*	forward (v)
Beförderung (f)	*(beh-FER-duh-unk)*	handling, promotion
Befrachtung (f)	*(beh-frahKH-tunk)*	charter (mercantile lease)
Befreiung (f)	*(beh-frEYE-unk)*	exemption
befristete Einlage (f)	*(beh-frIS-teh-teh EYEn-laa-geh)*	time deposit
Begleitbrief (m)	*(beh-glEYEt-brEEf)*	cover letter
begleitete Waren (pl)	*(beh-glEYEt-eh-teh VAAr-en)*	accompanied goods
Begünstigter (m)	*(beh-gEWns-tig-tuh)*	beneficiary
Begünstigungstarif (m)	*(beh-gEWns-tig-unks-tah-rIF)*	preferential tariff
Behälter (m)	*(beh-hEHlt-uh)*	container
bei Börsenöffnung	*(beye BEWr-sen-EWf-noong)*	at the opening
bei Börsenöffnung kaufen	*(beye BEWr-sen-EWf-noong kOW-fen)*	buy on opening (v)
bei Börsenschluß	*(beye BEWr-sen-shlUS)*	at the close
bei Börsenschluß kaufen	*(beye BEWr-sen-shlUS kOW-fen)*	buy on close (v)
bei Sicht	*(beye sikht)*	at sight

beifügen	*(beye fEW-gen)*	attach (v) (affix, adhere)
Beilage (f)	*(bEYE-lah-geh)*	insert
Beirat (m)	*(BEYE-raat)*	advisory council
Belastung (f)	*(beh-lAHs-tunk)*	encumbrance
Beleg (m)	*(beh-lAYg)*	voucher
Belegschaft (f)	*(beh-lAYg-shahft)*	labor force, personnel
Beleihung (f)	*(beh-lEYE-unk)*	hypothecation
Beleihungswert (m)	*(beh-lEYE-unks-vEHRt)*	loan value
Belohnung (f)	*(beh-lOHn-unk)*	reward
Benachrichtigungs-schreiben (n)	*(beh-nAKH-reekh-tee-gunks-shrEYE-ben)*	advice note
benutzerfreundlich	*(beh-nU-tsuh-frOYNd-likh)*	user-friendly
Benzin (n)	*(ben-tsEEn)*	gasoline
Benzintank (m)	*(ben-tsEEn-tahnk)*	gasoline tank
Benzinverbrauch (m)	*(ben-tsEEn-fuh-brOWkh)*	gas consumption
Benzol (n)	*(BEHN-tsol)*	benzene
Beobachtungskup-pel (f)	*(beh-OH-bahkh-tungs-kUP-pel)*	cupola
beraten	*(buh-rAAT-en)*	advise (v)
Berater (m)	*(buh-rAA-tuh)*	consultant
Beratungsdienst (m)	*(buh-rAA-tungs-deenst)*	advisory service
berechtigt sein	*(beh-rehkh-tIGT seyen)*	authority, to have (v)
Bereitstellungfonds (m)	*(beh-rEYEt-shtEHL-lunk-fOH)*	appropriation
bergen	*(BAYr-gehn)*	salvage (v)
Bergungskosten (pl)	*(BAYr-gunks-kOS-ten)*	salvage charges
Bergungswert (m)	*(BAYr-gunks-vEHRt)*	salvage value (recovery)
Bericht (m)	*(beh-rIKHt)*	report
berichtigen	*(beh-rIKH-tee-gen)*	adjust (v) (correct)
berichtigter cif-Preis (m)	*(beh-rIKH-tig-tuh TSAY-ee-ehf-prEYEs)*	adjusted CIF price
Berichtigungsbu-chung (f)	*(beh-rIKH-tee-gunks-bOO-khunk)*	adjusting entry

B

B

Berichtigungskon-to (n)	*(beh-rIKH-tee-gunks-kON-toh)*	adjustment account
Beruf (m)	*(beh-rOOf)*	occupation, profession
Berufsrisiko (n)	*(beh-rOOfs-rEE-see-koh)*	occupational hazard
Beruhigungsmittel (n)	*(beh-rOO-I-gungs-mit-tel)*	sedative
Beschaffung (f)	*(beh-shAF-funk)*	procurement
Bescheinigung (f)	*(beh-shEYEn-igunk)*	attestation, certificate
Beschlagnahme (f)	*(beh-shlAHg-nAA-meh)*	garnishment
beschlagnahmen	*(beh-shlAHg-nAA-men)*	attach (v), impound (v)
beschleunigen	*(beh-shlOY-ni-gen)*	speed up (v)
Beschluß (m)	*(beh-shlUS)*	resolution
Beschlußfähigkeit (f)	*(beh-shlUS-fAY-hig-keyet)*	quorum
beschränkte Haf-tung (f)	*(beh-shrAYnk-teh hAHf-tunk)*	limited liability
Besitz (m)	*(beh-zITs)*	ownership, property
Besitzdauer (f)	*(beh-zITs-dOW-uh)*	holding period
Besitzer (m)	*(beh-zITs-tsuh)*	holder, owner
Besitzwechsel (m)	*(beh-zITs-vEHk-sehl)*	note receivable
Bestand (m)	*(beh-shtahnt)*	inventory
Bestand an Fertig-waren (m)	*(beh-shtahnt ahn fAYr-tig-vaar-en)*	finished goods inventory
Bestandsüberwa-chung (f)	*(beh-shtahnts-EWb-uh-vAAkh-unk)*	inventory control
Bestandteil (m)	*(beh-shtuhnd-teyel)*	component
bestätigen	*(beh-shtAY-tigen)*	acknowledge (v)
bestätigter Scheck (m)	*(beh-shtAY-tikh-tuh shehk)*	certified check
Bestätigung (f)	*(beh-shtAY-ti-gunk)*	certificate
Bestechung (f)	*(beh-shtEHKH-unk)*	graft
bestellen	*(beh-shtEHL-len)*	order (v)
Bestellnummer (f)	*(beh-shtEHL-nUm-uh)*	order number
Bestellschein (m)	*(beh-shtEHL-sheyen)*	order form
Bestellung (f)	*(beh-shtEHL-lunk)*	order, purchase order
bestenfalls	*(beh-sten-fahls)*	at best

bestens kaufen	*(beh-stens kOW-fen)*	at or better, buy at best (v)
Besteuerung (f)	*(beh-shtOY-uh-runk)*	assessment, taxation
Besteuerungs-grundlage (f)	*(beh-shtOY-uh-runks-grUNd-laa-geh)*	tax base
bestimmen	*(beh-shtIM-men)*	earmark (v)
bestimmte Zeit-dauer (f)	*(beh-shtIM-teh tsEYEt-dOW-uh)*	fixed term
Betäubungsmittel (n)	*(beh-tOY-bungs-mit-tel)*	anaesthetic, narcotic
Beteiligter (m)	*(beh-tEYE-lig-tuh)*	partner
Beteiligung an Kapitalgesell-schaften (f)	*(beh-tEYE-li-gunk ahn kah-pi-tAAL-geh-zEL-shahf-ten)*	equity investments
Beteiligungsanleihe (f)	*(beh-tEYE-li-gunks-AHN-leye-eh)*	participation loan
Beteiligungsgebühr (f)	*(beh-tEYE-li-gunks-geh-bEWr)*	participation fee
Betrag (m)	*(beh-trAHk)*	amount
Betrauter (m)	*(beh-trOW-tuh)*	fiduciary
betreffs	*(beh-trehfs)*	with regard to
betriebliche Lei-stungsfähigkeit (f)	*(beh-trEEp-likh-eh lEYEs-tungs-fAY-hig-keyet)*	plant capacity
Betriebsbilanz (f)	*(beh-trEEps-bEE-laants)*	working balance
Betriebsbudget (n)	*(beh-trEEps-bew-tshEH)*	operating budget
Betriebseinheit (f)	*(beh-trEEps-eyen-heyet)*	operating unit
Betriebseinkom-men (n)	*(beh-trEEps-EYEn-kOM-mehn)*	operating income
Betriebsergebnis-rechnung (f)	*(beh-trEEps-ayr-gAYb-nis-rEHKH-nunk)*	operating statement
Betriebsführung (f)	*(beh-trEEps-fEW-runk)*	management, operations management
Betriebsführung durch Zielvorga-be (f)	*(beh-trEEps-fEW-runk durkh tsEEl-FOHR-gaa-beh)*	management by objectives
Betriebsführungs-schaubild (n)	*(beh-trEEps-fEW-runks-show-bild)*	management chart
Betriebsgewinn (m)	*(beh-trEEps-geh-vIN)*	operating profit

B

Betriebsjahr (n)	*(beh-trEEps-yaar)*	financial year
Betriebskapital (n)	*(beh-trEEps-kah-pi-tAAL)*	working capital
Betriebskosten (pl)	*(beh-trEEps-kOS-ten)*	carrying charges, operating expenses
Betriebsleiter (m)	*(beh-trEEps-lEYE-tuh)*	plant manager
Betriebsleitung (f)	*(beh-trEEps-lEYE-tunk)*	business management
Betriebsmittel (pl)	*(beh-trEEps-mit-tEL)*	working funds
Betriebspolitik (f)	*(beh-trEEps-po-li-tEEk)*	business policy, company policy
Betriebstätigkeits- prüfung (f)	*(beh-trEEps-tAY-tig-keyets- prEW-funk)*	operations audit
Betriebstreuhand- versicherung (f)	*(beh-trEEps-trOY-hahnd- fuh-ZIKH-eh-runk)*	fidelity bond
Betriebsverlust (m)	*(beh-trEEps-fuh-lUst)*	operating loss
Betriebsvermögen (n)	*(beh-trEEps-fuh-mER-gen)*	working assets
Betriebsversicher- ung (f)	*(beh-trEEps-fuh-ZIKH-eh- runk)*	industrial insurance
Betriebszentrale (f)	*(beh-trEEps-tsen-trAA-leh)*	operations headquarters
Betrug (m)	*(beh-trOOg)*	fraud
Betrügerei (f)	*(beh-trEW-guh-rEYE)*	double dealing
bevollmächtigter Händler (m)	*(beh-fol-mAYKH-tig-tuh hEHn-dluh)*	authorized dealer
Bevollmächtigung (f)	*(beh-fol-mAYKH-ti-gunk)*	proxy
bevorrechtigte Forderungen (pl)	*(beh-FOHR-rehkh-tIG-teh FOHR duh-run-gen)*	preferential debts
bevorstehende Änderung (f)	*(beh-FOHR-shtay-hen-deh EHn-deh-runk)*	impending change
bewegliche Preis- skala (f)	*(beh-wAYg-li-kheh prEYEs- skAA-lah)*	sliding price scale
bewegliche Sache (f)	*(beh-wAYg-li-kheh zAAkh- eh)*	chattel
Beweglichkeit (f)	*(beh-vAYg-likh-keyet)*	mobility of labor
Bewegung (f)	*(beh-wAYg-unk)*	motion
bewerten	*(beh-vEHR-ten)*	appraise (v), assess (v)
Bewertung (f)	*(beh-vEHR-tunk)*	appraisal, estimate

Bewilligung (f)	*(beh-vIL-ee-gunk)*	approval
bezahlter Feiertag (m)	*(beh-tsAAl-tuh fEYE-uh-taak)*	paid holiday
Bezahlung (f)	*(beh-tsAA-lunk)*	disbursement
bezeugen	*(beh-tsOY-gen)*	witness (v)
Beziehungen zu den Anlegern (pl)	*(beh-tsEE-hun-gen tsoo dehn AHN-lAY-guhn)*	investor relations
Bezirksleiter (m)	*(beh-tsIRKs-lEYE-tuh)*	area manager
Bezogener (m)	*(beh-tsOH-gen-uh)*	drawee
Bezugsoption (f)	*(beh-tsOOgs-op-tsEEohn)*	call option
Bezugspreis (m)	*(beh-tsOOgs-prEYEs)*	subscription price (periodicals)
Bezugsrecht (n)	*(beh-tsOOgs-REHKHT)*	preemptive right
Biber (m)	*(bEE-buh)*	beaver
bieten	*(BEE-ten)*	offer (v)
Bilanz (f)	*(bee-lAHnts)*	balance, balance sheet
Bilanzabschluß (m)	*(bee-lAHnts-AHB-shlUS)*	financial statement
Bilanzierungsricht-linien (pl)	*(bee-lAHnts-EEr-unks-rikht-lEEn-ee-ehn)*	accounting principles
Bilanzperiode (f)	*(bee-lAHnts pay-ree-OH-deh)*	financial period
Bilanzprüfung (f)	*(bee-lAHnts-prEWf-unk)*	auditing balance sheet
Bilanzverschleie-rung (f)	*(bee-lAHnts-fuh-shlEYE-uh-runk)*	window dressing (balance sheet)
Bildschirm (m)	*(Bild-SHIrm)*	screen
billig	*(BIl-ikh)*	cheap
billigen	*(BIl-li-gen)*	approve (v)
binäre Zahlendar-stellung (f)	*(bee-nAYr-eh tsAA-len-dAAr-shtEHL-lunk)*	binary notation
Binärkode (m)	*(bee-nAYR-koh-deh)*	binary code
Binärschreibung (f)	*(bee-nAYr-shrEYE-bunk)*	binary notation
Binnenmarkt (m)	*(BIN-nehn-mAHrkt)*	home market
Biochemie (f)	*(BEE-o-KHAY-mee)*	biochemistry
Biologe (m)	*(BEE-o-LOH-geh)*	biologist
Biologie (f)	*(BEE-o-LOH-gee)*	biology

B

biologische Entsäuerung	*(bee-oh-LOHG-ish-eh ent-ZOY-eh-runk)*	biological deacidizing
biologischer Anbau (m)	*(bee-oh-LOHG-ish-ehr-AHN-bow)*	organic farming
Blankoakzept (n)	*(blAHN-koh-ahk-tsEPt)*	general acceptance
Blankoauftrag (m)	*(blAHN-koh-OWf-trAHk)*	blanket order
Blatt (n)	*(blAHT)*	sheet
Blaupause (f)	*(blOW-pOW-zeh)*	blueprint
Blut (n)	*(blOOT)*	blood
bluten	*(blOO-ten)*	bleed (v)
Bodenreform (f)	*(BOH-den-reh-fOHrm)*	land reform
Bodenschätze (pl)	*(BOH-den-shAY-tseh)*	natural resources
Bonitätsprüfung (f)	*(bon-i-tAYts-prEW-funk)*	credit rating
Bootsverleih ohne Mannschaft und Verpflegung (m)	*(bohts-vAYr-leye ohneh mAAn-shahft unt fuh-pflAY-gunk)*	bareboat charter
borgen	*(bohr-gen)*	borrow (v)
Börse (f)	*(bER-seh)*	market (stock market), stock exchange
Börsenbericht (m)	*(bER-zen-beh-rIKHT)*	market report
Börsenbrief (m)	*(bER-zen-brEEf)*	market letter
börsenfähige Effekten (pl)	*(bER-zen-fAY-hi-geh ef-fAYk-ten)*	negotiable securities
Börsenfernschreiber (m)	*(bER-zen-fayrn-shrEYE-buh)*	ticker (stock prices)
börsengängige Werte (pl)	*(bER-zen-gAYng-igeh vEHR-teh)*	marketable securities
Börsenindex (m)	*(bER-zen-IN-dex)*	market index, stock index
Börsenmakler (m)	*(bER-zen-mAHk-luh)*	stockbroker, market-maker
Börsenmakler in kleinen Mengen (m)	*(bER-zen-mAHk-luh in klEYE-nen mAYn-gen)*	odd lot broker
Börsenmarkteinstufung (f)	*(bER-zen-mAHrkt-eyen-shtUf-unk)*	market rating
Börsensaal (m)	*(bER-zen-zaal)*	floor (stock exchange)
Börsenschluß (m)	*(bER-zen-shlUS)*	market closing
Börsenspezialist (m)	*(bER-zen-shpay-tsee-ah-lISt)*	specialist (stock exchange)

Börsentermingese- **häft (n)**	*(bER-zen-tayr-mEEn-ge-* *shehft)*	option (put or call options)
Börsentip (m)	*(bER-zen-tip)*	tip (inside information)
Börsenvollmacht **(f)**	*(bER-zen-fOHl-mahkht)*	stock power
Börsenwert (m)	*(bER-zen-vEHRt)*	exchange value (on stock exchange)
botanisch	*(bo-tAA-nish)*	botanic
Botendienst (m)	*(BOH-ten-dEEntst)*	courier service
Boykott (m)	*(boy-KOT)*	boycott
Branche (f)	*(brAHN-sheh)*	line of business
Bremse (f)	*(brEHM-zeh)*	brake
Bremspedal (n)	*(brEHMs-PEH-dahl)*	brake pedal
Brief (m)	*(brEEf)*	letter
Brief und Geld	*(brEEf unt GEHLT)*	bid and asked
Briefkurs (m)	*(brEEf-koors)*	asked price, offered rate
Brieftasche (f)	*(brEEF-tAH-SHeh)*	billfold, purse
Briefwechsel (m)	*(brEEf-vEHk-sel)*	correspondence
Brillenetui (n)	*(brIL-len-e-tuEE)*	eyeglass case
broschiert	*(bro-shEERt)*	sewn
Broschüre (f)	*(bro-shEW-reh)*	pamphlet
Brotkorb (m)	*(brOT-korb)*	breadbasket
Bruttoanlageninve- **stition (f)**	*(BRU-toh-AHN-laa-gen-in-* *vehs-ti-tsi-OHn)*	gross investment
Bruttoeinkaufs- **preis (m)**	*(BRU-toh-eyen-kOWfs-* *prEYEs)*	invoice cost
Bruttoeinkommen **(n)**	*(BRU-toh-eyen-kOM-mehn)*	gross income
Bruttoeinnahmen **(pl)**	*(BRU-toh-eyen-nAA-men)*	gross receipts
Bruttoertrag (m)	*(BRU-toh-uh-trAHk)*	gross yield
Bruttogewinn (m)	*(BRU-toh-geh-vIN)*	gross profit
Bruttogewinnspan- **ne (f)**	*(BRU-toh-geh-vIN-shpAHn-* *neh)*	gross margin
Bruttopreis (m)	*(BRU-toh-prEYEs)*	gross price
Bruttopreisunter- **schied (m)**	*(BRU-toh-prEYEs-un-tuh-* *shEEd)*	gross spread

B

Bruttosozialpro-dukt (n)	*(BRU-toh-zoh-tsEE-aal-proh-dUKt)*	gross domestic product, gross national product
Bruttoumsatz (m)	*(BRU-toh-um-zAHts)*	gross sales
Bruttoverlust (m)	*(BRU-toh-fuh-lUst)*	gross loss
Buch (n)	*(bOOKH)*	book
Buchforderungen (pl)	*(bOOkh-FOHR-duh-run-gen)*	accounts receivable
Buchführung der bar durchge-führten Geschäf-te (f)	*(bOOkh-fEWr-unk duh baar dURKH-geh-fEWr-ten geh-shEHF-teh)*	cash-basis accounting
Buchgewinn (m)	*(bOOkh-geh-vIN)*	paper profit
Buchhalter(m)	*(bOOkh-hAAl-tuh)*	accountant
Buchhaltung (f)	*(bOOkh-hAAl-tunk)*	accounting department, bookkeeping
Buchhaltungsleiter (m)	*(bOOkh-hAAl-tunks-lEYE-tuh)*	chief accountant
Buchhülle	*(bOOkh-hewl-leh)*	jacket (book)
Buchinventar (n)	*(bOOkh-in-fehn-tAAr)*	book inventory
Buchprüfer (m)	*(bOOkh-prEWf-uh)*	auditor
Buchrücken (m)	*(bOOKH-rEW-ken)*	spine
Buchschulden (pl)	*(bOOkh-shOOl-dehn)*	accounts payable
Buchstabe (m)	*(bOOKH-shtah-beh)*	letter
Buchungsmethode (f)	*(bOO-khungs-may-tOH-deh)*	accounting method
Buchungszeitraum (m)	*(bOO-khungs-tsEYEt-rowm)*	accounting period
Buchwert (m)	*(bOOkh-vEHRt)*	book value, carrying value
Buchwert pro Aktie (m)	*(bOOkh-vEHRt pro ak-tsEE-eh)*	book value per share
Budget (n)	*(bew-djEH)*	budget
Bukett (n)	*(bU-ket)*	bouquet
Bürgschaft (f)	*(bEWrg-shahft)*	guarantee, warrant (surety)
Büro (n)	*(bEW-roh)*	office
Büroangestellter (m)	*(bEW-roh-AHN-geh-shtEHL-tuh)*	white-collar worker
Bürokrat (m)	*(bew-roh-krAAt)*	bureaucrat
Bürokratie (f)	*(bew-roh-kraa-tEE)*	red tape

Büroleitung (f)	*(bEW-roh-lEYE-tunk)*	office management
Butterdose (f)	*(BUTuh-do-zeh)*	butter dish
Byte (n)	*(beyet)*	byte

C

Champagnerglas (n)	*(shahm-pAHN-yuh-glAAs)*	champagne glass
Charakter (m)	*(kah-rAHK-tuh)*	character
Chemie (f)	*(KHAY-mee)*	chemistry
chemisch	*(KHAY-mish)*	chemical
Chlorid (n)	*(khlOH-rit)*	chloride
Chloroform (n)	*(khlOH-ro-FOrm)*	chloroform
Chrom (n)	*(khrOHm)*	chromium
Computer (m)	*(kom-pyU-tuh)*	computer
Computerausdruck (m)	*(kom-pyU-tuh-OWs-druk)*	printout
Computereingabe (f)	*(kom-pyU-tuh-eyen-gaa-beh)*	computer input
Computerergebnis (n)	*(kom-pyU-tuh-ayr-gAYb-nis)*	computer output
Computerprogramm (n)	*(kom-pyU-tuh-proh-grAHm)*	computer program, software
Computersprache (f)	*(kom-pyU-tuh-shprAA-kheh)*	computer language
Computerterminal (n)	*(kom-pyU-tuh-tayr-mEE-nahl)*	computer terminal
Container (m)	*(kon-tAYnuh)*	container
Couturier (m)	*(ku-tEW-ree-ay)*	high fashion designer

D

Dachgesellschaft (f)	*(dahKH-geh-zEL-shahft)*	holding company, parent company
Damenunterwäsche (pl)	*(DAA-men-UN-tuh-vEH-sheh)*	lingerie
daneben	*(daa-nAY-ben)*	alongside

Darlehn (n)	*(dAAr-layn)*	loan
Darlehnsvertrag (m)	*(dAAr-layns-fuh-trAHk)*	loan agreement
Daten (pl)	*(dAA-ten)*	data
Datenbank (f)	*(dAA-ten-bahnk)*	data bank
Datenerwerb (m)	*(dAA-ten-ayr-vAYrb)*	data acquisition
Datenspeicherung (f)	*(dAA-ten-shpEYE-keh-runk)*	computer storage
Datenverarbeitung (f)	*(dAA-ten-fuh-ahr-bEYE-tunk)*	data processing
Datenverarbeitung verbunden (m)	*(dAA-ten-fuh-ahr-bEYE-tunk fuh-bOOn-den)*	on line
Datenverarbei- tungszentrale (f)	*(dAA-ten-fuh-ahr-bEYE-tungs-tsen-trAA-leh)*	computer center
Dauer eines Paten- tes (f)	*(dOW-uh EYE-nehs pah-tEHn-tes)*	life of a patent
Dauerauftrag (m)	*(dOW-uh-OWf-trAHk)*	standing order
dauerhafte Ver- brauchsgüter (pl)	*(dOW-uh-hahf-teh fuh-brOWkhs-gEW-tuh)*	durable goods
dazwischentreten	*(dah-tsvISHen-trEH-ten)*	intervene (v)
Debetposten (m)	*(deh-beht-pOS-ten)*	debit entry
Deckung (f)	*(DEK-kunk)*	collateral
Deckungsbeitrags- rechnung (f)	*(DEK-kunks-beye-trAAgs-rEHKH-nunk)*	breakeven analysis
Deckungsverhält- nis (n)	*(DEK-kunks-fuh-hEHLt-nis)*	cover ratio
Defizit (n)	*(DEH-fi-tsIT)*	deficit
Defizitfinanzierung (f)	*(day-fITS-it-fee-nahn-tsEE-runk)*	deficit financing
Deflation (f)	*(day-flAA-tsEE-ohn)*	deflation
dehnbarer Zollta- rif (m)	*(dAYN-baar-uh-tsOL-tah-rIF)*	flexible tariff
Dehnbarkeit (f)	*(dAYN-baar-kEYET)*	malleability
Delikthandlung (f)	*(deh-lIkt-hAHnd-lunk)*	tort
dem Preis entspre- chen	*(dehm prEYEs ehnt-shprAY-khen)*	meet the price (v)
demographisch	*(dAY-moh-grAA-fish)*	demographic

den Geschäftsge-winn wieder anlegen	*(dehn ge-shEHfts-geh-vIN vee-duh AHN-lay-gen)*	plow back earnings (v)
den Verlust auffangen	*(dehn fuh-lUst OWf-fahng-en)*	absorb the loss (v)
Deponie (f)	*(DEH-poh-nee)*	landfill
Deport (m)	*(day-pOHrt)*	backwardation
Depositenkonto (n)	*(deh-poh-zIT-en-kON-toh)*	deposit account
Depositenschein (m)	*(deh-poh-zIT-en-shEYEn)*	certificate of deposit
Depositenzertifikat (n)	*(deh-poh-zIT-en-tsEHR-ti-fi-kaat)*	certificate of deposit
Depot (n)	*(day-pOH)*	depository
Depression (f)	*(deh-preh-sEE-ohn)*	depression
depressionshem-mend	*(deh-pres-sI-ONs-hEHM-ment)*	antidepressant
Desinvestition (f)	*(days-in-vehs-ti-tsi-OHn)*	divestment
Dessertteller (m)	*(duh dehs-sEHah-tel-luh)*	dessert plate
Detailgeschäft (n)	*(deh-tEYE-geh-shEHft)*	retail
Detailverkauf (m)	*(deh-tEYE-fuh-kOWf)*	retail trade
Devisen (pl)	*(deh-vEE-zen)*	foreign currency, foreign exchange
Devisenausländer (m)	*(deh-vEE-zen)*	nonresident
Devisengelder (pl)	*(deh-vEE-zen-gEL-duh)*	monetary credits
Devisenkontrolle (f)	*(deh-vEE-sen-kon-trOL-leh)*	exchange control
Dezimalsystem (n)	*(deh-tsee-mAAl-zew-stAYm)*	metric system
Diagramm	*(dee-ah-grAHm)*	graph
Dichte (f)	*(DIKH-teh)*	density
Dieberei (f)	*(dEE-buh-rEYE)*	pilferage
Dienstalter (n)	*(dEENst-AAl-tuh)*	seniority
Dienstvertrag (m)	*(dEENst-fuh-trAHk)*	service contract
Differenz (f)	*(di-feh-rEHnts)*	spread
digital	*(di-gi-tAAl)*	digital
digitale Jahres-summenab-schreibung (f)	*(di-gi-tAA-leh yAAr-ehs-zu-men-AHB-shrEYE-bunk)*	sum-of-the-years digits

D

Digitalrechner (m)	*(dee-gee-tAAl-rEHKH-nuh)*	digital computer
direkt verkaufen	*(di-REHKT fuh-kOW-fen)*	sell direct (v)
Direktabsatz (m)	*(di-REHKT-AHB-zATS)*	direct selling
direkte Auslagen (pl)	*(di-REHKT-eh-OWs-lah-gen)*	direct expenses
direkte Kosten (pl)	*(di-REHKT-eh kOS-ten)*	direct cost
direkte Kursnotierung (f)	*(di-REHKT-koors-noh-tEE-runk)*	direct quotation (stocks)
direkte Preisangabe (f)	*(di-REHKT-eh prEYEs-AHN-gaa-beh)*	direct quotation
direkte Verschiffung (f)	*(di-REHKT-eh-fuh-shIF-funk)*	drop shipment
Direktinvestition (f)	*(di-REHKT-in-vehs-ti-tsi-OHn)*	direct investment
Direktor (m)	*(di-REHK-tohr)*	director, management
Direktplazierung (f)	*(di-REHKT-plAA-tsEE-runk)*	private placement
Direktverkauf (m)	*(di-REHKT-fuh-kOWf)*	direct selling
Direktverkauf an der Haustür (m)	*(di-REHKT-fuh-kOWf ahn duh hOWs-tEWr)*	house-to-house selling
dirigieren	*(di-ri-gEE-ren)*	manage (v)
Diskette (f)	*(dis-kEH-teh)*	floppy disk
Diskont (m)	*(dIS-kont)*	discount
Diskontbank (f)	*(dIS-kont-bahnk)*	acceptance house
Diskontierung (f)	*(dIS-kon-tEE-runk)*	discounting
Diskontsatz (m)	*(dIS-kont-zΛΛts)*	discount rate
Diskontwertpapiere (pl)	*(dIS-kont-vEHRt-pah-pEE-reh)*	discount securities
Disposition (f)	*(dIS-po-zi-tsEE-ohn)*	table of contents
Diuretikum (n)	*(dEE-U-reh-ti-kum)*	diuretic
Diversifikation (f)	*(dee-vayr-si-fi-kah-tsEE-ohn)*	diversification
Dividende (f)	*(di-vi-dEHN-deh)*	dividend
Dividendenertrag (m)	*(di-vi-dEHN-deh-uh-trAHk)*	dividend yield
dividendlos	*(di-vi-dEHN-deh-lohs)*	ex dividend
Dockempfangsschein (m)	*(DOK-em-pfahnks-shEYEn)*	dock (ship's) receipt

Dockgebühren (pl)	*(DOK-geh-bEW-ren)*	dock handling charges
Dokument (n)	*(dok-OO-mehnt)*	document
Doppelbesteuerung (f)	*(DOP-pel-beh-shTOY-uh-runk)*	double taxation
doppelte Buchfüh-rung (f)	*(DOP-pel-teh-bOOkh-fEW-runk)*	double-entry bookkeeping
Doppelverdienst (m)	*(DOP-pel-fuh-dEEnst)*	moonlighting
Doppelzüngigkeit (f)	*(DOP-pel-tsEWng-ig-keyet)*	double dealing
Dosierung (f)	*(doh-ZEE-runk)*	dosage
Dotation (f)	*(doh-tah-tsEE-ohn)*	endowment
Dragée (n)	*(drah-SHAY)*	pellet
Draht (m)	*(drAAt)*	wire
Drahtüberweisung (f)	*(drAAt-EW-buh-vEYE-zunk)*	cable transfer
drapieren	*(drah-PEE-ren)*	drape (v)
Drehbuch (n)	*(dRAY-bOOkh)*	script
Drehmoment (m)	*(drAY-mo-ment)*	torque
dringend	*(drING-ent)*	urgent
Drittexporteur (m)	*(drit-ex-pOHR-tEWr)*	third-party exporter
Droge (f)	*(drOH-geh)*	drug
Druck (m)	*(drUK)*	pressure
Druck (m)	*(drUK)*	print
Druck (m)	*(drUK)*	printing
Drucklauf (m)	*(drUK-lowf)*	print run
Drucksache (f)	*(drOOk-zahkh-eh)*	printed matter
Dumping (n)	*(dum-pink)*	dumping (goods in foreign market)
Duopol (n)	*(doo-oh-pOHl)*	duopoly
Durchsatz (m)	*(dURKH-zAHts)*	throughput
Durchschnitt (m)	*(dURKH-shnIT)*	mean, average
durchschnittliche Einheitskosten (pl)	*(dURKH-shnIT-li-kheh eyen-heyets-kOS-ten)*	average unit cost
durchschnittliche Lebensdauer (f)	*(dURKH-shnIT-li-kheh lAY-bens-dOW-uh)*	average life

D

Durchschnittsko-sten (pl)	*(dURKH-shnITs-kOS-ten)*	average cost
Durchschnittspreis (m)	*(dURKH-shnITs-prEYEs)*	average price

E

Echtheitsbeschein-igung für Anti-quitäten (f)	*(eKHT-heyets-beh-shEYE-ni-gunk fEWr ahnti-kvee-tAY-ten)*	antique authenticity certifi-cate
Echtzeit (f)	*(eKHT-tsEYEt)*	real time
Effekten (pl)	*(eh-fEHK-ten)*	securities
Effektenbörse (f)	*(eh-fEHK-ten-bER-zeh)*	stock market
Effektenüberträger (m)	*(eh-fEHK-EW-buh-trAY-guh)*	transfer agent
Effektiveinnahmen (pl)	*(eh-fEHK-tEE-feh-EYEn-nAA-men)*	actuals
effektiver Geld-wert (m)	*(eh-fEHK-tEE-fuh GEHLT-vEHRt)*	actual cash value
Effektivpreis (m)	*(eh-fEHK-tEEf-prEYEs)*	real price
Effektivverzinsung (f)	*(eh-fEHK-tEEf-fuh-tsINs-zunk)*	effective yield, yield to maturity
Effizienz (f)	*(ef-fi-tsEE-ents)*	efficiency
Eidechsenleder (n)	*(EYE-dekh-sen-lAY-duh)*	lizard (skin)
eidesstattliche Erklärung (f)	*(EYEd-ehs-shtAAt-likh-eh ayr-klAY-runk)*	affidavit
eigener Wagen-park (m)	*(EYE-gen-uh VAA-gen-paark)*	private fleet
Eigenkapital (n)	*(EYE-gen-kah-pi-tAAL)*	equity, net asset worth
Eigenkapitalanteil (m)	*(EYE-gen-kah-pi-tAAL-AHN-teyel)*	equity share
Eigenkapitalver-wässerung (f)	*(EYE-gen-kah-pi-tAAL-fuh-vEHS-seh-runk)*	dilution of equity
Eigentum (n)	*(EYE-gen-tOOm)*	ownership, property
Eigentum der öffentlichen Hand (n)	*(EYE-gen-tOOm duh EWf-ent-lIKH-en)*	public property
Eigentümer (m)	*(EYE-gen-tEWm-uh)*	proprietor

D

Eigentümer ohne Leitungsfunktion (m)	*(EYE-gen-tEWm-uh ohneh lEYE-tungs-foonk-tsEE-ohn)*	absentee owner
Eigentumstitel (m)	*(EYE-gen-tOOms-tI-tel)*	title
Eigentumsvorbehalt des Verkäufers (m)	*(EYE-gen-tOOms-FOHR-beh-hahlt dehs fuh-kOY-fehrs)*	vendor's lien
Eigenwechsel (m)	*(EYE-gen-vEHK-sel)*	promissory note
Eilauftrag (m)	*(EYEl-OWf-trAHk)*	rush order
ein Angebot machen	*(eyen AHN-geh-boht mAA-khen)*	put in a bid (v)
ein Schiff außer Dienst stellen	*(eyen shIF OW-suh dEEnst shtEHL-en)*	lay up (v)
einbringen	*(EYEn-bRIN-gehn)*	yield (v)
eine Emission begeben	*(EYE-neh eh-mi-see-OHn beh-gAY-ben)*	float (v) (issue stock)
eine Interessengemeinschaft bilden	*(EYE-neh in-tayr-rEHs-sens-geh-mEYEn-shahft bil-den)*	pooling of interests
einen Auftrag erteilen	*(EYE-neh-en OWf-trAHk ayr-tEYE-len)*	place an order (v)
einen Fehler beseitigen	*(EYE-nehn fAY-luh beh-sEYE-ti-gen)*	debug (v) (computers)
einen konkurrenzfähigen Preis festsetzen können	*(EYE-nehn kon-kOO-rents-fAY-hi-gen prEYEs fEHst-zeh-tsen kERn-nen)*	meet the price
einen Preis ansetzen	*(EYE-neh-en prEYEs AHN-zeh-tsen)*	price
Einfluß (m)	*(EYEn-flus)*	leverage
Einfuhr (f)	*(EYEn-foor)*	import
Einfuhrdeklaration (f)	*(EYEn-foor-deh-klah-rah-tsEE-ohn)*	import entry
Einfuhrdepots (pl)	*(EYEn-foor-day-pOHs)*	import deposits
einführen	*(EYEn-fEW-ren)*	import (v)
Einfuhrerklärung (f)	*(EYEn-foor-ayr-klAY-runk)*	import declaration
Einfuhrerlaubnis (f)	*(EYEn-foor-ayr-lOWb-nis)*	import license
Einfuhrquote (f)	*(EYEn-foor-kvOH-teh)*	import quota

E

Einfuhrsteuer (f)	*(EYEn-foor-shtOY-uh)*	import tax
Einführung (f)	*(EYEn-FEWR-runk)*	introduction
Einfuhrvorschriften (pl)	*(EYEn-foor-FOHR-shriften)*	import regulations
Einfuhrzoll (m)	*(EYEn-foor-tsOL)*	import duty, import tariff
Eingabe (f)	*(EYEn-gaa-beh)*	input
Eingaben-Ausgaben Analyse (f)	*(EYEn-gAA-ben-OWs-gAA-ben ah-nah-lEW-zeh)*	input-output analysis
eingefrorene Guthaben (pl)	*(EYEn-ge-frOH-reh-neh gOOt-hAA-ben)*	frozen assets
eingegliedertes Führungssystem (n)	*(EYEn-geh-glEE-dayr-tehs fEW-runks-zew-stAYm)*	integrated management system
eingelöster Scheck (m)	*(EYEn-geh-lEWs-tuh shek)*	cancelled check
eingeschränktes Indossament (n)	*(EYEn-geh-shrAYnk-tes in-dos-ah-mEH)*	qualified acceptance endorsement
eingetragener Scheck (m)	*(EYEn-geh-trAA-gen-uh shek)*	registered check
eingetragener Vertreter (m)	*(EYEn-geh-trAA-gen-uh fuh-trAY-tuh)*	registered representative
eingetragenes Lagerhaus (n)	*(EYEn-geh-trAA-gen-es LAA-guh-hOWs)*	regular warehouse
eingetragenes Warenzeichen (n)	*(EYEn-ge-trAA-gen-es vAA-ren-tsEYE-khen)*	registered trademark
eingezahlte Anteile (pl)	*(EYEn-ge-tsAAl-teh AHN-teye-leh)*	paid up shares
einheitlicher Satz (m)	*(EYEn-heyet-likh-uh zAH-ts)*	flat rate
Einkaufsleiter (m)	*(EYEn-kOWfs-lEYE-tuh)*	purchasing agent, purchasing manager
Einkaufstasche (f)	*(EYEn-kOWfs-tAH-SHeh)*	tote bag
Einkommen (n)	*(EYEn-kOM-mehn)*	income
Einkommensobligation (f)	*(EYEn-kOM-mehnz-ob-li-gah-tsEE-ohn)*	revenue bond
Einkommensstufe (f)	*(EYEn-kOM-mehnz-shtU-feh)*	income bracket
Einkommensteuer (f)	*(EYEn-kOM-mehnz-stOY-uh)*	income tax

E

Einlage (f)	*(EYEn-laa-geh)*	deposit
Einlage (f)	*(EYEn-laa-geh)*	insert
Einlösungsprämie (f)	*(EYEn-lER-zoongz-prAY-mee-eh)*	redemption premium
Einlösungsvergütung (f)	*(EYEn-lER-zoongz-fuh-gEW-tunk)*	redemption allowance
einmalige Summe (f)	*(EYEn-maa-lee-geh tsum-meh)*	lump sum
Einnahme (f)	*(EYEn-nAA-meh)*	revenue, earnings
einreichen	*(EYEn-reye-khen)*	file (v) (submit forms)
Einreisebewilligung (f)	*(EYEn-reye-zeh-beh-vIL-lee-gunk)*	entry permit
Einschreibepost (f)	*(EYEn-shrEYE-beh-pOSt)*	registered mail
Einschußkonto (n)	*(EYEn-shUs-kON-toh)*	marginal account
Einsparung (f)	*(EYEn-shpAA-runk)*	cutback
Einspritzdüse (f)	*(EYEn-shprITS-dew-zeh)*	injector
Einspruch (m)	*(EYEn-shprUKH)*	veto
einstellen	*(EYEn-shtel-len)*	tune (v)
Einstellung (f)	*(EYEn-shtEHL-lunk)*	abatement (suspension)
Einstellung ungelernter Arbeitskräfte (f)	*(EYEn-shtEHL-lunk un-geh-lAYrn-tuh AHR-beyets-krehf-teh)*	dilution of labor
Einstellungsquote (f)	*(EYEn-shtEHL-lunks-kvOH-teh)*	accession rate
einstweilig	*(EYEnst-vEYE-likh)*	interim
Eintrag (m)	*(EYEn-traag)*	item
einwandfreie Überbringung (f)	*(EYEn-vahnd-frEYE-eh EW-buh-brING-unk)*	good delivery
Einzelfertigungsbetrieb (m)	*(EYEn-tsehl-fAYr-tee-gunks-beh-trEEp)*	job shop
Einzelfirma (f)	*(EYEn-tsehl-fIR-mah)*	sole proprietorship
Einzelhandel (m)	*(EYEn-tsehl-hAHn-dehl)*	retail, retail trade
Einzelhandelspreis (m)	*(EYEn-tsehl-hAHn-dehls-prEYEs)*	retail price
Einzelhandelsumsatzsteuer (f)	*(EYEn-tsehl-hAHn-dehls-um-zAHts-shtOY-uh)*	retail sales tax
Einzelhandelsverkaufsstelle (f)	*(EYEn-tsehl-hAHn-dehls-fuh-kOWf-shtEHL-leh)*	retail outlet

E

Einzelhandelswaren (pl)	*(EYEn-tsehl-hAHn-dehls-vAA-ren)*	retail merchandise
Einzelkosten (pl)	*(EYEn-tsehl-kOS-ten)*	direct cost
einzeln aufführen	*(EYEn-tsehln OWf-fEW-ren)*	itemize (v)
Einzelverkauf (m)	*(EYEn-tsehl-fuh-kOWf)*	retail
einziehen	*(EYEn-tsEE-hen)*	call (v)
Einziehungszeit (f)	*(EYEn-tsEE-unks-tsEYEt)*	collection period
Eisen (n)	*(EYE-zen)*	iron
Eisenbahn (f)	*(EYE-zen-bAAn)*	railroad
Eisenbahnbetriebs-mittel (pl)	*(EYE-zen-bAAn-beh-trEEps-mit-tEL)*	rolling stock
Eisenbitterkalk (m)	*(EYE-zen-bIT-tuh-kahlk)*	limestone
Eisenerz (n)	*(EYE-zen-EHRTS)*	iron ore
Eisenguß (m)	*(EYE-zen-gUS)*	cast iron
Eisenlegierungen (f)	*(EYE-zen-leh-gEE-run-gen)*	ferroalloys
Eisenwaren (pl)	*(EYE-zen-vAA-ren)*	hardware
Elastizität (f) von Angebot (n)	*(eh-lahs-ti-tsee-tAYt fon AHN-geh-boht)*	elasticity
Elekrizität (f)	*(eh-lEHk-tri-tsee-TAYt)*	electricity
Elektrode (f)	*(eh-lEHk-tROH-deh)*	electrode
Elektrolyse (f)	*(eh-lEHk-tro-LEW-zeh)*	electrolysis
Elektrolyseprozeß (m)	*(eh-lEHk-tro-LEW-zeh-pRO-tsehs)*	electrolytic process
Elektron (n)	*(eh-lEHk-trOIIN)*	electron
elektronisch	*(eh-lEHk-trOH-nish)*	electronic
elektronisches Weissbrett (n)	*(eh-lehk-trOH-nish-es vEYEs-breht)*	electronic whiteboard
elektrostatisch	*(eh-lEHk-tro-stAH-tish)*	electrostatic
Elektrotechnik (f)	*(eh-lehk-troh-tEHKH-nik)*	electrical engineering
Element (n)	*(eh-leh-MENt)*	element
Emission (f)	*(eh-mi-see-OHn)*	stock issue
Emissionsbank (f)	*(eh-mi-see-OHns-bahnk)*	investment bank, underwriter (securities)
emittieren	*(ay-mee-tEE-ren)*	issue (v)

E

Empfang (m)	*(em-pfAHnk)*	receipt (reception)
Empfänger (m)	*(em-pfEHN-guh)*	consignee
Empfehlungs-schreiben (n)	*(em-pfAY lunks-shrEYE-ben)*	letter of introduction
Enderzeugnis (n)	*(EHNt-uh-tsOYg-nis)*	end product
Endprodukte (pl)	*(EHnd-Pro-dUk-teh)*	finished products
Energiequelle (f)	*(e-ner-GEE-kvEL-eh)*	energy source
Energieverbrauch (m)	*(e-ner-GEE-fuh-browkh)*	energy consumption
englische Tonne (f)	*(AYN-glish-eh tON-neh)*	long ton
Enteignung (f)	*(ehnt-AYg-nunk)*	expropriation
Enteisungsanlage (f)	*(ent-EYE-zunks-AHN-lah-geh)*	defroster
Entfroster (m)	*(ent-frOS-tuh)*	defroster
Entgeld (n)	*(EHNt-GEHLT)*	consideration (contract law)
entladen	*(EHNt-lAA-den)*	unload (v)
entlassen	*(EHNt-lAH-sen)*	discharge (v), fire, lay off(v)
Entlassungsabfindung (f)	*(EHNt-lAH-sunks-AHB-fIN-dunk)*	severance pay
entmutigender Faktor (m)	*(EHNt-mOO-ti-gehn-duh fAAK-tOHr)*	disincentive
entschädigen	*(EHNt-shAY-di-gen)*	reimburse (v)
Entschädigung (f)	*(EHNt-shAY-di-gunk)*	compensation, indemnity
Entsorgung (f)	*(ehnt-ZOHR-goong)*	waste disposal
entstandende Abschreibung (f)	*(EHNt-shtAAnt-endeh AHB-shrEYE-bunk)*	accrued depreciation
entwerfen	*(ent-vER-fen)*	design (v)
Entwerfer (m)	*(ent-vEHR-fuh)*	designer
Entwicklung eines neuen Produkts (f)	*(ehnt-vIK-lunk EYE-nes noy-en proh-dUkts)*	new product development
Entwicklungs-länder (pl)	*(EHNt-vIK-lunks-lAYn-duh)*	underdeveloped nations
Entwicklungsricht-ung (f)	*(EHNt-vIK-lunks-rIKH-tunk)*	trend
entzündungshem-mend	*(ent-tsEWn-dungs-hEHM-ment)*	anti-inflammatory

E

Enzym (n)	*(ehn-TSEWm)*	enzyme
Erbschaft (f)	*(AYrb-shahft)*	estate
Erbschaftssteuer (f)	*(AYrb-shahfts-shtOY-uh)*	inheritance tax
Erdgas (n)	*(AYrd-gaas)*	natural gas
Erdöl (n)	*(AYrd-ERl)*	petroleum
Erdöldollars (pl)	*(AYrd-erl-dOH-laars)*	petrodollars
Erfahrung (f)	*(ayr-fAA-runk)*	know-how
Erfüllungsorte (pl)	*(ayr-fEW-lunks-sOHr-teh)*	delivery points
Ergonomie (f)	*(AYr-goh-noh-mEE)*	ergonomics
ergonomisch	*(AYr-goh-nOH-mish)*	user-friendly
Erhaltungsspanne (f)	*(ayr-hahl-tOOnks-spAH-neh)*	maintenance margin
erhöhte Abschrei- bung (f)	*(ayr-hER-teh AHB-shrEYE-bunk)*	accelerated depreciation
Erhöhung (f)	*(ayr-hER-unk)*	increase
erlauben	*(ayr-lOW-ben)*	allow (v)
Erlaubnis (f)	*(ayr-lOWb-nis)*	license, permit
Erlös (m)	*(AYr-lERs)*	proceeds
ermächtigen	*(ayr-mAYkh-tigehn)*	authorize (v)
Ernennung (f)	*(ayr-nEHN-nunk)*	appointment (nomination)
erneuern	*(ayr-nOY-uhn)*	renew (v)
Eröffnungskurs (m)	*(ayr-ERf-nunks-koors)*	opening price
Ersatzreifen (m)	*(ayr-zAHTS-rEYE-fen)*	spare tire
Ersatzteile (pl)	*(AYr-zats-tEYE-leh)*	replacement parts
ersetzbar	*(ayr-zEHts-baar)*	fungible
Ersparnisse (pl)	*(ayr-shpAAr-nIS-seh)*	savings
erstklassiges Wert- papier (n)	*(ayrst-klAS-si-gehs vEHRt-pah-pEEr)*	blue-chip stock
Ertrag (m)	*(ayr-trAHk)*	outturner, yield
Ertragsergebnis (n)	*(ayr-trAHks-AYr-gAYb-nis)*	earnings yield
Ertragskonto (n)	*(ayr-trAHks-kON-toh)*	income account
Ertragsleistung (f)	*(ayr-trAHks-lEYEs-tunk)*	earnings performance

Ertragsobligation (f)	*(ayr-trAHks-ob-li-gah-tsEE-ohn)*	revenue bond
Ertragswert (m)	*(ayr-trAHks-vEHRt)*	going concern value
Erwerb (m)	*(ayr-vAYrb)*	acquisition
Erwerb der Aktienmehrheit (m)	*(ayr-vAYrb duh ak-tsEE-en-mayr-heyet)*	stock takeover
erwerben	*(ayr-vAYr-ben)*	acquire (v)
Erwerbskosten (pl)	*(ayr-vAYrbs-kOS-ten)*	original cost
Erwerbungsprofil (n)	*(ayr-vAYr-bunks-proh-fEEl)*	acquisition profile
erwirken	*(ayr-vEEr-ken)*	take out (v) (patent)
erworbene Rechte (pl)	*(ayr-vOHr-beneh rehkh-teh)*	acquired rights
erwünschtes Ergebnis (n)	*(ary-vEWnsh-tes ayr-gAYb-nis)*	expected result
Erz (n)	*(AYRTS)*	ore
Erzeugerabfüllung (f)	*(AYR-tsOY-guh-ahb-fewl-lunk)*	estate bottled
Erzeugnis (n)	*(ayr-tsOYg-nis)*	product, output
Espressotasse (f)	*(ehs-prEHS-so-TAHs-seh)*	espresso cup
Eßbesteck (n)	*(EHS-beh-shtek)*	cutlery
Eßlöffel (m)	*(EHS-lERF-fel)*	tablespoon
Etat (m)	*(AY-tah)*	budget
Etikett (n)	*(eh-TI-ket)*	label
Euroanleihe (f)	*(OY-roh-AHN-leye-eh)*	Eurobond
Eurodollar (m)	*(OY-roh-dOHl-laar)*	Eurodollar
Europäische Wirtschaftsgemeinschaft (f)	*(OY-roh-pAY-ish-eh vEErt-shahfts-geh-mEYEn-shahft)*	common market (European Common Market)
Eventuellverbindlichkeit (f)	*(eh-fEN-tOO-el-fuh-bINd-likh-keyet)*	contingent liability
Exemplar (n)	*(ehx-ehm-plAAR)*	copy
Experiment (n)	*(EHX-peh-RI-mehnt)*	experiment
experimentell	*(EHX-peh-RI-mehn-tel)*	experimental
Export-Import Bank (f)	*(ehx-pOHrt-im-pOHrt baank)*	Export-Import bank
Exportgeschäft (n)	*(ehx-pOHrt-geh-shEHft)*	export house

Exportmakler (m)	*(ehx-pOHrt-mAHK-luh)*	export middleman
Exportverkaufs- vertrag (m)	*(ehx-pOHrt-fuh-kOWfs-fuh- trAHk)*	export sales contract

---

F

Fabrik (f)	*(fah-brEEk)*	factory
Fabrikarbeiter (m)	*(fah-brEEk-ahr-bEYE-tuh)*	blue-collar worker
Fabriklage (f)	*(fah-brEEk-laa-geh)*	plant location
Facharbeiter (pl)	*(fAKH-ahr-bEYE-tuh)*	skilled labor
fachgemäß	*(fAKH-geh-mAYs)*	technical
Fachmann (m)	*(fAKH-mahn)*	professional
Faden (m)	*(FAH-den)*	thread
Fahnenabzug (m)	*(fAA-nen-ahb-tsOOk)*	galley proof
Fahrer (m)	*(fAA-ruh)*	driver
Fahrgestell (n)	*(fAAR-geh-shtel)*	chassis
Fahrnis (f)	*(fAAR-nis)*	chattel
Fahrplan (m)	*(fAAR-plAAn)*	timetable (trains)
Faktor (m)	*(FAHK-tohr)*	factor (component, element)
Faktorenanalyse (f)	*(FAHK-tohr-en-ah-nah- lEW-zeh)*	factor analysis
Faktorenbewer- tung (f)	*(FAHK-tohr-en-beh-vEHR- tunk)*	factor rating
Faktoring (n)	*(fEHK-toh-ring)*	factoring
Faktura (f)	*(fAHK-tOO-rah)*	invoice
Fakturenpreis (m)	*(fAHK-tOO-ren-prEYEs)*	invoice cost
Fälligkeit (f)	*(fEHl-likh-keyet)*	maturity
Fälligkeitsklausel (f)	*(fEHl-likh-keyets-klOW-zel)*	acceleration clause
Fälschung (f)	*(fEHl-shunk)*	counterfeit, forgery
Falte (f)	*(fAHL-teh)*	pleat
Farbauszug (m)	*(fAHRb-OWs-tsOOk)*	color separation
Farbe (f)	*(fAHR-beh)*	color, paint
färben	*(fAYR-ben)*	dye (v)
Faserung (f)	*(fAH-zeh-runk)*	grain

E

Faß (n)	*(fAHS)*	cask, vat
Faßbinder (m)	*(fAHS-bin-duh)*	cooper
Faulfracht (f)	*(fOWl-frahkht)*	dead freight
Feder (f)	*(fAY-duh)*	spring
Federzeichnung (f)	*(fAY-duh-tsEYEKH-nunk)*	line drawing
Feedback (n)	*(FEED-behk)*	feedback
Fehler (m)	*(fAY-luh)*	bug (computers), error
fehlerhaft	*(fAY-luh-hahft)*	defective
feilhalten	*(fEYEl-hahl-ten)*	offer for sale
Feinheitgehaltsbe- stimmung (f)	*(feyen-heyet-geh-hAHlts- beh-shtIM-munk)*	assay
Feinwäsche (f)	*(fEYEN-vEH-sheh)*	lingerie
Fernmeldetechno- logie (f)	*(fEHrn-mel-deh-tehkh-noh- loh-gEE)*	telecommunications
Fernmeldewesen (n)	*(fEHrn-mel-dEH-vay-zen)*	telecommunications
Fernschreiber (m)	*(fEHrn-shrEYE-buh)*	telex
Fernsehbandauf- nahme (f)	*(fEHrn-zay-band-OWf-nAA- meh)*	video cassette recording
Fernsehen (n)	*(fEHrn-zay-hen)*	television
Fernsprecher (m)	*(fEHrn-shprehkh-uh)*	telephone
Fernvertrieb (m)	*(fEHrn-fuh-trEEp)*	telemarketing
Fertighaus (n)	*(fEHr-tig-hOWs)*	prefabricated house
fertigmachen	*(fEHr-tig-mAAkh-en)*	finalize (v)
Fertigprodukt (n)	*(fEHr-tig-prOH-dukt)*	end product
Fertigung (f)	*(fEHr-tig-unk)*	production
Fertigungsgemein- kosten (pl)	*(fEHr-tig-unks-geh-MEYEn- kOS-ten)*	factory overhead, indirect expenses
Fertigungskosten (pl)	*(fEHr-ti-gunks-kOS-ten)*	production costs
Fertigungslöhne (pl)	*(fEHr-tig-unks-lER-neh)*	direct labor cost
Fertigungslohnko- sten (pl)	*(fEHr-tig-unks-lOHn-kOS- ten)*	direct labor
Fertigungsplan (m)	*(fEHr-tig-unks-plAAn)*	production schedule
Fertigungssteue- rung (f)	*(fEHr-tig-unks-shtOY-uh- runk)*	industrial engineering, pro- duction control

F

Fertigungsverfahren (n)	*(fEHr-tig-unks-fuh-fAA-ren)*	production process
feste Anlage (f)	*(FEHs-teh AHN-laa-geh)*	fixture
fester Pachtzins (m)	*(FEHs-tuh pAHKHt-tsINs)*	dead rent
fester Wechselkurs (m)	*(FEHs-tuh vEHk-sel-koors)*	fixed rate of exchange
festgelegte Frist (f)	*(FEHst-geh-layg-teh frist)*	fixed term
festgesetztes Eigenkapital (n)	*(FEHst-geh-zEHts-tes EYE-genkah-pi-tAAL)*	legal capital
Festkosten (pl)	*(FEHst-kOS-ten)*	fixed charges
Festobligation (f)	*(FEHst-ob-li-gah-tsEE-ohn)*	term bond
festverzinsliches Wertpapier (n)	*(FEHst-fuh-tsINs-likh-es vEHRt-pah-pEEr)*	fixed income security
Fettdruck (m)	*(fET-drUK)*	boldface
feuern	*(fOY-uhn)*	fire (v)
Filiale (f)	*(fi-lEE-ah-leh)*	branch office
Filialgeschäft (n)	*(fi-lEE-ahl-geh-shEHft)*	chain store
Filter (m)	*(FIL-tuh)*	filter
Finanzanalyse (f)	*(fee-nAHnts-ah-nah-lEW-zeh)*	financial analysis
Finanzberater (m)	*(fee-nAHnts-buh-rAA-tuh)*	investment adviser
Finanzbewertung (f)	*(fee-nAHnts-beh-vEHR-tunk)*	financial appraisal
Finanzdienstleistungen (pl)	*(fee-nAHnts-dEEnst-lEYEs-tun-gen)*	financial services
Finanzdirektor (m)	*(fee-nAHnts-di-REHK-tohr)*	financial director
Finanzfluß (m)	*(fee-nAHnts-flus)*	cash flow
finanzielle Höhepunkte (pl)	*(fee-nahn-tsee-EHl-leh hER-eh-pUnk-teh)*	financial highlights
finanzieller Anreiz (m)	*(fee-nahn-tsee EHl-luh AHN-rEYEts)*	financial incentive
finanzieren	*(fee-nahn-tsEE-ren)*	finance (v)
Finanzierungsgesellschaft (f)	*(fee-nahn-tsEE-runks-geh-zEL-shahft)*	finance company
Finanzierungskosten (pl)	*(fee-nahn-tsEE-runks-kOS-ten)*	front-end financing
Finanzkontrolle (f)	*(fee-nAHnts-kon-trOL-leh)*	financial control

F

Finanzplanung (f)	*(fee-nAHnts-plAA-nunk)*	financial planning
Finanzstatus (m)	*(fee-nAHnts-stAH-toos)*	financial statement
Finanzverwaltung (f)	*(fee-nAHnts-fuh-vAHl-tunk)*	financial management
Firma (f)	*(fIR-mah)*	company, firm
Firmenmitglied (n)	*(fIR-men-MIT-gleed)*	member of a firm
Firmenpolitik (f)	*(fIR-men-po-li-tEEk)*	company policy
Firmenwerbung (f)	*(fIR-men-vAYr-bunk)*	institutional advertising
Firmenzeichen (n)	*(fIR-men-tsEYE-khen)*	logo
Fixkosten (pl)	*(fIX-kOS-ten)*	fixed costs, standing costs
Flasche (f)	*(flAH-sheh)*	bottle
Flaschenhals (m)	*(flAH-shen-hahls)*	neck (of bottle)
Flaute (f)	*(flOW-teh)*	downswing, downturn, slump
Fliege (f)	*(fLEE-geh)*	bow tie
Fließband (n)	*(flEEs-bahnt)*	assembly line
Flöte (f)	*(FLER-teh)*	flute
Flugplan (air-planes) (m)	*(flOOg-plAAn)*	timetable
flüssige Anlagen (pl)	*(flEW-si-geh AHN-laa-gen)*	quick assets
Flüssigkeitsver-hältnis (n)	*(flEW-sig-keyets-fuh-hEHLt-nis)*	acid-test ratio
Folgerung (f)	*(fol-geh-runk)*	implication (conclusion)
Fonds (m)	*(fOH)*	fund
Förderband (n)	*(FER-duh-bahnt)*	conveyor belt
Förderer (m)	*(fER-duh-ruh)*	sponsor (of a fund or partnership)
Fördergerät (n)	*(FER-duh-geh-rEHt)*	conveyor
fördern	*(fER-duhn)*	advance (v) (promote)
Forderung (f)	*(FOHR-duh-runk)*	claim, demand
Förderung (f)	*(FER-duh-runk)*	promotion
Format (n)	*(fohr-mAAt)*	format
Formbarkeit (f)	*(FORm-baar-kEYET)*	malleability
Formel (f)	*(FOR-mehl)*	formula
Forschung (f)	*(FOR-shunk)*	research

F

Forschung und Entwicklung (f)	*(FOR-shunk unt ent-vIK-lunk)*	research and development
Frachltliste (f)	*(fRAHKHT-lIS-teh)*	manifest
Fracht (f)	*(frahkht)*	cargo, freight
Fracht gegen Nachnahme (f)	*(fRAHKHT gAY-gen nAHKH-nAA-meh)*	freight collect
Fracht gestattet	*(fRAHKHT geh-shtAH-tet)*	freight allowed
Fracht inbegriffen	*(fRAHKHT in-beh-grIF-fen)*	freight included
Frachtbetrieb (m)	*(fRAHKHT-beh-trEEp)*	freight all kinds
Frachtbrief (m)	*(fRAHKHT-brEEf)*	bill of lading, consignment note, waybill
Frachtführer (m)	*(fRAHKHT-fEW-ruh)*	freight forwarder
Frachtkostenrük- kerstattung möglich	*(fRAHKHT-kOS-ten-rEWK- uh-shtAHt-tunk mER- glikh)*	freight allowed
Frachtvertragsa- gent (m)	*(fRAHKHT-fuh-trAAgs-aa- gENT)*	charterparty agent
frci Eisenbahn	*(frEYE EYE-zen-baan)*	free on rail
frei Schiff	*(frEYE shIF)*	free on board (fob)
frei Seeschiffsseite	*(frEYE zAY-shIFs-zEYE-teh)*	free alongside ship
frei von besonderer Havarie	*(frEYE fon beh-zON-duh- ruh hah-fah-rEE)*	free of particular average
freie Marktwirt- schaft (f)	*(frEYE mAHrkt-vEErt-shaft)*	free enterprise
Freieexemplar (n)	*(frEYE-ex-em-plAAr)*	complimentary copy
freier Kurs (m)	*(frEYE-uh koors)*	floating rate
freier Markt (m)	*(frEYE-uh mAHrkt)*	free market
freier Wettbewerb (m)	*(frEYE-uh vet-beh-vAYfb)*	laissez-faire
freigestellt	*(frEYE-geh-shtehlt)*	optional
Freihafen (m)	*(frEYE-hAA-fen)*	free port
Freihandel (m)	*(frEYE-hAHn-dehl)*	free trade
Freihandelszone (f)	*(frEYE-hAHn-dehls-tsOH- neh)*	free trade zone
freihändig	*(frEYE-hAYn-dig)*	over the counter
freihändiger Kurs (m)	*(frEYE-hAYn-di-guh koors)*	over-the-counter quotation
Freiliste (f)	*(frEYE-lIS-teh)*	free list

F

Freiperiode (f)	*(frEYE-pay-ree-OH-deh)*	grace period
freischaffender Schriftsteller (m)	*(frEYE-shAHF-en-duh shrift-shtEHL-luh)*	freelance writer
Freiverkehr (m)	*(frEYE-fuh-kAYr)*	open market
freiwillig	*(frEYE-vil-lig)*	voluntary
Freizeit (f)	*(frEYE-tsEYEt)*	free time
Fremdenverkehr (m)	*(frehmd-en-fuh-kAYr)*	tourism
Fremdwährungswechsel (m)	*(frehmd-vAY-runks-vEHK-sel)*	foreign bill of exchange
Frequenz (f)	*(frEH-kvehnts)*	frequency
Frequenzkurve (f)	*(freh-kvENTS-kOOr-veh)*	frequency curve
Frequenzmodulation (f)	*(frEH-kvehnts-moh-DU-lah-TSIohn)*	frequency modulation (FM)
Fristablauf (m)	*(FRIST-ahb-lowf)*	deadline
Frontantrieb (m)	*(front-AHN-treeb)*	front-wheel drive
fruchtig	*(frUKH-tik)*	fruity
Fuchs (m)	*(fUKS)*	fox
führen	*(fEW-ren)*	manage (v) (direct)
Führer (m)	*(fEW-ruh)*	leader
Führungsgruppe (f)	*(fEW-runks-grUP-peh)*	management group
Füllung (f)	*(fEW-lunk)*	stuffing
Funktionsanalyse (f)	*(funk-tsEE-ohns-ah-nah-lEW-zeh)*	functional analysis
Fusion (f)	*(foo-zEE-ohn)*	amalgamation, merger
Futter (n)	*(fUT-tuh)*	lining

G

Gabel (f)	*(GAA-bel)*	fork
Galvanisierung (f)	*(gahl-vAA-nEE-zEE-runk)*	galvanizing
Gangschaltung (f)	*(gAHnk-shahl-tunk)*	gearshift
Garantie (f)	*(gah-rahn-tEE)*	guarantee, warrant (guarantee)
Garantieschein (m)	*(gah-rahn-tEE-sheyen)*	guaranty bond

Garn (n)	*(Gahrn)*	thread, yarn
Gärung (f)	*(gAY-runk)*	ferment
Gas (n)	*(gaas)*	gas
Gebiet (n)	*(geh-bEET)*	country, territory, zone
Gebietsfremder (m)	*(geh-bEEts-frEHM-duh)*	nonresident
Gebietsleiter (m)	*(geh-bEEts-lEYE-tuh)*	area manager
Gebrauchsabnutzung (f)	*(geh-brOWkhs-AHB-nU-tsunk)*	wear and tear
Gebrauchssteuer (f)	*(geh-brOWkhs-shtOY-uh)*	use tax
Gebühr (f)	*(geh-bEWr)*	duty (fee)
Gebühren (pl)	*(geh-bEW-ren)*	charges
gebührenfreier Investmentfonds (m)	*(geh-bEW-ren-frEYE-uh in-vehst-mEHnt-fOH)*	no-load fund
Gebührennachlaß (m)	*(geh-bEW-ren-nAHkh-lahs)*	remission of a customs duty
gebundene Hilfe (f)	*(geh-bUn-dehn-eh hIL-feh)*	tied aid
Gedeck (n)	*(geh-dEHk)*	cover charge
gedruckte Schaltung (f)	*(geh-drUK-teh shAHL-tunk)*	printed circuit
Gefahr (f)	*(geh-fAAr)*	risk
Gefälligkeitsakzept (n)	*(geh-fEH-lig-keyets-ahk-tsEPt)*	accommodation paper
Gefälligkeitsindossament (n)	*(geh-fEH-lig-keyets-in-dos-uh-mEH)*	accommodation endorsement
Gefälligkeitskredit (m)	*(geh-fEH-lig-keyets-kray-dIT)*	accommodation credit
Gefälligkeitsparität (f)	*(geh-fEH-lig-keyets-paa-rEE-tayt)*	accommodation parity
Gefälligkeitsplattform (f)	*(geh-fEH-lig-keyets-plAAt-fohrm)*	accommodation platform
Gefälligkeitswechsel (m)	*(geh-fEH-lig-keyets-vEHK-sel)*	accommodation bill
gefaltet	*(geh-fAHL-teht)*	pleated
gegen alle Gefahren	*(gAY-gen AHl-le geh-fAA-ren)*	against all risks

G

Gegenakkreditiv (n)	*(gAY-gen-ah-kreh-di-tEEf)*	back-to-back credit
Gegengerinnungs- mittel (n)	*(gEH-gen-geh-rin-nungs- mit-tel)*	anticoagulant
Gegenleistung (f)	*(gAY-gen-lEYEs-tunk)*	consideration (contract law)
gegenseitig sich ausschließende Gattungen (pl)	*(gAY-gen-zEYE-tig sikh OWs-shlEE-zen-deh gAHt-tun-gen)*	mutually exclusive classes
gegenseitige Aus- bildung (f)	*(gAY-gen-zEYE-tig-eh OWs- bil-dunk)*	reciprocal training
Gehalt (m)	*(geh-hahlt)*	body
Gehalt (n)	*(geh-hahlt)*	compensation, salary
Gehälterliste (f)	*(geh-hEHl-tuh-lIS-teh)*	payroll
geheftet	*(geh-hEHF-tet)*	sewn
Geld (n)	*(GEHLT)*	currency, money
geldähnliche For- derung (f)	*(GEHLT-AYn-likh-eh FOHR-duh-runk)*	near money
Geldanweisung (f)	*(GEHLT-ahn-vEYE-zung)*	money order
Geldbestand (m)	*(GEHLT-beh-shtANt)*	cash balance, money supply
Geldbörse (f)	*(gELt-bER-zeh)*	purse
Geldentwertung (f)	*(GEHLT-ehnt-vEHR-tunk)*	depreciation of currency
Geldkurs (m)	*(GEHLT-koors)*	bid price
Geldladen (m)	*(GEHLT-lAA-den)*	money shop
Geldmakler (m)	*(GEHLT-mAHk-luh)*	money broker
Geldmarkt (m)	*(GEHLT-mAHrkt)*	money market
Geldmenge (f)	*(GEHLT-mAYng-eh)*	monetary base
Geldpolitik (f)	*(GEHLT-po-li-tEEk)*	monetary policy
Geldschein (m)	*(GEHLT-shEYEn)*	bill (currency)
Geldsperre (f)	*(GEHLT-shpEH-reh)*	blockage of funds
Geldstrafe (f)	*(GEHLT-shtrAA-feh)*	fine (penalty)
Geldumlaufge- schwindigkeit (f)	*(GEHLT-um-lOWfs-geh- shvIN-dikh-keyet)*	velocity of money
Geldumlaufzu- wachs (m)	*(GEHLT-OOm-lowf-tsOO- vahkhs)*	incremental cash flow
Geldversorgung (f)	*(GEHLT-fuh-zOR-gunk)*	money supply
Geldverwalter (m)	*(GEHLT-fuh-vAHl-tuh)*	money manager
Geldwechsel (m)	*(GEHLT-vEHk-sel)*	currency exchange

G

Gelegenheitskauf (m)	*(geh-lAY-gen-heyets-kOWf)*	bargain
gelenkte Wirtschaft (f)	*(geh-lAYnk-teh vEErt-shaft)*	managed economy
gelernte Arbeitskräfte (pl)	*(geh-lAYrn-teh AHR-beyets-krehf-teh)*	skilled labor
Gemeindesteuer (f)	*(geh-mEYEn-deh-shtOY-uh)*	local tax
Gemeingut (n)	*(geh-mEYEn-gOOt)*	public domain
Gemeinkosten (pl)	*(geh-mEYEn-kOS-ten)*	indirect costs, overhead
Gemeinkostenlöhne (pl)	*(geh-mEYEn-kOS-ten-lER-neh)*	indirect labor
Gemeinkostensatz (m)	*(geh-mEYEn-kOS-ten-zahts)*	burden rate
gemeinnützig	*(geh-mEYEn-nEW-tsig)*	nonprofit (not-for-profit)
Gemeinpunkt in Übersee (m)	*(geh-mEYEn-pUnkt)*	overseas common point
gemeinsame Rechnung (f)	*(geh-mEYEn-zAA-muh rEHKH-nunk)*	joint account
gemeinsamer Besitz (m)	*(geh-mEYEn-zAA-muh beh-zITs)*	joint estate
gemeinsamer Markt (m)	*(geh-mEYEn-zAA-muh mAHrkt)*	common market
gemeinschaftliche Computerbenutzung (f)	*(geh-mEYEn-shahft-likh-eh kom-pyU-tuh-beh-nU-tsunk)*	time sharing
gemeinschaftliches Konto (n)	*(geh-mEYEn-shahft-likh-es kON-toh)*	joint account
gemeinschaftliches Unternehmen (n)	*(geh-mEYEn shahft likhes un-tuh-nAY-men)*	joint venture
Gemeinschaftswerbung (f)	*(geh-mEYEn-shahfts-vAYr-bunk)*	cooperative advertising
gemietete Abteilung (f)	*(geh-mEE-teh-teh AHB-tEYE-lunk)*	leased department
Gemisch (n)	*(geh-mISH)*	compound
genannter Ausfuhrort (m)	*(geh-nAAn-tuh OWs-foor-ohrt)*	named point of exportation
genannter Bestimmungsort (m)	*(geh-nAAn-tuh beh-shtIM-mungs-ohrt)*	named point of destination
genannter Einfuhrhafen (m)	*(geh-nAAn-tuh EYEn-fOOr-hAA-fen)*	named port of importation

G

genannter Ursprungsort (m)	*(geh-nAAn-tuh OOr-shprOOngs-ohrt)*	named point of origin
genannter Versandhafen (m)	*(geh-nAAn-tuh fuh-zAHND-hAA-fen)*	named port of shipment
genehmigen (v)	*(geh-nAY-mi-gen)*	authorize (v)
genehmigte Aktien (pl)	*(geh-nAY-mig-teh ak-tsEE-en)*	authorized shares
genehmigte Wertpapiere (pl)	*(geh-nAY-mig-teh vEHRt-pah-pEE-reh)*	approved securities
genehmigtes Lagerhaus (n)	*(geh-nAY-mig-tehs LAA-guh-hOWs)*	licensed warehouse
Generaldirektor (m)	*(gen-eh-rAAl di-REHK-tohr)*	general manager, president
Generalkosten (pl)	*(gen-eh-rAAl -kOS-ten)*	fixed charges, overhead
Generalstreik (m)	*(gen-eh-rAAl -shtreyek)*	general strike
Generalversammlung (f)	*(gen-eh-rAAl-fuh-zAM-lunk)*	general meeting
Generalversicherung (f)	*(gen-eh-rAAl -fuh-ZIKH-eh-runk)*	open cover
generell	*(gen-eh-rEHL)*	across the board
Genossenschaft (f)	*(gen-OS-sen-shahft)*	cooperative
geplante Überalterung (f)	*(geh-plAAn-teh EW-buh-AAl-tuh-runk)*	planned obsolescence
gerben (Leder)	*(gEHR-ben [lAY-duh])*	tan (v)
Gerber (m)	*(gEHR-buh)*	tanner
Gerberei (f)	*(gEHR-beh-rEYE)*	tannery
Gerbsäure (f)	*(gEHRb-ZOY-reh)*	tannin (tanin)
gerichtlich entscheiden	*(geh-rIKHt-likh ent-shEYE-den)*	adjudge (v)
gerichtliche Anordnung (f)	*(geh-rIKHt-likh-eh AHN-ord-nunk)*	injunction
Gerichtsbefehl (m)	*(geh-rIKHts-beh-fAYl)*	writ
Gerichtsbezirk (m)	*(geh-rIKHts-beh-tsEErk)*	jurisdiction
Gesamtangebot (n)	*(geh-zAHmt-AHN-geh-boht)*	aggregate supply
gesamte Industrie (f) betreffend	*(geh-zAHm-teh in-dus-trEE beh-trEH-fehnt)*	industrywide
Gesamtkapital (n)	*(geh-zAHmt-kah-pi-tAAL)*	total capital
Gesamtkosten (pl)	*(geh-zAHmt-kOS-ten)*	all in cost

Gesamtkosten für importierte Waren (pl)	*(geh-zAHmt-kOS-ten fEWr im-pOHr-tEEr-teh vAA-ren)*	landed cost
Gesamtlänge (f)	*(geh-zaHMT-LEHN-geh)*	footage
Gesamtnachfrage (f)	*(geh-zAHmt-nAKH-frah-geh)*	aggregate demand
Gesamtrisiko (n)	*(geh-zAHmt-REE-zee-koh)*	aggregate risk
gesamtschuldnerische Haftung (f)	*(geh-zAHmt-shUlt neh-rish-eh hAHf-tunk)*	joint liability
Gesamtverlustverhältnis (n)	*(geh-zAHmt-fuh-lUst-fuh-hEHLt-nis)*	loss-loss ratio
Geschäft (n)	*(geh-shEHft)*	store, transaction
Geschäftsbank (f)	*(geh-shEHfts-bahnk)*	retail bank
Geschäftsbereich (m)	*(geh-shEHfts-beh-rEYEkh)*	line of business
Geschäftsbogen (m)	*(geh-shEHfts-bOH-gen)*	letterhead
geschäftsführender Vorstand (m)	*(geh-shEHfts-fEW-ren-duh FOHR-stahnd)*	executive committee
Geschäftsführer (m)	*(geh-shEHfts-fEW-ruh)*	director, executive director, manager
Geschäftsjahr (n)	*(geh-shEHfts-yAAr)*	financial year, fiscal year
Geschäftskarte (f)	*(geh-shEHfts-kAAr-teh)*	business card
Geschäftsleitungstabelle (f)	*(geh-shEHfts-lEYE-tungs-tah-bEHl-leh)*	management chart
Geschäftslokal (n)	*(geh-shEHfts-loh-kAAl)*	place of business
Geschäftsnummer (f)	*(geh-shEHfts-nU-muh)*	reference number
Geschäftsplan (m)	*(geh-shEHfts-plAAn)*	business plan
Geschäftsstrategie (f)	*(geh-shEHfts-straa-teh-gEE)*	business strategy
Geschäftstagebuch (n)	*(geh-shEHfts-tAAgeh-bOOkh)*	journal
Geschäftstätigkeit (f)	*(geh-shEHfts-tAY-tig-keyet)*	business activity
Geschäftsumsatz (m)	*(geh-shEHfts-um-zAHts)*	turnover
Geschäftszentrum (n)	*(geh-shEHfts-tsEHN-troom)*	shopping center

G

geschriebener Text (m)	*(geh-shrEE-ben-uh tehxt)*	hard copy
Geschwindigkeits- messer (m)	*(geh-shvIN-dig-kEYETs- MEHS-suh)*	speedometer
Geselle (m)	*(geh-sEL-leh)*	journeyman
Gesellschaft (f)	*(geh-zEL-shahft)*	company
Gesellschaft mit beschränkter Haftung (GmbH) (f)	*(geh-zEL-shahft mit beh- shrAYnk-tuh hAHf-tunk) (GAY-EM-BAY-HAH)*	corporation
gesellschaftlich organisieren	*(geh-zEL-shahft-likh ohr- gaa-nee-zEE-ren)*	incorporate (v)
Gesellschaftsbild (n)	*(geh-zEL-shahfts-bilt)*	corporate image
Gesellschaftspla- nung (f)	*(geh-zEL-shahfts-plAA- nunk)*	corporate planning
Gesellschaftsstruk- tur (f)	*(geh-zEL-shahfts-shtrOOk- toor)*	corporate structure
Gesellschaftsziel (n)	*(geh-zEL-shahfts-tsEEl)*	company goal
Gesetz (n)	*(geh-zEHts)*	law
Gesetz vom abneh- menden Ertrag (n)	*(geh-zEHts fom ab-nAY- men-den uh-trAHk)*	law of diminishing returns
gesetzlich geschützt	*(geh-zEHts-likh geh- shEWtst)*	proprietary
gesetzliche Abhilfe (f)	*(geh-zEHts-likh-eh ab-hIL- feh)*	remedy (law)
gesetzliche Rück- lage (f)	*(geh-zEHts-likh-eh rEWk- laa-geh)*	legal reserve (banking)
gesetzliche Verjäh- rungsschriften (pl)	*(geh-sEHts-likh-eh fuh-yAY- runks-shrif-ten)*	statute of limitations
gesetzlicher Feier- tag (m)	*(geh-zEHts-likh-eh fEYE-uh- taak)*	legal holiday
gesetzliches Mono- pol (n)	*(geh-zEHts-likh-es mo-noh- pOHl)*	legal monopoly
gesetzliches Zah- lungsmittel (n)	*(geh-zEHts-likh-es tsAA- lungs-mit-tEL)*	legal tender
gesetzwidrig	*(geh-zEHts vEE-drig)*	illegal

G

gesetzwidrige Sendungen (pl)	*(geh-zEHts-vEE-dri-geh-zEN-dun-gen)*	illegal shipments
gesicherte Haftung (f)	*(geh-ZIKH-uh-teh hAHf-tunk)*	secured liability
gesicherte Konten (pl)	*(geh-ZIKH-uh-teh kon-tEN)*	secured accounts
gesicherte Obligation (f)	*(geh-ZIKH-uh-teh ob-li-gah-tsEE-ohn)*	guaranty bond
gespaltene Wechselkurse (pl)	*(geh-shpAAl-ten-eh vEHk-sel-koor-zeh)*	multiple exchange rate
gespaltener Markt (m)	*(geh-shpAAl-teh-nuh mAHrkt)*	two-tiered market
gestaffelte Steuer (f)	*(geh-shtAHf-fel-teh shtOY-uh)*	graduated tax
Gestalt (n)	*(geh-shtAHlt)*	form
Gestaltungsskizze (f)	*(geh-shtAHl-tunks-ski-tseh)*	layout
Gestehungskosten (pl)	*(geh-shtAY-unks-kOS-ten)*	prime costs
gestiegene Kosten (pl)	*(geh-shtEE-gen-eh kOS-ten)*	increased costs
gestrichenes Papier (n)	*(geh-shtRI-KHeh-nehs pah-pEER)*	coated paper
gestundete Zahlungen (pl)	*(geh-shtun-deh-teh tsAA-lun-gen)*	deferred charges
getätigter Verkauf (m)	*(geh-tAY-tig-tuh fuh-kOWf)*	negotiated sale
Getreide (n)	*(geh-trEYE-deh)*	grain
Gewächse (pl)	*(geh-vEHKH-seh)*	plants
Gewähr (f)	*(geh-vAYr)*	warrant (guarantee), warranty
Gewährleistungsgarantie (f)	*(geh-vAYr-lEYEs-tungs-gah-rahn-tEE)*	performance bond
Gewebe (n)	*(geh-vAY-beh)*	fabric
Gewerbeausstellung (f)	*(geh-vAYr-beh-OWs-shtEHL-lunk)*	trade fair
Gewerbehaus (n)	*(geh-vAYr-beh-hOWs)*	trade house
Gewerbesteuer (f)	*(geh-vAYr-beh-shtOY-uh)*	excise tax
Gewerbetechnik (f)	*(geh-vAYr-beh-tEHKH-nik)*	industrial engineering

G

gewerbliche Schiedsgerichtsbarkeit (f)	*(geh-vAYrb-likh-eh shEEds-geh-rIKHts-baar-keyet)*	industrial arbitration
Gewerkschaft (f)	*(geh-vEHrk-shahft)*	labor union, trade union
Gewerkschaftsetikett (n)	*(geh-vEHrk-shahfts-ti-keht)*	union label
gewerkschaftsfreier Betrieb (m)	*(geh-vEHrk-shahfts-frEYE-uh beh-trEEp)*	open shop
Gewerkschaftsführer(m)	*(geh-vEHrk-shahfts-fEW-ruh)*	labor leader
Gewicht (n)	*(geh-vIkht)*	weight
Gewinde (n)	*(geh-vIN-deh)*	coil
Gewinn (m)	*(geh-vIN)*	profit
Gewinn pro Aktie (m)	*(geh-vIN pro ak-tsEE-eh)*	earnings per share
Gewinn- und Verlustrechnung (f)	*(geh-vIN unt fuh-lUst-rEHKH-nunk)*	income statement, profit-and-loss statement
Gewinnanteilprozentsatz (m)	*(geh-vIN-AHN-teyel-proh-tsEHnt-zahts)*	percentage of profit
Gewinnbericht (m)	*(geh-vIN-beh-rIKHt)*	earnings report
Gewinnbeteiligung (f)	*(geh-vIN-beh-tEYE-li-gunk)*	profit sharing
gewinnen	*(geh-vIN-nen)*	acquire (v)
Gewinnfaktor (m)	*(geh-vIN-FAHK-tohr)*	profit factor
Gewinnnprognose (f)	*(geh-vIN-prog-nOH-zeh)*	profit projection
Gewinnobligationen (pl)	*(geh-vIN-ob-li-gah-tsEE-ohn-ehn)*	income bonds
Gewinnrealisierung (f)	*(geh-vIN-ray-aal-li-zEE-runk)*	profit-taking
Gewinnschwelle (f)	*(geh-vIN-shvEL-leh)*	break-even point
Gewinnschwelle erreichen (f)	*(geh-vIN-shvEL-leh ayr-rEYE-khen)*	break even (v)
Gewinnspanne (f)	*(geh-vIN-shpAA-neh)*	profit margin
Gewinnwirkung (f)	*(geh-vIN-vEEr-kunk)*	profit impact
gewogener Durchschnitt (m)	*(geh-vOH-gen-uh dURKH-shnIT)*	weighted average
Gewohnheit (f)	*(geh-vOHn-heyet)*	practice

G

gezogener Wechsel (m)	*(geh-tsOH-gen-uh vEKH-sel)*	direct paper
Gießerei (f)	*(gEE-seh-rEYE)*	foundry
Giftkunde (f)	*(gIFT-kun-deh)*	toxicology
Giftstoff (m)	*(gIFT-shtOF)*	toxin
Girat (m)	*(djEE-rAAt)*	endorsee
Giro (n)	*(djEE-rOH)*	endorsement
Girokonto (n)	*(djEE-rOH-kON-toh)*	checking account
Girozentrale (f)	*(djEE-rOH-tsen-trAA-leh)*	clearinghouse
glänzend	*(glEHN-tsent)*	glossy
Glas (n)	*(glAAs)*	glass
glatt	*(glAHT)*	glossy
Gläubiger (m)	*(glOY-bi-guh)*	creditor
gleicher Lohn für die gleiche Arbeit (m)	*(glEYE-kheh LOHN fEWr dee glEYE-kheh ahr-bEYEt)*	equal pay for equal work
Gleichheit (f)	*(glEYEkh-heyet)*	parity
Gleichstrom (m)	*(glEYEKH-shtrOHm)*	direct current
gleitender Durchschnitt (m)	*(glEYE-ten-duh dURKH-shnIT)*	moving average
gleitender Wechselkurs (m)	*(glEYE-ten-uh vEHk-sel-koors)*	floating exchange rate
Glockenkurve (f)	*(glok-en-kOOr-veh)*	bell-shaped curve
Goldbestände (pl)	*(GOLT-beh-shtEHn-deh)*	gold reserves
Goldklausel (f)	*(GOLT-klOW-zel)*	gold clause
Goldpreis (m)	*(GOLT-prEYEs)*	gold price
Grad (m)	*(graht)*	degree
gradlinig	*(grAHd-li-nig)*	linear
Grammolekül (n)	*(grAM-mo-leh-kEWL)*	mole
graphische Darstellung (f)	*(grAH-fish-eh dAAr-shtEHL-lunk)*	graph
Gratifikation (f)	*(graa-ti-fEE-kah-tsEE-ohn)*	gratuity, bonus
grauer Markt (m)	*(grOW-uh mAHrkt)*	gray market
gravieren	*(grah-vEE-ren)*	engrave (v)
greifbare Vermögenswerte (pl)	*(grEYEf-baar-uh fuh-mER-gens-vEHR-teh)*	tangible assets

G

Grenze (f)	*(grEHN-tseh)*	border
Grenzertrag (m)	*(grEHNts-uh-trAHk)*	marginal revenue
Grenzkosten (pl)	*(grEHNts-kOS-ten)*	incremental costs, marginal cost
Grenzproduktivität (f)	*(grEHNts-prOH-duk-ti-vee-tAYt)*	marginal productivity
Grenzsteuerberichtigung (f)	*(grEHNts-shtOY-uh-beh-rIKH-ti-gunk)*	border tax adjustment
großangelegt	*(grOHs-AHN-geh-laygt)*	large-scale
Großbuchstabe (m)	*(grOS-bOOKH-shtah-beh)*	capital
Größe (f)	*(gRER-seh)*	size
großes Faß (n)	*(grO-Sehs fAHS)*	vat
Großhandel (m)	*(grOHs-hAHn-dehl)*	wholesale market, wholesale trade
Großhandelspreis (m)	*(grOHs-hAHn-dehls-prEYEs)*	wholesale price
Großhändler (m)	*(grOHs-hEHn-dluh)*	wholesaler, distributor
Grossist (m)	*(groh-SISt)*	jobber
Großkonzern (m)	*(grOHs-kon-tsAYrn)*	conglomerate
Großlieferant (m)	*(grOHs-LEE-fuh-rahnt)*	rack jobber
größte Zahlung (f)	*(grERs-teh tsAA-lunk)*	balloon payment (loan repayment)
Großvertrieb (m)	*(grOHs-fuh-trEEp)*	mass marketing
Grundbesitz (m)	*(grUNd-beh-zITS)*	real estate
Grundbesitzer (m)	*(grUNd-beh-zIT-suh)*	landowner
Grundbuchung (f)	*(grUNd-bOO-khunk)*	original entry
gründen	*(grEWn-den)*	incorporate (v)
Grundkapital (n)	*(grUNd-kah-pi-tAAL)*	principal (capital)
gründlich besprechen	*(grEWnd-likh beh-shprEKH-en)*	jawbone (v)
Grundpreis (m)	*(grUNd-prEYEs)*	base price
Grundsatz (m)	*(grUNd-zAHts)*	policy (principle)
Grundsteuer (f)	*(grUNd-shtOY-uh)*	land tax
Grundstück (n)	*(grUNd-shtEWk)*	premises
Grundstücksverwalter (m)	*(grUNd-shtEWks-fuh-vAHl-tuh)*	estate agent

G

Grundtarif (m)	*(grUNd-tah-rIF)*	base rate
Gründungsfinanzierung (f)	*(grEWn-dunks-fee-nahn-tsEE-runk)*	front-end financing
Gründungsurkunde (f)	*(grEWnd-unks-OOr-kun-deh)*	certificate of incorporation
Grundvermögen (n)	*(grUNd-fuh-mER-gen)*	real assets
Grundwährung (f)	*(grUNd-vAY-runk)*	base currency
Gruppendynamik (f)	*(grUP-pen-dew-nAAm-ik)*	group dynamics
Gruppenführer (m)	*(grUP-pen-fEW-ruh)*	foreman
Gruppenmanagement (n)	*(grUP-pen-mehn-EHdj-ment)*	team management
Gruppenpolice (f)	*(grUP-pen-po-lee-sAY)*	fleet policy
Gruppenversicherung (f)	*(grUP-pen-fuh-ZIKH-eh-runk)*	group insurance
gültig	*(gEWl-tikh)*	valid
Gültigkeitsverlängerung (f)	*(gEWl-tikh-keyets-fuh-lAYn-guh-runk)*	rain check
Gürtel (m)	*(gEWR-tel)*	belt
Gürtelreifen (m)	*(gEWR-tel-rEYE-fen)*	radial tire
Gußblöcke (pl)	*(gUS-bLER-keh)*	ingots
Gußeisen (n)	*(gUS-EYE-zen)*	cast iron, pig iron
Gußform (f)	*(gUS-FORm)*	ingot mold
Gußhaut (f)	*(gUS-hOWT)*	scale
Gut (n)	*(gOOt)*	estate (or chateau)
gut und schlecht verkaufte Artikel	*(goot unt shlekht fuh-kOWf-teh ahr-tIK-el)*	leads and lags
Güter (pl)	*(gEW-tuh)*	goods, merchandise
Gütertransport (m)	*(gEW-tuh-trahns-pOHrt)*	movement of goods
Guthaben in konvertierbarer Währung (n)	*(gOOt-haa-ben in kon-fuh-tEEr-bAA-ruh vAY-runk)*	Eurocurrency
gutschreiben	*(gOOt-shrEYE-ben)*	credit (v)
Gutschriftsanzeige (f)	*(gOOt-shrifts-AHN-tseye-geh)*	credit note

G

H

Hafengebühren (pl)	*(hAA-fen-geh-bEW-ren)*	harbor dues
Haftpflichtversicherung (f)	*(hAHft-pflKHt-fuh-ZIKH-eh-runk)*	liability insurance
Haftung (f)	*(hAHf-tunk)*	liability
Halbfabrikate (pl)	*(hAHlb-fah-brEE-kAA-teh)*	work in progress
Halbleben (n)	*(hAHlb-lAY-ben)*	half-life
Halbleiter (m)	*(hAIILb-leye-tuh)*	semiconductor
Halbstiefel (pl)	*(hAHLb-shtEE-fel)*	ankle boots
Haltezeit (f)	*(hAHl-teh-tsEYEt)*	holding period
hamstern	*(hAHm-stehrn)*	hoard (v)
Handarbeiter (m)	*(hAHNd-ahr-bEYE-tuh)*	manual worker
handbemalt	*(hAHNd-beh-maalt)*	hand-painted
Handel (m)	*(hAHN-dehl)*	commerce, deal (transaction)
handeln	*(hAHN-dehln)*	trade (v)
Handelsabkommen (n)	*(hAHN-dehls-AHB-kOM-mehn)*	trade agreement
Handelsagentur (f)	*(hAHN-dehls-ah-gen-tOOR)*	mercantile agency
Handelsakzept (n)	*(hAHN-dehls-ahk-tsEPt)*	trade acceptance
Handelsbank (f)	*(hAHN-dehls-bahnk)*	commercial bank, merchant bank, retail bank
Handelsbedingungen (pl)	*(hAHN-dehls-beh-dINg-unk-en)*	terms of trade
handelsbezogen	*(hAHN-dehls-beh-tsOH-gen)*	mercantile
Handelsbilanz (f)	*(hAHN-dehls-bee-lAHnts)*	balance of trade
Handelsdatum (n)	*(hAHN-dehls-DAA-tum)*	trade date
Handelsgesellschaft (f)	*(hAHN-dehls-geh-zEL-shahft)*	trading company
Handelsgesetz (n)	*(hAIIN-dehls-geh-zEHts)*	mercantile law (a specific law)
Handelsgrenze (f)	*(hAHN-dehls-grEHn-tseh)*	trading limit
Handelshaus (n)	*(hAHN-dehls-hOWs)*	trade house
Handelskammer (f)	*(hAHN-dehls-kAHM-muh)*	chamber of commerce, merchant guild

H

Handelskommis-sion (f)	*(hAHN-dehls-koh-mi-sEE-ohn)*	trade commission
Handelskredit (m)	*(hAHN-dehls-kray-dIT)*	trade credit
Handelsmarke (f)	*(hAHN-dehls-mAHR-keh)*	trademark
Handelsrechnung (f)	*(hAHN-dehls-rEHKH-nunk)*	commercial invoice
Handelsrecht (n)	*(hAHN-dehls-REHKHT)*	mercantile law (in general)
Handelsschranke (f)	*(hAHN-dehls-shrAAn-keh)*	trade barrier
Handelssperre (f)	*(hAHN-dehls-shpEH-reh)*	embargo
handelsübliche Qualität (f)	*(hAHN-dehls-EWb-likheh kvah-li-tAYt)*	commercial grade
Handelsverband (m)	*(hAHN-dehls-fuh-bAHnd)*	trade association
Handelsvertrag (m)	*(hAHN-dehls-fuh-trAHk)*	trade agreement
Handelsware (f)	*(hAHN-dehls-vAAreh)*	commodity
handgeblasenes Glas (n)	*(hAHNd-geh-bLAA-zeh-nehs gLAAs)*	hand-blown glass
Händler (m)	*(hEHnd-luh)*	dealer, merchant, trader
Händlerrabatt (m)	*(hEHnd-luh-rah-bAAt)*	trade discount
Handlung (f)	*(hAHnd-lunk)*	dealership
Handlungsplan (m)	*(hAHnd-lunks-plAAn)*	plan, action
Handlungsreisen-der (m)	*(hAHnd-lunks-rEYE-zen-duh)*	manufacturer's representa-tive
Handschuhe (pl)	*(HAHNd-shOO-eh)*	gloves
Handtasche (f)	*(HAHNd-tAH-SHeh)*	handbag, pocketbook
Hardcover (n)	*(hart-kah-vah)*	hardcover
Hardware (f)	*(hAHrt-vayr)*	hardware (computer)
harntreibendes Mittel (n)	*(hAHRn-trEYE-ben-dehs mit-tel)*	diuretic
Härtung (f)	*(HEHR-tunk)*	annealing
Hartwährung (f)	*(hAHrt-vAY-runk)*	hard currency
Hase (m)	*(hAA-zeh)*	rabbit
häufiger Stellen-wechsler (m)	*(hOY-fi-guh shtEHL-len-vEHKHs-luh)*	job hopper
Hauptausfuhrwa-ren (f)	*(hOWpt-OWs-foor-vAA-ren)*	key exports

H

Hauptbuch (n)	*(hOWpt-bOOkh)*	ledger
Hauptbucheintra-gung (f)	*(hOWpt-bOOkh-EYEn-traa-gunk)*	ledger entry
Hauptbuchkonto (n)	*(hOWpt-bOOkh-kON-toh)*	ledger account
Hauptbüro (n)	*(hOWpt-bEW-roh)*	head office
Haupteinkäufer (m)	*(hOWpt-eyen-kOY-fuh)*	chief buyer
Hauptmarkt (m)	*(hOWpt-mAHrkt)*	primary market
Hauptrechner (m)	*(hOWpt-rEKH-nuh)*	mainframe computer
Hauptsendezeit (f)	*(hOWpt-zEN-deh-tsEYEt)*	prime time
Hauptsitz (m)	*(hOWpt-zITs)*	headquarters
Haushalt (m)	*(hOWs-hahlt)*	budget
Haushaltsjahr (n)	*(hOWs-hahlts-yaar)*	financial year
Haushaltsmittelbe-reitstellung (f)	*(hOWs-hahlts-mit-tEL-beh-rEYEt-shtEHL-lunk)*	budget appropriation
Haushaltsvoran-schlag (m)	*(hOWs-hahlts-FOHR-ahn-shlAHk)*	budget forecast
Haussebörse (f)	*(hOWs-seh-bER-seh)*	bull market
Haussemarkt (m)	*(hOWs-seh-mAHrkt)*	upmarket
Haussespekulant (m)	*(hOWs-seh-shpEHk-OO-lahnt)*	bull
Hausverkauf (m)	*(hOWs-fuh-kOWf)*	door-to-door sales
Hebelwirkung (f)	*(hAY-behl-vEEr-kunk)*	leverage
Hefe (f)	*(hay-feh)*	dregs, yeast
Heilmittel (pl)	*(hEYEL-mit-tel)*	remedies
Heimfall einer Erbschaft an den Staat (m)	*(hEYEm-fahl eye-nuh AYrb-shahft ahn dehn shtAAt)*	escheat
heißes Geld (n)	*(hEYEs-sehs GEHLT)*	hot money
Hektar (n)	*(hehk-tAAR)*	hectare
Hemd (n)	*·(hEHmt)*	shirt
hemmender Faktor (m)	*(hEHm-mehn-duh FAHK-tohr)*	disincentive
Herabsetzung (f)	*(hAYr-ahb-zET-tsunk)*	abatement (reduction), writedown
herabziehen	*(hAYr-ahb-tsEE-hen)*	drawdown

H

herausgeben	*(heh-rOWs-gay-ben)*	edit (v)
herausnehmen	*(hAYr-OWs-nAY-men)*	take out (v)
Herkunftsbeschei- **nigung (f)**	*(hAYr-kUnfts-beh-shEYE-ni-* *gunk)*	certificate of origin
Hersteller (m)	*(hAYr-shtEHL-luh)*	manufacturer
Herstellervertreter **(m)**	*(hAYr-shtEHL-luh-fuh-trAY-* *tuh)*	manufacturer's agent
Herstellung (f)	*(hAYr-shtEHL-lunk)*	production
Herstellungskapa- **zität (f)**	*(hAYr-shtEHL-lunks-kah-* *pah-tsee-tAYt)*	manufacturing capacity
herumgehen	*(hAYr-um-gAY-hehn)*	go around (v)
High-Fidelity (f)	*(HEYE fi-dEH-li-ti)*	high fidelity
hinauswerfen	*(hin-OWs-vAYr-fehn)*	fire (v)
Hinterachse (f)	*(hIN-tuh-akh-seh)*	rear axle
Hinterlegungs- **schein (m)**	*(hIN-tuh-lAY-gunks-* *shEYEn)*	trust receipt
Hochkonjunktur **(f)**	*(hOHkh-kon-yunk-tOOr)*	boom
Hochofen (m)	*(hOHKH-ohfen)*	blast furnace
Höchstgrenze (f)	*(hERkhs-grEHN-tseh)*	ceiling
Höchstpreis (m)	*(hERkhst-prEYEs)*	top price
Hoheitsgewässer **(n)**	*(HOH-heyets-geh-vEH-suh)*	territorial waters
höhere Gewalt (f)	*(hER-uh-reh geh-vAAlt)*	act of God
Holdinggesellschaft **(f)**	*(hohl-dEEngs-geh-zEL-* *shahft)*	holding company
Holzhammerme- **thode (f)**	*(hOHlts-hAAm-muh-meh-* *tOH-deh)*	hard sell
Homogenität (f)	*(homo-gehnI-tAYT)*	homogeneity
horten	*(hOHr-ten)*	hoard (v)
Hubraum (m)	*(hOOb-rOWm)*	displacement
Huckepackverkehr **(m)**	*(hU-keh-pahk-fuh-kAYr)*	piggyback service
Hundertaktien- **paket (n)**	*(hOOn-duht-ak-tsEE-en-* *paa-kAYt)*	round lot
husten	*(hUS-ten)*	cough (v)
Hustensaft (m)	*(hUS-ten-sahft)*	cough syrup

H

Hustentropfen (m)	*(hUS-ten-trOP-fen)*	cough drop
Hüttenwerk (n)	*(hEWT-ten-vehrk)*	steel mill
Hybridrechner (m)	*(hEW-brid-rEKH-nuh)*	hybrid computer
Hydrolyse (f)	*(HEW-dro-LEW-zeh)*	hydrolysis
Hypertonie (f)	*(hEW-puh-to-nee)*	hypertension
Hypothek (f)	*(hew-poh-tAYk)*	mortgage
Hypothekenbank (f)	*(hew-poh-tAYk-en-bahnk)*	mortgage bank
Hypothekenbrief (m)	*(hew-poh-tAYk-en-brEEf)*	mortgage bond
hypothekenfrei	*(hew-poh-tAYk-en-frEYE)*	free and clear (unmortgaged)
Hypothekenpfand-brief (m)	*(hew-poh-tAYk-en pfAHnd-brEEf)*	mortgage debenture
Hypothekenschein (m)	*(hew-poh-tAYk-en-shEYEn)*	mortgage certificate
Hypothekenschuld (f)	*(hew-poh-tAYk-en-shUlt)*	encumbrance

I

Iltishaar (n)	*(IL-tIS-hAAR)*	fitch hair
Iltishaarbürste (f)	*(IL-tIS-hAAR-bEWR-steh)*	fitch hair brush
im Börsenhandel eingetragener Verein	*(im bER-zen-hAHN-dehl eyen-geh-trAA-gen-uh fuh-EYEn)*	member firm
im Debet	*(im deh-bAYt)*	in the red
im Einzug (f)	*(im EYEn-tsOOk)*	float (outstanding checks)
im Umlauf	*(im um-lowf)*	afloat (in circulation)
im voraus einge-gangene Erträge (pl)	*(im FOHR-ows EYEn-geh-gAHN-geh-neh AYr-tray-geh)*	deferred income
immaterielle Werte (pl)	*(im-mah-tayr-ree-EL-leh vEHR-teh)*	intangible assets
Impfstoff (m)	*(IMpf-shtOF)*	vaccine
Import (m)	*(im-pOHrt)*	import
importieren	*(im-pOHr-tEE-ren)*	import (v)
Importlizenz (f)	*(im-pOHrt-lee-tsEHnts)*	import license

Impulskauf (m)	*(im-pUls-kOWf)*	impulse purchase
in Kommission	*(koh-mis-sEE-ohn)*	on consignment
in unabhängiger Datenverarbei- tung	*(in OOn-ab-hEHn-gi-guh dAA-ten-fuh-ahr-bEYE- tunk)*	off line
Index (m)	*(IN-dehx)*	index
Indexierung (f)	*(IN-dehk-sEE-runk)*	indexing
Indexoption (f)	*(IN-dehks-op-tsEE-ohn)*	index option
indirekte Steuer (f)	*(in-di-REK-teh shtOY-uh)*	indirect tax
indirekter Anspruch (m)	*(in-di-REK-tuh AHN- shprUKH)*	indirect claim
Indossament (n)	*(in-dos-ah-mEH)*	endorsement
Induktion (f)	*(IN-duk-TSI-On)*	induction
Induktionsofen (m)	*(IN-duk-TSI-Ons-ohfen)*	induction furnace
Industrie (f)	*(in-dus-trEE)*	industry
Industriegenossen- schaft (f)	*(in-dus-trEE-geh-nOS-sen- shahft)*	trade association
Industriegewerk- schaft (f)	*(in-dus-trEE-geh-vEHrk- shahft)*	industrial union
Industrieplanung (f)	*(iin-dus-trEE-plAA-nunk)*	industrial planning
Industrieprodukte (pl)	*(in-dus-trEE-prOH-duk-teh)*	industrial goods
ineffizient	*(in-ehf-fi-tsEE-ehnt)*	inefficient
Inflation (f)	*(in-flah-tsee-OHn)*	inflation
inflationär	*(in-flah-tsee-oh-nAYr)*	inflationary
Informationswege (pl)	*(in-fohr-mah-tsee-OHnz- vAY-geh)*	mass media
Infrastruktur (f)	*(in-fraa-strook-tOOr)*	infrastructure
Ingenieur (m)	*(in-sheh-NEE-er)*	engineer
Ingenieurwesen (n)	*(EEn-shen-EEewr-vAY-zen)*	engineering
Inhaber (m)	*(IN-haa-buh)*	bearer, holder, owner, pro- prietary
Inhaberobligation (f)	*(IN-hah-buh-ob-li-gah-tsEE- ohn)*	bearer bond
Inhaberpapier (n)	*(IN-hah-buh-pah-pEEr)*	bearer security
Inhalt (m)	*(IN-hahlt)*	content

I

Inhaltsverzeichnis (n)	*(IN-hahlts-fuh-tsEYEKH-nis)*	table of contents
inländische Gesellschaft (f)	*(in-layn-dISH-eh geh-zEL-shahft)*	domestic corporation
inländische Steuern und Abgaben (pl)	*(in-layn-dISH-eh shtOY-uhn unt AHB-gAH-ben)*	internal revenue tax
inländischer Frachtbrief (m)	*(in-lAYn-dish-uh frAHKHt-brEEf)*	inland bill of lading
Inlandserzeugnis (n)	*(IN-lahnds-ayr-tsOYg-nis)*	native produce
Inlandwechsel (m)	*(IN-land vEHk-sel)*	domestic bill
Innenfinanzierung (f)	*(IN-nen-fee-nahn-tsEE-runk)*	internal funding
inner	*(IN-nuh)*	internal
innerbetriebliche Beziehungen (pl)	*(IN-nuh-beh-trEEp- beh-tsEE-hun-gen)*	employee relations
innerbetriebliche Revision (f)	*(IN-nuh-beh-trEEp-likh-eh rAY-vEE-zee-ohn)*	internal audit
innerer Wert (m)	*(IN-nuh-ruh vEHRt)*	intrinsic value
insolvent	*(IN-sohl-vehnt)*	insolvent
Inspektion (f)	*(in-spehk-tsEE-ohn)*	inspection
Inspektor (m)	*(in-spEHK-tohr)*	inspector
instandhalten	*(in-shtAHnt-hahl-ten)*	service (v)
Instandhaltung (f)	*(in-shtAHnt-hahl-tunk)*	maintenance
Instandhaltungsvertrag (m)	*(in-shtAHnt-hahl-tunks-fuh-trAHk)*	maintenance contract
institutioneller Investor (m)	*(in-stEE-too-tsEE-oh-nEL-luh in-vEHS-tohr)*	institutional investor
integrierter Schaltkreis (m)	*(in-teh-gREER-tuh shAHLt-krEYES)*	integrated circuit
Interesse (n)	*(in-tayr-reh-sEH)*	interest (general)
Interessenausgleich (m)	*(in-tayr-rEHs-sen-OWs-gleyekh)*	interest parity
Interessenkonflikt (m)	*(in-tayr-rEHs-sen-kon-flIkt)*	conflict of interest
interimistisch	*(in-teh-rim-mIS-tish)*	interim
intern	*(in-tAYrn)*	internal

I

Internationale Entwicklungsstelle (f)	*(in-tayr-nah-tsee-oh-nAA-leh ent-vIK-lunks-shtEHL-leh)*	International Development Agency
Internationale Wiederaufbaubank (f)	*(in-tayr-nah-tsee-oh-nAA-leh vEE-duh-OWf-bow-bahnk)*	World Bank
internationale Datumsgrenze (f)	*(in-tayr-nah-tsee-oh-nAA-leh DAA-tums-grEHn-tseh)*	International Date Line
interne Rendite (f)	*(in-tAYr-neh ren-di-teh)*	internal rate of return
interne Zinsflußrechnung (f)	*(in-tAYr-neh tsINs-floos-rEHKH-nunk)*	discounted cash flow
Interview (n)	*(in-tayr-fEEoo)*	interview
Inventar (n)	*(in-vehn-tAAr)*	inventory
Inventarstück (n)	*(in-vehn-tAAr-stEWk)*	fixture
investieren	*(in-vAY-stEE-ren)*	invest (v)
Investition (f)	*(in-vehs-ti-tsi-OHnz)*	investment
Investitionsanalyse (f)	*(in-vehs-ti-tsi-OHnz-ah-nah-lEW-zeh)*	investment analysis
Investitionsausgabe (f)	*(in-vehs-ti-tsi-OHnz-OWs-gAA-beh)*	capital expenditure
Investitionsbudget (n)	*(in-vehs-ti-tsi-OHnz-bew-tshEH)*	capital budget, investment budget
Investitionseinstufung und Bewertung (f)	*(in-vehs-ti-tsi-OHnzeyen-shtOO-funk unt beh-vEHR-tunk)*	investment grade
Investitionsgüter (pl)	*(in-vehs-ti-tsi-OHnz-gEW-tuh)*	capital goods, industrial goods
Investitionskriterien (pl)	*(in-vehs-ti-tsi-OHnz-krEE-tay-rEE-ehn)*	investment criteria
Investitionsliste (f)	*(in-vehs-ti-tsi-OHnz-lIS-teh)*	legal list (fiduciary investments)
Investitionspolitik (f)	*(in-vehs-ti-tsi-OHnz-po-li-tEEk)*	investment policy
Investitionsprogramm (n)	*(in-vehs-ti-tsi-OHnz-proh-grAHm)*	investment program
Investitionsstrategie (f)	*(in-vehs-ti-tsi-OHnz-staa-teh-gEE)*	investment strategy
Investmentfonds (m)	*(in-vehst-mEHnt-fOH)*	mutual fund

Investmentfonds mit begrenzter Emissionshöhe (m)	*(in-vehst-mEHnt-fOH mit beh-grEHNts-tuh eh-mi-see-OHn-hER-heh)*	closed-end fund
Investmentgesell-schaft (f)	*(in-vehst-mEHnt-geh-zEL-shahft)*	investment company, mutual fund
Investmenttreu-handgesellschaft (f)	*(in-vehst-mEHnt-trOY-hahnd-geh-zEL-shahft)*	investment trust
irreführend	*(EEr-reh-fEW-rent)*	misleading
Irrtum (m)	*(EEr-toom)*	error
Isolator (m)	*(EE-zo-LAA-tor)*	insulator
Isotop (n)	*(EE-zo-tohp)*	isotope
Istkosten (pl)	*(ISt-kOS-ten)*	actual costs

J

Jacke (f)	*(yAH-Keh)*	jacket
Jäger auf Nach-wuchskräfte (m)	*(yAY-guh OWf nAHKH-vUkhs-krehf-teh)*	headhunter
Jahr (n)	*(yaar)*	year
Jahresabrechnung (f)	*(yAAr-ehs-AHB-rEHKH-nunk)*	annual accounts
Jahresabschluß (m)	*(yAAr-ehs-AHB-shlUS)*	year-end
Jahresbericht (m)	*(yAAr-ehs-beh-rIKHt)*	annual report
Jahresprüfung (f)	*(yAAr-ehs-prEW-funk)*	annual audit
Jahresrente (f)	*(yAAr-ehs-rAYn-teh)*	annuity
jahreszeitlich	*(yAAr-ehs-tsEYEt-likh)*	seasonal
Jahrgang (m)	*(yAAR-gahnk)*	vintage year
jährlich	*(yAYr-likh)*	annual
Jasonsklausel (f)	*(yAH-sohns-klOW-zehl)*	Jason clause
Jod (n)	*(yOHt)*	iodine
Journal (n)	*(djoor-naal)*	journal
Juniorpartner (m)	*(djOO-neeohr pAHrt-nuh)*	junior partner
juristische Person (f)	*(yoo-rIS-tish-eh payr-zOHn)*	legal entity
justieren	*(yus-tEE-ren)*	justify (v)

K

Kabel (n)	*(kAA-behl)*	cable
Kabelfernsehen (n)	*(KAA-bel-fehrn-zay-hen)*	cable television
Kabriolett (n)	*(kahb-ri-o-LET)*	convertible
Kaffeepause (f)	*(kAH-fay-pOW-zeh)*	coffee break
Kaffekanne (f)	*(kahf-fAY-kAHN-neh)*	coffeepot
Kai (m)	*(keye)*	wharf
Kaigebühren (pl)	*(kEYE-geh-bEW-ren)*	wharfage charges
Kalbsleder (n)	*(kAHLbs-lAY-duh)*	calfskin
Kalkstein (m)	*(kahlk-shTEYEn)*	limestone
Kaltwalzen (n)	*(kAHLT-vAL-tsen)*	cold rolling
Kamelhaar (n)	*(kah-mAYL-HAAr)*	camel's hair
Kanal (m)	*(kah-nAAL)*	channel
Kaninchen (n)	*(kah-nEEN-khen)*	rabbit
Kanne (f)	*(KAHN-neh)*	pitcher
Kapazität (f)	*(kah-pah-tsee-tAYt)*	capacity
Kapazitätsausnut-zung (f)	*(kah-pah-tsee-taAYts-OWs-nU-tsunk)*	capacity utilization
Kapazitätsausnut-zungsgrad (m)	*(kah-pah-tsEE-tayts-OWs-nU-tsunks-grAAt)*	load factor
Kapital (n)	*(kah-pi-tAAL)*	capital
Kapital blockieren	*(kah-pi-tAAL blo-kEE-rehn)*	lock in
Kapitalanlage (f)	*(kah-pi-tAAL-AHN-laa-geh)*	investment
Kapitalanlage ohne geborgte Mittel (f)	*(kah-pi-tAAL-AHN-laa-geh ohneh geh-bOHrg-teh mit-tEL)*	gearless
Kapitalaufbrin-gung (f)	*(kah-pi-tAAL-OWf-brINg-unk)*	raising capital
Kapitalaufwand (m)	*(kah-pi-tAAL-OWf-vahnt)*	capital expenditure
Kapitalaufwendun-gen (pl)	*(kah-pi-tAAL-OWf-vehn-dOOng-ehn)*	capital spending
Kapitalausfuhr (f)	*(kah-pi-tAAL-OWs-foor)*	capital exports
Kapitalerhöhung (f)	*(kah-pi-tAAL-uh-hER-unk)*	capital increase

Kapitalertrag (Kapitalverlust) (m)	*(kah-pi-tAAL-uh-trAHk [kah-pi-tAAL-fuh-lUst])*	capital gain (loss)
Kapitalflußrechnung (f)	*(kah-pi-tAAL-flus-rEHKH-nunk)*	cash flow statement
kapitalintensiv	*(kah-pi-tAAL-in-ten-zEEf)*	capital-intensive
Kapitalisierung (f)	*(kah-pi-tAAL-EE-zEE-runk)*	capitalization
Kapitalismus (m)	*(kah-pi-tAA-lis-mus)*	capitalism
Kapitalkoeffizient (m)	*(kah-pi-tAAL-koh-ayf-fEE-tsEE-ehnt)*	capital-output ratio
Kapitalkonto (n)	*(kah-pi-tAAL-kON-toh)*	capital account
Kapitalkosten (pl)	*(kah-pi-tAAL-kOS-ten)*	cost of capital
Kapitalmarkt (m)	*(kah-pi-tAAL-mAHrkt)*	capital market
Kapitalrendite (f)	*(kah-pi-tAAL-ren-dEE-teh)*	return on capital
Kapitalrückflußdauer (f)	*(kah-pi-tAAL-rEWk-floos-dOW-uh)*	payout period
Kapitalstruktur (f)	*(kah-pi-tAAL-strook-tOOr)*	capital structure
Kapitalüberschuß (m)	*(kah-pi-tAAL-EW-buh-shus)*	capital surplus
Kapitalverzinsung (f)	*(kah-pi-tAAL-fuhr-tsINs-zunk)*	return on investment
Kapitel (n)	*(kah-PI-tel)*	chapter
Kapsel (f)	*(kAP-sel)*	capsule
Kapuze (f)	*(kah-PU-tseh)*	hood
Karaffe (f)	*(kah-rAHF-feh)*	decanter
Karosserie (f)	*(kah-ros-seh-REE)*	body
Kartell (n)	*(kahr-tEHL)*	cartel, combination
Kartellgesetze (pl)	*(kahr-tEHL-geh-zEHt-seh)*	antitrust laws
Kaschmirwolle (f)	*(kah-shmEER-vOL-leh)*	cashmere
Käsebrett (n)	*(KAY-zeh-breht)*	cheese-tray
Kassabuch (n)	*(kAH-saa-bOOkh)*	cash book
Kassamarkt (m)	*(kAH-saa-mAHrkt)*	spot market
Kassaskonto (n)	*(kAH-saa-kON-toh)*	cash discount
Kasse (f)	*(kAH-seh)*	fund
Kassenbestand (m)	*(kAH-sehn-beh-shtAHnd)*	cash balance
Kasseneintrag (m)	*(kAH-sehn-eyen-trAHk)*	cash entry

K

Kassenhaltung (f)	*(kAH-sehn-hAAl-tunk)*	cash management
Kassenreserven (pl)	*(kAH-sehn-reh-zAYr-fehn)*	primary reserves
Kassenscheck (m)	*(kAH-sehn-shehk)*	cashier's check
Kassenvoranschlag (m)	*(kAH-sehn-FOHR-AHN-shlAHk)*	cash budget
Kassette (f)	*(kah-SEH-teh)*	cassette
Kassierer für Aus-zahlungen (m)	*(kah-sEE-ruh fEWr OWs-tsAA-lun-gen)*	paymaster
Katalog (m)	*(kah-tah-lOHg)*	catalog
Katalogisierung (f)	*(kah-tAA-loh-gEE-sEE-runk)*	listing
Katalysator (m)	*(kah-tah-LEW-zah-tohr)*	catalytic converter
Katalysator (m)	*(kah-tah-LEW-zah-tohr)*	catalyst
Kathode (f)	*(kah-TOH-deh)*	cathode
Kaufauftrag (m)	*(kOWf-OWf-trAHk)*	purchase order
Kaufbrief (m)	*(kOWf brEEf)*	deed of sale
kaufen	*(kOW-fen)*	purchase (v)
Käufer (m)	*(kOY-fuh)*	buyer
Käuferaufgeld (n)	*(kOY-fuh-OWf-GEHLT)*	buyer's premium
Käufermarkt (m)	*(kOY-fuh-mAHrkt)*	buyer's market
Käuferoption (f)	*(kOY-fuh-ohp-tsEE-ohn)*	buyer's option
Kaufhaus (n)	*(kOWf-hOWs)*	department store
Kaufinteressent (m)	*(kOWf-in-tayr-rehs-sENT)*	potential buyer
Kaufkraft (f)	*(kOWf-krahft)*	purchasing power
Kaufmann (m)	*(kOWf-mahn)*	merchant
kaufmännisch	*(kOWf-mAY-nish)*	mercantile
Kaufmannsinnung (f)	*(kOWf-mahns-sIn-nunk)*	merchant guild
Kaufpreis (m)	*(kOWf-prEYEs)*	purchase price
Kaufvertrag (m)	*(kOWf-fuh-trAHk)*	bill of sale
Kaution (f)	*(kow-tsEE-ohn)*	deposit
Kautionsversicher-ungsgesellschaft (f)	*(kow-tsEE-ohns-fuh-ZIKH-eh-rungs-geh-zEL-shahft)*	guaranty company, surety company
kein Problem	*(keyen prOH-blaym)*	no problem

K

Kelter (f)	*(kEL-tuh)*	winepress
kennzeichnen	*(kEHN-tsEYE-khen)*	earmark (v)
Kernkraftwerk (n)	*(kern-kraft-verk)*	nuclear power station
Kerzenständer (m)	*(kuh-tsen-shTEHN-duh)*	candlestick
Keynessche Wirt-schaftslehre (f)	*(kEHNs-sheh vEErt-shahtfs-lAY-reh)*	Keynesian economics
Kilometerzähler (m)	*(KI-loh-mAY-tuh-tsAY-luh)*	odometer
Kilowatt (n)	*(KI-loh-vaht)*	kilowatt
Kiste (f)	*(kIS-teh)*	case
Klage (f)	*(klAA-geh)*	lawsuit, legal action
Klang (m)	*(klAnk)*	tone
Klappe (f)	*(klAHP-peh)*	valve
Klartext (m)	*(klAAr-text)*	hard copy
Kleid (n)	*(klEYEt)*	dress
Kleidung (f)	*(klEYE-dunk)*	apparel
Kleinaktie (f)	*(klEYEn-ak-tsEE-eh)*	penny stock
Kleinanzeige (f)	*(klEYEn-AHN-tseye-geh)*	classified advertisement, want-ad
Kleinbetrieb (m)	*(klEYEn-beh-trEEp)*	small business
Kleinbuchstaben (pl)	*(klEYEn-bOOKH-shtah-behn)*	lower case
kleiner Diebstahl (m)	*(klEYEn-uh dEEb-shtaal)*	pilferage
Klima (n)	*(kLEE-mah)*	climate
knapp bei Kasse	*(knahp beye kAH-seh)*	short of cash
Knappheit (f)	*(knAHp-heyet)*	short supply
Knopf (m)	*(knOpf)*	button
Knopfloch (n)	*(knOpf-lOKH)*	buttonhole
Koaxialkabel (n)	*(ko-ahxi-AAL-KAA-bel)*	coaxial cable
Kodizill (n)	*(koh-dee-tsIL)*	codicil
Koffer (m)	*(kOF-fuh)*	suitcase, trunk
Kohle (f)	*(KOH-leh)*	coal
Kohlehydrat (n)	*(KOH-le-hEW-draat)*	carbohydrate
Kohlenstoff (m)	*(KOH-len-shtOF)*	carbon

K

Kohlenstoffstahl (m)	*(KOH-len-shtOF-shtAAL)*	carbon steel
Kohlenwasserstoff (m)	*(KOH-len-vAHS-suh-shtOF)*	hydrocarbon
Kolben (m)	*(kOL-ben)*	piston
Kollege (m)	*(koh-lAY-geh)*	colleague
Kollektivversicherung (f)	*(koh-lehk-tEEf-fuh-ZIKH-eh-runk)*	blanket insurance
Kommanditgesellschaft (f)	*(koh-mAHn-dit-geh-zEL-shahft)*	limited partnership
Kommissionär (m)	*(koh-mee-sEE-oh-nAYr)*	factor (agent)
kommissionsweise	*(koh-mee-sEE-OHns-vEYE-seh)*	on consignment
Kommunalobligation	*(ko-moo-nAAl-ob-li-gah-tsee-ohn)*	municipal bond
Kommunalsteuer (f)	*(ko-moo-nAAl-shtOY-uh)*	local tax
Kompensationshandel (m)	*(kohm-pehn-zaa-tsEE-OHns-hAHn-dehl)*	compensation trade
Komponente (f)	*(kom-PO-nen-tEH)*	component
Kondensator (m)	*(kon-den-ZAA-tor)*	condensor
Konferenzraum (m)	*(kon-fayr-rEHnts-rOWm)*	conference room
Konflikt (m)	*(kon-flIKT)*	dispute
Konjunkturindikatoren (pl)	*(kon-yunk-tOOr-in-dee-kAA-toh-rehn)*	economic indicators
Konjunkturspritze (f)	*(kon-yunk-tOOr-shprI-tseh)*	pump priming
Konjunkturzyklus (m)	*(kon-yunk-tOOr-tsEW-kloos)*	business cycle
Konkurrent (m)	*(kon-koor-rEHnt)*	competitor
Konkurrenz (f)	*(kon-koor-rEHnts)*	competition
konkurrenzfähiger Preis (m)	*(kon-koor-rEHnts-fAY-hi-guh prEYEs)*	competitive price
Konkurrenzstudie (f)	*(kon-koor-rEHnts-shtoo-di-eh)*	competitor analysis
Konkurs (m)	*(kon-kOOrs)*	bankruptcy, failure
Können (n)	*(kER-nen)*	know-how

K

Konnossementsga-rantie (f)	*(kon-no-seh-mEHnts-gah-rahn-tEE)*	letter of indemnity
konsolidierte Bilanz (f)	*(kon-soh-lee-dEE-rer-teh bee-lAHnts)*	consolidation
konsolidierter Finanzbericht (m)	*(kon-soh-lee-dEEr-tuh fee-nAHnts-beh-rIKHt)*	consolidated financial statement
Konsortium (n)	*(kon-zOHr-tEE-um)*	consortium, syndicate
Konsulatsfaktura (f)	*(kon-soo-lAAts-fahk-tOO-raa)*	consular invoice
Konsumentenkredit (m)	*(kon-soo-mEHn-ten-kray-dIT)*	consumer credit
Konsumgüter (pl)	*(kon-sOOm-gEW-tuh)*	consumer goods
Kontingent (n)	*(kon-tin-gEHnt)*	quota
Kontingentierungs-system (n)	*(kon-tin-gEHn-tEE-runks-zew-stAYm)*	quota system
kontinuierliche Walztraße (f)	*(kon-TEE-noo-EER-li-kheh vALTS-shtrAA-seh)*	continuous mill
Konto (n)	*(kON-toh)*	account
Kontoauszug (m)	*(kON-toh-OWs-tsOOk)*	bank statement, statement of account
Kontokorrentgut-haben (n)	*(kON-toh-kor-rEHnt-gOOt-haa-behn)*	compensating balance
Kontokorrentkon-to (n)	*(kON-toh-kor-rEHnt-KON-toh)*	open account
Kontokorrentkre-ditlinie (f)	*(kON-tohkor-rEHnt-kray-dIT-lee-nEE-eh)*	demand line of credit
Kontonummer (f)	*(kON-toh-num-muh)*	account number
Kontostand (m)	*(kON-toh-shtahnt)*	account balance
Kontrahent (m)	*(kON-trah-hEHnt)*	party
kontrollieren	*(kON-troh-lEE-rehn)*	manage (v) (control)
kontrollierte Kosten (pl)	*(kON-troh-lEEr-teh kOS-ten)*	managed costs
kontrollierter Kas-senvorschuß (m)	*(kON-troh-lEEr-tuh kah-sEHn-FOHR-shoos)*	managed float
Kontrolliste (f)	*(kon-trohl-lIS-teh)*	checklist
konvertierbare Obligationen (pl)	*(kon-fuh-tEEr-baa-reh ob-li-gah-tsEE-ohn-nehn)*	convertible debentures

konvertierbare Vorzugsaktie (f)	*(kon-fuh-tEEr-bAA-reh FOHR-tsoogs-ak-tsEE-eh)*	convertible preferred stock
Konzentration (f)	*(kon-tsen-trAH-TSI-on)*	concentration
Konzern (m)	*(kon-tsAYrn)*	combination
Konzernabschluß (m)	*(kon-tsAYrn-AHb-shlUS)*	consolidation, group account
Konzerngesellschaft (f)	*(kon-tsAYrn-geh-zEL-shahft)*	affiliate, subsidiary
Konzernunternehmen (n)	*(kon-tsAYrn-un-tuh-nAY-men)*	associate company
Konzessionsbetrieb (m)	*(kon-tsehs-sEE-OHns-beh-trEEp)*	franchise
Kooperationsabkommen (n)	*(koh-oh-peh-rah-tsEE-OHns-ahb-kOM-mehn)*	cooperation agreement
Kopfjäger (m)	*(KOpf-yay-guh)*	headhunter
Kopie (f)	*(ko-PEE)*	copy
Kopplungsgeschäft (n)	*(kOP-lungs-geh-shEHft)*	package deal
Korken (m)	*(kor-ken)*	cork
Korkenzieher (m)	*(kor-ken-tsEE-huh)*	corkscrew
Korn (n)	*(kohrn)*	grain
körperliche Inventur (f)	*(kER-puh-likh-eh in-vehn-tOOr)*	physical inventory
Körperschaftssteuer (f)	*(kER-puh-shahfts-shtOY-uh)*	corporate tax
Korrekturlesen (n)	*(kor-rehk-tOOR-lay-zen)*	proofreading
Korrespondenz (f)	*(koh-rehs-pon-dEHnts)*	correspondence
Korrespondenzbank (f)	*(koh-rehs-pon-dEHnts-bahnk)*	correspondent bank
Kosmetiktäschchen (n)	*(kos-mAY-tik-tEHSH-khen)*	makeup case
Kosten (pl)	*(kOS-ten)*	cost
Kosten und Fracht	*(kOS-ten unt frAHKHt)*	cost and freight
Kostenanalyse (f)	*(kOS-ten-ah-nah-lEW-zeh)*	cost analysis
Kostenaufteilungsverfahren (n)	*(kOS-ten-OWf-tEYE-lungs-fuh-fAA-rehn)*	absorption costing
Kostendeckung (f)	*(kOS-ten-DEK-kung)*	recovery of expenses

K

Kostendeckungs-punkt (m)	*(kOS-ten-DEK-unks-pUnkt)*	break-even point
Kosteneinsparung (f)	*(kOS-ten-EYEn-shpAA-runk)*	cost reduction
Kostenfaktor (m)	*(kOS-ten-FAHK-tohr)*	cost factor
kostenintensiv	*(kOS-ten-in-ten-zEEf)*	cost effective
Kostennutzenana-lyse (f)	*(kOS-ten-nU-tsen-ah-nah-lEW-zeh)*	cost-benefit analysis
Kostenpreisschere (f)	*(kOS-ten-prEYEs-shAY-reh)*	cost-price squeeze
Kostenrechnung (f)	*(kOS-ten-rEHKH-nunk)*	cost accounting
Kostenüberwa-chung (f)	*(kOS-ten-EWb-uh-vAAkh-unk)*	cost control
Kostenzuteilung (f)	*(kOS-ten-tsoo-tEYE-lunk)*	allocation of costs
Kotflügel (m)	*(kot-flEW-gel)*	fender
Krachverfahren (n)	*(KRAHKH-fuh-fAA-ren)*	cracking
Kraft (f)	*(krAHft)*	power
Kraftfahrzeug (n)	*(krAHft-fAAR-tsOYK)*	car
Kraftfahrzeugsam-melpolice (f)	*(krAHft-faar-tsoygs-zAAm-mehl-poh-lee-sAY)*	fleet policy
Kragen (m)	*(kRAH-gen)*	collar
Krämer (m)	*(krAY-muh)*	merchant
Krankheit (f)	*(KRAHNK-heyet)*	disease
Krankheitsurlaub (m)	*(krAHnk-heyets-OOr-lowb)*	sick leave
Krawatte (f)	*(kRAH-vAT-teh)*	necktie
Kredit (m)	*(kray-dIT)*	credit
Kreditanstalt (f)	*(kray-dIT-ahn-shtAAlt)*	credit bureau
Kreditbank (f)	*(kray-dIT-bahnk)*	credit bank
Kreditbedingungen (pl)	*(kray-dIT-beh-dEEn-gunk-ehn)*	credit terms
Kreditbrief (m)	*(kray-dIT-brEEf)*	letter of credit
Krediteinschät-zung (f)	*(kray-dIT-EYEn-shEHts-tsunk)*	credit rating
Kreditkarte (f)	*(kray-dIT-kAAr-teh)*	credit card
Kreditkäufer (m)	*(kray-dIT-kOY-fuh)*	credit buyer

K

Kreditkonto (n)	*(kray-dIT-kON-toh)*	charge account
Kreditkontrolle (f)	*(kray-dIT-KON-trol-leh)*	credit control
Kreditkündigung mit Geldforde- rung (f)	*(kray-dIT-kEWn-di-gunk mit GEHLT-FOHR-deh-runk)*	margin call
Kreditlinie (f)	*(kray-dIT-lEE-nee-eh)*	credit line
Kreditreferenz (f)	*(kray-dIT-reh-feh-rEHnts)*	credit reference
Kreditsaldo (m)	*(kray-dIT-zAAl-doh)*	credit balance
Kreditsicherungs- grenze (f)	*(kray-dIT-zikh-eh-runks- grEHN-tseh)*	lending margin
Kreditüberschrei- tung (f)	*(kray-dIT-EW-buh-shrEYE- tunk)*	overdraft
Kreditverein (m)	*(kray-dIT-fuh-EYEn)*	credit union
Kreditversiche- rung (f)	*(kray-dIT-fuh-ZIKH-eh- runk)*	credit insurance
Kreditverwaltung (f)	*(kray-dIT-fuh-vAHl-tunk)*	credit management
Kreisdiagramm (n)	*(krEYEs-dee-ah-grAHm)*	pie chart
Kreislaufwirtschaft (f)	*(KREYES-lahf-veert-shahft)*	recycling economy
Krise (f)	*(krEE-seh)*	depression
Kristallglasherstel- lung (f)	*(kris-tAHL-glAAs-huh- shTEL-lunk)*	crystal glass manufacturing
Kristallisierung (f)	*(kris-tAHL-li-ZEE-runk)*	crystallization
Krug (m)	*(krUk)*	pitcher
Küfer (m)	*(kEW-fuh)*	cooper
Kühlerschutzgitter (n)	*(kEW-luh-shuts-git-tuh)*	grille
Kukuruz	*(ku-ku-rOOts)*	maize
Kulturbesitz (m)	*(kul-tOOr-beh-zITs)*	cultural property
kumulativ	*(koo-moo-lah-tEEf)*	cumulative
kumulative Vor- zugsaktie (f)	*(koo-moo-laa-tEE-feh FOHR-tsoogs-ak-tsEE- eh)*	cumulative preferred stock
kündbare Obliga- tion (f)	*(kEWnd-bAA-reh ob-li-gah- tsEE-ohn)*	redeemable bond
Kunde (m)	*(kUN-deh)*	customer
Kundenbetreuer (m)	*(kUN-dehn-beh-tOY-uh)*	account executive

K

Kundendienst (m)	*(kUN-dehn-dEEnst)*	after-sales service, customer service
Kundenkredit (m)	*(kUN-dehn-kray-dIT)*	consumer credit
kündigen	*(kEWn-di-gehn)*	call (v), terminate (v) (employment)
Kündigungsklausel (f)	*(kEWn-di-gunks-klOW-zehl)*	call feature
Kündigungspreis (m)	*(kEWn-di-gunks-prEYEs)*	call price
Kündigungsregel (f)	*(kEWn-di-gunks-rAY-gehl)*	call rule
Kündigungsschutz (m)	*(kEWn-di-gunks-shuts)*	call protection
Kündigungstarif (m)	*(kEWn-di-gunks-tah-rIF)*	call rate
Kunjunkturab- schwung (m)	*(koon-yoonk-tOOr-ab- shvOOng)*	downswing
Kunst (f)	*(kUNst)*	art
künstliche Fasern (pl)	*(kEWnst-likh-eh fAA-zuhn)*	manmade fibers
Kunstseide (f)	*(kUNst-zeYE-deh)*	rayon
Kunststoffe (pl)	*(kUNst-shtOF-feh)*	manmade materials
Kupfer (n)	*(kup-fEHR)*	copper
Kupplung (f)	*(kUP-lunk)*	clutch
Kupplungspedal (n)	*(kUP-lunks-peh-dahl)*	clutch pedal
Kurbelstange (f)	*(kUR-bel-shtAHN-geh)*	connecting rod
Kurbelwelle (f)	*(kUR-bel-vEL-leh)*	crankshaft
Kurier (m)	*(koo-REER)*	courier
Kurs (m)	*(koors)*	rate
Kurs-Ertrag Ver- hältnis (n)	*(koors-uh-trAHk fuh-hEHLt- nis)*	price/earnings (p/e)
Kursfestsetzer (m)	*(koors-fehst-zEHts-uh)*	market-maker
kursiv	*(kur-zEEF)*	italic
Kurssicherung (f)	*(koors-zikh-uh-runk)*	forward cover
Kursstützung (f)	*(koors-shtEW-tsunk)*	pegging
Kursverlust (m)	*(koors-fuh-lUst)*	exchange loss
Kurswert (m)	*(koors-vEHRt)*	market value (stocks)

K

kurze Ärmel (pl)	*(KUr-tseh AYR-mel)*	short sleeves
kurze und mittel-fristige Verbind-lichkeiten (pl)	*(kURts-eh unt mit-tEL-frist-ti-geh fuh-bINd-likh-keye-ten)*	accounts payable
kurzfristig	*(kURts-fris-tikh)*	above-the-line (short term)
kurzfristige Finan-zierung (f)	*(kURts-fris-tikh-eh fee-nahnts-tsEE-runk)*	short-term financing
kurzfristige Ver-bindlichkeiten (pl)	*(kURts-fris-tikh-eh fuh-bINd-likh-keye-ten)*	current liabilities
kurzfristige Ver-schuldung (f)	*(kURts-fris-tikh-eh fuh-shUl-dunk)*	short-term debt
kurzfristiges Kapi-talkonto (n)	*(kURts-fris-tikh-ehs-kah-pi-tAAL-kON-toh)*	short-term capital account
kurzfristiges Umlaufvermö-gen (n)	*(kURts-fris-tikh-ehs OOm-lOWf-fuh-mER-gen)*	current assets, floating assets
kurzlebiges Wirt-schaftsgut (n)	*(kURts-lAY-bi-gehs vEErt-shahfts-gOOt)*	wasting asset
Kurzversicherung (f)	*(kURts-fuh-ZIKH-eh-runk)*	term insurance
Kurzwelle (f)	*(KUrts-vEL-leh)*	short wave

L

Labor (n)	*(lah-bOHR)*	laboratory
Labortechniker (m)	*(lah-bOHR-tehkh-ni-kuh)*	laboratory technician
Laden (m)	*(LAA-dehn)*	store
Ladenbesitzer (m)	*(LAA-dehn-beh-zIT-suh)*	merchant
Ladung (f)	*(LAA-dunk)*	cargo
Ladungsfähigkeit (f)	*(LAA-dunks-fAY-hig-keyet)*	tonnage
Ladungsriemen (pl)	*(LAA-dunks-rEE-men)*	strapping
Lageraufseher (m)	*(LAA-guh-OWf-zAY-uh)*	warehousekeeper
Lagerhaus (n)	*(LAA-guh-hOWs)*	warehouse
Lagerkosten (pl)	*(LAA-guh-kOS-ten)*	carrying charges

K

Lagerumschlag (m)	*(LAA-guh-um-shlAHk)*	inventory turnover, stock turnover
Lagerumschlag des Grossisten (m)	*(LAA-guh-OOm-shlAHk dehs groh-sIS-ten)*	jobber's turn
Lagerung (f)	*(LAA-geh-runk)*	storage
Land (n)	*(lahnd)*	land, country
Land-Seewegver- kehr (m)	*(LAHnd-zAY-vAYg-fuh- kAYr)*	fishyback service
Landungsgebühren (pl)	*(LAHn-dunks-geh-bEW-ren)*	landing charges
Landwirtschaft (f)	*(LAHnd-vEErt-shahft)*	agriculture
landwirtschaftliche Erzeugnisse (pl)	*(LAHnd-vEErt-shahft-likh- eh AYr-tzOYg-nis-seh)*	agricultural products
landwirtschaftli- ches Akzept (n)	*(LAHnd-vEErt-shahft-likh- ehs ahk-tsEPt)*	agricultural paper
Landzuteilung (f)	*(LAHnd-tsOO-teye-lunk)*	land grant
lange Ärmel (pl)	*(LAHN-geh AYR-mel)*	long sleeves
lange diskutieren	*(lAHn-geh dis-koo-tEE-ren)*	jawbone (v)
lange Hose (f)	*(LAHN-geh hOH-zeh)*	slacks
Länge (f)	*(LEHN-geh)*	length
langfristig	*(lAHng-fris-tikh)*	below the line
langfristige Pla- nung (f)	*(lAHng-fris-tikh-eh plAA- nunk)*	long-range planning
langfristige Schuld (f)	*(lAHng-fris-tikh-eh shUlt)*	long-term debt
langfristige Ver- bindlichkeit (f)	*(lAHng-fris-tikh-eh fuh- bINd-likh-keyet)*	fixed liability
langfristige Ver- mögenswerte (pl)	*(lAHng-fris-tikh-eh fuh- mER-gens-vEHR-teh)*	noncurrent assets
langfristige Verzin- sung (f)	*(lAHng-fris-tikh-eh fuh- tsINs-zunk)*	long interest
langfristiger Ter- minkauf (m)	*(lAHng-fris-tikh-eh tayr- mEEn-kOWf)*	long hedge
langfristiges Kapi- talkonto (n)	*(lAHng-fris-tikh-ehs kah-pi- tAAL-kON-toh)*	long-term capital account
langlebige Gebrauchsgüter (pl)	*(lAHng-lAY-bi-geh geh- brOWkhs-gEW-tuh)*	durable goods

L

Laser (m)	*(LAA-zuh)*	laser
lastenfrei	*(lAHs-ten-frEYE)*	free and clear (unencumbered)
Lastschrift (f)	*(lAHst-shrift)*	debit entry
Lastschriftanzeige (f)	*(lAHst-shrift-AHN-tseye-geh)*	debit note
Lastwagenladung (f)	*(lAHst-vAA-gehn-lAA-dunk)*	truckload
laufende Ausgaben (pl)	*(lOW-fehn-deh OWs-gAA-behn)*	fixed expenses
laufende Kosten (pl)	*(lOW-fehn-deh kOS-ten)*	standing charges
laufende Rendite (f)	*(lOW-fehn-deh ren-dI-teh)*	current yield
laufende Unkosten (f)	*(lOW-fehn-deh OOn-kOS-ten)*	running expenses
laufendes Konto (n)	*(lOW-fehn-dehs kON-toh)*	open account
laut Bericht	*(lowt beh-rIKHt)*	as per advice
Lauterkeit des Wettbewerbs (f)	*(lOW-tuh-keyet dehs VEHt-beh-vAYrbs)*	fair trade
Lautsprecher (m)	*(LOWt-shpreh-khuh)*	speaker
Layout (n)	*(LAY-owt)*	layout
Lebensdauer (f)	*(lAY-behnz-dOW-uh)*	life cycle, product life
Lebenshaltungsindex (m)	*(lAY-behnz-hAAl-tunks-IN-dehx)*	consumer price index
Lebenshaltungskosten (pl)	*(lAY-behnz-hAAl-tunks-kOS-ten)*	cost of living
Lebenslauf (m)	*(lAY-behnz-lOWf)*	curriculum vitae
Lebensmittel (pl)	*(lAY-behnz-mit-tEL)*	foodstuffs
Lebensstandard (m)	*(lAY-behnz-shtahn-dahrd)*	standard of living
Lebensversicherungspolice (f)	*(lAY-behnz-fuh-ZIKH-eh-rungs-poh-lee-sAY)*	life insurance policy
Leckage (f)	*(lehk-AAdj)*	leakage
Leder (n)	*(lAY-duh)*	leather
Lederjacke (f)	*(lAY-duh-yAH-Keh)*	leather jacket
Lederwaren (pl)	*(lAY-duh-VAAren)*	leather goods

L

Leerfracht (f)	*(lAYr-frAHKHt)*	dead freight
Leerverkauf (m)	*(lAYr-fuh-kOWf)*	short sale
Leerverkaufsposition (f)	*(lAYr-fuh-kOWfs-po-zi-tsEE-OHN)*	short position
Legierstahl (m)	*(leh-gEEr-shtAAL)*	alloy steel
Lehrling (m)	*(lAYr-ling)*	apprentice
Lehrmodell (n)	*(lAYr-moh-dEL)*	mock-up
Leibrentenempfänger (m)	*(lEYEb-rEHn-ten-em-pfAYng-uh)*	annuitant
Leinen (n)	*(LEYE-nen)*	linen
Leistungsfähigkeit (f)	*(lEYEs-tungs-fAY-hig-keyet)*	efficiency
leiten	*(lEYE-tehn)*	manage (v)
leitender Angestellter (m)	*(lEYE-tehn-duh AHN-geh-shtEHL-tuh)*	executive
Leiter (m)	*(lEYE-tuh)*	leader, manager
Leiter der Exportabteilung (m)	*(lEYE-tuh duh ehx-pOHrt-AHB-tEYE-lunk)*	export manager
Leiter der Finanzabteilung (m)	*(lEYE-tuh duh fee-nAHnts-AHB-tEYE-lunk)*	treasurer
Leiter des Rechnungswesens (m)	*(lEYE-tuh dehs rEHKH-nungs-vAY-zens)*	controller
Leitkurs (m)	*(lEYEt-koors)*	central rate
Leitung (f)	*(lEYE-tunk)*	management
Leitung durch Röhren (f)	*(lEYE-tunk dURKH rER-rehn)*	pipage
Leitungsschicht (f)	*(lEYE-tungs-shikht)*	management team
Leitzinssatz (m)	*(lEYEt-tsINs-zAHts)*	prime rate
Lernkurve (f)	*(lAYrn-kOOr-feh)*	learning curve
letzter Termin (m)	*(lEHts-tuh tayr-mEEn)*	deadline
Lichtmaschine (f)	*(LIKHT-mah-SHEE-neh)*	generator
Lieferant (m)	*(lee-fuh-rAHnt)*	supplier
Lieferpreis (m)	*(LEE-fuh-prEYEs)*	delivery price
Lieferschein (m)	*(LEE-fuh-shEYEn)*	delivery notice
Liefertermin (m)	*(LEE-fuh-tayr-mEEn)*	date of delivery
Lieferung (f)	*(LEE-feh-runk)*	delivery

Lieferungsangebot (n)	*(LEE-feh-rungs-AHN-geh-boht)*	tender offer
Liegegeld (n)	*(LEE-geh-GEHLT)*	demurrage (fee for)
Liegetage (pl)	*(LEE-geh-tAA-geh)*	laydays
Liegezeit (f)	*(LEE-geh-tsEYEt)*	lay time
limitierte Börsenorder (f)	*(li-mee-tEEr-teh bER-zehn-OR-duh)*	limit order
limitierter Börsenauftrag (m)	*(li-mee-tEEr-tuh bER-zehn-OWf-trAHk)*	stop-loss order
lineare Bedingungen (pl)	*(lin-ay-AA-reh beh-dEEng-unk-ehn)*	linear terms
lineare Programmierung (f)	*(lin-ay-AA-reh proh-grAHm-mEE-runk)*	linear programming
lineare Schätzung (f)	*(lin-ay-AA-reh shEH-tsunk)*	lineal estimation
Linie (f)	*(LEE-ni-eh)*	line
Liniendirektor (m)	*(LEE-nee-ehn-di-REHK-tohr)*	line executive
Linienmanagement (n)	*(LEE-nee-ehn-mehn-EHdj-mehnt)*	line management
Liquidität (f)	*(li-kvi-dee-tAYt)*	cash flow, liquidity
Liquiditätsbevorzugung (f)	*(li-kvi-dee-tAYts-FOHR-tsoo-gunk)*	liquidity preference
Liquiditätsgrad (m)	*(li-kvi-dee-tAYts-grAAd)*	current ratio, liquidity ratio
Listenpreis (m)	*(lIS-tehn-prEYEs)*	list price
Liter (m)	*(LEE-tuh)*	liter
Lizenz (f)	*(lee-tsEHnts)*	license
Lizenzaustausch (m)	*(lee-tsEHnts-OWs-tOWsh)*	cross-licensing
Lizenzbetrieb (m)	*(lee-tsEHnts-beh-trEEp)*	franchise
Lizenzgebühr (f)	*(lee-tsEHnts-geh-bEWr)*	royalty (patent)
Lizenzgebühren (pl)	*(lee-tsEHnts-geh-bEW-ren)*	license fees
LKW-Ladung (f)	*(EL-KAA-VAY lAA-dunk)*	truck-load
Locher (m)	*(lOKH-uh)*	keypuncher
Lochkarte (f)	*(lOKH-kAAr-teh)*	punch card
Lochstreifen (m)	*(lOKH-shtrEYE-fehn)*	paper tape

L

Lockartikel (m)	*(lOK-ahr-tIK-el)*	leader, loss leader
Lockvogelangebot (n)	*(lOK-foh-gehl-AHN-geh-boht)*	loss leader
Löffel (m)	*(LERF-fel)*	spoon
Logistik (f)	*(loh-gIS-tik)*	logistics
Lohn (m)	*(lohn)*	wage
Lohn-Preis-Spirale (f)	*(LOHN-prEYEs-shpEE-rAA-leh)*	wage-price spiral
Löhne (pl)	*(lER-neh)*	wages
Lohnempfänger (m)	*(LOHN-emp-fAYng-uh)*	wage earner
lohnintensiv	*(LOHN-in-ten-zEEf)*	labor-intensive
Lohnliste (f)	*(LOHN-lIS-teh)*	payroll
Lohnniveau (n)	*(LOHN-nee-voh)*	wage level
Lohnrichtung (f)	*(LOHN-rIKH-tunk)*	wage drift
Lohnrückstand (m)	*(LOHN-rEWk-shtAHnd)*	back pay
Lohnskala (f)	*(LOHN-skAA-lah)*	wage scale
Lohnsteuer (f)	*(LOHN-shtOY-uh)*	payroll tax
Lohnstopp (m)	*(LOHN-shtop)*	wage freeze
Lohnstreit (m)	*(LOHN-streyet)*	wage dispute
Lohnstruktur (f)	*(LOHN-strUk-toor)*	wage structure
Lohnunterschied (m)	*(LOHN-un-tuh-sheed)*	wage differential
Lohnzuschlag (m)	*(LOHN-tsOO-shlAHk)*	double time
Lombardwert (m)	*(lom-bAArd-vEHRt)*	loan value
Los (n)	*(lohs)*	lot
Löscher (m) (Tinten)	*(lERSH-uh [TIN-Ten])*	blotter
Löschkosten (pl)	*(lERsh-kOS-ten)*	landing costs
Löschschein (m)	*(lERsh-shEYEn)*	landing certificate
Löschungskosten (pl)	*(lERsh-unks-kOS-ten)*	wharfage
Löschzeit (f)	*(lERsh-tsEYEt)*	laydays
Löslichkeit (f)	*(LEWS-likh-kEYET)*	solubility
Lösung (f)	*(LER-zunk)*	solution
Lösungsmittel (n)	*(LER-zunks-mit-tel)*	solvent

Lotsengeld (n)	*(lOt-zehn-GEHLT)*	pilotage
Luchs(pelz) (m)	*(LUKHs [pELTS])*	lynx
Luftexpress (m)	*(LOOft-EX-prehs)*	air express
Luftfilter (m)	*(LUFT-FIL-tuh)*	air filter
Luftfracht (f)	*(LOOft-frAHKHt)*	air freight
Luftfrachtsendung (f)	*(LOOft-frAHKHt-zEN-dunk)*	air shipment
lustloser Markt (m)	*(lUst-loh-zuh mAHrkt)*	thin market
Luxussteuer (f)	*(LOOks-us shtOY-uh)*	luxury tax
Luxuswaren (pl)	*(LOOks-us-vAAr-ehn)*	luxury goods

M

Magnetband (n)	*(mahg-nAYt-bahnd)*	magnetic tape
Magnetplatte (f)	*(mahg-nAYt-plAA-teh)*	disk
Magnetplattenan-trieb (m)	*(mahg-nAYt-plAA-tehn-AHn-trEEp)*	disk drive
Magnetspeicher (m)	*(mahg-nAYt-shpEYE-khuh)*	magnetic memory
Mahlen (n)	*(mAA-len)*	grinding
mahnen	*(mAA-nehn)*	dun (v)
Mais (m)	*(meyez)*	maize
Makler (m)	*(mAHk-luh)*	broker
Maklerdarlehen (n)	*(mAHk-luh-dAAr-layn)*	day loan
Makroökonomie (f)	*(mak-roh-ew-ko-noh-mEE)*	macroeconomics
Management (n)	*(meh-nEHdj-mehnt)*	management
Mandat (n)	*(mahn-dAAt)*	mandate
Manganeisen (n)	*(mahn-gAAN-EYE-zen)*	ferromanganese
Manganerz (n)	*(mahn-gAAN-EHRTS)*	manganese ore
Mangel (m)	*(mAHng-ehl)*	shortage
mangelhaft	*(mAHng-ehl-hahft)*	defective
Manschettenknopf (m)	*(mAHN-shET-ten-knOpf)*	cuff link

L

Mantel (m)	*(mAHN-tel)*	coat
Manteltarifabkommen (n)	*(mAHn-tehl-tah-rIF-AHB-kOM-mehn)*	master agreement
Mantelvertrag (m)	*(mAHn-tehl-fuh-trAHk)*	collective agreement
Manuskript (n)	*(mAHn-oo-skrIpt)*	script
Mappe (f)	*(mAHP-peh)*	portfolio
Marge (f)	*(mAHrdj)*	spread
marginale Preisfestsetzung (f)	*(mahr-gee-nAA-leh prEYEs-fehst-zEHts-unk)*	marginal pricing
Marke (f)	*(mAHR-keh)*	brand
Markenanerkennung (f)	*(mAHR-ken-ahn-ayr-kEHn-unk)*	brand recognition
Markenimage (n)	*(mAHR-ken-EE-maa-djeh)*	brand image
Markentreue (f)	*(mAHR-ken-trOY-eh)*	brand loyalty
Marketing (n)	*(mAHR-keh-tING)*	marketing
Markt (m)	*(mAHrkt)*	market
Marktanteil (m)	*(mAHrkt-AHN-teyel)*	market share
Marktbericht (m)	*(mAHrkt-beh-rIKHt)*	market report
Marktdurchdringung (f)	*(mAHrkt-durkh-drING-unk)*	market penetration
Marktdynamik (f)	*(mAHrkt-dew-nAAm-ik)*	market dynamics
Markteinschätzung (f)	*(mAHrkt-eyen-shEH-tsunk)*	market appraisal
Marktforschung (f)	*(mAHrkt-fOHr-shunk)*	market research
Marktkonzentration (f)	*(mAHrkt-kon-tsEHN-trah-tsEE-OHn)*	market concentration
Marktkräfte (pl)	*(mAHrkt-krehf-teh)*	market forces
Marktlage (f)	*(mAHrkt-lAA-geh)*	market position
Marktleitung (f)	*(mAHrkt-lEYE-tunk)*	market management
Marktplan (m)	*(mAHrkt-plAAn)*	market plan
Marktplatz (m)	*(mAHrkt-plahts)*	marketplace
Marktpotential (n)	*(mAHrkt-po-ten-tsEE-AAL)*	market potential
Marktpreis (m)	*(mAHrkt-prEYEs)*	market price
Marktprognose (f)	*(mAHrkt-prog-nOH-zeh)*	market forecast
Marktsättigung (f)	*(mAHrkt-sEH-tee-gunk)*	market saturation
Marktstudie (f)	*(mAHrkt-shtoo-di-eh)*	market survey

Markttendenzen (pl)	*(mAHrkt-tehn-dEHn-tsehn)*	market trends
Marktübersicht (f)	*(mAHrkt-EW-buh-zikht)*	market survey
Marktwert (m)	*(mAHrkt-vEHRt)*	market value (general)
Masche (f)	*(mAH-sheh)*	stitch
Maschinenbau (m)	*(mah-shEE-nen-bOW)*	mechanical engineering
Maschinenpark (m)	*(mah-shEE-nen-pAArk)*	machinery
Maschinenschreiber (m)	*(mah-shEE-nen-shrEYE-buh)*	typist
Maß (n)	*(maas)*	ratio
Maßanalyse (f)	*(MAAS-aa-naa-LEW-zeh)*	titration
Massenabsatz (m)	*(MAHS-ehn-AHB-zATS)*	mass marketing
Massenkommunikation (f)	*(MAHS-ehn-ko-moo-ni-kah-tsEE-ohn)*	mass communications
Massenmedien (pl)	*(MAHS-ehn-mAY-dee-ehn)*	mass media
Massenproduktion (f)	*(MAHS-ehn-proh-dOOk-tsEE-ohn)*	mass production
Maßstab (m)	*(mAAs-shtahp)*	yardstick
Materialien (pl)	*(maa-tay-ree-AAl-EE-ehn)*	materials
mathematisches Modell (n)	*(mah-teh-mah-tISH-ehs moh-dEL)*	mathematical model
Matrixbilanz (f)	*(maa-trIKs-bee-lAHnts)*	spreadsheet
Matrize (f)	*(ma-TRI-tseh)*	matrix
Matrizenüberwachung (f)	*(maa-trEEts-eh-EW-buh-vakh-unk)*	matrix management
Medien (pl)	*(mAY-dee-ehn)*	media
Medikament (n)	*(meh-di-KAH-ment)*	drug
Medizin (f)	*(meh-di-tsEEN)*	medicine
medizinische Behandlung (f)	*(meh-di-tsEE-ni-sheh beh-hAHN-dlunk)*	medication
Mehrfachbesteuerung (f)	*(mAYr-fakh-beh-shtOY-uh-runk)*	multiple taxation
Mehrprogrammverarbeitung (f)	*(mAYr-proh-grAHm-fuh-ahr-bEYE-tunk)*	multiprogramming
mehrseitiger Handel (m)	*(mAYr-zEYE-ti-guh hAHn-dehl)*	multilateral trade

M

mehrseitiges Abkommen (n)	*(mAYr-zEYE-ti-gehs AHb-kOM-mehn)*	multilateral agreement
Mehrumsatz (m)	*(mAYr-um-zAHts)*	add-on sales
Mehrwertssteuer (f)	*(mAYr-vEHRt-shtOY-uh)*	value-added tax (VAT)
Meilenlänge (f)	*(mEYE-lehn-LEHN-geh)*	mileage
Meinungsbeein-flussung (f) der Abgeordneten	*(mEYE-nunks-beh-EYEn-flus-sunk duh AHB-ge-ORd-neh-ten)*	lobbying
Meinungsfor-schung (f)	*(mEYE-nunks-fOHr-shunk)*	public opinion poll
meistbegünstigtes Land (n)	*(mEYEst-beh-gEWns-tig-tehs lAHnd)*	most-favored nation
Meistbietende (m) (f)	*(mEYEst-bEE-ten-deh)*	highest bidder
Meldung (f)	*(mEHl-dunk)*	report
Menge (f)	*(mAYng-eh)*	quantity
Mengenrabatt (m)	*(mAYng-ehn-rah-bAAt)*	quantity discount, volume discount
messen	*(mehs-sehn)*	measure (v)
Messer (n)	*(MEHS-suh)*	knife
Metalle (pl)	*(meh-tAHl-leh)*	metals
Metallplatten (pl)	*(meh-tAHL-plaht-ten)*	slabs
Metallwaren (pl)	*(meh-tAHl-vAAr-ehn)*	hardware
Methode (f)	*(meh-tOII-deh)*	method
Metrifikation (f)	*(meh tri fi-kah -tsEE-ohn)*	metrification
Miete (f)	*(MEE-teh)*	rent
mieten	*(MEE-tehn)*	lease (v), rent (v) (rent from)
Mieter (m)	*(MEE-tuh)*	lessee, tenant
Mietsvertrag mit Bestimmungen für Ankauf (m)	*(MEEts-fuh-trAHk mit beh-shtIM-mun-gen fEWr AHN-kOWf)*	leveraged lease
Mietvertrag (m)	*(MEEt-fuh-trAHk)*	lease
Mikrochip (m)	*(mEE-kroh-ship)*	chip, microchip
Mikrocomputer (m)	*(mEE-kroh-ckom-pyU-tuh)*	microcomputer
Mikrofiche (n)	*(mEE-kroh-feesh)*	microfiche
Mikrofilm (m)	*(mEE-kroh-film)*	microfilm

M

Mikrofon (n)	*(mee-kroh-fOHN)*	microphone
Mikroprozessor (m)	*(mEE-kroh-pro-tsehs-sOHr)*	microprocessor
Mikrowelle (f)	*(mee-kroh-vEL-leh)*	microwave
Minderheitsanteil (m)	*(MIN-duh-heyets-AHN-teyel)*	minority interest
Minderlieferung (f)	*(MIN-duh-LEE-feh-runk)*	short delivery
Mindersendung (f)	*(MIN-duh-zEN-dunk)*	short shipment
minderwertig	*(MIN-duh-vEHR-tik)*	second rate
Mindestbetrag (m)	*(MIN-dehst-beh-trAHk)*	cover charge
Mindesteinschuß (m)	*(MIN-dehst-EYEn-shUs)*	margin
Mindestlohn (m)	*(MIN-dehst-lohn)*	minimum wage
Mindestpacht (f)	*(MIN-dehst-pAHKHt)*	dead rent
Mindestreserven (pl)	*(MIN-dehst-reh-zAYr-fehn)*	minimum reserves
Minicomputer (m)	*(mI-nee-kom-pyU-tuh)*	minicomputer
Mischindex (m)	*(MISH-in-dehx)*	composite index
Mischkonzern (m)	*(MISH-kon-tsayrn)*	conglomerate
Mischkosten (pl)	*(MISH-kOS-ten)*	mixed costs
Mißerfolg (m)	*(MIS-ayr-folg)*	failure
mißlingen	*(mis-lING-en)*	fail (v)
Mißverständnis (n)	*(MIS-fuh-shtEHnd-nis)*	misunderstanding
mit Bindestrich schreiben	*(mit BIN-deh-shtrIKH shrEYE-ben)*	hyphenate (v)
mit Dividende	*(mit di-vi-dEHN-deh)*	cum dividend
mit Durchschnitts-berechnung	*(mit dURKH-shnITs-rEHKH-nunk)*	with average
mit Latten versehen	*(mit lAH-tehn fAYr-zeh-en)*	batten fitted
mit Vorrechten ausgestattete Wertpapieremission (f)	*(mit FOHR-rehkh-ten OWs-geh-shtah-teh-teh vEHRt-pah-pEEr-eh-mi-see-OHn)*	senior issue
Mitarbeiter (m)	*(MIT-ahr-bEYE-tuh)*	colleague
Miteigentum (n)	*(MIT-eye-gehn-tOOm)*	co-ownership
Miteigentümer (m)	*(MIT-eye-gehn-tEW-muh)*	joint owner

Mitglied auf Lebenszeit (n)	*(MIT-gleed OWf lAY-behnz-tsEYEt)*	life member
Mitgliedsfirma (f)	*(MIT-gleeds-fIR-mah)*	member firm
mittelfristig	*(mit-tEL-fris-tig)*	medium term
Mittelmanagement (n)	*(mit-tEL-meh-nEHdj-mehnt)*	middle management
Mittelmann (m)	*(mit-tEL-mahn)*	middleman
Mittelstand (m)	*(mit-tEL-shtahnd)*	small business
Mittelverwendung (f)	*(mit-tEL-fuh-vEHn-dunk)*	resource allocation
mittlere Führungs-schicht (f)	*(MIT-luh-reh FEW-runks-shikht)*	middle management
mitverbunden	*(mit-fuh-bOOn-dehn)*	on line (computer)
Mitversicherung (f)	*(MIT-fuh-ZIKH-eh-runk)*	coinsurance
Mobiliarhypothek (f)	*(moh-bi-lee-AAr-hew-poh-tAYk)*	chattel mortgage
Mode (f)	*(mOH-deh)*	fashion
Modell (n)	*(moh-dEL)*	model
Modem (m)	*(moh-dEM)*	modem
modernisieren	*(moh-dayr-ni-zEE-ren)*	streamline (v)
Modeschöpfer (m)	*(mOH-deh-shER-PFer)*	designer
modifizieren	*(moh-di-fi-tsEE-ren)*	renegotiate (v)
modisch	*(mOH-dish)*	fashionable
Möglichkeiten (pl)	*(mER-glikh-keye-ten)*	facilities (possibilities)
Moireseide (f)	*(moh-EER-zeYE-deh)*	moiré
Molkereiprodukte (pl)	*(MOl-kuh-reye-prOH-duk-teh)*	dairy products
Molybdän (n)	*(mo-LEWB-dAYN)*	molybdenum
Monopol (n)	*(mo-noh-pOHl)*	monopoly
Monopsonie (f)	*(mo-nohp-soh-nEE)*	monopsony
Montage (f)	*(mohn-tAA-djeh)*	assembly
Montagebahn (f)	*(mohn-tAA-djeh-baan)*	assembly line
Monte Carlo Methode (f)	*(MON-tay kAAr-loh meh-tOH-deh)*	Monte Carlo technique
montieren	*(mon-tEE-ren)*	assemble (v) (things)

M

Moratorium (n)	*(moh-rah-tOH-ree-um)*	moratorium
Morphium (n)	*(mOR-fi-um)*	morphine
Motivationsstudie (f)	*(moh-ti-vah-tsEE-OHnz-shtoo-di-eh)*	motivation study
Motor (m)	*(mOH-tor)*	engine
Müdigkeit nach dem Flug (f)	*(MEW-dikh-keyet nakh dehm flOOg)*	jet lag
Müll (m)	*(mewl)*	garbage
Müllabfuhr (f)	*(MEWL-ahp-foor)*	garbage collection
Müllabladepatz (m)	*(Mul-ahp-lahd-eh-PLAHTS)*	garbage dump
Müllerei (f)	*(MEWl-luh-reye)*	milling
multinationale Gesellschaft (f)	*(MUL-tee-nah-tsee-oh-nAA-leh geh-zEL-shahft)*	multinational corporation
Multiplikator (m)	*(mul-tee-pli-kAA-tohr)*	multiplier
Multiwährung (f)	*(MuL-tee-vAY-runk)*	multicurrency
mündelsichere Anlage (f)	*(MEWn-dehl-zikh-eh-reh AHN-laa-geh)*	gilt-edged investment
mündlich bestätigter Scheck (m)	*(MEWnd-likh beh-shtAY-tikh-tuh shek)*	voiced check
Münzamt (n)	*(MEWnts-AHmt)*	mint
Murmeltier (n)	*(mur-mEL-tEER)*	marmot
Muster (n)	*(MUS-tuh)*	design, model, pattern
Musterbrief (m)	*(MUS-tuh-brEEf)*	form letter
Musterkollektion (f)	*(MUS-tuh-kol-layk-tsEE-OHn)*	sample line
Muttergesellschaft (f)	*(MU-tuh-geh-zEL-shahft)*	parent company
Mutterschaftsurlaub (m)	*(MU-tuh-shahfts-OOr-lowb)*	maternity leave

N

nach Sicht Akzept (n)	*(nakh zikht ahk-tsEPt)*	after-sight
Nachahmung (f)	*(nAKH-ah-munk)*	counterfeit, imitation
nachbestellen	*(nAKH-beh-shtEHL-len)*	reorder (v)

M

Nachbestellung (f)	*(nAKH-beh-shtEHL-lunk)*	repeat order
nachbörsliche Umsätze (pl)	*(nAKH-bERz-lIKH-eh um-zAY-tseh)*	after-hours trading
nachdatieren	*(nAKH-daa-tee-rehn)*	afterdate (v)
nachdatiert	*(nAKH-daa-teert)*	postdated
nachfassen	*(nAKH-fahs-sen)*	follow up (v)
Nachflugerschöpfung (f)	*(nAKH-floog-ayr-shERp-funk)*	jet lag
Nachfrage (f)	*(nAKH-frah-geh)*	demand
nachhängender Konjunkturindikator (m)	*(nAKH-hehn-gen-duh kon-yunk-tOOr-in-di-kah-tOH-ren)*	lagging indicator
Nachkaufsmietung (f)	*(nAKH-kOWfs-mEE-tunk)*	sell and lease back
Nachlaß (m)	*(nAKH-lahss)*	estate (testamentary)
nachlässig	*(nAKH-leh-sig)*	negligent
Nachlaßsteuer (f)	*(nAKH-laas-shtOY-uh)*	estate tax, inheritance tax
Nachnahme (f)	*(nAKH-nAA-meh)*	collect on delivery
Nachnahmesendung (f)	*(nAKH-nAA-meh-zEN-dunk)*	cash on delivery
nachrangige Hypothek (f)	*(nAKH-rahng-igeh hew-poh-tAYk)*	second mortgage
Nachricht (f)	*(nAKH-rikht)*	report
nachsenden	*(nAKH-zEN-den)*	forward (v)
Nachtdepot (n)	*(nAKHt-day-POH)*	night depository
Nachteil (m)	*(nAKH-teyel)*	drawback (disadvantage), handicap
Nadel (f)	*(nAA-del)*	needle
nähen	*(NAY-hen)*	sew(v)
Nähmaschine (f)	*(NAY-mah-SHEE-neh)*	sewing machine
Nahrungsmittel (pl)	*(nAA-runks-mit-tEL)*	foodstuffs
Nähtäschchen (n)	*(nAY-tEHSH-khen)*	sewing kit
Namenspapier (n)	*(nAA-menz-pah-pEEr)*	registered security
Namensscheck (m)	*(nAA-menz-shek)*	registered check
Narkotikum (n)	*(nahr-kOH-ti-kum)*	narotic
Nationalbank (f)	*(nah-tsee-oh-nAAl-bahnk)*	government bank

N

Nationalismus (m)	*(nah-tsee-oh-naa-lIIS-mus)*	nationalism
Naturgas (n)	*(nah-TOOR-gaas)*	natural gas
Naturschätze (pl)	*(naa-tOOr-shEH-tseh)*	natural resources
neben	*(nAY-behn)*	alongside
Nebenausgaben (pl)	*(nAY-behn-OWs-gAA-ben)*	incidental expenses
Nebenbetrieb (m)	*(nAY-behn-beh-trEEp)*	ancillary operation
Nebeneinkünfte (pl)	*(nAY-behn-EYEn-kEWnf-teh)*	perks
Nebenprodukt (n)	*(nAY-behn-prOH-dukt)*	by-product
Nebenvergütungen (pl)	*(nAY-behn-fuh-gEW-tunk-ehn)*	fringe benefits
Nebenvertrag (m)	*(nAY-behn-fuh-trAHk)*	subcontract
negativ	*(nay-gah-tEEF)*	negative
negativer Zahlungsstrom (m)	*(nAY-gaa-tee-fuh tsAA-lungs-shtrOHm)*	negative cash flow
Nennertrag (m)	*(NEHN-uh-trAHk)*	nominal yield
Nennwert (m)	*(NEHN-vEHRt)*	face value, par value
nennwertlose Aktie (f)	*(NEHN-vEHRt-lOH-zeh ak-tsEE-eh)*	no par value
Nerz (m)	*(nEHRTS)*	mink
netto	*(nEH-toh)*	net
Nettoänderung (f)	*(nEH-toh-EHn-deh-runk)*	net change
Nettobargeldstrom (m)	*(nEH-toh-baar-GEHLT-shtrOHm)*	net cash flow
Nettobarwert (m)	*(nEH-toh-bAAr-vEHRt)*	net present value
Nettobetriebskapital (n)	*(nEH-toh-beh-trEEps-kah-pi-tAAL)*	net working capital
Nettoeigenkapital (n)	*(nEH-toh-EYE-gehn-kah-pi-tAAL)*	net equity assets
Nettoeinkommen (n)	*(NEH-toh-EYEn-kOM-mehn)*	net income
Nettofremdkapitalreserven (pl)	*(nEH-toh-frehmd-kah-pi-tAAL-reh-zAYr-fehn)*	net borrowed reserves
Nettogehalt (n)	*(nEH-toh-geh-hAHlt)*	take-home pay
Nettogewinn (m)	*(nEH-toh-geh-vIN)*	net profit
Nettogewinnspanne (f)	*(nEH-toh-geh-vIN-shpAHn-neh)*	net margin

Nettoinvestition (f)	*(nEH-toh-in-vehs-ti-tsi-OHn)*	net investment
Nettostand eines Maklers (m)	*(nEH-toh-shtahnd EYE-nehs mAHk-luhs)*	net position of a trader
Nettoumsatz (m)	*(nEH-toh-um-zAHts)*	net sales
Nettowert (m)	*(nEH-toh-vEHRt)*	net worth
Netz (n)	*(nets)*	network
neu verhandeln	*(noy fuh-hAHn-dehln)*	renegotiate (v)
Neuausgabe (f)	*(NOY-OWs-gAA-beh)*	new issue
neubestellen	*(NOY-beh-shtEHL-len)*	reorder (v)
Neubestellung (f)	*(NOY-beh-shtEHL-lunk)*	repeat order
Neubewertung (f)	*(NOY-beh-vEHR-tunk)*	revaluation
Neuerung (f)	*(NOY-AYr-runk)*	innovation
neues Geld (n)	*(NOY-ehs GEHLT)*	new money
Neufinanzierung (f)	*(NOY-fee-nahn-tsEE-runk)*	recapitalization
Neugestaltung (f)	*(NOY-geh-shtAHl-tunk)*	reorganization
nicht auf Gewinn ausgerichtet	*(nIKHt OWf geh-vIN OWs-geh-rIKH-teht)*	non-profit
nicht ausgeschütte-te Dividende (f)	*(nIKHt OWs-geh-shEW-teh-teh di-vi-dEHN-deh)*	passed dividend
nicht eingetragen	*(nIKHt EYEn-geh-trAA-gehn)*	unlisted
nicht entnomme-ner Gewinn (m)	*(nIKHt ehnt-nOM-mehn-uh geh-vIN)*	paid-in surplus
nicht frei konver-tierbare Wäh-rung (f)	*(nIKHt frEYE kon-fayr-tEEr-baa-reh vAY-runk)*	blocked currency
nicht honorieren	*(nIKHt on-oh-rEE-rehn)*	dishonor
nicht sonst im Namenregister verzeichnet	*(nIKHt zonst im nAA-men-ray-gIS-tuh fuh-tsEYEkh-neht)*	not otherwise indexed by name
nicht verdienter Wertzuwachs (m)	*(nIKHt fuh-dEEn-tuh vEHRt-tsOO-vahkhs)*	unearned increment
nicht verzeichnet	*(nIKHt fuh-tsEYEkh-neht)*	unlisted
Nichterfüllung (f)	*(nIKHt AYr-fEWl-lunk)*	nonfeasance
nichtig	*(nIKH-tik)*	void

N

nichtkumulative Vorzugsaktie (f)	*(nIKHt-koo-moo-laa-tEE-feh FOHR-tsoogs-ak-tsEE-eh)*	noncumulative preferred stock
Nichtmitglied (n)	*(nIKHt-MIT-gleed)*	nonmember
Nickel (m)	*(ni-KEl)*	nickel
Nickeleisen (n)	*(ni-KEl-EYE-zen)*	ferronickel
niedrige Einkommenstufe (f)	*(nEE-dri-geh EYEn-kOM-mehn-shtOO-feh)*	low income
niedrigverzinsliche Darlehen (pl)	*(nEE-drikh-fuh-tsINs-likh-eh dAAr-lAY-hen)*	low-interest loans
niedrigverzinsliche Obligationen (pl)	*(nEE-drikh-fuh-tsINs-likh-eh ob-li-gah-tsEE-ohn-nehn)*	low-yield bonds
niesen	*(nEE-zen)*	sneeze (v)
noch nicht erledigter Auftrag (m)	*(nOHKH nIKHt AYr-lAY-dig-tuh OWf-trAHk)*	back order
noch rechtskräftiger Vertrag (m)	*(nOHKH REHKHTs-krehf-ti-guh fuh-trAHk)*	outstanding contract
Nockenwelle (f)	*(nOK-ken-vEL-leh)*	camshaft
Nominalpreis (m)	*(no-mi-nAAl-prEYEs)*	nominal price
Norm (f)	*(norm)*	norm
Normalzeit (f)	*(nor-mAAl-tsEYEt)*	standard time
Normung (f)	*(NOR-mung)*	standardization
Notar (m)	*(noh-tAAr)*	notary
Notbehelf (m)	*(NOHt-beh-hehlf)*	makeshift
Notenausgabe ohne Deckung (f)	*(NOHt-OWs-gAA-beh ohneh dEHK-unk)*	fiduciary issue
notieren	*(noh-tEE-ren)*	take down (v)
Notierung (f)	*(noh-tEE-runk)*	quotation (stock exchange)
Novation (f)	*(noh-vAA-tsee-ohn)*	novation
null und nichtig	*(nUl unt nIKH-tik)*	null and void
Nutriafell (n)	*(nOO-triah-fEL)*	nutria skin
Nutzlast (f)	*(nUts-lahst)*	payload
Nutzung noch nicht realisierter Gewinne (f)	*(nUts-unk nOHKH nIKHt ray-aal-lee-zEEr-tuh geh-vIN-neh)*	pyramiding
Nutzungsdauer (f)	*(nUts-ungs-dOW-uh)*	life cycle

O

obenerwähnt	*(OH-behn-AYr-vAYnt)*	above mentioned
oberste Führungs-schicht (f)	*(OH-buh-steh FEW-runks-shikht)*	top management
Obligation (f)	*(ob-li-gah-tsEE-ohn)*	bond, debebture
Obligation ohne aufgelaufene Zinsen (f)	*(ob-li-gah-tsEE-ohn ohneh OWf-geh-lOWf-ehneh tsIN-zen)*	flat bond
offene Handelsge-sellschaft (f)	*(OF-feh-neh hAHn-dehl-geh-zEL-shahft)*	general partnership
offener Güterwa-gen (m)	*(OF-feh-nuh gEW-tuh-vAA-gehn)*	flatcar
Offenmarkt (m)	*(OF-fen-mAHrkt)*	open market
öffentliche Arbei-ten (pl)	*(ERf-fehnt-likh-eh ahr-bEYE-ten)*	public works
öffentliche Mei-nungspflege (f)	*(ERf-fehnt-likh-eh mEYE-unks-pflAY-geh)*	public relations
öffentliche Mittel (pl)	*(ERf-fehnt-likh-eh mit-tEL)*	public funds
öffentliche Verstei-gerung (f)	*(ERf-fehnt-likh-eh fuh-shtEYE-guh-runk)*	public auction
öffentlicher Bereich (m)	*(ERf-fehnt-likh-uh beh-rEYEkh)*	public sector
öffentlicher Lager-betrieb (m)	*(ERf-fehnt-likh-uh LAA-guh-beh-trEEp)*	regular warehouse
öffentlicher Ver-kauf (m)	*(ERf-fehnt-likh-uh fuh-kOWf)*	public sale
öffentliches Ange-bot (n)	*(ERf-fehnt-likh-ehs AHN-geh-boht)*	public offering
öffentliches Ver-kehrsunterneh-men (n)	*(ERf-fehnt-likh-ehs fuh-kAYrs-un-tuh-nAY-mehn)*	common carrier
Öffentlichkeitsar-beit (f)	*(ERf-fehnt-likh-keyets-ahr-bEYEt)*	public relations
Offsetdruck (m)	*(OFF-seht-drOOk)*	offset printing
Offshore-Gesell-schaft (f)	*(OFF-shohr-geh-zEL-shahft)*	offshore company
ohne Dividende	*(oh-neh di-vi-dEHN-deh)*	ex dividend

ohne Geschäfts-bucheintragung	*(ohneh geh-shEHfts-bOOkh-EYEn-trAAg-unk)*	off-the-books
ohne Rechte	*(ohneh REHKH-teh)*	ex rights
ohne Testament	*(ohneh tehs-tah-mEHnt)*	intestate
Ökonometrie (f)	*(ER-ko-noh-meh-trEE)*	econometrics
Oligopol (n)	*(o-li-go-pOHl)*	oligopoly
Oligopsonie (f)	*(o-li-gop-zoh-nEE)*	oligopsony
Ölversorgung (f)	*(ERL-fuh-sor-gunk)*	lubrication
Opium (n)	*(OH-pi-um)*	opium
Opossum (n)	*(o-pOS-sum)*	opossum
Opportunitätsko-sten (pl)	*(op-por-too-ni-tAYts-kOS-ten)*	opportunity cost
Option (f)	*(op-tsEE-ohn)*	option
optisch	*(OP-tish)*	optic
Orderlimit (n)	*(OR-duh-lI-mit)*	position limit
Organisation (f)	*(ohr-gah-ni-zah-tsee-OHn)*	organization
Organisationssche-ma (n)	*(ohr-gah-ni-zah-tsee-OHnz-shay-mah)*	organization chart
organisch	*(or-gAA-nish)*	organic
organische Chemie (f)	*(or-gAA-ni-she KHAY-mee)*	organic chemistry
Ortsgebräuche (pl)	*(OHrts-geh-brOYkh-eh)*	local customs
Oszillator (m)	*(os-tsi-LAH-tor)*	oscillator
Otterfell (n)	*(OT-tuh-fEL)*	otter skin
Otterpelz (m)	*(OT-tuh-pELTS)*	otter fur
Ozonloch (n)	*(O-tsohn-lokh)*	hole in ozone layer

P

Pacht (f)	*(pAHKHt)*	lease
pachten	*(pAHKH-tehn)*	lease (v)
Pächter (m)	*(pEHKH-tuh)*	lessee
Packkiste (f)	*(PAHk-kIS-teh)*	packing case
Packzettel (m)	*(PAHK-tsEH-tehl)*	packing list
Paginierung (f)	*(pah-gi-nEE-runk)*	pagination

Paketpost (f)	*(paa-kAYt-pOSt)*	parcel post
Palette (f)	*(pah-lEH-teh)*	pallet
palettierte Ladung (f)	*(pah-leh-tEEr-teh lAA-dunk)*	palletized freight
Pantoffel (pl)	*(pAHN-tOF-fel)*	slippers
Panzerkasten (m)	*(PAHn-tsuh-kAHs-tehn)*	safe deposit box
Paperback (n)	*(pEH-puh-bEHK)*	paperback
Papier (n)	*(pah-pEER)*	paper
Papierband (n)	*(pah-pEEr-bahnd)*	ticker tape
Parallelschaltung (f)	*(pah-rah-LEL-shahl-tunk)*	parallel circuit
pari	*(pah-rEE)*	par
Parität (f)	*(pah-ri-tAYt)*	parity
Paritätseinkom- menverhältnis (n)	*(pah-ri-tAYts-EYEn-kOM- mehn-fuh-hEHLt-nis)*	parity income ratio
Paritätspreis (m)	*(pah-ri-tAYts-prEYEs)*	parity price
Pariwert (m)	*(pah-rEE-vEHRt)*	par value
Partieware (f)	*(pahr-tEE-vAA-reh)*	job lot
Parzellierung (f)	*(pahr-tseh-lEE-runk)*	acreage allotment
Paßetui (n)	*(pAHS-e-tuEE)*	passport case
Passierschein (m)	*(pahs-sEEr-sheyen)*	entry permit
pasteurisiert	*(pahs-tOY-REE-zEErt)*	pasteurized
Patent (n)	*(pah-tEHnt)*	patent
Patentabgabe (f)	*(pah-tEHnt-AHB-gaa-beh)*	patent royalty
Patentanmeldung (f)	*(pah-tEHnt-mEHl-dunk)*	patent application
patentiertes Ver- fahren (n)	*(pah-tehn-tEER-tes fuh-fAA- rehn)*	patented process
Patentrecht (n)	*(pah-tEHnt-REHKHT)*	patent law
Patentverletzung (f)	*(pah-tEHnt-fuh-lEHts-unk)*	patent infringement
Pattsituation (f)	*(PAHT-si-too-ah-tsEE-ohn)*	deadlock
Pauschalbetrag (m)	*(pow-shAAl-beh-trAHk)*	flat yield, lump sum
Pauschale (f)	*(pow-shAA-leh)*	flat rate

P

Pauschalversiche-rung (f)	*(pow-shAAl-fuh-ZIKH-eh-runk)*	floater
Peitsche (f)	*(pEYE-tSHEH)*	whip
Penizillin (n)	*(peh-ni-tsi-LEEN)*	penicillin
Pensionskasse (f)	*(pen-zee-OHns-kAH-seh)*	pension fund
perfekte Bindung (f)	*(puh-fehk-teh BIN-dunk)*	perfect binding
Periode (f)	*(pay-ree-OH-deh)*	period
periodische Bestandsaufnah-me (f)	*(pay-ree-OH-dish-eh beh-shtAHnds-OWf-nAA-meh)*	periodic inventory
permanente Buchinventur (f)	*(payr-mah-nEHn-teh bOOkh-in-vehn-tOOr)*	perpetual inventory
Personal (n)	*(payr-zoh-nAAl)*	personnel
Personalabteilung (f)	*(payr-zoh-nAAl-AHB-tEYE-lunk)*	personnel department
Personalausweis (m)	*(payr-zoh-nAAl-OWs-vEYEs)*	pass (written permit)
Personalbestand (m)	*(payr-zoh-nAAl-beh-shtAHnt)*	manpower
Personalleitung (f)	*(payr-zoh-nAAl-lEYE-tunk)*	personnel management
Personalwechsel (m)	*(payr-zoh-nAAl-vEHk-sehl)*	labor turnover
personenbezogene Aktiengesell-schaft (f)	*(payr-zohn-nen-beh-tsOH-geh-neh ak-tsEE-en-geh-zEL-shahft)*	closely held corporation
Personengesell-schaft (f)	*(payr-zohn-en-geh-zEL-shahft)*	partnership
persönliche Ein-kommensteuer (f)	*(payr-zERn-likh-eh EYEn-kOM-mehn-shtOY-uh)*	personal income tax
persönliche Haft-pflicht (f)	*(payr-zERn-likh-eh hAHft-pflIKHt)*	personal liability
persönlicher Abzug (m)	*(payr-zERn-likh-uh AHB-tsOOk)*	personal deduction
persönlicher Frei-betrag (m)	*(payr-zERn-likh-uh frEYE-beh-trAHk)*	personal exemption
Persönlichkeits-prüfung (f)	*(payr-zERn-likh-keyets-prEW-funk)*	personality test
petrochemisch	*(peh-troh-KHAY-mish)*	petrochemical

Petrodollars (pl)	*(peh-troh-dOHl-laars)*	petrodollars
Petroleum (n)	*(peh-trOH-lay-um)*	petroleum
Pfand (n)	*(pfahnt)*	pledge
Pfandbriefe (pl)	*(pfAHnt-brEE-feh)*	backup bonds
Pfandrecht (n)	*(pfAHnt-REHKHT)*	lien
Pfeffermühle (f)	*(pfEHF-fuh-mEW-leh)*	pepper mill
Pfefferstreuer (m)	*(pfEHF-fuh-shtROY-uh)*	pepper shaker
Pferdestärke (f)	*(pfEHR-deh-shtEHR-keh)*	horsepower
Pflanzen (pl)	*(pflAHN-tsen)*	plants
Pflicht (f)	*(pflikht)*	duty (obligation)
pflichtwidrige Unterlassung (f)	*(pflIKHt-vI-dri-geh un-tuh-lAH-sunk)*	nonfcasance
pharmazeutisch	*(fahr-ma-tsOY-tish)*	pharmaceutical
Phosphat (n)	*(FOS-faht)*	phosphate
Pica (f)	*(pi-kah)*	pica
Pigment (n)	*(PIG-ment)*	pigment
Pille (f)	*(pIL-leh)*	pellet, pill
Pistolenhalfter (n)	*(pis-tOH-len-hAHLf-tuh)*	holster
Plan (m)	*(plAAn)*	plan
planen	*(plAA-nen)*	project (v)
Plankosten (pl)	*(plAAn-kOS-ten)*	standard costs
Planwirtschaft (f)	*(plAAn-vEErt-shahft)*	managed economy
Platte (f)	*(plAHT-teh)*	plate
Platzlieferung (f)	*(plahts-LEE-fuh-runk)*	spot delivery
Plenarsitzung (f)	*(plehn-AAr-zIT-sunk)*	plenary meeting
Pleuelstange (f)	*(plOY-el-shtAHN-geh)*	connecting rod
Police (f)	*(poh-lee-sAY)*	policy (insurance)
Policeinhaber (m)	*(poh-lee-sAY-IN-hah-buh)*	policyholder
Politik (f)	*(po-li-tEEk)*	policy (action)
Politik der offenen Tür (m)	*(po-li-tEEk duh OF-fe-nen tEWr)*	open door policy
polymere Körper (pl)	*(po-lEW-meh-reh KER-puh)*	polymer
Popelin (m)	*(po-pEH-lin)*	poplin
Portefeuille (n)	*(port-fOY)*	portfolio

Portefeuilletheorie (f)	*(port-fOY-tAY-oh-rEE)*	portfolio theory
Portefeuilleverwaltung (f)	*(port-fOY-fayr-vAAl-tunk)*	portfolio management
Porzellan (n)	*(por-TSEl-lahn)*	china
Porzellanwaren (pl)	*(por-TSEl-lahn-VAAren)*	chinaware
positiv	*(po-zi-tEEF)*	positive
positiver Zahlungsstrom (m)	*(poz-ee-tEE-fuh tsAA-lungs-shtrOHm)*	positive cash flow
Postanweisung (f)	*(pOSt-ahn-vEYE-zunk)*	money order
Posten (m)	*(pOS-ten)*	item, lot
Postleitzahl (f)	*(pOSt-lEYEt-tsAAl)*	ZIP code
Postversand (m)	*(pOSt-fuh-zAHnt)*	mail order
Postversandliste (f)	*(pOSt-fuh-zAHnt-lIS-teh)*	mailing list
Postversandwerbung (f)	*(pOSt-fayr-zAHnt-vAYr-bunk)*	direct mail
potentieller Kunde (m)	*(po-tehn-tsee-EL-luh kUn-deh)*	potential buyer
potentieller Umsatz (m)	*(po-tehn-tsee-EL-luh um-zAHts)*	potential sales
Praktik (f)	*(PRAHk-tik)*	practice
Praktikant (m)	*(prahk-ti-kAHnt)*	trainee
praktisch	*(PRAHK-tish)*	practical
Prämie (f)	*(PRAY-mee-eh)*	bonus (premium)
Prämienzahlung (f)	*(PRAY-mee-ehn-tsAA-lunk)*	premium payment
Präparate (pl)	*(prAY-pah-rAA-teh)*	compounds
Präsident (m)	*(pray-zee-dEHnt)*	president
Preis (m)	*(prEYEs)*	price
Preis-Einnahmen Verhältnis (n)	*(prEYEs- EYEn-nAA-mehn fuh-hEHLt-nis)*	price/earnings (p/e) ratio
Preis-Gewinn Verhältnisse (pl)	*(prEYEs-geh-vIN fuh-hEHLt-nis-seh)*	multiples
Preisaufschlag (m)	*(prEYEs-OWf-shlAHk)*	markup
Preisbindung (f)	*(prEYEs-bIN-dunk)*	fair trade, price fixing
Preiselastizität (f)	*(prEYEs-eh-lahs-ti-tsee-tAYt)*	price elasticity

Preiserhöhung (f)	*(prEYEs-uh-hER-unk)*	price increase
Preisgabe (f)	*(prEYEs-gaa-beh)*	abandonment
Preisgrenze (f)	*(prEYEs-grEHN-tseh)*	price limit
Preisherabsetzung (f)	*(prEYEs-huh-AHB-zeht-tsunk)*	markdown
Preisindex (m)	*(prEYEs-IN-dehx)*	price index
Preiskrieg (m)	*(prEYEs-krEEg)*	price war
Preislage (f)	*(prEYEs-lAA-geh)*	price range
Preisliste (f)	*(prEYEs-lIs-teh)*	price list
Preisnachlaß (m)	*(prEYEs-nAKH-lahs)*	price abatement, rebate
Preissenkung (f)	*(prEYEs-zAYn-kunk)*	markdown, price cutting, rollback
Preisskala (f)	*(prEYEs-skAA-laa)*	price range
Preisstop (m)	*(prEYEs-stop)*	price freeze
Preisstützung (f)	*(prEYEs-shtEW-tsunk)*	pegging, price support
Preisunterschied (m)	*(prEYEs-un-tuh-shEEd)*	price differential
Preisverzeichnis (n)	*(prEYEs-fuh-tsEYEkh-nis)*	catalog, price list
Preiszettel (m)	*(prEYEs-tsEH-tehl)*	price tag
Pressebuch (n)	*(prehs-seh-bOOKH)*	press book
Primärreserven (pl)	*(pree-mAYr-reh-zAYr-fehn)*	primary reserves
Priorität (f)	*(pree-ohr-ree-tAYt)*	priority
Privateigentum (n)	*(pree-vAAt-EYE-gehn-tOOm)*	personal property
Privatflotte (f)	*(pree-vAAt-flOT-teh)*	private fleet
Privatmarke (f)	*(pree-vAAt-mAHR-keh)*	private label (or brand)
Privatplazierung (f)	*(pree-vAAt-plah-tsEE-runk)*	private placement (finance)
Privatwirtschaft (f)	*(pree-vAAt-vEErt-shahft)*	free enterprise
pro Anteil	*(proh AHN-teyel)*	per share
pro Kopf	*(proh kopf)*	per capita
pro Tag	*(proh tAAk)*	per diem
Probe (f)	*(pROH-beh)*	sample
Probeband (m)	*(pro-beh-bahnt)*	dummy

P

Probebilanz (f)	*(pROH-beh-bee-lAHnts)*	trial balance
probieren	*(pROH-bEE-rehn)*	sample (v)
Problem (n)	*(proh-blAYm)*	problem
Problemanalyse (f)	*(proh-blAYm-ah-nah-lEW-zeh)*	problem analysis
Problemlösung (f)	*(proh-blAYm-lER-zunk)*	problem solving
Produkt (n)	*(pro-dUkt)*	product
Produktdynamik (f)	*(proh-dUKt-dew-nAAm-ik)*	product dynamics
Produktentwick-lung (f)	*(proh-dUKt-ehnt-vIK-lunk)*	product development
Produktgestaltung (f)	*(proh-dUKt-geh-shtAAl-tunk)*	product design
Produktgruppe (f)	*(proh-dUKt-grUP-peh)*	product group
Produktion (f)	*(Pro-duk-TSI-On)*	production
Produktion am laufenden Band (f)	*(proh-dUK-tsEE-ohn ahm lOW-fehn-dehn bahnt)*	production line
Produktionsauf-wand (m)	*(proh-dUK-tsEE-ohns-OWf-vahnt)*	production costs
Produktionskapa-zität (f)	*(proh-dUK-tsEE-ohns-kah-pah-tsee-tAYt)*	manufacturing capacity
Produktionslen-kung (f)	*(proh-dUK-tsEE-ohns-lAYnk-unk)*	production control
Produktionsmittel (pl)	*(proh-dUK-tsEE-ohns-mit-tEL)*	facilities (means of production)
Produktivität (f)	*(proh-dUK-ti-vee-tAYt)*	productivity
produktivitätsab-hängige Lei-stungsprämie (f)	*(proh-dUK-ti-vee-tAYts-ahb-hAYng-ikheh lEYEs-tungs-PRAY-mee-eh)*	accelerating premium
Produktivkapital (n)	*(proh-dUK-teev-kah-pi-tAAL)*	instrumental capital
Produktmanage-ment (n)	*(proh-dUKt-meh-nEHdj-mehnt)*	product management
Produktrentabili-tät (f)	*(proh-dUKt-rehn-tah-bi-lee-tAYt)*	product profitability
Produktsortiment (n)	*(proh-dUKt-sohr-tee-mEH)*	product line
Profileisen (n)	*(pro-fEEL-EYE-zen)*	structural shapes

Proformarechnung (f)	*(proh-FOHR-mah-rEHKH-nunk)*	pro forma invoice
Prognose (f)	*(prog-nOH-zeh)*	forecast
Programm (n)	*(proh-grAHm)*	program
Programmablauf (m)	*(proh-grAHm-ahb-lOWf)*	routine
programmieren	*(proh-grahm-mEE-rehn)*	program (v)
Projektplanung (f)	*(proh-yEHkt-plAA-nunk)*	project planning
Prospekt (m)	*(proh-spEHkt)*	prospectus
Protektionismus (m)	*(proh-tehk-tsee-oh-nIS-mus)*	protectionism
Protokolldatum (n)	*(proh-toh-kOL-DAA-tum)*	record date
protokollierter Importeur (m)	*(proh-toh-kol-lEE-tuh im-pohr-tEWr)*	importer of record
Provision (f)	*(proh-vi-zee-OHn)*	commission (fee)
Provision des Verladers (f)	*(proh-vi-zee-OHn dehs fayr-lAA-duhs)*	address commission
Provisionseinkünfte (pl)	*(proh-vi-zee-OHns-EYEn-kEWnf-teh)*	percentage earnings
Prozent (n)	*(proh-tsEHnt)*	percent
Prozentpunkt (m)	*(proh-tsEHnt-pUnkt)*	percentage point
Prozeß (m)	*(proh-tsEHs)*	lawsuit, legal action
prüfen	*(prEW-fehn)*	assay (v), audit (v)
Prüfung (f)	*(prEW-funk)*	inspection
Prüfungsbeamter (m)	*(prEW-funks-beh-AHm-tuh)*	inspector
Prüfungsweg (m)	*(prEW-funks-vAYk)*	audit trail
Publicitymanager (m)	*(pu-bli-sI-tee-mEHn-edj-uh)*	advertising manager
Publizität (f)	*(pu-bli-tsi-tAYt)*	publicity
Pullover (m)	*(PUL-ovah)*	sweater
Pulver (n)	*(pUL-fuh)*	powder
Puppe (f)	*(pUP-peh)*	dummy
Purifikation (f)	*(PU-ri-fi-kah-TSI-on)*	purification

P

Q

Qualifikation (f)	*(kvah-li-fi-kah-tsee-OHn)*	qualification
Qualitätskontrolle (f)	*(kvah-li-tAYts-kon-trOL-leh)*	quality control
Qualitätsschaumwein (m)	*(kvah-li-tehts-shOWm-vEYEN)*	classified sparkling wine
Qualitätswaren (pl)	*(kvah-li-tAYts-vAA-rehn)*	quality goods
Quantität (f)	*(kvahn-tee-tAYt)*	quantity
quasi-öffentlicher Betrieb (m)	*(kvaa-zEE-ER-fehnt-likh-uh beh-trEEp)*	quasi-public company
Quellensteuer (f)	*(kvEL-ehn-shtOY-uh)*	withholding tax
Quittung (f)	*(kvIT-tunk)*	receipt (paper)
Quote (f)	*(kvOH-teh)*	quota

R

Rabatt (m)	*(rah-bAAt)*	allowance, discount
Rabatt je Verladeeinheit (m)	*(rah-bAAt yay fuh-lAA-deh-EYEn-heyet)*	unit load discount
Rad (n)	*(raht)*	wheel
Raffinerie (f)	*(RAf-fi-neh-ree)*	refinery
raffinieren	*(RAf-fi-nee-ren)*	refine (v)
Ramschwaren (pl)	*(rAHmsh-vAA-rehn)*	job lot
Randmarkt (m)	*(rAHnt-mAHrkt)*	fringe market
Randmaschinen (pl)	*(rAHnt-mah-shEE-nehn)*	peripherals
Rangiergebühren (pl)	*(rAHn-djeer-geh-bEW-ren)*	switching charges
Rate (f)	*(rAH-teh)*	rate
rationalisieren	*(rah-tsee-oh-nah-lee-zEE-rehn)*	streamline (v)
Rationierung (f)	*(rah-tsee-oh-nEE-runk)*	rationing
Reagenzglas (n)	*(reh-AH-gents-glAAs)*	test tube
Realeinkommen (n)	*(ray-AAl-EYEn-kOM-mehn)*	real income

Realgewinn nach Steuern (m)	*(ray-AAl-geh-vIN nAKH shtOY-uhn)*	after-tax real rate of return
Realinvestition (f)	*(ray-AAl-in-vehs-ti-tsi-OHn)*	real investment
Reallöhne (pl)	*(ray-AAl-lER-neh)*	real wages
Realzeit (f)	*(ray-AAl-tsEYEt)*	real time
Rechenanlage (f)	*(reh-khen-AHN-lah-geh)*	computer
Rechenfehler (m)	*(rEH-khen-fAY-luh)*	miscalculation
Rechenschaft ablegen	*(rEH-khen-shahft AHB-lAY-gen)*	account for (v)
rechenschaftspflichtig	*(rEH-khen-shahfts-pflIKH-tikh)*	accountable
Rechner (m)	*(rEHKH-nuh)*	calculator
Rechnung (f)	*(rEHKH-nunk)*	bill, invoice
Rechnungsabschnitt (m)	*(rEHKH-nungs-AHB-shnIT)*	accounting period
Rechnungsjahr (n)	*(rEHKH-nungs-yaar)*	fiscal year
Rechnungsprüfer (m)	*(rEHKH-nungs-prEW-fuh)*	comptroller
Rechnungsschluß (m)	*(rEHKH-nungs-shlUS)*	end of period
Rechnungswesen für Betriebsführungsbedürfnisse (n)	*(rEHKH-nungs-vAY-zen fEWr beh-trEEps-fEW-runks-beh-dEWrf-nis-seh)*	management accounting
rechtmäßiger Inhaber (m)	*(REHKHT-mEH-si-guh IN-hah-buh)*	holder in due course
Rechtsanwalt (m)	*(REHKHTs-AHN-vahlt)*	attorney, lawyer
Rechtsbehelf (m)	*(REHKHTs-beh-hEHlf)*	remedy (law)
Rechtsmängelversicherung (f)	*(REHKHTs-mEHn-gehl-fuh-ZIKH-eh-runk)*	title insurance
Rechtsmittel (n)	*(REHKHTs-mit-tEL)*	remedy (law)
Rechtsstreit (m)	*(REHKHTs-shtEYEt)*	litigation
Rechtstitel (m)	*(REHKHTs-ti-tEHl)*	title
recyclingsfähig	*(ree-SEYEK-lings-FAY-ikh)*	recyclable
Redakteur (m)	*(re-dahk-tER)*	editor
redigieren	*(reh-di-gEE-ren)*	edit (v)
Rediskontsatz (m)	*(RAY-dis-kONt-zahts)*	rediscount rate
Reduktion (f)	*(reh-duk-TSI-On)*	reduction

Q

Refinanzierung (f)	*(RAY-fee-nahn-tsEE-runk)*	refinancing
Reflation (f)	*(RAY-flah-tsEE-ohn)*	reflation
Regelung (f)	*(RAY-geh-lunk)*	settlement
Regelungsauslöser (m)	*(RAY-geh-lunks-OWs-lER-suh)*	adjustment trigger
Regenmantel (m)	*(RAY-gen-mAHN-tel)*	raincoat
Regierung (f)	*(reh-gEE-runk)*	government
Regierungssektor (m)	*(reh-gEE-runks-sehk-tOHr)*	public sector
Regierungstelle (f)	*(reh-gEE-runks-shtEHL-leh)*	government agency
registrieren	*(ray-gis-trEEr ehn)*	index (v)
Regressionsanalyse (f)	*(ray-grehs-sEE-ohns-ah-nah-lEW-zeh)*	regression analysis
Regreßrecht (n)	*(ray-grEHs-REHKHT)*	right of recourse
Reichtum (m)	*(rEYEKH-toom)*	wealth
reif	*(rEYEF)*	ripe
Reife (f)	*(rEYE-feh)*	maturity (due debts)
Reifen (m)	*(rEYE-fen)*	tire
rein	*(reyen)*	net
reines Risiko (n)	*(REYEN-ehs REE-zFee-koh)*	pure risk
Reingewinn (m)	*(REYEN-geh-vIN)*	net profit
Reinigung (f)	*(REYE-ni-gunk)*	purification
Reinverlust (m)	*(REYEN-fuh-lUst)*	net loss
Reinvermögen (n)	*(REYEN-fuh-mER-gen)*	net assets
Reinvermögens- wert (m)	*(REYEN fuh-mER-genz-vEHRt)*	net asset value
Reisebüro (n)	*(REYE-zeh-bEW-roh)*	travel agency
Reisescheck (m)	*(REYE-zeh-shehk)*	traveler's check
Reißverschluß (m)	*(rEYES-fuh-shlUS)*	zipper
Reklame (f)	*(reh-klAA-meh)*	advertisement
Reklametext (m)	*(reh-klAA-meh-tehxt)*	copy (advertising text)
Rendite (f)	*(ren-dEE-teh)*	yield
Rentabilität (f)	*(ren-tah-bi-lee-tAYt)*	profitability
Rentabilitäts- analyse (f)	*(ren-tah-bi-li-tAYts-ah-nah-lEW-zeh)*	profitability analysis

R

Rentabilitätsrate (f)	*(ren-tah-bi-lee-tAYts-rAH-teh)*	rate of return
Reportprämie (f)	*(ray-pOHrt-PRAY-mee-eh)*	contango
Reproduktion (f)	*(reh-proh-duk-tsEE-ohn)*	reproduction
Reservefonds (m)	*(reh-zAYrv-eh-fOH)*	contingent fund
Resolution (f)	*(reh-zoh-loo-tsEE-ohn)*	resolution
Resonanz (f)	*(REH-zo-nahnts)*	resonance
Rest (m)	*(rehst)*	remainder
restaurieren	*(rehst-ow-rEE-ren)*	restore (v)
Restkaufgeldhypothek (f)	*(rehst-kOWf-GEHLT-hew-poh-tAYk)*	purchase money mortgage
Restposten (m)	*(rehst-pOS-ten)*	job lot
retten	*(REHT-tehn)*	salvage (v)
revolvierender Kredit (m)	*(reh-vol-vEE-ren-duh kray-dIT)*	revolving credit
revolvierendes Akkreditiv (n)	*(reh-vol-vEE-ren-dehs ah-kreh-di-tEEf)*	revolving letter of credit
Rezept (n)	*(reh-tsEHPt)*	prescription
Rezession (f)	*(reh-tseh-sEE-ohn)*	recession
richterliehe Verfügung (f)	*(RIKH-tuh-likh-eh fuh-fEW-gunk)*	injunction
Richtlinie (f)	*(RIKHT-lee-nee-eh)*	guideline
Richtpreis (m)	*(RIKHT-prEYEs)*	target price
Ries (n)	*(rees)*	ream
Rindsleder (n)	*(RINds-lAY-duh)*	cowhide
Risiko (n)	*(REE-zee-koh)*	risk
Risiko übernehmendes Land (n)	*(REE-zee-koh EW-buh-nAY-mehn-dehs lAHnd)*	country of risk
Risikoanalyse (f)	*(REE-zee-koh-ah-nah-lEW-zeh)*	risk analysis
Risikoeinschätzung (f)	*(REE-zee-koh-EYEn-shEH-tsunk)*	risk assessment
Risikokapital (n)	*(REE-zee-koh-kah-pi-tAAL)*	risk capital, venture capital
Rock (m)	*(rOK)*	skirt
roh	*(roh)*	crude
Rohgewicht (n)	*(ROH-geh-vIKHt)*	gross weight

R

Rohgewinn (m)	*(ROH-geh-vIN)*	gross profit
Röhrensystem (n)	*(REWr-en-zew-stAYm)*	pipage
Rohstoffe (f)	*(ROH-shtof-feh)*	raw materials
Rollgeld (n)	*(ROL-GEHLT)*	drayage
rostfreier Stahl (m)	*(rost-frEYE-uh shtAAL)*	stainless steel
Routine (f)	*(roo-tEE-neh)*	routine
Rückerstattung (f)	*(rEWk-uh-shtAA-tunk)*	refund, (money) drawback
Rückerstattung im voraus (f)	*(rEWk-uh-shtAA-tunk im FOHR-ows)*	advance refunding
Rückgang (m)	*(rEWk-gahnk)*	recession, slump
Rückgriff (m)	*(rEWk-grif)*	recourse
Rückgriffsanspruch (m)	*(rEWk-grifs-AHN-shprUKH)*	rights of recourse
Rückkaufswert (m)	*(rEWk-kOWfs-vEHRt)*	cash surrender value
Rücklage (f)	*(rEWk-lAA-geh)*	reserve
Rückstand (m)	*(rEWk-shtahnt)*	backlog
Rückstände (pl)	*(rEWk-shtEHn-deh)*	arrears
rückständiges Konto (n)	*(rEWk-shtEHn-dikh-ehs kON-toh)*	delinquent account
Rücktrittsklausel (f)	*(rEWk-trits-klOW-sehl)*	escape clause
Rückverkaufen (n)	*(rEWk-fuh-kOW-fen)*	back selling
Rückversicherer (m)	*(rEWk-fuh-ZIKH-eh-ruh)*	reinsurer
rückwirkend	*(rEWk-vEEr-kehnt)*	retroactive
rückwirkende Steuer (f)	*(rEWk-vEEr-ken-deh shtOY-uh)*	regressive tax
Rückwirkung (f)	*(rEWk-vEEr-kunk)*	feedback
rückzahlbare Staatsubvention (f)	*(rEWk-tsAAl-bAA-reh shtAAt-zub-vehn-tsEE-ohn)*	revolving fund
Rückzahlung (f)	*(rEWk-tsAA-lung)*	refund
Ruhestand (m)	*(rOO-heh-shtAHnt)*	retirement
Ruhetag (m)	*(rOO-heh-taak)*	holiday
Rundschreiben (n)	*(RUnt-shrEYE-ben)*	memorandum
Rundstange (f)	*(rund-shtAHN-geh)*	rod
Rüstkosten (pl)	*(REWst-kOS-ten)*	set-up costs
Rüstung (f)	*(REWS-tunk)*	armaments

R

S

Sachanlagen (pl)	*(zahkh-AHN-laa-gen)*	fixed assets
Sachanlagevermögen (n)	*(zahkh-AHN-laa-geh-fuh-mER-gen)*	tangible assets
Sachleistung (f)	*(zahkh-lEYEs-tunk)*	payment in kind
Saffianleder (n)	*(zahf-fi-AAn-lAY-duh)*	Morroco leather
saisonal	*(zay-zOH-naal)*	seasonal
Salatteller (m)	*(zah-lAAT-tel-luh)*	salad plate
Salbe (f)	*(zAHL-beh)*	ointment, salve
Salpetersäure (f)	*(zahl-PEH-tuh-ZOY-reh)*	nitric acid
Salz (n)	*(ZAHlts)*	salt
Salzsäure (f)	*(ZAHlts-ZOY-reh)*	hydrochloric acid
Salzstreuer (m)	*(ZAHlts-shtROY-uh)*	salt shaker
Sammelfonds (m)	*(zAH-mehl-fOH)*	pool of funds
Sanierung (f)	*(Zah-nee-ROONG)*	renovation
Sattel (m)	*(zaHT-tel)*	saddle
Sattler (m)	*(zaHT-tluh)*	saddler
Satzung (f)	*(zAH-tsunk)*	by-laws, charter (written instrument), statute
Säulendiagramm (n)	*(zOY-lehn-dee-ah-grAHm)*	bar chart
Saum (m)	*(zOWm)*	hem
Säure (f)	*(ZOY-reh)*	acid
Säuregehalt (m)	*(ZOY-reh-geh-hahlt)*	acid content
Schachtelaufsichtsrat (m)	*(shAHKH-tel-OWf-zikhts-raat)*	interlocking directorate
Schaden (m)	*(shAA-dehn)*	damage
Schaden aus allgemeiner Havarie (m)	*(shAA-dehn ows AHl-geh-mEYE-nuh hah-fah-rEE)*	general average loss
Schaden in besonderer Havarie (m)	*(shAA-dehn in beh-zON-duh-ruh hah-fah-rEE)*	particular average loss
Schadennachweis (m)	*(shAA-dehn-nAKH-vEYEs)*	proof of loss
Schafleder (n)	*(shAAF-lAY-duh)*	lamb

S

Schal (m)	*(SHAAl)*	scarf
Schale (f)	*(SHAA-leh)*	bowl
Schallplatte (f)	*(shAHL-plaht-teh)*	record
Schallplattenspieler (m)	*(shAHL-plaht-ten-shPEE-luh)*	record player
Schaltautomatik (f)	*(shAHLt-OW-to-mah-tik)*	automatic gearshift
Schalterbeamter (m)	*(shAHl-tuh-beh-AHm-tuh)*	teller
Schaltfeld (n)	*(shAHLt-felt)*	panel
Schaltung (f)	*(shAHL-tunk)*	circuit
Schamottesteine (pl)	*(shah-mOT-eh-shTEYE-neh)*	refractories
Schankkonzession (f)	*(shAAnk-kon-tseh-tsEE-ohn)*	excise license
schätzen	*(shEH-tsen)*	estimate (v)
Schatzmeister (m)	*(shahts-mEYE-stuh)*	treasurer
Schätzpreis (m)	*(shEHts-prEYEs)*	estimated price
Schätzung (f)	*(shEH-tsunk)*	appraisal, estimate
Schatzwechsel (pl)	*(shahts-vEHK-sel)*	treasury bills
Schaubild (n)	*(shOW-bilt)*	flow chart
Schaufensterdekorateur (m)	*(SHOW-fen-stuh-deh-ko-rah-TER)*	window dresser
Schaufensterdekoration (f)	*(shOW-fehn-stuh-day-koh-rah-tsEE-ohn)*	window dressing
Schaumwein (m)	*(shOWm-vEYEN)*	sparkling wine
Scheck (m)	*(shehk)*	check
Scheckkonto (n)	*(shEHk-kON-toh)*	checking account
Scheibenbremse (f)	*(shEYE-ben-brEHM-zeh)*	disc brake
Scheingewinn (m)	*(shEYEn-geh-vIN)*	paper profit
Scherenetui (n)	*(shAY-ren-e-tuEE)*	scissor case
Schicht (working hours) (f)	*(shikht)*	shift
Schiedsabkommen (n)	*(shEEds-AHb-kOM-mehn)*	arbitration agreement
Schiedsrichter (m)	*(shEEds-rIKH-tuh)*	arbitrator
Schiedsverfahren (n)	*(shEEds-fuh-fAA-ren)*	arbitration

Schiffahrtsvertrag (m)	*(shIF-fahrts-fuh-trAHk)*	maritime contract
Schiffsfrachtvertrag (m)	*(shIFs-frAHKHt-fuh-trAHk)*	affreightment
Schirmherr (m)	*(shIrm-hAYr)*	sponsor
Schlaftablette (f)	*(shlAAF-tah-bleh-teh)*	sleeping pill
Schlange stehen	*(shlAHn-geh shtAY-hen)*	stand in line (v)
Schlangenleder (n)	*(shlAHN-gen-lAY-duh)*	snakeskin
schlecht bezahlt	*(shlekht beh-tsAAlt)*	underpaid
Schleier (m)	*(shlEYE-uh)*	veil
Schleifen (n)	*(shlEYE-fen)*	grinding
Schleuderausfuhr (f)	*(shlOY-duh-OWs-foor)*	dumping (goods in foreign market)
Schlichfräser (m)	*(shLIKH-frAY-zuh)*	finishing mill
Schlichtungsverfahren (n)	*(shlIKH-tunks-fuh-fAA-rehn)*	grievance procedure
Schlüsseletui (n)	*(shlEWS-sel-e-tuEE)*	key case
schlüsselfertiger Vertrag (m)	*(shlEW-sehl-fuh-tI-guh fuh-trAHk)*	turn-key contract
Schlüsselstellungen (pl)	*(shlEW-sehl-shtEHL-lunk-ehn)*	key positions
Schlußkurs (m)	*(shlUS-koors)*	closing price
Schmelzgang (m)	*(shmEHLTS-gahnk)*	heat
Schmelztiegel (m)	*(shmEHLTS-tEE-gel)*	crucible
Schmiergeld (n)	*(shmEEr-GEHLT)*	kickback
Schmierung (f)	*(shmEE-runk)*	lubrication
Schmuck (m)	*(shmUK)*	jewelry
Schmuggelwaren (pl)	*(shmOOg-gehl vAA-rehn)*	prohibited goods
Schneeballverkaufssystem (n)	*(shnAY-bahl-fuh-kOWfs-zew-stAYm)*	pyramid selling
Schneider (m)	*(shnEYE-duh)*	tailor
Schnellspeicher (m)	*(shnEL-spEYEkh-uh)*	direct access storage
Schnittwaren (pl)	*(shnIT-vAA-ren)*	dry goods
Schriftführer (m)	*(shrIFt-fEW-ruh)*	secretary

S

schriftliche Verein- barung (f)	*(shrIFt-likh-eh fuh-EYEn- baa-runk)*	written agreement
schriftlicher Ver- trag (m)	*(shrIFt-likh-uh fuh-trAHk)*	written agreement
Schriftsatz (m)	*(shrIFT-zAHTS)*	composition, font
Schrottwert (m)	*(shrOt-vEHRt)*	salvage value (junk, scrap)
Schubverarbeitung (f)	*(SHUb-fuh-AHR-beye-tunk)*	batch processing
Schuh (m)	*(shOO)*	shoe
Schuld (f)	*(shult)*	debt
Schuldbetrag (m)	*(SHULT-beh-trAHk)*	amount due
schuldenfrei	*(SHUL-dehn-frEYE)*	afloat (debt-free), free and clear (debt-free)
Schuldentilgung (f)	*(SHUL-den-tiIL-gunk)*	retirement (debt)
Schuldschein (m)	*(SHULT-sheyen)*	promissory note
Schuldübernahme (f)	*(SHULT-EW-buh-nAA-meh)*	novation
Schuldverschrei- bung (f)	*(SHULT-fuh-shrEYE-bunk)*	bond, debenture
Schuldverschrei- bungsvollmacht (f)	*(SHULT-fuh-shrEYE-bungs- fOL-makht)*	bond power
Schüssel (f)	*(SHEWs-sel)*	dish
Schutentransport (m)	*(SHOO-ten-trAHnz-port)*	lighterage
schützen	*(shEW-tsehn)*	safeguard (v)
Schutzmarke (f)	*(shUts-mAHR-keh)*	trademark
schutzzollbedürf- tige Industrie (f)	*(shUts-tsOL-beh-dEWrf-ti- geh in-dus-trEE)*	infant industry
Schutzzollsystem (n)	*(shUts-tsOL-zew-stAYm)*	protectionism
schwacher Markt (m)	*(shvAA-khuh mAHrkt)*	thin market
schwankende Ein- fuhrabschöp- fung (f)	*(shvAHnk-ehn-deh EYEn- foor-AHB-shERp-funk)*	variable import levy
schwankender Kurs (m)	*(shvAHnk-ehn-duh koors)*	variable rate
Schwarzmarkt (m)	*(shvAArts-mAHrkt)*	black market

schwarzweiß	*(shvarts-vEYES)*	black and white
schwebende Belastung (f)	*(shvAY-behn-deh beh-lah-stunk)*	floating charge
schwebende Schuld (f)	*(shvAY-behn-deh shUlt)*	floating debt
Schwefelsäure (f)	*(shvay-fel-ZOY-reh)*	sulfuric acid
Schweinsleder (n)	*(shvEYEns-lAY-duh)*	pigskin
Schwemme (f)	*(shveh-meh)*	glut
Schwerarbeiter (m)	*(shvAYr-ahr-bEYE-tuh)*	manual worker
Schwergutaufschlag (m)	*(shvAYr-gOOt-OWf-shlAHk)*	heavy lift charge
Schwerindustrie (f)	*(shvAYr-in-dus-trEE)*	heavy industry
Schwingung (f)	*(shvIN-gunk)*	wave
schwören	*(shvER-ehn)*	swear (v)
Sechszylindermotor (m)	*(zEKHs-tsew-lin-duh-mOH-tor)*	six-cylinder engine
Seehundsfell (n)	*(ZAY-hunds-fEL)*	sealskin
Seemeile (f)	*(ZAY-mEYE-leh)*	knot (nautical)
Seetransportversicherung (f)	*(ZAY-trahns-pohrt-fuh-ZIKH-eh-runk)*	marine cargo insurance
Seeversicherer (m)	*(ZAY-fuh-ZIKH-eh-ruh)*	marine underwriter
Seidenfabrik (f)	*(zeYE-den-fah-brIK)*	silk factory
Seidenhersteller (f)	*(zeYE-den-huh-shTEL-luh)*	silk manufacturers
Seidenraupe (f)	*(zeYE-den-ROW-peh)*	silkworm
Seidenstoff (m)	*(zeYE-den-shtOF)*	silk
Seidenwaren (pl)	*(zeYE-den-VAAren)*	silk goods
Seitenaufmachung (f)	*(zEYE-ten-owf-mah-khunk)*	page makeup
Sekretärin (f)	*(zeh-kreh-tEH-rin)*	secretary
Sektglas (n)	*(zehkt-glAAs)*	champagne glass
selbständig	*(zehlbst-shtEHn-dikh)*	autonomous, self-employed
Selbstbedienung (f)	*(zehlbst-beh-dEE-nunk)*	self-service
selbstfinanzieren	*(zehlbst-fee-nahn-tsEE-rehn)*	plow back earnings (v)
Selbstkosten (pl)	*(zehlbst-kOS-ten)*	actual costs, prime costs
Selbstschätzung (f)	*(zehlbst-shEH-tsunk)*	self-appraisal

S

senden	*(zEN-den)*	broadcast (v)
Sender (m)	*(zEN-duh)*	transmitter
Sendung (f)	*(zEN-dunk)*	consignment, shipment
Serienanleihen (pl)	*(ZAY-ree-ehn-AHN-leye-en)*	serial bonds
Serienproduktion (f)	*(ZAY-ree-ehn-proh-duk-tsEE-ohn)*	batch production
Serienspeicherung (f)	*(ZAY-ree-ehn-shpEYEkh-uh-runk)*	serial storage
Serum (n)	*(zAY-rum)*	serum
Serviette (f)	*(zuh-VI-et-teh)*	napkin
Serviettenring (m)	*(zuh-VI-et-tehn-rINk)*	napkin ring
Servolenkung (f)	*(zEHR-vo-len-kunk)*	power steering
(sich gegen Verluste) sichern	*(zikh gAY-gehn fuh-lUs-teh zIKH-uhn)*	hedge (v)
(sich gegenseitig) beeinflussen	*(zikh gAY-gehn-zEYE-tikh beh-EYEn-flus-sen)*	interact (v)
(sich) anmelden	*(zikh AHN-mel-den)*	check in (v)
(sich) einmischen	*(zikh EYEn-mIsh-ehn)*	intervene (v)
(sich) sammeln	*(zikh zAA-mehln)*	rally (v)
Sicherheit (f)	*(zIKH-uh-heyet)*	collateral, security
Sicherheitskoeffizient (f)	*(zikh-ehr-heyets-koh-ehf-fee-tsEE-ehnt)*	margin of safety
sichtbare Handelsbilanz (f)	*(zikht-bAA-reh hAHn-dehls bee-lAHnts)*	visible balance of trade
Sichteinlage (f)	*(zikht-EYEn-lAA-geh)*	demand deposit
Sichtwechsel (m)	*(zikht-vEHK-sehl)*	bill of sight, sight draft
sieben	*(ZEE-behn)*	screen (v)
Silizium (n)	*(zi-LEE-tsi-um)*	silicon
simulieren	*(zi-moo-lEE-rehn)*	simulate (v)
Sinus (m)	*(zEE-nus)*	sinus
Sitz (m)	*(zITS)*	seat
Sitzung (f)	*(ZIts-unk)*	meeting
Sitzungsraum (m)	*(ZIts-unks-rOWm)*	boardroom
Sitzungssaal (m)	*(ZIts-unks-zAAl)*	conference room
Smoking (m)	*(smOH-king)*	tuxedo

so bald wie möglich	*(zoh bahld vEE mER-glikh)*	as soon as possible
so schnell wie möglich	*(zoh shnehl vEE mER-glikh)*	as fast as possible
Socken (pl)	*(ZO-ken)*	socks
Software (f)	*(soft-vAYr)*	software
Soll (n)	*(zol)*	debit
Sollsaldo (m)	*(zol-zAAl-doh)*	adverse balance
Sondermüll (m)	*(ZON-duh-mewl)*	toxic waste
sonstige Verbindlichkeiten (pl)	*(ZONS-ti-geh fuh-bIND-likh-keye-ten)*	other liabilities
sonstiges Vermögen (n)	*(ZONS-ti-gehs fuh-mER-gen)*	other assets
Soßenschüssel (f)	*(ZOH-sen-SHEWs-sel)*	gravy boat
Spanne (f)	*(shpAHn-neh)*	spread
Sparbuch (n)	*(shpAAr-bOOkh)*	passbook
Sparkasse (f)	*(shpAAr-kAH-seh)*	savings bank
Sparkonto (n)	*(shpAAr-kON-toh)*	savings account
Spediteur (m)	*(shpeh-dee-tEWr)*	carrier, forwarding agent, shipping agent
Speicher des Computers (m)	*(shpEYE-khuh deh kom-pyU-tuhs)*	computer memory
speichern	*(shpEYE-khuhn)*	store (computer)
Speicherung (f)	*(shpEYE-khuh-runk)*	storage (computer)
Spekulant (m)	*(shpeh-koo-lAHnt)*	speculator
Spekulativhändler (m)	*(shpeh-koo-lah-tEEf-hEHnd-luh)*	scalper
Spesen (pl)	*(shpAY-zehn)*	charges
Spesenkonto (n)	*(shpAY-zehn kON-toh)*	expense account
Spezialerzeugnisse (pl)	*(shpeh-tsee-AAl-AYr-tsOYg-ni-seh)*	specialty goods
Spezialstahl (m)	*(shpeh-tsIAAL-shtAAL)*	specialty steels
spezifizierte Rechnung (f)	*(speh-tsee-fee-tsEEr-teh rEHKH-nunk)*	itemized account
Spitze (f)	*(SHPIT-tseh)*	lace
Spitzenbelastung (f)	*(shpI-tsehn-beh-lAH-stunk)*	peak load

S

Spitzenpreisanset- **zung (f)**	*(shpI-tsehn-prEYEs-AHn-* *zEH-tsunk)*	premium pricing
Spitzenqualität (f)	*(shpI-tsehn-kvah-li-tAYt)*	top quality
Spontankauf (m)	*(shpon-tAHn-kOWf)*	impulse purchase
Spontanstreik (m)	*(shpon-tAAn-shtreyek)*	wildcat strike
Sportkleidung (f)	*(shpORT-klEYE-dunk)*	sportswear
Spritze (f)	*(shpRI-tseh)*	injection, syringe
sprunghafte Bör- **senmarktlage (f)**	*(shprOONG-hAAf-teh* *bEWr-sehn-mAHrkt-lAA-* *geh)*	volatile market
Sprungkosten (pl)	*(shprUNG-kOS-ten)*	semivariable costs
Spule (f)	*(shpOO-leh)*	coil
staatlicher Grund- **besitz (m)**	*(shtAAt-likh-uh grUNd-beh-* *zITs)*	public domain
Staatsanleihen (pl)	*(shtAAts-AHN-leye-en)*	government bonds, treasury bonds
Staatsbank (f)	*(shtAAts-bahnk)*	government bank, national bank
Staatseigentum (n)	*(shtAAts-EYE-gehn-toom)*	public property
Staatsobligationen **(pl)**	*(shtAAts-ob-li-gah-tsEE-* *ohn-ehn)*	treasury notes
Staatspapiere (pl)	*(shtAAts-pah-pEE-reh)*	government bonds
Staatsschuldver- **schreibung (f)**	*(shtAAts-shUlt-fuh-shrEYE-* *bunk)*	savings bond
Staatssozialismus **(m)**	*(shtAAts-soh-tsee-ah-lIS-* *mus)*	economic nationalism
Staatsverschul- **dung (f)**	*(shtAAts-fuh-shUl-dunk)*	national debt
Stab (m)	*(shtahp)*	staff
Stab und Linie	*(shtahp unt lEE-nee-eh)*	staff and line
Stabsassistent (m)	*(shtahps-as-sis-tENt)*	staff assistant
Stabsorganisation **(f)**	*(shtahps-ohr-gah-ni-zah-* *tsee-OHn)*	staff organization
Stadtausbreitung **(f)**	*(shtAHt-OWs-brEYE-tunk)*	urban sprawl
Stadterneuerung **(f)**	*(shtAHt-ayr-nOY-uh-runk)*	urban renewal
Staffelhypothek (f)	*(shtAH-fel-hew-poh-tAYk)*	variable rate mortgage

S

Staffeltarif (m)	*(shtAH-fel-tah-rIF)*	adjusted rate, flexible tariff
Stagflation (f)	*(shtAHg-flaa-tsEE-ohn)*	stagflation
Stahldraht (m)	*(shtAAL-drAAt)*	wire
Stahlkammer (f)	*(shtAAl-kAHm-muh)*	safe deposit box
Stahlwerk (n)	*(shtAAL-vehrk)*	steel mill
Stammaktie (f)	*(shtAHm-ak-tsEE-eh)*	capital stock, common stock
Stammkapital (n)	*(shtAHm-kah-pi-tAAL)*	corpus, ordinary capital
Standardabweichung (f)	*(shtahnd-dahrd-AHB-vEYE-khunk)*	standard deviation
Standardbrief (m)	*(shtAHn-dahrd-brEEf)*	form letter
Stangen (pl)	*(shtAHN-gen)*	bars
Stapelverarbeitung (f)	*(shtAHpl-fuh-ahr-bEYE-tunk)*	batch processing
Stärke (f)	*(shtEHR-keh)*	starch
starre Nachfrage	*(shtAHr-reh nAHKH-frAA-geh)*	inelastic demand
starres Angebot	*(shtAHr-reh-ehs AHN-geh-boht)*	inelastic supply
starten	*(shtAAr-ten)*	take off (v)
Statistik (f)	*(shtah-tIS-tik)*	statistics
Statut (n)	*(shtah-tOOt)*	charter (written instrument), law
Statuten (pl)	*(shtah-tOO-ten)*	by-laws
Stauerlohn (m)	*(shtOW-uh-lOHn)*	stowage charges
Staulücken (pl)	*(shtOW-lEW-ken)*	broken stowage
steigern	*(shtEYE-guhn)*	maximize (v)
Steigerungsklausel (f)	*(shtEYE-guh-runks-klOW-sel)*	escalator clause
Steingut (n)	*(shtEYEn-gOOt)*	stoneware
Stellage (f)	*(shtEHL-lAA-geh)*	straddle
Stellagegeschäft (n)	*(shtEHL-lAA-geh-geh-shEHft)*	put and call
Stellenbeschreibung (f)	*(shtEHL-en-beh-shrEYE-bunk)*	job description
Stellenvermittlung (f)	*(shtEHL-en-fuh-mIT-lunk)*	placement (personnel)

S

Stellenvermitt-	*(shtEHL-en-fuh-mIT-lunks-*	employment agency
lungsbüro (n)	*bEW-roh)*	
stellvertretender	*(shtEHL-fuh-trAY-ten-duh*	assistant general manager
Generaldirektor	*gehn-eh-rAAl-di-REHK-*	
(m)	*tohr)*	
stellvertretender	*(shtEHL-fuh-trAY-ten-duh*	assistant manager, deputy
Geschäftsführer	*geh-shEHfts-fEW-ruh)*	manager
(m)		
stellvertretender	*(shtEHL-fuh-trAY-ten-duh*	deputy chairman
Vorsitzender	*FOHR-zits-en-deh)*	
(m)		
stereophonisch	*(shtAY-reh-o-FO-nish)*	stereophonic
Steuer (f)	*(shtOY-uh)*	duty, tax
Steuerabzug (m)	*(shtOY-uh-AHB-tsOOk)*	tax deduction
steuerbegünstigte	*(shtOY-uh beh-gEWn-stig-*	tax shelter
Anlagemöglich-	*teh AHN-laa-geh-mER-*	
keit (f)	*glikh-keyet)*	
Steuerbremse (f)	*(shtOY-uh-brEHm-zeh)*	fiscal drag
Steuereinnehmer	*(shtOY-uh-EYEn-nAY-muh)*	tax collector
(m)		
steuerfrei	*(shtOY-uh-frEYE)*	tax-free
Steuerfreibetrag	*(shtOY-uh-frEYE-beh-*	exemption (tax exemption),
(m)	*trAHk)*	tax allowance
steuerfreies Ein-	*(shtOY-uh-frEYE-ehs*	tax-free income
kommen (n)	*EYEn-kOM-mehn)*	
Steuerhinterzie-	*(shtOY-uh-hin-tuh-tsEE-*	tax evasion
hung (f)	*unk)*	
Steuerknüppel (m)	*(shtOY-uh-knEWp-pehl)*	joystick
Steuerlast (f)	*(shtOY-uh-lAHst)*	tax burden
steuerliche Veran-	*(shtOY-uh-likh-eh fayr-AAn-*	assessed valuation
lagung (f)	*lAA-gunk)*	
Steuern erheben	*(shtOY-uhn AYr-hAY-behn)*	levy taxes (v)
Steuernachlaß (m)	*(shtOY-uh-nAKH-laas)*	remission of a tax, tax abate-ment
Steueroase (f)	*(shtOY-uh-oh-AH-zeh)*	tax haven
steuerpflichtig	*(shtOY-uh-pflIKH-tik)*	liable for tax
steuerpflichtiges	*(shtOY-uh-pflIKH-tik-ehs*	adjusted gross income
Bruttoeinkom-	*BRU-toh-EYEn-kOM-*	
men (n)	*mehn)*	
Steuerrad (n)	*(shtOY-uh-raht)*	steering wheel

S

Steuerrückstände (pl)	*(shtOY-uh-rEWk-shtAYn-deh)*	back taxes
Steuerschulden (pl)	*(shtOY-uh-shUl-dehn)*	accrued taxes
Steuerung (f)	*(shtOY-eh-runk)*	steering
Steuervergünstigung (f)	*(shtOY-uh-fuh-gEWns-ti-gunk)*	tax allowance, tax relief
Steuerzahler (m)	*(shtOY-uh-tsAA-luh)*	taxpayer
Steuerzuschlag (m)	*(shtOY-uh-tsOO-shlAHk)*	surtax
Stichart (m)	*(shtIKH-ahrt)*	stitch
Stichprobe (f)	*(shtIKH-proh-beh)*	random sample
Stichprobenprüfung (f)	*(shtIKH-proh-ben-prEW-funk)*	acceptance sampling
Stichprobenumfang (m)	*(shtIKH-pro-ben-OOm-fank)*	sample size
Stichtag (m)	*(shtIKH-taak)*	deadline
Stickstoff (m)	*(shtIK-shtOF)*	nitrogen
Stiefel (pl)	*(shtEE-fel)*	boots
Stiefelladen (m)	*(shtEE-fel-laa-den)*	boot shop
Stiefelmacher (m)	*(shtEE-fel-mahkh-uh)*	bootmaker
Stiftung (f)	*(shtIF-tunk)*	endowment
Stil (m)	*(shtEEL)*	style
Stilist (m)	*(shtEEL-ist)*	stylist
stille Reserve (f)	*(shtIL-leh reh-zAYr-veh)*	hidden asset
stiller Gesellschafter (m)	*(shtIL-luh geh-zEL-shahft-uh)*	silent partner
Stilliegen (n)	*(shtIL-lEE-gen)*	down period (factory)
stillschweigendes Einverständnis (n)	*(shtIL-shvEYE-gen-dehs EYEn-fuh-stehnd-nis)*	implied-agreement
stimmaktiviert	*(shtIM-ahk-tee-vEErt)*	voice-activated
Stimmrecht (n)	*(shtIM-REHKHT)*	voting right
Stimmrechtsermächtigung (f)	*(shtIM-REHKHTs-uh-mAYkh-ti-gunk)*	proxy
Stoff (m)	*(shtOF)*	fabric
Störung (f)	*(shtER-unk)*	bug (computers)

S

Störungen auffinden und beseitigen	*(shtER-ung-en OWf-fin-dehn unt beh-zEYE-ti-gehn)*	troubleshoot (v)
Stoßdämpfer (m)	*(shtOS-dEHm-pfuh)*	shock absorber
Stoßstange (f)	*(shtOS-shtAHN-geh)*	bumper
Strafklausel (f)	*(shtrAAf-klOW-sehl)*	penalty clause
Straftat (f)	*(shtrAAf-tAAt)*	tort
Strafverfahren wegen Unterschlagung (n)	*(strAAf-fuh-fAA-ren vAY-gen un-tuh-shlAH-gunk)*	penalty-fraud action
Strahlung (f)	*(shtRAA-lunk)*	beam
strategische Artikel (pl)	*(strah-tAY-gi-sheh ahr-tIK-el)*	strategic articles
Strauß (m)	*(shtrOWS)*	ostrich
Streikbrecher (m)	*(shtrEYEk-brehkh-uh)*	strikebreaker
streiken	*(shtrEYE-ken)*	strike (v)
Streikpostenkette (f)	*(shtrEYEk-pOS-ten-keh-teh)*	picket line
Streit (m)	*(shtreyet)*	dispute
streiten	*(shtrEYE-ten)*	dispute (v)
Streßbewältigung (f)	*(shtres-beh-vEHl-ti-gunk)*	stress management
Strom (m)	*(shtrOHm)*	current
Stromspannung (f)	*(shtrOHm-shpAN-nunk)*	voltage
Stromverbrauch (m)	*(shtOHm-fuh-brOWkh)*	power consumption
Strümpfe (pl)	*(shtrEWM-PFeh)*	stockings
Stück (n)	*(shtewk)*	part
Stückarbeit (f)	*(shtEWk-ahr-bEYEt)*	piecework
Stückgutfracht (f)	*(shtEWk-gOOt-frahkht)*	berth terms
Stückgutsendung (f)	*(shtEWk-gOOt-zEN-dunk)*	less-than-carload
Stückkosten (pl)	*(shtEWk-kOS-ten)*	unit costs
Stückpreis (m)	*(shtEWk-prEYEs)*	unit price
Stückzoll (m)	*(shtEWk-tsOL)*	specific duty
Studie (f)	*(shtoo-di-eh)*	analysis

S

stufenweise einführ-ren	*(shtOO-fen-vEYE-zeh EYEn-fEW-ren)*	phase in (v)
stufenweise einstel-len	*(shtOO-fen-vEYE-zeh EYEn-shtEHL-en)*	phase out (v)
Stundenlohn (m)	*(shtUn-den-lOHn)*	hourly earnings
Stundung (f)	*(shtun-dunk)*	moratorium
Stützpreis (m)	*(shtEWts-prEYEs)*	pegged price
Submissionsgaran-tie (f)	*(zub-mi-see-OHnz-gah-rahn-tEE)*	performance bond
Subunternehmer (m)	*(zub-un-tuh-nAY-muh)*	subcontractor
Subvention (f)	*(zub-vehn-tsee-OHn)*	price support, subsidy
Suchanzeige (f)	*(zOOkh-AHN-tseye-geh)*	want-ad
Suche nach Füh-rungskräften (f)	*(zOO-kheh nAHKH fEW-runks-krehf-ten)*	executive search
Sulfamid (n)	*(zul-fah-mEEt)*	sulphamide
Superlegierungen (pl)	*(zOO-puh-leh-gEE-run-gen)*	super alloys
Suppenteller (m)	*(ZUP-pen-tel-luh)*	soup dish
Syndikat (n)	*(zewn-di-kAAt)*	syndicate
Synthese (f)	*(sewn-tAY-seh)*	synthesis
synthetisch	*(ZEWN-teh-tish)*	synthetic
synthetische Stoffe (pl)	*(zEWn-tAY-ti-sheh shtOF-feh)*	manmade
Systemanalyse (f)	*(zew-stAYm-ah-nah-lEW-zeh)*	systems analysis
Systemerarbeitung (f)	*(zew-stAYm-uh-ahr-bEYE-tunk)*	systems engineering
Systemgestaltung (f)	*(zew-stAYm-geh-shtAHl-tunk)*	systems design
Systemsteuerung (f)	*(zews-tAYm-shtOY-uh-runk)*	systems management

---

T

Tablette (f)	*(tah-bleh-teh)*	tablet
Tafelsilber (n)	*(TAH-fel-zil-buh)*	silverware
Taft (m)	*(tahft)*	taffeta

Tagesauftrag (m)	*(tAA-gehs-OWf-trAHk)*	day order
Tagesbestellung (f)	*(tAA-gehs-beh-shtEHL-lunk)*	order of the day
Tagesgeld (n)	*(tAA-gehs-GEHLT)*	day loan
Tagesordnung (f)	*(tAA-gehs-ORd-nunk)*	agenda
Tagesordnungs-punkt (m)	*(tAA-gehs-ORd-nungs-pUnkt)*	point of order
täglich	*(tAYg-likh)*	daily
täglich kündbares Geld (n)	*(tEHg-likh kEWnd-bAAr-ehs GEHLT)*	call money
tägliches Geld (n)	*(tEHg-likh-ehs GEHLT)*	demand deposit
Tagung (f)	*(tAA-gunk)*	meeting
Tanker (m)	*(tAAnk-uh)*	tanker
Tannin (n)	*(tahn-nEEN)*	tannin
Tarif (m)	*(tah-rIF)*	tariff
Tarifstreitigkeit (f)	*(tah-rIF-shtrEYE-tikh-keyet)*	labor dispute
Tarifverhandlun-gen (pl)	*(tah-rIF-fuh-hAHnd-lunk-ehn)*	collective bargaining
Tarifvertrag (m)	*(tah-rIF-fuh-trAHk)*	collective agreement, union contract
Taschentuch (n)	*(tAH-SHen-TOOkh)*	handkerchief
Tasse (f)	*(TAHs-seh)*	cup
tatsächliche Haft-pflicht (f)	*(taht-sEHKH-likh-eh hAHft-pflikht)*	actual liability
tatsächlicher Gesamtverlust (m)	*(taht-sEHKH-likh-uh geh-zAAmt-fuh-lUst)*	actual total loss
tauschen	*(tOW-shen)*	barter (v), exchange (v)
Tauschmittel (n)	*(tOWsh-mit-tEL)*	medium of exchange
Tauschwert (m)	*(tOWsh-vEHRt)*	exchange value
technisch	*(tehkh-nIsh)*	technical
Technologie (n)	*(tehkh-noh-loh-gEE)*	technology
Teekanne (f)	*(TAY-KAHN-neh)*	teapot
Teelöffel (m)	*(TAY-lERF-fel)*	teaspoon
Teil (m)	*(teyel)*	part
Teilfracht (f)	*(tEYEl-frahkht)*	part cargo
Teilhaber (m)	*(tEYEl-hAA-buh)*	partner, shareholder

T

Teilhaberschaft (f)	*(tEYEl-hAA-buh-shahft)*	partnership
Teilladung (f)	*(tEYEl-lAA-dunk)*	part cargo
Teilwert (m)	*(tEYEl-vEHRt)*	going concern value
Teilzahlung (f)	*(tEYEl-tsAA-lunk)*	partial payment
Teilzahlungskredit (m)	*(tEYEl-tsAA-lungs-kray-dIT)*	installment credit
Teilzahlungsplan (m)	*(tEYEl-tsAA-lungs-plAAn)*	installment plan
Telefon (n)	*(tay-leh-FOHN)*	telephone
Telegramm (n)	*(tay-leh-grAHm)*	cable, telegram, wire
telegraphische Überweisung (f)	*(tay-leh-grAA-fish-eh EWb-uh-vEYE-zunk)*	cable transfer, wire transfer
Telekommunikation (f)	*(tay-leh-kom-moo-ni-kah-tsEE-ohn)*	telecommunications
Telex (n)	*(tay-lehx)*	telex
Teller (m)	*(tel-luh)*	plate, dinner plate, dish
Temperatur (f)	*(tehm-peh-rah-tOOR)*	temperature
Tendenz (f)	*(tehn-dEHnts)*	trend
Terminabschluß (m)	*(tayr-mEEN-AHB-shlUS)*	forward contract
Terminal (n)	*(tayr-mi-nAAl)*	terminal
Termindeckung (f)	*(tayr-mEEN-DEK-unk)*	forward margin
Termingeschäfte (pl)	*(tayr-mEEN-geh-shEHf-teh)*	futures
Terminkauf (m)	*(tayr-mEEN-kOWf)*	forward purchase
Terminmarkt (m)	*(tayr-mEEN-mAHrkt)*	forward market
Terminoption (f)	*(tayr-mEEN-op-tsEE-ohn)*	futures option
Terminsendung (f)	*(tayr-mEEN-zEN-dunk)*	forward shipment
Terrine (f)	*(tuh-rEEN-neh)*	tureen
Testament (n)	*(tehs-tah-mEHnt)*	will
Testamentsanhang (m)	*(tehs-tah-mEHnt-AHn-hahnk)*	codicil
Testamentseröffnung und Bestätigung (f)	*(tehs-tah-mEHnt-uh-ERf-nunk unt beh-shtAY-ti-gunk)*	probate
Testamentsvollstrecker (m)	*(tehs-tah-mEHnt-fol-shtrEH-kuh)*	executor (of an estate)

T

Textilien (pl)	*(tehks-tEE-lee-ehn)*	dry goods, soft goods
Textverarbeitungsgerät (n)	*(tehxt-fuh-ahr-bEYE-tunks-geh-rayt)*	word processor
Thermometer (n)	*(tEHR-mo-mEH-tuh)*	thermometer
thesaurieren	*(tay-zow-rEE-rehn)*	hoard (v)
thesaurierte Gewinne (pl)	*(tay-zow-rEEf-teh geh-vIN-neh)*	retained earnings
tilgen	*(tIL-gehn)*	pay off(v)
Tilgung (f)	*(tIL-gunk)*	amortization
Tilgungsfonds (m)	*(tIL-gunks-fOH)*	redemption fund, sinking fund
tilgungsfreie Zeit (f)	*(tIL-gunks-frEYE-eh tsEYEt)*	grace period
Tinte (f)	*(TIN-Teh)*	ink
(Tinten) Löscher (m)	*([TIN-Ten] lERSH-uh)*	blotter
Tischordnung (f)	*(TISH-ORd-nunk)*	place setting
Tischtuch (n)	*(TISH-TOOkh)*	tablecloth
Titan (n)	*(ti-tAAn)*	titanium
Titel (m)	*(TI-tel)*	title
Titrierung (f)	*(ti-trEE-runk)*	titration
Tochtergesellschaft (f)	*(tOKH-tuh-geh-zEL-shahft)*	affiliate, associate company, subsidiary
Ton (m)	*(tOHn)*	sound, tone
Tonbandgerät (n)	*(tOHn-bahnd-geh-rEHt)*	tape recorder
Tonnage (f)	*(ton-nAA-djeh)*	tonnage
Töpferware (f)	*(TERp-fuh-VAAreh)*	earthenware, pottery
Topmanagement (n)	*(tOP-meh-nEHdj-mehnt)*	management, top management
Tortenheber (m)	*(TOR-ten-hay-buh)*	pastry server
Totalverlust (m)	*(toh-tAAl fuh-lUst)*	total loss
Toxikologie (f)	*(to-xi-ko-loh-gee)*	toxicology
Toxin (n)	*(to-xEEN)*	toxin
tragen	*(trAA-gen)*	bear (v)
Tranche (f)	*(trAHn-sheh)*	tranche
Tranchiermesser (n)	*(trahn-shEER-MEHS-suh)*	carving knife

T

Transitkonnossement (n)	*(trahn-zeet-kon-nos-seh-mEH)*	through bill of lading
Transitlager (n)	*(trahn-zEEt-LAA-guh)*	bonded warehouse
transitorische Passiva (pl)	*(trahn-zEE-toh-rish-eh pas-SEE-vaa)*	unearned revenue
Transport (m)	*(trahns-pOHrt)*	transportation
Transporthaftung (f)	*(trahns-pOHrt-hAHf-tunk)*	carrier's risk
Transportunternehmer (m)	*(trahns-pOHrt-un-tuh-nAY-muh)*	carrier
Tratte (f)	*(trAH-teh)*	draft
Treibhauseffekt (m)	*(TREYEB-house-eh-fekt)*	greenhouse effect
Trennung (f)	*(trEHn-nunk)*	separation
treuer Gehilfe (m)/treue Gehilfin (f)	*(trOY-uh geh-hIL-feh /trOY-eh geh-hil-fEEn)*	man (gal) Friday
Treuhänder (m)	*(trOY-hEHnd-uh)*	fiduciary, trustee
treuhänderisches Darlehen (n)	*(trOY-hEHnd-uh-rish-ehs dAAr-lAY-en)*	fiduciary loan
Treuhandfonds (m)	*(trOY-hahnd-fOH)*	trust fund
Treuhandgesellschaft (f)	*(trOY-hahnd-geh-zEL-shahft)*	trust company
Treuhandkonto (n)	*(trOY-hahnd-kON-toh)*	escrow account
Treuhandverhältnis (n)	*(trOY-hahnd-fuh-hEHLt-nis)*	trust
Treuhandverhältnis unter Lebenden (n)	*(trOY-hAHnd-fuh-hEHLt-nis un-tuh lAY-ben-den)*	living trust
Treuhandvertrag (m)	*(trOY-hahnd-fuh-trAHk)*	deed of trust, escrow
trinken	*(trINK-en)*	drink (v)
trockener Wein (m)	*(tRO-keh-nuh vEYEN)*	dry wine
Trockenladung (f)	*(trOK-en-lAA-dunk)*	dry cargo
Tropfen (m)	*(trOP-fen)*	drop

T

U

über den Rand gedruckt	*(EWbuh den rAHNt geh-drUKt)*	bleed
über der Linie	*(EW-buh duh lEE-nee-eh)*	above-the-line
über Nacht	*(EW-buh nAHkht)*	overnight
über pari	*(EW-buh pah-rEE)*	above par
Überalterung (f)	*(EW-buh-ahl-tAY-runk)*	obsolescence
Uberangebot (n)	*(EW-buh-AHN-geh-boht)*	glut, oversupply
Überbetrag (m)	*(EW-buh-beh-trAHk)*	overage
überbewerten	*(EW-buh-beh-vEHR-ten)*	overvalue (v)
überbieten	*(EW-buh-bEE-ten)*	outbid (v)
Übereinkommen (n)	*(EW-buh-EYEn-kOM-mehn)*	understanding (agreement)
Übereinstimmung (f)	*(EW-buh-EYEn-shtIM-munk)*	agreement
überfällig	*(EW-buh-fEH-lig)*	overdue, past due
Überfluß (m)	*(EW-buh-flUs)*	overstock
überfordern	*(EW-buh-fOHr-duhn)*	overcharge (v)
übergreifen	*(EW-buh-grEYE-fen)*	overlap
übergroße Artikel (pl)	*(EW-buh-grOH-seh ahr-tIK-el)*	outsized articles
überhängen	*(EW-buh-hehn-gen)*	overhang
überkapitalisiert	*(EW-buh-kah-pi-tAA-li-zEErt)*	overcapitalized
überlappen	*(EW-buh-lAHP-pen)*	overlap
Überliegezeit (f)	*(EW-buh-lEE-geh-tsEYEt)*	demurrage (period of)
Ubermittler (m)	*(EWbuh-mIT-luh)*	transmitter
Übernahme (f)	*(EW-buh-nAA-meh)*	buyout, takeover
Übernahmeange-bot (n)	*(EW-buh-nAA-meh-AHN-geh-boht)*	takeover bid
Übernehmer (m)	*(EW-buh-nAY-muh)*	assignee
übernommene Verpflichtung (f)	*(EW-buh-nom-meh-neh fuh-pflIKH-tunk)*	assumed liability
Überraschungsan-ruf (m)	*(EW-buh-rAHsh-unks-AAn-rOOf)*	cold call

Überschlagsrech- nung (f)	*(EW-buh-shlAHgs-rEHKH- nunk)*	rough estimate
Überschrift (f)	*(EW-buh-shrIFT)*	headline
Übersetzer (m)	*(EW-buh-zEH-tsuh)*	translator
Überstunden (f)	*(EW-buh-shtun-den)*	overtime
Übertrag (m)	*(EW-buh-trAHk)*	transfer
übertragbar	*(EW-buh-trAHk-bAAr)*	negotiable (convertible, transferable)
übertragbare Wertpapiere (pl)	*(EW-buh-trAHk-bAA-reh vEHRt-pah-pEE-reh)*	negotiable securities
übertragen	*(EW-buh-trAA-gen)*	assign (v), carry forward (v), transfer (v)
Übertragungsur- kunde (f)	*(EW-buh-trAA-gunks-OOr- kun-deh)*	deed of transfer
überweisen	*(EW-buh-vEYE-zen)*	transfer
Überzahlung (f)	*(EW-buh-tsAA-lunk)*	overpayment
überzeichnen	*(EW-buh-tsEYEkh-en)*	oversubscribe (v)
Überziehung (f)	*(EW-buh-tsEE-unk)*	overdraft
üblicher Satz (m)	*(EWb-likh-es zAHts)*	going rate (going price)
übliches Verfahren (n)	*(EWb-likh-es fuh-fAA-ren)*	standard practice
Übrige (n)	*(EWb-ri-geh)*	remainder
Uhrenarmband (n)	*(OO-ren-ahrm-bahnt)*	watch strap
Ultrakurzwelle (f)	*(ultrah-KUrts-vEL-leh)*	microwave
Umfang (m)	*(um-fank)*	volume
umgekehrter Markt (m)	*(um-geh-kAYr-tuh mAHrkt)*	inverted market
Umhang (m)	*(UM-hahnk)*	cape
Umlagekosten (pl)	*(um-lAA-geh-kOS-ten)*	joint cost
Umlaufsvermögen (n)	*(um-lOWfs-fuh-mER-gen)*	working capital, liquid assets
Umorganisierung (f)	*(um-ohr-gah-ni-zEE-runk)*	reorganization
Umsatz (m)	*(um-zAHts)*	sales
Umsatzrendite (f)	*(um-zAHts-ren-di-teh)*	return on sales
Umsatzschätzung (f)	*(um-zAHts-shEH-tsunk)*	sales estimate

U

Umsatzselbstko-sten (pl)	*(um-zAHts-zehlbst-kOS-ten)*	cost of goods sold
Umsatzsteuer (f)	*(um-zAHts-shtOY-uh)*	sales tax
Umschaltung (f)	*(UM-shahl-tunk)*	switch
umschichten	*(um-shIKH-ten)*	restructure (v)
Umschlag (m)	*(um-shlAHk)*	turnover
Umschreibstelle für Effekten (f)	*(um-shrEYEb-shtEHL-leh fEWr ehf-fEHK-ten)*	transfer
umstrukturieren	*(um-strook-tOO-rEE-ren)*	restructure (v)
umwandeln in eine Aktiengesell-schaft	*(um-vahn-dEHln in EYE-neh ak-tsEE-en-geh-zEL-shahft)*	go public (v)
Umwandler (m)	*(UM-vAHN-dluh)*	transformer
Umweltforschung (f)	*(UM-velt-four-shoong)*	ecology
Umweltschutz (m)	*(UM-velt-shuts)*	environmental protection
Umwertung (f)	*(um-vEHR-tunk)*	revaluation
Umzugskosten (pl)	*(um-tsOOgs-kOS-ten)*	moving expenses
unabhängiger Arbeitsplatz (m)	*(un-ahb-hEHn-gi-guh AHR-beyets-plahts)*	stand-alone workstation
unbearbeitet	*(UN-beh-ahr-beye-tet)*	crude
unbefristete Order (f)	*(un-beh-frIS-teh-teh OR-duh)*	open order
unbegleitete Waren (pl)	*(un-beh-glEYE-teh-teh vAA-ren)*	unaccompanied goods
unbeschränktes Akzept (n)	*(un-beh-shrEHnk-tehs ahk-tsEPt)*	general acceptance
Unbeständigkeit (f)	*(un-beh-shtEHn-dikh-keyet)*	instability
unbezahlte Rech-nung (f)	*(un-beh-tsAAl-teh rEHKH-nunk)*	delinquent account
undurchführbar	*(un-durkh-fEWr-bAAr)*	unfeasible
uneinbringliche Forderung (f)	*(un-eyen-brING-likh-eh for-deh-runk)*	bad debt
uneinbringliche Forderungen (pl)	*(un-eyen-brING-likh-eh FOHR-duh-run-gen)*	uncollectible accounts
uneingeschränkte Urkunde (f)	*(un-eyen-geh-shrEHnk-teh OOr-kOOn-deh)*	clean document
unentwickelt	*(un-ehnt-vI-kehlt)*	undeveloped

unerwarteter Gewinn (m)	*(un-ayr-vAAr-teh-tuh geh-vIN)*	windfall profit
Unfallschaden (m)	*(un-fAHL-shAA-den)*	accident damage
Unfallversicherung (f)	*(un-fAHL-fuh-ZIKH-eh-runk)*	casualty insurance
unfermentierter Rebensaft (m)	*(UN-fuh-men-tEEr-tuh ray-ben-zahft)*	unfermented grape juice
unfundierte Schuld (f)	*(un-fun-dEEr-teh shUlt)*	floating debt
ungebleichtes Leinen (n)	*(UN-geh-blEYEKH-tehs LEYE-nen)*	unbleached linen
ungefähr schätzen	*(un-geh-fAYr shEH-tsen)*	guesstimate
ungelernte Arbeitskräfte (pl)	*(un-geh-lAYrn-teh AHR-beyets-krehf-teh)*	unskilled labor
ungenutzte Kapazität (f)	*(un-geh-nUts-teh kah-pah-tsee-tAYt)*	idle capacity
ungerade Menge (f)	*(un-geh-rAA-deh mEHn-geh)*	odd lot
ungesicherte Anleihe (f)	*(un-geh-zikh-uh-teh AHN-leye-eh)*	unsecured loan
ungesicherte Haftung (f)	*(un-geh-zikh-ehr-teh-zikh-ehr-teh hAHf-tunk)*	unsecured liability
ungleichartige Stichprobenauswahl (f)	*(un-glEYEkh-ahr-ti-geh shtIKH-proh-ben OWs-vaal)*	mixed sampling
ungültig	*(un-gEWl-tikh)*	void
ungültig machen	*(un-gEWl-tikh mAA-khen)*	invalidate (v)
ungünstig	*(un-gEWns-tig)*	unfavorable
unlauterer Wettbewerb (m)	*(un-lOW-tuh-ruh vEHt-beh-vAYrb)*	unfair competition
unlegierter Stahl (m)	*(UN-leh-gEEr-tuh shtAAL)*	carbon steel
unmittelbar geleistete Arbeitszeit (f)	*(un-mit-tEL-bAAr geh-lEYEs-teh-teh AHR-beyets-tsEYEt)*	direct labor
unmittelbare Aufwendungen (pl)	*(un-mit-tEL-bAA-reh OWf-vEHn-dunk-en)*	direct expenses
unreines Konnossement (n)	*(un-rEYE-nehs kon-nos-seh-mEH)*	foul bill of lading
Unreinheit (f)	*(UN-rEYEn-heyet)*	impurity

U

unseren Erwartungen entsprechend	*(un-zEHren AYr-vAAr-tunk-en ehnt-shprEKH-ent)*	up to our expectations
unsichtbar	*(un-zikht-bAAr)*	invisible
unter dem Strich	*(un-tuh dehm shtrIKH)*	below the line
unter der Norm	*(un-tuh duh nohrm)*	substandard
unter pari	*(un-tuh pah-rEE)*	below par
unterbewerten	*(un-tuh-beh-vEHR-ten)*	undervalue (v)
unterbezahlt	*(un-tuh-beh-tsAAlt)*	underpaid
unterbieten	*(un-tuh-bEE-ten)*	undercut (v)
unterkapitalisiert	*(un-tuh-kah-pi-taa-li-zEErt)*	undercapitalized
Unterlassungsversprechen (n)	*(un-tuh-lAA-sunks-fuh-shprEHKH-en)*	negative pledge
Unterlieferant (m)	*(un-tuh-LEE-feh-rahnt)*	jobber
Unternehmen (n)	*(un-tuh-nAY-men)*	enterprise
Unternehmensberater (m)	*(un-tuh-nAY-menz-buh-rAA-tuh)*	management consultant
Unternehmenswachstum (n)	*(un-tuh-nAY-men-vahkhs-tOOm)*	corporate growth
Unternehmer (m)	*(un-tuh-nAY-muh)*	entrepreneur
Unterpacht (f)	*(un-tuh-pAHKHt)*	sublease
Unterredung (f)	*(un-tuh-rAY-dunk)*	interview
unterrichten	*(un-tuh-rIKH-ten)*	instruct (v) (teach)
unterschätzen	*(un-tuh-shEH-tsen)*	underestimate (v)
Unterschlagung (f)	*(un-tuh-shlAH-gunk)*	embezzlement
Unterschrift (f)	*(un-tuh-shrIft)*	signature
Unterstützungstätigkeiten (pl)	*(un-tuh-shtEWt-tsungs-tAY-tikh-keye-ten)*	support activities
Untersuchung (f)	*(un-tuh-zOO-khunk)*	analysis, inspection
Untertasse (f)	*(UN-tuh-TAHs-seh)*	saucer
Untervermietung (f)	*(un-tuh-fuh-mEE-tunk)*	sublease
Unterversorgung (f)	*(un-tuh-fuh-zOR-gunk)*	short supply
unterwegs	*(un-tuh-vAYgs)*	in transit
unterzeichnet	*(un-tuh-tsEYEkh-net)*	undersigned

U

unvorhergesehene Ausgaben (pl)	*(un-FOHR-hehr-geh-zeh-heh-neh OWs-gAA-ben)*	contingencies
unvorteilhaft	*(un-FOHR-teyel-hAHft)*	unfavorable
unzulänglich	*(un-tsoo-lEHng-likh)*	inadequate
unzureichende Aktiva (pl)	*(un-tsoo-rEYEkh-en-deh ahk-tEE-vah)*	insufficient assets
Urheberrecht (n)	*(OOr-hay-beh-rehkht)*	copyright
Urkunde (f)	*(OOr-kun-deh)*	deed, document, instrument (document)
Urlaub (m)	*(OOr-lOWb)*	leave of absence
ursprüngliche Fälligkeit (f)	*(OOr-shprunk-lIKH-eh fEHl-lig-keyet)*	original maturity
Ursprungsland (n)	*(OOr-shprunks-lAHnt)*	country of origin
Ursprungszeugnis (n)	*(OOr-shprunks-tsOYg-nis)*	certificate of origin
Urteil (n)	*(OOr-teyel)*	adjudication

V

V8-Motor (m)	*(fOW AKHT mOH-tor)*	V8 engine
Vakuumschmelz-ofen (m)	*(vAA-ku-um-shmEHLTS-ohfen)*	vacuum melting furnace
Vakzine (f)	*(vak-tsEEN-neh)*	vaccine
validieren	*(vah-li-dEE-ren)*	validate (v)
Vanadium (n)	*(va-nAA-di-um)*	vanadium
variabler Erlösüberschuß (m)	*(vaa-ree-AHb-luh ayr-lERs-EW-buh-shUs)*	variable margin
Veloursleder (n)	*(veh-lOORs-lAY-duh)*	suede
Ventil (n)	*(ven-tEEL)*	valve
Verabredung (f)	*(fuh-AHb-rAY-dunk)*	appointment (engagement)
Veralten (n)	*(fuh-AHl-ten)*	obsolescence
veralteter Scheck (m)	*(fuh-AHl-teh-tuh shek)*	stale check
veränderliche Jahresrente (f)	*(fuh-EHn-duh-likh-eh yAAr-es-rEHn-teh)*	variable annuity
veränderliche Kosten (pl)	*(fuh-EHn-duh-likh-eh kOS-ten)*	variable costs

veränderliche Parität (f)	*(fuh-EHn-duh-likh-eh pah-ri-tAYt)*	moving parity, sliding parity
Veränderung (f)	*(fuh-EHndeh-runk)*	variance
Veranlagung (f)	*(fuh-AHn-lAA-gunk)*	assessment
verantwortlich	*(fuh-AHnt-vOHrt-likh)*	liable to (responsible)
Verantwortung des Käufers (f)	*(fuh-AHnt-vOHr-tunk dehs kOY-fuhs)*	buyer's responsibility
Verantwortungsverteilung (f)	*(fuh-AHnt-vOHr-tunks-fuh-tEYE-lunk)*	allocation of responsibilities
verarbeiten	*(fuh-ahr-bEYE-ten)*	process
Verband (m)	*(fuh-bahnt)*	dressing
verbessern	*(fuh-bEHs-uhn)*	improve upon (v)
Verbesserung (f)	*(fuh-bEHs-suh-runk)*	improvement
Verbindung (f)	*(fuh-BIN-dunk)*	compound
Verbindung (f)	*(fuh-BIN-dunk)*	liaison
Verbindungen (pl)	*(fuh-BIN-dun-gen)*	compounds
Verbraucher (m)	*(fuh-brOW-khuh)*	consumer
Verbraucherannahme (f)	*(fuh-brOW-khuh-ahn-nAA-meh)*	consumer acceptance
Verbraucherforschung (f)	*(fuh-brOW-khuh-fOHr-shung)*	consumer research
Verbraucherpreisindex (m)	*(fuh-brOW-khuh-prEYEs-IN-dehx)*	consumer price index
Verbraucherzufriedenstellung (f)	*(fuh-brOW-khuh-tsOO-frEE-den-shtEHL-lunk)*	consumer satisfaction
Verbrauchsabgabe (f)	*(fuh-brOWkhs-AHB-gaa-beh)*	excise duty
Verbrauchsgüter (pl)	*(fuh-brOWkhs-gEW-tuh)*	nondurable goods
Verbrauchssteuer (f)	*(fuh-brOWkhs-shtOY-uh)*	excise tax
Verbrennungshilfsstoff (m)	*(fuh-brEHN-nungs-hilfs-shtOF)*	reactant
verbriefte Rechte (pl)	*(fuh-brEEf-teh rehkh-teh)*	vested rights
verbriefte Schuld (f)	*(fuh-brEEf-teh shUlt)*	funded debt
verbuchen	*(fuh-bOO-khen)*	(bookkeeping) post (v)

V

Verdampfung (f)	*(fuh-dAHM-pfunk)*	evaporation
Verderb (m)	*(fuh-dAYrb)*	spoilage
Verdienst (m)	*(fuh-dEEnst)*	profit
Verdienstspanne (f)	*(fuh-dEEnst-shpAHn-neh)*	profit margin
verdrängen	*(fuh-drEHn-gen)*	supersede (v)
veredeln	*(fuh-AY-dehln)*	refine (v)
vereidigen	*(fuh-EYE-di-gen)*	swear
Vereinbarung (f)	*(fuh-EYEn-bAA-runk)*	agreement, settlement
Vereinbarung auf Treu und Glauben (f)	*(fuh-EYEn-bAA-runk OWf troy unt glOW-ben)*	gentleman's agreement
Vereinheitlichung (f)	*(fuh-EYEn-heyet-liKH-unk)*	standardization
Vereinigung (f)	*(fuh-EYE-ni-gunk)*	amalgamation, combination, merger
Verfahren (n)	*(fuh-fAA-ren)*	method
Verfahrensfrage (f)	*(fuh-fAA-renz-frAA-geh)*	point of order
Verfall (m)	*(fuh-fAHl)*	maturity
Verfalltag (m)	*(fuh-fAHl-taak)*	expiry date, maturity date
verfolgen	*(fuh-FOL-gen)*	follow up (v)
verfügbares Bargeld (n)	*(fuh-fEWg-baa-res bAAr-GEHLT)*	ready cash
verfügbares Einkommen (n)	*(fuh-fEWg-bAA-res EYEn-kOM-mehn)*	disposable income
Vergaser (m)	*(fuh-gAA-suh)*	carburetor
Vergleichsjahr (n)	*(fuh-glEYEKHs-yaar)*	base year
vergrößern	*(fuh-grER-sen)*	enlarge (v)
Vergrößerung (f)	*(fuh-gRER-seh-runk)*	blowup
Vergütung (f)	*(fuh-gEW-tunk)*	compensation, gratuity, remuneration
Vergütung für leitende Angestellte (f)	*(fuh-gEW-tunk fEWr lEYE-ten-deh AHN-geh-shtEHL-tuh)*	executive compensation
Verhältnis (n)	*(fuh-hEHLt-nis)*	ratio
verhandeln	*(fuh-hAHn-dehln)*	negotiate (v)
Verhandlung (f)	*(fuh-hAHnd-lunk)*	negotiation

V

verhandlungsfähig	*(fuh-hAHnd-lunks-fAY-hik)*	negotiable (subject to discussion)
Verhandlungspaket (n)	*(fuh-hAHnd-lunks-pah-kAYt)*	package deal
Verhandlungsstärke (f)	*(fuh hAHnd-lunks-shtEHr-keh)*	bargaining power
Verkauf (m)	*(fuh-kOWf)*	marketing
Verkauf durch Versandgeschäft (m)	*(fuh-kOWf durkh fuh-zAHn-geh-shEHft)*	mail-order sales
Verkauf durch Vertreter (m)	*(fuh-kOWf durkh fuh-trAY-tuh)*	door-to-door sales
Verkauf gegen Barzahlung und Selbstabholung (m)	*(fuh-kOWf gAY-gen bAAr-tsAA-lunkg unt zehlbst-AHB-hOH-lunk)*	cash-and-carry
verkaufen	*(fuh-kOW-fen)*	market, sell (v)
verkaufen und anschließend mieten	*(fuh-kOW-fen unt AHN-shlEE-sent mEE-ten)*	sell and lease back
Verkäufer (m)	*(fuh-kOY-fuh)*	vendor
Verkaufsagent (m)	*(fuh-kOWfs-aa-gEHnt)*	distributor
Verkaufsbedingungen (pl)	*(fuh-kOWfs-beh-dING-unk-en)*	terms of sale
Verkaufsförderung (f)	*(fuh-kOWfs-fER-duh-runk)*	sales promotion
Verkaufsgebühr (f)	*(fuh-kOWfs-geh-bEWr)*	load (sales charge)
Verkaufsoption (f)	*(fuh-kOWfs-op-tsEE-ohn)*	put option
Verkaufspersonal (n)	*(fuh-kOWfs-payr-zoh-nAAl)*	sales force
Verkaufsprognose (f)	*(fuh-kOWfs-prog-nOH-zeh)*	sales forecast
Verkaufspunkt (m)	*(fuh-kOWfs-pUnkt)*	point of sale
Verkaufsquote (f)	*(fuh-kOWfs-kvOH-teh)*	sales quota
Verkaufsstelle (f)	*(fuh-kOWfs-shtEHL-leh)*	outlet
Verkaufstermin (m)	*(fuh-kOWfs-tayr-mEEn)*	on-sale date
Verkaufsurkunde (f)	*(fuh-kOWfs-OOr-kun-deh)*	bill of sale

Verkaufsvolumen (n)	*(fuh-kOWfs-vol-OO-men)*	sales volume
Verkehrswesen (n)	*(fuh-kAYrs-vAY-zen)*	transportation
Verladekosten (pl)	*(fuh-lAA-deh-kOS-ten)*	shipping expenses
verlangen	*(fuh-lAHng-en)*	demand (v)
Verlängerungsabschnitt (m)	*(fuh-lEHng-uh-runks-AHB-shnIT)*	allonge
Verleger (m)	*(fuh-LAY-guh)*	publisher
Verleumdung (f)	*(fuh-lOYm-dunk)*	libel
Verlust (m)	*(fuh-lUst)*	loss
Verlustsaldo (m)	*(fuh-lUst-zAAl-doh)*	adverse balance
Verlustvortrag (m)	*(fuh-lUst-FOHR-trAHk)*	carryover
Vermächtnis (n)	*(fuh-mEHkht-nis)*	bequest, legacy
vermehren	*(fuh-mAY-ren)*	increase (v)
Vermehrung (f)	*(fuh-mAY-runk)*	increase
vermieten	*(fuh-mEE-ten)*	rent (v) (rent to)
Vermieter (m)	*(fuh-mEE-tuh)*	lessor
Verminderung (f)	*(fuh-mIN-duh-runk)*	cutback
Vermischtes	*(fuh-mISH-tehs)*	miscellaneous
Vermittler (m)	*(fuh-mIT-luh)*	intermediary, middleman
Vermittlung (f)	*(fuh-mIT-lunk)*	mediation
Vermögen (n)	*(fuh-mER-gen)*	wealth
Vermögensstück (n)	*(fuh-mER-gens-shtEWk)*	asset
Vermögensübertragung gegen Aktien (f)	*(fuh-mER-gens-EW-buh-trAA-gunk gAY-gen ak-tsEE-en)*	spin off
Vermögensumsatz (m)	*(fuh-mER-gens-um-zAHts)*	asset turnover
Vermögensverwalter (m)	*(fuh-mER-gens-fuh-vAHl-tuh)*	trustee
Vermögensverwaltung (f)	*(fuh-mER-gens-fuh-vAHl-tunk)*	portfolio management
Vermögenswert (m)	*(fuh-mER-gens-vEHRt)*	asset value
vermuten	*(fuh-mOO-ten)*	guesstimate (v), project (v)
verpachten	*(fuh-pAHKH-ten)*	farm out (v)

V

Verpackung (f)	*(fuh-PAHK-unk)*	packaging
Verpfändung (f)	*(fuh-pfEHn-dunk)*	hypothecation
Verpflichtung (f)	*(fuh-pflIKH-tunk)*	commitment, obligation
Verringerungskontrolle (f)	*(fuh-rIN-guh-rungs-kon-trOL-leh)*	depletion control
versammeln	*(fuh-zAHm-meln)*	assemble (v) (people)
Versammlung (f)	*(fuh-zAHM-lunk)*	assembly, meeting
Versand (m)	*(fuh-zAHndt)*	dispatch
Versandanweisungen (pl)	*(fuh-zAHndt-AHN-vEYE-zun-gen)*	shipping instructions
Versandbehälter (m)	*(fuh-zAHndt-beh-hEHl-tuh)*	shipping container
Versandhandel (m)	*(fuh-zAHndt-hAHn-dehl)*	mail order
Versandkosten (pl)	*(fuh-zAHndt-kOS-ten)*	shipping charges
Verschiedenes	*(fuh-shEE-dehn-ehs)*	miscellaneous
Verschleiß (m)	*(fuh-shlEYEs)*	wear and tear
verschneiden	*(fuh-shnEYE-den)*	blend (v)
Verschuldung (f)	*(fuh-shUl-dunk)*	indebtedness
Verseifung (f)	*(fuh-zEYE-funk)*	saponification
Versender (m)	*(fuh-zEN-duh)*	shipper, shipping agent
Versicherer (m)	*(fuh-zIkh-eh-ruh)*	insurance underwriter
versicherter Bote (m)	*(fuh-zIkh-ehr-tuh bOH-teh)*	bonded carrier
Versicherung (f)	*(fuh-zIkh-eh-runk)*	insurance
Versicherung auf Zeit (f)	*(fuh-zIkh-eh-runk OWf tsEYEt)*	term insurance
Versicherung für Personen in Schlüsselstellungen (f)	*(fuh-ZIKH-eh-runk fEWr payr-zOH-nen in shlEW-sehl-shtEHL-lunk-en)*	key man insurance
Versicherungsbeitrag (m)	*(fuh-ZIKH-eh-rungs-bEYE-trAHk)*	insurance premium
Versicherungsgesellschaft (f)	*(fuh-ZIKH-eh-rungs-geh-zEL-shahft)*	insurance company
Versicherungskasse (f)	*(fuh-ZIKH-eh-rungs-kAH-seh)*	insurance fund
Versicherungsmakler (m)	*(fuh-ZIKH-eh-rungs-mAHk-luh)*	insurance broker

Versicherungsma-thematiker (m)	*(fuh-ZIKH-eh-rungs-maa-teh-mAA-tee-kuh)*	actuary
Versicherungspo-lice (f)	*(fuh-ZIKH-eh-rungs-poh-lee-sAY)*	insurance policy
Versicherungs-schutz (m)	*(fuh-ZIKH-eh-rungs-shUts)*	coverage (insurance)
Versicherungsstati-stiker (m)	*(fuh-ZIKH-eh-rungs-shtAH-tis-ti-kuh)*	actuary
Versicherungswert (m)	*(fuh-ZIKH-eh-rungs-vEHRt)*	actual cash value
versieGEHLTes Angebot (n)	*(fuh-zEE-gehl-tehs ΛHN-geh-boht)*	sealed bid
versorgen	*(fuh-zOR-gen)*	service (v)
Versorgungsbe-trieb (m)	*(fuh-zOR-gunks-beh-trEEp)*	public utility, utility
Verstaatlichung (f)	*(fuh-shtAAt-likh-unk)*	nationalization
Verstärker (m)	*(fuh-shtEHR-kuh)*	amplifier
Verstauung (f)	*(fuh-shtOW-unk)*	stowage
verteilen	*(fuh-tEYE-len)*	allot (v)
Verteiler (m)	*(fuh-tEYE-luh)*	distributor
Verteilung (f)	*(fuh-tEYE-lunk)*	allotment
Verteilungsbogen (m)	*(fuh-tEYE-lunks-bOH-gen)*	spreadsheet
Verteilungsnetz (n)	*(fuh-tEYE-lungs-nets)*	distribution network
vertikale Verflech-tung (f)	*(fayr-ti-kAA-leh fuh-flEHKH-tunk)*	vertical integration
Vertrag (m)	*(fuh-trAHk)*	agreement (written), contract, covenant (promises), treaty
vertraglicher Frachtführer (m)	*(fuh-trAHk-likh-uh frAHKHt-fEW-ruh)*	contract carrier
vertragsgemäß arbeiten	*(fuh-trAHks-geh-mEHs ahr-bEYE-ten)*	work by contract
Vertragsmonat (m)	*(fuh-trAHKs-mOH-naht)*	contract month
Vertragspartei (f)	*(fuh-trAHks-pahr-tEYE)*	party (contract)
Vertragsurkunde (f)	*(fuh-trAHks-OOr-kun-deh)*	indenture
Vertrauensorder (f)	*(fuh-trOW-ens-OR-duh)*	discretionary order

V

vertraulich	*(fuh-trOW-likh)*	confidential
vertreiben	*(fuh-trEYE-ben)*	market (v)
vertretbar	*(fuh-trAYt-bAAr)*	fungible
Vertreter (m)	*(fuh-trAY-tuh)*	agent, representative
Vertreter des Fiskus (m)	*(fuh-trAY-tuh dehs fis-kUs)*	fiscal agent
Vertretung (f)	*(fuh-trAY-tunk)*	agency
Vertretungsgebühr (f)	*(fuh-trAY-tunks-geh-bEWr)*	agency fee
Vertrieb (m)	*(fuh-trEEB)*	distribution
Vertriebshändler (m)	*(fuh-trEEps-hEHnd-luh)*	distributor
Vertriebskosten (pl)	*(fuh-trEEps-kOS-ten)*	distribution costs
Vertriebsleitung (f)	*(fuh-trEEps-lEYE-tunk)*	sales management
Vertriebspolitik (f)	*(fuh-trEEps-po-li-tEEk)*	distribution policy
verwalten	*(fuh-vAHl-ten)*	manage (v) (administrate)
Verwalter (m)	*(fuh-vAHl-tuh)*	administrator, manager
Verwaltung (f)	*(fuh-vAHl-tunk)*	administration, management
Verwaltungsbehörde (f)	*(fuh-vAHl-tunkz-beh-hER-deh)*	government agency
Verwaltungsgebühr (f)	*(fuh-vAHl-tunkz-geh-bEWr)*	management fee
Verwaltungskosten (pl)	*(fuh-vAHl-tunk-zkOS-ten)*	administrative expenses
verwaltungsmäßig	*(fuh-vAHl-tunkz-mEH-sig)*	administrative
verweigerte Zahlung (f)	*(fuh-vEYE-gehr-teh tsAA-lunk)*	payment refused
Verwicklung (f)	*(fuh-vIK-lunk)*	implication (involvement)
verzeichnen	*(fuh-tsEYEkh-nen)*	index (v)
Verzeichnung (f)	*(fuh-tsEYEkh-nunk)*	listing
Verzichtsklausel (f)	*(fuh-tsIKHts-klOW-sehl)*	waiver clause
Verzichturkunde (f)	*(fuh-tsIKHts-OOr-kun-deh)*	quit claim deed
Verzinsung (f)	*(fuh-tsINs-zunk)*	interest (return on capital)
Verzinsungszeitraum (m)	*(fuh-tsINs-zunks-tsEYEt-rOWm)*	interest period

V

Verzögerung (f)	*(fuh-tsER-geh-runk)*	delay
Veto (n)	*(vAY-toh)*	veto
Videokasettengerät (n)	*(vEE-deh-o-kahs-SEHt-ten-geh-rEHt)*	videocassette player
vierfarbig	*(fEER-fAHR-bik)*	four-color
Vierzylindermotor (m)	*(fEER-tsew-lin-duh-mOH-tor)*	four-cylinder engine
Visitenkartentäschchen (n)	*(vi-zEE-ten-kahr-ten-tEHSH-khen)*	card case
Vitamin (n)	*(vi-tah-mEEn)*	vitamin
Vizepräsident (m)	*(vEE-tseh-pray-zi-dEHnt)*	vice-president
Volkswirtschaftslehre (f)	*(folks-vEErt-shahfts-lAY-reh)*	economics
voll bezahlt	*(fol beh-tsAAlt)*	paid in full
voll eingezahltes Kapital (n)	*(fol EYEn-geh-tsAAl-tes kah-pi-tAAL)*	paid up capital
volle Zahlung (f)	*(FOL-leh tsAA-lunk)*	payment in full
völlig gedeckte Anleihe (f)	*(fER-likh geh-dEHK-teh AHN-leye-eh)*	back-to-back loan
völliger Stillstand (m)	*(fER-likh-uh shtIL-shtAHnt)*	deadlock
Vollmacht (f)	*(FOL-mahkht)*	power of attorney
Vollmacht haben (f)	*(FOL-mahkht hAA-ben)*	authority, to have (v)
Vollmachtsformular (n)	*(FOL-mahkhts-for-mu-lAAr)*	proxy statement
Vollmachtsüberschreitung (f)	*(FOL-mahkhts-EW-buh-shrEYE-tunk)*	ultra vires act
vollständig bezahlen	*(FOL-shtEHn-dikh beh-tsAA-len)*	pay up (v)
vollständiger Ausgleich (m)	*(FOL-shtEHn-dikh-uh OWS-gleyekh)*	settlement in full
Vollversammlung (f)	*(FOL-fuh-zAM-lunk)*	plenary meeting
Volontär (m)	*(fol-on-tAYr)*	trainee
Volumen (n)	*(fol-U-mehn)*	volume
von der Stange	*(fon duh shtAHN-geh)*	ready-to-wear
Vorankündigung (f)	*(FOHR-ahn-kEWn-di-gunk)*	advance notice

V

Voranschlag (m)	*(FOHR-ahn-shlAHk)*	rough estimate
Vorarbeiter (m)	*(FOHR-ahr-bEYE-tuh)*	foreman
vorausbezahlte Fracht (f)	*(FOHR-OWs-beh-tsAAl-teh fRAHKHT)*	advance freight, freight pre-paid
Vorausbezahlung (f)	*(FOHR-OWs-beh-tsAA-lunk)*	cash in advance
vorausgezahlte Aufwendungen (pl)	*(FOHR-OWs-geh-tsAAl-teh OWf-vEHn-dunk-en)*	prepaid expenses (balance sheet)
voraussagen	*(FOHR-OWs-zAA-gen)*	forecast (v)
voraussichtliche Abfahrt (f)	*(FOHR-OWs-zIKHt-liKH-eh AHb-fAArt)*	estimated time of departure
voraussichtliche Ankunft (f)	*(FOHR-OWs-zIKHt-lIKH-eh AHn-kunft)*	estimated time of arrival
vorauszahlen	*(FOHR-OWs-tsAA-len)*	prepay (v)
Vorauszahlung (f)	*(FOHR-OWs-tsAA-lung)*	advance payment
vorbehaltich der Verfügbarkeit	*(FOHR-beh-hahlt-likh duh fuh-fEWg-bAAr-keyet)*	subject to availability
vorbehaltlos	*(FOHR-beh-hahlt-lohs)*	down the line
vorbeugende Instandhaltung (f)	*(FOHR-bOY-gen-deh in-stAHnt-hAHl-tunk)*	preventive maintenance
Vorbilanz (f)	*(FOHR-bee-lAHnts)*	trial balance
Vorbild (n)	*(FOHR-bilt)*	model
Vorentwurf (m)	*(FOHR-ehnt-vOOrf)*	rough draft
Vorfahrt (f)	*(FOHR-fAArt)*	right of way
Vorfertigung (f)	*(FOHR-ʃayr-tI-gunk)*	modular production, prefab-rication
vorgeben	*(FOHR-gAY-ben)*	simulate (v)
Vorhaben (n)	*(FOHR-hAA-ben)*	project
Vorindikator (m)	*(FOHR-in-di-kAA-tohr)*	leading indicator
Vorkaufsrecht (n)	*(FOHR-kOWfs-REHKHT)*	preemptive right
vorläufig	*(FOHR-lOY-fikh)*	temporary
Vorlaufzeit (f)	*(FOHR-lOWf-tsEYEt)*	lead time
Vorprospekt (m)	*(FOHR-pros-pEHkt)*	preliminary prospectus
Vorrang (m)	*(FOHR-rahng)*	priority
Vorrat (m)	*(FOHR-rAAt)*	inventory, stock

V

Vorratsaktien (pl)	*(FOHR-rAAts-ak-tsEE-en)*	treasury stock
Vorratskauf (m)	*(FOHR-rAAts-kOWf)*	stock purchase
vorsätzliche Ladungsbes-chädigung (f)	*(FOHR-zehts-lIKH-eh lAA-dunks-beh-shEH-di-gunk)*	barratry
Vorschau (f)	*(FOHR-shOW)*	forecast
vorschießen	*(FOHR-shEE-sehn)*	advance (v) (money)
Vorschrift (f)	*(FOHR-shrift)*	regulation
Vorschriften (pl)	*(FOHR-shrif-ten)*	by-laws
Vorschriften über die Anstellung von Frauen und Minoritäten (pl)	*(FOHR-shrif-ten EW-buh dee AHn-shtEHL-lung fon frOW-en unt mEE-noh-ree-tAY-ten)*	affirmative action
Vorstand (m)	*(FOHR-shtAHnt)*	board of directors, executive board
Vorstandsmitglied (n)	*(FOHR-shtAHnts-mIT-glEEd)*	director
Vorstandssitzung (f)	*(FOHR-shtAHnts-zI-tsunk)*	board meeting
Vorstandsvorsit-zender (m)	*(FOHR-shtAHnts-fohr-zI-tsen-duh)*	chief executive, chairman of the board
vortragen	*(FOHR-trAA-gen)*	carry forward (v)
vorübergehend	*(FOHR-EW-buh-gAY-hehnt)*	temporary
Vorvertrag (m)	*(FOHR-fuh-trAHk)*	binder
Vorwort (n)	*(FOHR-vort)*	preface
vorzeitig kündba-rer Kredit (m)	*(FOHR-tsEYE-tik kEWnd-bAA-ruh kray-dIT)*	call loan
Vorzugsaktie (f)	*(FOHR-tsoogs-ak-tsEE-eh)*	preferred stock
Vorzugsaktien erster Ausgabe (pl)	*(FOHR-tsoogs-ak-tsEE-en AYr-stuh OWs-gAA-beh)*	first preferred stock
Vorzugsrecht (n)	*(FOHR-tsoogs-REHKHT)*	priority
Vorzugszoll (m)	*(FOHR-tsoogs-tsOL)*	preferential tariff

W

Wachstuch (n)	*(VAHKs-TOOkh)*	oilcloth
Wachstum (n)	*(vAHkhs-toom)*	growth

Wachstumsaktie (f)	*(vAHkhs-tooms-ak-tsEE-eh)*	growth stock
Wachstumsgebiet (n)	*(vAHkhs-tooms-geh-bEET)*	growth area
Wachstumsindex (m)	*(vAHkhs-tooms-IN-dehx)*	growth index
Wachstumsindustrie (f)	*(vAHkhs-tooms-in-dus-trEE)*	growth industry
Wachstumspotential (n)	*(vAHkhs-tooms-poh-ten-tsI-AAL)*	growth potential
Wachstumsrate (f)	*(vAHkhs-tooms-rAH-teh)*	rate of growth
Wagen (m)	*(vAA-gen)*	car
Wagenladung (f)	*(vAA-gen-lAA-dunk)*	carload
Wagenpark (m)	*(vAA-gen-pAArk)*	rolling stock
Wagniskapital (n)	*(vAAg-nis-kah-pi-tAAL)*	venture capital
wahlfreier Speicherzugriff (m)	*(vAAl-frEYE-uh shpEYEkh-uh-tsOO-grif)*	random access memory
Währung (f)	*(VAY-runk)*	currency
Währungseinheit (f)	*(VAY-runks-eyen-heyet)*	monetary standard
Währungsgruppe (f)	*(VAY-runks-grUP-peh)*	currency band
Währungsklausel (f)	*(VAY-runks-klOW-sehl)*	currency clause
Währungskredite (pl)	*(VAY-runks-kreh-dI-teh)*	monetary credits
Währungsrisiko (n)	*(VAY-runks-ree-zEE-koh)*	exchange risk
Walzwerkbetrieb (m)	*(vALTS-vehrk-beh-trEEb)*	rolling mill
Wandelobligationen (pl)	*(vAAn-dehl ob-li-gah-tsEE-ohn-ehn)*	convertible debentures
Waren (pl)	*(vAA-ren)*	goods, merchandise
Waren ohne Gewähr (pl)	*(vAA-ren ohneh geh-vAYr)*	as is goods
Waren unter Zollverschluß (pl)	*(vAA-ren un-tuh tsOL-fuh-shlUS)*	bonded goods
Warenanalyse (f)	*(vAA-ren-ah-nah-lEW-zeh)*	product analysis
Warenbestand (m)	*(vAA-ren-beh-shtAHnt)*	stock-in-trade

W

Warenbörse (f)	*(vAA-ren-bEWr-seh)*	commodity exchange
Warenhaus (n)	*(vAA-ren-hOWs)*	department store
Warenüberschuß (m)	*(vAA-ren-EW-buh-shUs)*	surplus goods
Warenumsatz (m)	*(vAA-ren-um-zAHts)*	sales turnover
Warenwechsel (m)	*(vAA-ren-vEHK-sehl)*	trade acceptance
Warmwalzen (n)	*(vahrm-vAL-tsen)*	hot rolling
Wartekosten (pl)	*(vAAr-teh-kOS-ten)*	opportunity cost
Wartezeit (f)	*(vAAr-teh-tsEYEt)*	attended time
Wartung (f)	*(vAAr-tunk)*	maintenance
Wartungsvertrag (m)	*(vAAr-tunks-fuh-trAHk)*	maintenance contract
Waschbär(pelz) (m)	*(vahsh-bAYR [pELTS])*	raccoon
Wasserpumpe (f)	*(VAHS-suh-pUM-peh)*	water pump
Weber (m)	*(vEH-buh)*	weaver
Wechsel (m)	*(vEHk-sel)*	acceptance bill, bank draft, bill of exchange
Wechselbank (f)	*(vEHk-sel-bahnk)*	acceptance house
Wechseldiskont (m)	*(vEHk-sel-dis-kONT)*	exchange discount
Wechselkredit (m)	*(vEHk-sel-kray-dIT)*	acceptance credit
Wechselkurs (m)	*(vEHk-sel-koors)*	exchange rate
Wechselmakler (m)	*(vEHk-sel-mAHk-luh)*	bill broker
wechselnde Kosten (pl)	*(vEHk-seln-deh kOS-ten)*	controllable costs
Wechselprotest (m)	*(vEHk-sel-proh-tEHst)*	protest (banking, law)
Wechselreiterei (f)	*(vEHk-sel-reye-tuh-rEYE)*	kiting
Wechselstrom (m)	*(vEHk-sel-shtrOHm)*	alternating current
Wechselstromgenerator (m)	*(vEHk-sel-shtrOHm-geh-neh-rAH-tor)*	alternator
Wechselstube (f)	*(vEHk-sel-shtOO-beh)*	money shop
weiche Verkaufstour (f)	*(vEYE-kheh fuh-kOWfs-tOOr)*	soft sell
weiche Währung (f)	*(vEYE-kheh vAY-runk)*	soft currency

W

Wein (m)	*(vEYEN)*	wine
Weinart (f)	*(vEYEN-ahrt)*	type of wine
Weinbauer (m)	*(vEYEN-bow-uh)*	winegrower
Weinbeere (f)	*(vEYEN-bay-reh)*	grape
Weinberg (m)	*(vEYEN-behrk)*	vineyard
Weinernte (f)	*(vEYEN-EHRn-teh)*	vintage
Weinertrag (m)	*(vEYEN-ehr-trahk)*	yield
Weinhersteller (m)	*(vEYEN-huh-shTEL-luh)*	winemaker
Weinkeller (m)	*(vEYEN-kel-luh)*	wine cellar
Weinkellner (m)	*(vEYEN-kel-nuh)*	wine steward
Weinlese (f)	*(vEYEN-lay-zeh)*	grape harvest
Weinpresse (f)	*(vEYEN-prehs-zeh)*	winepress
Weinprobe (f)	*(vEYEN-pro-beh)*	tasting
Weinrebe (f)	*(vEYEN-ray-beh)*	grape, vine
Weinschlauch (m)	*(vEYEN-shlowkh)*	skin
Weintraube (f)	*(vEYEN-trOW-beh)*	grape bunch
Weise (f)	*(veye-seh)*	mode
Weiterverkauf (m)	*(VEYE-tuh-fuh-kOWf)*	resale
Weiterverkaufsge- winnler (m)	*(VEYE-tuh-fuh-kOWfs-geh- vIN-luh)*	scalper
Welle (f)	*(vEL-leh)*	wave
Weltbank (f)	*(VEHLT-bahnk)*	World Bank
Weltwährungs- fonds (m)	*(VEHLT-vAY-runks-fOH)*	International Monetary Fund
Werbeagentur (f)	*(vAYr-beh-ah-gen-tOOR)*	advertising agency
Werbebudget (n)	*(vAYr-beh-bew-djEH)*	advertising budget
Werbeforschung (f)	*(vAYr-beh-fOHr-shunk)*	advertising research
Werbekampagne (f)	*(vAYr-beh-kahm-pAHn-yeh)*	advertising campaign
Werbekosten (pl)	*(vAYr-beh-kOS-ten)*	advertising expenses
Werbeleiter (m)	*(vAYr-beh-lEYE-tuh)*	advertising manager
Werbesendung (f)	*(vAYr-beh-zEN-dunk)*	commercial (broadcasting)
Werbetext (m)	*(vAYr-beh-tEHxt)*	copy (advertising text)
Werbetextprüfung (f)	*(vAYr-beh-tEHxt-prEW- funk)*	copy testing

W

Werbeträger (pl)	*(vAYr-beh-trAY-guh)*	advertising media
Werbung (f)	*(vAYr-bunk)*	advertisement
Werkleiter (m)	*(vEHrk-lEYE-tuh)*	plant manager
Werkmeister (m)	*(vEHrk-mEYE-stuh)*	foreman
Werkstatt (f)	*(vEHrk-shtaht)*	workshop
Werkstoffe (pl)	*(vEHrk-shtOf-feh)*	materials
Werksvertreter (m)	*(vEHrks-fuh-trAY-tuh)*	manufacturer's agent
Werkzeuge (pl)	*(vEHrk-tsOY-geh)*	tools
Wert (m)	*(vEHRt)*	value
Wertanalyse (f)	*(vEHRt-ah-nah-lEW-zeh)*	value engineering
Wertberichtigung auf das Anlagevermögen (f)	*(vEHRt-beh-rIKH-ti-gunk OWf dahs AHN-laa-geh-fuh-mER-gen)*	accumulated depreciation
wertlos	*(vEHRt-lOHs)*	worthless
Wertpapier nachgeordneter Sicherheit (n)	*(vEHRt-pah-pEEr -geh-ORd-neh-tuh zikh-uh-heyet)*	junior security
Wertpapierberater (m)	*(vEHRt-pah-pEEr-buh-rAA-tuh)*	account executive
Wertpapiere	*(vEHRt-pah-pEE-reh)*	securities
Wertpapieremissionsanzeige (f)	*(vEHRt-pah-pEEr-eh-mi-see-OHn-AHN-tseye-geh)*	tombstone advertisement
Wertpapierhandel (m)	*(vEHRt-pah-pEEr-hAIIn-dehl)*	secondary market (securities)
Wertplanungstechnik (f)	*(vEHRt-plAA-nungs-tehkh-nik)*	value engineer
Wertsteigerung (f)	*(vEHRt-shtEYE-guh-runk)*	appreciation
Wertzoll (m)	*(vEHRt-tsOL)*	ad valorem duty
Wertzuwachs (m)	*(vEHRt-tsOO-vahkhs)*	appreciation
Weste (f)	*(vEH-steh)*	vest
Wettbewerbsstrategie (f)	*(vEHT-beh-vAYrbs-strAH-teh-gee)*	competitive strategy
Wettbewerbsvorteil (m)	*(vEHT-beh-vAYrbs-FOHR-teyel)*	competitive advantage
widerrufliches Treuhandverhältnis (n)	*(vi-duh-rOOf-likh-ehs trOY-hAHnd-fuh-hEHLt-nis)*	revocable trust

W

Widerstand (m)	*(VI-duh-shtahnt)*	resistance
wieder ausführen	*(vEE-duh OWs-fEW-ren)*	reexport (v)
wieder verwerten	*(vee-duhfuh-VEHR-ten)*	reutilize, recycle
wiederaufnehmen	*(vEE-duh-OWf-nAY-mehn)*	resume (v)
Wiederbeschaf-fungskosten (pl)	*(vEE-duh-beh-shAF-fungs-kOS-ten)*	replacement cost
Wiedererlangung (f)	*(vEE-duh-uh-lAHn-gunk)*	recovery
Wiederherstellung (f)	*(vEE-duh-hAYr-shtEHL-lunk)*	reproduction
Wiederholungsauf-trag (m)	*(vEE-duh-hOH-lunks-OWf-trAHk)*	repeat order
Wiederinbesitz-nahme (f)	*(vEE-duh-in-beh-zITS-nAA-meh)*	repossession
Wiederverkauf (m)	*(vEE-duh-fuh-kOWf)*	resale
wilder Streik (m)	*(vIL-duh shtreyek)*	wildcat strike
Wildleder (n)	*(vILd-lAY-duh)*	suede
Wildlederjacke (f)	*(vILd-lAY-duh-yAH-Keh)*	suede jacket
Wille (m)	*(VIL-leh)*	will
Windschutzscheibe (f)	*(vINd-shuts-shEYE-beh)*	windshield
Wink (m)	*(veenk)*	tip (inside information)
Winzer (m)	*(vIN-tsuh)*	vintner
Winzergenossen-schaft (f)	*(vIN-tsuh-geh-nos-sen-shahft)*	wine cooperative
wirken auf	*(vEEr-ken OWf)*	impact on (v)
wirkungslos	*(vEEr-kunks-lohs)*	inefficient
wirtschaftlich	*(vEErt-shahft-likh)*	economic
wirtschaftliche Lebensdauer (f)	*(vEErt-shahft-likh-eh lAY-behnz-dOW-uh)*	economic life
wirtschaftliche Unabhängigkeit (f)	*(vEErt-shahft-likh-eh un-ahb-hEHng-ig-keyet)*	autarchy
Wirtschaftslehre (f)	*(vEErt-shahfts-lAY-reh)*	economics
Wirtschaftsprüfer (m)	*(vEErt-shahfts-prEW-fuh)*	accountant (CPA), certified public accountant, chartered accountant

W

Wirtschaftsteil (m)	*(vEErt-shahfts-teyel)*	financial pages (newspaper)
Wissen (n)	*(vIS-sehn)*	know-how
wohlerworbene Rechte (pl)	*(vOHl-uh-vOHr-bEH-neh REHKH-teh)*	vested interests
Wohn- und Indu- striebaubestim- mungen (pl)	*(vohn unt in-dus-trEE bOW- beh-shtIM-mun-gen)*	zoning laws
Wohnungsamt (n)	*(vOH-nunks-AHmt)*	housing authority (residen- tial)
Wolfram (n)	*(volf-rAAM)*	tungsten
Wolle (f)	*(vOL-leh)*	wool
Wucher (m)	*(vOO-khuh)*	usury

Z

Zähigkeit (f)	*(TSAY-hig-kEYET)*	toughness
zahlbar bei Sicht	*(tsAAl-bAAr beye zIKHt)*	payable on demand
zahlen	*(tsAA-len)*	pay (v)
zahlenmäßige Steuerung (f)	*(tsAA-len-mAY-si-geh shtOY-uh-runk)*	numerical control
Zahler (m)	*(tsAA-luh)*	payer
Zahlung (f)	*(tsAA-lunk)*	payment
Zahlung bei Liefe- rung (f)	*(tsAA-lunk beye LEE-feh- runk)*	cash on delivery
Zahlung verwei- gern (f)	*(tsAA-lunk fuh-vEYE-gehrn)*	refuse payment (v)
Zahlungen einstel- len (pl)	*(tsAA-lun-gen EYEn- shtEHL-len)*	suspend payment (v)
Zahlungsanwei- sung (f)	*(tsAA-lungs-AHn-veye-zunk)*	money order
Zahlungsaufschub (m)	*(tsAA-lungs-OWf-shUb)*	moratorium
Zahlungsbestäti- gung (f)	*(tsAA-lungs-beh-stAY-ti- gunk)*	acknowledgement of pay- ment
Zahlungsbilanz (f)	*(tsAA-lungs-bee-lAHnts)*	balance of payments
Zahlungsempfän- ger (m)	*(tsAA-lungs-em-pfEHn-guh)*	payee

Z

Zahlungsfähigkeit (f)	*(tsAA-lungs-fAY-hig-keyet)*	ability-to-pay concept, solvency
Zahlungshaushalt (m)	*(tsAA-lungs-hOWs-hahlt)*	cash budget
Zahlungsmeister (m)	*(tsAA-lungs-mEYE-stuh)*	paymaster
zahlungsunfähig	*(tsAA-lungs-un-fAY-hikh)*	insolvent
zahlungsunfähig werden	*(tsAA-lungs-un-fAY-ikh VEHRD-en)*	default (v)
Zeichnungsangebot (n)	*(tsEYEkh-nunks-AHN-geh-boht)*	prospectus
Zeichnungspreis (m)	*(tsEYEkh-nunks-prEYEs)*	subscription price (securities)
Zeit- und Bewegungsstudie (f)	*(tsEYEt unt beh-vAY-gunks-shtoo-di-eh)*	time and motion study
Zeitplan (m)	*(tsEYEt-plAAn)*	schedule, timetable
Zeitraum (m)	*(tsEYEt-rOWm)*	period (time)
Zeitungspapier (n)	*(tsEYE-tungs-pah-pEER)*	newsprint
Zeitwechsel (m)	*(tsEYEt-vEHkh-sel)*	time bill of exchange
zeitweilig	*(tsEYEt-vEYE-lik)*	temporary
zeitweilig nicht einlösbare Aktiva (pl)	*(tsEYEt-vEYE-lik nIKHt EYEn-lERs-bAA-reh ahk-tEE-vah)*	deferred assets
Zeitzone (f)	*(tsEYEt-tsOH-neh)*	time zone
Zentiliter (m)	*(tsen-ti-LEE-tuh)*	centiliter
Zentralbank (f)	*(tsehn-trAAl-bahnk)*	central bank, government bank
Zentrale (f)	*(tsehn-trAA-leh)*	head office, headquarters
Zentralisierung (f)	*(tsehn-trAA-li-zEE-runk)*	centralization
Zentralrecheneinheit (f)	*(tsehn-trAAl-rEHkh-en-eyen-heyet)*	central processing unit
Zentralwert (m)	*(tsehn-trAAl-vEHRt)*	median
Zeuge (m)	*(tsOY-geh)*	witness
Zeugnis (n)	*(tsOYg-nis)*	certificate
Ziegenleder (n)	*(tsEE-gen-lAY-duh)*	kidskin
Zigarettenetui (n)	*(tsEE-gah-ret-ten-e-tuEE)*	cigarette case
Zink (n)	*(tsINK)*	zinc
Zins (m)	*(tsINs)*	interest

Z

Zinsabschnitt (m)	*(tsINs-AHB-shnIT)*	coupon (bond interest)
Zinsarbitrage (f)	*(tsINs-ahr-bi-trAAsh)*	interest arbitrage
Zinsaufwendungen (pl)	*(tsINs-OWf-vEHn-dunk-en)*	interest expenses
zinsbegünstigtes Darlehen (n)	*(tsINs-beh-gEWns-tig-tehs dAAr-lAY-en)*	soft loan
Zinsertrag (m)	*(tsINs-uh-trAHk)*	interest income
Zinseszins (m)	*(tsIN-zehs-tsins)*	compound interest
Zinsfuß (m)	*(tsINs-foos)*	rate of interest
Zinskoupon (m)	*(tsINs-koo-pon)*	coupon (bond interest)
Zinssatz (m)	*(tsINs-zAHts)*	interest rate, rate of return
Zivilklage (f)	*(tsee-vEEl-klAA-geh)*	civil action
Zivilunrecht (n)	*(tsee-vEEl-un-REHKHT)*	tort
Zobel (pelz) (m)	*(tsOH-bel [pELTS])*	sable
Zoll (m)	*(tsOL)*	customs, customs duty, tariff
Zoll (m)	*(tsOL)*	inch
Zollagent (m)	*(tsOL-ah-gEHnt)*	customs broker
Zollagerhaus (n)	*(tsOL-LAA-guh-hOWs)*	bonded warehouse
Zollangleichung (f)	*(tsOL-AHn-glEYE-khunk)*	tariff adjustment
Zolleinnehmer (m)	*(tsOL-EYEn-nAY-muh)*	customs collector
Zolleinstufung (f)	*(tsOL-EYEn-shtOO-funk)*	tariff classification
Zollerklärung (f)	*(tsOL-ayr-klAY-runk)*	customs entry
Zollerlaß (m)	*(tsOL-AYr-lahs)*	remission of a customs duty
zollfrei	*(tsOL-frEYE)*	dutyfree
Zollgebühr (f)	*(tsOL-geh-bEWr)*	customs duty, tariff charge
Zollkrieg (m)	*(tsOL-krEEg)*	tariff war
Zollpapier für vor-übergehende zollfreie Einfuhr (n)	*(tsOL-pah-pEEr fEWr FOHR-EW-buh-gAY-hehn-deh tsOL-frEYE-eh EYEn-fOOr)*	carnet
zollpflichtige Waren (pl)	*(tsOL-pflIKH-ti-geh vAA-ren)*	bonded goods
Zollschranken (pl)	*(tsOL-shrAHnk-en)*	tariff barriers
Zollspeicher (m)	*(tsOL-shpEYE-khuh)*	bonded warehouse
Zollunterschied (m)	*(tsOL-un-tuh-shEEd)*	tariff differential

Z

Zollverein (m)	*(tsOL-fuh-EYEn)*	customs union
Zollware (f)	*(tsOL-vAA-reh)*	tariff commodity
Zollwert (m)	*(tsOL-vEHRt)*	value for duty
Zone (f)	*(tsOH-neh)*	zone
zu den Akten legen	*(tsoo dehn AHk-ten lAY-gen)*	file (v) (papers)
zu pari	*(tsoo pah-rEE)*	at par
zu stark gekauft	*(tsoo shtAHrk geh-kOWft)*	overbought
zu stark verkauft	*(tsoo shtAHrk fuh-kOWft)*	oversold
Zuckerdose (f)	*(TSU-ker-do-zeh)*	sugar bowl
Zuckergehalt (m)	*(TSU-ker-geh-hahlt)*	sugar content
Zuerstentnahme der älteren Vorräte (f)	*(tsoo-AYrs-ehnt-nAA-meh duh EHl-tuh-rehn FOHR-rEH-teh)*	first in-first out (FIFO)
Zuerstentnahme der neuen Vorräte (f)	*(tsoo-AYrs-ehnt-nAA-meh duh nOY-en FOHR-rEH-teh)*	last in-first out (LIFO)
Zuführungsverhältnis (n)	*(tsoo-fEW-runks-fuh-hEHLt-nis)*	feed ratio
Zugabenangebot (n)	*(tsoo-gAA-ben-AHN-geh-boht)*	premium offer
Zugartikel (m)	*(tsOOg-ahr-tIK-el)*	loss leader
zugeschrieben	*(tsoo-geh-shrEE-behn)*	imputed
Zulassungsschein (m)	*(tsoo-lahs-soonks-shEYEn)*	permit
Zulieferant (m)	*(tsoo-lee-fayr-rAHnt)*	subcontractor
zum Bestkauf	*(tsum bEHst-kOWf)*	at or better
zum Marktpreis	*(tsum mAHrkt-prEYEs)*	at the market price
zum Nennwert	*(tsum nEHn-vEHRt)*	at par
zum Verkauf anbieten	*(tsum fuh-kOWf AHn-bee-tehn)*	offer for sale
Zündkerze (f)	*(tsEWnd-kuh-tseh)*	spark plug
Zündung (f)	*(tsEWnd-dunk)*	ignition
zur Ausfuhr	*(tsOOr OWs-foor)*	for export
zur Emissionszeit	*(tsOOr eh-mi-see-OHn-tsEYEt)*	when issued
zur Verfügung stellen	*(tsOOr fuh-fEW-gunk shtEHL-lehn)*	make available (v)

Zurichtung (f)	*(tsOO-rIKH-tunk)*	make-ready
zurückbehaltene Gewinne (pl)	*(tsOO-rEWk-beh-hAHl-teh-neh geh-vIN-neh)*	retained profits
Zurückbehaltungs-recht des Hand-werkers (n)	*(tsOO-rEWk-beh-hAHl-tungs-REHKHT dehs hAHnd-vEHr-kuhs)*	mechanic's lien
zurückbringen	*(tsOO-rEWk-brING-en)*	carry back (v)
zurückdatieren	*(tsOO-rEWk-dah-tEE-ren)*	back date (v)
zurückgestellte Steuerzahlung (f)	*(tsoo-rEWk-geh-shtEHL-teh shtOY-uh-tsAA-lunk)*	deferred tax
zurückkaufen	*(tsOO-rEWk-kOW-fen)*	buy back (v)
Zurücknahme (f)	*(tsOO-rEWk-nAA-meh)*	withdrawal
zurückrufen	*(tsOO-rEWk-ROO-fen)*	call back (v)
Zurückstufung (f)	*(tsOO-rEWk-shtOO-funk)*	demotion
zurücktragen	*(tsOO-rEWk-trAA-gen)*	carry back (v)
zurückzahlen	*(tsOO-rEWk-tsAA-len)*	reimburse (v), repay (v)
Zurückzahlungs-zeitraum (m)	*(tsOO-rEWk-tsAA-lungs-tsEYEt-rOWm)*	payback period
zusammenlegen	*(tsOO-zAHM-men-lAY-gen)*	pool (v)
Zusammensetzung (f)	*(tsu-zaHM-mehn-zet-tsunk)*	composition
zusammenstellen	*(tsOO-zAH-men-shtEHL-len)*	assemble (v) (things)
Zusatz (m)	*(tsOO-zAHts)*	addendum
Zusatzdividende (f)	*(tsOO-zAHts-di-vi-dEHN-deh)*	extra dividend
Zusatzklausel (con-tracts) (f)	*(tsOO-zAHts-klOW-zehl)*	rider
Zusatzleistungen (pl)	*(tsOO-zAHts-lEYEs-tun-gen)*	fringe benefits
Zusatzsteuer (f)	*(tsOO-zAHts-shtOY-uh)*	surtax
zuschneiden	*(tsOO-shnEYE-den)*	cut (v)
Zuschuß (m)	*(tsOO-shUs)*	allowance (subsidy)
Zustellung (f)	*(tsOO-shtEHL-lunk)*	delivery
Zustimmung (f)	*(tsOO-shtIM-munk)*	approval, endorsement (approval)
Zuteilungsschein (m)	*(tsOO-tEYE-lungs-shEYEn)*	allotment letter

Z

zuverlässige Quelle (f)	*(tsOO-fuh-lEH-si-geh kvEH-leh)*	reliable source
zuviel fordern	*(tsOO-vEEl fOHr-duhn)*	overcharge
Zuwachs (m)	*(tsOO-vahkhs)*	accretion
Zuwachsrate (f)	*(tsOO-vahkhs-rAA-teh)*	growth rate, rate of increase
zuweisen	*(tsOO-vEYE-zen)*	allot (v), assign (v)
Zuweisung (f)	*(tsOO-vEYE-zunk)*	allotment
zuzüglich aufgelaufener Zinsen	*(tsOO-tsEW-glikh OWf-geh-lOW-feh-nuh tsIN-zen)*	plus accrued interest
Zwang (m)	*(tsvAHng)*	duress
Zwangseinziehung (f)	*(tsvAHng-EYEn-tsee-unk)*	mandatory redemption
Zweck-Gebrauch Schein (m)	*(tsvEHk-geh-brOWkh sheyen)*	end-use certificate
zweckgebundene Anleihe (f)	*(tsvEHk-geh-bUn-dehn-eh AHN-leye-eh)*	tied loan
zweckmäßig	*(tsvEHk-mAY-sig)*	practical
Zweiggeschäft (n)	*(tsvEYEg-geh-shEHft)*	branch office
Zweigstellenunternehmen (n)	*(tsvEYEg-shtEHL-len-un-tuh-nAY-men)*	chain store group
Zweiquartflasche (f)	*(tsveye-kvAHRT-flah-sheh)*	magnum
zweistufiger Markt (m)	*(tsvEYE-stoo-fi-guh mAHrkt)*	two-tiered market
zweite Hypothek (f)	*(tsvEYE-teh hew-poh-tAYk)*	second mortgage
zweitrangig	*(tsvEYEt-rAHng-ig)*	second rate
zweitstellig	*(tsvEYE-shtEHL-lig)*	second position
zwischen Banken	*(tsvISH-en bahnk-en)*	interbank
Zwischenabschluß (m)	*(tsvISH-en AHB-shlUS)*	interim statement
Zwischenhändler (m)	*(tsvISH-en-hEHnd-luh)*	middleman, purchasing agent
Zwischenhaushalt (m)	*(tsvISH-en-hOWs-hAHlt)*	interim budget
zwischenstaatlicher Handel (m)	*(tsvISH-en-shtAAt-lIKH-uh hAHn-dehl)*	interstate commerce
Zwischenwaren (pl)	*(tsvISH-en-vAA-rehn)*	intermediary goods
zwischenzeitlich	*(tsvISH-en-tsEYEt-likh)*	interim

Z

KEY WORDS FOR KEY INDUSTRIES

The dictionary that forms the centerpiece of *German for the Business Traveler* is a compendium of more than 3,000 words that you are likely to use or encounter as you do business abroad. It will greatly facilitate fact-finding about the business possibilities that interest you, and will help guide you through negotiations as well as reading documents. To supplement the dictionary, we have added a special feature–groupings of key terms about eleven industries. As you explore any of these industries, you'll want to have *German for the Business Traveler* at your fingertips to help make sure you don't misunderstand or overlook an aspect that could have a material effect on the outcome of your business decision. The industries covered in the vocabulary lists are the following:

- chemicals
- chinaware and tableware
- electronics
- environment
- fashion
- iron and steel
- leather goods
- motor vehicles
- pharmaceutical
- printing and publishing
- winemaking

CHEMICALS

English to German

acetic acid	die Azetatsäure	*(dee Ah-TSEH-taht-ZOY-reh)*
acid	die Säure	*(dee ZY-reh)*
ammonia	das Ammoniak	*(dahs a-MOH-nee-ahk)*
analysis	die Analyse	*(dee a-naa-LEW-zeh)*
analytic chemistry	die analytische Chemie	*(dee a-naa-LEW-ti-sheh KHAY-mee)*
atom	das Atom	*(dahs a-TOHm)*
atomic	atomar	*(a-toh-MAAr)*
base	die Base	*(dee BAA-zeh)*
benzene	das Benzol	*(dahs BEHN-tsol)*
biochemistry	die Biochemie	*(dee BEE-o-KHAY-mee)*
biologist	der Biologe	*(duh BEE-o-LOH-geh)*
biology	die Biologie	*(dee BEE-o-LOH-gee)*
carbon	der Kohlenstoff	*(duh KOH-len-shtOF)*
catalyst	der Katalysator	*(duh kah-tah-lEW-zah-tohr)*
chemical	chemisch	*(KHAY-mish)*
chemistry	die Chemie	*(dee KHAY-mee)*
chloride	das Chlorid	*(dahs khlOH-rit)*
chloroform	das Chloroform	*(dahs khlOH-ro-FOrm)*
component	die Komponente	*(dee kom-PO-nen-tEH)*
composition	die Zusammensetzung	*(dee tsu-zaHM-mehn-zet-tsunk)*
compound	die Verbindung	*(dee fuh-BIN-dunk)*
concentration	die Konzentration	*(dee kon-tsen-trAH-TSI-on)*
cracking	das Krachverfahren	*(dahs KRAHKH-fuh-fAA-ren)*
crystallization	die Kristallisierung	*(dee kris-tAHL-li-ZEE-runk)*
degree	der Grad	*(duh graht)*
density	die Dichte	*(dee DIKH-teh)*
dosage	die Dosierung	*(dee doh-ZEE-runk)*
electrolysis	die Elektrolyse	*(dee eh-lEHk-tro-LEW-zeh)*

electron	das Elektron	*(dahs eh-lEHk-trOHN)*
element	das Element	*(dahs eh-leh-MENt)*
engineer	der Ingenieur	*(duh in-sheh-NEE-er)*
enzyme	das Enzym	*(dahs ehn-TSEWm)*
ethane	das Äthan	*(dahs AY-taan)*
ether	der Äther	*(duh AY-tuh)*
evaporation	die Verdampfung	*(dee fuh-dAHM-pfunk)*
experiment	das Experiment	*(dahs EHX-peh-RI-mehnt)*
experimental	experimentell	*(EHX-peh-RI-mehn-tel)*
formula	die Formel	*(dee FOR-mehl)*
homogeneity	die Homogenität	*(dee homo-gehnI-tAYT)*
hydrocarbon	der Kohlenwasserstoff	*(duh KOH-len-vAHS-suh-shtOF)*
hydrochloric acid	die Salzsäure	*(dee ZAHlts-ZOY-reh)*
hydrolysis	die Hydrolyse	*(dee HEW-dro-LEW-zeh)*
impurity	die Unreinheit	*(dee UN-rEYEn-heyet)*
inorganic chem- istry	die anorganische Chemie	*(dee ahn-or-gAA-ni-she KHAY-mee)*
isotope	das Isotop	*(dahs EE-zo-tohp)*
laboratory	das Labor	*(duhs lah-bOHR)*
mole	das Grammolekül	*(dahs grAM-mo-leh-kEWL)*
natural gas	das Naturgas	*(dahs nah-TOOR-gahs)*
nitric acid	die Salpetersäure	*(dee zahl-PEH-tuh-ZOY-reh)*
organic chemistry	die organische Chemie	*(dee or-gAA-ni-she KHAY-mee)*
petroleum	das Erdöl	*(dahs AYrd-ERl)*
phosphate	das Phosphat	*(dahs FOS-faht)*
polymer	die polymeren Körper	*(dee po-lEW-meh-ren KER-puh)*
product	das Produkt	*(dahs pro-dUkt)*
purification	die Reinigung	*(dee REYE-ni-gunk)*
reactant	der Verbrennungshilfsstoff	*(duh fuh-brEHN-nungs-hilfs-shtOF)*
reduction	die Reduktion	*(dee reh-duk-TSI-On)*
refine (v)	raffinieren	*(RAf-fi-nee-ren)*

refinery	die Raffinerie	*(dee RAf-fi-neh-ree)*
research	die Forschung	*(dee FOR-shunk)*
salt	das Salz	*(dahs ZAHlts)*
saponification	die Verseifung	*(dee fuh-zEYE-funk)*
solubility	die Löslichkeit	*(dee LEWS-likh-kEYET)*
solute	der aufgelöste Stoff	*(duh OWf-geh-LER-stehr shtOF)*
solution	die (Auf) Lösung	*(dee [OWf] LER-zunk)*
solvent	das Lösungsmittel	*(dahs LER-zunks-mit-tel)*
sulfuric acid	die Schwefelsäure	*(dee shvay-fel-ZOY-reh)*
test tube	das Reagenzglas	*(dahs reh-AH-gents-glAAs)*
titration	die Titrierung	*(dee ti-trEE-runk)*
yield (v)	einbringen	*(EYEn-bRIN-gehn)*

German to English

Ammoniak (n)	*(a-MOH-nee-ahk)*	ammonia
Analyse (f)	*(a-naa-LEW-zeh)*	analysis
analytische Chemie (f)	*(a-naa-LEW-ti-sheh KHAY-mee)*	analytic chemistry
anorganische Chemie (f)	*(ahn-or-gAA-ni-she KHAY-mee)*	inorganic chemistry
Äthan (n)	*(AY-taan)*	ethane
Äther (m)	*(AY-tuh)*	ether
Atom (n)	*(a-TOHm)*	atom
atomar	*(a-toh-MAAr)*	atomic
(Auf) Lösung (f)	*([OWf] LER-zunk)*	solution
aufgelöster Stoff (m)	*(OWf-geh-LER-stehr shtOF)*	solute
Azetatsäure (f)	*(Ah-TSEH-taht-ZOY-reh)*	acetic acid
Base (f)	*(BAA-zeh)*	base
Benzol (n)	*(BEHN-tsol)*	benzene
Biochemie (f)	*(BEE-o-KHAY-mee)*	biochemistry
Biologe (m)	*(BEE-o-LOH-geh)*	biologist
Biologie (f)	*(BEE-o-LOH-gee)*	biology
Chemie (f)	*(KHAY-mee)*	chemistry

chemisch	*(KHAY-mish)*	chemical
Chlorid (n)	*(khlOH-rit)*	chloride
Chloroform (n)	*(khlOH-ro-FOrm)*	chloroform
Dichte (f)	*(DIKH-teh)*	density
Dosierung (f)	*(doh-ZEE-runk)*	dosage
einbringen	*(EYEn-bRIN-gehn)*	yield (v)
Elektrolyse (f)	*(eh-lEHk-tro-LEW-zeh)*	electrolysis
Elektron (n)	*(eh-lEHk-trOHN)*	electron
Element (n)	*(eh-leh-MENt)*	element
Enzym (n)	*(ehn-TSEWm)*	enzyme
Erdgas	*(AYrd-gaas)*	natural gas
Erdöl (n)	*(EHrd-ERl)*	petroleum
Experiment (n)	*(EHX-peh-RI-mehnt)*	experiment
experimentell	*(EHX-peh-RI-mehn-tel)*	experimental
Formel (f)	*(FOR-mehl)*	formula
Forschung (f)	*(FOR-shunk)*	research
Gemisch (n)	*(geh-mISH)*	compound
Grad (m)	*(graht)*	degree
Grammolekül (n)	*(grAM-mo-leh-kEWL)*	mole
Homogenität (f)	*(homo-gehnI-tAYT)*	homogencity
Hydrolyse (f)	*(HEW-dro-LEW-zeh)*	hydrolysis
Ingenieur (m)	*(in-sheh-NEE-er)*	engineer
Isotop (n)	*(EE-zo-tohp)*	isotope
Katalysator (m)	*(kah-tah-lEW-zah-tohr)*	catalyst
Kohlenstoff (m)	*(KOH-len-shtOF)*	carbon
Kohlenwasserstoff (m)	*(KOH-len-vAHS-suh-shtOF)*	hydrocarbon
Komponente (f)	*(kom-PO-nen-tEH)*	component
Konzentration (f)	*(kon-tsen-trAH-TSI-on)*	concentration
Krachverfahren (n)	*(KRAHKH-fuh-fAA-ren)*	cracking
Kristallisierung (f)	*(kris-tAHL-li-ZEE-runk)*	crystallization
Labor (n)	*(lah-bOHR)*	laboratory
Löslichkeit (f)	*(LEWS-likh-kEYET)*	solubility
Lösungsmittel (n)	*(LER-zunks-mit-tel)*	solvent

Maßanalyse (f)	*(MAAS-aa-naa-LEW-zeh)*	titration
Naturgas (n)	*(nah-TOOR-gahs)*	natural gas
organische Chemie (f)	*(or-gAA-ni-she KHAY-mee)*	organic chemistry
Phosphat (n)	*(FOS-faht)*	phosphate
polymere Körper (pl)	*(po-lEW-meh-reh KER-puh)*	polymer
Produkt (n)	*(pro-dUkt)*	product
Purifikation (f)	*(PU-ri-fi-kah-TSI-on)*	purification
Raffinerie (f)	*(RAf-fi-neh-ree)*	refinery
raffinieren	*(RAf-fi-nee-ren)*	refine (v)
Raffinierung (f)	*(RAf-fi-nee-runk)*	refinery
Reagenzglas (n)	*(reh-AH-gents-glAAs)*	test tube
Reduktion (f)	*(reh-duk-TSI-On)*	reduction
Reinigung (f)	*(REYE-ni-gunk)*	purification
Säure (f)	*(ZOY-reh)*	acid
Salpetersäure (f)	*(zahl-PEH-tuh-ZOY-reh)*	nitric acid
Salz (n)	*(ZAHlts)*	salt
Salzsäure (f)	*(ZAHlts-ZOY-reh)*	hydrochloric acid
Schwefelsäure (f)	*(shvay-fel-ZOY-reh)*	sulfuric acid
Titrierung (f)	*(ti-trEE-runk)*	titration
Unreinheit (f)	*(UN-rEYEn-heyet)*	impurity
Verbindung (f)	*(fuh-BIN-dunk)*	compound
Verbrennungshilfs-stoff (m)	*(fuh-brEHN-nungs-hilfs-shtOF)*	reactant
Verdampfung (f)	*(fuh-dAHM-pfunk)*	evaporation
veredeln	*(fuh-AY-dehln)*	refine (v)
Verseifung (f)	*(fuh-zeYE-funk)*	saponification
Zusammensetzung (f)	*(tsu-zaHM-mehn-zet-tsunk)*	composition

CHINAWARE AND TABLEWARE

English to German

bone china	das feine Porzellan	*(dahs fEYE-neh por-TSEl-lahn)*
bowl	die Schale	*(dee SHAA-leh)*
breadbasket	der Brotkorb	*(duh brOT-korb)*
butter dish	die Butterdose	*(dee BUTuh-do-zeh)*
candlestick	der Kerzenständer	*(duh kuh-tsen-shTEHN-duh)*
carving knife	das Tranchiermesser	*(dahs trahn-shEER-MEHS-suh)*
champagne glass	das Champagnerglas	*(dahs shahm-pAHN-yuh-glAAs)*
cheese-tray	das Käsebrett	*(dahs KAY-zeh-breht)*
china	das Porzellan	*(dahs por-TSEl-lahn)*
chinaware	die Porzellanwaren	*(dee por-TSEl-lahn-VAAren)*
coffeepot	die Kaffekanne	*(dee kahf-fAY-KAHN-neh)*
crystal glass manu-facturing	die Kristallglasherstellung	*(dee kris-tAHL-glAAs-huh-shTEL-lunk)*
cup	die Tasse	*(dee TAHs-seh)*
cutlery	das Eßbesteck	*(dahs EHS-beh-shtek)*
decanter	die Karaffe	*(dee kah-rAHF-feh)*
dessert plate	der Dessertteller	*(duh dehs-sEHah-tel-luh)*
dinner plate	der Teller	*(duh tel-luh)*
dish	die Schüssel	*(dee SHEWs-sel)*
earthenware	die Töpferware	*(dee TERp-fuh-VAAreh)*
espresso cup	die Espressotasse	*(dee ehs-prEHS-so-TAHs-seh)*
flute	die Flöte	*(dee FLER-teh)*
fork	die Gabel	*(dee GAA-bel)*
glass	das Glas	*(dahs glAAs)*
gravy boat	die Soßenschüssel	*(dee ZOH-sen-SHEWs-sel)*
hand-blown glass	das handgeblasene Glas	*(dahs hAHNd-geh-bLAA-zeh-neh glAAs)*
hand-painted	handbemalt	*(hAHNd-beh-maalt)*
knife	das Messer	*(dahs MEHS-suh)*

lace	die Spitze	*(dee SHPIT-tseh)*
linen	das Leinen	*(dahs LEYE-nen)*
napkin	die Serviette	*(dee zuh-VI-et-teh)*
napkin ring	der Serviettenring	*(duh zuh-VI-et-tehn-rINk)*
oilcloth	das Wachstuch	*(dahs VAHKs-TOOkh)*
pastry server	der Tortenheber	*(duh TOR-ten-hay-buh)*
pepper mill	die Pfeffermühle	*(dee pfEHF-fuh-mEW-leh)*
pepper shaker	der Pfefferstreuer	*(duh pfEHF-fuh-shtROY-uh)*
pitcher	der Krug	*(duh krUk)*
place setting	die Tischordnung	*(dee TISH-ORd-nunk)*
plate	der Teller	*(duh tel-luh)*
pottery	die Töpferware	*(dee TERp-fuh-VAAreh)*
salad plate	der Salatteller	*(duh zah-lAAT-tel-luh)*
salt shaker	der Salzstreuer	*(duh ZAHlts-shtROY-uh)*
saucer	die Untertasse	*(dee UN-tuh-TAHs-seh)*
silverware	das Tafelsilber	*(dahs TAH-fel-zil-buh)*
soup dish	der Suppenteller	*(duh ZUP-pen-tel-luh)*
spoon	der Löffel	*(duh LERF-fel)*
stoneware	das Steingut	*(dahs shtEYEn-gOOt)*
sugar bowl	die Zuckerdose	*(dee TSU-ker-do-zeh)*
tablecloth	das Tischtuch	*(dahs TISH-TOOkh)*
tablespoon	der Eßlöffel	*(duh EHS-lERF-fel)*
teapot	die Teekanne	*(dee TAY-KAHN-neh)*
teaspoon	der Teelöffel	*(duh TAY-lERF-fel)*
thread	der Faden	*(duh FAH-den)*
tureen	die Terrine	*(dee tuh-rEEN-neh)*
unbleached linen	das ungebleichte Leinen	*(dahs UN-geh-blEYEKH-teh LEYE-nen)*

German to English

Brotkorb (m)	*(brOT-korb)*	breadbasket
Butterdose (f)	*(BUTuh-do-zeh)*	butter dish
Champagnerglas (n)	*(shahm-pAHN-yuh-glAAs)*	champagne glass

Dessertteller (m)	*(duh dehs-sEHah-tel-luh)*	dessert plate
Espressotasse (f)	*(ehs-prEHS-so-TAHs-seh)*	espresso cup
Eßbesteck (n)	*(EHS-beh-shtek)*	cutlery
Eßlöffel (m)	*(EHS-lERF-fel)*	tablespoon
Faden (m)	*(FAH-den)*	thread
Flöte (f)	*(FLER-teh)*	flute
Gabel (f)	*(GAA-bel)*	fork
Glas (n)	*(glAAs)*	glass
handbemalt	*(hAHNd-beh-maalt)*	hand-painted
handgeblasenes Glas (n)	*(hAHNd-geh-bLAA-zeh-nehs glAAs)*	hand-blown glass
Käsebrett (n)	*(KAY-zeh-breht)*	cheese-tray
Kanne (f)	*(KAHN-neh)*	pitcher
Kaffekanne (f)	*(kahf-fAY-KAHN-neh)*	coffeepot
Karaffe (f)	*(kah-rAHF-feh)*	decanter
Kerzenständer (m)	*(kuh-tsen-shTEHN-duh)*	candlestick
Kristallglasherstellung (f)	*(kris-tAHL-glAAs-huh-shTEL-lunk)*	crystal glass manufacturing
Krug (m)	*(krUk)*	pitcher
Leinen (n)	*(LEYE-nen)*	linen
Löffel (m)	*(LERF-fel)*	spoon
Messer (n)	*(MEHS-suh)*	knife
Pfeffermühle (f)	*(pfEHF-fuh-mEW-leh)*	pepper mill
Pfefferstreuer (m)	*(pfEHF-fuh-shtROY-uh)*	pepper shaker
Porzellan (n)	*(por-TSEl-lahn)*	china
Porzellanwaren (pl)	*(por-TSEl-lahn-VAAren)*	chinaware
Salatteller (m)	*(zah-lAAT-tel-luh)*	salad plate
Salzstreuer (m)	*(ZAHlts-shtROY-uh)*	salt shaker
Schale (f)	*(SHAA-leh)*	bowl
Schüssel (f)	*(SHEWs-sel)*	dish
Sektglas (n)	*(zehkt-glAAs)*	champagne glass
Serviette (f)	*(zuh-VI-et-teh)*	napkin
Serviettenring (m)	*(zuh-VI-et-tehn-rINk)*	napkin ring
Soßenschüssel (f)	*(ZOH-sen-SHEWs-sel)*	gravy boat

Spitze (f)	*(shPIT-tseh)*	lace
Steingut (n)	*(shtEYEn-gOOt)*	stoneware
Suppenteller (m)	*(ZUP-pen-tel-luh)*	soup dish
Tafelsilber (n)	*(TAH-fel-zil-buh)*	silverware
Tasse (f)	*(TAHs-seh)*	cup
Teekanne (f)	*(TAY-KAHN-neh)*	teapot
Teelöffel (m)	*(TAY-lERF-fel)*	teaspoon
Teller (m)	*(tel-luh)*	plate, dish, dinner plate
Terrine (f)	*(tuh-rEEN-neh)*	tureen
Tischordnung (f)	*(TISH-ORd-nunk)*	place setting
Tischtuch (n)	*(TISH-TOOkh)*	tablecloth
Töpferware (f)	*(TERp-fuh-VAAreh)*	earthenware, pottery
Tortenheber (m)	*(TOR-ten-hay-buh)*	pastry server
Tranchiermesser (n)	*(trahn-shEER-MEHS-suh)*	carving knife
Untertasse (f)	*(UN-tuh-TAHs-seh)*	saucer
ungebleichtes Leinen (n)	*(UN-geh-blEYEKH-tehs LEYE-nen)*	unbleached linen
Wachstuch (n)	*(VAHKs-TOOkh)*	oilcloth
Zuckerdose (f)	*(TSU-ker-dozeh)*	sugar bowl

ELECTRONICS

English to German

alternating current	der Wechselstrom	*(duh vEHk-sel-shtrOHm)*
amplifier	der Verstärker	*(duh fuh-shtEHR-kuh)*
amplitude modula- tion	(AM) die Amplituden- Modulation	*(dee ahm-pli-TOO-den-moh- DU-lah-TSI-ohn)*
beam	die Strahlung	*(dee shtRAA-lunk)*
binary code	der Binärkode	*(duh bee-nAYR-koh-deh)*
broadcast (v)	ausstrahlen	*(OWs-shtrAA-len)*
cable television	das Kabelfernsehen	*(dahs KAA-bel-fehrn-zay- hen)*
cassette	die Kassette	*(dee kahs-SEHt-teh)*
cathode	die Kathode	*(dee kah-TOH-deh)*
channel	der Kanal	*(duh kah-nAAL)*
circuit	die Schaltung	*(dee shAHL-tunk)*
coaxial cable	das Koaxialkabel	*(dahs ko-ahxi-AAL-KAA- bel)*
computer	die Rechenanlage	*(dee reh-khen-AHN-lah-geh)*
condensor	der Kondensator	*(duh kon-den-ZAA-tor)*
current	der Strom	*(duh shtrOHm)*
direct current	der Gleichstrom	*(duh glEYEKH-shtrOHm)*
electricity	die Elektrizität	*(dee eh-lEHk-tri-tsee-TAYt)*
electrode	die Elektrode	*(dee eh-lEHk-tROH-deh)*
electron	das Elektron	*(dahs eh-lEHk-trOHN)*
electronic	elektronisch	*(eh-lEHk-trOH-nish)*
electrostatic	elektrostatisch	*(eh-lEHk-tro-stAH-tish)*
filter	der Filter	*(duh FIL-tuh)*
frequency	die Frequenz	*(dee frEH-kvehnts)*
frequency modula- tion (FM)	die Frequenzmodulation	*(dee frEH-kvehnts-moh-DU- lah-TSI-ohn)*
high fidelity	die High-Fidelity	*(dee HEYE fi-dEH-li-ti)*
induction	die Induktion	*(dee IN-duk-TSI-On)*
insulator	der Isolator	*(duh EE-zo-LAA-tor)*
integrated circuit	der integrierte Schaltkreis	*(duh in-teh-gREER-tuh shAHLt-krEYES)*

kilowatt	das Kilowatt	*(dahs KI-loh-vaht)*
laser	der Laser (strahl)	*(duh LAA-zuh [shtRAAl])*
microphone	das Mikrofon	*(dahs mee-kroh-fOHN)*
microwave	die Mikrowelle	*(dee mee-kroh-vEL-leh)*
optic	optisch	*(OP-tish)*
oscillator	der Oszillator	*(duh os-tsi-LAH-tor)*
panel	das Schaltfeld	*(dahs shAHLt-felt)*
parallel circuit	die Parallelschaltung	*(dee pah-rah-LEL-shahl-tunk)*
power	die Arbeitsleistung	*(dee AHR-beyets-lEYEs-tunk)*
printed circuit	die gedruckte Schaltung	*(dee geh-drUK-teh shAHL-tunk)*
receiver	der Empfänger	*(duh ehm-pfEHN-guh)*
record	die Schallplatte	*(dee shAHL-plaht-teh)*
record (v)	aufnehmen	*(OWf-nay-men)*
record player	der Schallplattenspieler	*(duh shAHL-plaht ten-shPEE-luh)*
resistance	der Widerstand	*(duh VI-duh-shtahnt)*
resonance	die Resonanz	*(dee REH-zo-nahnts)*
scanning	die (Bild) Abtastung	*(dee [Bild] AHB-tahs-tunk)*
screen	der Bildschirm	*(duh Bild-SHIrm)*
semiconductor	der Halbleiter	*(duh hAHLb-leye-tuh)*
short wave	die Kurzwelle	*(dee KUrts-vEL-leh)*
silicon	das Silizium	*(dahs zi-LEE-tsi-um)*
sound	der Ton	*(duh tOHn)*
speaker	der Lautsprecher	*(duh LOWt-shpreh-khuh)*
stereophonic	stereophonisch	*(shtAY-reh-o-FO-nish)*
switch	die Umschaltung	*(dee UM-shahl-tunk)*
tape recorder	das Tonbandgerät	*(dahs tOHn-bahnd-geh-rEHt)*
telecommunica- tions	die Telekommunikation	*(dee tay-leh-kom-moo-ni-kah-tsEE-ohn)*
tone	der Ton	*(duh tOHn)*
transformer	der Umwandler	*(duh UM-vAHN-dluh)*
transmitter	der Übermittler	*(duh EWbuh-mIT-luh)*
tune (v)	einstellen	*(EYEn-shtel-len)*

videocassette player	das Videokasettengerät	*(dahs vEE-deh-o-kahs-SEHt-ten-geh-rEHt)*
voltage	die Stromspannung	*(dee shtrOHm-shpAN-nunk)*
wave	die Welle	*(dee vEL-leh)*
wire	der Draht	*(duh drAAt)*

German to English

Amplitudenmodulation (f)	*(ahm-pli-TOO-den-moh-DU-lah-TSI-ohn)*	amplitude modulation (AM)
Arbeitsleistung (f)	*(AHR-beyets-lEYES-tunk)*	power
aufnehmen	*(OWf-nay-men)*	record (v)
ausstrahlen	*(OWs-shtrAA-len)*	broadcast (v)
(Bild) Abtastung (f)	*([Bild] AHB-tahs-tunk)*	scanning
Bildschirm (m)	*(Bild-SHIrm)*	screen
Binärkode (m)	*(bee-nAYR-koh-deh)*	binary code
Computer	*(kom-pyu-tuh)*	computer
Draht (m)	*(drAAt)*	wire
einstellen	*(EYEn-shtel-len)*	tune (v)
Elekrizität (f)	*(eh-lEHk-tri-tsee-TAYt)*	electricity
Elektrode (f)	*(eh-lEHk-tROH-deh)*	electrode
Elektron (n)	*(eh-lEHk-trOHN)*	electron
elektronisch	*(eh-lEHk-trOH-nish)*	electronic
elektrostatisch	*(eh-lEHk-tro-stAH-tish)*	electrostatic
Empfänger (m)	*(ehm-pfEHN-guh)*	receiver
Fernmeldewesen (n)	*(fEHrn-mel-dEH-vay-zen)*	telecommunications
Filter (m)	*(FIL-tuh)*	filter
Frequenz (f)	*(frEH-kvehnts)*	frequency
Frequenzmodulation (f)	*(frEH-kvehnts-moh-DU-lah-TSIohn)*	frequency modulation (FM)
gedruckte Schaltung (f)	*(geh-drUK-teh shAHL-tunk)*	printed circuit
Gleichstrom (m)	*(glEYEKH-shtrOHm)*	direct current
Halbleiter (m)	*(hAHLb-leye-tuh)*	semiconductor
High-Fidelity (f)	*(HEYE fi-dEH-li-ti)*	high fidelity

Induktion (f)	*(IN-duk-TSI-On)*	induction
integrierter Schaltkreis (m)	*(in-teh-gREER-tuh shAHLt-krEYES)*	integrated circuit
Isolator (m)	*(EE-zo-LAA-tor)*	insulator
Kabelfernsehen (n)	*(KAA-bel-fehrn-zay-hen)*	cable television
Kanal (m)	*(kah-nAAL)*	channel
Kassette (f)	*(kahs-SEHt-teh)*	cassette
Kathode (f)	*(kah-TOH-deh)*	cathode
Kilowatt (n)	*(KI-loh-vaht)*	kilowatt
Klang (m)	*(klAnk)*	tone
Koaxialkabel (n)	*(ko-ahxi-AAL-KAA-bel)*	coaxial cable
Kondensator (m)	*(kon-den-ZAA-tor)*	condensor
Kraft (f)	*(krAHft)*	power
Kurzwelle (f)	*(KUrts-vEL-leh)*	short wave
Laser (m)	*(LAA-zuh)*	laser
Lautsprecher (m)	*(LOWt-shpreh-khuh)*	speaker
Mikrofon (n)	*(mee-kroh-fOHN)*	microphone
Mikrowelle (f)	*(mee-kroh-vEL-leh)*	microwave
optisch	*(OP-tish)*	optic
Oszillator (m)	*(os-tsi-LAH-tor)*	oscillator
Parallelschaltung (f)	*(pah-rah-LEL-shahl-tunk)*	parallel circuit
Rechenanlage (f)	*(reh-khen-AHN-lah-geh)*	computer
Resonanz (f)	*(REH-zo-nahnts)*	resonance
Schallplatte (f)	*(shAHL-plaht-teh)*	record
Schallplattenspieler (m)	*(shAHL-plaht-ten-shPEE-luh)*	record player
Schaltfeld (n)	*(shAHLt-felt)*	panel
Schaltung (f)	*(shAHL-tunk)*	circuit
Schwingung (f)	*(shvIN-gunk)*	wave
senden	*(zEN-den)*	broadcast (v)
Sender (m)	*(zEN-duh)*	transmitter
Silizium (n)	*(zi-LEE-tsi-um)*	silicon
stereophonisch	*(shtAY-reh-o-FO-nish)*	stereophonic
Strahlung (f)	*(shtRAA-lunk)*	beam

Strom (m)	*(shtrOHm)*	current
Stromspannung (f)	*(shtrOHm-shpAN-nunk)*	voltage
Telegramm (n)	*(tay-leh-grAHM)*	wire
Telekommunika-tion (f)	*(tay-leh-kom-moo-ni-kah-tsEE-ohn)*	telecommunications
Ton (m)	*(tOHn)*	sound, tone
Tonbandgerät (n)	*(tOHn-bahnd-geh-rEHt)*	tape recorder
Ubermittler (m)	*(EWbuh-mIT-luh)*	transmitter
Ultrakurzwelle (f)	*(ultrah-KUrts-vEL-leh)*	microwave
Umschaltung (f)	*(UM-shahl-tunk)*	switch
Umwandler (m)	*(UM-vAHN-dluh)*	transformer
Verstärker (m)	*(fuh-shtEHR-kuh)*	amplifier
Videokasettengerät (n)	*(vEE-deh-o-kahs-SEHt-ten-geh-rEHt)*	videocassette player
Wechselstrom (m)	*(vEHk-sel-shtrOHm)*	alternating current
Welle (f)	*(vEL-leh)*	wave
Widerstand (m)	*(VI-duh-shtahnt)*	resistance

ENVIRONMENT

English to German

catalytic converter	der Katalysator	*(duh kah-tah-LEW-zah-tohr)*
chemical	chemisch	*(KHAY-mish)*
cleanup (waste waters)	Abwasserreinigung	*(AHP-vahsser-reyen-igoong)*
ecology	die Umweltforschung	*(dee UM-velt-four-shoong)*
energy consumption	der Energieverbrauch	*(duh e-ner-GEE-fuh-browkh)*
energy source	der Energiequelle	*(duh e-ner-GEE-kvEL-eh)*
environmental protection	der Umweltschutz	*(duh UM-velt-shuts)*
exhaust	der Auspuff	*(duh OWS-pUF)*
garbage	der Müll	*(mewl)*
garbage collection	der Müllabfuhr	*(mewl-ahp-foor)*
garbage dump	der Müllabladeplatz	*(mewl-ahp-lahd-eh-PLAHTS)*
greenhouse effect	Treibhauseffekt	*(TREYEB-hows-eh-fekt)*
hole (in ozone layer)	Ozonloch	*(O-tsohn-lokh)*
landfill	das Deponie	*(dahs DEH-poh-nee)*
natural gas	das Erdgas	*(dahs AYrd-gaas)*
nuclear power station	das Kernkraftwerk	*(dahs kern-kraft-verk)*
organic farming	der biologische Anbau	*(duh bee-oh-LOHG-ish-eh AHN-bow)*
petroleum	das Erdöl	*(dahs AYrd-ERl)*
recyclable	recyclingsfähig	*(ree-SEYEK-lings-FAY-ikh)*
recycling economy	Kreislaufwirtschaft	*(KREYES-lowf-veert-shaft)*
renovation	die Sanierung	*(Zah-nee-ROONG)*
reutilize	wieder verwerten	*(vee-duhfuh-VEHRt-en)*
sewage	das Abwasser	*(AHB-vahs-sehr)*
toxic waste	Sondermüll	*(ZON-duh-mewl)*
waste disposal	Entsorgung	*(ehnt-ZOHR-goong)*

German to English

Abwasser (n)	*(AHB-vah-sehr)*	sewage
Abwasserreinigung (f)	*(AHP-vahsser-reyen-igoong)*	cleanup of waste waters
Auspuff (m)	*(OWS-pUF)*	exhaust
chemisch (m)	*(KHAY-mish)*	chemical
Deponie (f)	*(DEE-pon-ee)*	landfill
biologischer Anbau (m)	*(bee-oh-LOHG-ish-uh AHN-bow)*	organic farming
Energiequelle (f)	*(e-ner-GEE-kvel-leh)*	energy source
Energieverbrauch (m)	*(e-ner-GEE-fuh-browkh)*	energy consumption
Entsorgung (f)	*(ehnt-ZOHR-goong)*	waste disposal
Erdgas (n)	*(AYrd-gaas)*	natural gas
Erdöl (n)	*(AYrd-ERl)*	petroleum
Katalysator (m)	*(kah-tah-LEW-zah-tohr)*	catalytic converter
Kernkraftwerk (n)	*(kern-kraft-verk)*	nuclear power station
Kreislaufwirtschaft (f)	*(KREYES-lowf-veert-shaft)*	recycling economy
Müll (m)	*(mewl)*	garbage
Müllabfuhr (f)	*(mewl-ahb-foor)*	garbage collection
Müllabladepatz (m)	*(mewl-ahb-lahd-eh-PLAHTS)*	garbage dump
Ozonloch (n)	*(O-tsohn-lokh)*	hole in ozone layer
recyclingsfähig	*(ree-SEYEK-lings-FAY-ikh)*	recycled
Sanierung (f)	*(Zah-nee-ROONG)*	renovation
Sondermüll (m)	*(ZON-duh-mewl)*	toxic waste
Treibhauseffekt (m)	*(TREEB-house-ay-fet)*	greenhouse effect
Umweltforschung (f)	*(UM-velt-four-shoong)*	ecology
Umweltschutz (m)	*(UM-velt-shuts)*	environmental protection
wieder verwerten	*(vee-duh fuh-VEHR-ten)*	reutilize

FASHION

English to German

angora	die Angorawolle	*(dee ahn-GOH-rah-vOL-leh)*
belt	der Gürtel	*(duh gEWR-tel)*
bow tie	die Fliege	*(dee fLEE-geh)*
button	der Knopf	*(duh knOpf)*
buttonhole	das Knopfloch	*(dahs knOpf-lOKH)*
camel's hair	das Kamelhaar	*(dahs kah-mAYL-HAAr)*
cape	der Umhang	*(duh UM-hahnk)*
cashmere	die Kaschmirwolle	*(dee kah-shmEER-vOL-leh)*
coat	der Mantel	*(duh mAHN-tel)*
collar	der Kragen	*(duh kRAH-gen)*
color	die Farbe	*(dee fAHR-beh)*
cuff link	der Manschettenknopf	*(duh mAHN-shET-ten-knOpf)*
cut (v)	zuschneiden	*(tsOO-shnEYE-den)*
design (v)	entwerfen	*(ent-vER-fen)*
designer	der Modeschöpfer	*(duh mOH-deh-shER-PFer)*
drape (v)	drapieren	*(drah-PEE-ren)*
dress	die Kleidung	*(dee klEYE-dunk)*
fabric	der Stoff	*(duh shtOF)*
fashion	die Mode	*(dee mOH-deh)*
fashionable	modisch	*(mOH-dish)*
footage	die Gesamtlänge	*(dee geh-zaHMT-LEHN-geh)*
handkerchief	das Taschentuch	*(dahs tAH-SHen-TOOkh)*
hem	der Saum	*(duh zOWm)*
high fashion designer	der Couturier	*(duh ku-tEW-ree-ay)*
hood	die Kapuze	*(dee kah-PU-tseh)*
jacket	die Jacke	*(dee yAH-Keh)*
jewelry	der Schmuck	*(duh shmUK)*
length	die Länge	*(dee LEHN-geh)*

lingerie	die Feinwäsche	*(dee fEYEN-vEH-sheh)*
lining	das Futter	*(dahs fUT-tuh)*
long sleeves	die langen Ärmel	*(dee LAHN-gen AYR-mel)*
moiré	die Moireseide	*(dee moh-EER-zeYE-deh)*
necktie	die Krawatte	*(dee kRAH-vAT-teh)*
needle	die Nadel	*(dee nAA-del)*
out of style	außer Mode	*(OWs-suh mOH-deh)*
pattern	das Muster	*(dahs MUS-tuh)*
pleat	die Falte	*(dee fAHL-teh)*
pleated	gefaltet	*(geh-fAHL-teht)*
poplin	der Popelin	*(duh po-pEH-lin)*
print	der Druck	*(duh drUK)*
raincoat	der Regenmantel	*(duh RAY-gen-mAHN-tel)*
rayon	die Kunstseide	*(dee kUNst-zeYE-deh)*
ready-to-wear	von der Stange	*(fon duh shtAHN-geh)*
scarf	der Schal	*(duh SHAAl)*
sew (v)	nähen	*(NAY-hen)*
sewing machine	die Nähmaschine	*(dee NAY-mah-SHEE-neh)*
shirt	das Hemd	*(dahs hEHmt)*
shoe	der Schuh	*(duh shOO)*
short sleeves	die kurzen Ärmel	*(dee KUr-tsen AYR-mel)*
silk	der Seidenstoff	*(duh zeYE-den-shtOF)*
silk factory	die Seidenfabrik	*(dee zeYE-den-fah-brIK)*
silk goods	die Seidenwaren	*(dee zeYE-den-VAAren)*
silk manufacturers	die Seidenhersteller	*(dee zeYE-den-huh-shTEL-luh)*
silkworm	die Seidenraupe	*(dee zeYE-den-ROW-peh)*
size	die Größe	*(dee gRER-seh)*
skirt	der Rock	*(duh rOK)*
slacks	die lange Hose	*(dee LAHN-geh hOH-zeh)*
socks	die Socken	*(dee ZO-ken)*
sportswear	die Sportkleidung	*(dee shpORT-klEYE-dunk)*
stitch	der Stich	*(duh shtIKH)*
stockings	die Strümpfe	*(dee shtrEWM-PFeh)*

style	der Stil	*(duh shtEEL)*
stylist	der Stilist	*(duh shtEEL-ist)*
suede	das Wildleder	*(dahs vILd-lAY-duh)*
suit	der Anzug	*(duh AHN-tsook)*
sweater	der Pullover	*(duh PUL-ovah)*
synthetic	synthetisch	*(ZEWN-teh-tish)*
taffeta	der Taft	*(duh tahft)*
tailor	der Schneider	*(duh shnEYE-duh)*
thread	der Faden	*(duh FAH-den)*
tuxedo	der Smoking	*(duh smOH-king)*
veil	der Schleier	*(duh shlEYE-uh)*
vest	die Weste	*(dee vEH-steh)*
weaver	der Weber	*(duh vEH-buh)*
window dresser	der Schaufensterdekorateur	*(duh SHOW-fen-stuh-deh-ko-rah-TER)*
wool	die Wolle	*(dee vOL-leh)*
yarn	das Garn	*(dahs Gahrn)*
zipper	der Reißverschluß	*(duh rEYES-fuh-shlUS)*

German to English

Angorawolle (f)	*(ahn-GOH-rah-vOL-leh)*	angora
Anzug (m)	*(AHN-tsook)*	suit
außer Mode	*(OWs-suh mOH-deh)*	out of style
Ausfütterung (f)	*(OWs-ſEWT-teh-runk)*	lining
Couturier(m)	*(ku-tEW-ree-ay)*	high fashion designer
Damenunter-wäsche (pl)	*(DAA-men-UN-tuh-vEH-sheh)*	lingerie
drapieren	*(drah-PEE-ren)*	drape (v)
Druck (m)	*(drUK)*	print
elegant	*(eh-leh-gAHNt)*	fashionable
entwerfen	*(ent-vER-fen)*	design (v)
Faden (m)	*(FAH-den)*	thread
Falte (f)	*(fAHL-teh)*	pleat
Farbe (f)	*(fAHR-beh)*	color

Feinwäsche (f)	*(fEYEN-vEH-sheh)*	lingerie
Fliege (f)	*(fLEE-geh)*	bow tie
Futter (n)	*(fUT-tuh)*	lining
Garn (n)	*(Gahrn)*	yarn
gefaltet	*(geh-fAHL-teht)*	pleated
Gesamtlänge (f)	*(geh-zaHMT-LEHN-geh)*	footage
Gewebe (n)	*(geh-vAY-beh)*	fabric
Größe (f)	*(gRER-seh)*	size
Gürtel (m)	*(gEWR-tel)*	belt
Hemd (n)	*(hEHmt)*	shirt
Jacke (f)	*(yAH-Keh)*	jacket
Kamelhaar (n)	*(kah-mAYL-HAAr)*	camel's hair
Kapuze (f)	*(kah-PU-tseh)*	hood
Kaschmirwolle (f)	*(kah-shmEER-vOL-leh)*	cashmere
Kleid (n)	*(klEYEt)*	dress
Kleidung (f)	*(klEYE-dunk)*	dress
Knopf (m)	*(knOpf)*	button
Knopfloch (n)	*(knOpf-lOKH)*	buttonhole
Kragen (m)	*(kRAH-gen)*	collar
Krawatte (f)	*(kRAH-vAT-teh)*	necktie
Kunstseide (f)	*(kUNst-zeYE-deh)*	rayon
kurze Ärmel (pl)	*(KUr-tseh AYR-mel)*	short sleeves
Länge (f)	*(LEHN-geh)*	length
lange Ärmel (pl)	*(LAHN-geh AYR-mel)*	long sleeves
lange Hose (f)	*(LAHN-geh hOH-zeh)*	slacks
Manschettenknopf (m)	*(mAHN-shET-ten-knOpf)*	cuff link
Mantel (m)	*(mAHN-tel)*	coat
Masche (f)	*(mAH-sheh)*	stitch
Mode (f)	*(mOH-deh)*	fashion
Modeschöpfer (m)	*(mOH-deh-shER-PFer)*	designer
modisch	*(mOH-dish)*	fashionable
Moireseide (f)	*(moh-EER-zeYE-deh)*	moiré
Muster (n)	*(MUS-tuh)*	pattern

nähen	*(NAY-hen)*	sew (v)
Nähmaschine (f)	*(NAY-mah-SHEE-neh)*	sewing machine
Nadel (f)	*(nAA-del)*	needle
Popelin (m)	*(po-pEH-lin)*	poplin
Pullover (m)	*(PUL-ovah)*	sweater
Regenmantel (m)	*(RAY-gen-mAHN-tel)*	raincoat
Reißverschluß (m)	*(rEYES-fuh-shlUS)*	zipper
Rock (m)	*(rOK)*	skirt
Saum (m)	*(zOWm)*	hem
Schal (m)	*(SHAAl)*	scarf
Schaufensterde-korateur (m)	*(SHOW-fen-stuh-deh-ko-rah-TER)*	window dresser
Schleier (m)	*(shlEYE-uh)*	veil
Schmuck (m)	*(shmUK)*	jewelry
Schneider (m)	*(shnEYE-duh)*	tailor
Schuh (m)	*(shOO)*	shoe
Seidenfabrik (f)	*(zeYE-den-fah-brIK)*	silk factory
Seidenhersteller (f)	*(zeYE-den-hehr-shTEL-luh)*	silk manufacturers
Seidenraupe (f)	*(zeYE-den-ROW-peh)*	silkworm
Seidenstoff (m)	*(zeYE-deh-shtOF)*	silk
Seidenwaren (pl)	*(zeYE-den-VAAren)*	silk goods
Smoking (m)	*(smOH-king)*	tuxedo
Socken (pl)	*(ZO-ken)*	socks
Sportkleidung (f)	*(shpORT-klEYE-dunk)*	sportswear
Stich (m)	*(shtIKH)*	stitch
Stichart (f)	*(shtIKH-ahrt)*	stitch
Stil (m)	*(shtEEL)*	style
Stilist (m)	*(shtEEL-ist)*	stylist
Stoff (m)	*(shtOF)*	fabric
Strümpfe (pl)	*(shtrEWM-PFeh)*	stockings
synthetisch	*(ZEWN-teh-tish)*	synthetic
Taft (m)	*(tahft)*	taffeta
Taschentuch (n)	*(tAH-SHen-TOOkh)*	handkerchief
Umhang (m)	*(UM-hahnk)*	cape

Veloursleder (n)	*(veh-lOORS-lAY-duh)*	suede
von der Stange	*(fon duh shtAHN-geh)*	ready-to-wear
Weber (m)	*(vEH-buh)*	weaver
Weste (f)	*(vEH-steh)*	vest
Wildleder (n)	*(vILd-lAY-duh)*	suede
Wolle (f)	*(vOL-leh)*	wool
zuschneiden	*(tsOO-shnEYE-den)*	cut (v)

IRON AND STEEL

English to German

alloy steel	der Legierstahl	*(duh leh-gEEr-shtAAL)*
aluminum	das Aluminium	*(dahs ah-lu-mEE-nEE-um)*
annealing	das Ausglühen	*(dahs OWs-gLEW-en)*
bars	die Stangen	*(dee shtAHN-gen)*
billets	die Barren	*(dee bAHR-ren)*
blast furnace	der Hochofen	*(duh hOHKH-ohfen)*
carbon steel	der Kohlenstoffstahl	*(duh KOH-len-shtOF-shtAAL)*
cast iron	der Eisenguß	*(duh EYE-zen-gUS)*
chromium	das Chrom	*(dahs khrOHm)*
coil	das Gewinde	*(dahs geh-vIN-deh)*
cold rolling	das Kaltwalzen	*(dahs kAHLT-vAL-tsen)*
continuous mill	die kontinuierliche Walzstraße	*(dee kon-TEE-noo-EER-li-kheh vALTS-shtrAA-seh)*
conveyor	das Fördergerät	*(dahs FER-duh-geh-rEHt)*
conveyor belt	das Förderband	*(dahs FER-duh-bahnt)*
copper	das Kupfer	*(dahs kup-fEHR)*
crucible	der Schmelztiegel	*(duh shmEHLTS-tEE-gel)*
cupola	die Beobachtungskuppel	*(dee beh-OH-bahkh-tungs-kUP-pel)*
electric arc furnace electrodes	die Elektroden	*(dee eh-lEHk-tROH-den)*
electrolytic process	der Elektrolyseprozeß	*(duh eh-lEHk-tro-LEW-zeh-pRO-tsehs)*
ferroalloys	die Eisenlegierungen	*(dee EYE-zen-leh-gEE-run-gen)*
ferromanganese	das Manganeisen	*(dahs mahn-gAAN-EYE-zen)*
ferronickel	das Nickeleisen	*(dahs ni-KEl-EYE-zen)*
finished products	die Endprodukte	*(dee EHnd-Pro-dUk-teh)*
finishing mill	der Schlichfräser	*(duh shLIKH-frAY-zuh)*
foundry	die Gießerei	*(dee gEE-seh-rEYE)*
furnace	der Hochofen	*(duh hOHKH-ohfen)*

galvanizing	die Galvanisierung	*(dee gahl-vAA-nEE-zEE-runk)*
grinding	das Mahlen	*(dahs mAA-len)*
heat	der Schmelzgang	*(duh shmEHLTS-gahnk)*
hot rolling	das Warmwalzen	*(dahs vahrm-vAL-tsen)*
induction furnace	der Induktionsofen	*(duh IN-duk-TSI-Ons-ohfen)*
ingot mold	die Gußform	*(dee gUS-FORm)*
ingots	die Gußblöcke	*(dee gUS-bLER-keh)*
iron ore	das Eisenerz	*(dahs EYE-zen-EHRTS)*
limestone	der Eisenbitterkalk	*(duh EYE-zen-bIT-tuh-kahlk)*
malleability	die Dehnbarkeit	*(dee dAYN-buar-kEYET)*
manganese ore	das Manganerz	*(dahs mahn-gAAN-EHRTS)*
molybdenum	das Molybdän	*(dahs mo-LEWB-dAYN)*
nickel	der Nickel	*(duh ni-KEl)*
nitrogen	der Stickstoff	*(duh shtIK-shtOF)*
ore	das Erz	*(dahs EHRTS)*
pickling	das Abbeizen	*(dahs ahb-bEYE-tsen)*
pig iron	das Gußeisen	*(dahs gUS-EYE-zen)*
plate	die Platte	*(dee plAHT-teh)*
powder	das Pulver	*(dahs pUL-fuh)*
pressure	der Druck	*(duh drUK)*
process	der Arbeitsvorgang	*(duh ahr-bEYEts-fOHR-gahnk)*
refractories	die Schamottesteine	*(dee shah-mOT-eh-shTEYE-neh)*
rod	die Rundstange	*(dee rund-shtAHN-geh)*
rolling mill	der Walzwerkbetrieb	*(duh vALTS-vehrk-beh-trEEb)*
scale	die Gußhaut	*(dee gUS-hOWT)*
scrap	der Abfall	*(duh ahb-fAHL)*
sheet	die Platte	*(dee plAHT-teh)*
slabs	die Metallplatten	*(dee meh-tAHL-plaht-ten)*
specialty steels	der Spezialstahl	*(duh shpeh-tsIAAL-shtAAL)*
stainless steel	der rostfreie Stahl	*(duh rost-frEYE-uh shtAAL)*
steel mill	das Hüttenwerk	*(dahs hEWT-ten-vehrk)*

structural shapes	das Profileisen	*(dahs pro-fEEL-EYE-zen)*
super alloys	die Superlegierungen	*(dee zOO-puh-leh-gEE-run-gen)*
titanium	das Titan	*(dahs ti-tAAn)*
toughness	die Zähigkeit	*(dee TSAY-hig-kEYET)*
tungsten	das Wolfram	*(dahs volf-rAAM)*
vacuum melting furnace	der Vakuumschmelzofen	*(duh vAA-ku-um-shmEHLTS-ohfen)*
vanadium	das Vanadium	*(dahs va-nAA-di-um)*
wire	der Stahldraht	*(duh shtAAL-drAAt)*

German to English

Abbeizen (n)	*(ahb-bEYE-tsen)*	pickling
Abfall (m)	*(ahb-fAHL)*	scrap
Aluminium	*(ah-lu-mEE-nEE-um)*	aluminum
Arbeitsvorgang (m)	*(ahr-bEYEts-fOHR-gahnk)*	process
Ausglühen (n)	*(OWs-gLEW-en)*	annealing
Barren (pl)	*(bAHR-ren)*	billets
Beobachtungskuppel (f)	*(beh-OH-bahkh-tungs-kUP-pel)*	cupola
Chrom (n)	*(khrOHm)*	chromium
Dehnbarkeit (f)	*(dAYN-baar-kEYET)*	malleability
Druck (m)	*(drUK)*	pressure
Eisenbitterkalk (m)	*(EYE-zen-bIT-tuh-kahlk)*	limestone
Eisenerz (n)	*(EYE-zen-EHRTS)*	iron ore
Eisenguß (m)	*(EYE-zen-gUS)*	cast iron
Eisenlegierungen (f)	*(EYE-zen-leh-gEE-run-gen)*	ferroalloys
Elektroden (pl)	*(eh-lEHk-tROH-den)*	electric arc furnace electrodes
Elektrolyseprozeß (m)	*(eh-lEHk-tro-LEW-zeh-pRO-tsehs)*	electrolytic process
Endprodukte (pl)	*(EHnd-Pro-dUk-teh)*	finished products
Erz (n)	*(AYRTS)*	ore
Förderband (n)	*(FER-duh-bahnt)*	conveyor belt

Fördergerät (n)	*(FER-duh-geh-rEHt)*	conveyor
Formbarkeit (f)	*(FORm-baar-kEYET)*	malleability
Galvanisierung (f)	*(gahl-vAA-nEE-zEE-runk)*	galvanizing
Gewinde (n)	*(geh-vIN-deh)*	coil
Gießerei (f)	*(gEE-seh-rEYE)*	foundry
Gußblöcke (pl)	*(gUS-bLER-keh)*	ingots
Gußeisen (n)	*(gUS-EYE-zen)*	cast iron, pig iron
Gußform (f)	*(gUS-FORm)*	ingot mold
Gußhaut (f)	*(gUS-hOWT)*	scale
Härtung (f)	*(HEHR-tunk)*	annealing
Hochofen (m)	*(hOHKH-ohfen)*	blast furnace, furnace
Hüttenwerk (n)	*(hEWT-ten-vehrk)*	steel mill
Induktionsofen (m)	*(IN-duk-TSI-Ons-ohfen)*	induction furnace
Kalkstein (m)	*(kahlk-shTEYEn)*	limestone
Kaltwalzen (n)	*(kAHLT-vAL-tsen)*	cold rolling
Kohlenstoffstahl (m)	*(KOH-len-shtOF-shtAAL)*	carbon steel
kontinuierliche Walzstraße (f)	*(kon-TEE-noo-EER-li-kheh vALTS-shtrAA-seh)*	continuous mill
Kupfer (n)	*(kup-fEHR)*	copper
Legierstahl (m)	*(leh-gEEr-shtAAL)*	alloy steel
Mahlen (n)	*(mAA-len)*	grinding
Manganeisen (n)	*(mahn-gAAN-EYE-zen)*	ferromanganese
Manganerz (n)	*(mahn-gAAN-EHRTS)*	manganese ore
Metallplatten (pl)	*(meh-tAHL-plaht-ten)*	slabs
Molybdän (n)	*(mo-LEWB-dAYN)*	molybdenum
Nickel (m)	*(ni-KEl)*	nickel
Nickeleisen (n)	*(ni-KEl-EYE-zen)*	ferronickel
Platte (f)	*(plAHT-teh)*	plate, sheet
Profileisen (n)	*(pro-fEEL-EYE-zen)*	structural shapes
Pulver (n)	*(pUL-fuh)*	powder
rostfreier Stahl (m)	*(rost-frEYE-uh shtAAL)*	stainless steel
Rundstange (f)	*(rund-shtAHN-geh)*	rod
Schamottesteine (pl)	*(shah-mOT-eh-shtEYE-neh)*	refractories

Schleifen (n)	*(shlEYE-fen)*	grinding
Schlichfräser (m)	*(shLIKH-frAY-zuh)*	finishing mill
Schmelzgang (m)	*(shmEHLTS-gahnk)*	heat
Schmelztiegel (m)	*(shmEHLTS-tEE-gel)*	crucible
Spezialstahl (m)	*(shpeh-tsIAAL-shtAAL)*	specialty steels
Spule (f)	*(shpOO-leh)*	coil
Stahldraht (m)	*(shtAAL-drAAt)*	wire
Stahlwerk (n)	*(shtAAL-vehrk)*	steel mill
Stangen (pl)	*(shtAHN-gen)*	bars
Stickstoff (m)	*(shtIK-shtOF)*	nitrogen
Superlegierungen (pl)	*(zOO-puh-leh-gEE-run-gen)*	super alloys
Titan (n)	*(ti-tAAn)*	titanium
unlegierter Stahl (m)	*(UN-leh-gEEr-tuh shtAAL)*	carbon steel
Vakuumschmelzofen (m)	*(vAA-ku-um-shmEHLTS-ohfen)*	vacuum melting furnace
Vanadium (n)	*(va-nAA-di-um)*	vanadium
Walzwerkbetrieb (m)	*(vALTS-vehrk-beh-trEEb)*	rolling mill
Warmwalzen (n)	*(vahrm-vAL-tsen)*	hot rolling
Wolfram (n)	*(volf-rAAM)*	tungsten
Zähigkeit (f)	*(TSAY-hig-kEYET)*	toughness

LEATHER GOODS

English to German

ankle boots	die Halbstiefel	*(dee hAHLb-shtEE-fel)*
astrakan	der Astrachan	*(duh ahs-trah-khAHN)*
attaché case	die Aktentasche	*(dee AHk-ten-tAH-SHeh)*
beaver	der Biber	*(duh bEE-buh)*
belt	der Gürtel	*(duh gEWR-tel)*
billfold	die Brieftasche	*(dee brEEF-tAH-SHeh)*
blotter	der (Tinten) Löscher	*(duh [TIN-Ten] lERSH-uh)*
boot shop	der Stiefelladen	*(duh shtEE-fel-laa-den)*
bootmaker	der Stiefelmacher	*(duh shtEE-fel-mahkh-uh)*
boots	die Stiefel	*(dee shtEE-fel)*
briefcase	die Aktenmappe	*(dee ahk-tEN-mAHP-peh)*
calfskin	das Kalbsleder	*(dahs kAHLbs-lAY-duh)*
card case	das Visitenkartentäschchen	*(dahs vi-zEE-ten-kahr-ten-tEHSH-khen)*
cigarette case	das Zigarettenetui	*(dahs tsEE-gah-ret-ten-e-tuEE)*
cowhide	das Rindsleder	*(dahs RINds-lAY-duh)*
dye (v)	färben	*(fAYR-ben)*
eyeglass case	das Brillenetui	*(dahs brIL-len-e-tuEE)*
fitch hair	das Iltishaar	*(dahs IL-tIS-hAAR)*
fitch hair brush	die Iltishaarbürste	*(dee IL-tIS-hAAR-bEWR-steh)*
fox	der Fuchs	*(duh fUKS)*
gloves	die Handschuhe	*(dee HAHNd-shOO-eh)*
handbag	die Handtasche	*(dee HAHNd-tAH-SHeh)*
holster	das Pistolenhalfter	*(dahs pis-tOH-len-hAHLf-tuh)*
key case	das Schlüsseletui	*(dahs shlEWS-sel-e-tuEE)*
kidskin	das Ziegenleder	*(dahs tsEE-gen-lAY-duh)*
lamb	das Schafleder	*(dahs shAAF-lAY-duh)*
leather	das Leder	*(dahs lAY-duh)*
leather goods	die Lederwaren	*(dee lAY-duh-VAAren)*

leather jacket	die Lederjacke	*(dee lAY-duh-yAH-Keh)*
lizard (skin)	das Eidechsenleder	*(dahs EYE-dekh-sen-lAY-duh)*
lynx	der Luchs (pelz)	*(duh LUKHs[pELTS])*
makeup case	das Kosmetiktäschchen	*(dahs kos-mAY-tik-tEHSH-khen)*
marmot	das Murmeltier	*(dahs mur-mEL-tEER)*
mink	der Nerz	*(duh nEHRTS)*
Morroco leather	das Saffianleder	*(dahs zahf-fi-AAn-lAY-duh)*
nutria (skin)	das Nutriafell	*(dahs nOO-triah[fEL])*
opossum	das Opossum	*(dahs o-pOS-sum)*
ostrich	der Strauß	*(duh shtrOWS)*
otter fur	der Otterpelz	*(duh OT-tuh-pELTS)*
otter (skin)	das Otterfell	*(dahs OT-tuh-fEL)*
passport case	das Paßetui	*(dahs pAHS-e-tuEE)*
pigskin	das Schweinsleder	*(dahs shvEYEns-lAY-duh)*
pocketbook	die Handtasche	*(dee HAHNd-tAH-SHeh)*
portfolio	die Aktentasche	*(dee AHk-ten-tAH-SHeh)*
purse	die Geldbörse	*(dee gELt-bER-zeh)*
rabbit	das Kaninchen	*(dahs kah-nEEN-khen)*
raccoon	der Waschbär (pelz)	*(duh vahsh-bAYR [pELTS])*
sable	der Zobel (pelz)	*(duh tsOH-bel [pELTS])*
saddle	der Sattel	*(duh zaHT-tel)*
saddler	der Sattler	*(duh zaHT-tluh)*
scissor case	das Scherenetui	*(dahs shAY-ren-e-tuEE)*
sealskin	das Seehundsfell	*(dahs ZAY-hunds-fEL)*
sewing kit	das Nähtäschchen	*(dahs nAY-tEHSH-khen)*
slippers	die Pantoffel	*(dee pAHN-tOF-fel)*
snakeskin	das Schlangenleder	*(dahs shlAHN-gen-lAY-duh)*
suede	das Wildleder	*(dahs vILd-lAY-duh)*
suede jacket	die Wildlederjacke	*(dee vILd-lAY-duh-yAH-Keh)*
suitcase	der Koffer	*(duh kOF-fuh)*
tan (v)	(Leder) gerben	*([lAY-duh] gEHR-ben)*
tanner	der Gerber	*(duh gEHR-buh)*

tannery	die Gerberei	*(dee gEHR-beh-rEYE)*
tannin (tanin)	die Gerbsäure	*(dee gEHRb-ZOY-reh)*
tote bag	die Einkaufstasche	*(dee EYEn-kOWfs-tAH-SHeh)*
trunk	der Koffer	*(duh kOF-fuh)*
watch strap	das Uhrenarmband	*(dahs OO-ren-ahrm-bahnt)*
whip	die Peitsche	*(dee pEYE-tSHEH)*

German to English

Aktenkoffer (m)	*(AHk-tEN-kOF-fuh)*	attaché case
Aktenmappe (f)	*(AHk-tEN-mAHP-peh)*	briefcase
Aktentasche (f)	*(AHk-ten-tAH-SHeh)*	portfolio
Astrachan (m)	*(ahs-trah-khAHN)*	astrakan
Biber (m)	*(bEE-buh)*	beaver
Brieftasche (f)	*(brEEF-tAH-SHeh)*	billfold, purse
Brillenetui (n)	*(brIL-len-e-tuEE)*	eyeglass case
Eidechsenleder (n)	*(EYE-dekh-sen-lAY-duh)*	lizard (skin)
Einkaufstasche (f)	*(EYEn-kOWfs-tAH-SHeh)*	tote bag
färben	*(fAYR-ben)*	dye (v)
Fuchs (m)	*(fUKS)*	fox
Geldbörse (f)	*(gELt-bER-zeh)*	purse
gerben (Leder)	*(gEHR-ben [lAY-duh])*	tan (v)
Gerber (m)	*(gEHR-buh)*	tanner
Gerberei (f)	*(gEHR-beh-rEYE)*	tannery
Gerbsäure (f)	*(gEHRb-ZOY-reh)*	tannin (tanin)
Gürtel (m)	*(gEWR-tel)*	belt
Halbstiefel (pl)	*(hAHLb-shtEE-fel)*	ankle boots
Handschuhe (pl)	*(HAHNd-shOO-eh)*	gloves
Handtasche (f)	*(HAHNd-tAH-SHeh)*	handbag, pocketbook
Hase (m)	*(hAA-zeh)*	rabbit
Iltishaar (n)	*(IL-tIS-hAAR)*	fitch hair
Iltishaarbürste (f)	*(IL-tIS-hAAR-bEWR-steh)*	fitch hair brush
Kalbsleder (n)	*(kAHLbs-lAY-duh)*	calfskin
Kaninchen (n)	*(kah-nEEN-khen)*	rabbit

Koffer (m)	*(kOF-fuh)*	suitcase, trunk
Kosmetiktäschchen (n)	*(kos-mAY-tik-tEHSH-khen)*	makeup case
Leder (n)	*(lAY-duh)*	leather
Lederjacke (f)	*(lAY-duh-yAH-Keh)*	leather jacket
Lederwaren (pl)	*(lAY-duh-VAAren)*	leather goods
Löscher (m) (Tinten)	*(lERSH-uh [TIN-Ten])*	blotter
Luchs(pelz) (m)	*(LUKHs[pELTS])*	lynx
Murmeltier (n)	*(mur-mEL-tEER)*	marmot
Nähtäschchen (n)	*(nAY-tEHSH-khen)*	sewing kit
Nerz (m)	*(nEHRTS)*	mink
Nutriafell (n)	*(nOO-triah-fEL)*	nutria skin
Opossum (n)	*(o-pOS-sum)*	opossum
Otterfell (n)	*(OT-tuh-fEL)*	otter skin
Otterpelz (m)	*(OT-tuh-pELTS)*	otter fur
Pantoffel (pl)	*(pAHN-tOF-fel)*	slippers
Paßetui (n)	*(pAHS-e-tuEE)*	passport case
Peitsche (f)	*(pEYE-tSHEH)*	whip
Pistolenhalfter (n)	*(pis-tOH-len-hAHLf-tuh)*	holster
Rindsleder (n)	*(RINds-lAY-duh)*	cowhide
Saffianleder (n)	*(zahf-fi-AAn-lAY-duh)*	Morocco leather
Sattel (m)	*(zaHT-tel)*	saddle
Sattler (m)	*(zaHT-tluh)*	saddler
Schafleder (n)	*(shAAF-lAY-duh)*	lamb
Scherenetui (n)	*(shAY-ren-e-tuEE)*	scissor case
Schlangenhaut (f)	*(shlAHN-gen-hOWT)*	snakeskin
Schlangenleder (n)	*(shlAHN-gen-lAY-duh)*	snakeskin
Schlüsseletui (n)	*(shlEWS-sel-e-tuEE)*	key case
Schweinsleder (n)	*(shvEYEns-lAY-duh)*	pigskin
Seehundsfell (n)	*(ZAY-hunds-fEL)*	sealskin
Strauß (m)	*(shtrOWS)*	ostrich
Stiefel (pl)	*(shtEE-fel)*	boots
Stiefelladen (m)	*(shtEE-fel-laa-den)*	boot shop
Stiefelmacher (m)	*(shtEE-fel-mahkh-uh)*	bootmaker

Tannin (n)	*(tahn-nEEN)*	tannin (tanin)
(Tinten) Löscher (m)	*([TIN-Ten] lERSH-uh)*	blotter
Uhrenarmband (n)	*(OO-ren-ahrm-bahnt)*	watch strap
Visitenkartentäsch chen (n)	*(vi-zeE-ten-kahr-ten-tEHSH-khen)*	card case
Waschbär (pelz) (m)	*(vahsh-bAYR [pELTS])*	raccoon
Wildleder (n)	*(vILd-lAY-duh)*	suede
Wildlederjacke (f)	*(vILd-lAY-duh-yAH-Keh)*	suede jacket
Ziegenleder (n)	*(tsEE-gen-lAY-duh)*	kidskin
Zigarettenetui (n)	*(tsEE-gah-ret-ten-e-tuEE)*	cigarette case
Zobel(pelz) (m)	*(tsOH-bel[pELTS])*	sable

MOTOR VEHICLES

English to German

air filter	der Luftfilter	*(duh LUFT-FIL-tuh)*
alternator	der Wechselstromgenerator	*(duh vEHk-sel-shtrOHm-geh-neh-rAH-tor)*
assembly line	das Fließband	*(dahs flEES-bahnt)*
automatic gearshift	die Schaltautomatik	*(dee shAHLt-OW-to-mah-tik)*
automobile	das Auto	*(dahs OW-to)*
body	die Karosserie	*(dee kah-ros-seh-REE)*
brake	die Bremse	*(dee brEHM-zeh)*
brake pedal	das Bremspedal	*(dahs brEHMs-PEH-dahl)*
bumper	die Stoßstange	*(dee shtOS-shtAHN-geh)*
camshaft	die Nockenwelle	*(dee nOK-ken-vEL-leh)*
car	das Auto	*(dahs OW-to)*
carburetor	der Vergaser	*(duh fuh-gAA-suh)*
chassis	das Fahrgestell	*(dahs fAAR-geh-shtel)*
clutch	die Kupplung	*(dee kUP-lunk)*
clutch pedal	das Kupplungspedal	*(dahs kUP-lunks-peh-dahl)*
connecting rod	die Kurbelstange	*(dee kUR-bel-shtAHN-geh)*
convertible	das Kabriolett	*(dahs kahb-ri-o-LET)*
crankshaft	die Kurbelwelle	*(dee kUR-bel-vEL-leh)*
defroster	der Entfroster	*(duh ent-frOS-tuh)*
designer	der Entwerfer	*(duh ent-vEHR-fuh)*
disc brake	die Scheibenbremse	*(dee shEYE-ben-brEHM-zeh)*
displacement	der Hubraum	*(duh hOOb-rOWm)*
distributor	der Verteiler	*(duh fuh-tEYE-luh)*
driver	der Fahrer	*(duh fAA-ruh)*
engine	der Motor	*(duh mOH-tor)*
exhaust	der Auspuff	*(duh OWs-pUF)*
fender	der Kotflügel	*(duh kot-flEW-gel)*
four-cylinder engine	der Vierzylindermotor	*(duh fEER-tsew-lin-duh-mOH-tor)*

front-wheel drive	der Frontantrieb	*(duh front-AHN-treeb)*
gas consumption	der Benzinverbrauch	*(duh ben-tsEEn-fuh-brOWkh)*
gasoline	das Benzin	*(dahs ben-tsEEn)*
gasoline tank	der Benzintank	*(duh ben-tsEEn-tahnk)*
gearshift	die Gangschaltung	*(dee gAHnk-shahl-tunk)*
generator	die Lichtmaschine	*(dee LIKHT-mah-SHEE-neh)*
grille	das Kühlerschutzgitter	*(dahs kEW-luh-shuts-git-tuh)*
horsepower	die Pferdestärke	*(dee pfEHR-deh-shtEHR-keh)*
ignition	die Zündung	*(dee tsEWnd-dunk)*
injector	der Einspritzer	*(duh EYEn-shprIT-tsuh)*
lubrication	die Schmierung	*(dee shmEE-runk)*
mileage	die Meilenlänge	*(dee mEYE-lehn-LEHN-geh)*
odometer	der Kilometerzähler	*(duh KI-loh-mAY-tuh-tsAY-luh)*
paint	die Farbe	*(dee fAHR-beh)*
pinion	das Antriebsrad	*(dahs AHN-treebs-raht)*
piston	der Kolben	*(duh kOL-ben)*
power steering	die Servolenkung	*(dee zEHR-vo-len-kunk)*
radial tire	der Gürtelreifen	*(duh gEWR-tel-rEYE-fen)*
rear axle	die Hinterachse	*(dee hIN-tuh-akh-seh)*
seat	der Sitz	*(duh zITS)*
shock absorber	der Stoßdämpfer	*(duh shtOS-dEHm-pfuh)*
six-cylinder engine	der Sechszylindermotor	*(duh zEKHs-tsew-lin-duh-mOH-tor)*
spare tire	der Ersatzreifen	*(duh ayr-zAHTS-rEYE-fen)*
spark plug	die Zündkerze	*(dee tsEWnd-kuh-tseh)*
speedometer	der Geschwindigkeitsmesser	*(duh geh-shvIN-dig-kEYETs-MEHS-suh)*
spring	die Feder	*(dee fAY-duh)*
starter	der Anlasser	*(duh AHN-lahs-suh)*
steering	die Steuerung	*(dee shtOY-eh-runk)*
steering wheel	das Steuerrad	*(dahs shtOY-uh-raht)*

suspension	die Aufhängung	*(dee OWf-hehn-gunk)*
tire	der Reifen	*(duh rEYE-fen)*
torque	der Drehmoment	*(duh drAY-mo-ment)*
V8 engine	der V8-Motor	*(duh fOW AKHT mOH-tor)*
valve	das Ventil	*(dahs ven-tEEL)*
water pump	die Wasserpumpe	*(dee VAHS-suh-pUM-peh)*
wheel	das Rad	*(dahs raht)*
windshield	die Windschutzscheibe	*(dee vINd-shuts-shEYE-beh)*

German to English

Anlasser (m)	*(AHN-lahs-suh)*	starter
Anlasserwelle (f)	*(AHN-lahs-suh-vEL-leh)*	crankshaft
Antriebsrad (n)	*(AHN-treebs-raht)*	pinion
Aufhängung (f)	*(OWf-hehn-gunk)*	suspension
Auspuff (m)	*(OWs-pUF)*	exhaust
Auto (n)	*(OW-to)*	automobile, car
Benzin (n)	*(ben-tsEEn)*	gasoline
Benzintank (m)	*(ben-tsEEn-tahnk)*	gasoline tank
Benzinverbrauch (m)	*(ben-tsEEn-fuh-brOWkh)*	gas consumption
Bremse (f)	*(brEHM-zeh)*	brake
Bremspedal (n)	*(brEHMs-PEH-dahl)*	brake pedal
Drehmoment (m)	*(drAY-mo-ment)*	torque
Einspritzer (m)	*(EYEn-shprIT-tsuh)*	injector
Einspritzdüse (f)	*(EYEn-shprITS-dew-zeh)*	injector
Enteisungsanlage (f)	*(ent-EYE-zunks-AHN-lah-geh)*	defroster
Entfroster (m)	*(ent-frOS-tuh)*	defroster
Entwerfer (m)	*(ent-vEHR-fuh)*	designer
Ersatzreifen (m)	*(ayr-zAHTS-rEYE-fen)*	spare tire
Fahrgestell (n)	*(fAAR-geh-shtel)*	chassis
Fahrer (m)	*(fAA-ruh)*	driver
Farbe (f)	*(fAHR-beh)*	paint
Feder (f)	*(fAY-duh)*	spring

Fließband (n)	*(flEES-bahnt)*	assembly line
Frontantrieb (m)	*(front-AHN-treeb)*	front-wheel drive
Gangschaltung (f)	*(gAHnk-shahlt-tunk)*	gearshift
Geschwindigkeits- messer (m)	*(geh-shvIN-dig-kEYETs- MEHS-suh)*	speedometer
Gürtelreifen (m)	*(gEWR-tel-rEYE-fen)*	radial tire
Hinterachse (f)	*(hIN-tuh-akh-seh)*	rear axle
Hubraum (m)	*(hOOb-rOWm)*	displacement
Kabriolett (n)	*(kahb-ri-o-LET)*	convertible
Karosserie (f)	*(kah-ros-seh-REE)*	body
Kilometerzähler (m)	*(KI-loh-mAY-tuh-tsAY-luh)*	odometer
Klappe (f)	*(klAHP-peh)*	valve
Kolben (m)	*(kOL-ben)*	piston
Kotflügel (m)	*(kot-flEW-gel)*	fender
Kühlerschutzgitter (n)	*(kEW-luh-shuts-git-tuh)*	grille
Kupplung (f)	*(kUP-lunk)*	clutch
Kupplungspedal (n)	*(kUP-lunks-peh-dahl)*	clutch pedal
Kurbelstange (f)	*(kUR-bel-shtAHN-geh)*	connecting rod
Kurbelwelle (f)	*(kUR-bel-vEL-leh)*	crankshaft
Lichtmaschine (f)	*(LIKHT-mah-SHEE-neh)*	generator
Luftfilter (m)	*(LUFT-FIL-tuh)*	air filter
Meilenlänge (f)	*(mEYE-lehn-LEHN-geh)*	mileage
Motor (m)	*(mOH-tor)*	engine
Nockenwelle (f)	*(nOK-ken-vEL-leh)*	camshaft
Ölversorgung (f)	*(ERL-fuh-sor-gunk)*	lubrication
Pferdestärke (f)	*(pfEHR-deh-shtEHR-keh)*	horsepower
Pleuelstange (f)	*(plOY-el-shtAHN-geh)*	connecting rod
Rad (n)	*(raht)*	wheel
Reifen (m)	*(rEYE-fen)*	tire
Schaltautomatik (f)	*(shAHLt-OW-to-mah-tik)*	automatic gearshift
Scheibenbremse (f)	*(shEYE-ben-brEHM-zeh)*	disc brake
Schmierung (f)	*(shmEE-runk)*	lubrication

Sechszylindermotor (m)	*(zEKHs-tsew-lin-duh-mOH-tor)*	six-cylinder engine
Servolenkung (f)	*(zEHR-vo-len-kunk)*	power steering
Sitz (m)	*(zITS)*	seat
Steuerrad (n)	*(shtOY-uh-raht)*	steering wheel
Steuerung (f)	*(shtOY-eh-runk)*	steering
Stoßdämpfer (m)	*(shtOS-dEHm-pfuh)*	shock absorber
Stoßstange (f)	*(shtOS-shtAHN-geh)*	bumper
V8-Motor (m)	*(fOW AKHT mOH-tor)*	V8 engine
Ventil (n)	*(ven-tEEL)*	valve
Vergaser (m)	*(fuh-gAA-suh)*	carburetor
Verteiler (m)	*(fuh-tEYE-luh)*	distributor
Vierzylindermotor (m)	*(fEER-tsew-lin-duh-mOH-tor)*	four-cylinder engine
Wagen (m)	*(vAA-gen)*	car
Wasserpumpe (f)	*(VAHS-suh-pUM-peh)*	water pump
Wechselstromgenerator (m)	*(vEHk-sel-shtrOHm-geh-neh-rAH-tor)*	alternator
Windschutzscheibe (f)	*(vINd-shuts-shEYE-beh)*	windshield
Zündkerze (f)	*(tsEWnd-kuh-tseh)*	spark plug
Zündung (f)	*(tsEWnd-dunk)*	ignition

PHARMACEUTICAL

English to German

anaesthetic	das Betäubungsmittel	*(dahs beh-tOY-bungs-mit-tel)*
analgesic	das Analgetikum	*(dahs ahn-ahl-gAY-ti-kum)*
antacid	das Antiacidum	*(dahs AHN-ti-AH-tsidum)*
antibiotic	das Antibiotikum	*(dahs AHN-ti-BEE-o-ti-kum)*
anticoagulant	das Gegengerinnungsmittel	*(dahs gEH-gen-geh-rin-nungs-mit-tel)*
antidepressant	depressionshemmend	*(deh-pres-sI-ONs-hEHM-ment)*
anti-inflammatory	entzündungshemmend	*(ent-tsEWn-dungs-hEHM-ment)*
antiseptic	das Antiseptikum	*(dahs AHN-ti-sEHp-ti-kum)*
bleed (v)	bluten	*(blOO-ten)*
blood	das Blut	*(dahs blOOT)*
botanic	botanisch	*(bo-tAA-nish)*
capsule	die Kapsel	*(dee kAP-sel)*
compounds	die Präparate	*(dee prAY-pah-rAA-teh)*
content	der Inhalt	*(duh IN-hahlt)*
cough (v)	husten	*(hUS-ten)*
cough drop	der Hustentropfen	*(duh hUS-ten-trOP-fen)*
cough syrup	der Hustensaft	*(duh hUS-ten-sahft)*
crude	roh	*(roh)*
density	die Dichte	*(dee DIKH-teh)*
disease	die Krankheit	*(dee KRAHNK-heyet)*
diuretic	das Diuretikum	*(dahs dEE-U-reh-ti-kum)*
dose	die Dosis	*(dee DOH-zis)*
dressing	der Verband	*(duh fuh-bahnt)*
drop	der Tropfen	*(duh trOP-fen)*
drug	die Droge	*(dee drOH-geh)*
drugstore	die Apotheke	*(dee ah-po-tAY-keh)*
eyedrop	der Augentropfen	*(duh OW-gen-trop-fen)*
hypertension	die Hypertonie	*(dee hEW-puh-to-nee)*

injection	die Spritze	*(dee shpRI-tseh)*
iodine	das Jod	*(dahs yOHt)*
iron	das Eisen	*(dahs EYE-zen)*
laboratory technician	der Labortechniker	*(duh lah-bOHR-tehkh-ni-kuh)*
laxative	das Abführmittel	*(dahs ahb-fEWR-mit-tel)*
medicine	die Medizin	*(dee meh-di-tsEEN)*
medication	die medizinische Behandlung	*(dee meh-di-tsEE-ni-sheh beh-hAHN-dlunk)*
morphine	das Morphium	*(dahs mOR-fi-um)*
narcotic	das Betäubungsmittel	*(dahs beh-tOY-bungs-mit-tel)*
ointment	die Salbe	*(dee zAHL-beh)*
opium	das Opium	*(dahs OH-pi-um)*
organic	organisch	*(or-gAA-nish)*
pellet	die Pille	*(dee pIL-leh)*
penicillin	das Penizillin	*(dahs peh-ni-tsi-LEEN)*
pharmaceutical	pharmazeutisch	*(fahr-ma-tsOY-tish)*
pharmacist	der Apotheker	*(duh ah-po-tAY-kuh)*
physician	der Arzt	*(duh ARtst)*
pill	die Pille	*(dee pIL-leh)*
plants	die Pflanzen	*(dee pflAHN-tsen)*
prescription	das Rezept	*(dahs reh-tsEHPt)*
purgative	das Abführmittel	*(dahs ahb-fEWR-mit-tel)*
remedies	die Heilmittel	*(dee hEYEL-mit-tel)*
salts	das Salz	*(dahs ZAHlts)*
salve	die Salbe	*(dee zAHL-beh)*
sedative	das Beruhigungsmittel	*(dahs beh-rOO-I-gungs-mit-tel)*
serum	das Serum	*(dahs sAY-rum)*
sinus	der Sinus	*(duh sEE-nus)*
sleeping pill	die Schlaftablette	*(dee shlAAF-tah-bleh-teh)*
sneeze (v)	niesen	*(nEE-zen)*
starch	die Stärke	*(dee shtEHR-keh)*
stimulant	das Anregungsmittel	*(dahs AHN-reh-gungs-mit-tel)*

sulphamide	das Sulfamid	*(dahs zul-fah-mEEt)*
synthesis	die Synthese	*(dee sewn-tAY-seh)*
syringe	die Spritze	*(dee shpRI-tseh)*
tablet	die Tablette	*(dee tah-bleh-teh)*
thermometer	das Thermometer	*(dahs tEHR-mo-mEH-tuh)*
toxicology	die Toxikologie	*(dee to-xi-ko-loh-gee)*
toxin	das Toxin	*(dahs to-xEEN)*
tranquilizer	das Beruhigungsmittel	*(dahs beh-rOO-I-gungs-mit-tel)*
vaccine	die Vakzine	*(dee vak-tsEE-neh)*
vitamin	das Vitamin	*(dahs vi-tah-mEEn)*
zinc	das Zink	*(dahs tsINK)*

German to English

Abführmittel (n)	*(ahb-fEWR-mit-tel)*	laxative, purgative
Analgetikum (n)	*(ahn-ahl-gAY-ti-kum)*	analgesic
Anregungsmittel (n)	*(AHN-reh-gungs-mit-tel)*	stimulant
Antiacidum (n)	*(AHN-ti-AH-tsidum)*	antacid
Antibiotikum (n)	*(AHN-ti-BEE-o-ti-kum)*	antibiotic
Antiseptikum (n)	*(AHN-ti-sEHp-ti-kum)*	antiseptic
Apotheke (f)	*(ah-po-tAY-keh)*	pharmacy
Apotheker (m)	*(ah-po-tAY-kuh)*	pharmacist
Arzneimittel (n)	*(ahr-tsnEYE-mit-tel)*	medicine
Arzneiverordnung (f)	*(ahr-tsnEYE-fuh-ORd-nunk)*	medication
Arzt (m)	*(ARtst)*	physician
Augentropfen (m)	*(OW-gen-trop-fen)*	eyedrop
Beruhigungsmittel (n)	*(beh-rOO-I-gungs-mit-tel)*	tranquilizer, sedative
Betäubungsmittel (n)	*(beh-tOY-bungs-mit-tel)*	anaesthetic, narcotic
Blut (n)	*(blOOT)*	blood
bluten	*(blOO-ten)*	bleed (v)
botanisch	*(bo-tAA-nish)*	botanic

depressionshem-mend	*(deh-pres-sI-ONs-hEHM-ment)*	antidepressant
Dichte (f)	*(DIKH-teh)*	density
Diuretikum (n)	*(dEE-U-reh-ti-kum)*	diuretic
Dosis (f)	*(DOH-zis)*	dose
Dragée (n)	*(drah-SHAY)*	pellet
Droge (f)	*(drOH-geh)*	drug
entzündungshem-mend	*(ent-tsEWn-dungs-hEHM-ment)*	anti-inflammatory
Eisen (n)	*(EYE-zen)*	iron
Gegengerinnungs-mittel (n)	*(gEH-gen-geh-rin-nungs-mit-tel)*	anticoagulant
Gewächse (pl)	*(geh-vEHKH-seh)*	plants
Giftkunde (f)	*(gIFT-kun-deh)*	toxicology
Giftstoff (m)	*(gIFT-shtOF)*	toxin
harntreibendes Mittel (n)	*(hAHRn-trEYE-ben-dehs mit-tel)*	diuretic
Heilmittel (pl)	*(hEYEL-mit-tel)*	remedies
husten	*(hUS-ten)*	cough (v)
Hustensaft (m)	*(hUS-ten-sahft)*	cough syrup
Hustentropfen (m)	*(hUS-ten-trOP-fen)*	cough drop
Hypertonie (f)	*(hEW-puh-to-nee)*	hypertension
Impfstoff (m)	*(IMpf-shtOF)*	vaccine
Inhalt (m)	*(IN-hahlt)*	content
Jod (n)	*(yOHt)*	iodine
Kapsel (f)	*(kAP-sel)*	capsule
Kohlehydrat (n)	*(KOH-le-hEW-draat)*	carbohydrate
Krankheit (f)	*(KRAHNK-heyet)*	disease
Labortechniker (m)	*(lah-bOHR-tehkh-ni-kuh)*	laboratory technician
Medikament (n)	*(meh-di-KAH-ment)*	drug
Medizin (f)	*(meh-di-tsEEN)*	medicine
medizinische Behandlung (f)	*(meh-di-tsEE-ni-sheh beh-hAHN-dlunk)*	medication
Morphium (n)	*(mOR-fi-um)*	morphine
Narkotikum (n)	*(nahr-kOH-ti-kum)*	narcotic

niesen	*(nEE-zen)*	sneeze (v)
Opium (n)	*(OH-pi-um)*	opium
organisch	*(or-gAA-nish)*	organic
Penizillin (n)	*(peh-ni-tsi-LEEN)*	penicillin
Pflanzen (pl)	*(pflAHN-tsen)*	plants
pharmazeutisch	*(fahr-ma-tsOY-tish)*	pharmaceutical
Pille (f)	*(pIL-leh)*	pellet, pill
Präparate (pl)	*(prAY-pah-rAA-teh)*	compounds
Rezept (n)	*(reh-tsEHPt)*	prescription
roh	*(roh)*	crude
Salbe (f)	*(zAHL-beh)*	ointment, salve
Salz (n)	*(ZAHlts)*	salts
Schlaftablette (f)	*(shlAAF-tah-bleh-teh)*	sleeping pill
Serum (n)	*(sAY-rum)*	serum
Sinus (m)	*(sEE-nus)*	sinus
Spritze (f)	*(shpRI-tseh)*	injection, syringe
Stärke (f)	*(shtEHR-keh)*	starch
Sulfamid (n)	*(zul-fah-mEEt)*	sulphamide
Synthese (f)	*(sewn-tAY-seh)*	synthesis
Tablette (f)	*(tah-bleh-teh)*	tablet
Thermometer (n)	*(tEHR-mo-mEH-tuh)*	thermometer
Toxikologie (f)	*(to-xi-ko-loh-gee)*	toxicology
Toxin (n)	*(to-xEEN)*	toxin
Tropfen (m)	*(trOP-fen)*	drop
unbearbeitet	*(UN-beh-ahr-beye-tet)*	crude
Vakzine (f)	*(vak-tsEEN)*	vaccine
Verband (m)	*(fuh-bahnt)*	dressing
Verbindungen (pl)	*(fuh-BIN-dun-gen)*	compounds
Vitamin (n)	*(vi-tah-mEEn)*	vitamin
Zink (n)	*(tsINK)*	zinc

PRINTING AND PUBLISHING

English to German

acknowledgment	die Anerkennung	*(dee ahn-EHR-ken-nunk)*
art	die Kunst	*(dee kUNst)*
black and white	schwarzweiß	*(shvarts-vEYES)*
bleed	über den Rand gedruckt	*(EWbuh den rAHNt geh-drUKt)*
blowup	die Vergrößerung	*(dee fuh-gRER-seh-runk)*
boldface	der Fettdruck	*(duh fET-drUK)*
book	das Buch	*(dahs bOOKH)*
capital	der Großbuchstabe	*(duh grOS-bOOKH-shtah-beh)*
chapter	das Kapitel	*(dahs kah-PI-tel)*
circulation	die Auflage	*(dee OWf-lah-geh)*
coated paper	das gestrichene Papier	*(dahs geh-shtRI-KHeh-neh pah-pEER)*
color separation	der Farbauszug	*(duh fAHRb-OWs-tsOOk)*
composition	der Schriftsatz	*(duh shrIFT-zAHTS)*
copy	die Kopie	*(dee ko-PEE)*
copy (v)	Abzüge machen	*(ahb-tsEW-geh ma-khen)*
copyright	das Urheberrecht	*(dahs OOr-hay-buh-rehkht)*
crop	die Masse	*(dee MAHs-seh)*
distribution	der Vertrieb	*(duh fuh-trEEB)*
dummy	der Proband	*(duh pro-beh-bahnt)*
edit (v)	herausgeben	*(heh-rOWs-gay-ben)*
edition	die Ausgabe	*(dee OWs-gah-beh)*
editor	der Redakteur	*(duh re-dahk-tER)*
engrave (v)	gravieren	*(grah-vEE-ren)*
font	der Schriftsatz	*(duh shrIFT-zAHTS)*
form	die Gestalt	*(dee geh-shtAHlt)*
format	das Format	*(dahs for-mAAT)*
four-color	vierfarbig	*(fEER-fAHR-bik)*
galley proof	die Fahnenabzug	*(dee fAA-nehn-ahb-tsOOk)*
glossy	glänzend, glatt	*(glEHN-tsent), (glAHT)*

grain	die Faserung	*(dee fAH-zeh-runk)*
hardcover	das Hardcover	*(dahs hart-kah-vah)*
headline	die Überschrift	*(dee EW-buh-shrIFT)*
inch	der Zoll	*(duh tsOL)*
ink	die Tinte	*(dee TIN-Teh)*
insert	die Einlage, die Beilage	*(dee EYEn-laa-geh), (dee bEYE-lah-geh)*
introduction	die Einführung	*(dee EYEn-FEWR-runk)*
italic	kursiv	*(kur-zEEF)*
jacket	die Buchhülle	*(dee bOOkh-hewl-leh)*
justify (v)	justieren	*(yus-tEE-ren)*
layout	das Layout	*(dahs LAY-owt)*
letter	der Buchstabe	*(duh bOOKH-shtah-beh)*
line	die Linie	*(dee LEE-ni-eh)*
line drawing	die Federzeichnung	*(dee fAY-duh-tsEYEKH-nunk)*
lower case	Kleinbuchstaben	*(klEYEn-bOOKH-shtah-behn)*
matrix	die Matrize	*(dee ma-TRI-tseh)*
negative	negativ	*(nay-gah-tEEF)*
newsprint	das Zeitungspapier	*(dahs tsEYE-tungs-pah-pEER)*
page makeup	die Seitenaufmachung	*(dee zEYE-ten-owf-mah-khunk)*
pagination	die Paginierung	*(dee pah-gi-nEE-runk)*
pamphlet	die Broschüre	*(dee bro-shEW-reh)*
paper	das Papier	*(dahs pah-pEER)*
paperback	das Paperback	*(dahs pEH-puh-bEHK)*
perfect binding	die perfekte Bindung	*(dee puh-fehk-teh BIN-dunk)*
pica	die Pica	*(dee pi-kah)*
pigment	das Pigment	*(dahs PIG-ment)*
plate	die Platte	*(dee plAHT-teh)*
positive	das Positiv	*(dahs po-zi-tEEF)*
preface	das Vorwort	*(dahs FOHR-vort)*
press book	das Pressebuch	*(dahs prehs-seh-bOOKH)*
print run	der Drucklauf	*(duh drUK-lowf)*

printing	der Druck	*(duh drUK)*
proofreading	das Korrekturlesen	*(dahs kor-rehk-tOOR-lay-zen)*
publisher	der Verleger	*(duh fuh-LAY-guh)*
ream	das Ries	*(dahs rees)*
scanner	der Abtaster	*(duh AHB-tahs-tuh)*
sewn	geheftet, broschiert	*(geh-hEHF-tet), (bro-shEERt)*
sheet	das Blatt	*(dahs blAHT)*
size	die Größe	*(dee gRER-seh)*
spine	der Buchrücken	*(duh bOOKH-rEW-ken)*
table of contents	das Inhaltsverzeichnis	*(dahs IN-hahlts-fuh-tsEYEKH-nis)*
title	der Titel	*(duh TI-tel)*
title page	die Titelseite	*(dee TI-tel-zEYE-teh)*

German to English

Abtaster (m)	*(AHB-tahs-tuh)*	scanner
Abzüge (pl) machen	*(ahb-tsEW-geh ma-khen)*	copy (v)
Anerkennung (f)	*(ahn-EHR-ken-nunk)*	acknowledgment
Auflage (f)	*(OWf-lah-geh)*	circulation, print run, printing
Ausbeute (f) schneiden	*(OWs-boy-teh shnEYE-den)*	crop
Ausgabe (f)	*(OWs-gah-beh)*	edition
Beilage (f)	*(bEYE-lah-geh)*	insert
Blatt (n)	*(blAHT)*	sheet
broschiert	*(bro-shEERt)*	sewn
Broschüre (f)	*(bro-shEW-reh)*	pamphlet
Buch (n)	*(bOOKH)*	book
Buchhüle	*(bOOkh-hewl-leh)*	book
Buchrücken (m)	*(bOOKH-rEW-ken)*	spine
Buchstabe (m)	*(bOOKH-shtah-beh)*	letter
Druck (m)	*(drUK)*	printing
Drucklauf (m)	*(drUK-lowf)*	print run

Einführung (f)	*(EYEn-FEWR-runk)*	introduction
Einlage (f)	*(EYEn-laa-geh)*	insert
Exemplar (n)	*(ehx-ehm-plAAR)*	copy
Fahnenabzug (m)	*(fAA-nen-ahb-tsOOk)*	galley proof
Farbauszug (m)	*(fAHRb-OWs-tsOOk)*	color separation
Faserung (f)	*(fAH-zeh-runk)*	grain
Federzeichnung (f)	*(fAY-duh-tsEYEKH-nunk)*	line drawing
Fettdruck (m)	*(fET-drUK)*	boldface
Format (n)	*(for-mAAT)*	format
geheftet	*(geh-hEHF-tet)*	sewn
Gestalt (n)	*(geh-shtAHlt)*	form
gestrichenes Papier (n)	*(geh-shtRI-KHeh-nehs pah-pEER)*	coated paper
glänzend	*(glEHN-tsent)*	glossy
glatt	*(glAHT)*	glossy
gravieren	*(grah-vEE-ren)*	engrave (v)
Größe (f)	*(gRER-seh)*	size
Großbuchstabe (m)	*(grOS-bOOKH-shtah-beh)*	capital
Hard cover (n)	*(hart-kah-vah)*	hardcover
herausgeben	*(heh-rOWs-gay-ben)*	edit (v)
Inhaltsverzeichnis (n)	*(IN-hahlts-fuh-tsEYEKH-nis)*	table of contents
justieren	*(yus-tEE-ren)*	justify (v)
Kapitel (n)	*(kah-PI-tel)*	chapter
Kleinbuchstaben (pl)	*(klEYEn-bOOKH-shtah-ben)*	lower case
Kopie (f)	*(ko-PEE)*	copy
Korrekturlesen (n)	*(kor-rehk-tOOR-lay-zen)*	proofreading
Kunst (f)	*(kUNst)*	art
kursiv	*(kur-zEEF)*	italic
Layout (n)	*(LAY-owt)*	layout
Linie (f)	*(LEE-ni-eh)*	line
Masse	*(MAHs-seh)*	crop
Matrize (f)	*(ma-TRI-tseh)*	matrix

negativ	*(nay-gah-tEEF)*	negative
Paginierung (f)	*(pah-gi-nEE-runk)*	pagination
Paperback (n)	*(pEH-puh-bEHK)*	paperback
Papier (n)	*(pah-pEER)*	paper
perfekte Bindung (f)	*(puh-fehk-teh BIN-dunk)*	perfect binding
Pica (f)	*(pi-kah)*	pica
Pigment (n)	*(PIG-ment)*	pigment
Platte (f)	*(plAHT-teh)*	plate
positiv	*(po-zi-tEEF)*	positive
Pressebuch (n)	*(prehs-seh-bOOKH)*	press book
Probeband (m)	*(pro-beh-bahnt)*	dummy
Redakteur (m)	*(re-dahk-tER)*	editor
redigieren	*(reh-di-gEE-ren)*	edit (v)
Ries (n)	*(rees)*	ream
Schriftsatz (m)	*(shrIFT-zAHTS)*	composition, font
schwarzweiß	*(shvarts-vEYES)*	black and white
Seitenaufmachung (f)	*(zEYE-ten-owf-mah-khunk)*	page makeup
Tinte (f)	*(TIN-Teh)*	ink
Titel (m)	*(TI-tel)*	title
Titlseite	*(TI-tel-zEYE-teh)*	title page
über den Rand gedruckt	*(EWbuh den rAHNt geh-drUKt)*	bleed
Überschrift (f)	*(EW-buh-shrIFT)*	headline
Urheberrecht (n)	*(OOr-hay-buh-rehkht)*	copyright
Vergrößerung (f)	*(fuh-gRER-seh-runk)*	blowup
Verleger (m)	*(fuh-LAY-guh)*	publisher
Vertrieb (m)	*(fuh-trEEB)*	distribution
vierfarbig	*(fEER-fAHR-bik)*	four-color
Vorwort (n)	*(FOHR-vort)*	preface
Zeitungspapier (n)	*(tsEYE-tungs-pah-pEER)*	newsprint
Zoll (m)	*(tsOL)*	inch

WINEMAKING

English to German

acid content	der Säuregehalt	*(duh ZOY-reh-geh-hahlt)*
acre	die Anbaufläche	*(dee AHN-bow-flehkh-eh)*
aging	das Altern	*(dahs AHL-tehrn)*
alcohol	der Alkohol	*(duh AHL-ko-hol)*
alcoholic content	der Alkoholgehalt	*(duh AHL-ko-hol-geh-hahlt)*
biological deacidizing	die biologische Entsäuerung	*(dee bee-oh-LOHG-ish-eh ent-ZOY-eh-runk)*
blend (v)	verschneiden	*(fuh-shnEYE-den)*
body	der Gehalt	*(duh geh-hahlt)*
bottle	die Flasche	*(dee flAH-sheh)*
bouquet	das Bukett	*(dahs bU-ket)*
case	die Kiste	*(dee kIS-teh)*
cask (225 litres)	das Faß	*(dahs fAHS)*
centiliter	der Zentiliter	*(duh tsen-ti-LEE-tuh)*
character	der Charakter	*(duh kah-rAHK-tuh)*
classified sparkling wine	der Qualitätsschaumwein	*(duh kvah-li-tehts-shOWm-vEYEN)*
climate	das Klima	*(dahs kLEE-mah)*
cooper	der Küfer	*(duh kEW-fuh)*
cork	der Korken	*(duh kor-ken)*
corkscrew	der Korkenzieher	*(duh kor-ken-tsEE-huh)*
draw off	ausdestillieren	*(OWs-dehs-ti-lEE-ren)*
dregs	die Hefe	*(dee hay-feh)*
drink (v)	trinken	*(trINK-en)*
dry wine	der trockene Wein	*(duh tRO-keh-neh vEYEN)*
estate (or chateau)	das Gut	*(dahs gOOt)*
estate bottled	die Erzeugerabfüllung	*(dee AYR-tsOY-guh-ahb-fewl-lunk)*
ferment	die Gärung	*(dee gAY-runk)*
fruity	fruchtig	*(frUKH-tik)*
grape	die Weinrebe	*(dee vEYEN-ray-beh)*
grape bunch	die Weintraube	*(dee vEYEN-trOW-beh)*

grape harvest	die Weinlese	*(dee vEYEN-lay-zeh)*
hectare	das Hektar	*(dahs hehk-tAAR)*
label	das Etikett	*(dahs eh-TI-ket)*
liter	der Liter	*(duh LEE-tuh)*
magnum	die Zweiquartflasche	*(dee tsveye-kvAHRT-flah-sheh)*
neck (of bottle)	der Flaschenhals	*(duh flAH-shen-hahls)*
pasteurized	pasteurisiert	*(pahs-tOY-REE-zEErt)*
production	die Produktion	*(dee Pro-duk-TSI-On)*
region	das Gebiet	*(dahs geh-bEET)*
ripe	reif	*(rEYEF)*
skin	der Weinschlauch	*(duh vEYEN-shlowkh)*
sparkling wine	der Schaumwein	*(duh shOWm-vEYEN)*
sugar content	der Zuckergehalt	*(duh TSU-ker-geh-hahlt)*
tannin	das Tannin	*(dahs tahn-nEEN)*
tasting	die Weinprobe	*(dee vEYEN-pro-beh)*
temperature	die Temperatur	*(dee tehm-peh-rah-tOOR)*
type of wine	die Weinart	*(dee vEYEN-ahrt)*
unfermented grape juice	der unfermentierte Rebensaft	*(duh UN-fuh-men-tEEr-tuh ray-ben-zahft)*
vat	das große Faß	*(dahs grO-Seh fAHS)*
vine	die Weinrebe	*(dee vEYEN-ray-beh)*
vineyard	der Weinberg	*(duh vEYEN-behrk)*
vintage	die Weinernte	*(dee vEYEN-EHRn-teh)*
vintage year	der Jahrgang	*(duh yAAR-gahnk)*
vintner	der Winzer	*(duh vIN-tsuh)*
wine	der Wein	*(duh vEYEN)*
wine cellar	der Weinkeller	*(duh vEYEN-kel-luh)*
wine cooperative	die Winzergenossenschaft	*(dee vIN-tsuh-geh-nos-sen-shahft)*
winegrower	der Weinbauer	*(duh vEYEN-bow-uh)*
wine steward	der Weinkellner	*(duh vEYEN-kel-nuh)*
winemaker	der Weinhersteller	*(duh vEYEN-huh-shTEL-luh)*
winepress	die Weinpresse, die Kelter	*(dee vEYEN-prehs-zeh), (dee kEL-tuh)*

yeast	die Hefe	*(dee hay-feh)*
yield	der Weinertrag	*(duh vEYEN-ayr-trahk)*

German to English

Alkohol (m)	*(AHL-ko-hol)*	alcohol
Alkoholgehalt (m)	*(AHL-ko-hol-geh-hahlt)*	alcoholic content
Altern (n)	*(AHL-tehrn)*	aging
Anbaufläche (f)	*(AHN-bow-flehkh-eh)*	acre
ausdestillieren	*(OWs-dehs-ti-lEE-ren)*	draw off
biologische Entsäuerung	*(bee-oh-LOHG-ish-eh ent-ZOY-eh-runk)*	biological deacidizing
Bukett (n)	*(bU-ket)*	bouquet
Charakter (m)	*(kah-rAHK-tuh)*	character
Erzeugerabfüllung (f)	*(AYR-tsOY-guh-ahb-fewl-lunk)*	estate bottled
Etikett (n)	*(eh-TI-ket)*	label
Faß (n)	*(fAHS)*	cask (225 litres), vat
Faßbinder (m)	*(fAHS-bin-duh)*	cooper
Flasche (f)	*(flAH-sheh)*	bottle
Flaschenhals (m)	*(flAH-shen-hahls)*	neck (of bottle)
fruchtig	*(frUKH-tik)*	fruity
Gärung (f)	*(gAY-runk)*	ferment
Gebiet (n)	*(geh-bEET)*	region
Gehalt (m)	*(geh-hahlt)*	body
großes Faß (n)	*(grO-Sehs fAHS)*	vat
Gut (n)	*(gOOt)*	estate (or chateau)
Hefe (f)	*(hay-feh)*	dregs, yeast
Hektar (n)	*(hehk-tAAR)*	hectare
Herstellung(f)	*(hayr-shTEHL-lunk)*	production
Jahrgang (m)	*(yAAR-gahnk)*	vintage year
Kelter (f)	*(kEL-tuh)*	winepress
Kiste (f)	*(kIS-teh)*	case
Klima (n)	*(kLEE-mah)*	climate
Korken (m)	*(kor-ken)*	cork

Korkenzieher (m)	*(kor-ken-tsEE-huh)*	corkscrew
Küfer (m)	*(kEW-fuh)*	cooper
Liter (m)	*(LEE-tuh)*	liter
pasteurisiert	*(pahs-tOY-REE-zEErt)*	pasteurized
Produktion (f)	*(Pro-duk-TSI-On)*	production
Qualitätsschaum-wein (m)	*(kvah-li-tehts-shOWm-vEYEN)*	classified sparkling wine
reif	*(rEYEF)*	ripe
Säuregehalt (m)	*(ZOY-reh-geh-hahlt)*	acid content
Schaumwein (m)	*(shOWm-vEYEN)*	sparkling wine
Tannin (n)	*(tahn-nEEN)*	tannin
Temperatur (f)	*(tehm-peh-rah-tOOR)*	temperature
trinken	*(trINK-en)*	drink (v)
trockener Wein (m)	*(tRO-keh-nuh vEYEN)*	dry wine
unfermentierter Rebensaft (m)	*(UN-fuh-men-tEEr-tuh ray-ben-zahft)*	unfermented grape juice
verschneiden	*(fuh-shnEYE-den)*	blend (v)
Wein (m)	*(vEYEN)*	wine
Weinart (f)	*(vEYEN-ahrt)*	type of wine
Weinbauer (m)	*(vEYEN-bow-uh)*	winegrower
Weinbeere (f)	*(vEYEN-bay-reh)*	grape
Weinberg (m)	*(vEYEN-behrk)*	vineyard
Weinernte (f)	*(vEYEN-EHRn-teh)*	vintage
Weinertrag (m)	*(vEYEN-ayr-trahk)*	yield
Weinhersteller (m)	*(vEYEN-huh-shTEL-luh)*	winemaker
Weinkeller (m)	*(vEYEN-kel-luh)*	wine cellar
Weinkellner (m)	*(vEYEN-kel-nuh)*	wine steward
Weinlese (f)	*(vEYEN-leh-zeh)*	grape harvest
Weinpresse (f)	*(vEYEN-prehs-zeh)*	winepress
Weinprobe (f)	*(vEYEN-pro-beh)*	tasting
Weinrebe (f)	*(vEYEN-ray-beh)*	grape, vine
Weinschlauch (m)	*(vEYEN-shlowkh)*	skin
Weinstock (m)	*(vEYEN-shtOK)*	vine
Weintraube (f)	*(vEYEN-trOW-beh)*	grape bunch

Winzer (m)	*(vIN-tsuh)*	vintner
Winzergenossensch aft (f)	*(vIN-tsuh-geh-nos-sen-shahft)*	wine cooperative
Zentiliter (m)	*(tsen-ti-LEE-tuh)*	centiliter
Zuckergehalt (m)	*(TSU-ker-geh-hahlt)*	sugar content
Zweiquartflasche (f)	*(tsveye-kvAHRT-flah-sheh)*	magnum

V. GENERAL INFORMATION

ABBREVIATIONS

a.a.   always afloat
a.a.r.   against all risks
a/c   account
A/C   account current
acct.   account
a.c.v.   actual cash value
a.d.   after date
a.f.b.   air freight bill
agcy.   agency
agt.   agent
a.m.t.   air mail transfer
a/o   account of
A.P.   accounts payable
A/P   authority to pay
approx.   approximately
A.R.   accounts receivable
a/r   all risks
A/S, A.S.   account sales
a/s   at sight
at. wt.   atomic weight
av.   average
avdp.   avoirdupois
a/w   actual weight
a.w.b.   air waybill

bal.   balance
bar.   barrel
bbl.   barrel
b/d   brought down
B/E, b/e   bill of exchange
b/f   brought forward
B.H.   bill of health
bk.   bank
bkge.   brokerage
B/L   bill of lading
b/o   brought over
B.P.   bills payable
b.p.   by procuration
B.R.   bills receivable
B/S   balance sheet
b.t.   berth terms
bu.   bushel
B/V   book value

ca.   circa; centaire
C.A.   chartered accountant
c.a.   current account
C.A.D.   cash against documents
C.B.   cash book
C.B.D.   cash before delivery
c.c.   carbon copy
c/d   carried down
c.d.   cum dividend
c/f   carried forward
cf.   compare
c & f   cost and freight
C/H   clearing house
C.H.   custom house
ch. fwd.   charges forward
ch. pd.   charges paid
ch. ppd.   charges prepaid
chq.   check, cheque
c.i.f.   cost, insurance, freight
c.i.f. & c.   cost, insurance, freight, and commission
c.i.f. & e.   cost, insurance, freight, and exchange
c.i.f. & i.   cost, insurance, freight, and interest
c.l.   car load
C/m   call of more
C/N   credit note
c/o   care of
co.   company
C.O.D.   cash on delivery
comm.   commission
corp.   corporation
C.O.S.   cash on shipment
C.P.   carriage paid
C/P   charter party
c.p.d.   charters pay duties
cpn.   corporation
cr.   credit; creditor
C/T   cable transfer
c.t.l.   constructive total loss
c.t.l.o.   constructive total loss only
cum.   cumulative

cum div. cum dividend
cum. pref. cumulative preference
c/w commercial weight
C.W.O. cash with order
cwt. hundredweight

D/A documents against acceptance;
  deposit account
DAP documents against payment
db. debenture
DCF discounted cash flow
d/d days after date; delivered
deb. debenture
def. deferred
dept. department
d.f. dead freight
dft. draft
dft/a. draft attached
dft/c. clean draft
disc. discount
div. dividend
DL dayletter
DLT daily letter telegram
D/N debit note
D/O delivery order
do. ditto
doz. dozen
D/P documents against payment
dr. debtor
Dr. doctor
d/s, d.s. days after sight
d.w. deadweight
D/W dock warrant
dwt. pennyweight
dz. dozen

ECU European Currency Unit
E.E.T. East European Time
e.g. for example
encl. enclosure
end. endorsement
E. & O.E. errors and omissions
  excepted
e.o.m. end of month
e.o.h.p. except otherwise herein pro-
  vided
esp. especially
Esq. Esquire
est. established
ex out

ex cp. ex coupon
ex div. ex dividend
ex int. ex interest
ex h. ex new (shares)
ex stre. ex store
ex whf. ex wharf

f.a.a. free of all average
f.a.c. fast as can
f.a.k. freight all kinds
f.a.q. fair average quality; free
  alongside quay
f.a.s. free alongside ship
f/c for cash
f c. & s. free of capture and seizure
f.c.s.r. & c.c. free of capture,
  seizure, riots, and civil commotion
F.D. free delivery to dock
f.d. free discharge
ff. following; folios
f.g.a. free of general average
f.i.b. free in bunker
f.i.o. free in and out
f.i.t. free in truck
f.o.b. free on board
f.o.c. free of charge
f.o.d. free of damage
fol. following; folio
f.o.q. free on quay
f.o.r. free on rail
f.o.s. free on steamer
f.o.t. free on truck(s)
f.o.w. free on wagons; free on wharf
F.P. floating policy
f.p. fully paid
f.p.a. free of particular average
frt. freight
frt. pd. freight paid
frt. ppd. freight prepaid
frt. fwd. freight forward
ft. foot
fwd. forward
f.x. foreign exchange

g.a. general average
g.b.o. goods in bad order
g.m.b. good merchantable brand
g.m.q. good merchantable quality
G.M.T. Greenwich Mean Time
GNP gross national product

g.o.b. good ordinary brand
gr. gross
GRT gross register ton
gr. wt. gross weight
GT gross tonnage

h.c. home consumption
hgt. height
hhd. hogshead
H.O. head office
H.P. hire purchase
HP horsepower
ht. height

IDP integrated data processing
i.e. that is
I/F insufficient funds
i.h.p. indicated horsepower
imp. import
Inc. incorporated
incl. inclusive
ins. insurance
int. interest
inv. invoice
I.O.U. I owe you

J/A, j.a. joint account
Jr. junior

KV kilovolt
KW kilowatt
KWh kilowatt hour

L/C, l,c, letter of credit
LCD telegram in the language of
  the country of destination
LCO telegram in the language of
  the country of origin
ldg. landing; loading
l.t. long ton
Ltd. limited
l. tn. long ton

m. month
m/a my account
max. maximum
M.D. memorandum of deposit
M/D, m.d. months after date
memo. memorandum

Messrs. plural of Mr.
mfr. manufacturer
min. minimum
MLR minimum lending rate
M.O. money order
m.o. my order
mortg. mortgage
M/P, m.p. months after payment
M/R mate's receipt
M/S, m.s. months' sight
M.T. mail transfer
M/U making-up price

n. name; nominal
n/a no account
N/A no advice
n.c.v. no commercial value
n.d. no date
n.e.s. not elsewhere specified
N/F no funds
NL night letter
N/N no noting
N/O no orders
no. number
n.o.e. not otherwise enumerated
n.o.s. not otherwise stated
nos. numbers
NPV no par value
nr. number
n.r.t. net register ton
N/S not sufficient funds
NSF not sufficient funds
n.wt. net weight

o/a on account
OCP overseas common point
O/D, o/d on demand; overdraft
o.e. omissions excepted
o/h overhead
ono. or nearest offer
O/o order of
O.P. open policy
o.p. out of print; overproof
O/R, o.r. owner's risk
ord. order; ordinary
O.S., o/s out of stock
OT overtime

p. page; per; premium

P.A., p.a.   particular average; per annum

P/A   power of attorney; private account

PAL   phase alternation line

pat. pend.   patent pending

PAYE   pay as you earn

p/c   petty cash

p.c.   percent; price current

pcl.   parcel

pd.   paid

pf.   preferred

pfd.   preferred

pkg.   package

P/L   profit and loss

p.l.   partial loss

P/N   promissory note

P.O.   post office; postal order

P.O.B.   post office box

P.O.O.   post office order

p.o.r.   pay on return

pp.   pages

p & p   postage and packing

p. pro   per procuration

ppd.   prepaid

ppt.   prompt

pref.   preference

prox.   proximo

P.S.   postscript

pt.   payment

P.T.O., p.t.o.   please turn over

ptly. pd.   partly paid

p.v.   par value

qlty.   quality

qty.   quantity

r. & c.c.   riot and civil commotions

R/D   refer to drawer

R.D.C.   running down clause

re   in regard to

rec.   received; receipt

recd.   received

red.   redeemable

ref.   reference

reg.   registered

retd.   returned

rev.   revenue

R.O.D.   refused on delivery

R.P.   reply paid

r.p.s.   revolutions per second

RSVP   please reply

R.S.W.C.   right side up with care

Ry   railway

s.a.e.   stamped addressed envelope

S.A.V.   stock at valuation

S/D   sea damaged

S/D, s.d.   sight draft

s.d.   without date

SDR   special drawing rights

sgd.   signed

s. & h. ex   Sundays and holidays excepted

shipt.   shipment

Sig.   signature

S/LC, s. & l.c.   sue and labor clause

S/N   shipping note

s.o.   seller's option

s.o.p.   standard operating procedure

spt.   spot

Sr.   senior

S.S., s.s.   steamship

s.t.   short ton

ster.   sterling

St. Ex.   stock exchange

stg.   sterling

s.v.   sub voce

T.A.   telegraphic address

T.B.   trial balance

tel.   telephone

temp.   temporary secretary

T.L., t.l.   total loss

T.L.O.   total loss only

TM   multiple telegram

T.O.   turn over

tr.   transfer

TR   telegram to be called for

TR, T/R   trust receipt

TT, T.T.   telegraphic transfer (cable)

TX   Telex

UGT   urgent

u.s.c.   under separate cover

U/ws   underwriters

v.   volt

val.   value

v.a.t.   value-added tax

v.g.   very good
VHF   very high frequency
v.h.r.   very highly recommended

w.   watt
WA   with average
W.B.   way bill
w.c.   without charge
W.E.T.   West European Time
wg.   weight guaranteed
whse.   warehouse
w.o.g.   with other goods
W.P.   weather permitting; without prejudice
w.p.a.   with particular average

W.R.   war risk
W/R, wr.   warehouse receipt
W.W.D.   weather working day
wt.   weight

x.c.   ex coupon
x.d.   ex dividend
x.i.   ex interest
x.n.   ex new shares

y.   year
yd.   yard
yr.   year
yrly.   yearly

WEIGHTS AND MEASURES

U.S. UNIT	METRIC EQUIVALENT
mile	1.609 kilometers
yard	0.914 meters
foot	30.480 centimeters
inch	2.540 centimeters
square mile	2.590 square kilometers
acre	0.405 hectares
square yard	0.836 square meters
square foot	0.093 square meters
square inch	6.451 square centimeters
cubic yard	0.765 cubic meters
cubit foot	0.028 cubic meters
cubic inch	16.387 cubic centimeters
short ton	0.907 metric tons
long ton	1.016 metric tons
short hundredweight	45.359 kilograms
long hundredweight	50.802 kilograms
pound	0.453 kilograms
ounce	28.349 grams
gallon	3.785 liters
quart	0.946 liters
pint	0.473 liters
fluid ounce	29.573 milliliters
bushel	35.238 liters
peck	8.809 liters
quart	1.101 liters
pint	0.550 liters

TEMPERATURE AND CLIMATE

Temperature Conversion Chart

DEGREES CELSIUS	DEGREES FAHRENHEIT
-5	23
0	32
5	41
10	50
15	59
20	68
25	77
30	86
35	95
40	104

Average Temperatures for Major Cities

	JAN	APR	JULY	OCT
Bonn	38°F (3°C)	50°F (10°C)	68°F (20°C)	54°F (12°C)
Hamburg	32°F (0°C)	50°F (10°C)	68°F (20°C)	50°F (10°C)
Munich	25°F (−3°C)	48°F (9°C)	68°F (20°C)	48°F (9°C)
Vienna	29°F (−2°C)	52°F (11°C)	68°F (20°C)	52°F (11°C)
Zurich	30°F (−1°C)	50°F (10°C)	68°F (20°C)	52°F (11°C)

spring	der Frühling
summer	der Sommer
autumn	der Herbst
winter	der Winter
hot	heiß
sunny	sonnig
warm	warm
cool	kühl
windy	windig
snowing	(es) schneit
raining	(es) regnet

COMMUNICATION CODES

Telephones

The German telephone network is almost entirely automated. Coin-operated booths are located on the street with English instructions. International calls can be made from booths marked in green with a sign *Ausland*. Emergency telephone numbers in Germany are 110 (police) and 112 (fire). In Austria they are 133 and 122, and in Switzerland, 117 and 118.

Area Codes within Germany

Berlin	30	Hamburg	40
Bonn	228	Hannover	511
Cologne	221	Leipzig	41
Dresden	51	Munich	89
Düsseldorf	211	Stuttgart	711
Frankfurt	611		

Area Codes within Austria

Linz	723	Vienna	222

Area Codes within Switzerland

Berne	31	Basel	61
Geneva	22	Zurich	1

International Country Codes

Algeria	213	Mexico	52
Argentina	54	Morocco	212
Australia	61	Netherlands	31
Austria	43	New Zealand	64
Belgium	32	Norway	47
Brazil	55	Philippines	63
Canada	1	Poland	48
Chile	56	Portugal	351
Colombia	57	Russia	7
Denmark	45	Saudi Arabia	966
Finland	358	Singapore	65
France	33	South Africa	27
Germany	37	South Korea	82
Gibraltar	350	Spain	34
Greece	30	Sri Lanka	94
Hong Kong	852	Sweden	46
Hungary	36	Switzerland	41
Iceland	354	Taiwan	886
India	91	Thailand	255
Ireland	353	Tunisia	216
Israel	972	Turkey	90
Italy	39	United Kingdom	44
Japan	81	USA	1
Kuwait	965	Venezuela	58
Luxembourg	352	Yugoslavia	38
Malta	356		

POSTAL SERVICES

In Germany: Post offices handle mail, telephone calls, and telegrams. Hours are 8–6, Monday through Friday and 8–noon on Saturday. Some offices have night counters as well. The following are open 24 hours.

Berlin Central Post Office
Bahnhof Zoologischer Garten
(main railroad station in former West Berlin)

Dusseldorf Central Post Office
51 Immermannstrasse

Frankfurt Central Post Office
Hauptbahnhof (main railroad station)

Munich Central Post Office
1 Bahnhofplatz

In Austria: Hours for post offices are 8–6, Monday through Friday, with an hour's lunch break. There is a 24-hour counter in the Vienna central post office.

In Switzerland: The postal service is highly efficient and delivery of regular mail ordinarily takes one day. For more information, contact:

PTT
Generaldirektion
Viktoriastrasse 21
3030 Berne

TIME ZONES

The table on the following page gives the time differences among various countries and major cities of the world, based on Greenwich Mean Time. Remember that from April through September, Daylight Savings Time must be considered.

MAJOR HOLIDAYS
(Observed in all German-speaking areas unless noted)

January 1	New Year's Day	Neujahr
January 6	Epiphany (Austria)	Heilige drei Könige
May 1	Labor Day	Tag der Arbeit
June 15	Corpus Christi Day (Austria)	Fronleichnam
August 1	National Day	Nationalfeiertag

−8 HOURS	−6 HOURS	−5 HOURS	GREEN-WICH MEAN TIME	1 HOUR	2 HOUR	3 HOUR	ADDITIONAL HOUR
Los Angeles	Chicago	Boston	Great Britain	Austria	Finland	Turkey	Sydney (10 hours)
San Francisco	Dallas	New York	Iceland	Belgium	Greece	Moscow	New Zealand
	Houston	Washington, (D.C.)	Portugal	Denmark	Romania		(12 hours)
				France	South Africa		
				Germany			
				Hungary			
				Italy			
				Luxemburg			
				Malta			
				Monaco			
				Netherlands			
				Norway			
				Poland			
				Spain			
				Sweden			
				Switzerland			
				Yugoslavia			

August 15	Assumption Day (Austria)	Mariä Himmelfahrt
October 3	Day of German Unity	Tag der Deutsche Einheit
October 26	Flag Day	Nationalfeiertag
November 1	All Saints Day (Austria)	Allerheiligen
December 8	Immaculate Conception (Austria)	Unbefleckte Empfängnis
December 25	Christmas Day	1. Weihnachtstag
December 26	St. Stephen's Day	2. Weihnachtstag
March–April	Good Friday	Karfreitag
	Easter	Ostern
	Easter Monday	Ostermontag
40 Days after Easter	Ascension	Christi Himmelfahrt
7 Mondays after Easter	Whitmonday	Pfingstmontag
November	Prayer Repentance Day	Buß-und Bettag

CURRENCY INFORMATION

Major Currencies of the World

Andorra	French Franc, Spanish Peseta
Austria	Schilling
Belgium	Belgian Franc
Denmark	Danish Krone
Finland	Finnmark
France	Franc
Germany	Mark (DM)
Greece	Drachma
Hungary	Forint
Iceland	Krone
Ireland	Punt
Israel	Shekel
Italy	Lira
Liechtenstein	Swiss Franc
Luxembourg	Luxembourg Franc
Malta	Maltese Lira
Monaco	French Franc
Netherlands	Guilder
Norway	Norwegian Krone
Portugal	Escudo
Russia	Ruble
Spain	Peseta
Sweden	Swedish Krone
Switzerland	Swiss Franc

Turkey   Lira
United Kingdom   Pound Sterling

Major Commercial Banks

In Germany
 Deutsche Bank AG
 Taunusanlage 12
 Postfach 10 06 10
 6000 Frankfurt 1

 Commerzbank AG
 Neue Mainzer Strasse 32-36
 Postfach 100505
 6000 Frankfurt 1

 Dresdner Bank AG
 Jürgen-Ponto-Platz 1
 Postfach 11 06 61
 6000 Frankfurt 11

In Austria
 Z-Länderbank Bank Austria AG
 Am Hof 2
 A-1010 Vienna

 Creditanstalt-Bankverein
 Schottengasse 6
 A-1011 Vienna

 Girocredit u. Bank der
 Österreichischen Sparkassen
 Schubertring 5
 Postfach 255
 A-1010 Vienna

In Switzerland
 Union Bank of Switzerland (UBS)
 Bahnhofstrasse 45
 Postfach
 CH-8021 Zurich

 Swiss Bank Corporation
 Aeschenplatz, 6
 CH-4002 Basel

 Credit Suisse
 Paradeplatz 8
 Postfach
 CH-8021 Zurich

MAJOR BUSINESS PERIODICALS

The *International Herald Tribune* is the leading English-language newspaper sold in Europe. It is available at most hotels and newsstands. The *Journal of Commerce* is also widely available.

In Germany

Frankfurter Allegemeine Zeitung
Handelsbatt
Süddeutsche Zeitung
Die Welt
Kapital
Welthandel

In Austria

Wiener Zeitung
Kurier

Die Presse
Der Standard
Salzburger Nachrichten

In Switzerland

Blick
Tages Anzeiger Zürich
Neue Zürcher Zeitung
Schweiz. Handelszeitung
Finanz und Wirtschaft

STOCK EXCHANGES

Import securities trading centers in German speaking areas are:

Frankfurter Wertpapierbörse
Börsenplatz 4
D-6000 Frankfurt 1

Wiener Börsenkammer
Wipplingerstr. 34
A-1010 Vienna

Basler Börsen-Informations AG
Aeschenplatz 7
CH-4002 Basel
Effektenbörsenverein
Selnaustrasse 32
CH-8001 Zürich

SELECTED TRADE FAIRS

In Germany

For a complete list of events, contact the German-American Chamber of Commerce (40 West 57 Street, New York, NY 10019-4092).

Berlin
International Green Week (Food, Forestry, Wines, etc.) (January)
International Tourism Exchange (March)
Entertainment Technology Fair (June)
Import Fair "Partners For Progress" (June)
International Audio and Video Fair (August)
AAA Motor Show (October)

Düsseldorf
International Boat Show (January)
Fashion Trade Fair IGEDO (March and September)
International Shoe Fair (March and September)
Interpack—Packaging Technology (May)

Frankfurt
Household Textiles (January)
International Fair Ambiente For Consumer Goods (February)
Musical Instruments Fair (March)
Interstoff Fashion (April and October)
Frankfurt Book Fair (October)
Management and Marketing Services (October)

Hamburg
Catering and Kitchen Equipment (March)
Boat Show (October)

Hanover
Domotex-Floor Coverings (January)
Construction-Building Tradea Exhibition (February)
CeBiT Fair Office Communications Technology (March)

Hanover Trade Fair-Engineering and Electronics (April)
Interhospital—Electromedical Equipment (June)
Biotechnica (October)

Leipzig
Leipzig Trade Fair for Consumer Goods and Industrial Technologies (March
and September)

Munich
International Fashion Fair (February and August)
Light Industries and Handicrafts Fair (March)
Drinktec-Interbrau, World Fair For Beverage Technology (September and
October)

Nuremberg
International Toy Fair (February)
Interzoo—Pet Supplies (May)

For additional information, contact: Ausstellungs Messe-Ausschuss der
Deutschen Wirtschaft e.V. (AUMA), Lindenstrasse 8, D-5000, Cologne 1.
Telephone: (0221) 20 90 70; Fax: 0221/2090712

In Austria

Vienna
Ferien—International Tourism Fair (January)
ÖSM—Austrian Shoe Show (March and September)
Exquisit—Leather Goods, Luggage (March)
IFABO—Information Technology and Office Organization Software (April)
Juwelia—Clocks, Jewels (September)
Küche und Keller—Food and Wine (October)
PC-Expo—Personal Computers (November)
Gewinn—Capital Investment Congress (November)
Art and Antiques (November)

Salzburg
TexBo—Home Textiles and Floor Covering (January)
Tourf—Tourism and Leisure (February)
Souvenir-Crea'tisch—Handicrafts, Tableware, Toys, Gifts, Housewares
(March and September)
Fashions "Made in Austria" (March and September)
Austro Glas—Glassmaking, Machinery, Accessories (May)
ÖSFA—Sportswear, Sports Equipment (September)
Alles für den Gast—Hotel and Catering Industry (November)

Graz
Häuslbau—Do It Yourself Housebuilding (February)
International Trade Fair (Spring and Autumn)
Stamps, Coins, Classic Cars (June)

Klagenfurt
  Hotel Industry, Food, Tourism (March)
  International Timber Fair Lumber Industry (September)

Innsbruck
  Trade Fair (Spring and Autumn)

  For additional information, contact: Austrian Federal Economic Chamber, Wiedner Haupstr. 63. A-1045, Vienna; Tel: 501 05-36 57

In Switzerland

Basel
  Watch, Clock and Jewelry Fair (April)
  International Fair for Contemporary Graphics (April)
  20th Century Air Fair (June)
  Fibo—Fitness and Leisure Show (November)
  Orbit—Communications Technologies (September)
  Collectibles—Antiques, Coins, Stamps (October)

Berne
  Solarsalon—Solar Vehicles, Technology (February)
  Classic Vehicles, Parts, Accessories (March)
  International Furniture Fair (May)
  Interior Decoration (November)

Zürich
  Sports, Tourist, Leisure Show (January)
  Ornaris—Home Design, Novelties Exposition (January)
  Computer Graphics (January)
  Art and Antiques (April)
  Computer Technology (May)
  Environmental Technologies (June)
  International TV, Radio, HiFi Show (August)
  International Minerals Fair (October)
  Security Systems Technologies (November)

  For additional information on all Swiss Fairs, contact the Swiss Office for Trade Promotion, Schweizerische Zentrale für Handelsförderung Stampfenbachstr. 85, CH-8035 Zurich, Tel: 01/365 51 51, Fax: 01/365 52 21

TRAVEL TIMES

To Germany

  Although there are direct flights to other German cities, many flights land in Frankfurt. At Frankfurt, you can connect with flights to other German cities as well as flights to major European, Middle Eastern, and Asian destinations. Trains leave Frankfurt's Rhein/Main Airport every 15 minutes to reach the center of the city 10 km away.

To Austria

At Schwechat Airport, 18 km from Vienna, there are daily flights to other Austrian cities as well as connections with other European cities. Austrian Airlines offers frequent direct service between New York and Vienna.

To Switzerland

Zurich is the main entryway to Switzerland via air, and there are also a large number of domestic flights to Geneva, Berne, Basel, and Lugano. Kloten Airport is 11 km from the city, with a 10-minute train ride to Hauptbahnhof.

Approximate Flying Times to Key German-Speaking Cities

New York—Frankfurt	7 hours, 30 minutes
Chicago—Frankfurt	8 hours, 45 minutes
Los Angeles—Frankfurt	11 hours
Montreal—Frankfurt	6 hours
Toronto—Düsseldorf	7 hours
London—Berlin	1 hour, 30 minutes
London—Munich	1 hour, 40 minutes
Sydney—Munich	14 hours
New York—Vienna	8 hours, 30 minutes

Average Flying Times between Major German-Speaking Cities

Düsseldorf—Frankfurt	50 minutes
Munich—Hanover	1 hour, 10 minutes
Stuttgart—Hamburg	1 hour, 10 minutes
Cologne—Munich	1 hour
Munich—Frankfurt	1 hour
Frankfurt—Vienna	1 hour, 20 minutes
Frankfurt—Zurich	55 minutes

Lufthansa (with its subsidiaries Condor and City Line), is Germany's major airline. It serves many international destinations and all important German cities, including those in the former GDR. There are also smaller domestic airlines, such as Nürnberger Flugdienst. Lufthansa offers six flights a day between Frankfurt and Düsseldorf, in both directions, as well as two train connections. Reservations and information may be made at Lufthansa ticket offices, any IATA travel agency, or Lufthansa Information at the airport of arrival.

Most major airports have direct rail connections to neighboring cities. The rail network, Deutsche Bundesbahn (in old West Germany) and Deutsche Reichsbahn (in the former GDR), is dense and efficient.

There are three major airlines in Austria, listed below. Contact each for information on flights and reservations.

Austrian Airlines	Tyrolean Airways
Oesterreichischer	Luftfahrt Ges.m.b.H. & Co. KG
Luftverkehr AG	Flughafen Innsbruck
Fontanastrasse 1	Fuerstenweg 10
A-1107 Vienna	A-6020 Innsbruck

Lauda Air Luftfahrt AG
Opernring 6
A-1010 Vienna

Swissair is the national airline of Switzerland. For information, contact Swissair, Schweizerischer Luftverhehr AG, CH-8058 Zurich. For domestic flights, contact:

Balair AG
Flugplatz Basel-Mülhausen
CH-4002 Basel

Crossair
Postfach 6300
CH-8058 Zurich

CTA
Case Postale 110
CH-1215 Geneva

MAJOR HOTELS

All hotels listed here have at least one restaurant; many have several. Major credit cards are accepted in all these hotels and restaurants.

Berlin

Bristol-Hotel Kempinski
Kurfürstendamm 27 (B 15)
Tel: 88 43 40
Fax: 8836075

Maritim Grand Hotel
Friedrichstr. 158 (0-1080)
Tel: 2 32 70
Fax: 23273362

Grand Hotel Esplanade
Lützowufer 15 (B 30)
Tel: 26 10 11
Fax: 2651171

Berlin Hilton
Mohrenstr. 30
Tel: 2 38 20
Fax: 23824269

Palace
Budapester Str. 42
Tel: 2 50 20
Fax: 2626577

Metropol
Friedrichstr. 150 (0-1086)
Tel: 2 38 75
Fax: 23874209

Dresden

Maritim Hotel Bellevue
Grosse Meissner Str. 15
Tel: 5 66 20
Fax: 55997

Dresden Hilton
An der Frauenkirche 5
Tel: 4 84 10
Fax: 4841700

Düsseldorf

Breidenbacher Hof
Heinrich-Heine-Allee 36 (D 1)
Tel: 1 30 30
Fax: 1303820

SAS Royal Scandinavia Hotel
Karl Arnold Platz 5
Tel: 4 55 30
Fax: 4553110

Ramada-Renaissance Hotel
Nördlicher Zubringer 6
Tel: 6 21 60
Fax: 6216666

Steigenberger Parkhotel
Corneliusplatz I (D 1)
Tel: 1 38 10
Fax: 131679

Frankfurt

Arabella Grand Hotel
Konrad-Adenauer-Str. 7
Tel: 2 98 10
Fax: 2981810

Mövenpick Parkhotel
Wiesenhüttenplatz 28
Tel: 2 69 70
Fax: 26978849

Frankfurt Marriott Hotel
Hamburger Allee 2
Tel: 7 95 50
Fax: 79552432

Hamburg

Atlantic-Hotel Kempinski
An der Alster 72 (H 1)
Tel: 2 88 80
Fax: 247129

Vier Jahreszeiten
Neuer Jungfernstieg 9 (H 36)
Tel: 3 49 40
Fax: 3494602

Inter-Continental
Fontenay 10
Tel: 41 41 50
Fax: 41415186

Hanover

Kastens Hotel Luisenhof
Luisenstr. 1
Tel: 3 04 40
Fax: 3044807

Schweizerhof
Hunüberstr. 6
Tel: 3 49 50
Fax: 3495123

Maritim Stadthotel
Hildesheimerstr. 34
Tel: 1 65 31
Fax: 884846

Leipzig

Merkur
Gerberstr. 15
Tel: 79 90
Fax: 7991229

Gästehaus am Park
Schwägrichenstr. 14
Tel: 3 93 90
Fax: 326098

Munich

Vier Jahreszeiten Kempinski
Maximilianstr. 17 (M 22)
Tel: 23 03 90
Fax: 23039693

Rafael
Neuturmstr. (M 2)
Tel: 29 09 80
Fax: 222539

Excelsior
Schützenstr. 11 (M 2)
Tel: 55 13 70
Fax: 55137121

Königshof
Karlsplatz 25 (M 2)
Tel: 55 13 60
Telex: 523616
Fax: 55136113

Eden-Hotel-Wolff
Arnulfstr. 4 (M 2)
Tel: 55 11 50
Fax: 55115555

Stuttgart

Steigenberger Graf Zeppelin
Arnulf-Klett-Platz 7
Tel: 2 04 80
Fax: 2048542

Inter-Continental
Neckarstr. 60
Tel: 2 02 00
Fax: 202012

Relaxa Hotel Stuttgart
Am Solitudering
Tel: 6 86 70
Fax: 6867999

Vienna

Imperial
Kärntner Ring 16, A-1015
Tel: 50 11 00
Fax: 50110410

Plaza Wien
Schottenring 11, A-1010
Tel: 31 39 00
Fax: 31390160

Penta Hotel
Ungargasse 60, A-1030
Tel: 71 17 50
Fax: 7117590

Scandic Crown Hotel
Handelskai 269, A-1020
Tel: 2 17 77
Fax: 21777199

Bristol
Kärntner Ring 1, A-1015
Tel: 51 51 60
Fax: 51516550

Hotel im Palais Schwarzenberg
Schwarzenbergplatz 9, A-1030
Tel: 78 45 15
Fax: 784714

Salzburg

Österreichischer Hof
Schwarzstr. 5
Tel: 8 89 77
Fax: 8897714

Bristol
Marktplatz 4
Tel: 87 35 57
Fax: 8735576

Basel

Plaza
Riehenring 45, CH-4058
Tel: 692 33 33
Fax: 6915633

Trois Rois
Blumenrain 8, CH-4001
Tel: 261 52 52
Fax: 2612153

Euler
Centralbahnplatz 14, CH-4002
Tel: 272 45 00
Fax: 2715000

International
Steinentorstr. 25, CH-4001
Tel: 281 75 85
Fax: 2817627

Zürich

Dolder Grand Hotel
Kurhausstr. 65, CH-8032
Tel: 251 62 31
Fax: 2518829

Atlantis Sheraton
Döltschiweg 234, CH 8055
Tel: 463 00 00
Fax: 4630388

Ramada Renaissance (near airport)
Talackerstr. 1, CH-8152
Tel: 810 85 00
Fax: 8108755

Hilton (near airport)
Hohenbühlstr. 10, CH-8058
Tel: 810 31 31
Fax: 8109366

Schweizerhof
Bahnhofplatz 7, CH-8023
Tel: 211 86 40
Fax: 2113505

Baur au Lac
Talstr. 1, CH-8022
Tel: 221 16 50
Fax: 2118139

MAJOR RESTAURANTS

Berlin

Rockendorf's Restaurant—two stars
Dusterhaupstr. 1 (B 28)
Tel: 4 02 30 99

Alt Luxemburg—one star
Windscheidstr. 31 (B 12)
Tel: 3 23 87 30

Bamberger Reiter—one star
Regensburger Str. 7 (B 30)
Tel: 2 18 42 82

Opernpalais-Königin Luise
Unter den Linden 5
Tel: 2 00 22 69

Grand Slam
Gottfried-von-Cramm-Weg 47 (B 33)
Tel: 8 25 38 10

Hemingway's
Hagenstr. 18 (B 33)
Tel: 8 25 45 71

Dresden

Opernrestaurant
Theaterplatz 2
Tel: 4 84 25 00

Ratskeller
Dr.-Külz-Ring 19
Tel: 4 88 29 50

Kügelgenhaus
Hauptstr. 13
Tel: 5 45 18

Düsseldorf

Im Schiffchen—three stars
Kaiserswerther Markt 9 (1st floor)
Tel: 40 10 50

Hummerstübchen—two stars
Bonifatiusstr. 35
Tel: 59 44 02

Aalschokker—one star
Kaiserswerther Markt 9 (ground floor)
Tel: 40 39 48

Victorian—one star
Königstr. 3a
Tel: 32 02 22

Frankfurt

Weinhaus Brückenkeller—two stars
Schützenstr. 6
Tel: 28 42 38

Zauberflöte—one star
Opernplatz 1
Tel: 1 34 03 86

Humperdinck—one star
Grüneburgweg 95
Tel: 72 21 22

Hamburg

Landhaus Scherrer—two stars
Elbchaussee 130
Tel: 8 80 13 25

Cölln's Austernstuben—one star
Brodschrangen 1
Tel: 32 60 59

Tafelhaus—one star
Holstenkamp 71
Tel: 89 27 60

Hanover

Landhaus Ammann—one star
Hildesheimer Str. 185
Tel: 83 08 18

Schu's Restaurant—one star
Hinüberstr. 6 (in Schweizerhof
Hotel)
Tel: 3 49 52 52

Stern's Restaurant—one star
Herrenhäuser Kirchweg 20 (in
Georgenhof Hotel)
Tel: 70 22 44

Leipzig

Auerbachs Keller
Grimmaische Str. 2 (Mädler Passage)
Tel: 2 11 60 34

Stadtpfeiffer
Augustusplatz 8
Tel: 28 64 94

Munich

Aubergine—three stars
Maximiliansplatz 5
Tel: 59 81 71

Tantris—two stars
Johann-Fichte-Str. 7
Tel: 36 20 61

Hilton-Grill (Hotel Park Hilton)—
one star
Am Tucherpark 7
Tel: 3 84 52 61

Le Gourmet Schwarzwälder—one star
Hartmannstr. 8
Tel: 2 12 09 58

Stuttgart

Wielandshöhe—one star
Alte Weinsteige 71
Tel: 6 40 88 48

Herzog Carl Eugen—one star
In Solitude Castle
Tel: 6 99 07 45

Top Air—one star
Terminal One in Airport
Tel: 9 48 21 37

Vienna

Steirereck—two stars
Rasumofskygasse 2
Tel: 7 13 31 68

Gottfried—one star
Untere Viaduktgasse 45
Tel: 7 13 82 56

Restaurant Korso—one star
Kärntner Ring 1 (in Bristol Hotel)
Tel: 51 51 60

Zu den drei Husaren
Weihburggasse 4
Tel: 5 12 10 92

Salzburg

Mozart
Getreidegasse 22
Tel: 84 37 46

K u. K. Restaurant
("Medieval Dinner Theater")
Waagplatz 2
Tel: 84 21 56

Basel

Stucki—two stars
Bruderholzallee 42
Tel: 35 82 22

Les Quatre Saisons—one star
Clarastr. 43 (in Hotel Europe)
Tel: 691 80 80

Zürich

Petermann's Kunststube—two stars
Seestr. 160
Tel: 910 07 15

Gasthof zum Bären—one star
8309-Nürensdorf
Tel: 836 42 12

Baron de la Mouette (Mövenpick)
Beethovenstr. 32
Tel: 286 53 53

Ermitage—one star
Seestrasse 80
Tel: 910 52 22

Witschi's—one star
Unterengstringen 8103
Tel: 750 44 60

Ratings extracted from the *Red Michelin Guide, 1993*

USEFUL ADDRESSES

Associations/Commissions

In Germany

Association of German Chambers of
Industry and Commerce
Adenauerallee 148
D-5300 Bonn 1

Federal Association of German
Industry
Gustav-Heinemann-Ufer 84-88
Postfach 51 05 48
D-5000 Cologne 51

Central Association of German
Handicrafts
Johanniterstrasse 1
D-5300 Bonn

Federal Association of German
Wholesale and Foreign Trade
Kaiser-Friedrich-Strasse 13
Postfach 1349
D-5300 Bonn

National Association of German
Retailers
Sachsenring 89
D-5000 Cologne 1

Federal Association of German
Banks
Mohrenstrasse 35-41
Postfach 10 02 46
D-5000 Cologne

General Association of Insurance
Carriers
Ebertplatz 1
D-5000 Cologne 1

Federal Association of German
Market Researchers
Papenkamp 2-6
D-2410 Mölln

Federal Ministry of Economics,
Public Relations Division
Villemombler Str. 76
D-5300 Bonn 1

Federal Statistical Office
Gustav-Stresemann-Ring 11
D-6200 Wiesbaden

German Trade Union Federation
Hans-Bockler-Strasse 39
D-4000 Dusseldorf 30

In Austria

Ministry of Trade and Industry
Export/Import Licensing Office
Landstrasse Hauptstrasse 55-57
1030 Vienna

Federal Economic Chamber of
Commerce
Wiedner Hauptstrasse 63
A-1040 Vienna

Austrian Industries AG
Kantgasse 1
A-1010 Vienna

Austrian National Tourist Office
Margaretenstrasse 1
A-1040 Vienna

Association of Austrian Industrialists
Schwarzenbergplatz 4
A-1030 Vienna

In Switzerland

Federal Office for Industry, Crafts
and Labor
Bundesgasse 8
3003 Berne

Federation of Swiss Employers'
Organizations
Florastrasse 44
8034 Zurich

Swiss Federation of Commerce and
Industry
Börsenstrasse 26
8001 Zurich

Swiss National Tourist Office
Bellariastrasse 38
8027 Zurich

In The United States

German-American Chamber of
Commerce
40 West 57th Street
New York, New York 10019

German-American Chamber of
Commerce
104 South Michigan Avenue
Chicago, Illinois 60603

German-American Chamber of
Commerce
3250 Wilshire Boulevard
Los Angeles, California 90010

German-American Chamber of
Commerce
465 California Street
San Francisco, California 94104

German Convention Bureau
1640 Hempstead Turnpike
East Meadow, New York 11554

Austrian Trade Commission
150 East 52nd Street
New York, New York 10022

Austrian Trade Commission
500 North Michigan Avenue
Chicago, Illinois 10022

Austrian Trade Commission
11601 Wilshire Boulevard
Los Angeles, California 90025

Consulate General of Switzerland
665 Fifth Avenue
New York, New York 10022

In Canada and Great Britain

Canadian-German Chamber of
Industry and Commerce
1010 Sherbrooke Street, West
Montreal, Ouebec H3A 2R7

Canadian-German Chamber of
Industry and Commerce
480 University Avenue
Toronto, Ontario M5G 1V2

German Chamber of Industry and
Commerce
16 Buckingham Gate
London SW1 6LB